WITHDRAWN

BOOKS by RICHARD O'CONNOR

FICTION

Guns of Chickamauga   Officers and Ladies
Company Q   The Vandal

NONFICTION

PACIFIC DESTINY

PACIFIC
DESTINY

An Informal History of the U. S. in the Far East: 1776–1968

RICHARD O'CONNOR

Little, Brown and Company   *Boston*   ·   *Toronto*

LIBRARY OF CONGRESS CATALOG CARD NO.: 75–79362

FIRST EDITION

All illustrations courtesy of Brown Brothers
unless otherwise noted

Published simultaneously in Canada
by Little, Brown & Company (Canada) Limited

PRINTED IN THE UNITED STATES OF AMERICA

A Fool lies here who tried to hustle the East.

— RUDYARD KIPLING

Introduction

The widening involvement of the United States in Asia — the evolution of this country as a Pacific rather than an Atlantic power — may be considered one of the major turning points in modern history. Relatively little study has been applied to this crucial turnabout, though it began quite perceptibly from the moment the United States established its independence.

For two centuries the process has been forwarded by such Presidents as Thomas Jefferson, James K. Polk, Benjamin Harrison, William McKinley, the two Roosevelts and Lyndon B. Johnson; by men of far-ranging vision such as John Ledyard, Homer Lea and Captain Alfred T. Mahan; by men of action like Frederick Townsend Ward and Commodore Perry; by literary men of the Pacific faith; by men of ambition and greed and evangelistic passion, traders, pirates, soldiers of fortune, missionaries, poets and plunderers.

Not all of this westering procession was confined to the forces of expansion. Aside from the romantics and others who sought personal adventure across the blue Pacific world, however, most were transfixed by an image of the Orient as a continental treasure-house waiting to be exploited by men of determination. It is seldom realized how deep are the roots of this ambition to establish an American hegemony over eastern Asia and all that lies between, or how penetrating this thrust westward has been. In our hazy generalized picture of the American past we see a fleet of clipper ships scudding to distant ports and returning with sandalwood, tea, silk and lacquered chests; a valiant band of missionaries establishing their compounds in the heathen wilderness; the flutter of Madame Butterfly's fan as she pirouettes before a pink-cheeked Lieutenant Pinkerton.

Over such pleasant scenes, for the sake of realism, should be imposed the flashing guns of Dewey's fleet in Manila Bay, the American columns marching over Chinese and Korean and even Siberian highroads, the American machine guns rattling in the mountain jungles of Mindanao, the confrontation of the German and American navies in the Pacific almost a century ago, the American blackbirders kidnaping South Sea natives for forced labor on Australian sugar plantations.

Considering this long involvement across the Pacific, we probably should have adopted the sailing ship rather than the covered wagon as the national symbol of expansion. The United States had stationed a consul in China before it placed a President in the White House. We sent United States Marines to invade Korea during the Grant Administration. The first appeal for American help came from Viet Nam, then part of Indo-China, in 1873. The first "peace corps," ten thousand strong, was sent abroad at the turn of the century to ease our qualms about occupying, instead of merely liberating, the Philippines. Technically we invaded Asiatic Russia half a century ago when we sent an expeditionary force to Siberia.

Twenty years ago Kenneth Scott Latourette, brooding over the American turn toward the Pacific, observed that "Few Americans yet appreciate the significance of what has been taking place before their very eyes . . . The United States has been pursuing a course from which there seems to be no probability of withdrawal. Here is a glacier-like movement, which cannot be turned back. Or, to change the metaphor, here is a Greek tragedy. Actions have already been taken, indeed were begun decades ago, the major outlines of whose denouement are, because of them, so inescapable as to be inevitable. The outcome cannot but affect profoundly the United States, the Far East, and the world as a whole."

Moving by indirection, acting out of the subconscious as nations often do, rarely examining our motives but often consulting our ambitions, we have steadily turned from Atlantic to Pacific and always kept our eye on the main — the Asian — chance. The fluctuating tendency toward isolationism has always, at least until the last year or two, been centered on disengagement from European conflict. The longest-running debate in our political life, antedating even the question of how to deal with our Negro population, has involved what might be called the Atlanticists — the European-minded — and the Pacificists, those who would have us concentrate our political, economic and military attention on Asia.

As this book was being written, the long and irreconcilable conflict between them seemed to be approaching a climax. During World War II, that struggle was part of the strategic debate over whether the main military effort should be directed against the Japanese empire, which struck at us first, or against its European allies. The Atlanticists, insisting on the prior destruction of Nazi Germany, won that argument. With considerable reluctance they went along with the massive U.S. contribution to the United Nations intervention in Korea five years later. But the American interposition in South Viet Nam was a different matter, without U.N. approval, without any significant show of sympathy from our European allies. The Arab-Israeli war of June 1967 also sharply illumined the conflicting attitudes of Atlanticists and Pacificists. Much of the present ambivalence is rooted in the fact that, both diplomatically and militarily, there is little space for maneuver in Europe compared with vaster territories of the Pacific relatively open to such opportunity.

Since the founding of the Republic, those who have opposed intervention in Europe have often favored expansion in Asia. The issue has split the political parties, never more divisively than during the American conquest of the Philippines when a liberal Republican, Carl Schurz, was denouncing it as "a story of deceit and brutal treachery" while a Republican President was sending fresh divisions to the islands. It has divided the forces of isolationism, pacifism and internationalism. It has diverted American attention from what geographically, if not geopolitically, would be its true sphere of influence — the contiguous lands of South America — to islands and areas ten thousand miles across the Pacific.

This book is an effort to explore the forces which finally brought us to a situation which can only be called imperial. If it is not a Pax Americana which has been extended to the Indian Ocean, placing a huge American army in South Viet Nam, American infantry divisions on the truce-line in South Korea, American task forces patrolling the Formosan straits and the Gulf of Tonkin, American squadrons flying from bases in Laos and Thailand, an American occupation force on Okinawa, and American proconsuls ruling thousands of Pacific islands "in trust," then any other name for it is a semantic evasion.

In a seemingly offhand way, almost as though it had been thrust upon us, we have acquired an empire. Whether this is "good" or "bad" in the sense of international morality, whether it happened by accident or design, whether America will destroy herself through overextension as other empires have, whether imperial systems of whatever amiable design can endure in a neocolonialist world, it is a fact. Arguing the fact is a job for moralists and formal historians.

This is a narrative of the impulses and forces, and the men and women who embodied them, that urged us on our Western way. It attempts to assemble on one stage the splendidly diverse cast of characters who participated, often unwittingly, in that effort. Every drama is a collective biography, and undoubtedly a more solemn and scholarly producer-director would assemble a statelier and more pompous company. I have yielded to casting those whose fascination sometimes exceeded their importance, admittedly have studied the career of Bully Hayes at greater length than Hamilton Fish's, and can only plead that history is made more tolerable by its picaroons than by its personages.

Contents

Book I. Destiny Made Manifest

Book II. Destiny Takes Root

Book III. The Pest of Glory

Book IV. The Blunted Sword

List of Illustrations

I. Destiny Made Manifest

1

America's Marco Polo

Long before American civilization had spread beyond the Alleghenies there were men who regarded the Pacific littoral as merely a springboard to Asia, the Far West a stepping-stone to the Far East. We had within our grasp the richest of continents, the resources to make us the richest nation in the world, yet we were dazzled by visions of wealth lying across the warm seas to the west. We had inherited the spirit of the Elizabethan trader-adventurers and thus were possessed by their lust for all that "the Indies" stood for.

The Indies, both East and West, were a synonym for all that was most alluring and precious in the way of worldly goods. A scent of incense, spice, perfumed women, sandalwood and opium drifted from the Orient to the Occident.

The Indies became the most compelling of legends, a paradise of the senses waiting to be possessed. The theme runs through the works of Shakespeare, who referred time after time to the wealth and glory of the

Indies (Falstaff chuckling over the fancy of making Mrs. Page and Mrs. Ford serve as his East and West Indies). By the time they were ready to send out their own argosies, Americans as well as Englishmen were indoctrinated with the tradition that only foreign trade could be dignified as "commerce," that domestic buying and selling was only "business."

Thus it was a great day in the countinghouses of lower Manhattan when, in 1784, five years before the inauguration of George Washington, the *Empress of China* sailed from the port of New York for Canton. America had entered the race for the riches of the East. Before that, however, had come the remarkably ill-starred but incredibly venturesome career of the man his contemporaries called "the Great American Traveler" and "America's Marco Polo."

His name was John Ledyard, and if it is seldom celebrated in the history books perhaps that is because the men who benefit from prophecies usually win more fame than those who make them. At the end of his short life, in a last letter to Thomas Jefferson, he paid his respects to the historians who, he was convinced, would ignore him in preference to his more consequential contemporaries: "I think all historians have written more to satisfy themselves than others. I am certainly very angry with those who have written of other countries where I have travelled as well as this [Egypt], and of this particularly. They have all more or less deceived me, and I am (I suppose like others) inclinable by the common operations of the imagination to deceive myself in reading history, and therefore stand in double need of truth. In some cases it is perhaps difficult to determine which does the most mischief: the self-love of the historian, or the curiosity of the reader." By that time the Connecticut Yankee had seen more of the world, in his thirty-seven years, than anyone then living; he had wandered from Lapland to the islands of the South Seas, and by word and example he had influenced his country's destiny more than he could know.

John Ledyard was born in Groton, Connecticut, in 1751. His father was a sea captain who died at sea when the boy was ten years old. His mother remarried and John was brought up by his paternal grandfather, a coldly pious leading citizen of Hartford. An early taste for rebellion was encouraged in the boy by the fact that he and two orphaned cousins were forced to live in the attic of the big house, while the lower and more comfortable rooms were occupied by the children of his grandfather's second marriage.

His sturdy sense of nonconformity was also nurtured by the fact that he spent his formative years in the suffocating respectability of Hartford. During his teens he presented himself as an unruly, untidy and entirely disagreeable youth to his grandfather, Squire Ledyard. He refused to wear a hat, a cravat, or the tight breeches then fashionable, preferring loose-fitting homespun pants more suitable to his active but unfashionable career as a lover of horses, dogs and — worse yet — Indians. Squire Ledyard simply could not comprehend John's interest in Indians as human beings. Decent white people had gone to a lot of bother and expense to reduce the Indian population of Connecticut. Those who survived, in the squire's opinion, should be vigorously Christianized, taught their place and set to work as indentured servants. John argued with all the insolence of undisciplined youth that the Indians deserved something better. But Squire Ledyard had the last word. He died when John was twenty, having taken the precaution, as a lawyer, to disinherit him in his will.[1]

At twenty, John was cut loose with sixty-odd pounds to his name, and encouraged the rest of the family to disavow him by refusing to follow his grandfather's footsteps into a law office. Just then he was invited by the Reverend Eleazar Wheelock, the founder of Dartmouth College, to come up to New Hampshire and attend his school for the training of missionaries to the Indians. Working with the Indians appealed to John, though it was doubtful whether he could ever have been much of a success as a sower of the Christian faith among them.

A memorial tree known as the Ledyard Pine was dedicated to John Ledyard much later on the Dartmouth campus, with a tablet proclaiming, "This was the Dartmouth spirit." If so, it was a troublesome spirit. John, a tall, husky, fair-haired youth with a devilish glint in his blue eyes, simply didn't fit into the life of a student missionary. He got along well with his fellow students, both Indian and white, and was particularly friendly with an Indian youth named Samson Occom. To young Ledyard, Samson was a sterling example of the noble savage ruined by civilization. The young Indian would drink too much rum, which at Dartmouth was rationed with a liberal hand, get into brawls with his fellow students and the faculty, and make even more of a nuisance of himself with the groaning repentance that followed. To Wheelock, however, John Ledyard was equally a constant problem. Instead of concerning himself with theological studies, he flung himself into amateur theatricals. Impatient of academic and religious discipline, he often disappeared on long trips into the woods and lived with the Indians of the Six Nations, not as a missionary but more as a fugitive from Wheelock's admonitions. His style of clothing also dismayed the president, who reported that Ledyard insisted on wearing "enormously large, loose Turkish breeches." Soon Wheelock was freely predicting the "utter ruin of a vain, foolish boy who might have become a good scholar."[2]

There was a dispute over payment of Ledyard's tuition and living expenses — the sixty pounds he had when he left Hartford was exhausted by expenditures for rum, tobacco and other frivolities — and in the spring of 1773 he terminated his education in a characteristic manner. With the help of several of his classmates he secretly built a dugout canoe in the woods. One day shortly after the ice on the Connecticut broke up, he launched himself and his canoe on the river and disappeared forever from the academic life.

He disembarked far down the river to pay a visit to his family, which waited with arms locked against him. The elder Ledyards proclaimed him a disgrace to the family and flourished letters which Wheelock had written charging him with pride, vanity, high temper and other of the seven deadly sins. Ledyard responded by writing a furious letter to Wheelock, inquiring, in part: "Who's this, that assumes the part of compassion, kindness, benevolence, and charity, to write as he writes?" On the back of the letter from his ex-student, Wheelock wrote the comment, "Saucy enough."[3] This verdict might have served as the epigraph for the young man's subsequent career.

Hastily quitting the granite-faced uncles and scornful cousins in Hartford, Ledyard made the transition from divinity student to wide-roving seaman, from theology under Cromwell to adventure under George III, with one eager bound. Sailing before the mast was a rough life, but he had decided to devote seven years to that calling before settling down. It was apparent from the beginning of his vagabondage that staying in one place more than a few days would never appeal to the fair-haired young man, one of the first of the new breed of American, that most restless of races. He sailed out of New London with a ship consigned to picking up a cargo of mules on the Barbary Coast. For the next two years he was rarely in port. In 1776, now twenty-five years old, he wound up on the London docks wondering what to do next. He loved England and the English with an uncolonial passion, and for the oddest of reasons (for so unconventional a fellow): "The English think and act with a heavenly propriety."

While wandering among the grogshops and doss houses of East London, Ledyard heard that Captain James Cook was preparing for his third voyage to the South Seas. Naturally he was determined to join the expedition. What Marco Polo started, Captain Cook with his voyages of discovery in the South Pacific was finishing, and at the same time ushering in what became known as the Age of the Pacific. Until his expeditions little was known of the wide Pacific world; almost half the earth was still terra incognita. Western America was unexplored, eastern Asia north of the port of Canton was a land as vast in mystery as it was in space. The European traders had penetrated only to the spice islands of southern Asia. The Great South Sea was occasionally traversed by the Spanish and Portuguese, but they kept the other maritime nations out. Even the far-roving Spanish had little interest in the area except for the lane followed by the treasure galleons from Manila to Acapulco. On his voyages Captain Cook had placed Australia and New Zealand on the maps and incidentally found the cure for scurvy; he also explored the island world of Polynesia.

Ledyard sought out Captain Cook at his lodgings and applied for a place on the roster of the expedition, which would include the newly built *Discovery* and her sister ship *Resolution*. Cook was sufficiently impressed by Ledyard's enthusiasm to enroll him as a corporal of Marines attached to his own ship, *Discovery*. Ledyard was the only American to accompany the expedition.

Resolution and *Discovery* sailed from Plymouth, bound for the South Seas by way of the Cape of Good Hope, on July 12, 1776. The American Revolution had broken out but word of it had not yet reached England. Even if it had, it may be doubted that the news would have caused Ledyard to rip off his red coat; he had not much more use for the narrower forms of patriotism than he did for organized religion. What drove him was an intense curiosity about the world, the whole world, and chauvinism was a piddling thing compared to that burning ambition to see and experience everything under the stars.

Discovery, not Dartmouth College, was his real alma mater. From Captain Cook and the scientists who accompanied him Ledyard was to receive a unique but thorough education. Among those aboard were William Bayley, the astronomer; David Nelson, the botanist; Dr. William Anderson, the surgeon and naturalist, who had made preliminary study of the Polynesian languages, and John Webber, the artist who would make the first engravings of the North Pacific peoples. And the head of this seagoing faculty was Captain Cook, geographer and marine surveyor. The son of a Yorkshire farm laborer, Cook was self-educated and had risen through the ranks. He had not only, in his plodding way, made himself into a great navigator but developed the talents of a physician. To prevent scurvy, which killed more British seamen than enemy guns or storms at sea, he saw to it that his crews were regularly given oranges, lemons, vinegar, sweet-wort (a form of malt), vegetables and two or three pounds of sauerkraut a week.

Aboard the sister ship *Resolution* were two other interesting gentlemen, her captain, William Bligh, a rough-mannered man who was to command the *Bounty* on his next and less fortunate trip to the Pacific, and Lieutenant James Burney. The latter was a member of the noted literary family, and Fanny Burney, the best-selling novelist, was his niece. He became a friend of Ledyard's. "Ledyard had the most romantic enthusiasm for adventure, perhaps of any man of his time," James Burney wrote many years later when he was the center of a literary group which included Hazlitt, Coleridge, Lamb and Southey.[4] Also aboard *Resolution* was Omai, a native of the Society Islands whom Captain Cook had picked up on his previous voyage, and who had been spoiled and petted by Mayfair society and invited to dine with Samuel Johnson until now he was returning home with what Ledyard called a "proud, empty, ambitious heart."

From the beginning Ledyard kept a careful record of Captain Cook's third voyage, at first on his own hook, later as official "historiographer" of the expedition. The results of his work were later published as *A Journal of Captain Cook's Last Voyage to the Pacific Ocean*. The two ships proceeded from the Cape of Good Hope, paused off Kerguelen Land in the

Antarctic, visited Tasmania and New Zealand, and finally dropped anchor in the bay of Tongatabu in the Friendly Islands, where the expedition stayed twenty-six days loading fresh water and stores.

Ledyard, as the first of a long line of American adventurers in the South Seas, and one of the best behaved, was enchanted by the tropical paradise, the carefree natives, the sound of flutes drifting across the moonlit lagoon. With his natural enthusiasm for anything new and beautiful, in fact, he was considered by his shipmates a little too colonial in his exuberant appreciation, a little too outgoing in all his responses. "His ideas were thought too sentimental" (as James Burney later wrote) "and his language was too florid. No one, however, doubted that his feelings were in accord with his expressions; and the same is to be said of the little that remains of what he has since written more worthy of being preserved, and which its worthiness will preserve."[5]

Ostensibly for the "amusement" of the thousands of natives ringing their encampment ashore at Tongatabu, Captain Cook held a fireworks display: "flower-pots, horizontal wheels, roses, water rackets, crackets, serpents, etc." It was "hard to say whether they were on the whole more terrified or delighted." Several thousands of the natives, in fact, fled from the scene in terror. Ledyard believed that Captain Cook ordered the display to keep them in line. "Our only defense was certainly our imaginary greatness," as Ledyard noted, "and this would unavoidably decline if not preserved by some studied means."[6] The demonstration of British majesty was well calculated considering Captain Cook's high-handed manner of dealing with the natives. When a peacock and hen were stolen from the collection of birds and animals aboard the *Discovery,* Cook immediately placed King Poulaho under house arrest until the birds were returned to him. Matters were smoothed over by the time *Discovery* and *Resolution* sailed away from the bay of Tongatabu after Captain Cook made up in part for his diplomatic lapses by presenting the people with a bull and cow, three goats, a horse and mare, a ram and two ewes and a pair of rabbits.

The ships weighed anchor for Tahiti, where they were loaded with all the stores they could hold. Captain Cook then revealed to his officers and crews the true purpose of his third voyage. Parliament had secretly offered a prize of twenty thousand pounds for the discovery of a Northwest Passage through the ice at the top of the American continent. If they pushed to within one degree of the Pole, they would receive an additional five thousand pounds. The money would be divided among all the men of the expedition.

In search of the long-dreamed-of shortcut to China, the expedition sailed across the Pacific and arrived off the American coast on March 7, 1778. Winter gales were blowing, but the weather soon cleared and Ledyard and others went ashore at Nootka Sound on Vancouver Island. Ledyard was overcome by a sense of homecoming, a shock of recognition of himself as an American, not merely an English subject. At that moment even the Indians, though different in appearance from those of the Six Nations, seemed like fellow citizens. "I had no sooner beheld these Americans," as he wrote five years later, "than I set them down for the same kind of people that inhabit the opposite side of the continent."

From that moment, perhaps, he began thinking of what Cook's discoveries could and should mean to his own country. The feeling of kinship wrenched at him in a way he found it difficult to explain to himself: "This was the first fair opportunity I had of examining the appearance of those unknown aborigines of North-America. It was the first time too that I had been so near the shores of that continent which gave me birth; and though more than 2000 miles distant from the nearest part of New-England I felt myself painfully affected. All the affectionate passions incident to natural attachments and early prejudices played round my heart, and I indulged them because they were prejudices. I was harmonized by it."[7]

Charting the waters as they went, the voyagers sailed north along the Canadian and Alaskan coasts seeking a passage to the Atlantic. Their next landfall was at Unalaska, where evidence of other white visitors — an old pair of plush breeches and a black waistcoat — served as the first hint that Russian fur traders had arrived before them. Until now the Russians had wisely kept secret the fact that they had found a bonanza in the fur trade along the northwestern coast of North America. Ledyard volunteered to go with native guides in search of whatever white men might be in the neighborhood. Unarmed, carrying brandy and bread to sustain him, Ledyard followed the guides over rough country until they came to a small bay on which were located several huts. At that moment two white civilizations, for good or ill, were about to meet at the top of the world.

Two men came out of the huts and escorted him to one of them. Under the lamplight within, "I discovered that the two men who held me by each arm were Europeans, fair and comely, and concluded from their appearance that they were Russians, which I soon found to be true . . ." The Russians overwhelmed him with hospitality, insisted that he change out of his wet uniform into garments of blue silk, fur robe and boots. "We had supper which consisted of boiled whale, halibut fried in oil, and broiled salmon." From his hosts, mostly through the use of sign language, he learned that about thirty fur traders came over to the Alaskan coast every year from Kamchatka to pick up the winter's catch.[8] He also caught a glimmering of the wealth waiting to be exploited in this traffic, and the first nudgings of his great and obsessive idea — the opening of trade between America and China. Along the Alaskan coast were trapped sables, foxes, ermines, beavers, sea otters. Pelts which could be bought from the natives for a few cents worth of iron were sold for sixty dollars on the Siberian market, a hundred dollars on the Chinese. Soon this trade, with its enormous profits, would attract the attention of all the great mercantile nations. But Ledyard began to see how it could especially benefit the Americans: pelts to China, where every mandarin must robe himself in fur, and Chinese products in exchange for them.

The Russians on Unalaska Island realized immediately what the intrusion of the English voyagers meant. They hastened back to their Siberian trading posts to send word to the provincial capital at Irkutsk warning that other nations would soon be invading the hunting and trapping grounds of the North Pacific, and thus caused Imperial Russia to expand westward in hopes of warding off the invasion.

Meanwhile *Discovery* and *Resolution* were sailing off to the Sandwich (later Hawaiian) Islands, where tragedy awaited. Cook had called there before and was regarded as a god by the natives, but his attitude toward them was frankly stated by Ledyard in his published journal: "Cook's conduct was wholly influenced by motives of interest." The presumed theft of a ship's boat enraged Cook, who did not understand the Pacific islanders' carefree attitude toward property rights, and he reacted in the same way as he did in the Society Islands when the peacock was stolen. Subsequently it was learned that the ship's carpenter had moved the boat under the bows without telling anyone, and Cook released the chief he had placed under arrest. However, the bad feelings that arose over the incident could not be smoothed away. "It was evident," wrote Ledyard later, "that our former friendship was at an end, and that we had best hasten our departure to some different island where our vices were not known, and where our extrinsic virtues might gain us another short space of being wondered at, or as our tars expressed it, of being happy by the month."[9]

The theft of *Resolution*'s cutter touched off the final, and fatal, explosion of Captain Cook's temper. He led a shore party consisting of himself and six Marines, including Corporal Ledyard, to the native town on Karakakooa Bay with the intention of taking the king into custody until the cutter was returned. A crowd gathered menacingly around the royal pavilion as Cook led the king out of his quarters. "Some of the crowd," Ledyard recalled, "now cried out that Cook was going to take their king from them and kill him." The natives began attacking with stones, spears and daggers as Cook's shore party reached the water. The king was released, but that didn't placate his subjects. The Marines opened fire and were quickly engulfed as they struggled toward their boat. Four of Ledyard's comrades were killed, and Cook himself was stabbed to death with an iron dagger he had presented to one of the chiefs. Under a heavy cannonade from *Discovery* and *Resolution,* Lieutenant Molesworth Phillips, Corporal Ledyard and a private managed to escape. That night the Marine guard was given an extra round of grog and sent ashore to recover Cook's body. They returned with a few scraps of flesh, possibly Cook's, left over from a cannibal feast in the hills.

The expedition continued under new leadership to Kamchatka, down the Russian Asiatic coast, and called in at Macao and the port of Canton, where there was a narrow strip along the Pearl River in which the foreign merchants had their "factories." It was the only territory in all of China that was open to foreign trade.

The members of the expedition soon learned that the sea-otter skins they had obtained through barter with the people of Nootka Sound on Vancouver Island were eagerly sought by the Chinese traders, who paid one hundred and twenty dollars for a good pelt which the sailors had bought for a few pence worth of iron. Ledyard and his comrades were not allowed off their ships, since all trading had to be done through the East India Company's factors and accredited Chinese merchants. The British East India Company then held a monopoly in that area. Ledyard did, however, catch glimpses of the splendor and opulence ashore. The vision of what trade with China could mean to his country was forming with clarity and force in his mind.

Discovery and *Resolution* sailed for England and dropped anchor at Plymouth in October of 1780 after being at sea for four years and three months. Ledyard then learned that his native land had been at war for more than four years with the British. His dilemma, apparently, was that he could not hate the British hard enough to take arms against them, nor would he fight against his own countrymen. "I do not know what to write or what I ought to write," he informed a cousin in Hartford. In a subsequent letter he declared that he intended "as soon as possible . . . once more to see America." For the next two years he paced the flagstones of a Marine barrack yard, more or less an honored guest for his services on Cook's last voyage. Late in 1782 he asked for a transfer to the American station, probably with the idea of deserting. He was aboard a frigate which anchored in Huntington Bay, Long Island. Slipping away from the man of war, he suddenly appeared at the tavern in nearby Southold kept by his widowed mother. From there he made his way to Groton, where one of his uncles was in command of Fort Griswold. The surrender at Yorktown occurred a few weeks later, sparing Ledyard the painful duty of bearing arms against the British. Later that year his book *A Journal of Captain Cook's Last Voyage to the Pacific* was published. The British admiralty would take another year to publish its own voluminous records of that voyage.

Now thirty-two years old, Ledyard found himself something of a notable in post-Revolutionary America, referred to as "the Great American Traveler," listened to (but not immediately heeded) by men of growing power, wealth and influence in the newly independent nation. He was blazing with great schemes, eager to push out the sea frontiers of America before the land was fairly won. His plan was to obtain the captaincy of a ship going around the Horn, then up the Pacific coasts of South and North America to Nootka Sound, where he would trade for furs, dispose of them in China, and bring tea, spices, silks and other commodities for the American market. He would stop off in Hawaii to pick up stores and repair any storm damage to his ship. Once he gained enough money from that fur-trading venture to finance himself, he would lead an expedition across the American continent to the Pacific coast and establish a trading post at Nootka Sound. It was essentially the concept that made other men rich and famous, which sent the United States into the China trade, inspired the Lewis and Clark Expedition and led to the establishment of John Jacob Astor's multimillion-dollar fur-trading post at Astoria, Oregon. But the time was not ripe, and John Ledyard was a luckless fellow. It would be a long time before his countrymen realized that he moved forward, against all obstacles, with "his country's future like a pillar of fire before him."

At the moment, however, the new republic's maritime industry as well as its financial structure were debilitated by the Revolution. The trading fleet had been outfitted as privateers and the ships which returned to their home ports of Boston, New York, Salem and New London from that arduous service were now hardly seaworthy. Britain naturally enough had cut off its commerce with the former colonies. The French, recently our allies, were blocking the Caribbean markets to American trade. The new government had so little money that soldiers were rioting for their back pay, and Robert Morris, the Philadelphia banker, was trying to resign as Superintendent of Finance because he was convinced that it was impossible for Congress to pay its debts.

Yet it was the cautious and longheaded Morris to whom Ledyard first recited his plans. The Philadelphian was pessimistic and tightfisted, but he was the only man in the country, Ledyard believed, with the resources to finance his trading venture. There could hardly have been a wider contrast between two Americans of their time: Ledyard, the enthusiast, visionary and adventurer, and Morris, the sedentary naysayer who believed in risking nothing without one hundred percent collateral. Yet it seemed to Ledyard that they hit it off extraordinarily well. He wrote his cousin Isaac, to whom he confided so many of his hopes and disillusionments, that he had talked to Morris twice and expected the banker's conclusive agreement at a third meeting. "What a noble hold he instantly took of the enterprise." He was drawing up estimates of the cost of outfitting a ship for the venture, and was pleased by the fact that he had come up with a figure two thousand pounds less than Morris had believed would be necessary. "I take the lead of the greatest commercial enterprise that has ever been embarked on in this country, and one of the first moment, as it respects the trade of America. If the affair is concluded, as I expect it will be, it is probable that I shall set off for New England to procure seamen, or a ship, or both. Morris is wrapped up in the idea of Yankee sailors."

Later in the same letter, in an appeal that was to characterize so much of his correspondence, he added, "Send me some money for Heaven's sake, lest the laurel now suspended over the brows of your friend, should fall irrecoverably into the dust."[10]

For all the high hopes he roused in Ledyard, the Philadelphia financier withdrew his support several months later. Perhaps Morris was dismayed by the harum-scarum element in Ledyard's character, the wild glint in his eye when the young man spoke of millions and concealed his frayed cuffs. Perhaps Morris decided to appropriate what seemed feasible in Ledyard's idea and discard its proponent, who, after all, could contribute only his mind and body, not the cold cash which convinces a banker that a man means what he says. The only explanation that Ledyard passed along was that Morris "shrunk behind a trifling obstruction" in withdrawing from the proposed voyage.

Instead Morris financed the dispatch of the first American trading vessel in the China trade — the *Empress of China* — with thirty tons of ginseng and furs obtained from American trading posts. Cautiously, with much less chance of profit but also less risk, Morris would send *Empress* around the Cape of Good Hope to Canton instead of around the Horn to Nootka Sound as Ledyard had proposed. When *Empress* sailed on February 12, 1784, from the Battery, a large group of lower Manhattan merchants and shipping men gathered to see her off, and as a newspaper reported, "All hearts seemed glad, contemplating the new source of riches which may arise to this city, from a trade to the East-Indies." Philip Freneau, the "poet of the Revolution," composed an ode for the occasion, which concluded:

> *Thus commerce to our world conveys*
> *All that varying taste can please;*
> *For us, the Indian looms are free*
> *And Java strips her spicy tree.*

The occasion could not have been nearly so heartwarming to John Ledyard, who was then scurrying around the commercial and banking district trying to convince shippers and merchants that the only sensible plan was to send ships to Nootka Sound, pick up furs and take them to China. The Chinese were interested in only one American product then available: furs. Anything else, with the exception of the rare ginseng root valued in Chinese pharmacology, was a waste of cargo space. The money men of lower Manhattan listened, pondered, even read Ledyard's *Journal* but money was too scarce at the moment for anyone to take the large risks he proposed. They turned him down, and he wrote in bitter disappointment that "the flame of enterprise I kindled in America terminated in a flash . . . Perseverance was an effort of understanding which twelve rich merchants were incapable of making."[11]

He decided to take his hopes and dreams to Europe and for the next several years was abroad as a kind of traveling salesman for the China trade. En route to Brest he wrote the faithful Isaac Ledyard: "You see the business deserves the attention I have endeavoured, and still am striving to give it; and had not Morris shrunk behind a trifling obstruction, I should have been happy, and America would this moment be triumphantly displaying her flag in the most remote and beneficial regions of commerce. I am tired of my vexations."

Somehow Ledyard managed to live off those hopes and vexations. In the winter of 1784–1785 he was making do with a subsidy granted him by merchants in the French port of Lorient who were interested in his proposals. Their interest flickered out — so they told Ledyard — but a year later, with the grant of a trade monopoly, they established a post on the island of Mauritius to facilitate trade with the East. By then Ledyard had moved on to Paris, taking a room in St. Germain. He was conscious that he was regarded as "the mad, romantic, dreaming Ledyard" but still determined to make an impression on hardheaded men of business and trade.

Paris just before the Revolution was plentifully supplied with men living by their wits. In this center of knaves, adventurers, tricksters and schemers, Ledyard somehow managed to scrounge a living for himself, though he was vague, in his letters to Isaac, as to just how he raised the rent and food money. "You wonder by what means I exist, having brought with me to Paris, this time twelve months, only three louis d'ors. Ask vice-consuls, consuls, ministers, and plenipotentiaries, all of whom have been tributary to me. You think I joke. No, upon my honour, and however irreconcilable to my temper, disposition and education, it is nevertheless strictly true." He mentioned other penniless Americans living off the land, of whom he had few illusions: "Such a set of moneyless villains have never appeared since the epoch of the happy villain Falstaff. I have but five French crowns in the world, Franks has not a sol, and the Fitz Hughs cannot get their tobacco money."[12]

As a professional diner-out, he was befriended by such sympathetic compatriots as Benjamin Franklin, Thomas Jefferson and Captain John Paul Jones. On the whole they were more impressed by Ledyard than were the men of business and finance. "That excellent man," Ledyard wrote of Franklin, "exhibited all the cheer of good health, the gay philosopher and friendly countryman."

Even warmer was his friendship with the angular, red-haired Jefferson, whom he addressed as "my friend, my brother, my father." There was no doubt that Ledyard exercised a great influence on Jefferson and his later actions as President of the United States. Jefferson, nine years older than Ledyard and ten times as important, being accredited to the French government as United States minister, wrote in his autobiography: "While at Paris I became acquainted with John Ledyard of Connecticut, a man of genius, of some science, of fearless courage and enterprise. He had accompanied Captain Cook on his voyage to the Pacific, had distinguished himself on several occasions by an unrivalled intrepidity, and published an account of that voyage, with details unfavourable to Cook's deportment towards the savages, in the hope of forming a company to engage in the fur trade of the Western coast of America."

Another semipatron to whom Ledyard was extravagantly grateful was the Marquis de Lafayette. "If I find in my travels a mountain as much elevated above other mountains as he is above ordinary men, I will name it *Lafayette.*" He never found a mountain suitable to being named Mont de Lafayette, but it was one of the lesser unfulfilled promises he made to himself.

Judging from extracts of his letters home, Ledyard might have better occupied himself with developing his literary flair, which would have won him more fame and money as a travel writer than as a propagandist for the China trade whose ideas could be appropriated by more cunning and well-heeled contemporaries. Some of the witty candor of his style was indicated in a letter home: "I find at our minister's [Jefferson's] table between fifteen and twenty Americans, inclusive of two or three ladies. It is very remarkable that we are neither despised nor envied for our love of liberty, but very often caressed."[13]

For a time in that hopeful summer of 1785 it seemed Ledyard had found the man who could help him realize those promises, a man whose daring equaled his own and whose resources and influence far exceeded his, Captain John Paul Jones. Probably he was introduced to the naval hero by either Jefferson or Franklin. Under the authority of Congress, Jones was staying in France to collect the prize money he was supposed to share from captured British ships sold by the French admiralty court. Jones's imagination was immediately ignited by Ledyard's proposals, though it was frequently distracted by affairs with duchesses and by other fervent attentions of Parisian society. (Twice, Ledyard reported in letters home, Jones appeared at the Paris Opera with laurel crowning his freckled republican brow.) In their initial discussions, it was agreed they would fit out a ship of 250 tons and man it with forty-five French seamen, with Jones himself as master; would set sail on October 10, 1785, around the Horn and proceed to Hawaii for stores before heading to Unalaska.

The two men, mutually inspiring each other, decided two ships would be necessary. One would be left behind with Ledyard at Nootka Sound as a station ship while Jones with the other would sail for China with their first cargo of furs. Furthermore, Captain Jones, small, softspoken but persuasive, would obtain the necessary financing from Louis XVI. On the return voyage they would import China tea, porcelain and silks which, Ledyard averred, could be sold on the French market at a thousand percent profit. Ledyard wrote Isaac:

"My affairs stand exactly thus. The celebrated Captain John Paul Jones has embarked with me in my expedition; he advances all the outfit himself except the two ships, one or both of which he is now at Lorient endeavouring to procure as lent or chartered by the King of France. He tells me he thinks he shall succeed, and his character is to speak and act with great caution. If he should not succeed, he has with the same caution intimated to me that he will reduce the outfits within the limits of his own private fortune and make the whole independently. Two or three weeks will determine the matter."

A prospectus written by Jones in French detailed for the benefit of the king's advisers and any other interested parties how they estimated a profit of a hundred and eighty thousand dollars. It must have seemed an outrageously optimistic figure, yet a few years later ships in the same trade made that much and more. Jones's optimism matched Ledyard's but it was tempered, as Ledyard noted, by his "great caution." The hero received thirty-five thousand dollars in prize money from the French admiralty but his dash among duchesses and his daring at sea far exceeded his recklessness with money. Jones made a thorough investigation of all the probabilities, found that outfitting a ship would cost three times what he and Ledyard had estimated, learned that two English merchantmen were embarking on the same mission, sought advice on the venture from Robert Morris and was discouraged by him, and even sounded out Spain's attitude to their plan. The American chargé d'affaires in Madrid, Jones said, indicated that "Spain is too jealous to permit any commercial speculation in the neighborhood of California."[14]

The firm of Ledyard & Jones broke up on that discouraging note, and Ledyard once again was bitterly disappointed. "I die with anxiety," he wrote his cousin Isaac, "to be on the back of the American states, after having either come from or penetrated to the Pacific Ocean. There is an extensive field for the acquirement of honest fame. A blush of generous regret sits on my cheek when I hear of any discovery there which I have no part in, and particularly at this auspicious moment. The American Revolution invites to a thorough discovery of the continent. . . . It was necessary that a European should discover the existence of that continent, but in the name of Amor Patriae, let a native explore its resources and boundaries. It is my wish to be that man. I will not yet resign that wish."[15]

Just then another somewhat eccentric sponsor showed up in Paris, the young Sir James Hall, who had heard of Ledyard's project and was enthusiastic about it. Sir James, who became the pioneer in experimental geology, "expressed the highest opinion of the tour I was determined to make, and said he would, as a citizen of the world, do anything in his power to promote it; but I had no more idea of receiving money from him than I have at this moment from Tippee Sahib."

Sir James was a man of his word and found a place for Ledyard on a

British trading vessel which was bound for the northwest coast of North America. In addition, he gave Ledyard twenty guineas to outfit himself for the voyage. Ledyard, displaying that notably feckless strain in his character, used the money for the purchase of two dogs for companionship, an Indian pipe and a hatchet; with these and his immense self-confidence he was ready to tackle the sub-Arctic. "My want of time as well as of money," he explained in a letter to Thomas Jefferson, "will prevent my going otherwise than indifferently equipped for such an enterprise."

The daring of Ledyard's new plan was breathtaking, as described by Colonel William Stephens Smith, secretary to the American legation in London, in a letter to Secretary of State John Jay. Ledyard would land on the northwest coast, "from which he means to attempt a march through the Indian nations to the back parts of the Atlantic states, for the purpose of examining the country and its inhabitants." His solitary trek would be the reverse of the Lewis and Clark Expedition which the United States government later mounted at enormous expense.

But once again his plans were thwarted by circumstances. The frigate *Trumbell* on which Ledyard was sailing for America was just clearing the mouth of the Thames when a revenue cutter came out from the customs house. The ship had departed without settling certain customs fees and was forced to return to her dock, with everything on board seized. "Everything, all my little baggage, shield, buckler, lance, dogs, squire — all gone. I only am left — left to what?" he lamented in a letter to cousin Isaac.[16]

He was stripped of his possessions, except the dogs which were returned to him, but his incredible determination remained. Taking up a suggestion made by Jefferson during their talks in Paris, Ledyard now proposed — all but penniless as he was — to make his way across Europe to St. Petersburg, then across Russia to Kamchatka, where he hoped to board a fur-trading vessel for the Alaskan coast. Ledyard had jumped at the idea, as Jefferson related. "I suggested to him the enterprise of exploring the western part of our continent, by passing through St. Petersburg to Kamchatka, and procuring a passage thence in some of the Russian vessels to Nootka Sound, whence he might make his way across the continent, and I undertook to have the permission of the Emperor of Russia solicited. He eagerly embraced the proposition."

Driven on by his monomania, Ledyard departed from London in December 1786 after writing a last letter to his cousin. "I dare not write you more, nor introduce you to the real state of my affairs. Farewell! Fortitude! Adieu." He had little more than a letter of introduction from Jefferson to the French minister in St. Petersburg which characterized Ledyard as a man of "much singularity of character" of the kind necessary to "undertake the journey he proposes." His purse contained less than ten guineas.

Undismayed by the grim winter of northern Europe, he journeyed to

Hamburg, then to Stockholm, determined to take the shortcut across the ice from Sweden to Finland; the alternative was to wait until spring and cross by boat, but Ledyard was obsessed by the need to hurry, convinced that other nations would win the riches of the Pacific trade and the territories of the Northwest if he did not stake out the American claim. (Jefferson, of course, shared in this view.) He got halfway across the Gulf of Bothnia on the ice when open water yawned before him.

Still he would not give up. He returned to Stockholm and began walking over icebound trails the twelve hundred miles to St. Petersburg, up through Swedish Lapland, through Swedish Finland and finally through Russian Finland until finally he reached his goal seven weeks later, early in March 1787. On the journey he was sustained by a diet of bread, milk and salt herring and the hospitality of the few people he met along the way. His spirits apparently were undiminished by the ordeal. "I had a letter from Ledyard lately," Jefferson wrote a friend three months later. "He had but two shirts, and yet more shirts than shillings. Still he was determined to obtain the palm of being the first circumnambulator of the earth. He says, that having no money, they kick him from place to place, and thus he expects to be kicked around the globe."

After weeks of waiting around the Russian capital, he finally obtained a passport of sorts allowing him to travel toward the Russian Maritime Provinces. The first stage of the journey, three thousand miles to the trans-Ural province of Barnaoul, he traveled in a three-horse *kibitka* with a Scottish physician employed by Empress Catherine. From there to Irkutsk, the fur-trading center, he accompanied the government couriers, "driving with wild Tartar horses over a wild and ragged country; breaking and upsetting *kibitkas,* beswarmed with mosquitoes; all the way hard rains; and when I arrived in Irkutsk I was and had been for the last forty-eight hours wet through and through, and covered with one complete mass of mud." From Irkutsk he traveled down the Lena to Yakutsk with a government expedition.

In the journal he kept of his Siberian travels he noted the almost desperate quality of Russian hospitality, that "they crowd their tables with everything they have to eat and drink; and not content with that, they fill your wallet. I wish I could think them as honest as they are hospitable. The reason the commandant did not show his wife was because he was jealous of her." Wise commandant, in that Siberian garrison, because Ledyard was a formidable womanizer by all accounts.

For all his haste, it was September 18 by the time he reached Yakutsk, the Siberian winter was closing in and the first snows fell. Once again circumstance had sandbagged him, for he could never reach the Russian Pacific ports now. "This is the third time," he wrote in his journal, "that I have been overtaken and arrested by winter; and both the others, by giving time for my evil genius to rally his hosts about me, have defeated the enterprise. Fortune, thou hast humbled me at last, for I am at this moment the slave of cowardly solicitude, lest in the heart of this dread winter there lurk the seeds of disappointment to my ardent desire of gaining the opposite continent."[17]

Ledyard humbled? Not for more than a moment, while he reveled in his role as Fortune's Fool. He had a lively sense of melodrama, and a justifiable conviction that he was cast for a leading part in the world's affairs. Often, in his letters and journals, he stands back and views his own performance with a grave approval, at other times with a sardonic smile. Until the second Great American Traveler, John Lloyd Stephens, came along, no one carried off his misadventures with so much grace, so lively a humor as John Ledyard.

Early that spring he was dealt a blow which even his sense of humor found it difficult to sustain. On orders from Empress Catherine, he was arrested on a charge of being a French spy. "I had penetrated through Europe and Asia almost to the Pacific Ocean, but in the midst of my career I was arrested as a prisoner to the Empress of Russia . . . I was banished from the empire, and conveyed to the frontiers of Poland, six thousand versts from the place where I was arrested."

At the Marquis de Lafayette's request, the French ambassador to Russia, Comte Ségur, investigated the reasons for Ledyard's banishment, and wrote: "He was at first very well received, but the Empress, who spoke to me on the subject herself, observed that she would not further a journey so fraught with danger as that he proposed to undertake, across the unknown and savage regions of northwestern America. . . . Possibly this pretext of humanity advanced by Catherine only disguised her unwillingness to have the new possessions of Russia on the western coast of America, seen by an enlightened citizen of the United States."[18]

Ledyard almost collapsed from exhaustion from his hurried trip out of Russia, under armed escort, but (as he wrote cousin Isaac from London) "my liberty regained and a few days rest among the beautiful daughters of Israel in Poland" restored his health.[19]

Almost immediately after his return to London, he was enlisted on yet another exploration, this time African. He called on Sir Joseph Banks, the wealthy botanist and promoter of science and exploration, who sent the first colonists to Australia. Sir Joseph had befriended him on a previous stay in England, and wanted to know whether Ledyard was willing to give up his preoccupation with American ventures for the time being to take on an exploration being launched by the newly organized Association for Promoting the Discovery of the Interior Parts of Africa. Ledyard, always willing to take up a new venture, agreed.

"When can you be ready?" Sir Joseph asked.

"Tomorrow morning," replied the irrepressible Ledyard.

On funds raised by subscription by the association, Ledyard took on the assignment — the first of many solitary travelers Sir Joseph Banks sent to explore Africa, including the intrepid German John Lewis Burckhardt, most of whom lost their lives. On his sketchy map of the continent Sir Joseph traced a line of exploration from Cairo to the headwaters of the Nile to the Niger. Ledyard would proceed to Cairo and hire whatever natives, buy whatever supplies he thought necessary for the venture.

On his way east Ledyard stopped off in Paris to see Thomas Jefferson, who was bitterly disappointed that Ledyard was temporarily abandoning his efforts to explore America on foot from coast to coast. Jefferson was now as transported by Ledyard's dream as Ledyard himself, and evidently he spoke rather harshly to him about the new project undertaken under English auspices. Ledyard wrote him from Cairo recalling that "you thought hard of me for being employed by an English association, which hurt me very much while I was at Paris . . . You are not obliged to esteem me, but I am obliged to esteem you, or to take leave of my senses, and confront the opinions of the greatest and best characters I know of." Later Jefferson, swallowing hard on his disappointment, wrote James Madison that Ledyard "promises me, if he escapes through his [African] journey, he will go to Kentucky, and endeavour to penetrate westwardly to the South Sea."

Egypt under Turkish rule appalled Ledyard, but he was determined to carry out the directives given him by Sir Joseph Banks. On November 15, just before his thirty-seventh birthday, he wrote Jefferson again to report that he had completed plans for the first stage of his journey southward, and evidently for once he was not greatly confident of the result. "I travel from here Southwest about three hundred leagues to a Black King. Then my present conductors leave me to my fate — beyond (I suppose) I shall go alone. I expect to cut the continent across between the parallels of 12 and 20 North Latitude. I shall if possible write you from the kingdom of this black gentleman. If not, do not forget me . . . I shall not forget you. Indeed it would be a consolation to think of you in my last moments. Be happy."

The repeated delays in departure of the caravan which he was to accompany to Sennar enraged him — fatally, it seems from the fragmentary report of his death which reached Jefferson. "Mr. Ledyard took offense at the delay and threw himself into a violent rage with his conductors, which deranged something in his system that he thought to cure by an emetic, but he took the dose so strong as at the first or second effect of its operation to burst a blood vessel — in three days he was suffocated and died."

If he almost literally died of impatience, it was an ironically fitting end in its way. It was of a tragic piece with the rest of his life. In hot haste, in headlong impetuosity, he had tried to persuade his countrymen of the accuracy of his vision of what America could become. For the most part they had ignored him — but not his ideas. Other men benefited, and there was only Jefferson — and perhaps a few others of lesser renown — to testify that John Ledyard was not only a Great American Traveler, an adventurer whose feats have seldom been equaled in our history, but a forerunner of our Pacific destiny.

2

Opium for the Pipes of China

In the older era of imperialism, when people liked to think they conducted themselves in a businesslike way, men of affairs often hooked their thumbs in their vest pockets, cleared their throats and solemnly proclaimed, "Trade follows the flag." They had their priorities confused. The flag, in fact, often followed trade — and before trade usually came the solitary adventurer, the articulate man with a vision. It was John Ledyard's role to inspire the one man who could clothe his visions with the reality of achievement: Thomas Jefferson, who became President at the turn of the century which saw the general expansion of the West into Asia.

Ledyard made Jefferson see that there was a great pressure of time and events on bringing about American participation in the race for Eastern trade. Through his influence on Jefferson, he was able posthumously to "take the country by the shoulders and make it turn right-about-face, toward the West." Ledyard was a saltwater sailor while

Jefferson was instinctively a landlubber engrossed in his initial conception of the new States as a self-enclosed agrarian republic. Jefferson was an Anglophobe, with some of Washington's fear of involvement in the quarrels of the European nations. He hated the Atlantic as a "breeder of wars." This view was not measurably broadened by his service in Paris as a glorified consul-general arranging trade and friendship treaties. He had gone abroad with hopes of bringing about an Anglo-American reconciliation, but England's actions convinced him of her continuing enmity. He was glad of the Spanish outposts on the Mississippi if only because Spain was too weak to be a menacing neighbor.

Even before he met Ledyard, Jefferson, as a member of Congress, had given much thought to expansion of the United States's holdings on the American continent. In December of 1783, more than a year before he met Ledyard, he wrote General George Rogers Clark that he had heard reports that the English were planning explorative efforts west of the Mississippi and believed that the United States should move in the same direction. "I find they [the English] have subscribed a very large sum of money . . . for exploring the country from the Mississippi to California. They pretend it is only to promote knowledge. I am afraid they have thoughts of colonizing in that quarter. Some of us have been talking here in a feeble way of making the attempt to search that country, but I doubt whether we have enough of that kind of spirit to raise the money. How would you like to lead such a party?" Exactly twenty years later Jefferson, as President, was sending the general's younger brother William with Meriweather Lewis on the Lewis and Clark Expedition into the West.

During Jefferson's second term, a Chinese merchant visiting New York found it difficult to return to his homeland because of the current embargo and appealed to Jefferson personally for his help. President Jefferson, in the earliest known official opinion on relations between America and China, asked that the Chinese be given a special passport and gave as his reason the fact that such a favor would indicate to the Chinese that Americans were friendlier to them than the English. China, he wrote Secretary of the Treasury Albert Gallatin, thus would understand "the difference between us and the English, and separate us in its policy." It would also be "likely to bring lasting advantage to our merchants and commerce with that country."

Even more positively Jefferson worked to forge the trans-Pacific link through the Louisiana Purchase. The same year he acquired that million square miles of territory (1803) he was secretly urging on Congress the exploration of the land west of the Mississippi. He also persuaded John Jacob Astor, the German-born fur merchant, to establish a trading post in the Northwest. Private enterprise, he believed, must undertake those projects too expensive or risky for the government. In 1813 he wrote Astor a congratulatory letter on his activities, declaring them the "germ of a great, free and independent empire on that side of the continent" and predicting that "liberty and self-government from that as well as this side will ensure their complete establishment over the whole." Even that vast and imaginative concept was only part of his view of America spreading herself on the canvas wings of her trading vessels to span the Pacific.

Much as he owed him for that concept, Jefferson in later years wrote that Ledyard was "a person of ingenuity" but "unfortunately had too much imagination."[1] It was Ledyard's vision, however, which awakened American merchants and shippers to the possibilities of the China trade, particularly after the theories he expounded in his published journals were supported by publication of Captain Cook's official records of his last voyage. Until then America had never sent a ship around Cape Horn and into the Pacific, nor had any American ship made the much easier passage around Africa and the Cape of Good Hope. Americans had refrained from trading east of Suez because that was regarded as the preserve of the British East India Company. Victory in the Revolution meant that at last Americans could trade where they pleased, and in almost that moment Ledyard had come home from Captain Cook's last voyage to describe the Pacific in the most alluringly poetic terms and beyond that to indicate how that ocean and its shipping lanes could become America's *mare nostrum*.

The mercantile leaders of New York, Boston and Salem, having satisfied themselves that Ledyard's evangelizing was not the fever-dream of a madman, began plunging into the Oriental trade as soon as their ships were refitted from the privateering ventures they had undertaken during the Revolution. A group of Bostonians outfitted the *Columbia* and the *Lady Washington* and sent them around the Horn to Nootka Sound in the year Ledyard died in Egypt. Their presence on Vancouver Island among the English and Spanish trading ships in the sound was ignored in London and Madrid, but the viceroy of Peru saw those two American ships as the forerunners of a busy future. "We should not be surprised," he wrote. ". . . Much more wandering about may be expected from an active nation, which bases its hopes on navigation and trade; and in truth it could hold the riches of Great China and of India, if it succeeds in establishing a colony on the western coasts of America."[2] In the next season five more United States ships sailed for the Pacific Northwest, and within the decade five hundred thousand dollars worth of otter pelts were being taken to the Chinese market every year, just as Ledyard had urged.

The more direct trade with China was given a strong impetus by the voyage of the *Empress of China*. The 360-ton privateer refitted and financed by Robert Morris and his associates was sent to Canton, as Morris wrote, to "encourage others in the adventurous pursuit of commerce" as well to as bring back a satisfying profit. It took the *Empress* almost six months to reach Canton, even with the escort of two friendly French vessels from the Straits of Sunda. The *Empress* tied up at Wham-

Foreign Trade Zone at Canton (courtesy of Peabody Museum, Salem)

poa, the anchorage on the Canton River twelve miles below Canton, on August 28, 1784, and found the Chinese disposed to be hospitable toward the newest of the trading nations. The Chinese merchants were quick to note a difference between English and Americans even though they spoke the same language. Samuel Shaw, supercargo on the *Empress* and shortly thereafter the first United States consul in China, reported a conversation with one of the "hong" merchants authorized to deal with foreigners.

"You are not an Englishman?" the Chinese asked.

"No," Shaw said.

"But you speak English word," the Chinese said, "and when you first come, I no can tell difference; but now I understand very well. When I speak Englishman his price, he say, 'So much — take it — let it alone.' I tell him, 'No, my friend, I give you so much.' He look at me. 'Go to hell you damned rascal. What? You come here, set a price on my goods?' Truly, Massa Taipan, I see very well you no hap Englishman. All Chinamen very much love your country."

Shaw was gratified by the merchant's willingness to distinguish between the rude English and the amiable American, but the Chinese shrewdly added, "All men come first time China very good gentlemen, all same you. I think two three more time you come Canton, you make all same Englishman too."[3]

The *Empress* disposed of its ginseng and furs and took on a cargo of 2460 piculs of black tea, 562 piculs of green tea, twenty-four piculs of nankeens, 962 piculs of chinaware, 490 pieces of silk and twenty-one piculs of Chinese cinnamon on the homeward voyage.* On its arrival in New York on May 11, 1785, the *Independent Journal* characterized the venture as a "very prosperous achievement" for Robert Morris and his associates, and the New York *Packet* proclaimed that Providence itself was "countenancing our navigation to this new world." It was one of the first pronouncements, so frequently echoed in the next century, that God Himself looked favorably upon the operations of American business and finance.

Just as important as its cargo of tea, china and silk was the information the *Empress* brought back on the intricacies of doing business in China. The Chinese, regarding all foreigners as devils, barbarians and subhumans, made their transactions as difficult as possible for the merchantmen of the West. Every transaction was hedged with laws, permits, "chops" affixed by the proper authorities. In effect, they were voluntary prisoners during their stay on Chinese territory. They were permitted to set foot on only three tiny enclaves on the South China coast. The Portuguese had a leasehold on Macao, where permits were issued by the Chinese

---

* There were one hundred catties to a picul, and a catty was 1.36 of a pound. Thus a picul was 136 pounds.

government allowing foreign ships to proceed. Wives accompanying sea captains had to be dropped off at Macao; their presence on the Chinese mainland was regarded as intolerable.

The second barrier was the anchorage at Whampoa, above which the larger ships could not, in any case, have navigated. At Whampoa the ships paid their port charges, usually about four thousand dollars for an American vessel. A comprador and interpreter, through whom the captain and supercargo must transact his business with the Chinese merchants, also had to be engaged at Whampoa. Arrangements were then made for a hong merchant in Canton through whom the foreigner had to conduct all his business.

The cargo was transferred to smaller vessels and taken upriver to the compound outside the walls of Canton. There were located the long narrow two- or three-story buildings called factories, where all business was transacted and the captain and supercargo stayed during his brief visit, and the godowns or warehouses. The cargo was either sold or bartered for goods to be lightered downriver for the homeward voyage. No foreigners were permitted to leave the trading compound except on rare occasion to be rewarded with a visit across the Canton River, under escort of a Chinese host, to the flower gardens of Fati. The foreigners had to deal with a designated hong merchant, whether they liked or trusted him or not, whether or not they agreed with the prices for their goods fixed by the Chinese merchants' association (called the co-hong). Back of the co-hong stood the authority of the provincial officials, headed by the viceroy, and back of them was the awesome power of the Imperial Throne. No ship was permitted to leave the Whampoa anchorage without the final "grand chop" of the port authorities which testified that it had satisfied all the requirements of the Imperial government.

All this apparent meddling, the endless affixing of seals and inscription of chops, served the purpose of the Chinese government. It wanted the revenue from trade with the outside world, but even more it wanted to make sure that the trading nations did not expand their present tiny footholds on the Chinese mainland. The fears that prompted this exclusiveness, as history proved, were entirely justifiable.

For some years Americans landing below Canton would be given only the most tantalizing glimpses of Chinese life — the ancient guns anchored in the stone parapets of the Bogue forts protecting Canton, the ungainly junks used in the Chinese coastal trade, the sound of gongs and the smoke of joss papers drifting from the shore, the flower boats in which mandarins dallied with their concubines, the sampans floating by with whole families aboard — all unforgettably strange and exotic. They were as eager to break through the barriers of protocol, Imperial edict and the "pidgin English" behind which the Chinese retreated when foreigners pressed for greater intimacy, as the Chinese with their infinite sense of superiority were determined to keep them in their place.

One young American who defied the Imperial edicts and wandered, in or out of disguise, beyond the foreign compounds discovered a native city of unimaginable vitality, squalor and majesty. He told of "a shrine containing a huge wooden image of a female Buddha painted green," a temple on the grounds of which were "stone-lined tanks of water with immense lotus leaves of four or five feet diameter" and "four enormous statues in gilded wood representing Music, War, Justice and the Medical Art (one hand extended with a pill of the size of a pumpkin between the thumb and forefinger)," and of an impromptu street battle between young ruffians in which "brickbats, bits of wood, the most thoroughly worn-out old shoes, mud and pieces of broken pots" were used as missiles. Beyond the shrines and temples were crooked streets in which "peaceful Chinamen look at you in bewilderment . . . In turning a corner you come in contact with an itinerant seller of live fish in a tub of water suspended from a bamboo over his shoulder. The water from the tub as it capsizes drenches you and the seller, the fish are flopping about the street, the owner heaps upon you unheard of abuse . . . You see that a 'circumstance' is brewing, and away you go at a run."[4]

Such forbidden glimpses of the hidden mysteries of native life beyond the factories only sharpened Occidental appetites for wider privileges in the treaty port. Back home the increased imports from the Orient simultaneously imprinted on the American imagination a picture of barbaric luxury and exotic pleasures as vivid as anything in the *Arabian Nights*. Tangible evidence of that presumed richness — teakwood chests, lacquered tables, jade and ivory ornaments, feather brushes, fans mounted with mother-of-pearl, miniature gold-leafed pagodas — decorated many homes. And as China became less exclusive and foreign sailors and traders were permitted to mingle with the populace they brought back tales even more stimulating, many of which could not be retailed in mixed company. After Ledyard, word of mouth was the chief, unwitting instrument of Pacificist propaganda. It created an alluring picture, partly commercial, partly aesthetic, partly sexual, of what the Orient could mean to America.

1. *King Derby of Salem*

The first American to become a millionaire made his fortune largely in the China trade. Elias Hasket Derby, "King Derby of Salem," descendant of Dorset yeomanry, was the archetypal merchant-venturer of the post-Revolutionary period. He had the face of a Holbein portrait, long-nosed, firm-jawed, with eyes reluctantly lifted from the ledgers and charts on the table at which he posed for his own official portrait. The only eccentric

Countinghouse of a Canton "factory" (courtesy of Peabody Museum, Salem)

thing about him, and he must have regretted it because he had a distaste for anything faintly outlandish, was the inescapable fact that he had one brown eye and one blue. He was a man of caution and probity, with a mercantile reputation as stainless as the snowy white stock around his throat; the Salem counterpart of Houqua, the leading member of the Canton hong, whose integrity matched his own. The two men never met, rich as they got from trading with each other, because they shared an aversion for the sea from which they made their fortunes; both were content to stare out at the world from their countinghouse windows. What made them wealthy was their canny willingness to assume only the financial aspect of the risks connected with their business. That and the bonded value of their word. Elias Hasket Derby was so conscientious about his obligations, personal as well as commercial, that one of his descendants recalls finding in the old family Bible a copy of the codicil to his will, in which was provided: "I Elias Hasket Derby bequeath to my colored child Ebenezer the sum of 20 pounds sterling."[5]

He began accumulating his fortune — and attracting the envy of less able men — during the Revolution when the Derby privateers fattened the family enterprise on British shipping. "Those who five years ago were the meaner people are now, by a strange revolution become almost the only men of power, riches and influence," the Salem diarist Samuel Curwen wrote, with a touch of aristocratic jaundice, at the end of the war. "The Cabots of Beverly who, you know, had but five years ago a very moderate share of property, are now said to be by far the most wealthy in New England; Hasket Derby claims the second place on the list." Derby's province tax, Curwen added, was eleven thousand pounds, "and his neighbors complain that he is not taxed half enough."[6]

Elias Hasket Derby was not entirely a self-made man, though it was he who made the Derby holdings on land and sea swell tenfold on taking over their management. He was the son of Captain Richard Derby, who after profitably commanding ships for other men set himself up in business as a merchant in Salem and by 1775 had acquired a fleet of half a dozen brigs, sloops and schooners engaged in the Spanish and West Indies trade. Elias Hasket took over the management at the beginning of the Revolution after twenty-five years of learning the business in his father's shadow. At forty-four he became head of the House of Derby, and it may be presumed that he was ready, if not impatient, for the task. It was his capacity for detail, according to a Salem historian, which made him preeminent. "He had never been to sea, he never visited any foreign country, but few men in America were more intimately acquainted with the infinite details of foreign trade than he. Also he evidently had a keen instinct for selecting good men to help him. He trusted them, treated them generously, and stood behind them. In return they served him with an enthusiasm and loyalty that has not been forgotten even to this day by the descendants of his captains. He was strictly honest and honorable in all his dealings and fulfilled all his engagements to the letter, and he expected the same treatment from others."[7] Systematic to an unusual degree in an enterprise so full of risk and hazard, he established a school of navigation for young men who wanted to go to sea. Nathaniel Bowditch, who wrote the definitive manual on navigation, was one of his captains early in his career.

But Derby's capacity for detail, his systematizing of all his operations from countinghouse to the distant ports where his captains and supercargoes traded and brought back their cargoes, did not inhibit his appetite for risk-taking. During the Revolution, he expanded the Derby fleet and before the war was over he was owner or part owner of twenty-six privateers engaged in raiding English shipping. If risks must be taken in that chancy game, however, he was determined to minimize them as his letters of instructions to the captains of the Derby fleet suggest. "I have ordered Hallett to throw all Papers over in case he gets taken, but I do not think of losing her as the Schooner sails very fast. If not taken & if he meets an Easterly wind, as it will be the right season of the year for it, he will stand a good chance to get into some of the Harbours on the North Shore . . . At present I have not made Insurance home [that is, on the homeward voyage of the vessel under discussion] as suppose I cannot at this time get it done under 25 per ct. & shall not make any at present for by the last acct. from England it seems they are tired of this unnatural War . . . The times at present are such that I cannot determine what will be for the best, and must therefore leave it wholly to you, not doubting the business will be conducted with care. Should so large a fleet come on this coast in the spring as is talked of, I should think it not best to ship so much to the Northward or otherwise . . . I commit you to the Almighty's protection, not doubting that we shall once more carry on business at Salem in peace and safety."[8]

At the end of the Revolution, Salem was one of the six largest cities in the former colonies. Only New York, Boston, Philadelphia, Baltimore and Charleston had larger populations. The profits from privateering had made her prosperous, and Elias Hasket Derby was determined to preserve that prosperity by expanding from the West Indian trade into the more distant seas. Even before the war ended, he had commissioned the building of the first of the *Grand Turks*, a three-hundred-ton merchantman with twenty-eight gun-ports, fully rigged, manned by a crew of 120. On one privateering venture just before the war ended, the cost of the *Grand Turk* was recovered with the capture of two English schooners and a brigantine. Before it was converted to peaceful purposes the armed merchantman had taken sixteen English ships. Derby, with this profitable patriotism at an end, had to devise ways to employ his fleet. Some pioneered the American trade with Russia, others continued plying the routes to the West Indies. But a ship like the *Grand Turk* was built with larger schemes in mind.

Derby had absorbed the doctrine laid down by John Ledyard in his *Journal* and confirmed by the publication of the reports of Captain Cook's voyages.

He moved a little more deliberately than his rivals in New York, but his *Grand Turk* became the third American ship (after the *Empress of China* and the smaller *Experiment*) to enter the China trade. Scouring the New England countryside for his own cargo, rather than loading his ship with goods taken on consignment, Derby made careful preparations for the *Grand Turk*'s voyage to the Orient. In December 1785, the *Grand Turk* lifted its anchor out of Salem harbor and departed with a cargo valued at slightly more than seven thousand pounds: ten barrels of pitch, ten barrels of tar, seventy-five barrels of flour, six tierces of rice, thirty-five hogsheads of tobacco, forty-nine firkins of New York butter, twenty casks of claret, 483 bars of iron, twelve hogsheads of loaf sugar, fifty cases of oil, twenty boxes of chocolate, twenty-two boxes of prunes, twenty crates of earthenware, twenty-six casks of brandy, 163 barrels of beef, nine casks of ginseng, thirty puncheons of Granada rum, forty-two casks of cognac, seven casks of bacon and ham, seven boxes of English mold candles, fifty boxes of sperm candles, twenty-seven boxes of tallow candles, thirty-two boxes of soap, 478 firkins of New England butter, 579 boxes of cheese, 123 barrels of pork, thirty-eight kegs of beef, twenty-five baskets of aniseed, fourteen hogsheads of New England rum, twenty hogsheads of fish, forty-two barrels of beer, four tierces of bottled beer, four tierces of porter and nine kegs of pork.

The *Grand Turk* stopped off at the Isle of France (Mauritius) in the Indian Ocean, where part of the cargo was sold and replaced in the holds by ebony, ginseng, gold thread, cloth and betel nuts. On July 1, 1786, the *Grand Turk* proceeded to Canton, sailing under tropical skies past Java Head, negotiating the treacherous passage of the Sunda Straits between Java and Sumatra, through the archipelago whose drowsing beauty was to start a glow in so many Western imaginations before and after Conrad, across the South China Sea to the mouth of the Canton River where a Chinese pilot came aboard. At the narrows commanded by the Bogue forts a co-hong official in a long silken robe and pigtail came aboard to examine the ship's papers and share a bottle of Mr. Derby's finest Madeira with Captain West. The *Grand Turk* beat her way up the river to the anchorage at Whampoa, shouldering in among the towering decks of the British East India's merchantmen.

Even before the cargo was discharged Captain West and his crew were acquainted with the Eight Regulations, which haughtily set forth that the "foreign barbarians" were not permitted to leave the factories on shore "except on the 8th, 18th and 28th days of the moon," when "they may take the air in the company of a Linguist to visit the Flower Gardens and the Honam joss-house, but not in droves of over ten at one time"; that they were forbidden to "sell to rascally natives goods subject to duty, that these

may smuggle them and thereby defraud his Celestial Majesty's revenue";
and that "neither women, guns, spears, nor arms of any kind can be
brought to the factories."

The Hoppo, or chief port official, accompanied by his retinue, came
aboard the *Grand Turk* in short order and laid down the principals of the
"cumshaw" system. Cumshaw was known in the Latin American trade as
mordita, the little bite; it was simply a formula for bribing His Celestial
Majesty's officials in accordance with their rank and influence. Fifty percent of the duty to be paid to the emperor's treasury was the Hoppo's
cumshaw. Ten percent went to the superintendent of the treasury for his
goodwill. Another ten percent had to be allotted for "transport of the duty
to Peking and weighing in Government scales." Another seven percent was
added to cover the "difference in weights between Canton and Peking." All
these bits of cumshaw, Captain West was appalled to learn, added up to
thirty-five hundred dollars.

Cumshaw may have seemed a detestable practice to the straitlaced
Yankee skippers, but they paid willingly enough in anticipation of the
profits to be made on the homeward voyage. The *Grand Turk* was loaded
with cargo valued at slightly over twenty-three thousand pounds. Seventy-
five cases of chinaware ("sufficient to floor the ship," as the *Grand Turk*'s
supercargo informed Mr. Derby), 240 chests of Bohea tea, 175 half-chests
of Bohea tea, two chests of Hyson tea, fifty-two chests of Souchong, thirty-
two chests of Bohea Congo tea, 130 chests of Cassia tea.

The *Grand Turk* appeared off Salem one day in May 1787 and found
the whole port awaiting her in a holiday mood. Everyone seemed to realize
that her successful voyage signalized the beginning of great things for
Salem. As she rounded Baker's Island a salute thundered from the cannon
on shore. The *Grand Turk* dipped her sails in response. Practically the
whole population was on hand and cheering while she made her way to
Derby Wharf. Her owner, Elias Hasket Derby, watched the scene from an
office window. Not a cheer came from those thin lips, but he had the best
reason of all to celebrate. According to Salem historians he realized a profit
of more than a hundred percent on the voyage. A more lasting testimony to
the success of that voyage, the Derby fortune having mostly evaporated
with the succeeding generations, is the Grand Turk Punchbowl, which was
decorated with a painting of the ship under full sail and presented by the
Chinese the day before she left Canton, and which still celebrates the glory
of that venture in the Peabody Museum in Salem.[9]

The *Grand Turk*'s successful gamble set off a maritime rush for the
Orient, particularly after word of the size of Derby's profit got around.
There was room for all in the trade, but Derby remained the pace-setter.
By 1789 there were fifteen American ships regularly engaged in the China
trade, five of which came from Salem, and four of these were Derby's.

Now well into his fifties, his enterprises assured of success, Derby gave consideration to that most solemn of matters to the new tycoon: dynasty. The Derby fleet and its expanding establishment ashore must be guaranteed continuity. People had begun calling him "King" Derby, not because of any presumptuous arrogance in his manner but because of his dominance as a merchant-venturer. Certainly his dynastic hopes seemed to be assured by the eight children produced by his wife Elizabeth and by the Derbys' intermarriage with other leading Salem families. They were closely allied to the Crowninshields, the descendants of a German-born doctor, Johannes Casper von Richter von Crowninsheldt, who (according to family legend) was forced to migrate following the unfortunate results of a duel. Elias Hasket Derby, Sr.'s wife was a Crowninshield, and one of his sisters had also married into the same family. Captain George Crowninshield, his brother-in-law, headed the family shipping firm next in importance to the Derbys', but their cooperation in business matters ended acrimoniously over a lawsuit. The Crowninshield wharf, located next to Derby's, was built too far out into the channel, according to the Derby contention. A long court battle ensued, at the end of which Crowninshield was forced to cut twelve feet off the end of his wharf, and he and his brother-in-law stopped speaking. With or without the Crowninshields, Elias Hasket, Sr. felt that he and his family would be able to maintain their supremacy in commerce. Three of his five sons joined in the family enterprise, and all three of his daughters obligingly married Derby captains (Nathaniel West, John Prince and Benjamin Pickman).

The first of King Derby's sons to be propelled into the business was his eldest, Elias Hasket, Jr., who was graduated from Harvard in 1786. He journeyed to Europe as a passenger on the Derby ship *Astrea,* which was calling at Baltic ports, and spent a year on his grand tour. When he returned to Salem, his father introduced him to the tall desks and thick ledgers of the counting rooms, where he was given a short course in the House of Derby's methods of doing business in foreign parts. There was no nonsense about serving an apprenticeship when it came time for Elias Hasket, Jr., to assume executive status. He was given command of the *Grand Turk.* Her old captain, Ebenezer West, was offered the post of sailing master of the merchantman but declined the responsibility of navigating without the authority of full command, so the first mate, John Williamson, was given the job. Elias Hasket, Jr., was only twenty-two but he soon proved himself a shrewd and active trader.

He took the *Grand Turk* to Port Louis on Mauritius, arriving at the island in the Indian Ocean in February 1788 with a cargo of wine, sugar, candles, meat and fish, butter, cheese and rum valued at twenty-eight thousand dollars. Mauritius was now booming and trade was brisk. The young man not only disposed of his cargo at a good profit, but was offered thirteen thousand dollars for the *Grand Turk* by a French merchant on the island. Like all Derby captains, he was empowered by his father to act as

"Grand Turk I," pride of the Derby Fleet (courtesy of Peabody Museum, Salem)

he thought best in the interests of the House of Derby; and like most Derbys, he was not sentimental, not even about the pride of the Derby fleet. The *Grand Turk* may have been the capstone of the Derby fortune, but he sold her and used the proceeds to buy the ship *Peggy* and the brig *Sultana.* He loaded the two new ships with cargo and proceeded to Bombay, where he traded for cotton. Pirates raided the port while he was taking the cotton aboard and young Derby had to flee with his two ships half loaded. Returning to Mauritius, he sent the *Peggy* back to Salem with a full cargo of cotton. The *Sultana* was sold in Calcutta at a profit, and the crown prince of the House of Derby returned home, after three years learning his way around the shipping lanes, ports and trading centers of the Indian Ocean. There had been no immense profits on his ventures, but he had accomplished something more important by establishing the Derby interests in India and on Mauritius.[10]

It took iron nerves and a stout heart for a shipping magnate to survive in those times when communications were slow and a man's whole fortune might be "afloat on the Far Eastern seas." He was matching his comparatively frail ships against typhoons, pirates lurking off most of the chief Oriental ports, sudden decline in demand for his goods in faroff places where he could have no idea of market conditions, and many other factors. Derby, Sr., and other merchants shared the necessary risks as much as they could. His captains, in addition to their three-pounds-a-month salaries, were allowed to carry five tons of cargo to be traded on their own account. When Derby commissioned his second *Grand Turk* — a three-decker of 560 tons built along the lines of an East Indiaman — he loaded her hold with many tons of merchandise shipped on consignment by other Salem merchants on her first voyage direct to Calcutta. This varied cargo even included a phaeton complete with harness and trappings which a Salem carriage builder hoped might attract the eye of a maharajah in the Punjab. Derby also succeeded in obtaining insurance for six thousand pounds — only part of the value of the ship and its cargo — from a firm of New York underwriters.[11]

Wealthy as he was becoming, Derby continued to keep his eye on every detail of his ships' operations, and when the second *Grand Turk* was sent on her way under Captain Benjamin Hodges its master received a letter of instructions: "Never suffer any *spirit* to be drawn after night — nor at any time on deck . . . Make it a constant practice to have the Chimney of the Galley swept down least by this neglect it might set the Ship on fire . . . Keep the hatches open so as to keep the ship cool & have a wind sail if there is occasion, as heat in the hold will damage the Ship . . . The ship will I suppose load without much on the Gun Deck — let the Ginger, pepper & every light article be on that deck."[12]

When he sent the *Astrea,* commanded by James Magee, to Canton in 1789, he spent six months assembling a cargo for her holds — wine and lead imported from France, iron bars and hemp from the Baltic, fifty-six pipes of wine from France and Madeira, 8933 pounds of candles, 1792 gallons of rum, 32,000 pounds of butter, 6300 barrels of codfish and nine kegs of snuff made in nearby Newburyport, in addition to chests of silver amounting to thirty thousand dollars which three Bostonians were sending abroad (at nine percent commission to the shipper) for trading purposes. Other Salem and Boston merchants also shared in the risks of the voyage. "This system," as one historian of the China trade has written, "not only made it easier to raise the capital for such long voyages, but it created as nothing else could an interest in the products of the Far East. None was so poor but he could make some small speculation in the China trade." The *Astrea* stopped off at Batavia, where trade was conducted in a high-handed fashion by the Dutch, and then proceeded to Canton.

For the first time, in Canton, the House of Derby began dealing with the House of Houqua. The Derby captains and other Americans found Houqua "rather dear, loves flattery and can be coaxed." Nevertheless Houqua was so shrewd and successful a trader that he was rated the richest man in the world. Americans posted in China often recalled how he displayed his friendship and generosity toward a Boston merchant who went bankrupt. Houqua held the man's promissory note for seventy-two thousand dollars. "You and I are No. 1 old friends," Houqua told the American. "You belong honest man, only got no chance." With that Houqua tore up the note.[13] That spirit of amity was to be destroyed, largely because of the greed of the Western traders and adventurers, but not during Elias Hasket Derby's lifetime. They formed a lasting commercial relationship, conducted by intermediaries, that was immensely profitable to both men.

The succeeding voyage of the *Astrea,* in 1791, provided a graphic illustration of the hazards of trading in the Orient. She had returned to Salem with her holds bulging with tea, chinaware, silks and ivory carvings, which Derby and his associates disposed of at a sizable profit. Under Captain John Gibaut, the *Astrea* then was dispatched on another trading mission to the Far East. She stopped at the Cape of Good Hope, Mauritius and the Coromandel Coast of India. Then she proceeded to Colombo, called at Madras and picked up freight bound for Rangoon. The Burmese port was found — too late — to be in turmoil, and before the *Astrea* could lift anchor she was seized by the sultan of Pogu, who was hastily mounting an expedition against Siam. Captain Gibaut and his men were interned for the duration. More than a year later the *Astrea* was returned to him, but in such wretched condition that he could only sail her to Calcutta and sell her. The voyage was a total loss.

Fortunately for Derby, his family and associates, there were few such disasters. On some voyages they cleared profits of seven hundred percent. Derby himself, venturesome in imagination as he was sedentary by disposition, was always seeking new trade routes, new markets to be developed. In

1796 he decided to send his new *Astrea* with her unusually heavy masts, greater spread of canvas and stouter rigging beyond the Indies and China to Manila. He assigned one of his best captains, Henry Prince, to take command of the *Astrea,* and Captain Prince in turn nominated the young mathematician Nathaniel Bowditch to be taken along, nominally as super-cargo but actually as his consultant on navigation. No Salem ship had ever ventured to the Philippines, and Captain Prince felt that he had need of Bowditch's genius.

A new route was explored on this passage. Sailing out of Salem harbor in March 1796, the *Astrea* beat her way to Lisbon, where she took on a cargo of wine, supplies and water, then sailed around the Cape of Good Hope into the Indian Ocean. A favoring monsoon whipped her through the Indies and into the South China Sea, then to Manila, where she disposed of her cargo. It was an uneventful voyage of fourteen months, the *Astrea* returning to Salem in May 1797.

On that voyage, Bowditch, in addition to teaching classes in naviga-tion to the crew, for whom he drew diagrams and charts in chalk on the holystoned decks, developed his method for the accurate determination of longitude, the principles of which were published as *The New American Navigator* in 1802. Later he became a shipmaster and trader, president of the American Academy of Arts and Sciences and an Overseer of Harvard. On his death in 1838 ships in all ports of the world flew their flags at half-mast.[14]

During these years the Derbys, the Crowninshields and the Peabodys were not only merchant princes but "feudal overlords" of Salem, as one historian called them. Elias Hasket, Sr., stately in carriage and generally aloof from all but commercial affairs, remained a rather simple man for all that. One of his few pleasures was sleighing across the ice of Salem harbor with his three daughters. He was so absorbed in business that luxury and fashion had little appeal for him. Early in his career he lived with his family in a house only a few steps away from his countinghouse and Derby Wharf. When great prosperity came to the House of Derby he moved out of the small house on the waterfront to a mansion on Washington Street. Later, at the urging of Mrs. Derby and her daughters, who believed the family should live up to their place in the world, he built the great house on what became Derby Square.

To the end of his days, however, Derby's impassive though discon-certing gaze was fixed on the harbor and the cold gray seas beyond. For him the story of his life was bound up entirely in his ledgers and the logbooks of his ships — and perhaps the names inscribed from time to time in the family Bible. The sardonic title of "King" had little meaning for him; it was neither offensive nor flattering, because the social and civic life of the town back of his wharf and counting rooms was less real than the ships he sent to Rangoon, Calcutta, Canton, Manila, Batavia. Only his business correspondence survives him because that was all he conducted. Until the last day he walked from his mansion to the offices near Derby Wharf, every small boy in Salem knew that whoever spotted a Derby sail entering the harbor and ran to Derby first with the news would receive a new Spanish silver dollar. And if he left anything of worth, it was the careers of many of those small boys who grew up to become Derby captains, often before they were out of their teens: Joseph Peabody, Stephen Phillips, Jacob and George Crowninshield, Benjamin Hodges, Ichabod Nichols and Nathaniel Silsbee, who took command of Derby's *Benjamin* when he was nineteen years old and returned eighteen months later with a cargo sold for one hundred percent profit.

Elias Hasket Derby, Sr., died in 1799, and with him the House of Derby. His heirs divided up the estate and went their separate ways, thus destroying the power of his accumulated wealth. According to one contemporary account published after his death, he had been "the tyrant of his day . . . with his Washingtonian gait, his Sir Roger de Coverly coat and small-clothes, his ample vest and diamond buckles and his gold-headed cane."[15] Yet most people in Salem, while aware that he was wealthy, were surprised to learn that he had become America's first millionaire.

Almost half a century later Nathaniel Hawthorne obtained a sinecure as surveyor of the port of Salem when he settled down to write his novels of decadence, but that was a Salem foreign to Elias Hasket Derby. Salem, with its shallow harbor, soon lost its dominance as a major American port. Its brief hour was memorialized on the city seal, which displayed an East Indian with a parasol under a palm tree and bore the legend "To the farthest port of the rich East." That would have been too poetic a sentiment for Elias Hasket Derby, but it could properly have been carved on his tombstone.

2. *On the Pepper Coast*

By the turn of the nineteenth century scores of American vessels were making the regular run to the ports of the Far East, not only from Salem but New York, Boston, Philadelphia and Providence. The products they brought back from the Indies enlivened American cuisine, brightened interior decoration and influenced feminine dress; until then all had been characterized by a frontier homeliness and utility. Pepper and nutmeg and cinnamon flavoring their food, Oriental curios decorating walls and mantelpieces, silk shawls and gold buttons on ladies' dresses provided tangible evidence of that "richness" Americans imagined was part of all Oriental life, comfortably ignorant as they were of the poverty of the masses which produced them.

At first such luxuries were to be found only in the homes of the wealthy merchants of the seaboard cities, but they soon became available to humbler people as the volume of trade increased. Thus when the *Rising Sun* returned to its home port of Providence in 1793 an advertisement typical of many newspapers in the maritime cities appeared in the Providence *Gazette:* "Fresh Bohea tea of the first quality, in Chests, Half, and Quarter Chests, China, a great variety, Satins, Lutestrings, Persians, Taffetas, of different qualities, black and other Colours. A Variety of fashionable silks and silk and cotton for Gentleman's summer wear, Nankeens, Elegant Satin Shoe-Patterns, Pearl Buttons with Gold Figures, Superfine Lambskins, Ivory and lacquered ware, Tea-Caddies, A large assortment of lacquered Tea-Trays, Waiters, Bottle-stands, etc., etc. Silk Handkerchiefs, Hair Ribbons, Cinnamons and Cinnamon Buds, Black Peppers, 200 boxes excellent Sugar, etc."[16]

The search for distinction among Americans in the post-Revolutionary years naturally found an outlet in the acquisition of Oriental products for the drawing room and kitchen and for personal adornment. The mansions of the wealthy, particularly in the seaboard cities and towns, were turned into museums of Oriental curios. Chinoiserie became the rage as the trade with China increased. The fashion spread to the lower levels of society, and "few were the housewives," a historian of that trade has written, "who could resist the chance to get a lacquer tea-set, some Chinese scrolls, or at least a dozen dishes after the return of one of Derby's ships from the long eastward voyage."[17]

The Orient literally materialized for almost every American, as chinaware replaced pewter dishes, durable yellow-brown nankeens took the place of homespun, tea became a part of the daily life, and silks and satins and crepes — not to mention lutestrings — enlivened many households. A large variety of ornamental plants, including the gardenia, the Cherokee rose (as it was renamed) and the camellia, and of such exotic trees as the camphor and gingko were sent home by traders and missionaries. Benjamin Franklin had forwarded a package of soybean seeds from Paris, to which they had been shipped from China, and urged that American farmers try growing them, but the advice was ignored for almost a century.

A momentary sensation was caused in New York when a Chinese girl with tightly bound feet was placed on exhibition in a theater. In Philadelphia, Nathan Dunn established a Chinese museum in 1839 with displays showing the daily life of the people of Canton. There were life-sized mannequins dressed in Chinese costumes, reconstructions of streets and houses, scenes of farming and manufacturing, exhibitions of the work of Chinese artisans, which were viewed by thousands of Americans. American and British travelers' accounts of what they saw in China, the journals of sea captains and diplomats, were published and found a receptive audience.

The American merchants trading with the East obligingly functioned as the mail-order houses of the time and accepted the smallest commissions

"King" Derby of Salem
(courtesy of Peabody Museum, Salem)

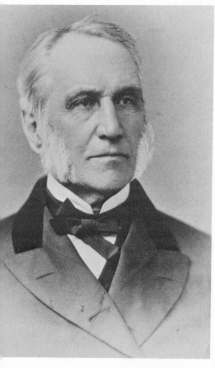

. Peter Parker, missionary-diplomat

Nathaniel Bowditch, master navigator

to satisfy the contemporary hunger for Oriental luxuries. Thus the captain of the *Messenger,* China-bound from Salem, carried with him such shopping lists as that of a Miss Harriet Elkins: "Please to purchase if at Calcutta two net bead with draperies; if at Batavia or any spice market, nutmegs, and mace, or if at Canton, two Canton Crape [*sic*] shawls of the enclosed colors at $5 per shawl. Enclosed is $10." In the same ship's papers at the Essex Institute, Salem, may be found the order of Mrs. Mary Townsend for "one Tureen, 14 by 10 inches, China."

The character of goods exported to and imported from the Far East soon changed and was expanded. This in turn enlarged the importance of the Pacific shores to Americans, widened our vision of that maritime traffic as a matter of national and political, as well as merely mercantile, significance. National pride became involved, the touchy self-esteem of a new country intent on taking its place among the great trading nations of the world, even after it was apparent that the newly united States would have to fight to obtain its self-apportioned share.

Despite the dangers of a renewed conflict with Great Britain over this attitude, and despite the extraordinary hazards then afflicting any American ship on the high seas, American-flag tonnage in the overseas trade increased to nearly a million tons (or by seven hundred percent) between 1789 and 1810, and foreign commerce carried in ships of American registry rose swiftly to the ninety percent level. American aggressiveness on the seas would be a major cause of the War of 1812.

Even while the Constitutional Convention was still sitting in Philadelphia, Phineas Bond, the British agent stationed there, was writing his government that United States ships were bringing tea not only to this country but to European markets the British had staked out as their own. Bond recommended that "an early check or restraint be thrown their way." possibly by "thwarting their credit," in an effort to "perfectly unhinge this trade." In accordance with his recommendations, the representatives of the British East India Company in Canton were instructed to "prevent the subjects of Great Britain from assisting or encouraging in any shape the American commerce."

The expansion of American trade in the Pacific and Indian oceans was not to be stopped by the mere issuance of a fiat. By the turn of the century American ships were plunging into the pepper and spice trade of the Indies, formerly the province of the Dutch and English, vigorously trading in the South Seas, and staking out a claim to Oregon bitterly contested by the British.

For a time Salem and the other American ports diverted their attention from Canton to the "pepper coast" of Sumatra. The demand for pepper and other spices from the East Indies provided a sudden bonanza, the exploitation of which found American traders seizing the initiative. The Dutch and the English each had a trading post on Sumatra, to which the natives brought their products for marketing. The Americans, however, went straight to the source, anchoring their ships in the native inlets and bargaining on the spot with Yankee ferocity, while the Dutch and English waited, with increasing futility, for the Sumatrans to haul their piculs of pepper over the jungle trails.

American merchants awakened to the possibilities of the pepper trade in 1797 when the Salem schooner *Rajah* and its skipper Captain Jonathan Carnes came into New York harbor loaded with the spice (along with an elephant's tooth, a double-stemmed Sumatran pipe and a goblet carved from rhinoceros horn). Captain Carnes realized a seven hundred percent profit on that venture and set off a rush from Salem, which became the capital of the world's pepper market for a time. American skippers naturally avoided the Dutch and British settlements — and the protection they afforded against Malay pirates — and went directly to the *datus* (chieftains) who sold the produce of their followers. It was an idyllic trade. Sumatra is mountainous in the interior, but the native villages on the white sands along the coasts, framed by palms, washed by a warm sea and ruffled by a gentle wind, had a dreamlike beauty.

On trading day, the American captain and his supercargo would go ashore and dicker with the *datu* until a price was agreed upon. A beam balance and weights were then brought ashore by the crew and the pepper was weighed. As Nathaniel Bowditch (commanding the ship *Putnam*, engaged in the pepper trade in 1803) described it, "On arrival at any of these ports you contract with the Datoo for the pepper and fix the price. If more than one vessel is in port, the pepper which comes daily to the scale is shared between them . . . The price in 1803 was ten to eleven dollars per picul; in former years it had been as low as eight, but the demand for it had risen the price considerably, there being near thirty sail of American vessels on the coast. The pepper season commences in January, when they begin to gather the small pepper at the bottom of the vines; in March, April and May is the height of the crop. The best pepper grows at the top of the vines, and is gathered the last . . . Some suppose it is all gathered in May, but I was in some of the gardens in July and found at the top of the vines large quantities which would be ripe in a few days . . . It is sold by the picul of one hundred catties, equal to 136 pounds American weight. What is weighed in the day is paid for in the evening, they being unwilling to trust their property in the hands of those they deal with, and they ought to be dealt with in the same manner, it not being prudent to pay in advance to the Datoo, as it would often be difficult to get either pepper or money of him again."[18]

Why the boom in pepper? Several millions of Americans, after all, couldn't use the hundreds of thousands of pounds imported annually. The records of the customs house at Salem show that much of it was transshipped to Europe, thus further irritating the English. Much was shipped directly from Salem to European ports, and much of the balance to other American ports, where it was used to make up cargoes for Europe. Nearly one hundred and fifty thousand pounds of the pepper brought to Salem by Stephen Phillips on the *Union,* for instance, was transshipped to Europe on two of his brigs, while another twenty-three thousand pounds was forwarded to Baltimore merchants who dispatched it to Leghorn and Trieste. The pepper was particularly valuable in trading with European merchants who disdained such New England products as dried codfish and barrel staves.

It wasn't all pleasure and profit, though, in the pepper trade. The traffic off the Sumatran coast attracted the attention of Malay pirates, who were adept at boarding a trading vessel armed with the short sword called a *kris* and attempting to slaughter the crew. Some of the Sumatrans reasoned that it was foolish to grow pepper, tend the vines, harvest the pods and haul them to a coastal village, when all that work could be avoided simply by capturing an American vessel, killing the crew and taking the money brought in the ship's safe for trading purposes. They manned their swift *praus* and fell upon any ship lulled into a false sense of security by the tranquil waters of a lagoon and the smiling faces of the natives ashore.

One day in 1806 Captain William Story was sitting in the cabin of the ship *Marquis de Somereulas* going over the accounts of several days of trading with the local *datu.* He heard a shout from his first mate on deck that the ship was under attack. The mate had been slashed with the marauders' *krises* and four members of the crew were swinging their cutlasses in defense of their ship. Captain Story grabbed a pistol and started up the companionway, only to be met by his first mate and the four seamen tumbling down the steps in retreat from the pirates swarming over the deck. Captain Story quickly ordered one member of the crew to stand by the powder magazine and blow up the ship if the Malays took it over. Then the captain and his men, armed with pistols and cutlasses, rushed up the companionway determined to fight it out. Unaccountably, however, the pirates had jumped back overboard and were making for the shore in their *praus.* The profits of the pepper trade made up for such risks. On that voyage the *Marquis de Somereulas* cleared $99,751.

Others trading on the pepper coast and up the Malay peninsula didn't get off so lightly. A ship that returned to its American port after a year in the Indian Ocean counted itself lucky if it hadn't been forced to beat off at least one pirate attack. The ship *Putnam,* of which Nathaniel Bowditch became part owner after turning over his command to Captain John Carleton, was lying off Bintang Island, near Singapore, after several days of trading. Captain Carleton was ashore settling his accounts with the local *datu* when a swarm of Malays swept over the *Putnam*'s deck. The second mate and five of the crew were killed; the first mate and several others were badly wounded, but managed to escape with the rest of the crew to a nearby English brig. The pirates sailed off with the *Putnam,* her cargo of pepper and everything else aboard, and she was never recovered.

By 1805 the American market, and its tributaries in Europe, were temporarily glutted with pepper. Captain George Crowninshield and his sons, who formed the second largest trading house in Salem, were threatened with financial disaster under the circumstances because they had sent out their large ship *America* under command of a slightly unreliable relative, Captain Ben Crowninshield. The latter had been ordered to proceed to Sumatra and pick up a full cargo of pepper, and not stop off to trade in other ports as he had made a habit of doing, often to the disadvantage of the firm.

In July, Captain George Crowninshield and his sons kept watching Salem harbor for the *America* to come beating around Baker's Island. One day she was sighted and the senior Crowninshield and his sons rowed out to meet her in the harbor, hoping for once that Captain Ben had disobeyed orders as usual. They caught a whiff of coffee on the warm breeze blowing from the incoming ship.

Captain George picked up his speaking trumpet and bellowed: "What's your cargo?"

Captain Ben, lounging at the rail of the quarterdeck, grinned and shouted back, "Pepper! Isn't that what you wanted?"

"You lie!" his uncle roared back. "I smell coffee!"

The family fortune was indeed saved. On the outward voyage to Mauritius Captain Ben had done enough research among the ships in the harbor and in the countinghouses ashore to determine that huge amounts of pepper were heading west on every vessel, but that not one of them was carrying coffee. Captain Ben disregarded his orders from Uncle George and instead of proceeding to Sumatra he had changed course for the coffee port of Mocha on the Red Sea.

With a similar mercantile agility and shrewdness, the Americans began invading the South Sea islands to satisfy the Canton market, which had been falling off because Westerners had not been able to supply a variety of the goods the Chinese wanted. The epicurean tastes of the mandarins had not been taken sufficiently into account. They wanted bird's nests, shark's fins and *bêche-de-mer* (the sea slug) for their rich soups; sandalwood for its delicate smell; tortoise shell and mother-of-pearl. This demand, the Yankee shippers learned, could be matched with the yearning of South Sea natives for trinkets and iron tools. Marquesans and Fiji islanders could be encouraged to collect the goods which brought a good price in Canton by trading off knives and hatchets made on ships' forges, carved whales' teeth, calico, needles, nails, mirrors, glass bottles. Sandalwood could be gathered in the Sandwich (Hawaiian) Islands, where the ships' crews cut the wood themselves at a cost of one cent a pound and took it to the Canton market for sale at thirty-four cents a pound.

And in addition to the profitability of trading voyages to the South Seas, there were the beauty of the islands and the lubricity of their women. The glamour of those seas was considerably enhanced for an American public by the memoirs of Captain Benjamin Morrell, a Stonington man who took the schooner *Antarctica* into the Pacific in search of *bêche-de-mer* and mother-of-pearl and found a lot more than he hoped for. In his frank account of his adventures, *A Narrative of Four Voyages,* published in 1832, he recalled that rumors of the beauty and availability of the women of the South Seas had decided him against taking his wife on the voyage. He gave in only after "she bathed her pillow with tears at night, and drooped all day like a fading lily."[19] There was much fever and sickness aboard the *Antarctica,* and Captain Morrell succeeded in persuading Mrs. Morrell to stop off in Manila while he proceeded on his way. Calling in at Bergh's Group and Young William's Group, he was inspired to poetic celebration of the island women. Their eyes sparkled, he noted, "like jet beads swimming in liquid enamel," their lips were "just the proper thickness for affection's kiss," and he found it just possible, and not at all onerous, to span "their naked waists with both my hands." And he delicately added that "imagination must complete the bewitching portrait."

Much as he admired the women, Captain Morrell was constantly aware that he was in enemy territory when his ship stopped at one of the islands. Those lips just thick enough for kissing were not untouched by roasted human flesh. Many of the South Sea islanders were cannibals, and the men, smiling and anxious to trade one day, might suddenly appear in force the next, with painted faces, war clubs and a howling determination to kill and feast off the white visitors. The *Antarctica* barely escaped capture at Young William's Group, and a more hazardous experience awaited Captain Morrell and his men on Massacre Island. Morrell set up a temporary trading post on the island, built drying sheds for the *bêche-de-mer* the natives agreed to collect, and had his ship's armorer set up a forge to fashion the axes and iron hoops he would trade for sea slugs.

The shore party of twenty-one men was suddenly attacked by three hundred natives armed with bows and clubs. They fought back with their cutlasses while a whaleboat was dispatched to their rescue from the *Antarctica.* Only seven of the shore party, four of them badly injured by war clubs, were taken off in the whaleboat. The natives pursued the rescue boat in their canoes, loosing flights of arrows until it reached the shelter of the ship's swivel gun, which drove them off. The schooner lay becalmed under windless skies, and Captain Morrell ordered that the ship's magazine be touched off if the natives succeeded in boarding and taking her. Instead, that night the smells of roasting flesh, provided by the fourteen men left presumably dead ashore that afternoon, were wafted over the calm waters to the quarterdeck of the *Antarctica.* During that long and agonizing night, Captain Morrell swore to himself that he would avenge the deaths of the men who involuntarily were providing the occasion for the feast ashore.[20]

He sailed back to Manila, recruited Filipinos to fill out his roster, and bought additional cannon and muskets. On his return to Massacre Island, he opened up on the native village without warning, swivel gun, cannon and muskets all blazing away until, ten minutes later, the village was leveled. Incredibly enough, he then landed at the site of the ruined village and built a fort to protect his men while they gathered sea slugs and cured them under the sun. They were so harassed by the natives, however, that Captain Morrell finally gave up and sailed away.

The *Antarctica* cruised around the South Seas until, somewhere along the way, Captain Morrell found a lovely group of islands to which he was determined to return. He kept the location of the islands to himself; only he knew their bearings, since he locked up the ship's navigational instruments and wouldn't allow any of his officers to use them. He sailed the *Antarctica* back to New York and persuaded a group of merchants to back him in a South Sea trading venture. His new ship was the *Margaret Oakley,* which he sailed out of New York in 1834 with an adventure-seeking young man named Thomas Jefferson Jacobs aboard.

The rest of Captain Morrell's strange story, which reads like the plot of James Hilton's *Lost Horizon* and the quest for Shangri-La, was told by Jacobs in his *Scenes, Incidents and Adventures in the Pacific Ocean.* Captain Morrell, he said, remained secretive about their destination. They cruised through the islands of Australasia until finally they reached the group Captain Morrell had been seeking. From Jacobs's account, they were the enchanted isles dreamed of by poets, with happy and hospitable natives, cool trade winds, lagoons filled with fish, trees dropping their fruit, birds singing all the day. For months the *Margaret Oakley* drifted through the island group, and evidently Captain Morrell had forgotten all about the golden promises he had made to his backers in New York. It almost seemed that he intended to spend the rest of his life cruising among the islands, a project which met with no objections from his passenger or crew. ("Who would change such a life," Jacobs wrote later, "for the toils, and cares, and constant miseries of a moneyed slave?") Finally, however, Morrell remembered his mission and collected a cargo, which he took to Canton. Jacobs left her there. Later he learned that the *Margaret Oakley* had been wrecked in a storm off Madagascar. Instead of returning to the States, Morrell took passage on a ship bound for the South Seas, evidently determined to go back to his paradise, but he died along the way. He was perhaps the first of many to be fatally enchanted by the dreaming, timeless islands of the tropical Pacific.[21]

There were many others who found the South Seas fatally unattractive, particularly if they fell among the Fiji islanders, who had notoriously keen appetites for human flesh, or among other groups where they were taken prisoner and enslaved. The brig *Union* lost its captain and a shore party on its first voyage to the Fijis. On its second visit to the islands the brig was tossed up on a reef during a heavy squall, and its entire company was either drowned or murdered by the natives. When the brig *Juno* ran aground June 20, 1808, the survivors were taken prisoner and enslaved. Most were probably eaten but one, Samuel Patterson, escaped by canoe after being so mistreated that he tried to hang himself with a length of bark. The entire crew of the *Oeno,* out of Nantucket, was massacred in 1827 when the ship was wrecked by a storm.

The high prices brought by *bêche-de-mer* in Canton continued to lure American ships despite these tales of horror. Captain Edmund Fanning, a veteran of the trade, wrote in his memoir that on one voyage he was able to collect enough goods in ninety days to obtain a full cargo of Chinese products in Canton and pay all the port charges. It was all a matter of constant vigilance — and luck — he wrote in *Voyages Around the World.* Every ship that beat its way around the coral reefs of the Fijis, he recalled, was surrounded by fleets of native canoes waiting to pounce if it ran aground, and "if we should be wrecked, immediate massacre was the destiny of all on board."[22]

The same drive for profits, uninhibited by occasional displays of native hostility, impelled American entry into the Northwest fur trade along the lines suggested by John Ledyard. The *Columbia* and the *Lady Washington,* financed by a group of six Bostonians, opened this trade in 1787, surviving a rough passage and an attempted ambush by the Indians (in which one man was killed) at Nootka Sound. By carrying the furs obtained in trade for trinkets to the Canton market, the *Columbia* proved the trade could be immensely profitable. In 1790 Captain Joseph Ingraham's *Hope* collected a cargo of sea-otter furs along the coast of what is now British Columbia, took them to Canton and sold them for thirty thousand dollars. This he invested in tea which he sent to Boston on another ship while he himself returned with *Hope* directly to the Northwest coast. Soon many other American trading ships had joined in the venture, even though every vessel had to be heavily armed and often had to repel Indian war parties. Trade one day, fight the next, seemed to be the formula. But the profits swelled as the ships grew larger.

Probably the largest profit ever turned in this trade was the voyage of the *Pearl* in 1805. Her captain was one of those God-fearing skippers who had risen from the forecastle. John Suter, born to Scottish parents in Norfolk, Virginia, was left an orphan at the age of eight. A Boston pilot took him in, taught him to read the Bible and drilled him in seamanship. Suter, at seventeen, shipped out before the mast. Eventually he worked his way up to mate, supercargo, then captain of the sizable trading vessel *Pearl.* In 1805 he sailed her to the Northwest coast, and on a cargo and ship together valued at about forty thousand dollars cleared a profit of two hundred and fifty thousand dollars. Once the Indians stormed the *Pearl* but he got away to Canton with a cargo of furs, plus sandalwood collected en route in Hawaii, which he traded for more than one hundred and fifty thousand dollars worth of Chinese goods — 480 tea sets (forty-nine pieces each), thirty boxes of enameled cups and saucers (fifty dozen to the box), one hundred chests of Souchong tea, 170,000 pieces of nankeens, ninety-two cases of silks, 235 chests of Hyson tea, fifty blue and white dining sets (172 pieces each), two hundred chests of Cassia and four hundred chests of other teas, and other items. This was sold at auction in Boston for $261,343, and the owners got their ship back in good condition. Captain Suter's share, or "primage" of five percent, was $12,960. He credited his good fortune to daily reading of the Bible, and after seven round-the-world voyages came ashore in Boston, settled down and raised a family.[23]

There were many others, less pious, certainly less fortunate, whose luck ran out and whose bones littered the shores of the fur-trading coast. When the ship *Boston* was wrecked in 1802, for instance, only two members of her crew survived the ensuing massacre.

In 1811 the profits of the trade finally attracted the attention of the first great American capitalist. John Jacob Astor, a butcher's son, migrated to America from Germany in 1783 at the age of twenty. Three years later he started a fur business in New York, and within a dozen years, aided by marriage into the Anglo-Saxon ascendancy, he was a prosperous merchant with scores of trappers and agents in the American hinterland. At the trading posts of his American Fur Company, where Indians brought their skins in exchange for whiskey, there was a "disgusting scene of drunkenness, debauchery and misery," as a United States Army officer reported to the Secretary of War, and whole tribes were demoralized.

Astor extended his operation to the Pacific Northwest by dispatching the ship *Tonquin* to the Columbia River with thirty-one men who were to establish a settlement called Astoria whose permanence would be guaranteed by construction of a log fort, warehouses and living quarters. Astoria, he wrote John Quincy Adams, would be a permanent depot for obtaining furs and "conducting a trade across the continent to that river [the Columbia], and from thence, on the range of the northwest coast to Canton, in China." A short time later, however, the first American outpost on the Pacific, with its link to China, came to grief. The War of 1812 broke out, and representatives of the British-owned Northwest Fur Company came to Astoria with a threat and an offer. The Americans could either sell out or be captured by a British naval sloop on its way to the Oregon coast. Astor's men sold out, but their failure was retrieved through vigorous American diplomacy. At the peace conference at Ghent, President Madison insisted that Astoria be restored to American possession. Oregon itself was still in dispute, attached to a fuse which threatened to explode another Anglo-American conflict in the years to come: the agreement to share possession of all territory bounded by the Russian-claimed land to the north, the Spanish to the south, and the country "westward of the Stony [Rocky] Mountains."

Once again the flag had followed trade.

3. The Opium War

If anyone doubts that history carries the sting of a scorpion, he need only consult that militarily insignificant but morally imperative conflict known as the Opium War. The importation of opium which the Western nations forced upon China a century and a half ago has been returned in kind — and more — through the smuggling of Communist Chinese heroin, opium twenty-five times distilled and twenty-five times more dangerous, to the Western world.

The war itself was largely a British affair, but Americans carried their share of responsibility. Originally the drug was brought to China for medicinal purposes only. Then the Chinese discovered its nonmedical use as an escape from the vexations of life. In 1800, by Imperial edict, the importation of opium was forbidden. Opium, said the edict, was "vile dirt." But so many Chinese had become addicted that the edict — reinforced in 1809 by a law requiring hong merchants to put up a bond guaranteeing they wouldn't handle opium — had no more effect than the Prohibition laws later enacted by the United States.

Ways were quickly found to circumvent the Imperial will. The British East India Company agreed, under pressure from the Chinese government, to give up bringing opium into the country, but continued to license the traffic by a subterfuge, operating through the so-called "country ships." East India Company officials protested that in any case the ten or twelve million dollars worth of opium imported by China annually could hardly ruin a population of two hundred and fifty million; as though the ruin of only a million or two was an inconsequential matter. The East India Company's "country ships" and others engaged in the trade simply anchored off the island of Lintin, at the mouth of the Pearl River; transferred their cargoes of Indian opium to storeships, and from these sold the opium to Chinese traders. In the year 1834–1835 it was reported that thirty-five opium ships were anchored off Lintin and that the money they received for their cargoes exceeded that of the ships engaged in legitimate trade at Whampoa. From Lintin the opium was smuggled upriver on large red junks manned by sixty or seventy oarsmen; these were called "smug boats" and were armed with swivel-guns and muskets to repel the Chinese river pirates. The opium was unloaded at Canton through the bribery of port officials, who in turn forwarded a share of the cumshaw to province officials and on up the line to Peking.

Determining the extent to which Americans were involved in this traffic is a complicated matter, in which statistics understandably are incomplete and contradictory. In his book *The Old China Trade,* Foster Rhea Dulles, basing his conclusions largely on reports of the Select Committee of the British East India Company, which kept a jealous eye on what they regarded as their monopoly, estimated that Americans handled five percent of the opium trade. Between 1818 and 1823 the British transported more than one hundred and four million dollars' worth of opium while the Americans, by British reckoning, sent a little less than five million dollars' worth of the drug. American competition in this respect was limited, not by the proddings of conscience but by the difficulty of obtaining large amounts of opium. The British monopolized the opium raised and processed in India. For Americans, obtaining the drug and shipping it to China was a complicated process, since they had to depend on a meager supply from Turkey.

American entry into the dope traffic began in 1805 when three brigs called in at Smyrna and obtained 124 cases and fifty-one boxes of opium. By 1823 the number of American vessels calling at Smyrna, the exit port for Turkish opium, had increased to eighteen carrying out 1741 chests. Unofficially the Americans established a monopoly on Turkish opium bound for China, and in addition many United States ships carried the stuff on consignment, by arrangement with the British East India Company, from India to Canton.

One authority is convinced that Americans were far more deeply involved in the traffic than any combing of bills of lading or customs declarations could show. "The existence of the trade itself conferred on them [the American traders] a direct commercial benefit, for it reduced the necessity for the importation of specie by the substitution of bills on London. Opium was sold in ever increasing quantities, and the Americans, as well as the English and other foreigners, used the bills thus obtained in place of specie to purchase their return cargoes. In this phase of the opium trade the Americans, all of them, benefited as much as, or more than, the other traders. As the supply of furs began to diminish, after 1820, and while the American cotton trade was in its infancy, the increased importation of opium from whatever country and by whomever transported, was a very important consideration. The system was vicious and short-sighted economically . . . The consumption of opium demoralized the producing and consuming powers of China, led to greatly increased importation of specie, and the ill-will of the people, but when the capital of the American merchants was still relatively small . . . the opium trade, like slaves and distilleries, entered into the foundation of many American fortunes."[24]

It was true enough that the seed-money for a number of early American fortunes was stigmatized by the "blood of the poppy." A Delano, the forbear of Franklin Delano Roosevelt, was captain of an opium packet. The American firms trading in China bearing the commercially and socially exalted names of Perkins, Peabody, Russell, Low, Forbes, all dealt in opium. It was simply good business, port taxes were avoided and the goods were paid for in advance. The American dealing in opium before 1839 was on to a good thing, as William C. Hunter, that oldest of Old China Hands, wrote in his memoir: "His sales were pleasantness and his remittances were peace. Transactions seemed to partake of the nature of the drug; they imparted a soothing frame of mind with three percent commission on sales, one percent on returns, and no bad debts!"

Hunter, who was connected with the Russell firm, provided a detailed description of how the opium trade was conducted with all its niceties and formalities. He sailed as a passenger on the schooner *Rose* in 1837 when she carried three hundred chests of opium. The first stop on the run up the China coast was at the island of Namoa, on the border between Kwangtung and Fukien provinces. A few minutes after the *Rose* dropped anchor she was boarded by a Chinese commodore who dutifully displayed a copy of the Imperial edict prohibiting any foreign vessel from "loitering" in those waters any longer than was necessary to take on supplies and fresh water.

Immediately after performing that duty, the commodore strode into the captain's cabin and inquired how much opium the *Rose* was carrying. The question of cumshaw immediately arose, and was settled in a gentlemanly manner.

The bribe paid, the Chinese official consented to a glass of wine and a cheroot with the captain. At his leisure, the commodore chatted for a few minutes and then was escorted to the deck, from which he descended to his gig. Then he was rowed back to his junk while servants held a silk umbrella over his head and fanned away the flies and mosquitoes.

No other craft dared to approach the *Rose* until that transaction had been completed, but the moment the commodore returned to his junk the schooner was surrounded by the barges of the opium buyers. Before the afternoon was over, the *Rose*'s supercargo had disposed of one hundred and fifty thousand dollars worth of merchandise.

One of the dominant figures in mercantile nineteenth-century Boston was that of Commodore Robert Bennet Forbes. In the post–Civil War years he was director of half a dozen railroad and insurance companies, chairman of the Board of Trade, chairman of the Humane Society, vestryman of King's Chapel, the very model of the Proper Bostonian. Behind it all was the hair-raising youthful career of Captain "Black Ben" Forbes, who went to sea at the age of thirteen in the barque *Canton Packet* owned by his uncles, the mercantile Perkins brothers. Black Ben became one of the most daring of the opium clipper captains, entering the trade in 1828 (when he was twenty-four years old) by taking the brig *Danube* to Smyrna and buying opium with the proceeds from the sale of his cargo of coffee, twenty thousand dollars in currency and a London letter of credit for sixty thousand pounds. He conveyed the opium to Gibraltar, where it was trans-

ferred to his uncles' ship, the *Bashaw*. A year later he took command of
the storeship *Tartar* stationed off Lintin Island to conduct opium transactions for his uncles' firm of J. & T. H. Perkins and the allied firm of Bryant
& Sturgis.

By the time he got around to writing his autobiography Captain
"Black Ben" had transmogrified into the esteemed Commodore Robert
Bennet Forbes, and was inclined to temporize on the morality of the opium
trade. Smoking opium, he asserted, was no worse than drinking hard
liquor; the practice "had a much less deleterious effect on the whole
country than the vile liquor made of rice, called 'samshue.'" The real
reason the Chinese Imperial government opposed it was "the large amount
of specie going out of the country to pay for it." Not quite able to utter a
personal *mea culpa,* he added:

"Dealing in opium was not looked upon by the British government,
by the East India Company, or by the merchants as a smuggling transaction; it was viewed as a legitimate business so long as the drug was sold on
the coast, outside of the professed jurisdiction of China. It was certainly
legitimate in India, where a large revenue was derived from it; it was
certainly legitimate at Singapore, at Manila, at Macao . . . and it would
have been very difficult to draw the line where it became smuggling.

"I shall not go into any argument to prove that I considered it right to
follow the example of England, the East India Company, the countries that
cleared it for China, and the merchants to whom I had always been accustomed to look up to as exponents of all that was honorable in trade — the
Perkins's, the Peabodys, the Russells, and the Lows."* 25

Forbes did not mention the fact that at least two American trading
firms in Canton refused to have anything to do with the "vile dirt." John P.
Cushing of Boston quit participating in any deal involving opium in 1821,
possibly at the urging of Houqua, who foresaw the trouble it was bringing,
and left China seven years later. The trading firm of Talbot, Olyphant &
Co. of New York also refused to touch any transaction involving the drug
traffic. This and its sponsorship of the endeavors of Christian missionaries
soon won for the company the jeering sobriquet of "Zion's Corner."

The strictly commercial love affair between the Chinese and the
Americans and other Westerners began curdling early in the 1820's. The
more the Chinese and their guests saw of each other, it seemed, the less
they liked what they saw. By then sailors, as well as ship's officers and

---

* At begging the question of the morality of the opium trade, Commodore
Forbes was easily outdone by a famous German missionary, the Reverend Charles
Gutzlaff. In 1832 he consented to act as interpreter aboard the opium ship *Sylph*
in exchange for his passage, admittedly after "a conflict in my own mind." Reverend
Gutzlaff explained that he did so because it gave him an "exceptional opportunity"
to distribute his missionary tracts along the coast — while the *Sylph* distributed its
opium. He did not seem to be aware of the fact that opium had become the religion of the people.

supercargoes, were allowed to go ashore and wallow in the grogshops of Hog Lane. *Samshu,* the fiery liquor distilled from rice, often caused riotous scenes. Western seamen assaulted the natives, particularly after they had been fleeced in one of the Hog Lane establishments, and Westerners wandering outside the proscribed area set aside for their entertainment ran the risk of being mobbed as "foreign devils." By Imperial edict, any foreigners who killed a Chinese were automatically to be executed. Extraterritorial rights for visiting nationals had not yet been proposed, but the idea was already being discussed by Westerners, who wanted the right to punish their own people.

Any residual goodwill was severely tested in 1821 when an American seaman, Francis Terranova of the *Emily,* out of Baltimore, was accused of having killed a Chinese woman who came out in a bumboat to trade with the men aboard the ship. The Chinese authorities demanded that Terranova be turned over to them for trial. Captain Cowpland of the *Emily* refused to surrender the man, and was backed in his refusal by other American captains in the port. The merchants in Canton, however, took a different view, fearing the Chinese government in its wrath might terminate their trading privileges. Finally the American residents in Canton arrived at a compromise: the issue would be decided by a committee formed by five captains, five supercargoes (presumed to be neutral) and five merchants. The committee came up with a plan whereby the Chinese would be allowed to hold their trial aboard the *Emily.*

A mandarin appointed as judge by the Chinese authorities padded up the *Emily*'s gangplank, immediately found Terranova guilty and demanded that he be turned over for execution of the sentence: death by strangulation. The Americans balked; the Chinese announced that all trading with Americans was suspended. In the contest between national pride and pursuit of the dollar, the latter was a quick and easy winner. Terranova was surrendered, and strangled. The British were appalled at what they considered American pusillanimity; you had to take a firm hand with the wogs or they'd walk all over you. The Select Committee of the East India Company condemned the Americans for "barbarously abandoning a man serving under their Flag to the sanguinary laws of this Empire without an endeavour to obtain common justice for him." The American merchants eased their consciences by issuing a rather bombastic statement which they asked Houqua to forward to the Chinese authorities:

"We consider the [Terranova] case prejudiced. We are bound to submit to your laws while we are in your waters, be they ever so unjust. We will not resist them. You have followed your ideas of justice, and have condemned the man unheard. But the flag of our country has never been disgraced. It now waves over you. It is no disgrace to submit to your power, surrounded as you are by overwhelming force, backed up by a great Empire. You have the power to compel us."[26]

The Terranova case later became a much-cited precedent in the controversy over the granting of extraterritorial concessions wherever the United States maintained military or commercial bases — a bitter one that has plagued American relations with the Philippines and other countries and has always provoked charges that such concessions are imperialistic. But the United States of the 1820's was not inclined, with its meager military and naval power, to enforce its opinions on distant nations. Washington took no official notice of the Terranova case. American subjects who insisted on doing business in distant parts of the world operated at their own risk. Twelve years after Francis Terranova was executed the United States negotiated a treaty with the kingdom of Siam in which it was agreed that "merchants of the United States trading in the Kingdom of Siam shall respect and follow the laws and customs of the country in all points."

About that time the *North American Review* published a long article reflecting on the lessons of the Terranova case and just how far the United States was justified in going to protect its national honor and any persons serving under its flag. The journal held that "as a question in the law of nations and casuistry, it would bear an argument whether the United States could rightfully go to war against the Chinese for administering their own laws on persons voluntarily coming within their jurisdiction."[27]

When the Opium War of 1839–1840 broke out, the Americans in Canton were swept along with the British into a sort of preview of the Boxer Rebellion at the end of the century. By all accounts, the Americans were more generous and tolerant toward the Chinese than the British, whose arrogance increased in exact proportion to the wealth they were gaining from the opium trade. But their white faces and round eyes, and their position in the Canton trading community, made the Americans prisoners of their situation. The Americans tried to conduct themselves in a manner calculated to win a preferred position for themselves; to disassociate themselves from the harsh and haughty methods of the British. To the Chinese, however, there was little difference, if any, between an American and a Briton. In times of trouble, the Americans would suffer with the British.

The trouble was foreshadowed for several years, during which one faction in Peking wanted to legalize the opium traffic and obtain revenue for the government while their more numerous opponents insisted that the opium trade be destroyed and the growing financial influence of the foreigners be reduced.

Late in 1838, the Manchu government made its decision in favor of wiping out the opium traffic. To signify that determination, on December 12, 1838, the Chinese authorities in Canton set up their apparatus for beheading a Chinese opium dealer in the square fronting on the foreign factories and godowns. English and Americans alike rushed out of their compounds and drove off the executioners with their prisoner. The prisoner was soon executed in another part of the city. Meanwhile an enraged mob of seven to eight thousand Chinese gathered in the square and was met by a barrage of bricks, stones and bottles from the Americans and English, who then fell back and barricaded themselves in their factories. A detachment of Chinese troops armed with whips dispersed the mob, and the American consul, Peter W. Snow, in his report to the State Department, blamed the incident on the "imprudence and fclly of a small number of English and American young men." Later Snow, in consultation with the French and Dutch consuls (but not the British), decided that their flags should be hauled down, evidently to avoid any more provocations.

That incident, however, was only the premonitory rumble of the storm to come. It arrived in the person of the stern and incorruptible Lin Tse-hsu, who had been appointed by the emperor as high commissioner in charge of suppressing the opium trade. He appeared in Canton in March 1839 and announced that he would immediately exercise the full powers granted him. Both foreign and Chinese dealers in opium were to cease their transactions. All opium, including that on the storeships anchored off Lintin Island, must be surrendered to the authorities. All foreign traders must provide bonds within three days guaranteeing that they would import no more drugs. "Let our ports once be closed against you," Lin Tse-hsu warned, "and for what profit can your several nations any longer look?" He added that violators would be given the death sentence.

Although United States Consul Snow considered Lin's proclamation a "just demand" in his report to the State Department, the Americans in Canton joined with the British and other Westerners in announcing their defiance of the edict.

In this deadlock, amounting to a state of semisiege for the Westerners in Canton, Commissioner Lin ordered all Chinese employees out of the foreign compounds and surrounded the enclave with a cordon of troops. The hong merchants who had been dealing with the foreigners, including the politically influential Houqua, were placed in chains and informed that they would be beheaded if they did not persuade the foreigners to comply with Lin's edict. Meanwhile, British diplomacy was at work. On second thought, the British superintendent of trade, Charles Elliott, informed Commissioner Lin, the British would be willing to surrender 20,283 chests of opium valued at ten million dollars. Lin was inclined to be reasonable but declared that until the opium was surrendered the Western enclave would remain incommunicado.

Robert Bennet Forbes, who had arrived in Canton a few months earlier to take over as manager of the Russell & Co. firm, provided a rather jolly account of the Americans sequestered in their compound. "I was called upon to organize the house for work; lots were drawn to settle who should cook, and who play the part of waiters, chambermen, etc. It fell to me to be chief cook. The first thing to be done was to clean out the kitchen, into which no white man had before entered; all hands went at it, and soon made things fit for my new work. My first effort was fried eggs and ham: all bore the color and partook of the consistency of dirty sole-leather. It was immediately voted to depose me, and to put Warren Delano in my place, and I assumed his duties, which were to look after the glass and silver; to this end I put upon the side-board a piece of sheeting, and when I required towels I had only to tear off a strip, wipe my utensils, and throw the strip into a corner. W. C. Hunter was lamp-trimmer, and all had something to do." Most of the besieged Americans accepted their hardships cheerfully, except for Consul Snow who complained to Forbes one morning, "Is this not too bad, Mr. Forbes, that a public official at my time of life, not owning a pound of opium, should be imprisoned, and compelled to do a chamber-maid's work?"

During the six weeks of negotiation between British and Chinese, Forbes recalled, a skylarking atmosphere prevailed in the American compound. "Terrier dogs being abundant as well as rats, the younger members of the community got up regular hunts, and killed many fine specimens. The Chinese guards outside filled the square, and they imagined we lived principally on rats and beer. Foot-races were organized, cricket and ball matches, and some of the sailors [off two American ships caught at Whampoa and interned with the other Americans] competed for prizes in climbing flagstaffs. Every one tried to be jolly."[28]

What they thought of as a typically Chinese exercise in melodrama was staged for the Westerners shortly before the British complied with Commissioner Lin's terms. "At a meeting of the chamber of commerce," Forbes wrote, "Houqua and one or two other principal Hong merchants appeared, with very lugubrious faces and with chains around their necks; but the chains were so very light, that I could not help thinking this was a farce got up to frighten their friends into compliance with Lin's demands."

Early in May, with delivery of the opium, Commissioner Lin lifted his siege of the Western enclave. Trade could not be resumed, however, until the merchants signed the bonds against dealing in opium as decreed in the second clause of his proclamation. The British decided to teach him a lesson and move out of Canton in a body, downriver to Macao, until the Chinese became less demanding. They urged the Americans to join them, at first politely, then threateningly. Superintendent of Trade Elliott himself begged Forbes, as manager of the Russell interests, to join in the boycott. "I replied," Forbes later recorded, "that *I had not come to China for health or pleasure, and that I should remain at my post as long as I could sell a yard of goods or buy a pound of tea;* that we Yankees had no Queen to guarantee our losses, etc. He asked if I was willing to do business with a chain about my neck, and said he would soon make Canton too hot for us. I rejoined that the chain was *imaginary,* the duty to constituents and the commission account were *real;* and that if he made Canton too warm I should go to Whampoa, retreating step by step, but buying and selling just as long as I found parties to operate with."[29]

The Americans remaining in Canton were reassured by a sudden flexing of naval muscle, an unexpected demonstration of support from Washington. The United States East India Squadron — actually two small warships, the *Columbia* and the *John Adams,* despite its grandiose title — arrived off Macao. It was stationed there when the British, taking alarm when the Chinese sank a Spanish vessel believing she was English, fled to the Portuguese outpost en masse. "The British residents," Commander George C. Read of the United States squadron wrote the Navy Department, "are evidently displeased with the course our countrymen have adopted."[30]

The British did not stay displeased. As their cold war against the Chinese continued, they used the American merchants in Canton as middlemen, and American ships as carriers, for the freight piling up at Macao. The next time Robert Bennet Forbes met Charles Elliott, the latter told him, "My dear Forbes, the Queen owes you many thanks for not taking my advice as to leaving Canton. We have got in all our goods, and got out a full supply of teas and silk. If the American houses had not remained at their post, the English would have gone in. I had no power to prevent them from going. Now the trade of the season is over, and a large force at hand, we can bring the Chinese to terms."

Possibly because they were in a weaker position, the Americans behaved with greater circumspection than the British, who felt their national power cresting. The traders in Canton memorialized Congress May 25, 1839, to help "establish commercial relations with this [Chinese] empire upon a safe and honorable footing," with a treaty to include stationing of an American envoy at Peking, establishment of a fixed tariff, and agreement with the Chinese on a clearly understood scale of punishment for foreign nationals convicted of crimes on Chinese territory.

Meanwhile, Britain and China edged closer to a shooting war when sailors from an English ship got in a drunken brawl with villagers on Kowloon and a Chinese was killed. The Chinese sent a fleet of forty-nine war junks against the English merchant fleet anchored off Hong Kong and demanded that the murderer be turned over to them. The British opened fire, sank four junks, and the overt phase of the Opium War began. Commissioner Lin addressed Queen Victoria in highly insulting language: "You savages of the further seas have waxed so bold, it seems, as to defy and insult our mighty empire . . . If you continue in your path of obstinate delusion, your three islands will be laid waste and your people pounded into mincemeat."

Queen Victoria's answer was to send out a fleet of sixteen men of war, twenty-seven troopships, auxiliary vessels and four thousand troops, which in June of 1840 blockaded Canton, Ningpo and the mouth of the Yangtze. During the next year, the British exerted their full military force against the Manchu empire, capturing Canton and the river forts protecting it, struck north, south and west, and advanced wherever they pleased. The Chinese, with neither the weapons nor the discipline to fend off the invaders, fought back with suicidal courage; at Chapu twelve thousand were killed either by the British or by falling on their own swords when the garrison fell. British bayonets had slashed away the last pretensions of the Manchus of being a "mighty" empire. Peking surrendered, and the peace terms imposed by the British were harsh. The Chinese were forced to cede Hong Kong, to open Amoy, Shanghai, Ningpo and Foochow to trade, to abolish the hong system of maintaining a trade monopoly, and to pay an indemnity of twenty-one million dollars. Nothing was said about the importation of opium in the treaty; even the British were shamefaced enough about that to avoid mentioning it in diplomatic correspondence, but the opium traffic was resumed, the only difference being that Peking now would receive duties paid on its import.

America's role during all this was that of a not entirely innocent bystander. Her main concern when the Anglo-Chinese conflict ended was to secure for herself the privileges obtained by the British. In doing so, in sharing the spoils but not the fighting, she could not claim to be unstained by the bloody humiliation inflicted on the Chinese. American public opinion appeared to be neutral; certainly there was no overwhelming sentiment for joining the British in their military and naval operations. The leading war hawk was John Quincy Adams, who had been Secretary of State during the Terranova affair. In an address before the Massachusetts Historical Society, which the *North American Review* refused to publish because it considered Adams's opinions ran counter to the prevailing anti-British sentiment of other Americans, Adams declared that the real cause of the Opium War was not opium but China's feeling of superiority over other nations, her haughty exclusiveness.

The Chinese, Adams complained, felt "no obligation to hold commercial intercourse with others. China utterly denies the equality of other nations with itself . . . It holds itself to be the center of the terraqueous globe, equal to the heavenly host." Her refusal to trade openly and willingly was an "enormous outrage upon the rights of human nature." The Chinese resentment of the opium traffic was a "mere incident to the dispute . . . no more the cause of war than the throwing overboard of the tea in the Boston harbor was the cause of the North American Revolution." Adams insisted that "the cause of the war is the *kowtow!* — the arrogant and insupportable pretensions of China, that she will hold commercial intercourse with the rest of mankind, not upon terms of equal reciprocity, but upon the insulting and degrading forms of relation between lord and vassal."

John Quincy Adams's broadside, echoing the British doctrine that a great trading nation had the right to force its commercial ethics on any other country, including the importation of opium or any other product the inhabitants craved, found little support in the young republic. Revolutionary memories still were too fresh for America openly to emulate Britain. Americans were content with the terms of the Treaty of Wanghia, which granted them most-favored-nation status, and to look to the glowing promise of the future. A Southern Congressman put it in the homely terms his countrymen could understand and approve of, when he hymned the growing market for American goods in China and rhetorically inquired whether "anyone can tell how much of our tobacco might be chewed there, in place of opium."[31]

3

"To Establish on Earth the Noblest Temple"

We are a nation of human progress — and who will, who can set the limits to our onward march?

— JOHN L. O'SULLIVAN

More than a century ago Thoreau advised his contemporaries to "probe the earth and see where your main roots run." The America of the 1840's had barely extended itself to the Mississippi and was faced with the problem of pacifying and exploiting a vast fertile continent, yet even then Americans were looking to the imagined riches beyond their borders. The gold of the seven buried cities of Cibola was always more alluring than the rich black earth of Illinois.

Americans simply had no roots to explore. Like any amphibious creatures, we regarded our own land as a base, a safe harbor to which we could always return.

We began expanding long before we had the people to occupy the territory we acquired. The object was to engulf Oregon and California, not for their intrinsic value, or even because they were part of the American continent, but because they gave us a jumping-off place for the Far East. Once the Pacific coast was secure, we began worrying about Hawaii, then Samoa, then the Philippines — and soon the national consciousness was swarming with villains, not only British but German, Russian and Japanese. There was a feverish religiosity about the majority opinion on our presumed necessity to move out, look westward, join the scramble for trading rights and later for territory to occupy. Throughout the nineteenth century the feeling grew that America must expand or be suffocated, a feeling embodied in the policies of Republican and Democratic administrations alike (though never, of course, simultaneously). That this thrust us into competition with other and more powerful imperialisms was a danger to be borne with equanimity.

The rival expansion of Germany and Russia finally became a critical problem for the twentieth century but the United States began colliding with German and Russian aspirations in the Pacific more than a century ago. In 1805 the czar's chamberlain visited the Pacific coast, recommended that San Francisco be occupied as an outpost of Russian America and urged that the czar "make use of any favorable turn in European politics to include the coast of California in the Russian possessions." Germany was slower in entering the Pacific but equally aggressive.

There was always the pressure of time urging America to make the most of her geographic opportunities; the realization, as foreseen by various theorists of military and naval strategy, that the American destiny — even her survival — might depend on the swiftness with which she moved into the Pacific world. An America whose interests ended on the Pacific shore would be a limited power in every respect; at worst subject to the encroachments of more enterprising nations.

1. *"Its Floor Shall Be a Hemisphere"*

Not at all by accident the bastard art form of advertising first flowered and still flowers most abundantly on the American continent. The manufacture of slogans, which are the distillate of propaganda, began long before Betsy Ross stitched together the first American flag. We are too restless and impatient to absorb a philosophy; our minds begin to wander the moment a sentence grows qualifying clauses, and we have always given our greatest attention to the political leaders who make the least demands on it. Presidents with an advertising man's ability to simplify, to make his pitch in a few pungent words or with a graphic word picture, have always commanded the American ear.

The surging expansionism of the 1840's had its advance men and drumbeaters, and most of all it had an advertising slogan, resounding and reassuring if lacking in precision or depth, whose lengthy reverberations testify to its semimystic appeal. The electrifying and sometimes hypnotizing phrase was "Manifest Destiny." It was a shelter for all sorts of motives; it had just the ripeness and roundness to issue throbbingly from an oratorical mouth. If it had been phrased "Our Plain Duty," for instance, it would have died like a dragonfly on a summer's noon. A *manifest* duty, somehow, sounded like a call from on high.

Even before that decade and its outward movements began, with its clamoring of "Fifty-four Forty or Fight" and "On to Mexico City," two Irishmen named Kelley and O'Sullivan, both endowed with the Celtic talent for phrase-making, were busy propagandizing for an enlarged United States, regardless of the claims of Britain in the Northwest and the legal possessions of the Mexicans, as inheritors of Spain, to the South and West.

Fifteen years before it became a fact, Hall J. Kelley, formerly a Boston schoolteacher, was advocating the detachment of Oregon from British rule. Erratic but singleminded, he constantly toured the country carrying the banner for the acquisition of Oregon, speaking wherever he could gather a crowd, publishing many pamphlets prophecying and urging the expansion of the United States to the Pacific. Not only must Oregon be settled by Americans but California must be annexed to bring about an unbreakable commercial alliance with China. Furthermore the "liberal, refined and free" United States must shatter the "monopolies, vexations and the bondage of the East India Company." Kelley envisioned the day when the "spirit of American enterprise" would gain supremacy on the Pacific coast and communications from the Mississippi Valley would be opened to the Gulf of Mexico and the Pacific — a day he lyrically described as "opening *new channels* which across the bosom of a widespread ocean, and intersecting islands, where health fills the breezes and comforts spread the shores, would conduct the full tide of a golden traffic into the reservoir of our national finance."[1]

A much more prominent and eloquent publicist of the expansionist movement was John L. O'Sullivan, who came over from Ireland with a sound education, a reputation as a scholar and a magnificent talent for sloganeering. A bluff, energetic man, he attached himself to the Democratic Party as the one with the most room for new citizens and the most capacity for expanding the nation at a time when immigration from Ireland and Germany was rapidly increasing. He was one of the founders of the *Democratic Review,* which began publishing in Washington in 1837, moved to New York City and continued as a theoretical organ of the Democratic Party until 1859. For the first fifteen years of its existence O'Sullivan was intermittently its publisher and most of the time its editor-in-chief. It spoke for the Northern wing of the party, and was a literary as well as a political monthly. Among its more distinguished contributors were Lewis Cass, George Bancroft, Samuel J. Tilden, William Cullen Bryant, Nathaniel Hawthorne and Edgar Allan Poe.

O'Sullivan was a prolific writer, an eloquent advocate of expansionism and an astute political observer, but his talents as an editor were occasionally questioned. Particularly by Edgar Allan Poe, who referred to him as "that ass O'Sullivan," because the latter had reviewed a book Poe felt should have been turned over to him.[2] Poe had better reason for questioning O'Sullivan's literary taste when the editor of the *Democratic Review* rejected "The Fall of the House of Usher."[3]

From 1843 on, O'Sullivan wore two hats as editor of the *Democratic Review* and of the New York *Morning News*. The wealthy and politically ambitious Samuel J. Tilden was persuaded to establish the *Morning News* because the city lacked a respectable and influential Democratic morning paper. Tilden agreed to publish the paper with the editorial supervision of O'Sullivan who, according to Tilden's biographer, "was very anxious to connect himself with the daily press, but who had neither the means nor the political influence to warrant him in attempting to found a new paper alone." The success of the Democratic ticket in 1844, and in part the election of James K. Polk to the presidency, was attributed to the vigor of O'Sullivan's editorial campaigning. Tilden got his candidate elected to the governorship and wanted no more of the newspaper business, so he turned his interest in the *Morning News* over to O'Sullivan.

In both the *Democratic Review* and the New York *News* O'Sullivan made his voice heard, his influence felt, his mark on history (though it was only as indelible as the scattered files of his two publications). During the crucial years of American expansion, in the mid-1840's, his jeremiads were read, quoted and cribbed from by the politicians whose voices were magnified by their offices. The phrase "manifest destiny" is often attributed to Daniel Webster, but its true author was John L. O'Sullivan.[4] In 1859, the *Democratic Review,* some years after O'Sullivan's departure as its editor, boasted with justification that it had "from its birth until the present moment advocated the 'manifest destiny' of the American Republic." An editorial written by O'Sullivan for the November 1839 issue first hinted at formation of the phrase under the title "The Great Nation of Futurity":

"The far-reaching, the boundless future will be the era of American greatness. In its magnificent domain of space and time, the nation of many nations is *destined to manifest** to mankind the excellence of divine principles; to establish on earth the noblest temple ever dedicated to the worship of the Most High — the Sacred and the True. Its floor shall be a hemisphere — its roof the firmament of the star-studded heavens, and its congregation a Union of many Republics, comprising hundreds of happy

---

* The italics are mine.

millions, calling, owning no man master, but governed by God's natural and moral law of equality, the law of brotherhood — of 'peace and good will amongst men.' "

Then and later O'Sullivan rang just the right changes on his dominating theme. The question at the moment was forcing Great Britain to settle the Oregon boundary dispute, and, baldly put, to snatch Texas and California away from Mexico, whose right to those territories was indisputable. Brandishing America's growing power against those two nations was not a project of the highest morality, and it troubled many Americans who believed this country should not acquire by force what it could not gain by diplomacy. To satisfy the self-righteous strain in the American character, which was almost as strong as the instinct for self-aggrandizement, the brutality of the American government's proposed course of action had to be clothed in pseudoreligious explanations.

O'Sullivan did not raise the mailed fist or summon up a vision of conquering armies, but spoke instead of the American mission to build the "noblest temple" and spread the brotherhood of man. If the roof of that temple had to be extended over property belonging to others, if brotherhood had to be offered at bayonet point to unwilling Mexicans, those were necessary expediencies to be forgiven in the process of demonstrating to the unenlightened "the excellence of divine principles."

In the July-August 1845 issue of the *Democratic Review*, O'Sullivan used the famous phrase in denouncing opposition to the last step in annexing Texas. Since other nations had tried to interfere with that design, he proclaimed, all Americans should unite against those who were "thwarting our policy and hampering our power, limiting our greatness and checking the fulfillment of our manifest destiny to overspread the continent allotted by Providence for the free development of our yearly multiplying millions."

He hammered away at the urgency of taking Oregon as well as Texas all that year, and on December 27 wrote in a New York *Morning News* editorial headed "The True Title":

"Our legal title to Oregon, so far as law exists for such rights, is perfect. There is no doubt of this. Mr. Calhoun and Mr. Buchanan have settled that question, once and for all. Flaw or break in the triple chain of that title, there is none. Not a foot of ground is left for England to stand upon, in any fair argument to maintain her pretensions.

"And yet, after all, unanswerable as is the demonstration of our legal title to Oregon — and the whole of Oregon, if a rood! — we have a still better title than any that can ever be reconstructed out of all these antiquated materials of old black-letter international law. Away, away with all these cobweb tissues of rights of discovery, exploration, settlement, continuity, etc. To state the truth at once in its neglected simplicity, we are free to say that were the respective cases and arguments of the two parties, as to all these points of history and law, reversed — our claim to Oregon would still be best and strongest. And that claim is by the right of manifest destiny to overspread and to possess the whole of the continent which Providence has given us for the development of the great experiment of liberty and federated self-government entrusted to us. The God of nature and of nations has marked it for our own; and with His blessing we will firmly maintain the incontestable rights He has given, and fearlessly perform the high duties He has imposed."

The O'Sullivan editorials provided source material for the congressional debates which erupted over President Polk's aggressive policies. "Manifest destiny," with all its splendid vacuity, was picked up and thundered across the floors of House and Senate as though it composed a mandate handed down to the new Moses as an Eleventh Commandment in the burning bush of lower Manhattan. None of the congressional plagiarists mentioned the source by name, and only an opponent of the administration's policy, unable to believe that God was ordaining the new subdividing of the continent, indicated that journalism was providing the fuel for partisan politics.

One week after the *Morning News* editorial announcing that Providence had adjusted the national boundaries in our favor, Representative Robert C. Winthrop of Massachusetts told the House that he was afraid that other nations would consider that explanation lacking in juridical force. "There is one element . . . to which I may not have done entire justice," he declared on January 3, 1846. "I mean that new revelation of right which has been designated as the right of our manifest destiny to spread over this whole continent. It has been openly avowed in a leading Administration journal that this, after all, is our best and strongest title — one so clear, so pre-eminent, and so indisputable that if Great Britain had all our other titles in addition to her own, they would weigh nothing against it. The right of our manifest destiny! There is a right for a new chapter in the law of nations; or rather, in the special laws of our own country; for I suppose the right of a manifest destiny to spread will not be admitted to exist in any nation except the universal Yankee nation!"

The popularity of the catchphrase grew as only the well-packaged half-truth can on American soil. It grew in proportion to the continued need for justification of this country's policies in the Pacific and elsewhere. Only a few days after Winthrop's speech, in fact, O'Sullivan defended its inherent chauvinism on the ground that "an immense democratic population" he foresaw would need *lebensraum.*[5] Americans found the idea less palatable when German and Japanese expansionists echoed it as an excuse for their own actions. Even so, it continued to serve political orators as a handy cliché for generations, and in some quarters there is still a sneaking fondness for the idea it embodies.

During the decade of his greatest influence O'Sullivan saw his country taking giant strides south and west, but he was convinced that the potential for expansion was still not exhausted. There were islands beyond which might benefit from Americanization. Not only a divinely inspired destiny called for it but the fact that we represented "human progress" at its highest pitch of excellence — "and who will, who can," he demanded, "set limits to our onward march?"

The seminal influence of O'Sullivan's editorials could be detected at the Wheeling Congress of 1852, though by now it spoke with a definite German accent. The congress brought together delegates representing German revolutionary societies from all over the United States, who formed the People's League of the Old and New Worlds. Germans had been flooding into the United States by the hundreds of thousands during the past decade, many of them intellectuals stifled by the repressive atmosphere of their homeland. Some were pioneer Communists, many were Socialists; and almost all of them were utopians, to whom America represented the starting point of a worldwide democracy. Their proposals showed that "manifest destiny" was a portmanteau phrase capable of lengthy extension indeed. They were stated in a pamphlet titled *The New Rome, or the United States of the World,* in which it was suggested that it was the American destiny to annex all the other civilized nations of the world, with Washington as the capital of the world state. Force was not prescribed, nor was it prohibited, but the German-American theorists stated their hope for "an American Empire that is at the same time a Democracy." In that expression of faith in the purity of American character they exceeded even O'Sullivan.[6]

2. *"What a Country This Might Be!"*

The national enthusiasm for acquiring California as well as Oregon and Texas was spurred on, though less deliberately, by literature as well as journalism. More than half of Richard Henry Dana, Jr.'s *Two Years Before the Mast* was devoted to descriptions of the California coast under Mexican rule; they were realistic, nothing like the later effusions of the All-Year Club of California, but they made the place picturesquely attractive. His months along the California coast as a member of the crew of a ship in the hide and tallow trade convinced him that California could be a garden spot under more diligent stewardship. "In the hands of an enterprising people," as Dana put it, "what a country this might be!" He echoed another traveler of the time who urged that "the eastern and middle states pour into it their thousands of emigrants, until magnificent cities would rise on the shores of every inlet along the coast, while the wilderness of the interior would be made to blossom like a rose."[7]

The lure of the golden coast on the other side of the continent was most strikingly pictured by Dana, a nineteen-year-old Harvard dropout who from August 14, 1834, to September 21, 1836, sailed before the mast of the 180-ton brig *Pilgrim,* weathering the roaring gales around the Horn, enduring the harsh life of the forecastle, luxuriating in the hide ports of California and returning to Boston to publish his superb account of that voyage. *Two Years Before the Mast* was recognized as a classic the moment it was published in 1840, when Dana had finished his education at Harvard and was twenty-five years old. The book was many things — to Dana a protest against the flogging of seamen and harsh treatment of men in the forecastle, to Herman Melville an "unmatchable" sea story with its chapters on rounding Cape Horn "written with an icicle," and to later generations the best American account of a sailor's life under canvas. But to many of his contemporaries it was a glowing testimonial to a part of the continent, still perversely Mexican territory, which sounded very much as though it belonged under the American flag, in the keeping of men of vigor and enterprise who would know what to do with it.

Few books, in so many ways, proved to be so influential in more than the literary sense. It made young Dana famous within months; edition after edition appeared here and abroad (more than a hundred altogether). The book was placed in the libraries of all the ships of the British navy, and Samuel Plimsoll, the English philanthropist, used it as a prime source in his successful campaign to persuade Parliament to enact laws safeguarding the human rights of all seamen.

From the moment the brig *Pilgrim* anchored off Santa Barbara, Dana's account of California before the gold rush made it apparent that the Sundown Sea could be the end of the rainbow for Americans, a dreamland awaiting development by a less slothful people. The *Pilgrim* landed off Santa Barbara in January (1835) but "It was a beautiful day, and so warm that we wore straw hats, duck trousers and all the summer gear. As this was midwinter, it spoke well for the climate; and we afterwards found that the thermometer never fell to the freezing-point throughout the winter, and that there was very little difference between the seasons." The settlement of Santa Barbara, dominated by its mission and presidio, was built in a crescent around the bay. There and at ports up the coast the *Pilgrim* lingered for days and weeks as the captain and supercargo bargained for the bags of tallow and stacks of iron-hard bullocks' hides which were to be transported back to the East Coast.

The bay of Monterey was even more beautiful, "its houses being of whitewashed adobe, which gives a much better effect than those of Santa Barbara, which are mostly left of a mud colour. The red tiles, too, on the roofs, contrasted well with the white sides and the greenness of the lawn, upon which the houses — about a hundred in number — were dotted about, here and there, irregularly . . . We felt as though we had got into a Christian (which in the sailor's vocabulary means a civilised) country."

At the beginning of a long stay in Monterey, the *Pilgrim* displayed its wares from the cargo hold — casks of spirits, teas, coffee, sugar, spices, raisins, molasses, hardware, crockery, tinware, cutlery, clothing, boots and shoes, silks, calicoes and cottons, furniture, and even Chinese fireworks — for sale or trade to the inhabitants. These, for reasons he soon made apparent, met with the young Bostonian's disfavor.

"The Californians are an idle, thriftless people and can make nothing for themselves. The country abounds in grapes, yet they buy, at great price, bad wine made in Boston . . . and retail it among themselves at a *real* [twelve and a half cents] by the small wine-glass. Their hides, too, which they value at two dollars in money, they barter for something which costs seventy-five cents in Boston; and buy shoes (as like as not made of their own hides, which have been carried twice around Cape Horn) at three and four dollars, and 'chicken-skin' boots at fifteen dollars a pair. Things sell, on an average, at an advance of nearly three hundred percent upon the Boston prices. This is partly owing to the heavy duties which the government, in their wisdom, with an idea, no doubt, of keeping the silver in the country, has laid upon imports."[8]

He conceded that the women were attractive enough, but "their complexions are various, depending — as well as their dress and manner — upon the amount of Spanish blood they can lay claim to, which also settles their social rank. Those who are of pure Spanish blood, having never intermarried with the aborigines, have clear brunette complexions, and sometimes even as fair as those of English women . . . These form the upper class, intermarrying, and keeping up an exclusive system in every respect . . . From this upper class they go down by regular shades, growing more and more muddy and dark, until you come to the pure Indian, who runs about with nothing upon him but a small piece of cloth, kept up by a wide leather strap drawn round his waist."

Men and women of all classes, he noted, had such fine voices, speaking in a Creole drawl, that he loved to listen to their liquid Spanish even before he could understand what they were saying. "A common bullock-driver, on horseback, delivering a message, seemed to speak like an ambassador at a royal audience."

Fine speech and manners, however, did not make up for the Californians' inability or unwillingness to develop their country. Most of the trading and shopkeeping was monopolized by Englishmen or Americans who had married native women and joined the Catholic Church. The native men seemed to spend most of their lives on horseback, at bull-baiting and other amusements. "Monterey is also a great place for cock-fighting, gambling of all sorts, fandangoes, and various kinds of amusement and knavery." One of the local enterprises followed with a rare enthusiasm was trimming fur trappers and traders who came down from the Rockies and "wasted their opportunities and their money, and then go back, stripped of everything." Monterey was rich in soil and water and had a good harbor, and "nothing but the character of the people prevents it from becoming a large town."

The *Pilgrim* journeyed down to the Pueblo de los Angeles, the future city of Los Angeles and its port of San Pedro, and though it was the center of a cattle country providing the ship with many hides, Dana and his shipmates agreed it was the most desolate place they had come across, "the worst place we had seen yet." Sailing southward, they found that San Diego was decidedly the best place in California, with great potentialities as a port. "The harbour is small and land-locked; there is no surf; the vessels lie within a cable's length of the beach, and the beach itself is smooth, hard sand, without rocks or stones." They went ashore on Easter Sunday and were delighted by the festive atmosphere. "There, everything wore the appearance of a holiday. The people were dressed in their best; the men riding about among the houses, and the women sitting on carpets before the doors. Under the piazza of a *pulqueria* two men were seated, decked out with knots of ribbons and bouquets, and playing the violin and Spanish guitar." Even death was treated lightly by the natives. Dana came across a house in which a child had died the day before and from which the funeral procession would begin in an hour. "I found a large room, filled with young girls, from three or four years of age up to fifteen and sixteen, dressed all in white, with wreaths of flowers on their heads, and bouquets in their hands. Following our conductor among these girls, who were playing about in high spirits, we came to a table, at the end of the room, covered with a white cloth, on which lay a coffin."

With a censorious eye he noted that the walls were stained from wine and food thrown about at the wake of the night before. Once the funeral was over the townsmen settled into their holiday routine of bull-baiting, cockfights and horse racing. The Easter holiday, in fact, roared on for two more days.

"So much for being Protestants," Dana dourly observed. "There's no danger of Catholicism spreading to New England, unless the Church cuts down her holidays; Yankees can't afford the time."[9]

He was capitivated by San Juan Capistrano — was the first to point out what later became a prime tourist attraction — and it was only fitting that Dana Cove and Dana Point were later named for him along that stretch of coast. "The country here for several miles is high table-land, running boldly to the shore, and breaking off into a steep cliff, at the foot of which the waters of the Pacific are constantly dashing. For several miles the water washes the very base of the hill, or breaks upon ledges and fragments of rock which run out into the sea . . . There was a grandeur in everything around, which gave a solemnity to the scene, a silence and solitariness which affected every part! Not a human being but ourselves for miles, and no sound heard but the pulsations of the great Pacific!" For the first time in his life, the nineteen-year-old Bostonian felt that "everything was in accordance with my state of feeling, and I experienced a glow of pleasure at finding that what of poetry and romance I ever had in me had not been entirely deadened by the laborious life, with its paltry, vulgar associations, which I had been leading."

By far the most attractive specimens of human life Dana found along the California coast were "Sandwich-Islanders," Hawaiians who had established a small colony at San Diego, which they used as headquarters between sailing on ships plying between California and Hawaii. Bearing the colorful English names of "Pelican," "Foretop," "Banyan," "Lagoda Jack" and "California Bill," they were, he said, "the most interesting, intelligent, and kind-hearted people that I ever fell in with. I felt a positive attachment for almost all of them."

He stayed ashore for several months at San Diego, taking charge of a hide-curing operation, and got to understand the sociology of the settlement. The kingpins were an assortment of forty or fifty Europeans mostly engaged in the hide trade, and at wassail nights "A German gave us 'Ach! mein leiber Augustin!'; the three Frenchmen roared through the Marseilles Hymn; the English Scotchmen gave us 'Rule, Britannia' and 'Wha'll be King but Charlie?'; the Italians and Spanish screamed through some national affairs; and we three Yankees made an attempt at the 'Star-Spangled Banner.' "[10]

The California settlements were ruled, he observed, by "strangers sent from Mexico, having no interest in the country . . . for the most part men of desperate fortunes — broken-down politicians and soldiers — whose only object is to retrieve their condition in as short a time as possible." Obviously California needed the evenhanded benefits of Yankee governmental efficiency. "The government of the country is an arbitrary democracy, having no common law, and nothing that we should call a judiciary. Their only laws are made and unmade at the caprice of the legislature, and are as variable as the legislature itself." Revolutions broke out frequently and were carried on with a southern indolence.

One uprising was staged while Dana was at San Diego and it was a deplorably slack affair. "A general with titles enough for a hidalgo was at San Gabriel, and issued a proclamation as long as the foretop-bowline, threatening destruction to the rebels, but never stirred from his fort; for forty Kentucky hunters, with their rifles, and a dozen of Yankees and Englishmen, were a match for a whole regiment of hungry, drawling, lazy half-breeds." The authorities bestirred themselves to vigorous action only when an Indian committed a crime, upon which he was usually shot with hardly a pretense of legal proceedings.

On more intimate association, he found that his first impression of the native Californian was all too accurate. The women were unfaithful wives, once they escaped the "sharp eyes of a duenna" assigned to protect their virtue in girlhood. "The men are thriftless, proud, extravagant, and very much given to gaming; and the women have but little education, and a good deal of beauty, and their morality, of course, is none of the best . . . One vice is set over against another; and thus something like a balance is obtained. If the women have but little virtue, the jealousy of their husbands is extreme, and their revenge deadly and almost certain. A few inches of cold steel have been the punishment of many an unwary man."

Later Dana and the *Pilgrim* sailed up the coast to San Francisco Bay. The settlement was nothing compared to San Diego, but its surroundings, especially the Bay and its natural harbors, were magnificent. The view, however, was blighted by the presence of one other ship anchored in the Bay — a Russian brig down from Sitka trading for tallow and grain. The Russians, according to Dana, were a scruffy lot, and he went into considerable detail about their wretched seamanship, their appearance, manners and customs. "Such a stupid and greasy-looking set I never saw before . . . They had brutish faces, looked like the antipodes of sailors, and apparently dealt in nothing but grease. They lived upon grease; ate it, drank it, slept in the midst of it, and their clothes were covered with it. To a Russian, grease is the greatest luxury. They looked with greedy eyes upon the tallow-bags as they were taken into the vessel, and, no doubt, would have eaten one up whole, had not the officer kept watch over it . . . If they were to go into a warm climate, they would melt and die of the scurvy."[11]

If the Americans didn't move swiftly to secure the Western coast of their continent, it was obvious that California would either be snatched by the barbarous Russians and turned into a vast depot for collecting grease, or left in the careless hands of the Mexicans. As he sailed for home, Dana reflected on what he had seen along the sun-drenched shore, the good harbors, the fine forests in the north, the waters filled with fish, the coastal plain covered with grazing herds, the climate "than which there can be no better in the world" and a soil so rich that "corn yields seventy to eighty-fold." Yankee energy could transform the place, yet he was certain that living in such a place would change the Yankee even more, that he would succumb to the lassitude, the lotus-eating atmosphere. Americans and Englishmen were prospering in the larger towns through their willingness to work and accumulate, but he had noticed that "their children are brought up Mexicans in most respects, and if the 'California fever' (laziness) spares the first generation, it is likely to attack the second."

His fears, as it turned out, were groundless. He returned to California, a middle-aged and distinguished maritime lawyer, a little less than a quarter-century later and found that American rule had transformed the sleepy pueblos of his youth without noticeably eroding the American character.

3. *"To Plunder Ye Like Sin"*

Before America could move out in force on the world stage, she had to become the indisputed master in her own house, which she now regarded as extending from the Rio Grande to the Canadian border, from the Atlantic to the Pacific. In 1846, the United States made a breathtaking series of moves toward that end. President Polk gave fair warning of them in his annual message: "It is due alike to our safety and our interests that the efficient protection of our laws should be extended over our whole territorial limits, and that it should be distinctly announced to the world as our settled policy that no future European colony or dominion shall with our consent be planted or established on any part of the American continent."[12]

The President was not usually so unambiguous; his was an enigmatic personality, and in his career was noted one of the first great "credibility gaps" that were to plague a much later President. But it was the uninspiring Polk who advanced our frontiers in several amazing bounds. He was riding a tide of jingoism and would not be swept away by it, nor would he be carried under its surface.

Two years before, he had run for the presidency on the Democratic campaign slogan, regarding Oregon, of "Fifty-four Forty or Fight." Ostensibly the United States claimed all of Oregon Territory up to the limits of Russian Alaska: 54 degrees 40 minutes north latitude. But that was mostly a bargaining point for United States diplomats, and the more sensible, though unstated policy had been to settle for a United States–Canadian boundary at the 49th Parallel. The question of Oregon was vexatious, complicated, a running sore for decades in Anglo-American relations. Britain claimed Oregon because she got there first; the United States maintained the territory belonged to her because she settled it. A year before Polk took office, in fact, a group of American settlers at Champoeg announced that they would govern themselves "until such time as the United States of America extend their jurisdiction over us."

Whatever the terms, the United States wanted the Oregon question settled immediately. President Polk knew that Britain would not surrender all of the Northwest, and quietly advanced the 49th Parallel as a reasonable boundary line. The British at first rejected this solution, then changed course and found it acceptable. Polk requested the advice and consent of the Senate, which finally concurred in the settlement. The treaty was signed June 15, 1846, with the United States in possession of the Columbia Valley and Puget Sound and Great Britain retaining Vancouver Island.

Next question: the resolution of the Texas boundary. Texas, after fighting for her independence from Mexico, was admitted as a state of the Union shortly after Polk's inauguration. Its southwest boundary, however, was still in dispute. Texans insisted that their state extended to the Rio Grande. Mexico maintained that the Nueces River was the boundary.

President Polk was not inclined to extend to Mexico the same niceties of fairly patient diplomacy as he did Britain, though he sent a commissioner to Mexico City to offer that government forty million dollars for the territories of New Mexico and California. The sum was not only ridiculous, but the offer itself an affront to the Mexican sense of honor. She also had reason to be concerned over American intrigue in her rich province of California, now being vigorously colonized by Americans.

Once he was fairly certain that France and Britain would not intervene on the Mexican side, Polk launched his military offensive against Mexico. One force led by General Zachary Taylor advanced to the Rio Grande, where it was attacked by Mexican troops. On May 11, 1846, Polk declared that a state of war existed with Mexico. Overland and by sea another expeditionary force under General Winfield Scott struck out for Mexico City and marched toward its objective against a desperate but unavailing Mexican army. General Taylor occupied Monterey in northern Mexico. Easy conquests. A brisk little war, with rich rewards in territory, of the sort needed by a nation newly conscious of its power and no longer unwilling to exercise it against weaker neighbors.

But the real objective was not Mexico City or the strip of territory between the Nueces and the Rio Grande, it was the golden prize of California. Secretary of State James Buchanan urged President Polk at a Cabinet meeting to proclaim that this country had no intention of seizing Mexican territory other than the strip of Texas. "I told him," Polk confided to his diary, "that we had not gone to war for conquest; yet it was clear that in making peace we would if practicable obtain California." For California he was willing to fight "either England or France or all the Powers of Christendom" and would "stand and fight until the last man amongst us fell in the conflict."[13]

In his secretive way, Polk had already advanced upon that objective. Captain John C. Frémont, "the great pathfinder" and son-in-law of the expansionist Senator Benton, had been dispatched on what was called an exploring mission to the valley of the Sacramento. The Mexican authorities ordered him to leave with his fellow explorers, but he refused. Meanwhile President Polk had sent an army lieutenant scurrying to the American consul in Monterey with secret dispatches. Consul Thomas O. Larkin was advised that the United States did not mean to encourage Americans living under the Mexican flag in California to throw off the yoke. "But," Polk added, "if the people should desire to unite their destiny with ours, they

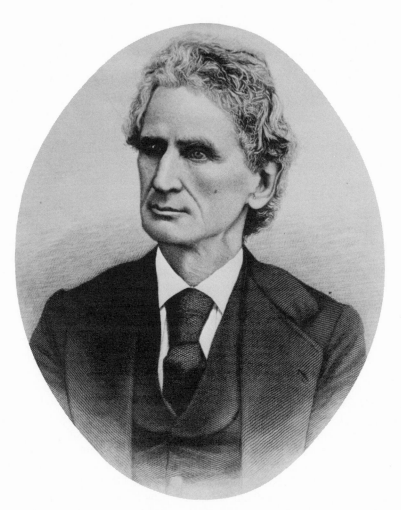

Richard Henry Dana: First Hymns to California

would be received as brethren; whenever this can be done without affording Mexico any just cause of complaint."

It was really a masterpiece of maneuvering, both in Washington and in California, and it was accomplished because all parties concerned understood each other without having to commit politically dangerous thoughts to writing. War with Mexico officially began May 11, but Polk's helpers in California were on the move long before they learned of it. An "independent" Bear Republic, flag and all, was proclaimed by a small number of American settlers, who proceeded to capture Sonora. The independence of California was announced June 14. On July 7, Commodore John Sloat raised the American flag over Monterey, and everyone conveniently forgot about the Bear Republic.

Dismembered Mexico signed a peace treaty by which New Mexico, Arizona and California were ceded to the United States. The American writ ran clear across the continent. From the great natural harbor of San Francisco, the United States now had its window on the Pacific. The vision of another empire across those seas, in a vast area in which there seemed to be a vacuum of power and the prospect of immeasurable wealth to be gained through aggressively promoted trade, was now clear in outline. The imperialism which revolutionary America had foresworn had, within just seven decades, assumed the compulsive aspects of a destiny made manifest.

4. *The Second Great American Traveler*

Everything seemed to conspire to bear out the prophecies of the expansionists in the dozen years preceding the Civil War. A year after California became a Union territory gold was discovered there and inspired the migration of thousands overland and by sea to the Pacific coast. Almost at the same time hundreds of thousands of immigrants came flooding across the Atlantic from the Ireland of the potato famines and the Germany of political oppression, all helping to fill up the continent. And the same year he relieved Mexico of her northern provinces, President Polk, a man of more vision than he was ever given credit for, signed a little-noticed treaty with New Granada (later Colombia) giving the United States the right to build a railway and/or canal across its province of Panama, the narrow waist joining North and South America.

One man who took note of that obscure treaty was John Lloyd Stephens, who like John Ledyard was often referred to as the Great American Traveler, like Ledyard envisioned an America stretching out from its continental limits, like Ledyard roamed the world in search of adventure and knowledge, but unlike Ledyard had the money to make his dreams come true. He was one of the most famous Americans of his day, and the last great ambition of his foreshortened life was to build a railway across the Isthmus of Panama. The future of America, he believed, lay far west of its Pacific shore, and as a supporter of Polk's policies he was willing to lay down what was left of his health and fortune in furthering that cause.

New Jersey–born, Stephens was a lawyer, diplomat, writer and archeologist whose discovery and description of the Mayan ruins of Central America and southern Mexico (recorded in some of the best travel books ever written) have kept his fame alive ever since. But that was only one phase of a protean career. He set out on a life of unremitting hazard and adventure by traveling in Turkish disguise over the hostile Arabian desert to the "rose-red city" of Petra. The result was the first of many bouts with malaria and dysentery which eventually drained away his life, and also the first of a series of best-selling volumes on what he saw going to and coming from Petra. On his way back to New York in 1836 Stephens, who had been educated for the law but rarely practiced it, met an artist-architect named Frederick Catherwood. Instead of going back to his law office as he had promised his father, he was inspired by Catherwood, himself an amateur archeologist, to consider the idea of a joint exploration of the jungle-covered and long-buried ruins of the Mayas. For the next several years Stephens and Catherwood explored the mountain jungles of Central America and Mexico and uncovered the ancient cities of Copan, Palenque, Uxmal and Chichen Itza, collaborated on their *Incidents of Travel in Central America and Yucatán,* and demonstrated to a hitherto unbelieving world that the Western hemisphere had once been the center of a great civilization.

In between the archeological ventures Stephens, acting as the "confidential agent" of the United States State Department, also found time to inspect possible routes for a canal across Central America. The survey inflamed his imagination as Ledyard's service aboard Captain Cook's *Discovery* inspired him to become a missionary for trade with China. To cut a canal joining the Atlantic and the Pacific, Stephens wrote, would be "glory surpassing the conquest of kingdoms," and he urged his countrymen to "make this greatest enterprise ever attempted by human hands entirely our own work."[14]

On his return to the United States, Stephens worked for Polk's candidacy because he believed a Democratic President would help the United States become the great maritime and trading power Stephens believed she was destined to be. It would also further his plans for bridging the Isthmus. If the cost of a canal was too great, the route could be covered by a railroad across Panama with the new, bigger and faster ships carrying passengers and freight from New York to the Atlantic terminus, then from the Pacific terminus up the coast to San Francisco. It was also his belief in the potentialities of American trade that led him to invest some of the sizable profits from his books in the Ocean Steam Navigating Company, of which he became a vice president and director. Steam-driven vessels, uneconomic at the moment, would only hasten American supremacy on the seas. He sailed with the company's first ship, the S.S. *Washington,* on her maiden voyage to Europe.

One of his purposes in journeying to Europe was to arrange an interview with the aging Alexander von Humboldt, the geographer, naturalist and explorer, colleague of Goethe, "the most famous man in Europe after Napoleon Bonaparte." The old man received Stephens at his Potsdam house and listened to his plans for speeding and enlarging American trade because "the closer we could be drawn together the better it would be for both countries" — a theory which developed historic flaws. Humboldt also enthused over Stephens's Central American plans and told him it was essential that the United States gain a shorter route between her coasts and expand her influence in eastern Asia.

Greatly inspired, Stephens hastened back to the United States to push his plans for the Panamanian railway. As always he returned to his father's house in New York — he would never marry an American woman of his class, as his writings clearly show, because they showed up so poorly, so unattractively in comparison with the disheveled natural beauty of the native girls he had pursued, tweaked, fondled and probably seduced from rose-red Petra to Chichen Itza. He told his father that he intended to drop out of sight for a while, and the senior Stephens was simply to tell anyone who asked that his son was "out of town."

Stephens disappeared for six months, having secretly gone to Panama to survey a route for his railroad with James Baldwin and Colonel G. W. Hughes of the army engineers. Secrecy and surprise were essential to his project because the British had just occupied the Mosquito Coast of Nicaragua to counteract American influence in that region and because there would be political objections to reawakening the old rivalry with England.

He popped up in New York again in November 1848 and began evangelizing among the capitalists for funds to carry out his project. He was quick to quote Goethe, even to self-made money men who thought the name rhymed with teeth; particularly the passage in *Conversations with Eckermann* — "It is absolutely indispensable for the United States to effect a passage from the Mexican Gulf to the Pacific Ocean; and I am certain that they will do it. Would that I might live to see it!" He soon acquired the backing of two financiers, William H. Aspinwall, the president of the Pacific Mail Steamship Company, and Henry Chauncey, who had considerable mining interests in South America.

On December 11, 1848, a "memorial" composed by the three men was presented to Congress announcing the plans to build a railway over the Cordilleras, the mountain spine of Panama, from the Atlantic to the Pacific ports. "The route over it is probably worse now than in the early days of

Spanish domination. No wheeled carriage has ever attempted to cross it in the present mode." The memorial pointed out that thousands of Americans were then braving the "storms of Cape Horn" to reach the California gold fields while overland others were risking their lives in wagon trains traveling through Indian country in hopes of arriving in California. To provide quicker and safer transportation linked to their railroad, they would arrange for "a monthly mail steamer from New York to Chagres" on the Atlantic side of the Isthmus and "on the Pacific side, to California and Oregon." The railroad would be built under United States government "auspices" but with entirely private financing.

With the approval of Congress — and a last-minute warning from the White House that Stephens could count on the government's moral support but any bill providing money for the railroad would be vetoed — Stephens returned to Panama in the spring of 1849. He was now in his mid-forties, and the various fevers and parasites which afflicted a venturesome traveler of his time had sapped his health and vitality. His next step was to sign an agreement with the Republic of New Granada permitting construction of the railroad through its province of Panama. Getting to the capital, Bogota, required a heroic effort in itself. He had to take an old sidewheel steamer up the Rio Magdalena to the end of navigation at the town of Honda, and from there travel on muleback to the capital. Halfway to Bogota a rock-slide frightened his mule, which bolted and tossed Stephens on a nearby ledge. One of his lower vertebrae was chipped and a nerve center was blocked, temporarily paralyzing him from the waist down. His native porters had to carry him the rest of the way on a litter. He was still on a stretcher when he and the president signed their agreement at the presidential palace on June 20, 1850.

Still paralyzed, Stephens had to be carried down the trails to the Rio Magdalena and the steamer which took him back to Panama. He convalesced on the island of Jamaica and was able to walk again. He refused to believe his health was breaking down, despite constant bouts with the fever, and the only concession he would make was to give up smoking the long black cigars he had puffed on since his youth. And Panama was one of the unhealthiest places in the world, swarming with tarantulas, scorpions, stinging ants, praying mantises, poisonous snakes, and worst of all the clouds of mosquitoes bearing yellow fever and malaria. Such a variety of fevers were epidemic in Panama that they were all lumped together under the title of "Chagres fever," after the river which coursed across the Isthmus.

Stephens supervised the work of hundreds of workmen — natives, Negroes, Germans and Irish — as they hacked westward through the jungle. The workmen had been recruited through advertisements promising them "money, adventure and women," but most found only disease and death. It took almost a year to lay the first section of track eight miles across a mangrove swamp to the first station on the line, Gatun, where the dam was later built for the Panama Canal. The construction costs were running at an average of three hundred and fifty thousand dollars a mile, and money became a problem. The Panama Railway's stock kept sinking on the New York Stock Exchange, and the project was now referred to as Stephens's Folly. Perhaps it would have been, except for the luck which had favored Stephens all his adventurous life.

Just when the treasury was depleted, the floodtide of gold-rushers bound for California began landing on Limon Bay, the eastern terminus of the Panama Railway. From there they had to make their way up the Chagres on boats poled by recalcitrant natives, then on foot over the Cordilleras to the Pacific shore, where another ship would take them to California. Even those eight miles of completed track looked like luxury to men impatient to reach the gold-bearing creeks. They begged Stephens to open up service to Gatun. Stephens finally agreed, under travel-at-your-own-risk terms, at a rate of one dollar a mile. They rode on flatcars, over trestles hammered together out of green timber, and often were knocked off their perches by overhanging tree limbs or jolted off by the rough roadbed, but none was killed or seriously injured. What Stephens called his "emergency measure," taken against the advice of his engineers, brought in so much revenue that the New York bankers offered all the credit the company needed and the price of its stock again shot up.*

Stephens still had to contend with all the troubles of pioneer railroad-building in the tropics — the rockslides, engineering problems encountered on the steep slopes of the Cordilleras, difficulties with both native and imported labor, and endemic banditry along the trail westward. As the line was pushed slowly inland, he established himself in a mountain cottage thirty miles up the Chagres, about halfway between the Atlantic and Pacific. From this promontory, one of America's foremost Pacificists caught the only glimpses he would have of the ocean which inspired so much of his labors. He imported a Texas Ranger named Ran Runnels to organize what the newspapers called the "ragged regiment" to hunt down the *cimarrones* who robbed and killed his workmen. He built hospitals for his men and saw to it that they were dosed daily with quinine, newly discovered to be a specific against malaria. Friends from the States who made the Panama journey — including General John C. Frémont and his wife — took alarm at his haggard appearance, his sweating face and trembling hands, and begged him to go back home.

Stephens was determined to stick it out, to live long enough to see his

---

* The Panama Railway, completed after Stephens's death, was a greater bonanza than most of the gold-rushers found in California. It cost a total of eight million dollars but took in twelve million dollars during the first ten years of operation, and later was sold to the French-owned Panama Canal Company for twenty-five million dollars.

trains running to the Pacific terminus. But his body, for once, betrayed his urgent spirit. One day late in February 1852, he was found lying unconscious under a tree near his cottage. The Panama Railway was three years short of completion, but he was carried in a litter down the mountain trails to Limon Bay. Still in a coma, he was placed aboard a steamer bound for New York.

He regained consciousness on the voyage back to New York, but the debility brought on by tropical diseases made him so weak that he could barely lift his hand. All that summer he lingered on, his life only a flicker, gazing wordlessly out of a window in his father's house. A new Pacific Mail steamer named the S.S. *John L. Stephens* was launched but he had to be represented at the launching ceremony by his aged father. That same day, in fact, he fell into another coma. Three weeks later, only forty-seven years old, he died. The minute-bells tolled in the steeples of lower Manhattan's churches, for unlike John Ledyard he was fully appreciated, and fully honored, in his own time. He belongs in the first rank of those who turned America Pacificward.

5. *The Yankee Clippers*

In mid-August 1859, Richard Henry Dana returned to California for the first time since he had visited the former Mexican province serving before the mast of a hide-trading ship, and the moment his luxurious steamship *Golden Gate* sailed into the Bay he saw confirmation of his belief that American industry could transform the place. They anchored in the evening, in the glow of the city's lighted hills. Twenty-three years ago it had been settled by a few dispirited Indians, visiting Russians and Mexicans, but now, "flickering all over with the lamps of its streets and houses, lay a city of one hundred thousand inhabitants. Clocks tolled the hour of midnight from its steeples, but the city was alive from the salute of our guns, spreading the news that the fortnightly steamer had come, bringing mails and passengers from the Atlantic world."

Already San Francisco was the great entry port for the Asiatic trade: "Clipper ships of the largest size lay at anchor in the stream, or were girt to the wharves; and capacious high-pressure steamers, as large and showy as those of the Hudson or Mississippi, bodies of dazzling light, awaited the delivery of our mails, to take their cruises up the bay, stopping at Benicia and the United States Naval Station, and then up the great tributaries — the Sacramento, San Joaquin and Feather Rivers — to the far inland cities of Sacramento, Stockton and Marysville."[15]

There were more ships in its harbor than in London's or Liverpool's, he proudly noted; the city had become "one of the capitals of the American Republic, and the sole emporium of a new world, the awakened Pacific."

The only glimpses of life that displeased him in the new and prosperous city were the Cathedral of St. Mary, "more like one of our stifling Irish Catholic churches in Boston or New York, with intelligence in so small a proportion to the number of faces," and the "strangely solitary" Mission Dolores with its ancient walls surrounded by "the most uncongenial rapidly growing modernisms."

He journeyed down the coast and found Santa Barbara "not still a lifeless Mexican town," and Los Angeles a flourishing city of twenty thousand. Returning to San Francisco, he could only marvel at how the city had grown from its one adobe house in 1836, and at the development of huge ranches, vineyards and mines in the hinterland. He was candid enough to note that San Francisco had just passed through "its season of heaven-defying crime, violence, and blood," from which it had been rescued by the drastic actions of the Vigilance Committee. Americans, it seemed, brought not only prosperity but violent change and violent disorder wherever they appeared in force — a characteristic dismayingly evident now, as then.[16]

The Pacific world had indeed been "awakened," and quickened, by the massive appearance of the Americans along its littoral and among its islands. Once they had been well behaved and mild-mannered in contrast to the arrogance of the British, but now they had taken on the airs of conquistadors and had acquired a contempt for everything and everyone not American (or possibly, in a lesser degree, English or European). The Chinese found that the ports they had opened to the United States as a "most-favored" nation were now disorderly by day and riotous by night from the presence of hundreds of hard-bitten American losers — luckless adventurers who had been washed out by the California gold rush and drifted over to the China coast, and sailors who had been crimped in San Francisco and beached in Shanghai. A glimpse of what the American presence, in part, meant to the Chinese was provided in a scarifying report to Washington by Humphrey Marshall, the United States commissioner in Shanghai:

"There are now in this port at least one hundred and fifty sailors ashore, men of all nations, who go into the Chinese city and drink and riot and brawl, daily and nightly." He made it clear that most of them were Americans. "They presume to defy all law, because they have tried the jail and find that they cannot be confined in it. No other punishment has been inflicted on them yet besides confinement. They have no money from which to collect a fine. I earnestly request the President to give the authority to lease a lot of ground in this vicinity on which to erect a jail with a yard attached thereto, in which sailors may have air and exercise, and that Congress shall be urged to make an appropriation for the purpose of erecting a jail thereon. The marshall can reside in the tenement, and the fines and forfeitures will probably pay for a guard to attend the premises.

"The United States having assumed jurisdiction over their own citizens in China, are expressly bound to compel them to keep the peace, and this cannot be done as long as there is no place to confine the delinquents in, except a loathsome hole inhabited by the foulest lepers, and in itself so weak that a man of American energies can kick his way out in a few minutes."[17]

American energies, more usefully and respectably employed, had also been channeled into the construction of a fleet of magnificent clipper ships. In a way, they epitomized the America of the years just preceding the Civil War with the almost arrogant beauty of their passage, the speed with which a combination of wind, sail and the genius of naval architecture could carry their cargo to the most distant ports, the venturesomeness of their captains and the ruggedness of their crews, which matched that of their country in forcing its way into the world's affairs. Those who love the sea say that the American model of the clipper was the "greatest aesthetic achievement of the American genius."[18] Under full sail, with a favoring wind, the American clipper seemed to skim just over the waves, half bird, half fish, traveling on canvas wings.

On those spreading wings, for about twenty years from 1840 to 1860, the American clippers made the Pacific and its farthest ports seem just around the corner. They monopolized even the transportation of tea to England, for a time, because they could deliver their cargoes in a shorter time and a fresher condition. (In those years England was concentrating on the conversion to steam and was struggling to maintain its monopoly on the North Atlantic steamship traffic between Europe and America.) Americans' self-esteem soared as they read in their newspapers of the records set by the clippers and their "driving" masters, who cared more about elapsed time than the men under them, who lived under inhuman hardships in the narrow forecastles of those lean, taut ships.

All of the pride of American workmanship went into the clippers, and "the long-suppressed artistic impulse of a practical, hard-worked race burst into flower," as Samuel Eliot Morison (*The Maritime History of Massachusetts*) has written. "Never, in the United States, has the brain of man conceived, or the hand of man fashioned, so perfect a thing as the clipper ship . . . The *Flying Cloud* was our Rheims, the *Sovereign of the Seas* our Parthenon, the *Lightning* our Amiens."

They were constructed of the best oak and other seasoned woods, and finished with all the skill and polish of some of the finest shipwrights in the world. Their topsides were planed and sandpapered as smooth as a baby's skin and then painted to bring out their lines "like a black velvet dress on a beautiful woman." The pine decks were holystoned to a creamy white, the deck fittings shone with brass and the bright work was of mahogany and rosewood. Many clipper ships boasted staterooms and paneled cabins more luxurious than the great passenger liners that followed in the era of steam, and the *Mastiff* contained a library with twelve hundred dollars worth of books.

Some of these comforts undoubtedly were introduced for the benefit of the captains' wives, who often accompanied their husbands and who frequently deserved such amenities. Typical of those heroic wives was the nineteen-year-old bride of Captain Patten of the *Neptune's Car*. Captain Patten came down with brain fever while the clipper was driving through a Cape Horn gale; his first mate was in irons for insubordination and the second mate had never studied navigation. Young Mrs. Patten took command, nursed her husband and brought the ship into San Francisco safely fifty-two days later.

In 1851, the *Flying Cloud,* that most perfect example of the ship-wright's craft, made the passage around the Horn from New York to San Francisco in eighty-nine days, a record never surpassed and only twice equaled by sailing vessels. In this and 425 other American clippers built between 1846 and 1855, American shipwrights refined and combined all the best features which had emerged from two centuries of building privateers, packets, smugglers, trading schooners and slavers. The size of the clippers increased from about six hundred tons for those built in the mid-1840's to more than two thousand tons a half-dozen years later. Ten years later they had climbed toward the tonnage of the lordliest of them all, the *Great Republic* designed by Donald McKay, which was registered at 4555 tons. Even the bigger clippers, designed to carry more cargo faster than any sailing ship afloat, retained the lean hulls and lofty spars of the early models. The more notable clipper captains and their achievements were regarded then with the same awe and admiration as astronauts are today.*

The day of the clippers was as brief as it was glorious; steam soon made them uneconomical. But during the 1850's they embodied all the bursting hopes, pride and ambition of Americans who believed we should turn firmly and irrevocably to the Pacific. They carried tens of thousands to California, and to the gold some of them found at the end of the continental rainbow, and when the gold petered out there was the even more shimmering prospect of direct trade between the American West and the Asian East.

---

* Literally flogged into giving their last ounce of effort, the crews of the American clippers were responsible for some amazing records. In 1849 the *Sea Witch* made it from New York to Hong Kong in seventy-four days, fourteen hours. The *Witch of the Wave* skimmed the seas from Calcutta to Boston in eighty-one days in 1853, and the *Sweepstakes* sailed from Bombay to New York in the same elapsed time in 1856. In 1856 the 1961-ton clipper *Young America* ran from New York to Cape Horn in forty-nine days and from Liverpool to Melbourne in seventy-one days two years later. A record for twenty-four hours sailing, from noon to noon, was established in 1854 by the *Champion of the Seas,* which covered 465 miles in that time.

Soon steamships would travel the clipper lanes to the Far East. Steam meant coaling stations would have to be established along those routes. Coaling stations would require ports and other facilities. Both the shipping lanes and ports, in turn, would have to be protected by naval bases and squadrons of warships. The ruts of imperialism ran deeper than most Americans had suspected, as became apparent when they were told that coaling stations and naval bases would have to be protected, in their turn, by land forces. Even then there was talk of annexing the Hawaiian Islands, and an American diplomat was suggesting the seizure of Formosa, which he apparently regarded as an offshore island of California.

4 🌿

"The Curse of a People Calling Themselves Christians"

The ascendancy of a junta of ignorant and designing Methodist elders in the councils of a half-civilised king, ruling with absolute sway over a nation just poised between barbarism and civilization . . . was not precisely calculated to impart a healthy tone to the policy of the government.

— HERMAN MELVILLE in the appendix to *Typee*.

Even in the hopefully bustling America of the mid-nineteenth century, with the Civil War as yet the remotest of threats to ordinary Americans, there was an uneasy tendency toward escapism. Even in that relatively untroubled time Americans became obsessed with a dreamlike conception of the South Seas largely fathered by reading accounts of Captain Cook's voyages or, a little later, the tremendously popular South Seas romances of Herman Melville. From such sources, and the less literary but equally vivid tales brought home by young men who had gone to sea, they conjured a lovely vision of mirrorlike lagoons bordered by grass huts and reflecting the swaying brown bodies of native girls wearing little more than a string of beads. It was hard to say which stimulant was the more powerful, the literary or the aphrodisiac, but whichever it was Americans were powerfully attracted to the island world of the Pacific as well as the commercial world of its continental shores.

A glimpse of the reasons for Americans to be restless and dissatisfied may be found in Lewis Mumford's summation of social conditions in the mid-nineteenth century, in which he noted that "this mixture in society of old and new, provincial and metropolitan, vital and mechanical, was still a turbid one: the elements had not yet settled; contrast and comparison were difficult; and people stood for one or the other, chiefly by intuition, while perhaps a good part of the population wanted both; they wanted the old privileges of birth and the new ones of opportunity, the old stability and order, and all the new fields to conquer and the new positions to occupy," with few intimations of the "chaos and dissolution that was to come."[1]

During the 1840's there was a sense of expectancy and a ferment of diverse but original intellects — Emerson lecturing his contemporaries, Thoreau experimenting at Walden Pond, Fourier discoursing on socialism, and on a lower level Bronson Alcott and Dr. Graham creating controversy and high expectations with their near-holy crusades for the consumption, respectively, of sun-dried fruit and bread made from bran. Ordinary people, of course, were not greatly affected by seethings of the intellect, but they were intensely conscious of a change in the American climate. The old provincial culture, agrarian as the plow and harrow, was being obliterated by a new order. America was quickly changing from a patchwork of farms and villages to a complicated and powerful state based on imperialistic enterprise and its necessary military and naval expeditions.

The Northern industrialism that provided the base for the victorious armies of the Mexican and Civil Wars was already established, and quickly changing the quality of life. It was responsible for such changes in the American character as may be noted, in a literary way, in the differences between Melville, a member of the Mexican War generation, and Mark Twain of the Civil War generation; both were youthful adventurers and wanderers, but the variance between Melville's romantic accounts of his adventures in the Marquesas and Twain's casual cynicism about his travels in the Hawaiian Islands is so marked in feeling and attitude that they might have been writing on separate planets.

For the American youth who did not feel capable of devoting his life to making or selling things, of committing himself to success and respectability, there was still the possibility of escaping across the far horizons. Running away to sea was the traditional remedy; the sailing ships provided a quick but not easy exit, and swallowed up malcontents, misfits, romantics and rebels by the thousands. Those who didn't like that rough and hazardous life could drop out once more by jumping ship. Thus the ports of eastern Asia and the islands of the South Seas were littered with those who rejected the growing complications of American life, who couldn't abide the floggings and salt horse and hardtack and brutal routine of life on a merchant ship, who had rushed to California for gold and panned nothing but gravel and could only keep going west.

Awaiting them was a world which would be the worse for their coming. Already many of the islands, the more accessible ones, knew only grief and bitterness in their contact with the newcomers. "It has been said that the greatest curse to each of the South Sea Islands was the first man who discovered it," Richard Henry Dana wrote, describing the Hawaiian seamen's colony near San Diego in 1836. Two of his friends among the Kanakas were young men "wasting away under a disease which they would never have known but for their intercourse with people from Christian America and Europe." One, apparently suffering from tuberculosis, was "the most dreadful object I had ever seen in my life — his eyes sunken and dead, his cheeks fallen in against his teeth, his hands looking like claws; a dreadful cough, which seemed to rack his whole shattered system; a hollow, whispering voice, and an entire inability to move himself."[2]

Americans and other white men, he said, had "brought in diseases before unknown to the islanders, which are now sweeping off the native population of the Sandwich Islands at the rate of one-fortieth of the entire population annually. They seem to be a doomed people. The curse of a people calling themselves Christians seems to follow them everywhere."

1. *The Semi-Idyll of Herman Melville*

"If by any possibility," wrote Herman Melville in *Moby Dick,* "there be any as yet undiscovered thing in me; if I shall ever deserve any real repute in that small but high hushed world which I might not unreasonably be ambitious of; if hereafter I shall do anything that, upon the whole, a man might rather have done than have left undone; if, at my death, my executors or more properly my creditors find any precious mss. in my desk, then here I prospectively ascribe all the honour and the glory to whaling; for a whale ship was my Yale College and my Harvard."

The man who wrote that tribute to the whaling ship *Acushnet* was looking back on his impressionable youth. Like so many other of America's greatest literary men, he began his career, unwittingly, by leaving home and seeking a life of adventure; it was the opening theme in the lives of Dana, Twain, Bret Harte, Jack London, and on down to Ernest Hemingway and many of those he influenced. After the breakaway from a bourgeois home, the several years of youthful adventure fix the pattern for years of writing, and thus the vigor, the youthfulness — and possibly some of the immaturity — of the American novel.

"With a philosophical flourish Cato throws himself upon his sword; I quietly take to the ship," Melville wrote in the opening chapter of *Moby Dick*. Like many of his contemporaries he was overcome by desperation at the thought of living out his life as part of the American success machine. Unlike many of them, he was well born and would not have had to adapt himself to menial labor. His father was an importer in New York City, and young Melville could easily enough have made himself part of a comfortable and prosperous life. Instead, at eighteen, he shipped out as a cabin boy on a ship bound for England. He taught school for a few years, and then at twenty-one evidently was encouraged to break away again by reading Dana's *Two Years Before the Mast*.

A handsome, strapping youth, he sailed with the whaler *Acushnet* the next year, in 1841, on a long voyage to the South Seas. What he brought back with him, besides his education in the University of the Forecastle, was the material for a series of romances which made him famous before he was thirty. In the five books he wrote about the South Seas, he made the warm blue Pacific an irresistibly alluring place for his countrymen — a lasting enchantment that almost fifty years later inspired young Jack London to ship out with a Pacific sealer and later to explore the scenes of Melville's *Typee* on his own boat.

Melville was prepared for the hardships of sailing before the mast through his own service as a cabin boy and reading Dana's account of sailing around the Horn, but not for the brutality of the *Acushnet's* master, Valentine Pease, or the moral squalor of his fellow seamen. The whaler rounded the Horn, stopping off at Rio de Janeiro and the Galapagos Islands, and then headed into the southern Pacific. The misery of serving aboard the *Acushnet,* and what he imagined life on a South Sea island would be like, encouraged thoughts of desertion even before the whaler sailed into the Marquesas. In the opening chapter of *Typee,* he describes the vision he had of the beauty and horror he expected to find in the Marquesas: "Lovely houris — cannibal banquets — groves of coca-nuts — coral reefs — tatooed chiefs — and bamboo temples; sunny valleys planted with bread-fruit trees — carved canoes dancing on the flashing blue waters — savage woodlands guarded by horrible idols — *heathenish rites and human sacrifices*."

He felt an "irresistible curiosity" about those islands, not merely to see them while the *Acushnet* took on fresh water and food but to sample the delights of the Stone Age as he had heard of and read about them. He already doubted that Western civilization was the greatest of human blessings, a doubt first implanted by a seaman he met in Liverpool several years before, who railed at the curse of what he called "snivelization." As Melville remembered the diatribe: "Snivelized chaps only learns the way to take on about life and snivel . . . You don't see any damned beggars and pesky constables in Madagasky [Madagascar]. Blast Ameriky, I say."[3]

Thus it took no great wrench of loyalties for Melville to jump ship in the harbor of Nuka-hiva in the Marquesas with the intention of hiding in the interior and catching another ship for Australia or home. His first glimpse of the anchorage was dramatic: "bold rockbound coasts, with the surf beating high against the lofty cliffs." The night after they dropped anchor a "band of sylphs" came aboard to entertain the crew of the *Acushnet*. Melville was shocked at the ensuing "riot and debauchery." The Marquesans, he learned, had already been "contaminated" by a French naval fleet which had raised its flag over the islands and claimed their possession.[4]

Hoping to find part of the population unspoiled by the appearance of the white man, Melville jumped ship and made his way to the valley of the Typee, a tribe said to practice cannibalism. Among the Typee, however, he found nothing but kindness and hospitality. They gave him a hut, servants, "several young damsels" for decoration, and medical treatment for a leg injury he had sustained in his flight to the interior.

His favorite among the girls was Fayaway, as lyrical in grace and form as her name. His descriptions of that free spirit, the naked brown Eve of Melville's Eden, undoubtedly were largely responsible for the book's success. That and the utopian aspects of life among the Typees, for whom there were "none of those thousand sources of irritation that the ingenuity of civilized man has created to mar his own felicity . . . no cross old women, no cruel step-dames, no withered spinsters, no lovesick maidens, no sour bachelors, no inattentive husbands, no melancholy young men, no blubbering youngsters and no squalling brats. All was mirth, fun, and high good humor."[5]

It was apparent from his observations, set down with the exactitude of an anthropologist, that the carefree aspects of Typee society could be explained partly by the food that dropped from the breadfruit trees and the tappa bark that provided their clothing, both eliminating the necessity for competition. The whole tribe was a permanent leisure class. Their serenity was helped along, according to Melville, by a completely permissive attitude toward sex. Their taboos governed social, but not sexual, conduct. During his four-month stay in the valley, Melville affirmed, he never witnessed a quarrel or heard an unkind word. There was no possessiveness in the love the Typees felt for each other. "The natives appeared to form one household, whose members were bound together by ties of strong affection . . . Where all were treated as brothers and sisters, it was hard to tell who were actually related to each other by blood."[6]

Only the necessity of seeking treatment for his infected leg, he claimed, could have torn him away from the Elysian valley. He heard that an Australian ship was lying offshore and decided to embark with her as a matter of survival. Leaving the brown arms of Fayaway, his almost constant companion for months, was a wrenching experience he may often have regretted in cold New England. The last he saw of her she was clutching a piece of calico he had given her as a parting consolation. Years later an American traveler named Henry A. Wise, backtracking on Melville's account in *Typee,* found a woman named Fayaway drudging as a servant in the commissary of the French garrison at Nuku-heva.

Aboard the Australian whaler *Julia* he found himself under the command of a cockney landlubber whom the crew called Paper Jack. The ship's doctor, incredibly named Dr. Long Ghost, managed to heal up Melville's infected wound. Dr. Ghost also served as his tutor in the ways of the more sophisticated world. "He had certainly at some time or other spent money, drunk burgundy, and associated with gentlemen . . . He quoted Virgil, and talked of Hobbes of Malmesbury . . . In the easiest possible way he could refer to an amour he had in Palermo, his lion-hunting before breakfast among the Caffres [Kaffirs], and the quality of the coffee he had drunk in Muscat."

When the ship reached Papeete, in Tahiti, Melville and Ghost jumped ship, desertion then being a form of tourism. There was a flotilla of French warships in the harbor, whose commander had just succeeded in deposing the Tahitian queen. Melville and Ghost, in their roles of Candide and Pangloss, offered their services to the deposed queen but they were rejected. They drifted from isle to isle, beachcombers living on the kindness of the natives. The dreamlike quality of those hand-to-mouth days later worked its way into the texture of *Typee* and *Omoo* and *Mardi.* One unpleasant contrast he found to life in the Marquesas was the presence of missionaries. Christianity, he believed, would be the ruination of the Tahitians.

Melville drifted on to Hawaii, where he again was depressed by the effects of Christianization. In 1843, when he arrived in Honolulu, the Americans and the English had just begun their long contest for the islands. In an appendix to *Typee,* he vented all his heartfelt disgust at United States colonialism, with guile and hypocrisy its chief weapons rather than the overt display of thirty-two-pounders favored by the French and British. He inveighed against "the ascendancy of a junta of ignorant and designing Methodist elders . . . ruling with absolute sway over a nation just poised between barbarism and civilization." Puritanical laws had been imposed upon a people unaware of any connection between sex and guilt and "the most innocent freedoms between the sexes are punished with fine and imprisonments . . . In consequence of this, the fort at Honolulu was filled with a great number of young girls, who were confined there doing penance for their slips from virtue."[7]

After serving a year aboard the frigate *United States,* he returned to New York in 1844, a bronzed and bearded young man of twenty-five determined to put adventure behind him and make literary capital of his experiences. *Typee* was published in 1846, when the American imagination dwelled as never before on what lay beyond the Mississippi. In the next several years he published in rapid succession *Omoo, Mardi, Redburn* and *White-Jacket,* all based on his seafaring experiences. Neither *Moby Dick* (1851) nor any of his other books until *Billy Budd,* published in the year of his death, 1891, recaptured the audience his youthful accounts of roaming in the South Seas had won for him. His books about the South Pacific came at a time and were written in a manner that coincided happily with the nation's booming confidence in itself and in its reach for the seas he described with all the freshness and vigor of youth.

Yet there was also a warning implicit in what he observed as there was in the writings of his predecessors, Ledyard and Dana. Americans were spoilers as well as the self-conscious bearers of civilization. Ledyard saw that whites ruined the natural grace and snatched away the freedoms of the natives, and Dana, from a distance, observed how the white man's diseases spread among a people without immunity to either the viruses or the vices of civilization. To Melville, Christianity as presented to and enforced upon the Pacific islanders was itself a viral form of depredation; he considered himself a Christian, but the bitter honesty and self-knowledge that compelled him to write *Moby Dick,* when another romance would have kept him rolling along with the success machine, made him suspect that Trade, Cross and Flag was less than a holy trinity.

In a passage which his publishers persuaded him to eliminate in later editions of *Typee,* he described Honolulu as "a community of disinterested merchants, and devoted self-exiled heralds of the Cross, located on the very spot that twenty years ago was defiled by the presence of idolatry. What a subject for an eloquent Bible-meeting orator! . . . But when these philanthropists send us such glowing accounts of one-half of their labors, why does modesty restrain them from publishing the other half of the good they have wrought? — Not until I visited Honolulu was I aware of the fact that the small remnant of the natives had been civilised into draught horses and evangelized into beasts of burden. But so it is. They have been literally broken into the traces and are harnessed to the vehicles of their spiritual instructors like so many dumb brutes."[8] The pity was that after Melville there were no writers with his power and moral indignation to convey to Americans what their presence meant to the peoples involved in the great westering movement; the greater pity is that it probably wouldn't have mattered.

2. *The Legend of Bully Hayes*

The hard, salt-rimed men who peopled the books of Melville and Dana were gentle folk compared to the legendary one-eared rascal named William Henry Hayes, better known as Bully, who was America's leading entry in the annals of piracy. Literary-minded Americans had their view of the Pacific world through the prismatic vision of their great writers, but the semiliterate masses who read little but the newspapers could glimpse a raffish seascape of blackbirders, slavers, smugglers, pearl-hijackers, opium-runners, ship-scuttlers and gun-runners through the ardently reported career of Bully Hayes. The midcentury newspapers recounted his exploits in column after column, well aware of their readers' fascination with an uneducated runaway boy from the Middle West who became a South Seas buccaneer so long after piracy was supposed to have disappeared from the modern world.

No writer would have dared to invent him, nor to have cast his career as fiction. Not even an age that accepted melodrama straight and unrefined could have believed in Bully Hayes as a fictional character. Yet his life can be traced, and some of his incredible exploits verified, in newspaper accounts, memoirs and the vexed dispatches of officials charged with trying to tame him. He was outsized in his villainy, and even Robert Louis Stevenson, studying his career from his home on Samoa, did not dare create from it a literary companion for his Long John Silver. "Talk in the South Seas," Stevenson noted more than a dozen years after Hayes met his overdue death, "is all upon one pattern; it is a wide ocean, indeed, but a narrow world: you shall never talk long and not hear the name of Bully Hayes, a naval hero, whose exploits and deserved extinction left Europe cold."

True enough, Europe by then was fed up with the romance of piracy and wary of the hyperbolic American of the adventure legends. Bully was simply unbelievable to Europeans, but to Americans he was a real-life, seagoing Mike Fink or Paul Bunyan; a disgraceful fellow really, but a matter of sneaking pride in the way he outwitted all those foreigners all those years out in the Pacific. As one admirer put it, he managed to "bamboozle" the British, the Germans, the French, the Spanish, the Maoris, the Dutch, everyone unfortunate enough to cross his path. "They never caught him out, did they? They would never have got Hayes stumbling down the stone steps of the Pirates' stairs at Wapping before being slung in chains at Blackwall Point — no, nor would he have sat biting his nails at Newgate like that plucked crow, Captain Kidd, waiting and waiting in vain for the King's pardon which never came. Bully Hayes would have fooled his jailer; taken tea with the Governor of the prison; asked the chaplain to pray for him, emptied the prison safe and then vamoosed with the Governor's daughter — and what's more, he'd have dropped a donation into the poor-box before leaving."[9]

That was an accurate and succinct description of Bully Hayes's personality and methods. The rascal who is both bold and charming has more than his share of luck, and Hayes was beguiling enough, when the mood was upon him, to charm the birds out of the sky, the fish out of the sea and women out of their virtue. He had the physical appearance ascribed in fiction, but rarely encountered in reality, of the all-American hero: tall, muscular, blond, blue-eyed, always smiling, apparently eager to please. One acquaintance especially remembered the look in his honest blue eyes which seemed to be saying, "I'm jest achin' to do yew a service." The service, often, was cutting your throat or stranding you on a rock in the middle of the South Pacific. A shellbacked British admiral who knew him while stationed at Hong Kong as a young midshipman also remembered him as an irresistible fellow, "one of those men who almost always had a twinkle in his eye and a grin around his mouth, however things were stacking up — and whether with men, women or children he had such a hearty 'put it there' sort of way with him, all geniality and good manners, that never a soul could resist his blandishing mode of carrying on — even the toughest of desperadoes became clay in his hands."[10]

There were in fact several of him careering around the Pacific, the well-born but much put-upon William Henry Hayes, a victim of cruel fate, as he pictured himself; the spectacular rogue portrayed in the newspapers; the charmer that a number of women knew, usually to their regret; the horrible Bully Hayes who kidnaped and slaughtered the natives of the islands he visited — all the contradictions of a living legend.

Much of what was written about him by his contemporaries was colored by rage, sorrow, fear and indignation, but the bulk of his career and the man himself was summed up most adequately in the dispassionate naval prose of Commander A. E. Dupuis of H. M. *Rosario* in a report to Commodore J. G. Goodenough, commanding the Australian station. His warship had recently cruised among the islands and in the waters in which Bully Hayes had been operating, and Commander Dupuis could only conclude from the information he gathered that Hayes was "a most unprincipled but shrewd man, one who has (I now have no doubt) committed many shocking acts of violence on the natives . . . yet so clever is he in methods of proceeding, and so much has his name got to be feared by both natives and white residents on the islands, that though it was evident that at nearly all the islands I visited he was well known, yet it was impossible to find out much about him or his deeds. I was perfectly convinced that nearly the whole of the whites and natives were afraid to speak out."[11]

Commander Dupuis wrote of "a case of shockingly brutal treatment of a young girl whom he brought from the island of Pingelap," of "another case of rape and shocking cruelty on the person of a young native girl," of visiting Hayes's settlement at South Harbour, where "no less than five young women or girls were living in his house, who had all, with one exception, been living on board the *Leonora* with him." Philandering, of course, was the least of the crimes charged against him. Commander Dupuis heard whispers of murder, robbery, kidnaping, and a whole catalogue of crimes on land and sea, but admitted that "thinking the case over quietly afterwards, I cannot see how I could have arrested Hayes."

To his sole biographer, Basil Lubbock, he was somewhat traduced in the accounts of his contemporaries and was more of a conman than a buccaneer, "a past-master at obtaining something for nothing. Sometimes that something was a pretty girl . . . at other times it was a ship . . . he was equally successful in conjuring golden sovereigns or Mexican dollars from the pockets of hard-headed American, Colonial, and even Chinese business men." Often he would be stranded in some Oriental port, penniless and wanted by the police, yet "with consummate nerve and effrontery he would at once proceed to borrow sufficient from a new victim to provide himself not only with a new vessel but with sea stock for that vessel, and even a valuable cargo."[12]

And there was the testimony of Louis Becke, an Australian who sailed with Hayes for almost two months as his supercargo and later wrote some of the finest South Sea tales, who recalled that when Hayes signed him on he was told, "I give you my word that I won't ask you to join in anything doubtful; the traders round here are the greatest scoundrels unhung, and I have to treat them as they treat me." For a time Becke was a hero-worshiper, and retained a certain reluctant admiration for him even after his disillusionment.

Becke, of course, had reason to be grateful to the memory of William Henry Hayes because his adventures on Hayes's brig *Leonora* provided the basis for his best-known work, *A Modern Buccaneer,* published in 1894. A leading character in that novel is William Henry Hayston, who is Bully Hayes in all his menace as well as his courage and charm. Scoundrels are always sociable, as Schopenhauer noted, but Becke in his fictional analysis showed the psychosis underlying that genial smile.

Hayes first appeared in the Pacific in the early 1850's, when he was in his early twenties. By his own dubious account, his background was both romantic and melancholy. As he told it, he was descended from a distinguished naval family and himself became a lieutenant in the United States Navy, serving under Captain Farragut. He fell in love with the sweetheart of a brother officer, a scandal ensued, and he was forced to resign his commission. Much against his natural inclinations, he was cast into lowly company and eventually he drifted to the Far East to start life anew.

The few facts available on his early years are somewhat grimier. In 1859, a Honolulu newspaper made its own investigation. The *Advertiser* learned that Hayes was born in Cleveland, in 1829, the son of a lakefront saloonkeeper. Early in his teens he was cut loose by his family and served as "loblolly boy" on a Great Lakes schooner, on which he was seasoned as a brawler among the mallet-fisted Irishmen who sailed those ships. He quickly acquired their life-style: rather drink than eat, rather fight than drink. He was still in his teens when he married his first wife. Without legally discarding her, he gave the unhappy title of Mrs. William Henry Hayes to a second woman. Intervals ashore apparently were disastrous for him, because at the age of twenty he was accused of stealing a horse, a curious charge to be lodged against a sailor. Rather than face trial for bigamy and horse-thievery, he headed out west with Mrs. Hayes number two in the first wave of the gold rush. It was characteristic of him that instead of heading for the diggings in the foothills he became a professional gambler on the theory that it was easier mining gold out of miners' pockets than in a mountain creek. Apparently he left San Francisco — and along with it the second Mrs. Hayes and one of his ears, which evidently was detached in a knife fight over the gaming table — at the urgent request of the Vigilance Committee. To cover the missing ear he wore his tawny hair long, and turned nasty whenever anyone asked him about it.[13]

Then came one of those blank spaces in his record. All that is known for certain is that he popped up in Singapore on July 11, 1853, in command of the ship *Canton,* which he sold a week later. American consular records show that he bought the ship *Otranto* with the proceeds. On March 10, 1856, he returned to Singapore, sold the *Otranto,* bought back the *Canton* and renamed her the *C. W. Bradley* — a series of transactions which mystified the more sedate businessmen but which were in keeping with his sleight-of-hand disposition. Not shown in the consular records, but discovered by his biographer, was a hair-raising account of the six months he spent away from the Singapore waterfront.

He had joined up with the British navy, probably for the prize money involved, in its attempt to clean out the *pilongs* — Chinese pirates — who infested the coastal creeks and were led by a young renegade Yankee named Eli Boggs. Using his *Otranto* as a scout vessel, Hayes learned that the pirate junks were based in a creek flowing into the Gulf of Leotung. He boarded the British warship *Bittern* to guide the way to the creek. The *pilongs* had trapped more than a hundred merchant junks upriver off the city of Newchang.

Shortly before the *Bittern* arrived on the scene, the *pilongs* had sent ashore a basket containing the drawn-and-quartered body of a mandarin, along with a note demanding one hundred thousand dollars ransom for the merchant fleet. A swarm of thirty to forty pirate junks attacked the *Bittern* as she came up the Gulf of Leotung at daybreak. The pirate fleet came on full tilt, lobbing stinkpots (clay vessels which burst on deck loosing a cloud of noxious smoke — an early form of tear-gas grenades), launching iron-pointed rocket arrows and firing cannon and musket balls.

Bittern's tiers of well-serviced guns roared at the flimsy junks, and within half an hour the pirate fleet was scattered, many of the junks sunk or in flight. Bully Hayes insisted that the pursuit be kept up until the junk captained by Eli Boggs was run down. Boggs's junk was cornered in a creek at the south end of the gulf, when Hayes spotted a white man jumping overboard and trying to make his escape. Hayes jumped in after him, caught up with him in the shallows, knocked him out and dragged him aboard the *Bittern*. The reward for his services included two chests of silver, cases of furs, chests of tea, boxes of silk, curios, opium and two jade idols. He sold the lot and went on a monumental spree in Hong Kong, possibly to wipe out the memory of the first and last time he fought on the side of the law. He drank up the prize money, and more, then sailed back to Singapore in the *Otranto* followed by the wails of bilked merchants.[14]

For the next twenty years his exploits as a highbinder on land and sea were the leading topic of conversation from Honolulu to Singapore and made him a sort of hero, regarded with a concealed admiration by his countrymen, through newspaper accounts in the States. To Europeans and Asians he was simply a dangerous criminal, but to Americans a high-spirited lad with, perhaps, a little more than his share of enterprise. His career was marked not only by financial success but an amatory prowess that spoke well for the American libido.

It may have been true, as Bully himself inferred, that business rivals blackened his name unduly and blamed every atrocity that occurred in the South Seas on him to conceal their own roguery, just as financiers back in the States blamed Jay Gould every time large numbers of investors were wiped out in the stock market. But even from the certifiable facts the elusive W. H. Hayes had a lot to answer for. Late in 1856 he took a full cargo on consignment for merchants in Singapore, sold it in Batavia, Java, and refilled his hold with another cargo from Dutch merchants, who were also swindled out of the proceeds. From the Indies he bustled into the coolie-smuggling trade out of Swatow, on the Chinese coast, to Australia, where the forcibly migrated Chinese were sold to slave on the plantations. Even from this profitable traffic Bully managed to squeeze extra dividends. A coolie transport was supposed to pay a poll tax of fifty dollars a head when it landed in Australia. On his last trip to Sydney, Bully decided to evade the tax. As he arrived in the harbor he suddenly hoisted distress signals indicating he had sprung a leak. A fleet of rescue ships came out and was persuaded to take his "passengers" — one hundred coolies — to safety on land on the plea that he would have to beach his sinking craft. Bully then piled on sail and scuttled away, leaving the rescuers to pay the poll tax on the Chinese they had "saved." It saved Bully five thousand dollars. As his biographer commented, "There was some stubborn kink in Bully Hayes's constitution which prevented him from ever paying a bill — even when ready money was available."[15]

With the proceeds from various recent ventures encouraging a spell of leisure, Captain Hayes spent most of 1857 as an ornament of refined circles in Fremantle, on the west coast of Australia, which not too long before had been colonized by convicts from Britain. Perhaps they had uncertain standards by which to judge a newcomer, possibly they were completely taken in by the cloak of respectability in which Hayes now wrapped himself. He dressed well, was more courteous to women than their rough-mannered consorts, and sang beautifully at musicales. And he spoke often of "settling down," of hoping to find a good woman, the sort of talk which quickly endeared him to local matrons and attracted the attention of a pretty young widow, Mrs. Amelia Littleton, the daughter of the local harbor master. His courtship was undoubtedly hastened by two conditions: Mrs. Littleton had money, and Bully had just been deprived of most of his when agents of the Singapore merchants he had swindled caught up with him and threatened to expose him if he refused to pay up. Mrs. Littleton agreed to marry him, unaware that he had been twice married and not once divorced.

Mr. and Mrs. Hayes next turned up in San Francisco, where Bully evidently was again forced to live by his wits, judging by the story in a San Francisco newspaper detailing his means of departure. He had somehow talked a shipowner into giving him command of the brig *Ellenita.* "The brig *Ellenita,* Captain Hayes, ran off on Sunday night without clearing papers, and leaving creditors to the amount of several thousand dollars in the lurch. The captain pretended that he was about to sail for Melbourne, and obtained credit for the repair of the vessel and large amounts of stores, besides the baggage of intending passengers, with all of which he put off on an unknown and unlawful voyage." Behind him on the waterfront he left the third Mrs. Hayes, who later made her way to Apia, Samoa, and spent the rest of her life there.[16]

The *Ellenita* began taking water off Samoa and finally foundered in heavy seas. Sixteen crew members floated away on a makeshift raft, which was picked up twenty days later by a British warship, while Captain Hayes and four others made off in the lifeboat and reached the island of Savaii.

Bully had hardly reached Australia and sobered up from celebrating his narrow escape when the leading newspaper in Sydney published a cautionary column advising no one to trade, take passage or even shake hands with Captain Hayes. The story was headed THE CAREER OF A REMARKABLE SCOUNDREL and described him as a large solidly built bucko "of rather plausible, bluff exterior, which with many, it would seem, has enabled him to pass off, until a settlement came, as a very honest jolly seaman, and he is a man who at times spends his money, or the money in his possession, very liberally . . . The success of this enormous mercantile humbug (he having possessed himself probably to the amount of $20,000, or to the value thereof, without any equivalent but impudence and promises) is the more singular from the fact that he is a man of the most meager education, and possessing no particular qualities, except rare cunning, attended by an unlimited command of impudence, and a somewhat more than average degree of physical power."[17]

Despite such bulletins published in newspapers throughout the

Pacific, Hayes continued to find a victim for plucking whenever he needed a ship, a drink, or a cargo on consignment. In 1862 he popped up in the new gold fields at Arrowtown, New Zealand, convinced by his experience as a California gold-rusher that gold is easier extracted from miners' pokes than in the comfortless diggings. He took a quick look around and decided that show business was his best bet at the moment. The Buckingham Variety Troupe was providing the only entertainment available at the time, and its star was the widowed Mrs. Rona Buckingham, described as "good-looking in the florid buxom style." Most of the troupe consisted of other members of the family: her daughter Rona, with a voice so powerful she could sing "Annie Laurie" in competition with a brass band, and her four sons who were billed as the Masters Buckingham. Bully took over as Mrs. Buckingham's suitor and manager of the troupe, but soon became dissatisfied with the percentage of profits received from the theater. He moved the troupe into a jerrybuilt establishment calling itself the United States Hotel, where it performed in the barroom. It was a bad move, because another troupe took over the Arrowtown theater and offered vigorous competition. Bully was soon embroiled in a feud with the rival troupers, who bribed a cockney barber to find out why Hayes wore his hair shoulder-length. The barber discovered that an ear had been lopped off, and the town roared with ribald speculation over how Hayes had lost it. The rival troupe plastered the place with three-sheets announcing it would present a farce titled *The Barbarous Barber,* and made it plain that the career of W. H. Hayes had provided the inspiration. Hayes rounded up a gang of mining-camp toughs and raided the theater on opening night, only to be repelled by an enraged audience. Bully then disappeared from Arrowtown with the Buckinghams in tow. With his usual gallantry he made Rona the fourth Mrs. Hayes.

In 1864, he obtained command of the coal schooner *Black Diamond,* out of Sydney, and sailed up the coast with a full cargo and with his wife, their thirteen-month-old daughter and his brother-in-law aboard. The *Black Diamond* sprang a leak and had to put in at Croixelles Bay, off South Island, for repairs. To while away the time, Hayes took his wife and baby daughter out for a cruise on a borrowed yacht. The yacht sank, his wife and daughter were drowned, and Hayes swam ashore alone. Most people familiar with his career were convinced that he scuttled the boat and thus rid himself of the complications of family life.[18]

The tragedy apparently left him undaunted. Several months later a New Zealand paper reported that Hayes had made off with a young Irish girl. "It appears that Hayes, commander of the cutter *Wave,* 10 tons, put in last month at Akaroa, and in a hotel at that place met a young girl named Helen Murray, 16 or 17 years old, a native of Ireland, a well-educated and intelligent girl, who had lost both parents. Having prevailed on her 'by fraud and persuasion,' which constitute the crime of abduction, to accompany him in his cutter to Lyttleton, for the purpose, as he falsely stated, of there joining several other girls and young women whom he had engaged to go to China as part of a theatrical company he was then organising . . . he induced the girl to embark." There were several other passengers aboard, according to this account, and all were horrified by Hayes's heavyhanded attempts to seduce the girl.

"All Hayes's persuasions and entreaties could not induce the girl to share the [cabin] occupied by him. During wet and stormy nights she remained on deck, and one night in particular, when the waves were washing over the cutter, she sometimes clung to the mast, and during a temporary lull would cling to one of the men, entreating him to save her." Thwarted and enraged, Bully finally put the girl off his cutter in a small boat and she drifted ashore on Long Island with her virtue intact.[19]

After that, with police or creditors watching for him at every sizable port in the South Pacific, Hayes made few attempts at pretending to be respectable. The jolly roger was up on every ship he sailed; his theme song, roared out from the bridge in his booming baritone when he felt in the mood, was entirely suitable:

> *My name is Racketty Jack*
> *A noisy swell am I,*
> *I care not how the world may wag,*
> *I will never say die.*

> *Hi! Ho! Hi! Stop!*
> *Here, waiter! Fizz! Pop!*
> *I'm Racketty Jack, and no money I lack;*
> *Oh, I'm the boy for a spree!*

The rest of his career, accordingly, read like a police blotter, one large enough to accommodate the offenses of a dozen renegades. He ran guns to the Maoris rebelling against the white government of New Zealand, in a brig he sentimentally named the *Rona* for the fourth Mrs. Hayes, whom he may or may not have murdered. He obtained a seventy-one-ton schooner, the *Shamrock,* and made himself prominent in the blackbirding trade, more politely called "labor recruiting," in which natives were kidnaped from their islands or bought from their chiefs.

The blackbirders were the worst scoundrels in the South Pacific, according to one missionary who had tried to deal with Bully Hayes. "When we preached peace they led in war; when we deprecated the lack of clothing they went native in their dress; when we frowned on *kava* drinking they brewed sugar toddy; and finally, many of them actually joined in the terrible cannibalistic feasts and even boasted that they enjoyed eating 'long pig' as they called human flesh." He did not claim to have seen Hayes gorging himself at a cannibal banquet, but he did charge that Hayes passed himself off as a missionary to lure Kanakas aboard the *Shamrock* and sell them to the Australian plantations as slave labor, and that the murder of Bishop Patteson on Nukapu Island, of the Swallow group, was in revenge for a kidnaping performed by Hayes in the guise of a missionary. Usually, however, Hayes preferred to deal with the chiefs, who took trade goods in return for the "black ivory" worked to death on the copra plantations and the guano islands off Peru.[20]

Every year added something new and horrible to the legend of Bully Hayes. Once his ship foundered on the reef near Manihiki, and the natives helped him and his crew build a boat. Bully rewarded them by taking them off their island at gunpoint and selling them to the planters of Samoa. He was only one of about fifty blackbirders "recruiting" labor in the South Seas, a traffic which around 1870 became very important to the development of the Queensland sugar plantations, but he was easily the most notorious. It became an issue in the more civilized parliaments of the world, and the British finally assigned five small gunboats to intercept blackbirding vessels, but they proved ineffectual, as did certain halfhearted gestures on the part of the Australian government.

Around that time Hayes went into partnership with the man noted for being his near-equal in degradation. He was Ben Pease, former lieutenant in the United States Navy, who had deserted the naval service in favor of commanding a Chinese gunboat charged by the Imperial government with protecting the mercantile junks against pirates. Pease demanded almost as high a price for protection as the pirates. Later he became a blackbirder in the Solomons, where he traded human heads with the chiefs for live human merchandise. Hayes was then cruising the Solomons pretending to be a missionary bishop and snatching his "converts" off to slavery. The two men met and decided to go into partnership — an odd couple indeed, the outsize, hearty Hayes and the small, cruel-eyed Pease with his silky little beard, gentle voice, womanish hands and tittering laugh.

They acquired a heavy armed brig, the *Pioneer,* and sallied forth to various forms of piracy. Their most profitable venture was raiding various islands and looting the traders' copra and coconut oil sheds. Once they came across a Portuguese gunboat grounded on a reef, offered to help float her off, instead stripped her guns and left the crew stranded.

The firm of Hayes & Pease broke up, predictably enough, over a girl. Pease bought a young beauty from a chief on Pelew Island for two hundred and fifty dollars. Hayes complimented his partner on his excellent taste, then appropriated the girl for himself. Wild with rage, Pease drew his revolver, which Hayes wrenched away from him. The unhappy voyage continued to Shanghai. A few days after the *Pioneer* docked a squad of Shanghai police came aboard and took Pease away on charges of piracy. There were few who disbelieved the report that Bully had tipped off the police. Well aware of his ex-partner's vengeful disposition, Hayes slipped away from Shanghai in the *Pioneer,* which he discreetly renamed the *Leonora.*

For a time he made his headquarters on Kusaie in the western Carolines, a lovely island he soon made horrible with his depredations. He was specifically charged by King Togusa of Kusaie, in a complaint to the British naval authorities, with having raped a ten-year-old girl and having held a chief as hostage for two girls and seven thousand coconuts. The corvette *Rosario* steamed up to investigate after Commander Dupuis received a letter from the king stating, "I am glad to see your ship to my island at this time. I think because you come Kaptin Hayes he go . . . We think Kaptin Hayes one bad man . . . I like very much you take him on board your ship and carry him off."

Commander Dupuis arrested Hayes and charged him, according to Louis Becke, who had accompanied Hayes to Kusaie, with "everything but leprosy."

"The inquiry was a farce," Becke wrote later. "Of seven witnesses against Hayes, stranded and dissolute white traders who had professed themselves anxious to give evidence, only two were game to appear, and they so contradicted themselves that the commander told them to clear out." Commander Dupuis advised the king that he could detain Hayes and hand him over to an American warship, but the "king and his people were too mortally afraid of him to attempt such a course." Hayes grandly sailed away from Kusaie in a small boat with an American beachcomber for a companion.[21]

In the spring of 1875 Hayes turned up on Spanish-ruled Guam, got into a scrape and was promptly arrested by the Spanish military, who sent him in chains to Manila for trial. The court sentenced him to nine months in prison, where he professed to repent his scabrous past. He was visited in prison by Captain Joshua Slocum, who was making his famous solitary voyage around the world in the *Spray.*

"When I called upon Hayes in the Manila jail," Slocum wrote, "I found him in the midst of the governor's family on the veranda, discussing religious matters . . . Hayes became a chum of the governor of the prison, and also struck up a warm friendship with the priest, who baptized him in the Roman Catholic faith . . . Now that he was converted to the true faith, Hayes found an all-powerful friend in the Bishop of Manila. The buccaneer was a penitent and he made a most impressive and moving figure. . . . The light free spring of his gait was gone, and he was the picture of the shuffling monk.

"To behold the old freebooter, penniless, reduced by sickness, tall, gaunt, with flowing white beard half a fathom long, marching barefooted at the head of a religious procession, and carrying the tallest candle of them all, softened the hearts of his enemies . . . His accusers retracted their charges . . . After his release, Hayes obtained passage home from Manila on the ship *Whittier,* bound for San Francisco. The U.S. consul vouched for him as a destitute citizen. He found himself in clover on the *Whittier.* Parcels containing comforts and knick-knacks of various kinds were sent to him from ships in the harbour, and the captain of the *Whittier,* being of a religious turn of mind, treated the reformed buccaneer like a brother."[22]

Reformed? If true, a choir of angels would have hovered over that ship plowing back to America with one of her unruliest sons.

Once back in San Francisco, Hayes, now bald and close to fifty but still full of juice, proved himself a backslider. He talked a well-to-do San Franciscan named Moody, who had a pretty wife as well as a nest egg, into buying the small schooner *Lotus,* on which they would sail to the South Seas and make their fortune off a cargo of five thousand dollars worth of trade goods. The rest of the company would include a mate and a Scandinavian cook named Dutch Pete.

Bully then made one of his famous getaways. The *Lotus* sailed suddenly with himself, his mate, cook and cargo — and Mrs. Moody. Her husband was left behind, having been sent on an errand by Hayes just before the *Lotus* upped anchor. According to his mate, it was a fairly happy voyage; Mrs. Moody did not seem to object to her fate, and it was smooth sailing until they left the island of Jaluit at the end of March 1877. One night Hayes and the cook got into a fight on deck. Hayes drew his gun but Dutch Pete was quicker and swung a boathook at him.

Down went Bully Hayes, for the last time. His body was thrown overboard.[23] The *Lotus* returned to Jaluit, where Dutch Pete was acclaimed a hero. Several months earlier, in a Dakota saloon, a similar long-haired, middle-aged golden boy named Wild Bill Hickok was shot in the back of the head by a moronic youth. Hayes and Hickok had both outlived the time for legend-making, whether on land or sea. Freebooting henceforth would be undertaken in a more prosaic and businesslike fashion.

5

Onward Christian Soldiers, Sailors and Marines

Multiply your ships and send them forth to the East.
— SENATOR WILLIAM H. SEWARD

During the decade preceding the American Civil War the international rivalry over eastern Asia greatly resembled a cutthroat poker game on a Mississippi riverboat. Gathered around the green baize were Great Britain whose naval power made her the toughest player of the lot; France with her many colonial frustrations, mostly caused by Britain; Imperial Russia with her great and persevering ambition to move down from the cold seas of the north; and a number of lesser but equally cunning participants including the United States, Portugal, Germany and Spain. The table stakes were trade and territorial concessions, naval bases and commercial treaties to be wrung out of the comparatively defenseless nations of China, Japan and Korea.

A later name for the game was "gunboat diplomacy," but it was a pious age and the players were required to mask their intentions with talk of ushering the Far Eastern countries into "the family of nations." Their chancelleries spoke in parables of bringing Christianity to the heathen East, but those were only code words for the movement of gunboats and landing parties, the imposition of most-favored-nation treaties, and the spreading of Western influence where it would do the most commercial good.

With stakes so high, the contending Western nations worked and plotted against each other with a furious energy, despite the pretense that they were all brothers-in-Christ, the propaganda that their sole united aim was bearing peace, prosperity and Western civilization to the Orient. They succumbed to brotherly love only when their interests were mutually threatened by ungrateful resistance from the subjects of their ministrations. In such circumstances the resentful French could cooperate with the contemptuous British, the aggressive Germans with the suspicious Russians, the ex-colonial Americans with their old masters from the British Isles. Thus in 1854 the United States and Britain sent a joint landing force ashore at Shanghai to drive off a body of Chinese troops who had inconvenienced the local foreign colony by camping out on the race track.*

Farsighted Americans were increasingly absorbed by the problem of expanding our interests in the Far East. The industrial economy had reached the takeoff point by the mid-Fifties, the domestic market was saturated by its products, and the price index was falling at an alarming rate. The solution to a growing economic problem was to send manufactured goods that could not be consumed at home to the developing markets of the Far East; it was taken for granted that the Oriental nations would not industrialize themselves but would be content to supply raw materials, just as Africa is now regarded as a supplier and buyer but not a maker.

The American Congress, urged on by the mercantile lobbyists, was constantly alert to the opportunities offered by trade with the Orient. As early as 1848, the House's Committee on Naval Affairs introduced a recommendation that steamship routes be opened between California, Hawaii and China. Regarding communication between the United States and China, the committee report asserted that swifter ships would "bring these two great nations nearer together, to give them a more perfect knowledge of each other, develop their resources, and build up a commerce more extensive than has probably ever heretofore existed between two nations. The improved condition of our relations with that country under the new treaties, and the extension of our territorial possessions to the Pacific, have placed it in our power *ultimately* to communicate with China almost as rapidly as we now do with Europe. To accomplish this, however, we must

* That operation was made doubly ironic by the fact that the American shore party was led by a Commander Kelly, who performed his duty with enthusiasm.

extend telegraphic wires across the continent, and establish a line of steamers from San Francisco, or Monterey, to Shanghai and Canton."[1]

Appended to this document was a report by Lieutenant Matthew F. Maury of the Naval Observatory which pointed out that with the adoption of the "great circle route" the United States was, in effect, three thousand miles closer to China. This was accomplished by elimination of the stopoff at the Hawaiian Islands. Accordingly, Lieutenant Maury emphasized, New Orleans was three thousand miles closer to China than Panama was by way of Honolulu, and from Monterey to Japan was not as far as from Panama to the Hawaiian Islands. If he fudged a little on his geography lesson for the congressional scholars, there was no one to dispute his reckoning.[2]

Five years later Secretary of the Navy John P. Kennedy, in the closing months of the Pierce Administration, urgently requested that the government establish its own steamship line across the Pacific if private enterprise could not be encouraged to take that step. He also recommended that coaling stations be set up on the Pacific islands to supply both naval and mercantile steamships. Such depots, Kennedy said, could be maintained at a low cost by developing the tobacco trade with China, encouraging the Chinese to lay aside their opium pipes in favor of briars and cigars, and an import trade of guano from the Pacific islands.

Morality had nothing to do with his proposal, nor any belief that tobacco was less dangerous to the consumer than opium, but Kennedy did not hesitate to drag Christianity into the argument. "The use of opium in China has been the great cause of preventing the extension of commerce into that country, while at the same time, many believe, it has almost entirely shut out the lights and advantages of Christianity. If, by any means that our government shall employ, a trade between us and China shall be opened, there is reason to suppose that our tobacco will be generally received there as a substitute for this poisonous drug. This article, now so abundantly produced in our tobacco-growing states, will then become the pioneer of our trade, and open the way for our manufactures of cotton, wool, and particularly of cutlery and other manufactures of iron — in which latter articles the trade between Great Britain and China is now very large.

"These two articles of tobacco and guano would alone, without any other commodities, afford the means of opening a rapid and profitable intercourse with China. The production of tobacco would be increased in a measure corresponding to the increased demand of the two hundred millions of Chinese consumers, and thus our national wealth would be greatly augmented."[3]

Simpler and more striking was the formula of the Senator from New York, William H. Seward, who was to be one of the chief engineers of the Pacific movement: "Multiply your ships and send them forth to the East."

American optimism has never burned brighter than when it envisions the potential wealth of the Asian market — no less now, for all the dismal but unheeded lessons of the statistics, than during the less sophisticated 1850's. Regarding the evergreen promise of the Asian market, Akira Iriye, the young Japanese-American historian, has written: "The longer it failed to materialize, the greater the need would be to overcome the frustrations and paint a picture of what might have been and what might yet be . . . American exports to China and Japan never grew in proportion to the growth rate of American export trade as a whole. Imports from these countries always surpassed exports to them, though in over-all American trade the reverse was almost always the case after 1875. Besides, China and Japan continuously bought natural products from the United States, such as cotton, wheat, and tobacco, and not manufactured goods as Americans hoped. For these the Asian purchasing power was excessively low, even without higher tariffs."[4] But always an excuse could be found for the disparity between hope and reality; the opening of the Suez Canal in 1869, for instance, and the increased competition from Europe that resulted.

In all phases of the American relationship with eastern Asia a similar wishfulness, if not downright hypocrisy, shaped our attitudes. The great shibboleth, by no means destroyed even under the impact of twentieth-century actualities, was the concept that commerce is peaceful, therefore it will bring peace among nations — a theory that attempts to conceal the fact that commerce also brings about rivalry among the competing nations, that competition develops into a search for military as well as trade alliances, and military alliances often serve their ultimate purpose. It was an idea borrowed from eighteenth-century Europe, but American statesmen have always been particularly fond of it, even while they attributed more sinister motives to the European activity in Asia.

There was also the official attitude, dating back to the first years of the China trade, that American merchants acted as private individuals, that their activities were not the direct concern of Washington; yet the United States government made it a policy to open consulates almost everywhere the British did and later to build a navy capable of protecting the trade routes, bases and ports in which that business was transacted. This policy and its proclaimed passiveness left American representatives in Asia to act on their own initiative, particularly during the years when it took almost a year to exchange messages between Washington and eastern Asia, and contributed much to the venality which often characterized our Asian performance.

Some of the conspiratorial ardor with which these representatives performed their duties was exemplified by Dr. Peter Parker, D.D., M.D., who went to China as a medical missionary before the Opium War and soon decided that his talents were more necessary to the diplomatic service than to God's work among the heathen. By 1856 he had risen from interpreter and adviser attached to various diplomatic missions to United States commissioner in China. He, too, belongs in the first rank of Pacificists, for his ambitions if not his achievements.

In 1856 the Manchu rulers of China were proving reluctant to make any more trade concessions to Great Britain and France and both nations were considering the use of force against Peking. Policy was supposed to be made in Washington, with Dr. Parker its instrument, but he saw an opportunity for a masterstroke of aggressive diplomacy. The Manchus could be brought to their knees, he declared in consultation with the French and British representatives in China, if more of their territory was detached. Therefore he proposed that the United States occupy Formosa, the coal deposits of which would make the island a valuable naval station, while the French and British nibbled elsewhere at the Chinese carcass. The French and British indicated their agreement with the plan, and Dr. Parker hastened from Hong Kong to Macao for a conference with Commodore James Armstrong, the commander of the United States naval squadron on station there. The commodore thought it was an excellent idea, but insisted he would need reinforcements on the possibility the Chinese resisted his landing forces.

On February 12, 1857, Parker wrote the State Department urging the seizure of Formosa on the grounds that "the subject of Formosa is becoming one of great interest to a number of our enterprising fellow-citizens, and deserves more consideration from the great commercial nations of the West than it has yet received; and it is much to be hoped that the Government of the United States may not *shrink* from the *action* which the interests of humanity, civilization, navigation, and commerce impose upon it in relation to Tai-Wan, particularly the southeastern portion of it, at present inhabited by savages, to whose depraved cruelties we have every reason to believe many Europeans, and among them our own friends and countrymen, have fallen victims."[5]

That dispatch landed on State Department desks with a dull thud. Apparently Secretary of State William H. Marcy was so taken aback by the ex-missionary's uninhibited exercise of diplomacy that it took him a long time to formulate a reply. In any case, Commissioner Parker and Commodore Armstrong, no matter how feverish their thirst for adventure, would not be able to make a move without the reinforcement of the Far East naval squadron. Also Dr. Parker's commission would soon expire, and with it his grandiose design for the American occupation of Formosa. Shortly before the Pierce Administration ended, however, Marcy wrote Parker coolly disavowing any sanction for the proposal and pointing out that "even if our relations with China warrant the 'last resort' you speak of . . . the military and naval forces of the United States could be used only by the authority of Congress." The squadron on the China station would be reinforced, he added, but not for "aggressive purposes." An even sharper implied rebuke to Parker was contained in a letter of instruction to his successor: "This country, you will constantly bear in mind, is not at war with the Government of China, nor does it seek to enter into that empire for any other purpose than those of lawful commerce, and for the protection of the lives and property of its citizens."[6]

Actually Dr. Parker might have been forgiven his enthusiasm for aggrandizement, if not his presumption in going so far to arrange it without consulting Washington. By the time he had formulated his plans for the seizure of Formosa, the United States had provided the example, under a previous administration, by forcibly opening the ports of Japan to American trade.

1. *Four Black Ships*

A heavyset, bearlike man with an equally ursine temperament was chosen for the delicate task of "opening the door to Japan." That a naval hero nicknamed "Old Bruin" and famed for his salty disposition was nominated for this semidiplomatic, semimilitary role was indicative of the determination with which the United States was prepared to proceed against the Japanese. The dispatch of Commodore Matthew Calbraith Perry with his squadron of four ships painted black (a Freudian slip, perhaps) was ordered in 1852 as a measure of meeting the competition with Britain, a means of securing a United States counterpart of Hong Kong. In a dispatch from Madeira on his way to the Far East, Commodore Perry made it clear enough that this was the real purpose of his expedition: "When we look at the possessions in the east of our great maritime rival, England, and of the constant and rapid increase of their fortified ports, we should be admonished of the necessity of prompt measures on our part . . . Fortunately the Japanese and many other islands in the Pacific are still left untouched by this unconscionable government; and, as some of them lay in a route of commerce which is destined to become of great importance to the United States, no time should be lost in adopting active measures to secure a sufficient number of ports of refuge."[7]

As a veteran of the War of 1812, as a squadron commander during the Mexican War, as the commander of the navy's first steam vessel, Perry was eminently qualified for such an independent mission. He possessed further influence and prestige through his brother Oliver Hazard Perry, one of the few heroes of the War of 1812 (for his exploits in Lake Erie) and through the marriage of his daughter to August Belmont, the German-born financier and American representative of the Rothschilds, who was pre-eminent in venture capitalism and the financing of the Far East trade. Thus, as Tyler Dennett has pointed out, the initial American policies in Japan were "framed by not more than three or four people and executed by only one — Commodore Perry."[8] And Matthew Calbraith Perry was not a man to shy from responsibility or acting on his own initiative.

The instructions given Perry by the State Department on November 5, 1852, would not, in any case, have tended to inhibit him. They referred to the Japanese as a "weak and semi-barbarous people." (The city of Yedo, as Tokyo was then called, had a population of a million and a half and was one of the world's largest, and the intricate structure of Japanese society need not be dwelled upon.) The mandate continued that the mistreatment of shipwrecked sailors by the Japanese placed her in the category of nations which "may justly be considered as the common enemy of mankind." Protecting American seamen who might be cast up on Japanese shores was a matter that "can no longer be deferred." The State Department conceded that "every nation undoubtedly has the right to determine for itself the extent to which it will hold intercourse with other nations," but "the exercise of such a right imposes duties which cannot justly be disregarded." Accordingly Perry was to secure the agreement of the Japanese to the protection of American seamen, to the opening of one or more ports for provisioning and trade and the establishment of coaling depots. In return he was to assure the Japanese that the United States had no intention of interfering with their religion, that she was acting quite independently of Great Britain, and that "the President desires to live in peace with the Emperor."

One significant paragraph contained the first official statement of policy in the Pacific: "Recent events — the navigation of the ocean by steam, the acquisition and rapid settlement by this country of a vast territory on the Pacific, the discovery of gold in that region, the rapid communication established across the Isthmus which separates the two oceans — have practically brought the countries of the east in closer proximity to our own; although the consequences of these events have scarcely begun to be felt, the intercourse between them has already greatly increased and *no limits can be assigned to its future extension.*"* [9]

The letter of instructions invested Perry with "large discretionary powers," and before leaving on his mission he made no secret of his determination to exercise them. Nor did he maintain any sort of secrecy about the expedition itself when he appeared as the guest of honor at the banquet given him by a G Street club in Washington, at which, according to his first biographer, who was present, he expanded on "the clear and well-defined plans of his proposed operations . . . in response to the various queries."[10] Without any apprehension that Great Britain might attempt to checkmate the expedition to Japan by mounting one of its own from Hong Kong, the plans were broadcast in Washington, by others as well as Perry, and soon were receiving the alarmed attention of American

---

* The italics are mine.

and English newspapers and of the opposition party, the Whigs, which had just been succeeded in the White House by the Democratic President Franklin Pierce.

There was little interest in the United States in ventures so far from home. The Eastern newspapers, in fact, reflected an antipathy for the Perry expedition and its purposes that almost matched the outrage in the British press. The London *Times* wondered whether "the Emperor of Japan would receive Perry with most indignation or most contempt," and the American correspondent of the English-owned *China Mail* warned that the United States was setting out on the path of conquest, that Japan's "brilliant and populous capital already glares on the eye of ambition and inflames the heart of cupidity." *Punch* commented that "Perry must open the Japanese ports even if he has to open his own."[11]

The Baltimore *Sun* was discomfited by the scorn with which Perry's plans were viewed abroad and insisted that the government must abandon "this humbug, for it has become a matter of ridicule abroad and at home." James Gordon Bennett's New York *Herald,* which under his son and successor would become the most vociferous of Pacific-minded journals, mordantly voiced his opposition, possibly because Bennett was enraged by the fact that his leading rival, the New York *Tribune*, was being allowed to send its correspondent, Bayard Taylor, on the expedition. "The Japanese expedition," commented a Bennett editorial, "is to be merely a hydro-graphical survey of the coast. The 32-pounders are to be used merely as measuring instruments in the triangulations; and the cannon balls are for procuring the base lines. If any Japanese is foolish enough to put his head in the way of these meteorological instruments, of course nobody will be to blame if he should get hurt."[12]

Even Bayard Taylor, commissioned as a master's mate to bring him under Commodore Perry's discipline (and censorship), was inclined privately to view the expedition with a sardonic eye. His temporary commission, he wrote home, "will ruin forever my small reputation as a poet, I fear, for the world believes that a poet can never be anything but a poet, least of all a naval officer . . . Think of me hereafter as wearing a blue coat, a gilt anchor on the front of my cap, and a terrible sword by my side. I belong to the great American Navy — that glorious institution which scatters civilization with every broadside and illuminates the dark places of the earth with the light of its rockets and bombshells."[13]

Another civilian who joined the expedition when it reached China was S. Wells Williams, one of the great missionary scholars, who somewhat against his wishes was attached to the expedition as interpreter. Williams, though unordained, was sent to Canton in 1834 by the American Board of Commissioners for Foreign Missions to take charge of its printing press and journal, the *Chinese Repository.* A linguist and historian, he published a Chinese dictionary and translated the Bible into Japanese, and later produced the erudite and authoritative three-volume *The Middle Kingdom*. When the Perry expedition arrived at Canton, he was busy compiling a dictionary in the Cantonese dialect. The fact that he had a side job as secretary and interpreter at the American legation, which paid him twenty-five hundred dollars a year, overrode his qualms about leaving his desk in Canton for the hazards of a naval expedition.

The purposes of the expedition, he wrote his brother in the States, were "glorification of the Yankee nation, and food for praising ourselves," no matter what noble aims were outlined by the State Department. Yet his vocation as a nominal missionary persuaded him that the armed mission to Japan was part of a heavenly design. Behind the worldly and materialistic motives of the expedition, he wrote, "lie God's purposes of making known the Gospel to all nations . . . I have a full conviction that the seclusion policy of the nations of Eastern Asia is not according to God's plan of mercy to these peoples, and their government must change them through fear or force, that the people may be free."[14] And that righteous expression of sentiment could stand for more than a century as the moral shield of the American conscience.

On its way to Japan the Perry expedition stopped off at Okinawa and the Bonin Islands, both Japanese possessions, for the purpose of establishing coal facilities and showing the flag. Perry immediately got off a dispatch to Washington proposing that an American protectorate be established over the islands. "It is self-evident that the course of coming events will ere long make it necessary for the United States to extend its jurisdiction beyond the limits of the western continent, and I assume the responsibility of urging the expediency of establishing a foothold in this quarter of the globe, as a measure of positive necessity to the sustainment of our maritime rights in the east."

The reply from Washington was chillingly discreet: Perry was authorized to set up coal depots where he saw fit, but not to make any moves toward annexation.

On July 8, 1853, his squadron sailed into Tokyo Bay with her decks cleared for action and her guns double-shotted for bombardment of the Japanese land batteries in case of resistance. The commodore intended to make two visits to Japan, presenting the President's letter to the emperor on his first call, then entering into negotiations on his second. Their reception was unfriendly, if not actively hostile. A vice governor came aboard the flagship and ordered the American ships to proceed to Nagasaki, which Perry indignantly refused to do. The Japanese official then declared that guard boats would be posted around the American squadron, to which Perry replied, in effect, that he would blow them out of the water if they did not withdraw. The vice governor waved his fan as a signal for the small craft to leave the scene.

It was a touchy situation, but the commodore was certain the

Japanese were bluffing and would permit him to come ashore and present the President's letter to a suitable authority — if not the emperor himself, then someone close to the throne. To show his contempt for the lack of hospitality with which the American squadron was received, Perry sent armed survey boats around the bay but out of range of the Japanese shore batteries. The Japanese asked that the survey boats return to their mother ships. Perry not only refused but sailed the flagship *Mississippi* further up the bay and closer to Tokyo, explaining that surveys were necessary because he intended to return in the spring with a "larger force."

The Japanese got the point, and several days later Perry was received ashore with appropriate ceremony by suitable personages, "the Prince of Idzu, first counsellor of the Emperor, and his coadjutor, the Prince of Iwami." (Actually the two emissaries from the shogun, who handled all affairs of state, were provincial governors and not princes. Perry was playing the same game himself. He styled himself as Admiral Perry to make a greater impression on the Japanese. No harm was done, since each side accepted the pretenses of the other.) After handing over the message from President Pierce, the commodore received what was described as "an Imperial receipt" from his hosts. Actually it was an Imperial rebuff, and concluded, "As this is not the place wherein to negotiate with foreigners, so neither can conferences, nor entertainment, be held. Therefore, as the letter has been received, you can depart."

Perry digested this, then announced through his interpreter that he intended to return in the spring.

"Will the Admiral return with all four vessels?" the Japanese inquired.

"All of them, and probably more," Perry bluffed, "as these are only a portion of the squadron."

On the way back to their ships the Americans passed through a double file of Japanese soldiers, whose officers, according to J. W. Spalding, a clerk with the expedition, looked as though "they were perhaps thinking how agreeable a thing it would be to hold one of those Americans on the end of one of their blades, as a fork, and hack him with the other as a knife; if they only dared to try."[15]

"Thus," recorded Interpreter Williams in his journal, "closed an eventful day on which the key was put into the lock and a beginning was made to do away with the long seclusion of this nation."[16] A few days later the squadron raised its anchors and departed from Tokyo Bay. Perry and his black ships returned to the port of Naha on Okinawa and spent part of the summer superintending the construction of a coal shed with a capacity of five hundred tons. Later in the year the squadron moved on to the China station at Macao, then to the better anchorage at Hong Kong.

While lying off Hong Kong, Perry was enraged to learn that four Russian warships, short of coal, were permitted to refuel from the United States Naval Stores at Shanghai. Partly on American coal the Russian ships steamed for Nagasaki, stayed in that Japanese harbor for a month and delivered a message from the Russian foreign minister to the Japanese government. Perhaps it was this incident which caused the commodore to prophesy several years later that the Americans and Russians — or Saxons and Cossacks, as he put it — would become rivals for dominion over the Far East.

In an address before the American Geographical and Statistical Society, Perry predicted that "the people of America will, in some form or other, extend their dominion and their power, until they shall have . . . placed the Saxon race upon the eastern shores of Asia. And I think too that eastward and southward will her great rival in further aggrandizement [Russia] stretch forth her power to the coasts of China and Siam: and thus the Saxon and the Cossack meet.

"Will it be in friendship? I fear not! The antagonistic exponents of freedom and absolutism must thus meet at last, and then will be fought the mighty battle on which the world will look with breathless interest; for on its issue will depend the freedom of the world . . . I think I see in the distance the giants that are growing up for that fierce and final encounter; in the progress of events that battle must sooner or later be fought."[17]

A remarkable prophecy, considering it was uttered on March 6, 1856, when almost everyone else believed that Russia and America, separated by such vast distances, could not possibly arrive at a conflict of interests. Britain was then regarded as our greatest rival and most likely enemy. Within a few months the commodore's view of the world and America's strategic role had changed drastically. A sea change had occurred between Madeira, where he sent off the dispatch referring to England as "our great maritime rival," and the China station, where he came to the conclusion that Russia was our "great rival in further aggrandizement."

Fear of further Russian encroachments impelled him to hasten his return to Tokyo Bay, where the squadron again dropped anchor on February 13, 1854. During the months of his absence, a bitter debate was conducted over how to answer the Americans — how much to concede — when they called again. The first contact only confirmed the Japanese belief that the "Red Beards" were barbarians, but ones of superior power and military sophistication. The mikado, the shogunate (his regents, administrators, military leaders) and the bureaucracy were agreed on viewing the American presence as a national humiliation; the difference between them was that some believed such a mortification, and the reforms it would bring, was both inevitable and necessary.

Japan would be dragged into modernism, but only with the greatest resentment, suspicion and thirst for eventual revenge. The prince of Mito, who was supervising work on the coastal fortifications just in case the Americans tried to shoot their way to the Imperial Palace, expressed the

A SUPERB VIEW OF THE UNITED STATES JAPANESE SQUADRON, UNDER COMMAND OF COMMODORE PERRY, BOUND FOR THE EAST.

U.S. naval firepower introduced to Japan

Americans landing in Japan

conservative and pessimistic view of what surrendering to the American demands would mean. He counseled the shogunate to resist rather than be corrupted by Western civilization. "At first they will give us philosophical instruments, machinery, and other curiosities, will take ignorant people in, and trade being their chief object, will manage bit by bit to impoverish the country; perhaps behave with the greatest rudeness and insult us, and end by swallowing up Japan. If we don't drive them away now, we shall never have another opportunity. . . . We shall gnaw our navels afterward when it will be of no use."

When Perry arrived, however, the Japanese had decided to yield. They notified the commodore that they would open Nagasaki as a port of entry, and another port in five years; they would accord humane treatment to shipwrecked sailors. Perry wanted more ports opened, and quicker, but on the advice of Wells Williams he did not ask that extraterritorial rights be granted Americans while they were on Japanese soil. Williams's observation of the evils of such rights in China, by which Westerners arrogated to themselves the privilege of behaving as they liked on foreign land, convinced him it was one measure that a strong nation must not force upon a weaker one.

The gifts exchanged by the two nations when the treaty was signed late in March symbolized in their rueful way the cultural differences between the ritualistic old and the rough-edged new. From the President to the emperor went rifles, pistols, one hundred gallons of whiskey, eight baskets of potatoes and a locomotive. From the emperor and his officials to the United States government, gold-lacquered boxes and bookcases, bronze ornaments, porcelain goblets and four hundred assorted seashells.

Perry and his squadron sailed away home in triumph. At least one American, Bayard Taylor, foresaw the rapidity with which Japan would then cast off feudalism. "The Japanese is the most curious, inquiring person, next to a Yankee, in the world. He would be an inventor were it not for the policy of his government, which fears nothing so much as a new idea."

Within four decades, Japan would grow in power and ambition sufficiently to defeat China and Russia, and in four more to challenge the United States for hegemony over the western Pacific. Thus the United States Navy, to the extent that it acted as the instrument of its government's policy, created the monster which almost destroyed it at Pearl Harbor.

To the end of his days, with misgivings he did not trouble to conceal, Commodore Perry believed that American expansion into the Pacific was predestined. He preferred to think of any American acquisitions as "offshoots from us" rather than "strictly speaking, colonies." In one of his last public statements before his death in 1858, he considered the inevitability of making the Pacific an American sea, because "it is not to be supposed that the numberless islands which lie scattered throughout this immense ocean are always to remain unproductive, and under the mismanagement of savages. The history of the world forbids any such conclusion. How, and in what way, the aborigines will be disposed of," he could not say, but "that they are doomed to mingle with, or give way to some other race, is as certain as the melancholy fate of our own red brethren."[18]

He might also have pondered the "melancholy fate" of nations and leaders acting on the conviction that their deeds are an inescapable part of "destiny," and dictated by historical inevitability.

2. *The Isolation of Townsend Harris*

Socially, psychologically and culturally it has often seemed the Japanese and Americans were born to misunderstand each other. Of all the Westerners who appeared in Japan in large numbers, the Americans have made the least favorable impression, as individuals, on the Japanese people. With the British, the Germans and the French, for varying reasons, the Japanese generally feel a stronger current of sympathy and understanding. All the more ironic that during the various crises in modern Asian history the Japanese usually found themselves trying to cope, either as friends or enemies, with the mysterious and vexing American character. This is the conclusion of Fosco Maraini, an Italian scholar who has long lived in Japan and arrived at the judgment in his classic study *Meeting with Japan*.

The Japanese and British, according to Maraini, have a basis for understanding in their geographical status, their long history of centralization and their rigid social structure, and their relations have been characterized by "mutual esteem rather than warmth." The French and the Japanese get along well because both are "exquisitely pagan and sophisticated countries, made to understand each other." But it was with the Germans, their Prussian element a counterpart of the samurai tradition, that the Japanese found their Western soul-mates, largely because in each "there is an obscure, imperious need to live in a spirit of heroic self-dedication to something or somebody . . . a hankering for the terrible which borders on the tragic and sometimes descends to the ridiculous . . . German-Japanese accord is easier at all levels; I have the impression that the only mixed marriages that have any chance of success are Japanese-German."

Between the puritan American and the pagan Japanese, as Maraini sees it, there is small chance of a meeting of the minds, let alone the spirits. Americans are "straightforward, practical men without a true and constant interest in the arts, always ready to cut the Gordian knot," while the Japanese are "an extremely complicated people, full of ancient fears and new ambitions, extremely sensitive to all forms of beauty. intellectual values, emotional claims, always ready, when confronted with a Gordian knot, not to cut it, but to tie another, bigger one all round it and thus put it out of sight." It is an encounter between "two attitudes to life, two interior universes, which differ so profoundly that it is hard to think that a greater contrast could be possible."[19]

It may be presumed that since the American occupation of Japan — a second Reconstruction, in effect, equally as violent in its impact on Japanese traditions as that brought by Perry and his generation — there has been a greater understanding, if not a great increase in affection, between the two nations. Thousands of American servicemen living in their midst, and thousands of Japanese war brides who went back to the States, have accomplished that on the people-to-people level.

A century ago, however, the meeting between Japanese and Americans came as a cultural affront, a shock more damaging to Japanese sensibilities than to the bustling self-importance of their uninvited guests. The Japanese had closed off their islands to foreign intercourse, except for annual visits from Dutch traders, ever since the 1630's, largely out of fear that closer association with foreigners and the modern world would destroy the structure of their society. Yet they had not entirely closed their windows to the outside world, and their educated men took a keen interest in such subjects as the Napoleonic wars and the American Revolution. Perhaps it was significant that when the Japanese translated a Dutch biography of Napoleon in 1837 their scholars had great difficulty in finding a Japanese equivalent for the Dutch word *Vrijheid* — freedom.

From the turn of the nineteenth century on, particularly when the Opium War showed how defenseless an Oriental nation was against Western armaments and military methods, the Japanese, with a shuddering distaste, realized that a renewed and much more penetrating conjunction with the West was inevitable. "It is significant," Akira Iriye has written, "that the debate usually took the form of discussion on maritime security, a theme that would return again and again in the course of Japan's encounter with the West . . . Japanese feudal lords debated whether the country's defense needs were adequately met, whether the resumption of foreign contact would enhance or diminish the threat to national existence, and whether foreign trade would add to or deplete national wealth."[20]

Although initially unenthusiastic or uninformed about the Perry expedition, Americans naturally were more eager and hopeful about the Japanese contact once it was accomplished. A professed idealism overlay much of what was written about the penetration of those unknown and mysterious islands, as in the somewhat overconfident view of one writer, who commented, "The thirty millions of Japan await the key of the western Democrat to open their prison to the sun-light of social interchange." Often the American optimism regarding our relations with Japan reflected a belief that the Japanese were a superior breed compared with the Chinese and other Asian peoples. To the *Atlantic Monthly,* China, "so palsied, so corrupt, so wretchedly degraded, and so enfeebled by misgovernment as to be already more than half sunk in decay" stood in sharp contrast to the "vigor, thrift and intelligence" of the Japanese. The Japanese, said *Frank Leslie's Illustrated Newspaper,* were a "refined and enlightened" people while the Chinese were a race of "bird-nest and puppy-dog eaters." *Harper's Monthly* in 1860 declared that the Japanese had proved themselves superior to all other Asian peoples because of their "aptitude for acquiring the civilization of the West," and four years earlier the *North American Review* had informed its readers that it was a mistake to consider the Japanese a "Chinese subdivision of the human species," that "In language, in the method of writing, and in personal appearance, there is so great a diversity as to make it quite certain that the two nations belong to widely parted races."

In this atmosphere of American hopefulness and Japanese resentment, the figure of a remarkable American, the first diplomat to be sent to Japan with the responsibility of making the Perry treaty work, was of great importance to both countries. Diplomacy has raised few heroes in its history, but the stern solitary man named Townsend Harris, first United States consul-general to Japan, deserves consideration in that respect. To a large extent he was Japan's first instructor in Westernism, in Occidental values and the Anglo-Saxon code of conduct; and if he often mystified and outraged the Japanese by his unbending personality, he succeeded beyond any reasonable expectations in winning their respect. He did not hesitate to lecture his hosts, yet when he left them in 1862 after a six-year residence the shogun of Tokugawa wrote the President that Harris had brought "happiness" with him.

The face which Townsend Harris constantly showed the Japanese was that of a man of the firmest character. Actually it was a mask; the man behind it was psychologically flawed and deeply troubled enough to have acquired the reputation of being a near-hopeless drunkard less than ten years before he was sent to Japan. Born in 1804, of Welsh extraction, he got off to a fast start in the mercantile life in New York City. By his sixteenth birthday he was the proprietor of his own chinaware shop on Pearl Street in downtown Manhattan. The strongest influence on his life was that of his adoring, and adored, mother, to whom Harris was so attached that he found no room in his life for any other woman. He also had an older brother, John, a hardheaded merchant and real estate operator who had little affection for him. His father had died early in his boyhood and Townsend took his place as the head of a household that included his mother and two orphaned nieces.

By his early forties Townsend Harris was one of New York's most respected citizens. He and his brother had entered into a prospering partnership, he was a loyal Tammany Democrat and appointed as president of the board of education. Handsome, cultured, a Christian gentleman by all accounts, his life could have served as a model for the hundreds of thousands of immigrants flooding into New York.

What shattered him was his mother's death in 1847, when she was eighty-three and he was forty-three. Life suddenly lost its meaning when death broke the silver cord. The driving impulse of his career had been winning his mother's approval of his accomplishments. In his grief Harris took to drink, and being an inexperienced toper he succumbed to its perils with headlong haste. The chinaware business, in which he and his brother were partners, suffered accordingly. "He began drinking steadily and intemperately," it was noted, "and although his friends insisted that he never drank to such an extent as to be incapacitated for business, they admitted that he was usually noticeably under the influence of liquor in the afternoons when all respectable businessmen were cold sober and clear-headed."[21]

A bibulous chinaware merchant was not likely to prosper when most of his customers were respectable married women. Business soon fell off to the extent that his brother John, who was living in semiretirement in London, began investigating. John learned that Townsend had become a drunkard, wrote him a letter branding him the black sheep of the family and announced that he was returning to New York for a showdown.

Townsend was so alarmed at the prospect of being confronted by the always censorious John that he took what money he could scrape together and, at forty-five, ran away to sea. Opposite his name in the New York City Directory was the cryptic notation "gone to San Francisco." Actually he bought a half-interest in a sailing ship and set out with her on a long trading voyage to the Indian and Pacific oceans. With indifferent success, he traded on the Malay Peninsula, in the Philippines, in China and India, as a sort of seagoing peddler.

Four years later he went broke and washed up on the beach at Hong Kong, but by then he had cured himself of drinking. In desperate circumstances, he applied to the State Department for a consular appointment either at Hong Kong or Canton, but despite the influence of well-placed Democrats back in the States on his behalf, as well as that of Senator William H. Seward, he was rewarded in 1854 with the minor post at Ningpo, which paid only a thousand dollars a year plus fees.

When he heard that an American representative would be sent to Japan to see that the terms of the Perry treaty were carried out, he decided to press for the appointment with all the influence he could bring to bear. Aside from his influential friends, he possessed two qualifications for the post. The Japanese had insisted to Perry that they "wanted no women in Shimoda." The appointee would have to be a Democrat and a bachelor, and Harris was eminently both. He hastened back to America to apply in person. It was well he did, because the question of his former drinking habits was raised and both President Pierce and Secretary of State Marcy were dubious about him until his friends assured them that Harris had reformed completely. He also managed to secure the support of Senator Seward and Commodore Perry for the appointment. On August 4, 1855, he wrote the President:

"I have a perfect knowledge of the social banishment I must endure while in Japan, and the mental isolation in which I must live, and am prepared to meet it. I am a single man, without any ties to cause me to look anxiously to my old home or to become impatient in my new one. You may rely, Sir, that I will not ask for leave to visit my friends, or resign the place for any reasons of dislike of the country, but will devote myself, zealously, to the faithful discharge of my duties."[22]

President Pierce was sufficiently impressed by the letter to sign Harris's commission as consul-general for Japan the day he received it. Further, the President directed Harris to stop off in Siam on his way to Japan to negotiate a trade treaty. Reporting to the State Department on the success of that mission in June 1856, Harris wrote that Siamese officials had "expressed both fear and hatred of England. . . . They were most anxious to be taken under the protection of the United States. They plainly told me that if I would make a treaty of alliance they would give us all we could ask, even to a monopoly of the trade."[23] It was a symptom of the changing balance of power in the Far East, with the smaller nations looking to America to protect them from the aggressive methods of the British. Similarly, a fear of British or Russian encroachment would make his mission to Japan more palatable to the Japanese.

Yet when Harris arrived at Shimoda aboard the United States warship *San Jacinto* on August 21, 1856, he found the Japanese officials in a perverse mood. He had to bluster and bargain for hours before he was permitted to come ashore, the Japanese claiming that most of Shimoda had been destroyed in an earthquake and there were no suitable accommodations for an American plenipotentiary. It was true that a quake had destroyed much of Shimoda eighteen months earlier but the harbor town had since been rebuilt. Finally it was agreed that Harris and his Chinese servants would be permitted to occupy an abandoned temple in Shimoda. The Temple Rioshen, he noted in his journal, was "badly placed for hot weather . . . and is surrounded by stagnant pools." When they saw that Harris would accept it, the Japanese insisted that it wasn't suitable and he would have to make his permanent residence in a smaller abandoned temple in the fishing village of Kakizaki.[24]

The *San Jacinto* fired a thirteen-gun salute in his honor and then sailed away. For the next eighteen months Harris was cut off completely from communication with his homeland, left to his own devices as no other American diplomat before or since. It didn't bother Harris, particularly, because he was completely absorbed in learning the difficult ways of the Japanese. Several days before he was landed in Japan, he had confided to

his journal exactly what he expected of himself: "A people almost unknown to the world is to be examined and reported on in its social, moral
and political state; the productions of the country — animal, vegetable and
mineral — to be ascertained; the products of the industry of the country
found out; and its capacity for commercial intercourse, what are its wants,
and what it had to give in exchange. A new and difficult language to be
learned; a history, which may throw some light on that of China and
Korea, to be examined; and, finally, the various religious creeds of Japan
are to be looked at." His first official act was to raise his flag over the
temple, to the consternation of the Japanese. "I *hoist* the 'First Consular
Flag' ever seen in this empire. Grim reflections — ominous of change —
undoubted beginning of the end. Query — if for the real good of Japan?"[25]

He had already decided that the face he would show Japanese
officialdom would be one of impassive dignity, grim determination, complete candor and unfailing patience. Thus he would confront all the
vexations, lies and evasions with which the Japanese met him; the police
spies who questioned his visitors and bullied his Dutch interpreter and
Chinese servants, and the necessity of presenting to the Japanese officials
his list of groceries and supplies required, which they edited at their own
whims. He called the Japanese officials liars to their faces, and lectured
them, unavailingly, on the fact that "in my country a man who lied was
disgraced." One interview he described as a "rare scene of Japanese deceit,
falsehood, flattery and politeness."[26]

No matter how brusque his manner the Japanese kept coming to visit
him on various pretexts. What attracted them, he soon learned, was his
well-stocked sideboard and the Japanese thirst for hard liquor. He noted in
his journal that "at all these visits they readily drink all I offer them —
wine, cordials, brandy, whiskey, etc., etc. — and many of them drink more
than enough. Spirits of all kinds they drink raw." As an ex-drinking man
himself, he could only admire their capacity.

Within several months Harris felt he was beginning to win the confidence of the Japanese government and found that the ordinary people
living around him were friendly. As he began to study the law and customs
of the Japanese, he was appalled by the severity of their punishments.
"Imprisonment . . . is unknown. The punishments are either death or
whipping, and the accused is only in prison until he is tried. The Japanese
code is somewhat sanguinary. Death is inflicted for murder, arson, bur-
glary, grand larceny and for violent deportment towards a father."[27]

Remote as he was from the seat of even a provincial government,
Harris decided on October 25, 1856, that he must break through the
barriers put up by minor officials, no doubt on orders from the shogunate,
and he wrote the minister of foreign affairs in Tokyo that he proposed
delivering a letter from the President to the emperor. One immediate result
of the letter was an announcement that the law forbidding an Imperial

governor to visit any foreigner had been repealed, and not one but two governors, plus a vice-governor, would call on him at the consulate. Much to his surprise the governors did not "eat or drink to excess" and "their conduct during the whole visit was that of well-bred persons."

While he waited to hear from Tokyo, he suffered a number of illnesses, probably caused by improper diet, for which he could not obtain medical attention. "Ill, ill, ill," one January 1857 entry in his journal reads. "I have cured the 'Saint Anthony's Fire' but am constantly wasting away in the flesh." He was invited to the provincial governor's home, where all his puritan instincts and Christian orthodoxy were tested by the frank lasciviousness of the conversation. "The lubricity of these people passes belief. The moment business is over, the one and only subject on which they dare converse comes up. I was asked a hundred different questions about American females, as whether single women dressed differently from the married ones, etc., etc.; but I will not soil my paper with the greater part of them, but I clearly perceive that there are particulars that enter into Japanese marriage contracts that are disgusting beyond belief." He was genially informed by the governor that "one of the vice-governors was specially charged with the duty of supplying me with female society, and said if I fancied any woman the vice-governor would procure her for me, etc., etc., etc."[28] In a fog of et ceteras he concealed what his reply to the offer was, but it is clear that he didn't accept.*

Slowly and patiently Harris was winning the confidence of the Japanese and penetrating the higher echelons of their government. By February he was invited to attend a council of governors at Goyoshi, where he demanded and received the same coaling rights for American ships as the Russians had been granted at Nagasaki. "My next [demand] was that American ships in want of supplies and not having money, that goods should be taken in payment. They said this was already granted by our Treaty . . . My next was that Americans committing offences in Japan should be tried by the Consul and punished if guilty according to Japanese laws. To my great and agreeable surprise this was agreed to without demur."[29]

He continued to consider the Japanese authorities the "greatest liars on earth," but he doggedly exposed their falsehoods and insisted on dealing candidly with them on all questions. The Japanese provided him with a dictionary and other books, and requested with an eagerness that later generations would find significant that Harris send to America for "books on all branches of military and naval science, as taught at West Point and the Naval School."

In March 1857 the sailing vessel *Messenger Bird* arrived from San Francisco with newspapers telling of Buchanan's election to the presidency.

---

* When Hollywood made a film on Harris in Japan some years ago, it unerringly cast the lusty John Wayne as the prim Mr. Harris.

Buchanan was a Democrat, so Harris was safe in his post for another four years. Harris arranged the currency transactions connected with the sale of part of the *Messenger Bird*'s cargo, and talked with Americans for the first time in a year and a half.

He finally accomplished in June two of the more important objects of his mission to Japan, the granting of new concessions under a convention signed June 17 and an audience with the shogun, a privilege breathtaking in its rarity and Oriental ceremony. The shogun would receive the letter addressed to the emperor.

The concessions agreed to by the council of state included most-favored-nation status, opening Nagasaki as a port of call, extraterritorial rights for visiting Americans, the right to station a vice-consul at Hakodate, and pegging the exchange rate of the *ichibu* at thirty-four and a half cents instead of a dollar as originally provided in the Perry treaty. Harris would also be allowed to travel more freely beyond Shimoda.

Actually it took almost six months of bargaining, bickering and preparing for the ceremonial journey of less than a hundred miles from Shimoda to Tokyo. Full-dress negotiations were required for the question of how Harris would comport himself when admitted to the shogun's presence. Oriental custom required any person so honored by such a ranking personage to fall on the floor and knock his head against the floor three times. Harris indignantly replied that such obeisance was out of the question for a citizen of the American republic. It was finally agreed that Harris would bow three times from the waist.

While negotiations for the journey and the style in which it would be undertaken dragged on, Harris was depressed that he had not "received a single letter from the United States. As no direct communication is allowed by sea between Shimoda and Hakodate by Japanese junks, my supplies might as well be at Hongkong as there. I have been out of flour, bread, butter, lard, bacon, hams, sweet oil, and in fact out of every kind of foreign supply for more than two months. I am living on rice, fish and very poor poultry . . . My health is miserable, my appetite is gone, and I am so shrunk away that I look as though a vice-consul has been cut out of me. Where, oh! where is Commodore Armstrong?"* The isolation of his position in Shimoda, surrounded by the simplicity of a fishing village's daily life, began to weigh on him, and he felt that he was living in a prison, "a large one it is true — but still a prison."[30]

With much stamping of seals and affixing of ribbons, the exact details

---

* In his dispatch number seven to the State Department, June 18, 1857, he reminded Washington that a United States man-of-war was supposed to call at Shimoda every three months. He was informed by Commodore James Armstrong of the Far East Squadron, however, that no orders had come to that effect. Harris stressed the importance of "having the means to communicate with you" at least three times a year.[31]

of his journey to and reception by the shogun were finally documented. Rarely has an American representative traveled in the style enforced upon Townsend Harris. Forty-odd porters would carry his luggage, bedding and cooking equipment. In addition he would be accompanied by a retinue including twenty palanquin-bearers, twelve guardsmen, two standard-bearers, two shoe- and fan-bearers, two grooms and two commanders in charge of the procession. Palanquin-bearers and grooms would carry one sword, all others two, and the design and decoration of the silk robes worn by all were minutely set forth. As an afterthought, it was decreed that a huge ceremonial umbrella be carried in the procession. A great honor, as Harris later learned. Only princes of the highest rank were privileged to carry them.

The gorgeous procession set out from Shimoda on November 24 and arrived in Tokyo a week later. A great silent mass of people crowded the streets on the way from Sinawaga to the Great Castle of Yedo. "Not a shout or cry was heard. The silence of such a vast multitude had something appalling in it. Lord Byron called a silent woman *sleeping thunder.*" Harris later calculated that the throng numbered 185,000. The house set aside for him within the walls of the Great Castle, he learned, had formerly been known as "the Office for the Examination of Barbarian Books." Here a board of censors culled foreign publications and allowed those to be translated which would not conflict with government policy.[32]

On December 7, after days of wearying ceremonial visits, he was taken to the audience chamber of the castle by the prince of Shinano, who crawled on hands and knees toward the shogun while Harris walked at his side. He was presented with a box containing seventy pounds of bonbons, and handed over the presidential letter addressed to the emperor. It was the better part of diplomacy, he had decided, not to mention that the letter bore the signature of a President repudiated by his own party and now out of office.

While in residence on the grounds of the Great Castle, he took the greatest pride in the fact that, with his Dutch interpreter the only other Christian present, he celebrated the Second Sunday in Advent by reading "in an audible voice" the full Episcopal service for that observance. He reflected that the death penalty was still in effect for anyone conducting Christian services of any sort in Japan "and yet here have I boldly and openly done the very acts that the Japanese law punishes so severely. What is my protection? The American name alone . . . The first blow is now struck against the cruel persecution of Christianity by the Japanese . . ." He promised himself that he would persuade the Japanese to allow Christians to practice their religion openly and "I will also demand the abolition of the custom of trampling on the cross or crucifix, which the Dutch have basely witnessed for 230 years without a word of remonstrance."[33]

On December 12 he finally obtained an interview with Lord Hotta, the minister of foreign affairs, at which he launched into a lengthy discourse on the dangers confronting Japan from the imperialist powers — principally Britain, France and Russia — and the advantages of a close relationship between Japan and the United States. A three-cornered power struggle had begun in the Far East, with Britain maneuvering to thwart an expansionist Russia in the latter's moves to invade Manchuria and northern China, and Britain and France together scheming to divide China between themselves. In the event of a war between Russia and Britain, he warned, the British would attempt to use Japan as her main base of operations. It was also possible that Russia would try to use Japan for the same purpose.

By disposition and the logic of geography, America was a natural ally of the Japanese, particularly since the United States had foresworn any imperialist ambitions herself. Washington wanted free trade, not territory; open competition, not exclusive contracts. "I said the Islands of Japan are in the direct line between the West Coast of the United States and the East Coast of Asia and that a great and constantly increasing intercourse with Japan would arise thereby. I said that Japan would by the operation of these things be compelled to abandon her exclusive policy and that she might soon become a great and powerful nation by simply permitting her people to exercise their ingenuity and industry; that the resources of Japan when developed by the action of trade would show a vast amount of exchangeable values; that this production would not interfere with the production of the necessary food for the people but would arise from the employment given to the actual surplus labor of the country."[34]

Lord Motta apparently was not affronted at being lectured by the plainspoken American, nor even by his advocacy of religious freedom (or as Harris put it, "leaving men free to follow the dictates of their own consciences"). It was a highly successful visit to Tokyo. The eventual result was the treaty of 1858, which became the basis of Japan's foreign relations until the last decade of the century. Included in its terms were permission for a United States diplomatic agent to be stationed in Tokyo, Americans to be granted residence in the open ports, there to be free of "intervention of any Japanese officers," freedom of religious observance by American residents in Japan, three ports (Yokohama, Nagasaki and Hokodate) to be used as supply depots by the United States Navy.

The Japanese by then had decided to modernize their nation and make it capable of defending itself. But that process would take years, and she would need a Western protector until her army and navy were armed, trained and equipped to contend with a Western power. In the interim the United States, in effect, would act as her buffer against the world — or, in the words of the treaty, "at the request of the Japanese government" the United States would "act as a friendly mediator in such matters of difference as may arise between the Government of Japan and any European power." Japan would also be allowed to purchase warships, cannon, munitions and arms of all kinds from the United States and employ her citizens as military and naval instructors and advisers.

Within the feudal ruling circles of Japan, the treaty caused an uproar. Many of the provincial rulers opposed the treaty and insisted that Japan maintain her seclusion, and the Imperial Court was stirred by intrigues so involved they would have awed ancient Byzantium. For months during 1858 the Japanese government postponed signature of the treaty until the domestic power struggle was resolved.

Onrushing developments elsewhere terminated the dissension. A French and British naval expedition to northern China had defeated the Chinese forces resisting further concessions, and the Manchu government had been forced to sign a treaty agreeing to all of the victors' demands. The U.S.S. *Mississippi* steamed into Shimoda with the news, and was followed by the U.S.S. *Powhatan* with even more alarming dispatches. The French and British fleets were about to steam for Japan with demands that treaties with their nations be signed forthwith, and a Russian squadron which had been shadowing those fleets in North China waters was headed in the same direction with the same mission.

Obviously it was to the advantage of the Japanese to sign the American treaty first and use it as a model in negotiating with the British, French and Russians. They would also, by the terms of that treaty, have the "friendly mediation" of the United States; though the protection the *Mississippi* and *Powhatan* could offer against the powerful naval forces converging on Japan was not much greater than that of the huge umbrellas the Japanese carried in ceremonial processions.

It was marvelous how swiftly the feudal bureaucracy could move in a time of crisis. Two commissioners hastened from Tokyo to Shimoda and boarded the *Powhatan* at midnight, July 29, 1858, and the treaty was signed before dawn. Japanese and American flags were hoisted to the halyards and a twenty-one-gun salute was fired. With that cannonade Japan entered, with a resentment concealed by diplomatic smiles, the stage of the modern world. The American treaty did, as Harris and the Japanese foresaw, serve as a model in dealing with the more importunate British, French and Russians.

Harris stayed on in Japan for almost four more years despite the deterioration of his health and, in 1861, the murder of his Dutch interpreter and secretary. The Japanese internal struggle, as Harris quickly realized, was behind the murder. "Expel the barbarian" was still a popular cry as the antiforeign party agitated furiously for the overthrow of the shogunate and the restoration of his ancient absolute powers to the emperor. Harris's aide Heusken was killed as a means of embarrassing the shogunate and causing a panic in the foreign colony, with the possibility of driving out all Westerners. The French and British ministers fled from

Tokyo to Yokohama and made threats of reprisal from their Far Eastern naval forces. The more astute and coolheaded Harris took the incident for what it was and stayed at his post, which so annoyed his French and British colleagues that they broke off all relations with him.

As he explained his actions in a letter to an old family friend in New York, his refusal to flee with his colleagues to Yokohama "probably prevented some very aggressive measures from being adopted by the French and British," who believed the Heusken murder was the signal for a massacre. "My course has been approved by the foreign community both in Japan and China, and the Japanese are loud in their thanks to me, saying that I had prevented the horrors of war from being brought on them. The affair has broken off all intercourse between me and the French and English legations, which makes my position here a very isolated one. I go down to Kawagawa once in a while and visit the missionary ladies."[35]

When the Lincoln Administration took office, he expected to be recalled forthwith. He awaited it eagerly because of his failing health; several years before he had written that he did not expect to leave Japan alive. When the recall order did not come, he submitted his resignation, despite pleas from the Japanese government to the State Department that he be persuaded to remain at his post. Returning to New York, he lived in respectable obscurity until his death in 1878. Oddly enough the greatest compliment paid to his career was written by a British historian, J. H. Longford, who justly declared that his six years of service in Japan was a diplomatic achievement "not exceeded by any in the entire history of the international relations of the world."[36]

3. *"Younger Brother of Christ"*

> Do not ask where the hero comes from. The lotus rises from the mud,
> but does not smell of it.
>
> — Chinese proverb

Nothing enraged and horrified the nineteenth-century Christian so much as alien efforts to adapt his religion by the people he was attempting to convert. Christianity had to be accepted without modifications. Though itself bitterly divided on doctrine, it presented a united and militant front against tampering by the heathen. And so Christian armies would draw the sword on people who naively tried to use Christianity for their own purposes. This was true even on American soil at the end of the century when the Ghost Dance craze swept the Indian nations from Arizona to the Dakotas. The Ghost Dancers believed that an Indian Messiah was coming to bring back the buffalo and drive the whites from North America. Clearly an offshoot of Christian teachings, the cult, however, turned them inside out and made the white men representative of the anti-Christ. This was unbearable. The heresy was drowned in blood when United States cavalry regiments slaughtered hundreds of Ghost Dancers at the "battle" of Wounded Knee on the Dakota plain.

The Ghost Dancers and Dakota Territory were a long way from the Taiping rebels and China, but there were religious and psychological parallels between the two insurrections and the fury with which they were smashed. In the case of the Taiping rebellion — an uprising of Chinese Christians against the pagan Manchus — the West sided against their fellow Christians partly because they had the audacity to improvise their own mode of Christianity. "For the West," as one historian remarked, "this was the mercy killing of a horrifying mutant."

The Taiping movement erupted some years before Townsend Harris began trying to convince the Japanese to show a tolerance for Christianity which the Christians were demonstrating, across the South China Sea, they were unable to show each other. The founder of the Taiping (Heavenly Peace) movement was Hung Siu-tsuen, the son of a rice farmer near Canton. His family wanted him to be a scholar, sacrificed everything to keep him in school, and sent him to Canton to take the examinations for the provincial civil service. Hung Siu-tsuen failed the examinations repeatedly, perhaps because he did not have the money to bribe his examiners. Ill and impoverished, raging inwardly at the corruption of the Manchu bureaucracy, he was one of those dangerous young men, intellectuals in a limited sense, whose visions have caused more trouble in the world than all the premeditated villainies combined.

In 1842, at the age of twenty-nine, he began studying Christian tracts translated into Chinese, conceived himself as the instrument of heavenly wrath, and became one of the most fervent Christians ever taken into the fold. He lost his schoolmaster's job when he tore down Confucian tablets in the village where he was teaching and urged the visitors to destroy the idols in the local temple.[37]

Hung Siu-tsuen baptized himself and two fellow schoolmasters and set out with his disciples — both of whom became military and political "kings" in the Taiping government — to raise converts in Kwangsi province. After several years in the wilderness, they journeyed to Canton to study under the eccentric Baptist missionary, the Reverend Issachar J. Roberts, who had detached himself from the Baptist Mission headquarters in Hong Kong and with inherited money set up his own school and mission.

After a short course in theology as taught by Roberts, Hung Siu-tsuen returned to the mountains of Kwangsi and founded his own branch of Christianity with the aid of his two disciples. They formed the Association of Worshipers of God. Hung Siu-tsuen appropriated the title of Heavenly King of this movement and declared himself "the younger brother of Jesus." His membership in the Holy Family, he said, had been revealed to him in a divine trance. Other revelations commanded him to convert all of

China to his beliefs, with permission from God to draw the sword in that cause. He issued his own Ten Commands [*sic*], based on and expanded from those handed down to Moses.[38]

Politically, his Taipings were given the heavenly directive to drive the Manchus from power and replace them in Peking with the Ming dynasty, which had been deposed two centuries earlier. Both the political and religious implications of the movement struck fire among the peasant masses. By 1850 Hung Siu-tsuen had gathered thousands of followers willing to fight and die in his cause. The Manchus launched military expeditions to snuff out the Taipings, but the Chinese Imperial Army was as inefficient against the spears, halberds and ancient muskets of the Taipings as the modern arms of European armies.

Hung Siu-tsuen then announced the accession of the Great Peaceful Heavenly Dynasty and began an insurrection that took twenty million lives in the next nine years. Rich on booty, the "younger brother of Jesus" traveled in the wake of his armies in a huge palanquin carried by sixteen of his officers and followed by his thirty wives in sedan chairs. His revolutionary forces succeeded largely because the Imperial Army made a practice of marching into a city abandoned by the Taipings and slaughtering most of the populace on the grounds they had sided with Hung Siu-tsuen. Much of the killing, in fact, was done by the Manchu armies in a frenzy of frustration. The Taipings marched north, overran six hundred cities and towns, took Nanking (from which the Heavenly King ruled for the next nine years) and all the cities along the Yangtze River; along the way they burned Buddhist and Taoist temples, converted the people from Confucius to Christ and distributed Bibles in the wreck of burning towns. By 1860 they controlled more than half of China.

At first the movement was viewed with sympathy and understanding in Britain and the United States. The Taipings might be a little confused in their doctrine, but they were converting the heathen Chinese in the name of Christ. One of their early supporters was the Anglican bishop of Victoria who wrote: "Throughout their long line of march for fifteen hundred miles over fertile and populous districts, plunder, murder, and rape — the usual attendant curses of Asiatic warfare — were denounced and punished by death. With more than Puritanical strictness, they waged an internecine war with the most dearly cherished sensual habits of their countrymen. The ten moral rules of the Decalogue (Hung Siu-tseun's Ten Commands) were enforced and a stricter interpretation attached to its terms. Amorous glances, libidinous songs, and all the common incentives to profligacy were prohibited and abandoned. The drinking of wine, the smoking of tobacco, gambling, swearing, lying, and, above all, the indulgence in the fumes of opium, were denounced and abolished with a moral determination that permitted no half measures."[39]

When the Heavenly King established himself in a palace in Nanking with his thirty wives and countless concubines, the western Christians began having second thoughts about this exotic overseas branch of their religion. If it swept all of China, what use would the Chinese have for the austere Western version of Christianity? Also the missionaries were closely allied with the merchants and traders, who viewed the Taiping uprising as a threat to business.

It was a complex situation for all concerned. The Second Anglo-Chinese War had just been concluded with the Manchu capitulation at Tientsin. When the Taiping rebels appeared in force outside the walls of Shanghai, thereby posing a threat to the biggest of the Western trading ports, the Westerners realized they had to make a choice: ally themselves with the recently defeated Manchu enemy or allow the empire to fall apart and disrupt the newly expanded trade arranged in the peace treaty with Peking.

Suddenly the Christianized Taipings were viewed as a plundering barbaric horde, especially when seen close-up. The Shanghai organ of the British traders reported that the Taipings were burning, looting and massacring in the villages on the outskirts. "They continued advancing towards Shanghai, when on the third day their flaunting flags were seen within a mile of the outskirts; while at night lurid flames flashed over the horizon from the buildings and farmsteads set on fire. All was commotion in the [Shanghai] settlement. Only a few Indian troops and English soldiers could be assembled to form outposts for defence." A thirty-inch snowstorm, however, held off the anticipated attack.[40]

The British hurriedly negotiated a treaty with the Imperial government agreeing to support it against the Taipings, and plans were rushed for an international army of white mercenaries to take over the fighting against the rebels.

In this situation the United States preferred to play a passive role. So far, in China, it had won a preferred position by staying neutral, letting the British and French do the fighting, and sharing in the concessions which always resulted. Covertly, however, the United States sided against the Taipings. The outbreak of the Civil War caused the withdrawal of most of the Far East Squadron, and there was little it could contribute officially to the quelling of the rebellion. But it did supply the first leader of the mercenary army — unofficially — and many of the men who fought under him, including his second-in-command. This free-lance warrior, Frederick Townsend Ward, was one of the more remarkable products exported by Salem, Massachusetts. Born of a respectable seafaring family in 1831, he yearned for a West Point appointment and a conventional military career. The appointment went to one of *the* Crowninshields of Salem, however, and young Ward shipped out as second-mate of a clipper captained by a relative. He spent two years at Norwich (Vermont) University, a military academy, where he picked up whatever knowledge of tactics he later found useful in China. By his own account Ward then spent an adventurous ten years as mate on a clipper, California gold-miner and member of William Walker's filibustering expedition to Nicaragua. In 1859 he turned up on the China coast and signed on as mate of the *Confucius,* a gunboat chartered by the Chinese Committee of Patriotic Merchants of Shanghai to protect their shipping against the pirates on the lower Yangtze.[41]

The twenty-eight-year-old Ward, slight of build, mild of manner, somehow managed to impress the Chinese merchants and bankers that he was the man to raise and lead a mercenary force to take the offensive against the Taipings in their semicircular front around Shanghai. The only forces then in the field against the Taipings were several divisions of provincial "Green Flag" troops of dubious loyalty. Ward and a newly acquired comrade-in-arms, Henry A. Burgevine, a South Carolinian, were each given a nominal salary and the promise of prize money for each town or city they recaptured from the Taipings. The merchants would also pay and supply any force Ward and Burgevine managed to organize.

In June of 1860, with Napoleonic audacity, Ward and Burgevine launched themselves at the head of a raffish band of European and American recruits against Sunkiang, a walled city thirty miles southwest of Shanghai. Waving the cane which became his hallmark, Ward directed a night attack against Sunkiang. Most of his followers were so drunk they could hardly clamber up the scaling ladders, and once over the wall they were met by a withering fire from the Taipings. Badly shot up, Ward's force withdrew in haste and returned to Shanghai.

Ward managed to persuade his Chinese backers that the first venture had miscarried because it was undermanned, and to give him the money to recruit a new "army" along the Shanghai waterfront. He enlisted more than three hundred American, English, Irish, French and Scandinavian beachcombers, plus six British marine noncoms whom he talked into deserting from their ships in the harbor. He also raised a second battalion of Filipinos — "Manilamen" as they were then known — to serve as auxiliaries; bought ten artillery pieces, machetes, axes, brass knuckles, and a large supply of stinkpots for close-quarter assaults.

This was the nucleus of what the soon-interested British called "Ward Force," the exploits of which, under Ward's daring leadership, with his flair for partisan warfare, convinced Westerners in Asia that "one white man can whip ten Wogs." The success of his campaigning was due not only to "General" Ward's tactical genius but to the fact that the Taipings were becoming demoralized and the spiritual leadership, the ideological passion with which their Heavenly King had provided them were no longer rationed from Nanking; Hung Siu-tsuen now secluded himself in the palace with his wives and concubines, where the atmosphere was more that of Venusberg than the Mount of Olives.

On July 16, Ward again attacked Sunkiang, used his artillery to blow down the city gates and managed to take the city after a nightlong battle. The Taipings put up a stiff resistance and Ward Force was almost wiped out by the victory. Rocket signals brought in several thousand Green Flag troops to occupy Sunkiang, and Ward returned to Shanghai with only thirty-seven of his followers alive and on their feet.

His capture of Sunkiang made Shanghai safe from a Taiping offensive based on Hangchow and broke the ring of rebel strongholds around the city. Ward was awarded one hundred and thirty-three thousand dollars in prize money for the feat. But his success at Sunkiang almost ruined him. So many men deserted from British ships at Shanghai, twenty-nine from the Royal Navy alone, to join Ward Force and enrich themselves on the loot of Taiping-held cities that the British authorities were outraged and ordered his arrest.

There was a long lull in the fighting around Shanghai while the Western powers tried to decide what to do about Ward. Plainly he was a necessary evil. If a band of irregulars, largely composed of white soldiers of fortune, didn't clear the Shanghai area of the Taipings, the job would have to be done by French and British regular forces.

An agreement was reached under which Ward renounced his American citizenship and was accepted as a subject of China on orders from Peking. He was thereupon given the rank of mandarin fourth-class and appointed a major general in the Chinese army and an admiral of the Chinese navy. Thus at the age of thirty-one Ward became the only American ever to be a mandarin-general-admiral. At the same time Ward Force — renamed the Ever-Victorious Army at the request of the Chinese — was reconstituted. A review attended by Admiral Sir James Hope of the British navy, who was placed in charge of coordinating all the efforts against the rebels, demonstrated that his force had now been placed on a sound military basis. The ranks were filled by Chinese infantry, about two thousand men newly armed and retrained. At their head marched Ward and his collaborator, Burgevine; ten captains, twenty lieutenants and forty sergeants, all Americans or Europeans.

During the next several months Ward and his Ever-Victorious proved they were worth the $1,800,000 annual budget allotted by the Chinese government. In cooperation with a force of 336 British marines and sailors led by Admiral Hope and a similar French naval detachment of 160 led by Admiral Protet, they began a clearing operation in the thirty-mile arc around Shanghai. In February 1862, Ward's "army" captured the villages of Quang-fu-ling and Kachaiou and drove six thousand Taipings out of Tseedong.

The process of defeating the Taiping rebellion obviously had begun, and the United States covertly approved of the actions of its former citizen. The new American minister to China, Anson Burlingame, a Massachusetts politician who had served three terms in Congress, wrote to the State

Department that he was introduced to Ward by Admiral Hope shortly after his arrival in early 1862. He could promise neither Ward nor Admiral Hope any material assistance, but made it plain that he was extending American approval of the operations against the Taipings.

To Secretary of State William H. Seward, an ardent apostle of American expansion in Asia, Burlingame dispatched a lengthy explanation, which drew no reproof from Seward. "The treaty powers are represented here by men of modern ideas; by men who, in this land, where everything is to be done, do not choose to embarrass each other by sowing distrust in the Chinese mind, but who with an open policy and common action, deepen each other's confidence and win the respect of the Chinese. That the too sanguine hopes in relation of China of our more advanced civilization may be fully realized by any action we may take, ought not to be expected. The peculiar people we are among must be remembered; how hoary is their civilization, and how proud they are, and how ignorant of us they have always been, and how little their knowledge of some of us has tended to create in their minds a desire for change . . . The people are free to license, and, as in our own country, we find a portion of them in rebellion, because they have felt too little the influence of the central government."[42]

Equating the Taipings with the Confederates, and their rebellion with the American Civil War, was a vast oversimplification. Aside from its original religious motivations, the Taiping rebellion occurred precisely because the Chinese masses had endured the "influence" — the cruelty and corruption of the Manchu regime — all too long.

A minority of Americans in China opposed the undercover cooperation of their government with Peking in quelling the Taiping movement, among them Issachar J. Roberts, the eccentric Baptist missionary in Canton who had tutored Hung Siu-tsuen before he pronounced himself the younger brother of Christ. Sir Frederick Bruce, the senior British diplomat in China, indignantly reported to the Foreign Office that Roberts had joined the Taipings in Soochow: "He has described, in a letter which will no doubt be published, one of their religious meetings at which he attended, having previously dined with their leader Le. It consisted of the offering up of large provisions before an altar erected in honour of Shangti."[43]

The "offering of provisions" and the burning of prayer papers indicated that Chinese Christianity was undergoing heretical modifications more suitable for the Oriental temple than the Christian church, and Western orthodoxy accordingly was outraged; all of its suspicions of the Heavenly Peace movement now seemed to be justified.

Through the summer and early fall of 1862 Ward occupied himself with clearing the Taipings out of the countryside around Shanghai. His name was legend among the Chinese. Wounded several times, once in the jaw, he insisted on leading his Ever-Victorious Army in every engagement.

His blazing eyes, combined with a quiet friendly manner, also impressed his Chinese followers, who testified that he treated them as fairly as he did his white officers. His standing among the Chinese, if not the British and American colonies in Shanghai, was enhanced by his marriage to the daughter of Taki, the leader of the Shanghai bankers who were backing him.

The English were inclined to disparage Ward as a typical Yankee swashbuckler, whispered that he was already worth three hundred thousand dollars for his services as a Chinese patriot and that he kept his troops keyed up on plentiful rations of alcohol. William Chesney, an English blockade runner, trader and later a Shanghai magazine publisher, reinforced this impression when he recounted an orgiastic scene at the National Hotel: "As I passed the National the place was full of Ward's officers and expectant officers, one of whom rushed out after me and wished me to join them in their booze. I went in with him and shook hands with all of them. Several of them being lately up from Hongkong had known me there, and they had apparently just been enlisted by Ward, and were purposely being boozed, so as to get them off to Sungkiang, I believe. The house was being washed out with champagne at General Ward's expense."[44]

In September of 1862, Ward turned his attention to the old treaty port of Ningpo, which had been occupied by the Taipings the previous year. Supported by a gunboat, he began attacking the Taiping-held towns on the approaches to Ningpo. On September 21, he was directing the assault on the walled village of Tzeki when he was struck in the abdomen by a sniper's bullet. He died that night, shortly after making a verbal will leaving his wife fifty thousand taels, the rest of his estate to his brother and sister, a testament that was to be contested in various courts for the next forty years. In 1902 his brother's widow received $368,237 from the Chinese government, surely a generous stipend for two years of active service.

So great was Ward's fame in America by this time, even while the Union was fighting for its survival, that United States Minister Burlingame wrote a personal letter to President Lincoln reporting in emotional detail on Ward's death: ". . . Indeed, he taught the Chinese their strength, and laid the foundations of the only force with which their government can hope to defeat the rebellion. General Ward was a man of great wealth, and in a letter to me, the last he probably ever wrote, he proposed through me to contribute ten thousand taels to the government of the United States, to aid in maintaining the Union, but before I could respond to his patriotic letter he died. Let this wish, though unexecuted, find worthy record in the archives of his native land, to show that neither self-exile nor foreign service, nor the incidents of a stormy life, could extinguish from the breast of this wandering child of the Republic the fires of a truly loyal heart."[45]

President Lincoln, in the gloomy autumn of Antietam, must have regretted that Ward had not been graduated from West Point and devoted his military talents to a federal army that sorely needed them. He forwarded the letter to Congress in answer to a Senate resolution requesting all available information on Ward's death. Secretary of State Seward ordered Burlingame to thank the Chinese government for the elaborate funeral it gave Ward, and added, "He fell while illustrating the fame of his country in an untried, distant and perilous field. His too early death will, therefore, be deeply mourned by the American people."

Ward was succeeded by his second-in-command, Henry Burgevine, which turned out to be a bad mistake. While Ward had many of the more admirable soldierly qualities, his deputy was an unabashed freebooter, the sort that gave American filibustering a bad name. Burgevine was also arrogant, greedy and ill-tempered, and many of his Chinese sponsors suspected with good reason that he hoped to carve his own domain out of the shattered empire. His own successor, a young English captain named Charles George Gordon, later "Chinese" Gordon, still later Gordon of Khartoum, denounced him as a "man of large promises and few works." Early in January of 1863, after a successful assault on a fortified village, Burgevine marched into Shanghai with his bodyguard, broke into the house of one of the mercantile mandarins who supported the Ever-Victorious Army and bullied fifty thousand dollars out of him on the pretext that his unpaid troops were threatening mutiny. Summarily dismissed, he defected to the Taipings but was soon captured by his former comrades and exiled to Japan. The stubborn fellow slipped back into China in 1865, rejoined the Taipings, again was captured, and this time was tortured and killed. The job of finishing off the Taipings was briskly handled by Captain Gordon, who marched on Nanking with his combined forces in the spring of 1864. As they stormed his palace, the Heavenly King, Hung Siu-tsuen, elegantly committed suicide by swallowing goldleaf. His corpse was burned and the ashes scattered in the street.

The depth of the American involvement in crushing the Taiping movement, by then, could be measured by the fact that Burgevine's disastrous appointment to command the Ever-Victorious Army was engineered by United States Minister Burlingame, who insisted that an American should be kept in command of that force. Burlingame informed Washington that he had notified the Chinese government of his "desire" that Burgevine succeed Ward, despite "considerable opposition" from the British. Without Burgevine, he insisted, "his force might dissolve and be lost to the cause of order." He explained to the State Department: "I felt it was no more than fair that an American should command the foreign-trained Chinese on land, as the English . . . would command the same quality of force on sea. Do not understand by the above that in this, or in any case, I have pushed the American interests to the extent of angry disagreement."

History is crammed with bootless suppositions, with the ache of might-have-beens. Few convey such a raging sense of frustration as the question of what might have happened to China if the West had adopted a more flexible attitude toward the Taipings and their exotic transformation of Christian doctrine; if it had not been quite so obsessed with what the American minister called the "cause of order" and the "cause of civilization." There was something feverishly disordered in the concept that the Manchu usurpers, as incompetent as they were corrupt, represented the civilized values.

If the Western nations, however, had accepted the inventive religiosity of the Taiping movement and even suffered through the aberrations of its Heavenly King — taking into account their original idealism and determination to rule wisely and modernize China — that nation might be the foundation stone of an orderly Asia today. A great opportunity, never to be regained, was lost exactly a century ago.

II. Destiny Takes Root

6

Little Wars with the Heathen

Some indication of the depth of American interest in the Pacific and eastern Asia may be gathered from a brief survey of our interventions almost a century ago. Our first expeditionary force to Korea was dispatched shortly after the Civil War. In 1873 the Vietnamese asked our help against a foreign invader — the French. The strategic outpost of Midway, from which American air power was launched to destroy the Japanese carrier fleet in 1942 and dramatically reverse our fortunes, was acquired during the administration of Andrew Johnson. The first American President to offer his services as mediator in an Asian dispute was not Theodore Roosevelt but Ulysses S. Grant.

The extension of American power into the Pacific was undertaken by both the Republicans and Democrats, depending on which party controlled the executive branch of the government. The other party then assumed the burdens of opposition. On the political seesaw of expansionism, it was the

Democratic James K. Polk in the 1840's and succeeding Democratic administrations in the 1850's which enlarged our territories and expanded our influence. During the 1860's and 1870's it was the turn of the Republicans (Lincoln, Grant, Hayes — plus Andrew Johnson, a Democrat captive of the Republicans) to preside over our pre-imperial efforts abroad. Neither party, on regaining the seat of power, tried to shut off this alternating current generated by a strong young nation growingly conscious of what it believed to be its destiny. Only once in later years, during the Democratic administration of Grover Cleveland, was a determined effort made to halt the process.

Generally, in the period between the Civil and Spanish-American Wars, the spirit of expansionism was animated, or damped down, by the man who presided over the State Department. Lincoln was too preoccupied by the Civil War to spare much consideration for foreign affairs not touching on the war, and Grant, until he took his post-presidential world tour, was a provincial. The Secretary of State made foreign policy without much interference from the White House. The dynamism of a William H. Seward, lengthened our reach in the Pacific, committed us to enormous responsibilities, with a centripetal speed.

The Secretary of State a century ago could make foreign policy his personal responsibility, in consultation with the Senate Foreign Relations Committee, largely because the American people were too busy exploiting their own undeveloped land to lift their eyes beyond our shores.

That policy, to whoever examined it, seemed unexceptional and unaggressive, respectful of the rights of other nations. It was dictated both by a lack of naval force and a predisposition, derived from our own colonial experience, against imposing ourselves on other people. There was a gap between what our people thought of themselves and what they should be as a nation, and the ambitions of men who achieved national office; but the latter had to be respectful of our lingering anticolonialism. The foundation stone of our foreign policy was to attain most-favored-nation status, but never to acquire overseas territories or protectorates. This was incorporated in the treaties with both China and Japan. The United States would "sustain" both Asian countries and Siam against French, British or Russian assaults on their sovereignty. It could only be a moral sustenance. On the other hand we would cooperate with other Western nations in maintaining what was later called the "open door" and protecting the flow of commerce. It was this policy which Seward would bend to the extent that an expeditionary force against Korea was seriously considered in 1868 — and carried out several years later.

During those years of tentative contact with the Far East, the first of what would later be called cultural exchanges was promoted with China and Japan. One of the first Oriental students was Yung Wing, the son of a Cantonese merchant, who hoped that a Yale education would equip him to become a leader in his own government. When he returned with his degree, however, he found the Manchu bureaucracy unreceptive to anyone claiming a Western education. It was years before he obtained even a minor post, though he had enough influence to found the Yung Wing Mission, which sent other Chinese youth to American schools. In his frustration, Yung Wing subsequently returned to the United States, married an American girl and settled down here.

The Japanese, less self-sufficient in that respect, were much more eager to absorb what they needed or wanted from American culture, education, technology. The first Japanese student to come here was Niijima Shimeta, a member of the samurai class, who yearned so much to sample American political and religious freedom that in 1864 he smuggled himself aboard a ship leaving Japan. Shimeta spent ten years studying and observing in New England, fell in love with the democratic system, and finally returned to Japan to help modernize his country's educational establishment.[1]

In more direct ways the United States also sought to strengthen the impression that she was more liberal in her policy toward the Asian nations, that her political system should be the model for China and Japan. Missions, or embassies as they were called, were invited to tour the country; these were composed largely of Chinese and Japanese officials, and the effect was as much to educate Americans about the Orient as it was to indoctrinate the Orientals in the visible and audible virtues of the American people. Among the more progressive officials in China and Japan there was a feeling that the United States was the most sympathetic of the Western powers, that her brief history somehow equipped her to understand the problems of much older civilizations. As Tseng Kuo-fan, a prominent Chinese official, viewed the contending nations in 1861, "the English are the most crafty, the French next; the Russians are stronger than either the English or the French and are always struggling with the English barbarians, who are afraid of them. The Americans are of pure-minded and honest disposition and long recognized as respectful and compliant toward China . . . sincerely loyal to China."[2]

Anson Burlingame, as minister to Peking, brought over a Chinese delegation in 1868 partly to show them his country and partly to sign the "Burlingame Treaty," actually an American supplement to the Treaty of Tientsin, which provided that American schools could be established in China, that the United States disavowed "any intention or right to intervene in the domestic administration of China" in regard to the railroad and telegraph lines the French and British were insistent on building, and that Chinese could freely migrate to the United States. The immigration clause particularly pleased Secretary of State Seward, who believed that a fresh supply of cheap labor would help American industry compete successfully in foreign markets. The hope that it would also build respect between the two nations was soon deflated with ironic emphasis; pigtailed coolies were treated with greater contempt and brutality by Americans, particularly in the Western states, than the Negroes or Indians.

By now Burlingame, like many Americans who made the effort to know and understand the Chinese, was a passionate Sinophile. As shepherd of the visiting Chinese, he was a great success and so was the delegation itself; all across the country it was enthusiastically received. The previous impression in America that the Chinese were heathen savages with a sword in one hand, a stinkpot in the other, and possibly an opium pipe in the mouth, was greatly modified. Anyone who met the Chinese visitors was impressed by their courtesy, culture and intelligence. And everywhere they appeared Burlingame eloquently developed his theme that "China must be welcomed back into the family of nations."

He was a political orator and his words, read today, seem to convey more passion than logic. But his sincerity was obvious and transmitted itself to his audiences. One of his loftier flights took place at a dinner given in honor of the mission in New York, when he exhorted his fellow diners:

"China, seeing another civilization approaching on every side, has her eyes open. She sees Russia on the north, Europe on the West, America on the east. She sees a cloud of sail on her coast, she sees the mighty steamers coming from everywhere — bow on. She feels the spark from the electric telegraph falling hot upon her everywhere; she rouses herself, not in anger, but for argument . . . She tells you she is ready to take upon her ancient civilization the graft of your civilization. She tells you that she is willing to trade with you, to buy of you, to sell to you, to help you strike off the shackles from trade . . . For she is hospitable to fair argument . . .

"Let her alone; let her have her independence; let her develop herself in her own time and in her own way. She has no hostility to you. Let her do this and she will initiate a movement which will be felt in every workshop of the civilized world , . . All she asks is that you be as kind to her nationals as she is to your nationals . . . The imagination kindles at the future, which may be, and which will be, if you will be fair and just to China."[3]

Some of the more cynical merchants in his audience may have had second thoughts about that emotional plea, and any who had traveled to China would have disagreed that the Chinese had no hostility to outsiders, but they gave Burlingame so enthusiastic an ovation when he sat down that many must have believed Sino-American relations in the future would be an unending love feast. During that period, however, there was a genuine receptiveness between the two countries that might have flowered into something glorious, might really have opened the new era Burlingame envisioned.

Similarly two delegations of Japanese were warmly received and favorably impressed in 1860 and 1871. The first mission was composed of seventy-odd samurai dispatched by the shogunate to obtain ratification by the commercial treaty of 1858. A more concealed purpose was to find out just what elements in Western society made it capable of generating a power that could be extended so far from its shores; not only the technology but the spirit and intellect that developed it. The samurai inspected the railroad system, arsenals and military installations and factories. They marveled at the newly developed gaslight, and were politely amused by that contemporary triumph of American civilization, the flush toilet.

In 1871 the Iwakura Embassy, encouraged by American missionaries in Japan, came over to plead for revision of the treaty and also to study the American political and economic systems. It was made up mostly of political leaders in their thirties, and from their observations it was evident that they grasped at least one important idea: that a modern system of government, based on the popular will and enlisting the energy of the masses, was essential to rebuilding Japan. That would have to precede the construction of a powerful army and navy. The young Japanese politicians concluded in general that Japan should adopt Western methods without absorbing Western values — such as the desire for material comforts which produced indoor plumbing.

Two of the young men of the Iwakura Embassy, Okubo Toshimichi and Ito Hirobumi, were later responsible for much of the modernization accomplished in Japan. Okubo believed that the Japanese were not adaptable to a republican form of government, but that American educational methods must be transplanted, particularly in the style of textbooks and teaching. The textbooks subsequently produced in Japan stressed how America had grown "increasingly rich and strong" within a comparatively few years.

While abroad, members of the Iwakura Embassy learned of plans being completed back in their home islands for an invasion of Formosa. Their experience in the West, out of which grew the conviction that the Western nations would not allow Japan to seize Formosa without intervening themselves, urged them to protest the proposed venture, and in fact they succeeded in delaying it. Okubo wrote home that Japan lacked the money and resources for such an operation, or any other military or naval adventures. Similarly he argued against Japanese designs on Korea on the basis of what the Iwakura Embassy learned on its tour of America and later of Europe: "Of all the foreign powers Russia is the most to be feared, and her southward movement is well known; so that if Japan and Korea fight with one another, both will fall an easy prey to Russia. England is also a powerful nation, from whom Japan has already borrowed much money, so that if Japan and Korea fight and we cannot pay the interest in consequence of the war, she would make it a pretext for interfering in our internal affairs, thus making Japan another India." The goodwill of the

United States, however, was something Okubo believed could be taken for granted.[4]

Oddly, for peoples so suspicious of Westerners and so innately cynical about human motives, the Chinese and the Japanese both were prepared to accept American idealism as the innocence of the newborn, as Americans themselves did. Europeans were not so credulous. Your rival often knows you better than your victim.

1. *Seward and the "Great Hereafter"*

William H. Seward, with his leonine mane, commanding nose, polished manners and oratorical eloquence, looked so much more like a statesman that a large section of the Republican Party hoped he would be nominated for the presidency over Abraham Lincoln. He had the style and presence Lincoln lacked, yet there was more substance to him than a consequential manner acquired on the floor of the United States Senate. He was bold in the exercise of statecraft, and even bolder in his visions of what his country could and should become. He was not only the preeminent Pacificist of the post-Civil War period. In his actions and ambitions, if not the cautious prose of the State Department, he was an outright imperialist.

Actually he was as much a provincial as Lincoln; one was an upstate New York lawyer, the other a downstate Illinois lawyer. The world Seward knew was bounded on the east by Orange County, New York, and on the west by Washington, D.C. It wasn't until after his retirement in 1869 that he traveled to California and Alaska, then made an around-the-world tour a year before his death. He had risen from a Utica lawyer to Governor of New York in 1838 when he was thirty-seven years old. For the twelve years preceding his appointment as Secretary of State by Lincoln, he was the Senator from New York, first as a Whig, then as a member of the successor Republican Party.

Little as he actually knew of the world, his imagination easily encompassed it from the beginning of his two terms as Senator. He made the Foreign Relations Committee his natural element and became a vigorous advocate of American expansion even during the Democratic administrations when the Whig/Republican stance was at least nominally anti-expansionist.

The Nestorian declarations of Senator Seward on the American destiny were among the notable set pieces of congressional oratory in the decade preceding the Civil War. Against the mini-America of farmers and artisans Jefferson hoped for, he painted word pictures of a maxi-America, breaking out of the confines of its continent and imperially striding to the eastern shores of Asia, commanding the north Pacific, occupying islands as stepping-stones and planting herself irrevocably on the Asian mainland.

Townsend Harris, our man in Tokyo

A Japanese embassy explores the United States

Early in his career as a Senator he proclaimed that having snatched the prizes of the War of 1846 the American people were "destined to roll their resistless waves to the icy barriers of the north, and to encounter Oriental civilization on the shores of the Pacific."

Toplofty in its magniloquence, his speech on the future opened up by the prospective Perry Expedition was a classic. In majestic periods he proclaimed that it was the welcome fate of the American nation to renovate the "constitutions, laws, and customs in the land that is first greeted by the rising sun." America must turn westward to meet her destiny; Europe was the past, Asia the future. Europe had been drained white by her wars and revolutions. Asia was the land of promise. Soon European influence would markedly wane while "the Pacific Ocean, its shores, its islands, and the vast regions beyond, will become the chief theater of events in the world's great hereafter."[5]

But it would be a peaceful conquest, as he foresaw it. Unarmed steamers, not warships, would open Asia to American influence. It was the American destiny to replace military conquest with aggressive commerce (though he did not say what would happen if the client nations of Asia decided to shut out our trading ships). America's great contribution to Asia, as to Europe, would be political theory. When we made the Asians more like us, there would be no grounds for conflict. This influence would be "sublime and beneficient," he explained. And it could be exerted only by the United States. "Certainly no one expects the nations of Asia to be awakened by any other influence than our own from the lethargy into which they sunk nearly three thousand years ago. If they could be roused and invigorated now, would they spare their European oppressors and spite their American benefactors?"

Echoes of his senatorial orations would ring with irony even before he left office as Secretary of State. He would learn that "influence" could be extended only by the threat of force, and protected only by the omnipresence of a naval squadron based on South China, because there were other contestants in that arena. Nor were the Asians so quick to grasp the difference between "European oppressors" and "American benefactors," particularly since they all looked like white-eyed monsters peering over the sights of their twelve-pounders.

When he became Secretary of State, communication with Asia was speeded up and gave him firmer control over diplomacy in the Far East than his predecessors could exercise. The transcontinental telegraph system was completed in 1862 and more ships began traveling the sea lanes to China and Japan, which resulted in shortening the time it took a dispatch to reach Tokyo from six months to one. During his first five years in office, he was inhibited from pursuing a bold policy in the East because the war against the Confederacy claimed priority over any foreign ventures. Even after the Civil War ended, he complained, "The public attention . . . continues to be fastened upon the domestic questions which have grown out of our late civil war. The public mind refuses to dismiss these questions, even so far as to entertain the higher, but more remote, questions of national extension."[6]

His last several years at the State Department provided him with several opportunities for promoting "national extension," and he was quick to grasp each one. With his approval, the Navy Department introduced Americans to the vexations of Asian guerrilla war in the spring of 1867. The scene was the rugged interior of Formosa. The occasion was the wreck of the American bark *Rover* off the Formosan coast early in 1867 and the murder of her crew by the natives.

It was time, Seward and the Navy Department apparently decided, to show that the United States could brandish gunboats and punitive expeditions in defense of its citizens. Two ships of the China Squadron, *Wyoming* and *Hartford,* proceeded to the southern coast of Formosa. A landing party of 181 sailors and Marines led by a rear admiral went ashore on June 13, 1867. The Americans plunged into the rugged interior in pursuit of the hostile natives. The latter led them into ambushes, then faded away into the bush, then showed up on the ridge line again to lure on their pursuers. This could have gone on indefinitely, except that the landing party finally quit in frustration and total exhaustion. One American was killed and fourteen were laid low by sunstroke. One hundred years later the essential details were being repeated in South Viet Nam. During that century Americans would meet with the same maddening frustrations in Haiti, in Nicaragua, in northern Mexico, in the Philippines and elsewhere; not all the devices of their technology nor the cerebrations of war colleges and "think tanks" would provide a solution. The heavily armed Western legionary, with all the advantages of numbers and equipment, is still poised at long odds against the rebellious native, with his inferior weapon and a bag of rice, as he was in the southern Formosa mountains a century ago.

That same year Seward involved us in the tangled affairs of Korea, where both France and Russia were bitterly determined to achieve hegemony, and made two other moves to extend our power in the Pacific. In August 1867 we took possession of Midway, and the following month Seward served notice that this country considered the Sandwich Islands — Hawaii — within the American sphere of interest. He wrote the United States representative in Honolulu that "a lawful and peaceful annexation of the islands to the United States with the consent of the people of the Sandwich Islands is deemed desirable by this government." That project, however, could not be pushed at speed because Great Britain and other nations had their own aspirations in that quarter.

What might be called the First Korean War, so far as the United States was concerned, was touched off by a slow-burning fuse. For some years Korea, the "Hermit Kingdom," had resisted all efforts from the West to open trade with her. Any Western trading vessel which ventured to the Korean coast or up one of her rivers traveled at her own peril; often she would be fired upon. Early in 1867 the news reached the State Department that an American vessel had come to grief in Korea and all her crew murdered.

Seward studied the dispatches with a consuming interest. They were forwarded from Peking by S. Wells Williams, the missionary-historian and interpreter for Commodore Perry, who was chargé d'affaires in Peking during Minister Burlingame's absence on home leave. A French naval squadron had just returned from investigating reports that a number of French missionaries had been massacred by the Koreans. Not only was that report verified, the French informed Williams, but they had also collected information on the fate of the American trading schooner *General Sherman,* which had sailed to Korea in August 1866 with a cargo of cotton goods, tinplate and glass. The whole crew had been slaughtered by the Koreans.[7]

All the facts regarding the *General Sherman*'s venture were not ascertained until twenty years later, but its voyage was not as innocent as it first appeared. The trade goods were only a cover for more nefarious purposes. What the owner and crew of the *General Sherman* actually planned was to loot the tombs of Korean royalty and hold their contents for ransom. Only the trickiness of the Korean tidal rivers ruined this plot. The *General Sherman* worked her way up the mouth of the Ta-dong River on a rising tide. Suddenly the water fell, leaving the ship grounded. Her crew assumed a belligerent attitude toward the natives who approached; they were heavily armed for their tomb-looting project and confident they could handle any number of hostile natives. The Koreans, however, responded with cunning. Instead of directly attacking the *General Sherman* they floated fire rafts down the river toward her. The blazing rafts set the ship on fire, and her entire crew was killed as they scrambled ashore.

Seward was unaware of these facts; all he knew was that American citizens, peaceful traders, had been slaughtered by the Koreans. A second dispatch from Peking a month later informed him that the French were proposing to "march to the conquest of Korea" and establish a French protectorate. The French emperor, announced the French chargé d'affaires in Peking, had the "right and power to dispose, according to his good pleasure, of the country and the vacant throne." (Actually Napoleon III was having great difficulty extricating himself from Mexico at the time, and had little real power to dispose.) As he pondered the dispatches from Peking, Seward evidently decided that the great powers were now launched on the partition of Asia. Such a fragmentation had been threatening for a long time. The French were gobbling up Indo-China and wanted Korea. The British were supreme in China. The Russians wanted Manchuria. Even the Japanese were edging outward and hoping to annex Formosa.

Seward's suspicions in this regard were heightened by the fact that the French did launch a punitive expedition against Korea in November 1867 and destroyed the city of Kwanghoa, south of Seoul, but did not have the resources to occupy the peninsula and were forced to withdraw.

Before that futile gesture was made, however, Seward had almost committed the United States to participate in the imperialistic contest for spoils. Franco-American relations then were complicated by the touchy situation arising from American demands for a French withdrawal from Mexico. In essence, Seward was proposing to cooperate with the French empire in the Far East while frowning heavily on French imperialism in Mexico. The brief reign of Maximilian and Carlotta, who had been propped on the Mexican throne by Napoleon III, was coming to an end. To hasten the French withdrawal from Mexican affairs, a United States cavalry corps under General Philip H. Sheridan had been sent to the border to threaten intervention, and with him had gone secret orders to turn over Federal arms and ammunition to the Mexican resistance.

Even while the United States was secretly supplying Benito Juarez with thirty thousand muskets from the Baton Rouge arsenal, in the spring of 1867, Secretary of State Seward was blandly proposing a Franco-American venture in Korea. He called in M. Berthemy, the French minister in Washington, supposedly to discuss another matter.

Quite abruptly, Seward then proposed that the United States and France send a joint naval expedition to Korea to avenge the murder of the French missionaries and the crew of the *General Sherman,* with the further purpose of forcing the Koreans to open their ports to trade. The French declined the offer and acted on their own hook late that year.[8] Only French disdain, and possibly their bitterness over the Mexican situation, spared the United States from involvement in an unjustifiable invasion of the Asian mainland.

Undismayed by his rebuff from the French, Seward continued his efforts to break open Korea later that year. He had installed his nephew, George F. Seward, as United States consul at Shanghai. With his domination over President Johnson, it was easy enough to obtain the President's signature on a letter to Seward's nephew authorizing him to proceed to Korea, escorted by a naval task force, with a commercial treaty similar to that signed by the Japanese. The directive read:

"The design of this government is to render your visit a generous and friendly one, reserving the question of force, if found necessary, for ultimate consideration . . . you will be expected to practise discretion, prudence and patience, while firmly asserting the dignity and maintaining the demands of the United States. You will, however, give notice to the Korean Government, if you find it expedient, that this government cannot suffer the outrage committed in the case of the *General Sherman* to remain indefinitely without receiving proper guaranty of adequate and ample redress."

Thus Seward's nephew was to shoot his way into the hearts of the Korean people, if necessary, with the dual and conflicting purposes of persuading them to trade with Americans and of being punished for repulsing the invasion of a freebooting band of American adventurers. He may not have invented gunboat diplomacy but he was proving adept at lending new force to the meaning of the phrase.

The Seward Expedition to Korea, as it developed, never weighed anchor. It was called off at the last moment when intelligence reports indicated that more naval force than the Americans could muster in the Far East would be needed to blast their way into Korea's fortified ports.

But the question of trading with the Land of the Morning Calm continued to vex Washington, even after Seward left the State Department. There was an inevitable sequel to his determined plotting against Korea's national integrity, though it simmered for three years while the United States tried to effect a peaceful entry into the Hermit Kingdom. A capsule history of the sequel is contained in the raised bronze letters of a plaque placed in the wall of the chapel at the United States Naval Academy in Annapolis:

In memory of Hugh W. McKee

Lieut., U.S.N.

Born April 23, 1844

Died June 11, 1871

from wounds received the same day on the

parapet of The Citadel, Kanghoa Island,

Corea; while heroically leading the

assault of the Naval Battalion

of the U.S. Asiatic Fleet

In 1870, during the Grant Administration, Seward's successor, Hamilton Fish, ordered Frederick F. Low, the United States minister to China, to proceed to Seoul with units of the Asiatic Fleet. The expedition would be modeled after Commodore Perry's, with equal success anticipated in obtaining a commercial treaty.

A stout New Englander who had been governor of California from 1863 to 1867 and one of the founders of the University of California, Low proceeded to Nagasaki to join the fleet's commander, Rear Admiral John Rodgers, a veteran of the Seminole and Mexican Wars and commander of Union ironclads during the Civil War. Both were men of great determination. They would need that quality in mounting the expedition; sending thin-skinned warships against land batteries was then the riskiest of naval operations. Rodgers's squadron would consist of the flagship *Colorado,* a wooden frigate so frail that she couldn't fire a full broadside without springing her timbers, the corvettes *Alaska* and *Benicia,* and the gunboats *Monocacy* and *Palos* — a force totaling eighty-five guns and 1230 sailors and Marines. Late in May 1871 the squadron sailed from Nagasaki Bay to the mouth of the Han River, where it anchored and received a delegation of minor Korean officials.[9]

Obviously the Koreans were stalling, so the gunboats *Monocacy* and *Palos* were sent upriver on a surveying mission. When they appeared off the fortified lower end of Kanghoa Island, the gunboats were fired upon by the Korean batteries ashore. The Americans suffered little damage, and immediately opened fire with their eight-inch guns, which killed a considerable number of Koreans in the earthworks. Then they rejoined the rest of the squadron downriver. For several days the Americans and Koreans traded diplomatic insults while the United States commanders planned to give the natives a "good drubbing" and "kick their mud forts downhill." Unfortunately only the two gunboats had a shallow enough draft to steam back up to Kanghoa Island with a landing force. The *Monocacy*'s firepower was increased by the transfer of two nine-inch guns from the *Colorado.* Then the two gunboats, on June 10, returned to the fortified island upriver, hauling twenty longboats packed with the landing party of 546 sailors and 105 Marines armed with seven howitzers and with breech-loading carbines. At 1 P.M. the *Monocacy* bombarded Kanghoa Island and its garrison fled. While the landing party went ashore, the gunboats proceeded to attack a fort farther up on the island. The next day the naval battalion ashore marched to the northern end of the island to assault the main fort, called the Citadel, a formidable bastion crowning a 150-foot hill and menacing the countryside with 143 artillery pieces. It was defended by an elite Korean force called the Tiger Hunters, each member of which was supposed to have killed a tiger singlehanded.

The Americans charged uphill, supported by fire from the *Monocacy*'s batteries. They stormed over the parapet — Lieutenant McKee falling with a bullet in the groin and a spear in the thigh — and a bloody hand to hand combat followed, steel cutlasses (American) clashing with soft iron swords (Korean). Steel inevitably proved superior to iron. American sharpshooters cut down Koreans trying to flee. By midday the Stars and Stripes were raised over the Citadel. Three hundred and fifty Koreans had been killed to three American dead and ten wounded.

Superficially, "Our Little War with the Heathen," as it was headlined in the expansionist New York *Herald,* appeared to be a rousing victory. The American amphibious force stayed on Kanghoa Island long enough to level the fortifications, bury the dead and pose for photographs. Then it rejoined the squadron at the mouth of the Han, where the Americans stayed for another three weeks hoping that word of capitulation would come from Seoul. None came, and when the Americans offered to return twenty Tiger Hunters captured at the Citadel the Korean government replied with contempt, "Do as you please with them." The object of any military exercise is to convince the enemy that he has been beaten. This the Americans had failed to do. They weren't strong enough to attack the capital, so they dithered at the anchorage on the Han. Finally Minister Low presented his demands for a commercial treaty but the Koreans rejected them with scant courtesy. The American task force, lacking the ability to occupy any sizable part of the peninsula, was forced to sail away empty-handed. It took another eleven years of patient bargaining before Korea, succumbing to pressures from all sides, finally signed a trade treaty with the United States. Force had only delayed the process, and our First Korean War, initiated by Seward's aggressive policy, had to be written down as a humiliating defeat.

2. *Seward's Polar-Bear Garden*

According to the official Seward family version, the acquisition of the Territory of Alaska, or Russian America as it was then known, was a casual, homey affair transacted over a family whist session. The deal was arranged, without the knowledge of the Congress or the American people, while Seward was similarly and secretly negotiating with the French for a joint expedition to Korea. As his son Frederick W. Seward described it:

"On Friday evening, March 29, 1867, [twenty-seven days after he had proposed the Korean operation], Seward was playing whist in his parlor with some of his family, when the Russian minister was announced.

" 'I have a dispatch, Mr. Seward, from my Government by cable. The Emperor gives his consent to the cession. Tomorrow if you like, I will come to the department, and we can enter upon the treaty.' "

"Mr. Seward with a smile of satisfaction at the news, pushed away the whist table, saying:

" 'Why wait till tomorrow, Mr. Stoeckl? Let us make the treaty tonight.' "[10]

Baron de Stoeckl and Mr. Seward then adjourned to the State Department. Secretaries were summoned and, almost as an afterthought, the sympathetic Senator Charles Sumner, chairman of the Foreign Relations Committee, was called in to serve as a witness.

Before dawn rose over the capital, Seward and the Russian minister to Washington signed a document agreeing that the United States would acquire Alaska — more than half a million square miles, more than twice as big as Texas — in exchange for $7,200,000.

The story behind the Alaskan purchase was a lot more interesting than the Seward family legend, and a lot less inspiring than the version told in school history books. It involved the strange passivity, bordering on somnolence, of President Andrew Johnson. It was marked by the equally strange — from hindsight — eagerness of Russia to dispose of its holdings on the American continent, which constitutes one of the larger blunders of the czars. It was begrimed by the Russian bribery it took to persuade certain members of Congress to vote for the $7,200,000 appropriation. That it turned out to be an extremely lucrative bargain for the United States does not entirely mitigate the alarming high-handedness with which William H. Seward conducted the nation's foreign policy. From the standpoint of safeguarding constitutional government, it was all of a piece with his personal declaration of hostility on Korea.

Seward pushed his imperialism-now policy with unflagging zest, great boldness and shrewd manipulation of public and congressional opinion. The country was weary from four years of civil war, and the Congress reflected that weariness, yet Seward managed to guide them along the course of empire. Occasionally he over-reached, as when the Senate refused to comply with his demand that the Danish West Indies be purchased and the House prevented the annexation of Santo Domingo.

The "national extension" he advocated, however, was accomplished with little hindrance. Balked in his expansionist plans for the Caribbean, he was determined to make certain that the United States held a distant outpost line in the Pacific theater. The work of acquiring more island territory in the central Pacific would be taken up by his son, who was Undersecretary of State in the Hayes Administration. The northern sector of the Pacific, where American power would impinge on the Russian and Japanese, was equally important. Seward was resolved that Alaska would serve as the sub-Arctic anchor of our Pacific defenses. It would also serve as the capstone of his career.

Fortunately for that project Russia was simultaneously deciding that she couldn't afford to keep Alaska any longer. Her finances had been drained by the Crimean War. Ever since the sea otter had been hunted and slaughtered almost to extinction, the trade between Russia and its Alaska colony had run into yearly deficits. The decision to unload Alaska was taken at a council of ministers in 1866, and Baron de Stoeckl was instructed to promote the sale as quickly as possible.

Shortly after the Russian minister approached him, Seward took up the Alaskan proposal with the President and the rest of the Cabinet, which gave him its approval to proceed with the bargaining. Except for his friend Senator Sumner, it seemed as though Seward was the only enthusiast for the proposition. Even his own party, now carrying the expansionist banner, would support him reluctantly. In its reading of the country's mood, Congress sensed that the people were opposed to ventures of any kind outside their territorial limits; they wanted time to recover from the war, to conserve their remaining energies for subduing the Indians, occupying the

West, extending the railroads and other domestic projects. "In the general judgment of the people," as James G. Blaine accurately read their mood, "the last thing we needed was additional territory."[11]

The influential Senator Sumner supported Seward partly out of their old friendship and also because he was a strong advocate of friendship with Russia. It was his favorite among the nations, and he was willing to help her by foisting the Alaskan burden on his own country. The Alaskan purchase "tried me severely," he admitted. "Abstractly I am against further accessions of territory, unless by the free choice of the inhabitants. But this question was perplexed by considerations of politics and comity and the engagements already entered into by my Government. I hesitated to take the responsibility of defeating it." Taking Alaska off Russia's hands, as he saw it, would be a just repayment for her friendly attitude toward the Union during the Civil War.

"It is difficult to see," Sumner wrote in a pamphlet (*On the Cession of Russian America*) published in support of the project, "how we can refuse to complete the purchase without putting to the hazard the friendly relations which happily subsist between the United States and Russia."[12]

Without his support, and perhaps also the outlay of considerable sums of Russian money in Washington, the Alaskan purchase probably would have died in Congress. The American press greeted the proposal at first with incredulity, because it seemed such a swindle, and then with a drumfire of ridicule. In the newspapers it was often referred to as "Seward's Folly" and "Seward's Polar-Bear Garden." The Democratic press particularly denounced the proposed purchase as a colossal gold-brick scheme, unaware of how very real was the gold in the frozen gravel of the Yukon's tributaries; saluted the "shrewdness" of the Russians and the "silliness" of the administration. So little was known of the territory that most articles pictured Alaska as part of the North Pole, covered with ice and populated only by bears and wolves.

The general ignorance was modified, to some degree, by the propaganda pouring from Seward's office. He compared the projected acquisition of Alaska with the Louisiana Purchase — not unfairly, as it turned out — and supplied the few receptive newspapers with extracts from editorials denouncing the latter in terms comparable to the present journalistic campaign against his own scheme. Meanwhile Sumner was working on the apathy of his fellow Senators. Undoubtedly he was echoing Seward when he pointed to the strategic importance of the Alaskan coast in controlling the North Pacific, to the Aleutian Island chain "extending a friendly hand to Asia," to the possibility of opening up trade between the Alaskan ports and China and Japan.

Under his vigorous advocacy, the treaty sailed through the Senate with only two dissenting votes. In the House, however, there was much stronger opposition, and no countervailing force such as Sumner's in the

Senate. Among that body large amounts of Russian money would be needed to still doubts and arouse enthusiasm for the purchase. "The whole transaction," Foster Rhea Dulles has written, "was tainted with that aroma of corruption which was to become so familiar to post-war Washington."[13]

Baron de Stoeckl reported to his government that he spent most of the two hundred thousand dollars allotted him for "secret expenses" during the months of debate and horse-trading when the appropriation was being considered in the House. The baron was so disgusted by the corruptibility of the House of Representatives, in fact, that he pleaded with St. Petersburg, once the deal was made, to transfer him elsewhere so he could "breathe an atmosphere purer than that of Washington."

Incredible as it now seems, influential Congressmen had to be bribed to agree to the Alaskan purchase. Twenty thousand of the baron's secret fund went to Robert J. Walker, the Secretary of the Treasury in the Polk Administration, who acted as Stoeckl's lobbyist, but much of the balance was funneled into congressional pockets. In the day of the Crédit Mobilier and other scandals, taking money from a foreign country was a relatively innocent matter.

The bribery was partly spelled out in a memorandum found in the papers of the indiscreet Andrew Johnson. Secretary of State Seward was the authority, President Johnson noted, for the information that the Russian minister paid liberally for support of the Alaska treaty — thirty thousand dollars to John W. Ferney, twenty thousand dollars to F. P. Stanton, ten thousand dollars to Thaddeus Stevens and eight thousand dollars to Nathaniel P. Banks. The vitriolic Stevens was a leader of the Radical Republicans, so righteous about the slavery issue, so vindictive in "reconstructing" the former Confederacy. Banks was one of the war's less successful political generals, and had once commanded a Union army on his own with less than satisfactory results; now he commanded the House Foreign Relations Committee.* [14]

Neither the President nor his Secretary of State, who presumably got his information about the bribery from Baron de Stoeckl himself, saw fit to call off the deal or even rebuke the erring Congressmen. Corruption was taken for granted, or regarded as insignificant against the larger view, the visions of American greatness which preoccupied Seward.

In the case of Representative Banks, at least, the Russians got value for their money. He delivered a stem-winder of an oration on the subject of the nation's Pacific destiny and Alaska's role in the future. "That ocean,"

---

* Banks, an ex-"bobbin boy" who had worked his way up from the woolen mills of Massachusetts, was commissioned a major general largely because of his prewar congressional rank of Speaker of the House. His sluggish campaign in support of Grant's siege of Vicksburg resulted in the capture of Port Hudson, but afforded Grant little relief. Later he succeeded General Ben Butler as occupation commander in Louisiana.

declared Banks, "will be the theater of the triumphs of civilization in the future. It is on that line that are to be fought the great battles of the hereafter. It is there that the institutions of the world will be fashioned and its destinies decided. If this transfer is successful, it will no longer be an European civilization or an European destiny that controls us. It will be a higher civilization and a nobler destiny. It may be an American civilization, an American destiny of six hundred million souls."

Just how the half-billion Asian souls were to be brought under the direct influence of American civilization through the Alaskan purchase, Representative Banks did not explain, but he apparently believed that one could walk across the Aleutians from Alaska to Asia. The Aleutians, he said, constituted a "drawbridge between America and Asia" and were "stepping stones across the Pacific Ocean." (The Aleutian stepping-stone delusion lasted a long time. As late as 1908, the round-the-world automobile racers planned to drive their cars across the Aleutian chain from Valdez, Alaska to Siberia.)

Representative Horace Maynard of Tennessee, though his enthusiasm apparently was not rewarded by any grant from Baron de Stoeckl's secret fund, also proclaimed the day when "the civilization of this world will be transferred from the Atlantic to the Pacific." Alaska would be "but a part of our great Pacific system."

Other Congressmen similarly unrewarded by the Russian minister were less generous in their appraisals of Seward's deal. The theme of their complaints on the House floor was that we would be buying seven million dollars worth of snow, ice and frozen scenery. Representative C. C. Washburn of Wisconsin sarcastically suggested to the State Department that it "could have bought a much superior elephant in Siam or Bombay for one hundredth part of the money, with not a ten thousandth part of the expense incurred in keeping the animal in proper condition." Representative Orange Ferris of New York groused that Alaska was "an inhospitable, wretched and God-forsaken region, worth nothing, but a positive injury and encumbrance as a colony of the United States." Williams of Pennsylvania decried the proposition on the grounds that it was contrary to the wishes of the American people. "Not a sensible man among them had ever suggested it," he told the House. "The whole country exclaimed at once, when it was made known to it, against the ineffable folly, if not the wanton profligacy, of the whole transaction."

A more dispassionate, longheaded and reasoned view was taken in the opposition of Representative Samuel Shellabarger of Ohio. He pointed out that the new territory was separated from our continental limits by the Canadian provinces. Alaska, in a sense, would be an overseas colony. The most important factor in its purchase, Shellabarger told the House, was the fact that it would constitute a striking departure in American policy. He was concerned because this aspect had not even been considered in the congressional debate; because on its surface the purchase of Alaska seemed so quixotic it couldn't possibly be establishing a precedent.

"Is the United States prepared," Shellabarger demanded, "to step now for the first time upon the policy of acquiring possessions across the world?"

Congress finally appropriated the money for Alaska on July 14, 1868, more than a year after Seward committed the United States to buying it. That it was a strategic and financial bargain can hardly be doubted; purely as a real estate deal it may be compared with the purchase of the Virgin Islands, which cost more than three times as much half a century later. Fish, furs, gold, timber and oil have come streaming out, new Alaskans streaming in, and the value of the air and naval bases commanding the North Pacific and the transpolar air space is incalculable. Its military worth can be judged by considering what it would mean if Sitka were still a Russian provincial capital and Soviet missile sites dotted the tundra.

And Seward must be credited with foreseeing that aspect of its acquisition. It was part of his unstated dream of empire. If we had not bought it then, we would probably have had to seize it as a forward area against the Japanese in World War II — or the Japanese might have bought it from the Russians.

If our fate is imperial, if our destiny is Roman, then William H. Seward was a great man. No one has done more to shift the axis of American power and influence from East to West.

3. *The Team of De Long and Le Gendre*

French history glitters with figures celebrated for their exploits as imperial adventurers. The French who migrated to America, however, might have come from Lapland for all their contributions to historical glamour, and the French-Americans have been one of the quietest, most modest and self-effacing elements in the American mixture.

The necessary exceptions to the rule were a pair of high-handed American representatives in Asia (diplomatists they were not) who left their mark on American relations with the Far East in the early 1870's. They were Charles E. De Long, the United States minister to Japan during the Grant Administration, and C. W. Le Gendre, the United States consul at Amoy, both of whom behaved like direct descendants of Marshal Ney. Their brief essays in personal, independent diplomacy illustrated the continuing lack of control, despite the quickened communications, which the State Department was able to exert over its representatives in Asia. By then, of course, it was traditional for an American posted to an Asian consulate or legation to act without constant consultation with Washington.

The cable, and finally the instant communication afforded by Teletype and Telex machines, ended all that.

De Long was a picturesque character indeed to have attained ministerial status, especially before the American diplomatic service was curried into the neat, tight-lipped conformity of the British. When former Secretary of State William H. Seward appeared in Tokyo in 1871 on his round-the-world tour, his declining years may have been shortened by acceptance of De Long's hospitality. De Long drove him around the Japanese capital behind a pair of fast ponies, with a huge revolver bulging from his belt and a buggy whip with which he flailed at pedestrians who didn't scurry out of the way fast enough.[15]

When De Long came to Japan, he was met with the usual maneuvering by the authorities to prevent him from having an audience with the emperor. He insisted that he had to present his credentials to the emperor in person. The Court yielded a bit and said De Long would be admitted to the audience chamber but the emperor would receive him from behind silk screen. De Long insisted on a face-to-face encounter. Finally, after weeks of negotiation, the audience was granted.

As De Long recalled the occasion, he "threaded through corridors" of the palace "to the sound of the most weird and dismal music that ever saluted the ears of a man; and when finally I reached the audience chamber, I found the whole building filled with courtiers abasing themselves on the ground, with their hands upon their swords, his Majesty sitting on a throne, backed by a perfect arsenal of weapons immediately within his reach, and his sword-bearer having his sword about three inches out of his sheath."[16]

He believed that it was a testimonial to the confidence he had won among the Japanese that when he was recalled four years later, there were no weapons in evidence and the emperor received him "standing on the same level as ourselves, dressed in a uniform like that of a hussar in foreign service, with cocked hat and plume."

Despite his readiness to use whip or tongue in pursuit of his goals, De Long was an ardent admirer of the Japanese nation. Soon he was as much their ally and adviser as an envoy of the American government. In 1871 he was greatly alarmed by a draft treaty between China and Japan which he was shown by friends in the Japanese foreign office. One article provided for a defensive alliance, which De Long opposed because he was determined that the United States would be Japan's closest friend and ally.

Diplomacy may be the art of polite meddling in the affairs of another nation to the presumed advantage of your own, with the line between discreet influence and overt interference difficult to determine, but De Long was rarely bothered by fine distinctions. He exerted all his influence to have the article stricken from the proposed treaty on the curious grounds that the Japanese were temperamentally much different from the Chinese and a

Frederick Townsend Ward, scourge of the Taipings

William Seward, first-water Pacificist

A Chinese embassy ventures abroad

friendship between them would be "calamitous." America must remain Japan's number-one friend, he wrote the State Department, because the Japanese were "a power to be welcomed as an ally and dreaded as a foe by all civilized states should trouble occur with China, or our troubles with Korea enlarge and increase."[17]

Secretary of State Hamilton Fish replied that the Japanese should indeed be encouraged to "separate themselves as far as possible from the exclusive policy of the Chinese." Fish also believed the Japanese should "adopt the progressive policy of free commercial and social intercourse with the powers." The latter was a giddy misapprehension; apparently the Secretary of State did not know that all Westerners themselves discouraged "free social intercourse" with any Orientals and from the beginning had adopted a policy of excluding them from any social functions.

Many of De Long's subsequent actions could be ascribed only to an advanced case of what the Old Asia Hands later called "going Asiatic," which covered everything from running amok in a brothel to wearing a kimono and sleeping with your head on a wooden pillow.

He was exhilarated, as his dispatches to Washington indicate, by Japanese plans for an aggressive expansion in 1872. The Japanese were preparing to invade Korea, fearful that Russia or one of the other Western powers would beat them to that iron-rich peninsula; to launch an expedition to Formosa and subdue the aborigines; send a delegation to Peking which would *demand* an audience with the Manchu emperor, and threaten war against China if it was snubbed. Splendid ideas, De Long believed. He had become fascinated by the intrigues of the Imperial Palace and was eager to participate; conniving behind silk screens, dropping innuendoes from behind jeweled fans, all the muted melodrama of an Oriental court, were more to his taste than the politicking over cuspidors he had witnessed in America.

A kindred spirit dropped by in November 1872. C. W. Le Gendre, the consul at Amoy, was en route to the United States for home leave. Like the pistol-packing De Long, Charles Le Gendre was an activist. He had migrated to the United States in his youth, served in the Union Army, risen to the rank of brigadier general and lost one eye in the Battle of the Wilderness. America was too tame for him after the excitement of war, so he obtained the appointment as consul at Amoy in 1866. A year later he accompanied the United States naval expedition against Formosa, the humiliating consequences of which so rankled in him that he organized his own punitive force, including a Chinese gunboat and a battalion of mercenaries, then returned to Formosa prepared to tear the island apart. The Formosan authorities disappointed him by promising that American castaways would be protected in the future; Le Gendre had to sail away with his blood-thirst unslaked.

The two musketeers were delighted with each other. De Long introduced his new friend at the Foreign Office and the war ministry, suggesting that Le Gendre was just the man to help the Japanese launch their program of expansion. He had not only dealt with the Chinese on a diplomatic level but with the Formosans at gunpoint. Le Gendre forgot all about continuing on his way home when the Japanese agreed that he would be a valuable adviser. He would be attached to the embassy being sent to Peking as a counsellor (his official rank was that of an officer of the second rank with a salary equivalent to twelve thousand dollars a year), and to the proposed Formosan expedition as a military adviser. The fact that he was entering the employ of a foreign government while still a representative of the State Department on leave did not trouble him any more than launching his own invasion against Formosa on a Chinese gunboat flying the American flag.

His indifference to the prior claims of the State Department on his services was partly explained by a sudden infatuation with the Japanese way of life. Like De Long, he was undismayed by the feudal aspects of Japanese society. He doubted that Japan should adopt a Western political system since "a country is not necessarily free because it has a form of government similar to that of other nations whose people are free." Japan, he believed, should retain an authoritarian government because it seemed to suit the people. So much for democracy. What really interested him was Japanese adventurism, which to him was so much more flexible than the stodginess, the passivity of American policy in the Far East. Some years later, in 1878, he published a book titled *Progressive Japan* in which he proclaimed that it was the Japanese destiny to "form the advanced post of a transformed superior civilization."

The results of the De Long–Le Gendre collaboration with the Japanese were seriocomic. Filibustering was going out of style even in the Orient; massed armies and modern firepower were narrowing the field of opportunity for military adventurers and other romantics.

First came the belligerent embassy to Peking. A top-ranking Japanese diplomat, Soyeshima, and his delegation sailed off in March 1873 aboard two warships. With Counsellor Le Gendre at the head of his retinue, all togged out in morning coats and silk hats, Soyeshima swaggered into Peking. At first there was lengthy bickering over Soyeshima's exact status in the Peking diplomatic corps, who would bow to whom, whose rank was sufficient to be admitted to Soyeshima's presence. Le Gendre insisted that his chief must be hard-nosed about all these details, as well as the bellicose insistence on being received by the Chinese emperor.

The haggling over protocol went on for weeks before the Japanese were permitted to submit their proposals — that China agree to the Japanese occupation of the Ryukyus (including what is now called Okinawa), allow Japan to invade and occupy Formosa and yield to Japan its claims of sovereignty over Korea. On these matters the Chinese gave only evasive answers, which the Japanese were quick to take for assent.

An even touchier question was Soyeshima's demand for an audience with the emperor, who had never received the representative of a foreign country. The Chinese did not propose to break precedent solely for the blustering Japanese and their American counsellor. Nor did they want war with Japan. They solved the problem in the Chinese way, by inviting the whole diplomatic corps — but with Soyeshima at its head — to an audience with the emperor.

Le Gendre returned to Tokyo with the Soyeshima embassy, with his prestige intact. His supposedly expert advice was then taken on the Formosan question. The Japanese had Minister De Long's word for it that no one knew more about Formosa and its tangled relations with China than the former United States consul at Amoy. Le Gendre told the Japanese that the Chinese did not exercise sovereignty over that part of the island where a number of Ryukyu fishermen were killed by the aborigines — the pretext Japan intended to use for invading Formosa — and that only a small expeditionary force would be required to make a landing. In return for his expertise, Le Gendre was appointed to accompany the proposed expedition as a sort of ex-officio chief of staff; he was also promised that if war resulted from the venture he would be made a general in the Japanese army, and if Japan occupied all of Formosa he would be made governor of the island.

De Long was positively delighted at these developments, which he informed Washington would drive China and Japan farther apart and probably place both Korea and Japan under the "flag of a nation in sympathy with the western powers."[18] Apparently he never heard of the law forbidding American citizens to serve in foreign armies on pain of losing their American citizenship.

Despite their enthusiasm for the Formosan expedition, it was suspended on advice from the Iwakura Embassy touring America and Europe, and De Long and Le Gendre could only fume while the expansionist issue was fought out in the upper echelons of the Japanese government. Early in 1874 the Japanese again decided to invade the island, citing a clause in their treaty with China: "The raw barbarians of Formosa once unlawfully inflicted injury on the people *belonging to Japan,* and the Japanese Government with the intention of making the said barbarians answer for their acts sent troops to chastise them." That clause, in later negotiations, also established Japan's claim to the Ryukyu Islands.[19]

Once again the old firm of De Long & Le Gendre was in the thick of military preparations. Two other Americans — Lieutenant Commander Douglas Cassel, on a year's leave from the U.S.S. *Ashelot,* and Major James R. Wasson, a former United States Army engineer — were engaged to accompany the naval landing force as Le Gendre's advisers. Le Gendre himself had been transferred from the Foreign Office to the Department of

Colonization. The steamship *New York* was chartered from the Pacific Mail Steamship Company as a military transport.

Suddenly China became alarmed by reports of the preparations for the invasion of Formosa. In an attempt to remove the linchpin of the operation, the Chinese government offered Le Gendre a twenty-thousand-dollar-a-year post with the Chinese customs service, which Le Gendre, his samurai blood boiling, turned down. China then officially protested to Washington that its citizens were engaged in activities hostile to Chinese interests. The State Department was also receiving belated reports from its consuls along the China coast on just how seriously disruptive the Japanese involvement could be, particularly since it appeared to be sanctioned by the United States government.

The drowsy Washington of the Grant Administration was jarred into wakefulness. It ordered its citizens to disengage themselves from the Japanese expedition. De Long was summarily relieved of his post in Tokyo. Le Gendre's humiliation was even greater. He had indiscreetly journeyed to his old stamping ground at the port of Amoy to buy supplies. His replacement as United States consul there boarded his ship, placed him under arrest and sent him to Shanghai.

The plans De Long and Le Gendre had set in motion could not, however, be thrown into reverse. The expedition sailed off in April 1874 and landed on the eastern shore of Formosa to begin operations against the hostile Botan tribe in the jungle-covered mountains. Under a Japanese commander, with Commander Cassel and Major Wasson as advisers, the landing force bogged down. E. H. House, a New York *Herald* correspondent and a friend of Le Gendre's, wrote that the operation lacked the master's (Le Gendre's) touch and was ill-prepared for the severity of the jungle fighting, the heat, the tropical diseases. The Japanese finally managed to secure the eastern coast and settled down to occupy it. Cassel and Wasson were handsomely paid and discharged, Cassel dying at his Pennsylvania home a year later of a tropical disease.

For the next five years China and Japan, subsequently joined by Britain, quarreled and negotiated over whether Japan should be allowed to retain her foothold on the island. The British had intervened on behalf of the Formosan merchants, with whom they had established a lucrative trade. By 1879 the dispute had grown so heated that it appeared likely that Japan and China would go to war.

The adventurous Le Gendre, meanwhile, stayed out East. He returned to Japan for several years and became the first foreigner to be awarded the Order of the Rising Sun. Later he moved to Korea and became an adviser on that country's trade relations. As a Korean envoy he returned to Japan in 1891 to seek revision of the Korean-Japanese trade agreement. By then Japan, he said, had become arrogant to an impossible degree, and he wrote a friend in the States that "Japan has become perfectly hateful to me."[20]

Both De Long and Le Gendre faded into obscurity, but they had known their moment of glory in the affairs of a nascent empire. Picturesque though their methods were, they undoubtedly could be credited with having played considerable roles in Japan's eventual acquisition of Korea and Formosa and increasing the tensions in the Far East which were to result in wars between China and Japan, Japan and Russia, and eventually Japan and the United States. For that they deserve more than the footnote or two they receive, at most, in the history of their country's Asian involvement. The American diplomatic service would never see their like again.

4. *"Together in the Same Sampan"*

The two administrations of Ulysses S. Grant were distinguished mainly by exposures of the corruption at their roots. The former general-in-chief of the Union armies seemed to have used up all his energy in defeating the Confederacy. What little force he released in his presidential function was directed mostly at domestic problems, particularly the misnamed Reconstruction of the South and the sudden collapse of the economy in 1873. The period was aptly titled the Flash Age, a postwar era of rampant materialism. Whenever the general could spare a little time for foreign policy, he tried to promote interest in a scheme for occupying Santo Domingo, which he had inherited from Seward.

Thus it was only at the last moment that the capers of De Long and Le Gendre, as free-lance makers of history in the Orient, were summarily halted when it appeared that they might create a situation in which France, Britain or Russia would step between China and Japan and make off with Formosa or Korea. He had refused to use his influence to halt the French in their gouging at the underbelly of the Chinese empire. The Chinese had long held suzerainty over Indo-China. France, however, had been plotting for years to take over the area. In 1867 she had annexed three provinces of Cochin-China, and in the next dozen years she would expand her control over all of what then were called the Annamese; the prelude to a century of colonialism in its most brutal forms.

In 1873, the year before the French made their decisive grab, the Vietnamese sent an envoy to Washington to appeal for help from the Grant Administration against the French encroachments. Probably not a dozen men in Washington had the vaguest idea of where Indo-China was located, or even that it existed. Besides the administration was preoccupied by the financial panic brought on by the collapse of Jay Cooke's Philadelphia banking house. The envoy from Saigon was politely informed that the United States could do nothing to help his people.

On his way back home the Vietnamese envoy stopped off in Japan to visit the United States consul at Yokohama, an old friend of his. They discussed the probability that the United States in the future would be greatly involved in the affairs of all the Asian nations. Before the Vietnamese left Yokohama, he composed a poem which compressed his thoughts on the subject into a few lines. "Spiritual companion," read one line, "in what year will we be together in the same sampan?"*

Shortly after he concluded his second term as President, Grant and his family embarked on a leisurely tour of the world; so leisurely it took them almost two years to cover Europe, northern Africa and the Middle East. Then they sailed for India and the Far East. Accompanying them was John Russell Young, later the United States minister to China but presently a correspondent for the New York *Herald.* James Gordon Bennett, Jr., the publisher of the *Herald,* who had sent Stanley to find Livingston, had an uncanny instinct for such projects, even though they were costly and time-consuming. He guessed correctly that the reticent Grant, relaxing on shipboard, looking back over his career for the first time, might produce a lot of interesting copy for Young — and he was right. Young, in fact, filled hundreds of columns of the *Herald* and more than twelve hundred pages in the two volumes of *Around the World with General Grant.* The ex-President poured out his memories and reflections, and it was fascinating stuff. He told Young, for instance, that if Britain had joined the Confederacy in action against the Union, the North would have immediately seized all of Canada. "If Sheridan, with our resources, could not have taken Canada in thirty days he should have been cashiered . . . We could have thrown half a million men into their country, not militia but men inured to war."[22]

It was a pity, perhaps, that Grant had not taken his grand tour before he became President. He had been an expansionist, but a lethargic one, while in office. Now that he saw the world for himself his view changed from indifference — an attitude easily acquired from reading State Department prose — to one of compassion. It was a strange hegira, a voyage of discovery for the grubby little provincial who had sprung in less than three years from a leather store in Galena, Illinois, to commander of all the Union armies.

Grant and his party arrived in Tientsin at a critical stage in the relations between China and Japan. The two countries were on the verge of going to war over possession of the Ryukyus and other disputed territory. Grant began absorbing the facts about the conflict in the Far East between the Western imperialisms and the Asian nations, among the Westerners themselves, and between the Asian nations contending for control over their own continent. If he had been mildly imperialist, like most Americans

* President Lyndon B. Johnson retailed the anecdote at the conclusion of the Guam conference on Viet Nam late in March 1967, commenting, "Today we know the answer. We are together. And we know our destination."[21]

of his time, he now began to understand the human effects of conquest, subjugation and importunate rule by members of one race over those of another. As an about-face, executed with West Point precision, it ranks with the stern warning issued by President Eisenhower at the end of *his* second administration against the expanding power of the military-industrial establishment.

During gong-clanging ceremonies and lengthy banquets in Tientsin he became friendly with Viceroy Li Hung Chang, in effect China's Secretary of War, who compared his suppression of the Taiping Rebellion (though it was largely accomplished by Ward and other foreigners) with Grant's quelling of the Confederacy. "How funny," the viceroy commented, "that I should be named Li, and General Grant's opponent should be called Lee."[23]

Grant and his entourage then sailed upriver to Peking on the viceroy's private yacht, where he was immediately received by Prince Kung, the regent for the boy emperor. He was greeted, in fact, with an enthusiasm that indicated the Chinese government believed that a former President of the United States retained most of the power and influence of his former office. At a dinner party attended by the viceroy and Prince Kung as well as their womenfolk (a rare event in Chinese society, testifying to the eagerness of the Chinese to fall in with Western customs just this once) the Chinese were introduced to the waltz. Two ladies of the foreign colony performed the dance; a man and woman dancing together in public would have been too great a shock for the Chinese. "This revelation of barbarian customs created great astonishment, and when the dance stopped there was a chorus of approbation from the Chinese, as if they had discovered a new pleasure in the world, the hostess nodding and smiling with more energy of manner that she had shown during the evening. This performance was witnessed by the Viceroy, who perhaps had his own thoughts as a far-seeing statesman as to what China would become if German music ever found its way into Chinese households, and mothers and maidens gave way to the temptations of the waltz."

Once the ceremony and social mingling were out of the way, Prince-Regent Kung got down to business. Knowing that Grant was going to be received in the highest circles in Japan, he proposed, in brief, that the American act as a mediator between the two countries.

"For generations," the regent told Grant, "the Loochoo [the Ryukyu Islands] had recognized the sovereignty of China, not alone the present dynasty, but the dynasty of the Mings. The king of this island was taken to Japan and deposed, and the sovereignty was extinguished." Relations had grown so bitter, the regent added, that war seemed inevitable.

Grant replied that such a war would be a "measureless misfortune."

Prince Kung suggested that "you might be induced to use your good offices with Japan."

At first Grant, realizing the limitations of his unofficial position, was reluctant to take on the responsibility and emphasized that he was "only a traveler." The prince smiled in polite disbelief. Finally Grant told him, "I have no idea what their argument is. They, of course, have an argument. I do not suppose that the rulers are inspired by a desire wantonly to injure China. I will acquaint myself with the Chinese side of the case, as your Imperial Highness and the Viceroy have presented it, and promise to present it. I will do what I can to learn the Japanese side." Arbitration, he said, "may not satisfy either party at the time, but it satisfies the conscience of the world and must commend itself more and more as the means of adjusting international disputes."[24]

Grant, full of a sense of high purpose such as he had not known since Appomattox, sailed off to Japan with his party. They left China, as John Russell Young said, deeply impressed by a civilization which was "in some things a wonder to us, and in others a reproach . . . Ancient, vast, unyielding, impenetrable China sits enthroned in the solitude of Asia, remembering that she was in her splendor before the Roman empire was born, and that her power has survived the mutations of every age. What is her power today? That is the question of the nineteenth century, and it is a question which cannot be asked too seriously."

En route to Japan, Grant spoke of his abhorrence of the panoply of war, of militarism in all its manifestations. He had entered West Point only because his father wanted it, he had hated serving in the war against Mexico as a young officer. While visiting Versailles he had tried to appreciate the war murals but "they were disgusting." In England the Duke of Cambridge had invited him to attend a review at Aldershot but "I told his Royal Highness that the one thing I never wanted to see again was a military parade." The general made it clear that he had come to be the next thing to a pacifist. He had refused to accept General Lee's sword at Appomattox, he recalled bitterly, because "It would only have gone to the Patent Office to be worshipped by the Washington rebels."[25]

In this idealistic mood, Grant arrived with his party in Japan late in June 1879. It was reflected in a speech he made at the magnificent reception given him in Nagasaki:

"America has much to gain in the East — no nation has greater interests; but America has nothing to gain except what comes from the cheerful acquiescence of the Eastern people and insures them as much benefit as it does us. I should be ashamed of my country if its relations with other nations, and especially with these ancient and most interesting empires in the East, were based upon any other idea.

"We have rejoiced over your progress. We have watched you step by step. We have followed the unfolding of your old civilization and its absorbing the new. I hope it may continue, that it may long continue. America . . . is more affected by the eastern populations than any other power. She is your next neighbor . . .

"No nation needs from the outside powers justice and kindness more

than Japan, because the work that has made such marvelous progress in
the past few years is a work in which we are deeply concerned, in the
success of which we see a new era in civilization."²⁶

General and Mrs. Grant attended the Nagasaki Fair and planted trees
near the monument memorializing their visit, then attended a banquet of
fifty courses including seaweed, raw fish, duck, truffles, turnips, dried
bonito, aromatic shrubs, snipe, shrimp, raw carp, pickled and mashed and
powdered fish with plum juice and walnuts, red and white bean cake, and
sweetmeats. After that heroic performance, the Americans proceeded to
Tokyo, where Grant was saluted by the thunder of naval guns and shore
batteries. Despite his protests that he was traveling as a private citizen,
Young noted, the Japanese, like the Chinese, "insist upon regarding the
visit as official, as the coming of a ruler, as an embassy of the highest
rank." He and his party were quickly ushered into the presence of the
prime minister and all of the highest officials of the government, then the
emperor and empress. The emperor even advanced from his throne and
shook hands with Grant, "a thing never before known in the history of
Japanese majesty," as Young observed.

During their stay in Tokyo, the Grants were quartered in one of the
emperor's palaces, Enriokan, which lay behind a deep moat and high walls.
After his formal audience, Grant returned to the Imperial Palace for a long
conversation with the emperor through interpreters. No doubt his Imperial
host was gratified by Grant's statement that he found much that was good
in British rule over India, that British power could only be replaced by
anarchy, but "since I left India I have seen things that made my blood boil,
in the way that European powers attempt to degrade the Asiatic nations. I
would not believe such a policy possible. It seems to have no other aim
than the extinction of the independence of the Asiatic nations."

Citing the experience of Egypt and the independence she had surrendered to Britain, he warned against Japanese acceptance of foreign
loans. "Japan could not go into a European money market and make a
loan that would be of advantage to her."

In even stronger terms he warned both the emperor and the prime
minister against an aggressive policy toward China, which would only result in foreign intervention. As Young summed up his appeal, Grant
emphasized: "Other counsels would be given to His Majesty, because there
were powerful influences in the East fanning trouble between China and
Japan. Such a war would bring in foreign nations, who would end it to suit
themselves. The history of European diplomacy in the East was unmistakable on that point." In all his conferences, Young observed, Grant
spoke with "great earnestness," more engaged by his role as peacemaker
between China and Japan than by any previous effort in his career. It
seemed to Young that the Japanese appreciated the sincerity of this most
unusual of diplomats, this stumpy cigar-chewing little Middle Westerner.

The mikado had received English, Russian and German princes "as princes," but "he has treated General Grant as a friend."[27]

The upshot of Grant's personal, unaffiliated diplomacy was a letter drafted by Grant on August 18, 1879, and sent to Prince-Regent Kung after being approved by the emperor of Japan and his advisers. As the basis for a settlement of grievances between China and Japan, the general proposed that China withdraw certain dispatches which Japan had found offensive in letter and spirit, that each country appoint a commission to settle their differences, that no foreign power be allowed to participate in the deliberations of the two commissions, and that if the commissions did not agree they would name an arbitrator, whose decisions would be binding on both parties.

In essence, Grant then proposed that China and Japan form a defensive alliance directed at any Western powers which might try to interfere with their peaceful development: "In the vast East, embracing more than two thirds of the human population of the world there are but two nations even partially free from the domination and dictation of some one or other of the European powers, with strength enough to maintain their independence — Japan and China are the two nations. The people of both are brave, intelligent, frugal and industrious. With a little more advancement in modern civilization, mechanics, engineering, etc., they could throw off the offensive treaties, which now cripple and humiliate them, and could enter into competition for the world's commerce . . .

"Japan is now rapidly reaching a condition of independence, and if it had now to be done over, such treaties as exist could not be forced upon her. What Japan has done, and is now doing, China has the power — and I trust the inclination — to do. I can readily conceive that there are many foreigners, particularly those interested in trade, who do not look beyond the present and who would like to have the present condition remain, only grasping more from the East, and leaving the natives of the soil merely 'hewers of wood and drawers of water' for their benefit. I have so much sympathy for the good of their [the foreigners'] children, if not for them, that I hope the two countries will disappoint them."[28]

A revolutionary document, in every sense of the word. If General Grant's proposals had been accepted in good faith on both sides, if the Western powers could have foresworn their mercenary interest in keeping China and Japan weak, and above all at odds with each other, and if China and Japan had formed a strong alliance, history would have taken a very different course in Asia.

It almost seemed for a time that the Grant plan would work. China and Japan did appoint commissions and arrive at a division of influence over the Ryukyus, the sorest point of dispute. At the last minute China perversely delayed in signing the agreement. Within the next few years Japan quietly took over administration of the Ryukyus, and when China wanted to reopen the negotiations Japan pointed out that her annexation of the islands was a *fait accompli*. The chance for peace was lost.

Grant's farsighted embassy of goodwill was not greatly appreciated by his own government. If taken too seriously, American interests were likely to suffer as much or more than the European from a close associa- tion between China and Japan. The news of his letter to Prince-Regent Kung struck American trading firms in Japan and along the Chinese coast like a shock wave; nor was it anything but alarming to the financial powers back in the States deeply involved in those ventures, the same sophisticated gentlemen who had always regarded Grant as a splendidly thick-witted fellow to have in the White House. From Washington, accordingly, went a cautionary from the State Department to its representatives in the Orient stating that it feared China and Japan were using Grant's good offices under the misapprehension that he was acting on behalf of the United States government. United States consuls and ministers were to broadcast the fact that Grant was acting as a private citizen. Grant had already made that clear repeatedly and emphatically. The underlining from Washington was significant. It could only be taken as disapproval of Grant's attempt to arrange a peaceful settlement between China and Japan, and more par- ticularly, perhaps, of his proposal for a defensive alliance.[29]

In the splendor of their tomb overlooking the Hudson River, General and Mrs. Grant lie surrounded by the red battleflags of his victorious armies. There should be room for one small white banner signifying his great humanitarian effort of the summer of 1879. Failing that, his country- men might remember him for that magnificent failure as well as Shiloh, Vicksburg and the Wilderness.

His brief and impulsive effort at making peace between nations he had never seen before, motivated simply by what he had observed on his tour of the Orient, should have served as a warning to his own country. During the Civil War his staff officers had noted the peculiarities of his intellect. Often he seemed almost a stupid little man, yet at the critical moment his mind always penetrated straight to the heart of a problem. His letter to the prince-regent of China showed that he divined exactly what his countrymen, and others, had in mind for Asia, keeping their people, in his borrowing of the Biblical phrase, "hewers of wood and drawers of water." He also perceived that the victims of their policy would include their own children.

The account of his peacemaking efforts was widely read in the United States, both in book and newspaper form, but their meaning was widely ignored. The American people, so busy with other matters, would not halt the process, creeping in its effects, in the years when it was still possible to reverse the "course of empire."

7

The Furor of the Consuls

I can see but one way out — to follow the demand of the Samoan people that the Berlin Act be rescinded . . . the natives be let alone and allowed to govern the islands as they choose . . . The Samoans would continue fighting . . . but at least they would fight it out by themselves, without their wars being turned to the advantage of meddling foreigners.

— ROBERT LOUIS STEVENSON

The British and the French took the imperial way with a certain amount of style, adopting viceregal graces to clothe an often brutal efficiency, but when the United States and Germany finally ventured on the scene of power politics, meeting head-on in Samoa, they went at it like a pair of embattled real estate promoters. Nothing so sharply illumined the changing realities of nineteenth-century geopolitics as the fact that Bismarckian Germany and post–Civil War America did, in fact, collide and almost go to war over a tropical anchorage called Pago Pago. The scenario for that intermittent conflict might have been written by Gilbert and Sullivan. A comic-opera title for that confrontation of naval guns and diplomatic fusillades was provided by the alternately amused and enraged observer who lived in the hills above the arena. Robert Louis Stevenson called it the "Furor Consularis."

The Samoan "crisis" lasted more than twenty years while Germany and the United States, and to a lesser extent Great Britain, jockeyed for supremacy in the archipelago more than two thousand miles south of Hawaii. There were moments of high comedy, as when two German dignitaries named Conrad Cederkrantz and Baron von Pilsach disgraced themselves by quarreling with each other instead of the other foreigners; as when the Royal Navy of Hawaii — one leaky gunboat — sailed to conquer the islands under the drunkest captain who ever lurched across a quarterdeck; as when foreign-supported "kingdoms" rose and fell overnight. But thanks to the Anglo-German-American intervention there were also hundreds of people — mostly Samoans — killed in bush wars, and war between Germany and the United States seemingly was averted only by a tropical storm which wrecked six of the seven warships about to clear decks for action.

During those years of diplomatic intrigue and naval maneuver, two decades of plot and counterplot in Berlin, London and Washington as well as the drowsy ports of the archipelago, the American people took little notice of our involvement in Samoa. There was skimpy coverage of Samoan affairs in the newspapers, and even such liberal Democratic journals as Joseph Pulitzer's New York *World* paid little attention to the Pacific world until a Democratic administration (both of Grover Cleveland's terms) made something of a political issue of our policy toward the Pacific islands and nations.

Yet those were the years in which the United States, with Samoa as the laboratory for our first experiments, became an imperialist power. The nation itself became aware of our acquisitive tendency at the end of the century when American forces landed in the Philippines to "liberate" them, stayed to "pacify," and finally established themselves openly to "occupy." A large part of the electorate was shocked as it would not be again until the Viet Nam War; appalled when our true intentions were stripped of their verbal camouflage. In American history such moments of self confronting self have been very rare indeed; we are the least introspective of peoples, tending to seek our image as it is reflected by others, by what we call "world opinion," by which we are often mesmerized. But the real springboard for our massive penetration of the East was the long-drawn struggle for Samoa; it provided the precedent for further expansion; it led to the Philippines as the Philippines eventually led to Viet Nam.

The last quarter of the last century, a period in which superficially the nation was at peace (the Indians conquered, no foreign enemies to be engaged, the Negro question put back to sleep), seems like a long tranquil sunny afternoon. Even the Spanish-American War, so far as the fighting between American and Spanish forces was concerned, was barely an interruption. During that quarter-century, however, our industry was developing its gigantic power, and the appetite for markets abroad in which competition was negligible grew in sequence.

Only a few intellectuals applied themselves to the consideration of what American expansion westward, overseas, might mean. Until the Civil War they were full of the certainty that Western civilization was the high point of human history, and that the American development of that civilization would manifest the finest qualities of which mankind was capable. We were the hope of the earth, the successor to decadent Europe. We would avoid European sins against humanity, and share our method of making a better life with the backward nations. We were quite as quick to call the Chinese or Japanese barbarians, benighted heathen, as they were to size us up as clumsy, slow-witted, uncultured newcomers.

During the last quarter of the nineteenth century American intellectuals began to wonder aloud whether it wasn't the American mission, particularly in Asia, to advance civilization by force if necessary. If the missionary failed, he would have to be replaced by the soldier. Darwinism encouraged the view that the fittest survived, and we were the fittest of all. Perhaps it wasn't necessary to inspire, to provide an example for the backward East; not if there was a shortcut available through more forceful means. Darwinism applied to international relations encouraged the idea that the West must triumph over the East, rather than lead it by its little brown hand.

It seemed to many intellectuals, now that mankind's diversity had been studied for a century and more, that the success of Western civilization indicated that Caucasians must be a superior race. And if they were superior, didn't it follow that they were destined, by natural law, to dominate the inferior races? The prominent historian John Fiske declared in 1885 that there had been a constant struggle between East and West throughout history. The East, as he saw it, was characterized by a "barren and monotonous way of living and thinking"; the West was concerned with "making life as rich and fruitful as possible in varied material and spiritual achievement." The clash of the two cultures, Fiske stated, had resulted in a demonstrable superiority of Western values over Eastern.[1]

Already there were some doubts, however, that despite the professed moral and material superiority of the West, its organized and industrialized power would necessarily prevail in the long run. It had to be recognized that the white race was far outnumbered by the brown, black and yellow. In his essay "Some Aspects of Civilization in America," Charles Eliot Norton began by announcing that "Beginning the century as a small, weak people, we end it one of the greatest and most powerful nations that the earth has known." He ended on a despairing note: "Thus we are brought

face to face with the grave problem which the next century is to solve —
whether our civilization can maintain itself, and make advance, against the
pressure of ignorant and barbaric multitudes."[2]

Americans had been traveling to the Far East for a century now, but
the picture of the Orient as a teeming mass of near-savages was only
imprinted the more firmly on the American mind. The Orient summoned
up a picture of endless hordes of coolies trotting down the streets of a
thousand ramshackle cities. The weight of their numbers oppressed the
imagination. It was alleviated only by the helplessness and stupidity of
those masses.

The barbarous inferiority of the Oriental peoples was attested repeatedly by the missionaries, who were a principal source of information to
most Americans. On their return from Eastern missions, they would lecture
in the churches on what they had seen over the walls of their compounds,
and invariably it was a grim picture of hopeless misery, ignorance and
superstition. The plight of the Orientals was made even clearer by the
barrel which stood inside most church doors, in which parishioners were
asked to deposit castoff clothing for the multitudinous waifs of the East.

Even the scholarly S. Wells Williams, who went to China as a missionary, stayed on as a historian and diplomat and made himself the standard authority, added vigorous brush strokes to that image. In the three
volumes of his *The Middle Kingdom,* which he published in 1848, with a
revised edition in 1883, he claimed that he wanted to "show the better
traits" of the Chinese, to wipe out the "impression of ridicule" and to show
that the time was passing when "the people of the Flowery Land can fairly
be classified among the uncivilized nations." Even so, he could not conceal
his disgust at what he considered the depravity, often the viciousness of the
Chinese people. He wrote:

"With a general regard for outward decency, they are vile and
polluted in a shocking degree; their conversation is full of filthy expressions
and their lives of impure acts . . . There is nothing which tires one so
much when living among them as their disregard of the truth, and renders
him so indifferent as to what calamities may befall so mendacious a
race . . .

"Their better traits diminish in the distance and patience is exhausted
in its daily proximity and friction with this ancestor of all sins . . . Thiev-
ing is exceedingly common . . . The politeness which they exhibit seldom
has its motive in goodwill and consequently, when the varnish is off, the
rudeness, the brutality, and coarseness of the material is seen . . . Female
infanticide in some parts openly confessed and divested of all disgrace and
penalties . . . the universal practice of lying and dishonest dealings; the
unblushing lewdness of old and young; harsh cruelty toward prisoners by
officers and tyranny over slaves by masters — all form a full unchecked
torrent of human depravity, and prove the existence of a kind and degree

of moral degradation of which an excessive statement can scarcely be made or an adequate conception hardly be formed."

Despite the Christian charity he intended to display toward the people among whom he lived for most of his adult life, Williams could only conclude that "if there is something to commend" about the Chinese "there is more to blame." He conceded that they "have more virtues than most pagan nations." Obviously he was vexed by the intertwining of vice and virtue in the Chinese character as he found it. "Ostentatious kindness and inbred suspicion, ceremonious civility and real rudeness, partial invention and servile imitation, industry and waste, sycophancy and self-dependence, are, with other dark and bright qualities, strangely blended."[3]

Somewhat more humorous and perceptive were the observations of Arthur Smith in his *Chinese Characteristics,* which was also a standard work, particularly for the indoctrination of those recruited to serve in the Chinese missions. The Chinese, he wrote, should be viewed as resembling the bamboo. "It is graceful, it is everywhere useful, it is supple, and it is hollow. When the east wind blows, it bends to the west. When the west wind blows, it bends to the east. When no wind blows, it does not bend at all." For Williams's indignation at the "depravity" of the Chinese, Smith substituted a patient and rueful humor. "Many Chinese unconsciously adopt toward foreigners an air of amused interest combined with deprecia-tion, like that with which Mr. Littiner regarded David Copperfield, as if mentally saying perpetually, 'So young, sir, so young!' " Smith even be-lieved that Americans might adopt some of the better Chinese character-istics, such as their filial piety, their cheerfulness and "unlimited capacity for patient endurance."

Even Smith could not conceal his exasperation with their wayward-ness, however, as he fired off a series of epigrammatic observations. "All Chinese are gifted with an instinct for taking advantage of misunderstand-ings . . . The Chinese marry at a very early age and the desire for posterity is the one ruling passion . . . No extended experience of the Chinese is required to enable a foreigner to arrive at the conclusion that it is impossible, from merely hearing what a Chinese says, to tell what he means . . ." What the Chinese needed, he concluded, was "new life in every individual soul." True to his training, Smith was certain this could be supplied "permanently, completely, only by Christian civilization."[4]

In a century the Mysterious East had become the Horrible East. As Harold Isaacs (*Scratches on Our Minds*) has defined Western attitudes, the eighteenth century was the Age of Respect; it was followed by the Age of Contempt (1840–1905) and the Age of Benevolence (1905–1937). During the last quarter of the nineteenth century, Americans saw the Asian peoples and the Polynesians, Micronesians and Melanesians as faceless hordes to be managed, reformed, uplifted. There was no boggling at the fact that this might have to be accomplished at gunpoint. This was bluntly stated at the turn of the century in the slogan of the Americans bent on quelling the Philippine Insurrection: "Civilize 'em with a Krag [rifle]."

Japan was regarded with a little more respect, but a lot more condescension, as our very own client and protégé in the Far East, the one whose door we opened, the one Asian nation which flatteringly promised to westernize itself in the American style. In the 1880's, however, various American writers were warning against the idea that the Japanese resembled us in any qualitative sense. In *Soul of the Far East,* Percival Lowell noted that the striking difference between Americans and the Japanese was in their attitudes toward the individual. The individual counted for less the farther east you went, and "Ideas of ours which we deem innate find in them no home, while methods which strike us as preposterously unnatural appear to be their birthright . . . The sense of self grows more intense as we follow in the wake of the setting sun, and fades steadily as we advance into the dawn. America, Europe, the Levant, India, Japan, each is less personal than the one before."[5]

The facelessness, the iniquity, the general worthlessness of the Asian masses, even in their own eyes, appeared to Americans as encouragement to extend their sway westward. If a physical and moral vacuum existed, wasn't it the American destiny to fill it? Imperialism seemed less and less a pejorative term, if it was accompanied by American benevolence and good-will. Every schoolchild knew how American missionaries were making the heathen of the Pacific islands put on a decent amount of clothing, lay down the spear and take up the Bible, stop regarding human flesh as a staple commodity. Admittedly missionaries couldn't carry on by themselves; there were times when the natives foolishly resisted, and force was required to make them see the error of their ways.

To serve as the instrument of this mission, the United States Navy would obviously have to be enlarged and modernized. In the 1880's it became clear that the navy must be converted into a steam-driven, steel-hulled, heavy-gunned arm of American policy. The navy had been sadly neglected, compared to the naval forces of our chief rivals in the Pacific, Germany and Great Britain. In 1870 the Navy List included less than two hundred vessels with a total of less than two hundred thousand tons and mounting only thirteen hundred guns. Most of these were obsolete, and only fifty-two were actually in commission. There was no Pacific Fleet, only a pair of cruising task forces, the Far East (or China) Squadron and the Pacific Squadron. A handful of outmoded ships, mostly sailing vessels converted hastily to steam, to show the flag from San Francisco to Singapore. Those who wanted to modernize the navy had to contend with the reactionary old-line admirals who bitterly resisted efforts to replace sails with steam; also, in the Seventies, with the reluctance of the Grant and Hayes administrations to spend money on modern warships when the economy was barely recovering.[6]

Beginning with the Garfield Administration in 1881, American naval power began growing rapidly. The Navy League would not be organized until 1903, but the steel industry and Wall Street took an understandably benevolent attitude toward proposals that a new navy be built from the keel up. In 1883 the construction of four steel cruisers — classified as "protected" but "unarmored" — was authorized by Congress. The four ships — the *Chicago,* the *Boston,* the *Atlanta* and the *Dolphin* — were organized into the White Squadron as a symbol of the New Navy.

In the next several years, with William C. Whitney, the New York financier, as Secretary of the Navy in the Cleveland Administration, naval construction really boomed with a dozen fleet-size and fifteen smaller vessels going down the ways. Two battleships, the ill-omened *Maine* and the *Texas,* and an armored cruiser were among the capital ships ordered. By later standards, even the heaviest, the battleship *Texas,* was something less than a dreadnought, displacing less than seven thousand tons, carrying only two heavy (twelve-inch) guns and attaining a top speed of less than eighteen knots. Even more inhibiting, perhaps, was the fact that the navy would have to wait several more years for the formulation of the grand strategy under which far-ranging fleets would operate, the commandments of modern sea power as handed down by Captain Mahan. Most of its senior officers were well prepared to refight the Battle of Mobile Bay, but not to meet the Imperial German Navy in Samoan waters.

1. *"A New Conspiracy Every Day"*

One of the happiest residents of the Samoan archipelago was an Irishman, who apparently found that the incessant intrigue in the islands closely resembled that of his native village.

"I never saw so good a place," he told Robert Louis Stevenson, who had settled there with his American wife and family. "You can be in a new conspiracy every day!"[7]

That was true enough, according to Stevenson's own findings. "Should Apia ever choose a coat of arms," he wrote, "I have a motto ready: 'Enter Rumour painted full of tongues.' The majority of the natives do extremely little; the majority of the whites are merchants with some four mails in the month, shopkeepers with some ten or twenty customers a day, and gossip is the common resource of all. The town hums to the day's news, and the bars are crowded with amateur politicians. . . . Every one tells everything he knows; that is our country sickness. Nearly every one has been betrayed at times, and told a trifle more; the way our sickness takes the predisposed. And the news flies, and the tongues wag, and fists are shaken."[8]

That deleterious atmosphere, for which Stevenson and others held the

American and European residents chiefly responsible, was largely the result of the three-power collision of interests in Samoa. The islands were strategically located for any intruding nation which intended to gain supremacy over the Pacific world.

Those ambitions displayed themselves as the English, the Germans and the Americans made their separate appearances in the islands. American interest in the area developed slowly, with our chief aim the maintenance of a coaling station in the superb anchorage of Pago Pago on the island of Tutuila. Imperial Germany was then feeling a growing appetite for colonies under the chancellorship of Count Bismarck. As a latecomer to the colonial-power game, she found the avenues to expansion in Africa and Asia blocked by the claims staked out by France and Britain. The islands of Melanesia and Micronesia seemed fair game; Bismarck envisioned Germany spreading out from her extensive holdings on the Samoan island of Upola, on which the trading port of Apia was located, to all of the South Seas. But Germany couldn't feel safely and firmly established until she had elbowed her British and American rivals aside. Britain had moved into the Samoan arena mainly to checkmate Germany, because German hegemony in the Southwest Pacific would pose a threat to her Australian dominion and possibly to her dominant position in China.

Both as a liberal humanitarian and the owner of a cocoa plantation in the hills above Apia, Robert Louis Stevenson inveighed against the foreign interventions which kept his wind-cooled paradise stirred up and in an almost constant state of siege. He wrote a Honolulu newspaper that the Western powers should withdraw completely from Samoa and "the natives be let alone, and allowed to govern the islands as they choose . . . there would be internal dissensions covering a certain period . . . it might affect commerce, and certainly the present standing of all foreigners . . . but it is the patient and not the doctor who is in danger. If left alone, the Samoans would continue fighting, just as they do under the tripartite treaty . . . but at least they would fight it out by themselves, without their wars being turned to the advantage of meddling foreigners."[9]

American interest in Samoa was first aroused, in a minor way, when Commodore Charles Wilkes visited Samoa in 1839 on an exploring mission. His description of the islands, including a five-volume report on his expedition to the South Seas, was an idyllic passage in naval literature. English missionaries had diverted the natives from their warlike customs and taught them to play cricket. The islanders were prospering from trade in copra and coconut oil. On the shores of the serene bay of Pago Pago, Wilkes found an American trader whom he immediately appointed an agent of his government.[10]

Samoa slumbered on for three more decades, during which, however, German influence was steadily increasing. The Samoan capital of Apia, on Upolo, was the South Seas headquarters for the large and aggressive

Hamburg trading firm of Goddefroy, and the German consulate there was exerting a considerable influence over native politics. British influence meanwhile was diminishing.

In 1871 American shipping interests began exploring the possibility of establishing a regular mail, cargo and passenger service to Australia. Samoa seemed the logical way station on that route, so they sent a survey ship to the islands to determine whether a naval and coaling facility could be built there. The survey report was enthusiastic and described Pago Pago as "the most perfectly land-locked harbor that exists in the Pacific Ocean." Once again the flag would follow trade. A copy of the survey was sent to the Secretary of the Navy, who forwarded it to Rear Admiral John A. Winslow, commanding the Pacific Squadron. Admiral Winslow immediately dispatched Commander Richard W. Meade to Samoa under orders to arrange a treaty with the native chiefs of Tutuila. Commander Meade's orders noted that it might be necessary to "frustrate foreign [German] influence which is at present very active in this matter, seeking to secure the harbor [Pago Pago]." The German consul, in fact, had already suggested to Berlin that Germany annex the whole archipelago and establish a naval base. Chancellor Bismarck, however, was then preoccupied with dismantling the imperial pretensions of Napoleon III, besieged Metz was a lot closer to any Prussian heart than Apia, and the consul was instructed to avoid offending the United States.

Commander Meade set about his semidiplomatic mission with vigor and dispatch and by February 1872 had persuaded the leading chief of Tutuila to sign an agreement allowing the United States to take over the harbor of Pago Pago. A treaty embodying this agreement was presented somewhat hesitantly to the Senate by President Grant, who had adopted a cautious attitude toward overseas ventures since the Senate's recent rejection of his treaty for the annexation of Santo Domingo. In his message the President stressed that the agreement had been made without his knowledge, which every knowledgeable Senator was prepared to believe, but he concluded by recommending the Senate's approval. To the Senate, Samoa was more remote than the moon, and the treaty was not ratified.

American trading, shipping and naval interests, however, were determined that the flag would be planted at Pago Pago, with or without the consent of the United States Senate, with or without the formality of a treaty. They presented a petition from a group of Samoan chiefs who had been prevailed upon to appeal to the President to annex the islands. In response to the various pressures, Secretary of State Hamilton Fish appointed a special commissioner to investigate the Samoan situation. As hesitant about the venture as Grant himself, perhaps sensing the mare's nest of commercial and political intrigue into which any intervening party would become entangled, Fish instructed Special Commissioner A. B. Steinberger that "it is not unlikely that perhaps in the not distant future the interests of the United States may require not only a naval station in the Samoan group, but a harbor where their steam and other vessels may freely and securely frequent." After planting that hedge of qualifications, Fish ordered Steinberger to bring back a report which would "enable the government here to determine as to the measures which may be advisable toward obtaining that object."[11]

The Secretary of State would have been even more cautious in his directive if he had sensed the trickiness of his envoy's character and understood how the atmosphere of Samoa at that time — with German, American and English traders all plotting against each other and conniving with the Samoan chiefs, who were similarly maneuvering to cut each other's throats — was likely to lead astray the most straitlaced and dutybound visitor. A new conspiracy every day, as the delighted Irishman said.

Steinberger returned to Washington from his first visit to Samoa with a glowing report on how American influence would be welcomed in the islands. Just how ignorant the Samoans were of their proposed benefactor and protector was indicated by a letter Steinberger had persuaded a Samoan chief to write the Secretary of State. The chief wrote that he wanted the United States to annex Samoa because he was greatly touched by the "paternal care" our government had extended to its Indian minority.

Steinberger then requested that he be sent back to Samoa as a "labor of love," to extend American influence there. Fish should have been warned by the phrase, but agreed to Steinberger's proposal with an intuitive warning against taking any actions which would be "adverse to the usual traditions of the government."

That was a flexible cautionary indeed, which Steinberger, nursing his ambitions to build a small personal empire, proceeded to bend to his own purposes. The gifts he took for presentation to the Samoan chiefs were undoubtedly indicative of his private interpretation of the "labor of love" he was undertaking under State Department auspices. They included boxes of guns and ammunition, a hundred sailors' uniforms and three American flags.[12]

Within a month of Steinberger's return to Apia, the American consul there was reporting to the State Department that the activities of its special commissioner were causing alarm and arousing indignation in the foreign colony, especially its American and British sectors. Steinberger was running around telling the Samoan chiefs that the United States was about to establish a protectorate over the islands. He denied making any unauthorized promises, but in July of 1875, evidently irked at the unwillingness of Washington to follow his suggestions and angered by the resentment of his local compatriots, he announced that he was taking up new duties in Samoa. A. B. Steinberger henceforth was prime minister of the kingdom of Samoa. The American consul subsequently reported to Washington that Prime Minister Steinberger had entered into an agreement with Goddefroy of Hamburg to provide trading concessions for the Germans which would work to the disadvantage of the American firms there. Steinberger had turned in his resignation as United States special commissioner but neglected to disavow his American citizenship. That gave the American consul, at the urgent petitioning of other Americans there, the leverage to arrange for Steinberger's immediate deportation — ministerial portfolio and all.[13]

His departure, however, did not quiet the islands. Constant rumors circulated that either Germany or Britain was about to bring in a naval squadron and take possession. Twice the American consul raised the American flag — against instructions from Washington, which disavowed the actions — when he heard that the British were about to establish a protectorate. Both in Apia and Washington there was constant agitation for the United States to annex the group before Britain or Germany could make a similar move. The New Navy's advocates kept pointing out that Samoa was strategically located for an American base, on the shipping lane to Australia, 2300 miles south of Hawaii, 4100 miles southwest of San Francisco, 5600 miles west of Panama.

The campaign for American intervention was heightened by the dispatch of a two-man mission — one an American merchant, the other a Samoan official — to Washington. The Hayes Administration was only tepidly expansionist, but the burdens of extending American influence had now been taken up by Frederick W. Seward, son of William H., who was appointed Undersecretary of State. As Seward recalled in his autobiography, so informal was diplomacy in those days, the first he knew about the mission was when two men "from some Pacific Islands" appeared in front of his desk in the State Department. "One was an American merchant, who had been engaged in business at Apia Harbour. The other was a tall, fine-looking, swarthy-complexioned man, in ordinary American dress, who proved to be the Secretary of State and Minister of Foreign Affairs of the Samoan Islands."

Seward lost no time in introducing the Samoan to Secretary of State Evarts and President Hayes, who authorized Seward to negotiate with him. The Samoan representative explained, Seward wrote, that his people were "doubtful of their ability to maintain peaceful and stable existence" and "wished the United States to recognize and protect their independence . . . Having seen Pacific islands, one after another, eagerly seized by some European power, and having no wish to become subjects of any such power, they had decided to offer their islands to the United States. Of course they hardly anticipated that there would be any hesitation on our part of accepting such an offer." Seward had to explain that his country was in a withdrawn mood, though he believed "this dread of national expansion was a passing phase and an unreasonable and unnatural one."[14]

Hopeful that by careful maneuvering, by slowly building a base of support, he could ease a treaty with Samoa through the Senate this time, Seward drew up a cautiously phrased agreement by which the United States would be allowed to establish a naval base at Pago Pago and would also receive certain commercial and extraterritorial rights in return for mediating any differences Samoa might have with other powers. The "American merchant" who accompanied the Samoan foreign minister is not mentioned again in Seward's account but doubtless he was lurking at Willard's, as the representative of the American interests pulling for the treaty and the real motive force behind it, and "advising" his Samoan friend on the negotiations with Seward.

The Undersecretary of State performed with skill and diligence in obtaining ratification of his treaty, "sounding" the opinion of leading members of the Foreign Affairs Committees and the Republican leadership in both houses. He found that "practically all were agreed that the times were inauspicious for the consideration of any such project. The Senate would not consent to any treaty that involved expense or obligation, and the House, in which there was an anti-Administration majority, would vote it down as a matter of course."

Seward bitterly observed that "It seemed to be a mark of patriotism to oppose any addition to our own country," but persevered in proselytizing Congress. He wrote several drafts of the treaty to meet senatorial objections, finally got one through the Foreign Affairs Committee. It was ratified by the full Senate, signed by Secretary of State Evarts and Mr. Mamea, the Samoan representative. Seward, however, could feel no sense of triumph. "The press and public seemed to regard the matter with indifference, and the House refused any coal-yard for Pago Pago."

The whole idea of planting the United States flag in an area so remote from American concerns of the moment seemed faintly ridiculous; whoever heard of Pago Pago, and what was it? It became a vaudeville tagline, as Zamboanga did a few years later. The diplomatic corps in Washington, Seward said, was amazed at our indifference to what could be a giant stride toward acquiring primacy in the vast Pacific world. "For a nation of 'land-grabbers' as we were called in Europe, we seemed to be very slow and reluctant to take steps for our own aggrandizement." The growing number of Pacificist officers at the Navy Department were much more appreciative of Seward's singlehanded effort. Two years after the Samoan treaty was signed in the summer of 1878 Commodore Robert W. Shufeldt, a veteran of long duty in Far Eastern waters, was observing that the United States was now in a position to assert herself forcefully: "The acquisition of Alaska and the Aleutian Islands, the treaties with Japan, Sandwich Islands and Samoa are only corollaries to the proposition that the Pacific Ocean is to become at no distant day the commercial domain of the United States."[15]

A few months after the Samoan treaty was ratified Undersecretary Seward and Dr. von Schlozer, the German minister to the United States, held what Seward called a "cheerful" conversation at the State Department. As Seward described it:

" 'Aha,' said he. 'Also we have a harbour in Samoa. Not the best — no, you have the best. You have Pago Pago. But we have the next best.'

" 'What one have you, mein Herr?'

" 'Apia — Apia Harbour. It is a good harbour. It is where our people are, and the trade. We shall use our harbour now. You do not use yours — no. But you will, some day. Some day, you will."

"And in so saying the cheery Envoy proved himself a prophet."

The genial Dr. Schlozer's prophecy came true all too quickly. German, British and American warships soon rode high above native outriggers in the Samoan harbors. Britain and Germany moved swiftly to obtain the same rights as the United States had secured for herself, and Apia, the trading center of the islands, was to be ruled jointly by representatives of the three countries.

None was satisfied with one-third of the prize. German commercial interests, in particular, were restive; they claimed superiority on the grounds that their share of the trade was the largest. The British pointed out that they had landed on Samoa first. The Americans argued their own claims of priority on the basis that they had signed the first treaty with the Samoan chiefs.

Inevitably the contending powers began playing tribal politics, hoping to bolster their rival claims by enlisting "popular consent." If there was something ridiculous about portly white businessmen puffing up the trails to mountain villages to cajole native chiefs about the advantages of being ruled from Berlin or Washington, no one in the foreign colony seemed to realize it.

The American consul in Apia was Berthold Greenebaum, whose German ancestry did not prevent him from contending most aggressively with his German counterparts in the tribal intrigues. As a sideline, Greenebaum was the Samoan agent for a firm which manufactured overalls. His private dream was to see all the natives of Micronesia happily at work and clad in Greenebaum overalls, though the costume would surely have ruined the tourist business. Officially, however, he busied himself with attempting to block every move by the German consul. He would not be deterred by such experiences as occurred on his goodwill mission to Chief Malietoa, who was claiming the kingship over his rival Chief Tamasese. A native guide led Greenebaum to a large hut in the mountains, according to a contemporary account, and "paralyzed" him by announcing it was the royal palace. "Just as Greenebaum removed his hat and bowed his head to enter the low doorway, a big hog made a sudden rush from the interior, dashed between his legs and threw the disgusted consul into a heap of kitchen refuse by the side of the door."[16]

Despite this affront to his dignity, Consul Greenebaum backed the

claims of Chief Malietoa and arranged a deal by which Malietoa became
king-in-chief and Tamasese vice-king, with the agreement signed on board
the United States warship *Lackawanna*. The Germans then attempted to
subvert the agreement by forcing King Malietoa to sign a new document
which provided for a German adviser to his government and a council of
state on which Germans and Samoans, but not Americans, were to be
equally represented. Greenebaum strenuously objected, the Germans ran
up their own flag in Apia, and the languid air was charged with threats of
war.

The United States formally protested the flag-raising to Berlin, but
without vehemence. Grover Cleveland has assumed the presidency and was
opposed to annexation of any overseas territory. At the same time he made
it clear that he was equally opposed to any German annexations. Chancellor Bismarck replied that he too was against annexation, and what was
all the bad feeling about? Surely three great civilized powers could settle so
inconsequential a matter among themselves like gentlemen. The result of
Bismarck's publicly conciliatory attitude was an agreement by Washington,
Berlin and London to hold a conference in Washington at which a compromise would be hammered out. Meanwhile, however, Bismarck was
secretly encouraging his colonial officials and sending a squadron of four
warships to Apia; German diplomacy wore one mask in Washington, another in Berlin and still another in Apia. But it was the one in Apia that
counted.

2. *Royal Hawaii Intervenes*

In their attempts to emulate the major powers in pursuit of imperial glory,
the lesser ones occasionally provided a distorting mirror in which the
former might examine themselves. As in an amusement park funhouse, the
great expanding nations could see the pomp, pretense and vainglory of
their actions mirrored by Japan's clumsy lunges at Formosa and Korea,
and even more comically by the imperialistic upsurge of the then-inde-
pendent kingdom of Hawaii.

In 1887 Hawaii, under the rule of King Kalakaua, suddenly decided
to snatch Samoa out from under Germany, Great Britain and the United
States. It was something like Lichtenstein marching its army to Waterloo
and proclaiming the occupation of Belgium.

By then Hawaii was being thoroughly Americanized. The missionaries and their descendants had gone into business for themselves, once the
natives had been bullied into wearing clothes, and Honolulu had now
begun to take on the look of downtown Omaha. They allowed the
Hawaiians to keep their monarchy and usually managed to corrupt who-

ever was sitting on the throne. Thus the present king, Kalakaua, allowed the Americans to take over the vast sugar and pineapple plantations, receiving in return a plentiful supply of champagne, and an American adventurer named Walter Murray Gibson as his chief adviser.

After various adventures in Central America and the Dutch East Indies, Gibson had come to Hawaii as a Mormon missionary. He had soon displeased the authorities in Salt Lake City by selling apostleships at a hundred fifty dollars a head, and was promptly excommunicated. The failed missionary then turned to politics and became a member of the privy council and of the legislature, which under his domination conveyed a large tract on Maui to the American sugar magnate Claus Spreckels for ten thousand dollars and passed laws providing for the importation of opium and the sale of liquor to the natives.

King Kalakaua was a plump and stately man, a former Honolulu newspaper editor who had been helped to the throne by Gibson. He was a spendthrift with a touch of megalomania, who styled himself "The First Gentleman of the Pacific" but was more widely known as the Merry Monarch. His thirst for champagne was phenomenal, even by monarchial standards.

Together, in the middle 1880's, King Kalakaua and Walter Gibson dreamed up a policy they sonorously titled "Primacy of the Pacific." The white race would take over the whole Pacific world if not soon checked, and it was up to Hawaii to establish itself as the headquarters of a new Polynesian empire. Gibson pushed through a resolution in which the legislative assembly declared that "the Hawaiian kingdom by its geographic position and political status is entitled to claim a Primacy in the family of Polynesian States." As King Kalakaua and Walter Gibson saw it, the kingdom of Hawaii should immediately annex the Tonga group, the Gilberts and the Samoan archipelago. Certainly Hawaii had as much right to those islands as the United States, Germany or Britain — which is to say none — but what made the proposed venture ridiculous was Hawaii's lack of financial and naval muscle, not to mention her population's lackadaisical attitude toward empire-building. When the scheme was finally advanced, it had to be undertaken largely by white men acting supposedly in Hawaiian interests.

With considerable effort Gibson managed to persuade the legislative assembly to appropriate a total of $185,000 for equipping and manning an expeditionary force. Political opponents scoffed that Gibson's plans for territorial expansion were "a ridiculous farce for a one-horse kingdom." Gibson indignantly responded, "What was Rome but a one-horse state at its beginning? The Great Powers never think of us as a one-horse state!"

Nor was he dissuaded by the fact that his expeditionary force, for which Samoa was unwisely chosen as the first objective, would be sailing at the predictable displeasure of the American, British and German navies.

The first two could be counted on to take an indulgent, big-brotherly attitude, but the German temper, on land or sea, was a variable element. The Teutonic sense of humor could not be depended on to appreciate the Royal Hawaiian Navy.

That naval arm consisted of an old converted steamer launched in 1871, which Gibson fitted out as a gunboat with the addition of four muzzle-loading six-pounders which had been used to fire salutes at Iolani Barracks. Twenty-four of its crew were boys paroled for the purpose from the Oahu Reformatory School. Its captain was one George E. Gresley Jackson, who claimed to have served as an officer in the British navy but in recent years was known as the most incurable drunkard on the beach at Honolulu. The old guano-trade steamer was renamed His Hawaiian Majesty's Ship *Kaimiloa* and was to serve as a punitive threat to any islanders unwilling to acknowledge King Kalakaua's "Primacy in the Pacific."

Before unleashing H.H.M.S. *Kaimiloa* — which his political enemies sneered at as a "toy ship" for which Hawaii had "as much need as a cow has for a diamond necklace" — Gibson proposed to send an embassy to present Hawaiian demands on the king, vice-king and chiefs of Samoa. Its makeup was hardly calculated to give the impression of Polynesian solidarity. The leader, who was given the title of "Envoy Extraordinary and Minister Plenipotentiary to the King of Tonga and High Commissioner to the Sovereign Chiefs and Peoples of Polynesia," was John Edward Bush, a Caucasian-Hawaiian, and his two aides were both American, Henry Poor, a part-time politician who was designated secretary of the mission, and Joe Strong, an American artist who married Robert Louis Stevenson's stepdaughter and was assigned to capture its triumphs on canvas. The group, accompanied by Bush's guitar-strumming servants, left Honolulu on December 25, 1886, aboard the S.S. *Zeelandia*. It was to be followed to Apia by H.H.M.S. *Kaimiloa,* which Gibson's opponents sarcastically declared would "strike terror into the hearts of the natives, and teach the pigmy national ships of France, Germany and Great Britain a necessary lesson," as soon as its reform-school crew could be whipped into shape.

The story of the Hawaiian attempt to take over Samoa has been told in all its hilarious detail in Stevenson's *A Footnote to History*, which he drew from his son-in-law's account of its woebegone efforts on Samoan soil and in Samoan waters and published in 1892 to the dismay of all concerned. Bush, Poor and Strong sailed into Apia as naively confident as Winken, Blinken and Nod.

Certainly any South Seas romancer would have been fascinated by the Hawaiian embassy's first days on Samoan soil. Bush and his colleagues busied themselves with building a permanent Hawaiian legation. They decided to support King Malietoa's claim to the Samoan throne, presented him with the Grand Cross of the Royal Order of the Star of Oceania and confided their plan to unite Samoa with Hawaii, the Tonga and Cook Islands, the Gilberts and probably Tahiti in a Polynesian confederation under King Kalakaua. Malietoa and his chiefs then joined in all-night revelry with the Hawaiian delegation, which had brought along enough Holland gin to stupefy most of the archipelago's population for at least a year.

Malietoa finally agreed to sign a Treaty of Confederation on February 17, 1887, an event commemorated by a carousal that shocked even the hard-drinking foreign colony of Apia. In the Joe Strong account, Malietoa left the party early, but for those who stayed "all decency appears to have been forgotten; high chiefs were seen to dance; and day found the house carpeted with sleeping grandees, who must be roused, doctored with coffee and sent home. As a first chapter in the history of the Polynesian Confederation, it was hardly cheering, and Malietoa remarked to one of the embassy, 'If you have come here to teach my people to drink, I wish you had stayed away.' "

To the outrage of the Germans, the Hawaiian diplomats then proceeded to lure the father-in-law of their royal candidate, King Tamasese, into Malietoa's camp; then Tamasese's wife was "charmed with the guitar music" of one of the Hawaiian legation's servants and left the king to live with the scullion. Romance perfumed the air of the legation like frangipani, and King Malietoa offered to make Bush's daughter Queen Molly of Samoa, but she declined. Just as well, because, as her father reported to Honolulu in one extraordinary dispatch, Molly was living with his secretary, Henry Poor, and was pregnant. This situation, Ambassador Bush explained, was responsible for a new crop of troubles which had broken through the soil at the Hawaiian legation. His fatherly concern had caused him to be a little careless about the title to the ground on which the legation was built, and a lawsuit had ensued. Within a month, Bush and his followers had succeeded in making themselves contemptible to the English and the Americans, and downright detestable to the Germans.

All this was only complicated by the arrival of H.H.M.S. *Kamiloa* in Samoan waters in mid-June. The first eleven days of the voyage Captain Jackson had locked himself in his cabin with a dozen cases of square-face gin. On entering Apia harbor the *Kamiloa* was signaled by the German corvette *Adler* to identify herself. Captain Jackson, unaware of such standard naval usage, despite his claims to service in the British navy, kept right on coming, until the German ship fired a shot across his bow. From then on the *Kamiloa*, her captain and crew were in constant trouble. A mutiny took place one night early in July when a crew member returned to the ship in a drunkenly bellicose mood and announced he was going to open the magazine and blow her up. His shipmates mutinied when the officers tried to throw him into the brig.

The German corvette steamed up again, and her officers were so shocked at the indiscipline aboard the *Kamiloa* that they sent a party aboard to restore order. If the Hawaiian navy didn't behave itself, the *Adler*'s captain warned, he would place the *Kamiloa*'s officers and crew in irons and sail her back to Hawaii with a German crew. The threat of being returned to the Oahu Reformatory School quieted the *Kamiloa*'s crew for a few weeks, and there were only such minor scandals as Captain Jackson's drunken conduct ashore. Brooding over their situation, the reform-school contingent of his crew decided to jump ship en masse, fled into the hills above Apia, and were never heard of again. The remaining crew members bartered all the ship's muskets for pigs and liquor to sustain them in port.

Totally disenchanted by the naval support he had received, Ambassador Bush ordered the *Kamiloa* to return to Honolulu. He tried to put a good face on the summary action by throwing a party aboard the gunboat the night before she sailed, and King Malietoa was among the invited guests. The affair ended when Captain Jackson was overtaken by a violent spell of delirium tremens.[17]

On the way back to Honolulu, Captain Jackson anchored in the bay of Pago Pago long enough to sell the ship's silverware and lay in a stock of bananas and gin for the long voyage home. As a footnote to Stevenson's *Footnote to History,* it should be recorded that Jackson displayed himself later in various American ports, wearing a gorgeous uniform and identifying himself as the First Sea Lord of Hawaii, but belied his assumed position by complaining of the untrustworthy qualities of Hawaiian seamen on the grounds that "they are too fond of gin."

Ambassador Bush and his party sold all their possessions to pay for their passage back to Honolulu on the first available ship, and thus the "era of gin diplomacy," as foreign-colony wits in Apia called it, came to an abrupt and bedraggled conclusion. Both the Hawaiian embassy and the naval expedition cleared out of Samoa just in time. Eleven days after the "envoy extraordinary" and his party decamped, a squadron of four German warships arrived in Apia harbor with orders to blow the *Kamiloa* out of the water if she were still in Samoan waters and to arrest the Hawaiian embassy. The orders came from Chancellor Bismarck himself, and would undoubtedly have been carried out. Germany then warned Hawaii directly that she would invade the islands if any Hawaiian, in any guise, ever set foot on Samoa again.*

---

* Walter Gibson was kicked out of office a year later, not for the failure of his grandiose plans for "Primacy of the Pacific," but because of an opium scandal. He and his friends had taken a seventy-one-thousand-dollar bribe for an opium concession, but delivered it to a rival Chinese merchant who had paid eighty thousand dollars for the same privilege, and had unwisely refused to return the first bribe.

King Kalakaua, primate of the Pacific

3. *A Breaking of Sword Arms*

A new crisis arose in Samoa almost immediately after the Hawaiians decamped. While German commissioners amiably negotiated with the British and Americans in Washington over proposals for a tripartite rule of the islands, Germany was showing a more warlike disposition in Samoa itself. The four warships in Apia harbor, late in the summer of 1887, landed six guns and seven hundred sailors and marines to depose King Malietoa and replace him with Vice-King Tamasese. Malietoa was captured and deported, leaving behind him a memorial to the British and American consuls reminding them of their promises to protect the "lives and liberties of my chiefs and people."

The Americans, the British and most of the Samoan people refused to recognize Tamasese as the king. A revolt broke out, undoubtedly with the covert support of the British and Americans, with the aim of placing Chief Mataafa on the throne. Mataafa was a Catholic convert — a "Popee" as the natives called them — and was adjudged the ablest and least corruptible of the native leaders. In September 1888 his forces clashed with those of King Tamasese and routed them. The king's army did not halt its retreat, despite the pleas of German advisers, until they reached the cover of the German warships' guns in Apia harbor. The United States and Britain immediately recognized Mataafa as the king of Samoa.

But the Germans were not so easily disheartened, and at the moment they held the trumps of naval power on the scene. They sent a landing party of one hundred and forty ashore to disarm Mataafa's followers. And they paid dearly for underestimating the native powers of resistance. The German party, heavily armed and laden with equipment, was led on a chase through the bush, and finally into an ambush in which fifty-six were killed or wounded. Washington received an alarming dispatch cabled via Sydney from the American consulate in Samoa. GERMANS SWEAR VENGEANCE. SHELLING AND BURNING INDISCRIMINATELY, REGARDLESS OF AMERICAN PROPERTY. PROTESTS UNHEEDED. NATIVES EXASPERATED. FOREIGNERS' LIVES AND PROPERTY IN GREATEST DANGER. GERMANS RESPECT NO NEUTRAL TERRITORY.[18]

Things weren't quite that bad, though the Germans again hoisted their flag over Apia and proclaimed martial law throughout the islands. The shelling was mostly for purposes of demonstration and intimidation. American, British and German consuls fired off dispatches to their capitals describing the most horrible battles and atrocities in hope of persuading their governments to intervene more forcefully.

President Cleveland, however, had no intention of extending American power where he felt it didn't belong. As a firm anti-Pacificist, he would take only such actions as were required to maintain American integrity. With the greatest reluctance he allowed the Navy Department to dispatch three of its older warships to Samoan waters, meanwhile instructing Secretary of State Thomas F. Bayard to keep trying to work out a diplomatic solution. His hardest problem was how to keep Congress and the country damped down. Reports had been published that the Germans had not only torn down but torn up American flags while hoisting their own in Samoa, and public indignation was tempered only by the fact that few people had the slightest idea of where Samoa was or what the Germans and Americans were quarreling about in such a remote place. The wife of James G. Blaine, the man who was supposed to be knowledgeable enough about foreign affairs to take over the State Department in the next administration, wrote her son, "Your father is now looking up Samoa on the map."

The tripartite conference in Washington turned out to be long-winded, boring and indecisive. A member of the British delegation, Cecil Spring-Rice, graphically described the sessions: "The Secretary [Bayard] clears his throat and makes a speech in the senatorial style — very eloquent and rather long . . . Then the German says (in English) he will read a written statement. Of course wholly irrelevant to Bayard's speech. Then West [British Minister Sackville-West] reads a written statement. Then Bayard asks questions but is too deaf to hear the answers, and resumes his speech where he left it off . . . Then we all get hungry and yawn. Then the sitting is adjourned and we telegraph home. This has been going on for some days."[19]

The conferees exasperated, confounded and contradicted each other through the damp heat of a Washington summer, and then adjourned without having accomplished anything. Nor was the country's mood any less belligerent for the peace talks. Rudyard Kipling a short time later found Americans in a state of xenophobia, and in describing a banquet he attended in San Francisco he wrote, "It was my first introduction to the American Eagle screaming for all it was worth. I sat bewildered on a coruscating Niagara of blatherskite. It was stupendous."

The passionate outcries from Congress and the public made it impossible for President Cleveland to avoid taking vigorous action of some kind. Pacificist sentiment in the Senate particularly was aroused, with several Senators stridently insisting that the anchorages at Honolulu and Pago Pago were essential to safeguarding American interests in the Pacific.

In this mood Congress hastily made appropriations of five hundred thousand dollars to protect (in what way was not stated) American lives and property in Samoa and another one hundred thousand dollars to improve the harbor of Pago Pago. These actions were taken so hastily that the liberal, mostly Democratic opposition had little time to rally their forces. The *Nation* protested against "running this wild goose chase respecting a group of islands in the South Pacific Ocean more distant from

our shores than Berlin itself." The wisest course was to abandon everything
we owned in Samoa, and let Germany develop the islands as she pleased.
"The more the matter is looked into, the more plainly does it seem, on our
part, an outbreak of sheer jingoism and meddlesomeness in other people's
affairs." The editorial could have been used as a stereotype for anti-imperialist sentiment about the Philippines a decade later, and subsequently
about Korea and South Viet Nam.[20]

Just as Cleveland was ending his first term, a conciliatory message
was received from Berlin. Bismarck claimed that Germany had no interest
in seizing Samoa for herself, and proposed that the abortive conference of
commissioners be reconvened to settle the dispute.

As usual, however, smooth talk and diplomatic smiles in the contending capitals were contrasted by bellicose attitudes and actions on the
scene. Germans, Americans and Britons glowered at each other through
gunsights. The situation was so close to the flashpoint that any untoward
incident might have started an unauthorized war — a quarrel between
drunken sailors on shore leave, for instance. So far the Germans had fired
only on natives, and the British and Americans had refrained from any
kind of direct intervention. In naval strength the quarreling powers were
now almost evenly matched. Germany had three warships in the harbor of
Apia, the *Adler,* the *Eber* and the *Olga.* The American flag was flown by
the *Trenton,* the *Nipsic* and the *Vandalia,* all obsolete relics of the Old
Navy. In case of emergency the American warships would probably have
been supported by the sole British vessel in the harbor, the *Calliope.* All
were on the alert, with gun crews standing by.

Those guns, however, were never destined to be fired. On the clouded
horizon beyond Apia harbor the afternoon of March 15, 1889, a more
furious and destructive enemy than the combined broadsides of the seven
warships was advancing at a deliberate pace — a tropical storm of hurricane intensity. That night the barometer plunged to 29.11.

By first light the storm was driving mountainous seas into the bottle-
like harbor. "Day came about six," as Stevenson described it, "and
presented to those on shore a seizing and terrifying spectacle. In the pressure of the squalls, the bay was obscured as if by midnight, but between
them a great part of it was clearly if darkly visible amid driving mist and
rain. The wind blew into the harbour mouth. Naval authorities describe it
as of hurricane force. It had, however, few or none of the effects on shore
suggested by that ominous word, and was successfully withstood by trees
and buildings. The agitation of the sea, on the other hand, surpassed experience and description. Seas that might have awakened surprise and
terror in the midst of the Atlantic, ranged bodily and (it seemed to observers) almost without diminution into the belly of that flask-shaped
harbour; and the war-ships were alternately buried from view in the trough,
or seen standing on end against the breast of billows."

All seven warships were anchored fairly close together and threatened to collide. Their crews labored to keep the pressure up in the boilers and the pumps working. On deck the officers were unable to maintain any headway; the ships were entirely at the mercy of the roaring seas.

Actually the catastrophe about to descend on those ships might have been avoided if their commanders had not been more interested in keeping a jealous eye on each other and displaying bravado in refusing to haul up their anchors. They had delayed too long in seeking sea room, because each commander feared the other might steal a march on him. They risked making junk of millions of dollars worth of naval hardware, not to mention hundreds of lives, rather than sensibly sailing out of Apia when the storm's fury first developed.

The German gunboat *Eber* tore loose from her anchor chains and was hurled stern-first on a reef in the harbor. She went down by the stern in a matter of minutes, carrying all but four of her crew of eighty to the bottom with her.

Next went the *Nipsic,* American, which was driven happily enough onto a sandy beach and grounded. Most of her crew jumped to safety on the beach.

The German corvette *Adler* made for the same beach, but she was dashed against the very reef that knifed her sister ship, the *Eber,* and her keel was broken by the impact. While the storm raged on through March 16, her twenty survivors clung to the wreckage all that day and the following night while Samoans, charitably overlooking the fact that Germany had declared war on them, tried to reach them in small craft that bobbed like corks in the running seas.

The four ships still afloat were in greater danger from destroying each other with their prows, now, than with their gun batteries. The *Calliope* was driven against the *Vandalia* and almost sank her. The captain of the *Vandalia* then decided to attempt beaching her alongside the *Nipsic,* but his ship suddenly began sinking from the hundreds of tons of water taken through her leaking seams. He and forty-two members of his crew were swept off the deck by the pile-driving seas as she sank; the others found refuge on her masts and turrets.

The German ship *Olga* smashed into the American ship *Trenton* as she attempted to make her way out of the harbor and went careening against the shore. The *Olga* was beached without loss of life.

The *Trenton,* badly gored by the collision with the *Olga,* began sinking. Aboard the cruiser were 450 officers and men. Instead of going to the bottom, however, she was driven against the partially submerged *Vandalia,* and all but one of the men aboard reached shore safely.

The only ship still making seaway was the British *Calliope,* a tribute, undoubtedly, to superior British seamanship and also to the fact that her officers were less involved in the deadly eyeball-to-eyeball confrontation of the Germans and Americans. Their first concern had been the safety of the ship. Keeping up a good head of steam, *Calliope* had been slowly and cautiously maneuvering to gain the harbor entrance. She narrowly missed being snagged by the reef on her port side and the disabled, much heavier American cruiser *Trenton* on the other. Somehow she negotiated the narrow passage and steamed for the mouth of the harbor while the men aboard the *Trenton* cheered. The *Calliope* reached the open sea and rode out the rest of the storm.[21]

On the morning of March 17, the sun rose over Apia harbor and the wreckage of six ships, along with the broken hulks of many lesser craft. Hundreds of lives had been lost to the stubborn vanity, the obsessive rivalry on the quarterdecks of the German and American warships. But their mutual fear of seeming to back away from each other the slightest fraction was dictated not only by professional pride but the strident advice from their respective consuls ashore, whose prestige rested on those gray ships, and behind the consuls the furious competition between German and American commercial interests. The flag in this case had followed trade — to the reefs, beaches and sandy bottom of Apia harbor.

The surviving crews of the German and American warships had been hurled together on the same beach and were ready to settle with their fists the issues which the hurricane had prevented them from fighting out aboard the lost ships. Their commanders, however, ordered them into separate quarters of the town. In the American sector the United States authorities ordered all bars closed on pain of having their stocks confiscated if they refused, and also set up a shore patrol instructed to shoot any sailor attempting to leave that part of town. Thus the German and American sailors were prevented from battling in the streets. Eventually the castaways were all embarked on rescue ships of their respective navies and returned home.

The most immediate result of the ship-wrecking hurricane was that it made both Germany and the United States — and even their embattled citizens in Samoa — realize how futile their struggle was, how close they had come to war, how much they had already lost in ships and men, mostly out of an excess of national rivalry. Another and more portentous result was that it impressed on the United States the urgency of building a large modern navy to make the American presence in the western Pacific more credible and authoritative.

4. *An Entangling Alliance*

It took an Act of God, in the form of a hurricane, to bring the quarreling powers to their senses, but the shock of the naval disaster in Apia harbor persuaded them that there must be some better way to adjudicate their differences than by threatening each other with twelve-pounders. Surely three great Christian nations could decide at the conference table how they would jointly rule the Samoan islands, if possible with the consent of the native population, without being constantly harassed by complaints from their colonizers and merchants that they were being oppressed. A treaty defining the rights of each power would be drawn up in Berlin, starting with the suggestion of tripartite rule which was still under discussion when the Washington Conference was suspended two years before. And while their governments conferred in Berlin, the foreign colony on Samoa, for once, refrained from stirring up trouble among themselves but worked together, along with the natives, to repair the damage from the March hurricane.

James G. Blaine, Secretary of State in the current Harrison Administration, believed that three-power rule of the islands was the only possible solution, short of an American withdrawal. He was determined that Germany should not take over Samoa, and any agreement must be based on a return to the Samoans of internal self-government. This, of course, meant the restoration of the forcibly exiled King Malietoa. It also signified a break in American tradition, as Secretary Blaine realized. An agreement with Germany and Britain was not "in harmony with the established policy of this Government," as he put it. The proposed arrangement for condominium over Samoa raised the old specter of American foreign relations — an "entangling alliance." Even more importantly, though Blaine did not mention that factor, it would mark our entrance into the field of colonial administration. The country, of course, was not consulted on whether it wished its citizens to join the legion of sun-helmeted Caucasians who were carrying the torch of Western civilization, welcome or not, to so much of Africa, Asia and Oceania.

The American sentiment for cooperation was matched by the presently conciliatory attitude of Chancellor Bismarck, who announced that Germany would give up her insistence that the Samoan government have a German adviser only, that King Tamasese remain on the throne, that she must be repaid for the naval losses she had suffered in Apia harbor. Germany would also rein in her aggressive consular agents and agree to the return of King Malietoa. Bismarck may have delighted in the sobriquet of the Iron Chancellor but now, as on other occasions, he showed an un-Prussian ability to reverse himself completely.

The American commission to Berlin included three men of diverse views, John A. Kasson, sympathetic to the Germans; George H. Bates, who believed we should stand fast in Samoa because it was "the key to maritime dominion of the Pacific"; and William Walter Phelps, who was more or less neutral and simply wanted to see a treaty take shape.

Secretary of State Blaine supported Bates's views whenever there was a conflict between his three commissioners as they met with the British and German representatives in Berlin. Once Kasson cabled a warning to Blaine that the United States was "irritating" the other two powers by insisting, through Bates, on all its conditions for a Samoan settlement. Blaine sharply replied that British or German irritability was "not a determining factor with the Government of the United States."

A tripartite treaty was signed with surprisingly little difficulty, but once again it developed that an agreement reached in a foreign capital could not be so easily enforced in quarrelsome Samoa. After a few peaceful months, the situation grew even more complicated than before the Treaty of Berlin supposedly settled all disputes. Samoans fought Samoans, Germans quarreled with Germans, and even the Americans and the British could not find a basis for cooperation. Chief Mataafa, whose claims had not been considered in the settlement, staged an uprising and tried to set up a rival government. The treaty powers arrested a number of chiefs trying to smuggle arms to Mataafa, and placed dynamite charges under the jail in Apia when their followers threatened to rescue them by force. Mataafa eventually was deported, but years later, when an absolutely final settlement was reached and Germany took over western Samoa, he was brought back as the king of their islands, even though originally the Germans had opposed his attempts to depose King Tamasese. It really takes a sizable chart to follow all the twists and turnabouts of the intervening powers' policies in Samoa.

An even more ludicrous spectacle was the bungling and bickering of the tripartite administration. It really seemed as though the most gin-raddled native chiefs could have done better. German inflexibility, which worked well enough when imposed on their own people, coupled with the Germans' almost psychopathic obsession with the dignity of office, made for scenes which provided a constant entertainment for the residents.

The publication in 1892 of Stevenson's *A Footnote to History* was only one of a series of events which rocked colonial society in Apia and had their repercussions back home. Immediately afterwards, the German publishing firm of Tauschnitz was fined for bringing out a translation in Germany. Another uproar ensued in London as a result of Stevenson's reference in his book to a London Missionary Society official in Samoa who had political ambitions and according to Stevenson suggested a treacherous plot to the American consul by which Chief Mataafa (a Catholic) would be eliminated.

The book's anti-German tone naturally caused a certain amount of ill-feeling in Samoa, but it was nothing compared to the feud between the two highest German officials in the tripartite administration. They were Conrad Cederkrantz, the chief justice of the Samoan supreme court, and Baron Senfft von Pilsach, the president of the privy council. The two engaged in a bitter dispute over which ranked the other, which was granted precedence at banquets and other ceremonial functions, which had the ultimate power of decision over the actions of the government. Their vendetta not only interfered with the conduct of trade and commerce in the islands but almost brought the functioning of the government to a standstill, particularly after the natives, taking advantage of the confusion, refused to pay taxes or obey the writs of the supreme court. An embarrassed Berlin finally broke the impasse by recalling both Cederkrantz and Von Pilsach.

It was not quite so amusing when Mataafa and his followers staged a guerrilla uprising in the hills of Upolo, and there was bloody fighting between his partisans and the government troops. "I wish you could see my 'simple and sunny heaven' now," Stevenson wrote Mark Twain. "War has broken out, 'they' have long been making it, 'they' have worked hard, and here it is — with its concomitants of blackened faces, severed heads and men dying in hospital."[22] The insurgency was soon ended, however, with Mataafa and his leading chiefs exiled to the German-controlled Marshall Islands.

Repercussions from all these events reached the States and were regarded with unalloyed disgust by the new administration, Grover Cleveland's second term as President. Of all the Presidents, Cleveland was the most opposed to expansion in the Pacific or anywhere else. It was one of the ironies of the two Cleveland administrations that he unwillingly became involved in some of the more critical events in our advance on the Pacific world. Both Hawaii and Samoa clamored for his attention during his second term. The possession of both island groups was regarded as equally important by the Pacificists of the day, the New Navy's boosters, the newly intellectualized navy itself (now thinking in terms of fleets and grand strategy instead of remotely based squadrons and tactics), and others who believed America should look westward. Hawaii was to become of strategic importance, while Samoa has declined to the status of a tourists' paradise and a stopover for Presidents winging their way to Asian conferences, but in the 1890's Samoa figured importantly in our Pacific strategy. Pearl Harbor to the north, Pago Pago to the south would serve as the bastions of American power in the Central Pacific.

President Cleveland, citing the continuing turmoil in Samoa, pointing to the Treaty of Berlin as "signally illustrating the impolity of entangling alliances with foreign powers," asked Congress to consider ordering a complete withdrawal of American influence from Samoa. In their second terms, Presidents traditionally have a hard time exerting any control over Congress, and Cleveland was no exception. His request was ignored. Cleveland and Congress were embroiled from the beginning of his administration in the whole question of expansion in the Pacific.

Even as Cleveland was preparing to take office for a second term, Allan Nevins (*Grover Cleveland: A Study in Courage*) has written, "the United States was suddenly confronted with a choice not less momentous than that which the Roman Senate had to make when the Mamertines invited it to occupy part of Sicily, and thus abandon the policy of isolation which had hitherto confined Roman expansion to the peninsula." His predecessor, Benjamin Harrison, and Harrison's Secretary of State, James G. Blaine, both prime imperialists, had taken steps to establish a protectorate over Hawaii just before leaving office. Even more determined steps were taken by Cleveland to nullify that annexation, thus arousing a considerable controversy in Congress and the press. "It furnished the first great debate in American history," Nevins says, "over the merits of imperialism . . . it revealed the force of the economic and nationalist impulses that were pressing for expansion overseas."

Against a large segment of public opinion favoring Pacific naval bases to protect the proposed construction of a Panama canal, Cleveland posed a foreign policy "radically different from the Republican policy of Seward, Blaine and Hay [a later Republican Secretary of State] — a policy of unyielding opposition to imperialist tendencies, Latin-American or Pacific adventures, and overseas entanglements in general." Nor was he dissuaded from this policy by such Pacificist propaganda as the article titled "Hawaii and Our Future Sea-Power," written by the growingly influential navy captain Alfred T. Mahan and pointedly published just after Cleveland took office.[23]

Just before Cleveland returned to the White House, Queen Liliuokalani, poet, song-writer and autocrat, had been deposed from her Hawaiian throne by a coalition of American businessmen and native dissidents who styled themselves the Revolutionary Committee of Safety. Marines were landed in mid-January 1893 to protect the new provisional government, and a month later President Harrison hastily sent a treaty of annexation to the Senate. The untidy haste of the queen's dethronement and the measures to annex Hawaii were considered necessary because Liliuokalani had suddenly determined to eliminate American influence and return to native rule of her islands. Polynesian supremacy would have caused problems regarding the ethnic and economic organization of Hawaii. The Americans, top dog economically, numbered only two thousand. The Chinese and Japanese, who did most of the work, totaled thirty thousand. There were also nine thousand Portuguese, who intermarried with their usual vigor overseas. Against all these were balanced forty thousand Polynesians and half-castes.

On March 9, five days after taking office, Cleveland courageously decided to defy prevailing public opinion and recall the annexation treaty from the Senate, determined, as he said, to "vindicate national honor, conscience, and love of justice."

The kickback came as expected. "In ordering Old Glory pulled down at Honolulu," fulminated a leading expansionist journal, "President Cleveland turned back the hands on the dial of civilization. Native rule, ignorant, naked, heathen, is reestablished; and the dream of an American republic at the crossroads of the Pacific — a dream which Seward and Marcy and Blaine indulged, and the fulfillment of which the more enlightened of our 65,000,000 people awaited with glad anticipating — has been shattered by Grover Cleveland, a Buffalo liliputian! He has ordered his man Blount, a southern reactionary [he was sent by Cleveland as his special agent to investigate the rights and wrongs of Queen Liliuokalani's reign], to allow the gathering fabric of a stable government to fall to pieces. He has declared that the superstitious orgies of the heathen queen and her wild-eyed Kanakas may be resumed; that American property interests may no longer have the abiding protection that such men as Dole and Armstrong and Bishop [leaders of the Revolutionary Committee of Safety] declare is essential; that the Hawaiian islands should be tossed into the arena of national strife, for which the Japanese, the English, and heaven knows who else may scramble and quarrel."[24]

The theme of that editorial was expressed more succinctly and sardonically by a jingle which swept the country:

> *Queen Liliuokalani . . .*
> *Give us your little brown hannie!*

While Cleveland's special agent was running around the islands testing sentiment for and against annexation, the provisional president, Sanford Dole, consolidated himself in power. He was confident that American bayonets would not be used to restore Queen Liliuokalani, who damaged her own case when asked if she would grant amnesty to those who had dethroned her. No, replied the queen; she would chop off their heads and confiscate their property. Special Agent James H. Blount, in his report to the President in July 1893, declared that native sentiment was against annexation. People who had signed petitions to Washington for annexation did so under pressure from their employers, the American sugar planters. "I am satisfied that it [a vote on annexation] would be defeated by a vote of at least two to one. If the votes of persons claiming allegiance to foreign countries were excluded, it would be defeated by more than five to one."[25]

Cleveland was presented with a situation of the most wearying complexity. If he acted in defense of the popular will in Hawaii and deposed the provisional government, he would have to use American troops to fight expatriated Americans. Justice might demand that, but not political sanity. The American people sympathized with Queen Liliuokalani but not to the extent that they would favor her restoration behind a hedge of Marine bayonets. It was simply too late to throw out the provisional government. The best Cleveland could do was to block annexation. The rest he left to Congress, which decided to leave Dole and his fellow "revolutionaries" in control, in the knowledge that Britain, which had been scheming to take over Hawaii as Germany had been plotting to swallow up the Samoan Islands by herself, was now permanently thwarted. Cleveland's biographer, Allan Nevins, conceded that the President was "compelled, by a decided humiliation of the executive power, to ask Congress to furnish the leadership in solving a problem in foreign relations."

Much of the debate over Hawaii was to be repeated a few years later over the Philippines, mostly by the same people. Congressional refusal to turn Hawaii over to something like popular rule, with or without its strongminded queen, was viewed as the first irrevocable step in the formation of an American empire. Carl Schurz inveighed against it in a magazine article widely quoted as the anti-imperialists' statement of principles. Charles Francis Adams, Jr., wrote President Cleveland praising his "defiance of jingoism," adding, "It is not easy to see how the United States can protest against the policy of force pursued by England and France in their dealings with semi-civilized natives if we ourselves are quite unable to resist the temptation to have a hack at them on our own account."[26]

For the more acquisitive side, and particularly the modernized navy with its new capital ships, Admiral George E. Belknap spoke out against those who would keep the United States within her continental limits and thereby allow Great Britain to establish control of the Pacific. "Let the British lion once get its paw" on Hawaii, he warned, and "Honolulu would soon become one of the most important strongholds of Britain's power." Furthermore we must avoid sharing the islands with any other power. "We want none of that — no entangling alliances. We have had enough of such business at Samoa . . . Let the Monroe Doctrine stay not its hand until it holds Hawaii securely within its grasp."[27]

Admiral Belknap need not have worried, with Americans now secure in the political as well as economic control of Hawaii.

. . . And meanwhile Samoa simmered and stewed in its peppery juices of intrigue and international rivalry. It came to a boil in 1898 when King Malietoa died. His more or less legitimate successor, by Anglo-American reckoning, was a relative named Malietoa Tanu. *Nein,* said the Germans, who naturally opposed whatever the British and Americans proposed. They brought their old enemy, Chief Mataafa, back from the Marshall Islands, where they had exiled him years before. Once again it was the bad relations between the consuls that caused the rupture, and again it was mostly the Samoans who suffered.

Careless of past mistakes and disasters, the treaty powers assembled their warships in Apia harbor — three American, two British and one German. In other respects the situation had reversed itself. Now the Americans, with the expansionist President William McKinley in the White House, were the more aggressive, while the Germans, their colonial ambi-

Queen Liliuokalani, always alert to the White Peril

tions centered more on Africa than Asia, were slightly less so, and the British merely supported the Americans.

Admiral Albert Kautz sailed in aboard the cruiser *Philadelphia* and decided on a show of force. His big guns fired across Apia — some of the shells falling short and damaging German property — and into the hills back of the port where Chief Mataafa and his forces were threatening to take the town. Repeating the German mistake of a decade ago, Admiral Kautz sent a landing party inland, where it was promptly ambushed.

Fortunately the admiral's bellicosity was not reflected in the capitals concerned. The three powers at once agreed to send a commission to Samoa and settle the question of its sovereignty once and for all. Bartlett Tripp, the American commissioner, and his German and British colleagues arrived in Apia in the spring of 1899 to find United States Marines patrolling the streets, King Malietoa's followers guarding the outskirts, and three thousand of Chief Mataafa's warriors entrenched above the city. The commission acted with vigor and dispatch; abolished the monarchy, the succession to which had been used as the excuse for so much troublemaking, and persuaded both sides to disarm and disband.

Commissioner Tripp's dispatch to the State Department rang with the joy of accomplishment: "The chiefs and warriors have returned to their homes. The smoke is now ascending from the native cabins and plantations in every portion of the islands. The war song is discontinued, the war camp abandoned, and the happy joyous nature of this unrevengeful people manifests itself in the ready forgiveness of their enemies and their glad welcome of returning peace."[28]

On December 2, 1899, after further negotiating in the capitals of the treaty powers, the Samoan question was finally settled in the time-honored manner of the nineteenth-century imperialism. Germany got Upolo and Savaii, the United States won Tutuila (with the prized anchorage of Pago Pago) and several smaller islands, and Britain was satisfied by the German cession of the Tonga Islands, part of the Solomons, bits and pieces of West Africa, and extraterritorial rights formerly held in Zanzibar. This real estate deal — which could have been arranged years before, if overweening national pride had not been involved — left the three major powers fairly content. The wishes of the people being divided up along with their native lands were not consulted. They had to be satisfied with the declaration that it was all for their ultimate good.

8

"For Ways That Are Dark"

Dead, my reverend friends, dead, stoned to death in the streets of San Francisco, in the year of grace, 1869, by a mob of half-grown boys and Christian school children.

— BRET HARTE'S obituary of Wan Lee

A sensational crime sometimes sharply illumines social attitudes and bedrock public opinion as nothing else can — the Stanford White murder exposing Edwardian upper-class morality, for instance. A case several years later, much less celebrated among the connoisseurs of crime, was the murder of a well-bred young Caucasian social worker by her Chinese lover in 1909. It not only raised the specter of miscegenation but floodlighted for a moment the white American attitude toward the Asians in our midst, an attitude which in turn contributed toward shaping our relations with the Pacific world. It also demonstrated how in less than half a century the Chinese in America have assumed a different aspect to other Americans, from pigtailed subhumans good for building Western railroads to sinister representatives of the Yellow Peril.

We have always been adept at finding excuses for racism. Our treatment of the Chinese, and later the Japanese and other Orientals, has served as a simplistic diagram of the change in attitude toward the Negro, always with the aim of attempting to justify injustice and explain away prejudice. First the minority is regarded as inferior, by virtue of the inferiority imposed on it; then it is nominated as a danger to the American way of life.

The illuminating crime which highlighted our feelings about the Chinese was stated mostly succinctly on the blotter of the West 47th Street precinct house in New York City on June 18, 1909: "At 4:45 P.M. an unknown woman, white, about 33 years, five feet, 130 pounds, dark complexion and hair, partly dressed with white cotton underwear, was found dead in the room occupied by Leon Ling, in a trunk on the fourth floor, rear hall room at 728 Eighth Ave., with a sash cord tied about the neck. Body in badly decomposed condition."

The murder was committed in a room above what was then called a "chop suey parlor." What shocked New York and the rest of the country was the identity of the young woman whose body was found in that room: Miss Elsie Sigel, granddaughter of a newspaper editor, prominent politician and Civil War corps commander. Her grandfather, Major General Franz Sigel, was a leader of the German-American community so renowned that "I Fights mit Sigel" had been a Civil War slogan. Credited with being "a great factor uniting the German population of the North behind the Union," if not for his bumbling military campaigns, General Sigel edited a German-language paper and was collector of internal revenue in New York when he died in 1902.

That the body of his granddaughter should be found in a Chinese waiter's room in Hell's Kitchen was almost as shocking to respectable society as to her horrified family. Her father refused to identify the body in the morgue as his daughter's, and her aunt on viewing it declared, "My niece was a faithful member of the Audubon Society and would not wear a bird on her hat as this poor creature did." Three days later her father broke down and admitted the body was that of his daughter.

Because of the Sigel family's prominence, and the interracial aspects of the case reflected at a time when the exclusion of Oriental immigrants was a prime political issue, the details of Elsie's tragic love affair were described in newspapers from coast to coast. There was little doubt of the young woman's fascination with Chinese men after a friend of Leon Ling's was arrested and told the story of her death. Ling had strangled her because she wanted to leave him for the owner of a restaurant on Mott Street, in the lower Manhattan Chinatown. The police never did manage to find Ling.

The details of the murder were simple and sordid enough, but what fascinated millions of newspaper readers was just how a young woman of respectability could become involved with a Chinese waiter. The files of the New York *World,* a liberal Democratic paper, are especially instructive and illuminating; the *World* was as horrified as the China-baiting Hearst newspapers. Elsie Sigel, it seemed, viewed herself as a Salvation Nell and several years before had ventured into Chinatown to distribute Bibles and missionary tracts and plead with the Chinese to give up their amiable heathen gods. There she met Ling, who "made no secret among his companions of his infatuation for her." The *World* quoted a fellow social worker of Elsie's who warned against the "strong fascination of the Oriental character for young American girls." A preacher was interviewed on the subject and came up with the statement, "The number of mission workers ruined by their pupils would shock the country." The *World* thereupon published a front-page cartoon titled "The Real Yellow Peril" and showing several young white women staring with fascination into a Chinatown mission.

Poor Elsie was finally buried by her shamed family but the circumstances of her death haunted — and titillated — the American imagination, which for so long has imparted a sinister glamour to the Chinatowns and their mysterious tongs, their hatchetmen, singsong girls, opium dens and apothecary shops believed to be crammed with the most insidious aphrodisiacs. Respectable matrons whispered that once a young white woman fell into the lascivious clutches of a Chinaman . . .[1]

No element seemed so greatly at variance with the America of the little red schoolhouse and the white church on the hill. The various Chinatowns became notorious as centers of vice and depravity. An imagined aura of evil continued to hover over them until World War II. During the days of the silent film, nothing was quicker or more profitable to produce, with the aid of a few murkily lighted sets, than something that might be called *Sins of Chinatown.* Such a film would be a compendium of all the clichés shuddering Occidentals liked to believe about Orientals. "The mystery of Chinatown," sociologist Dorothy Jones has written about these cheapjack essays into folk culture, "was suggested by a whole series of visual clichés — the ominous shadow of an Oriental figure thrown against a wall, secret panels which slide back to reveal an inscrutable Oriental face, the huge shadow of a hand with tapering fingers and long pointed fingernails poised menacingly, the raised dagger appearing suddenly and unexpectedly from between closed curtains."[2]

In 1927 a Chinese student, quoted in a national magazine, laconically listed a large number of things many Americans believed about the Chinese in their midst. "The favorite delicacies of the Chinese are rats and snakes . . . The Chinese say yes for no and vice versa . . . They eat soup with chopsticks . . . Chinese men wear skirts and women pants . . . A Chinaman never gets drunk . . . A Chinese is properly a Chinaman and

the word 'Chinee' is singular for 'Chinese.' . . . The Chinese are a nation
of laundrymen yet have a highly developed civilization. . . . All Chinese
are cunning and crafty . . . All Chinese are honest and absolutely trustworthy . . . The Chinese never lose their tempers . . . The United
States is the friend and protector of China . . . All Chinese look alike
. . . The Chinese have no nerves and can sleep anywhere . . . They
have no souls because they are not Christians . . . The Chinese all hate
water and never bathe . . . They are a mysterious and inscrutable race
and do everything backwards . . ."[3]

With such a distorted image in the minds of their fellow Americans,
with their memory of being the first people to be specifically excluded from
migrating to America, it is little wonder that the Chinese have resisted
amalgamation more than any other national element. Excluded by law
and custom, they now exclude all others.

1. *Coming of the Yellow Slaves*

American hostility to the Chinese was based on something more than their
color, specifically the means of their arrival and their motive for coming
here. They came not to settle down and "grow up with the country," but to
make enough money to go back to China and live like mandarins. "The
forces that led to exclusion," Oscar Handlin has written, "reflected a novel
discrepancy between immigrants and Americans. The Chinese newcomers
differed significantly from other arrivals in the United States both in
motives and in experience. These people did not intend to form a permanent part of the American population, but were sojourners who expected
before long to return to the place of their birth . . . The mode of their
migration left them unfree and incapable of involving themselves in the life
about them."[4]

Many of the earlier Chinese immigrants came over as contract
laborers, a system closely resembling slavery. In return for their passage to
San Francisco, which cost about fifty dollars, they were forced to indenture
themselves to work for a stipulated number of years at a stipulated wage.*
Generally it took them five or six years to work off the cost of their
passage, so little did they receive in addition to shelter and food. Their
numbers increased in sequence to the need for their labor. In 1852, there
were about twenty-five thousand Chinese in America, which had doubled
by 1867. In 1882, there were 132,000, by which time they had become a
resented surplus on the labor market.

Their treatment in the United States bettered or worsened in exact

---

* Many Germans came to the United States under the similar redemptioner
system, but the conditions under which they worked out their years of indenture were
much gentler than for the Chinese.

relation to the need for their services. When California and the Western seaboard were being opened up, and the railroads were being built over the Rockies, they were welcomed with glad cries in the newspapers and from the politicians, if not the public. The *Daily Alta California* called them a "worthy integer" of the population on May 12, 1852, and declared, "The China boys will yet vote at the same polls, study at the same schools and bow at the same altar as our countrymen."

But the Chinese and other Orientals, like the Negroes, were marked men in a largely white America. The idea of white supremacy was firmly imbedded in all but a few Americans. Anglo-Saxons considered themselves top-drawer, with the peoples from northwestern Europe in the next compartment, Causasians of any kind in the next, and all other races a part of subhumanity. The only escape of the Chinese, as Harold Isaacs has written, was "until recently to try to disappear by withdrawing as far as he could into his tiny little communities and into himself."[5]

Anson Burlingame, who promoted the treaty of 1868 under which thousands of Chinese were permitted to "sojourn" in America, mostly as members of the railroad construction gangs, apparently sensed the hostility with which they would be met. In advance of their coming he pleaded for decent treatment, when he said of China, "All she asks is that you be as kind to her nationals as she is to your nationals."

The plea was not heeded. Until the depression of the 1870's, the Chinese were tolerated by most and even respected by a few, who took favorable notice of their thrift, industriousness and obedience to the law. They worked at whatever the white man considered too hard or degrading. Nine out of ten of the approximately ten thousand men working on the Pacific railroads in 1869 were Chinese. They were also hired on as cooks in the mining camps, stoop labor on the farms and ranches, servants and dishwashers and laundrymen in the cities. From mining gold they were excluded as rigorously as Germany for centuries had proscribed Jewish employment in certain occupations.

Once the railroads were built and the mining boom ended, the Chinese were harshly mistreated in an effort to persuade them to return to China; they were lynched, beaten, mobbed, burned out. From being tolerated they were regarded, as one survey showed, as " 'a distinct people,' 'unassimilable,' 'keeping to their own customs and laws.' They lowered 'the plane of living' . . . 'shut out white labor.' They were 'clannish,' 'dangerous,' 'criminal,' 'secretive in their actions,' 'debased and servile,' 'deceitful and vicious,' 'inferior from a mental and moral point of view,' 'filthy and loathsome in their habits.' . . . Every aspect of the invaders became unpleasant; their slant eyes bespoke slyness; their conversation among themselves frightful jabbering."[6]

Soon there were organized demonstrations against the Chinese as well as rioting and mob action. In San Francisco, a demagogue named Denis

Kearney organized the Workingmen's Party, one slogan of which was "The Chinese Must Go!" Mobs inflamed by his oratory rampaged through Chinatown, burning many buildings and beating up every Chinese they could lay hands on. Still not satisfied, Kearney urged his followers to store up dynamite, which was to be dropped from balloons on Chinatown. His excesses were regarded with a guarded sympathy by the city's two leading newspapers, the *Call* and the *Chronicle,* which apparently feared that his party would take over the state government. Until Kearney's influence finally waned, the city's 116,000 Chinese lived in constant fear. The anti-Chinese feeling spread elsewhere in the West, and there were riots in Tacoma, Seattle, and worst of all in Rock Springs, Wyoming, where many Chinese were killed and beaten. On the demand of the Chinese Imperial government, after much haggling, the United States was forced to pay China an indemnity of $276,000 for the cruelties inflicted upon a people whose migration was urged and pleaded for when their labor was needed.

Even more indignities were heaped on the Chinese in a succession of legislative acts discriminating against them. By 1876 both the Republicans and Democrats, responding to popular feeling, had adopted as part of their platforms a demand for legislation to exclude Chinese immigrants. A California state election in 1879 included a vote on Chinese exclusion, for which 154,638 marked their ballots in favor, only 883 against. And in 1882 Congress passed the Chinese Exclusion Act, even though the rights of Americans in China at the time were protected by extraterritorial provisions in the Sino-American Treaty. It was the first such discriminatory legislation passed in the United States, and in succeeding decades, instead of reconsidering it, Congress only reinforced its provisions. One of the crueller refinements was the Scott Act passed in 1888, which forbade Chinese back home on a visit to return to this country, regardless of whether they had left families and businesses on this side of the ocean.

And for many years the Chinese had to endure pain and humiliation on the streets of Western cities, particularly in San Francisco. The sight of a defenseless "John Chinaman" padding along in his felt-soled slippers was often the signal for an attack by streetcorner thugs or a pack of schoolboys on their way home. The Chinese were fair game, the sport of all the idle viciousness generated in city streets.

Their only defenders, it seemed, were some of the more civilized men from back East who now formed the "San Francisco school" of writing. They included Bret Harte, who had been chased out of a northern California town for daring to tell the truth about a massacre of helpless Indians by white settlers; Ambrose Bierce, the wounded veteran of the Union Army, who was writing the *News-Letter*'s "Town Crier" column, and Mark Twain, the mining-camp wandervogel who was just settling down to more serious writing. All decried the treatment of the Chinese in terms that most of their readers must have found offensive, if not unsettling to their prejudices.

A Harte vignette in the *Overland Monthly* served as the obituary of an obscure citizen named Wan Lee. "Dead, my reverend friends, dead, stoned to death in the streets of San Francisco in the year of grace 1869, by a mob of half-grown boys and Christian school children."

He also described the dangers of travel for an inoffensive Chinese: "On the road to Sacramento, he was twice playfully thrown from the top of a stagecoach by an intelligent but deeply intoxicated Caucasian, whose moral stature was shocked at riding with one addicted to opium-smoking. At Hangtown he was beaten by a passing stranger—purely an act of Christian supererogation. At Dutch Flat he was robbed by well-known hands from unknown motives. At Sacramento he was arrested on suspicion of something or other and discharged with a severe reprimand . . . At San Francisco he was freely stoned by children of the public schools, but by carefully avoiding the monuments of enlightened progress, he at last reached, in comparative safety, the Chinese quarter where his abuse was confined to the police and limited by the strong arm of the law."[7]

Ambrose Bierce, as the "Town Crier," also took note of the vulnerability of the Chinese whenever they ventured near the centers of Anglo-Saxon enlightenment. "On last Sunday afternoon," he observed in 1869, "a Chinaman passing guilelessly along Dupont Street was assailed with a tempest of bricks and stones from the steps of the First Congregational Church. At the completion of this devotional exercise the Sunday-scholars retired within the hallowed portals of the sanctuary, to hear about Christ Jesus, and Him crucified."

Bierce was also delighted to point out that the horrors of miscegenation were, in effect, a one-way street for the city's moralists. They were shocked whenever a Chinese married one of the local servant-girls, usually Irish or German immigrants, but didn't hesitate to sneak into Chinatown with hatbrims pulled down and collars pulled up to visit the beautiful but notorious Miss Atoy or some other courtesan. Bierce gleefully reported that when a fresh shipment of singsong girls arrived on the San Francisco docks, they were greeted not by their countrymen but a delegation of prominent white citizens. The girls were then escorted to the Occidental Hotel and shown the sights by the mayor and the full membership of the board of supervisors.[8] (That Caucasians did not mind mingling with the Chinese on their own terms has been observed by a historian of their first two decades in America: "The Chinese also found other groups sharing their life. Americans entered their employ, Germans occupied their dormitories, tents, and log cabins, Frenchmen sat at their tables, and Mexicans guided their pack horses through the Sierra. All these nationalities intermarried with the Chinese.")[9]

But it was Harte and Twain who exposed and flayed anti-Chinese prejudice with their bitterest satire. Harte described the observance of St. Patrick's Day in his mythical Slumgullion Gulch as the occasion on which the Irish boasted of their love of freedom by beating up a Negro and chasing several Chinese out of the camp. He paraphrased the slogan of the Fenians, the Irish freedom-fighters, to read "Ireland for the Irish, America for the Naturalized, and Hell for Niggers and Chinese."

In his solemn essay on the ordeal of the Chinese, Harte observed that in "John Chinaman" he saw "an abiding consciousness of degradation — a secret pain of self-humiliation in the lines of the mouth and eye . . . They seldom smile, and their laughter is of such an extraordinary and sardonic nature — so purely a mechanical spasm, quite independent of any mirthful attribute — that to this day I am doubtful whether I ever saw a Chinaman laugh." The life of the ordinary Chinese, he said, was a "torment" resulting from the "persecutions of the young and old of a certain class," and he concluded: "I don't know what was the exact philosophy that Confucius taught, but it is to be hoped that poor John in his persecution is still able to detect the conscious hate and fear with which inferiority always regards the possibility of even-handed justice, and which is the key note to the vulgar clamor about servile and degraded races."

Oddly and ironically, it was Bret Harte who confirmed much of what his fellow Americans believed about the Chinese in his widely read poem "Plain Language from Truthful James," the popularity and misapprehension of which he had failed to anticipate. He wrote those sixty lines of doggerel in the summer of 1870 while he was the editor of the *Overland Monthly*. When white space yawned in the September issue of that magazine, he exhumed the poem titled "Plain Language from Truthful James" but ever afterward called "The Heathen Chinee" and published it. Certainly he was unaware that white Americans would miss the satirical implications of the line "We are ruined by cheap Chinese labor" bleated by one of the whites outwitted at the card table by their intended victim.

The poem told of Ah Sin and how he outmaneuvered two whites bent on cheating him at euchre, upon which Truthful James comments:

> *Which I wish to remark —*
> *And my language is plain —*
> *That for ways that are dark*
> *And for tricks that are vain,*
> *The heathen Chinee is peculiar,*
> *Which the same I would rise to explain.*[10]

The public seized on the poem as a diatribe against the Chinese, entirely disregarding its satiric intentions. It was recited in parlors from coast to coast, anthologized as far away as England and Australia, reprinted in pirated editions sold on the streets. When an illustrated version was placed on sale in New York, hundreds mobbed the store. "In all our knowledge of New York," the New York *Globe* commented, "nothing like this has ever been seen on Broadway . . . We have been obliged to produce it twice in the *Globe* to answer the demands of the public, and we venture to say there is not a secular paper in the United States which has not copied it."

Mark Twain was equally biting in his references to the mistreatment of the Chinese in the late 1860's and early 1870's. In a series of newspaper articles published in 1870, Twain included the letters of a fictional Chinese who describes his experiences in America, where "all are free and all are equal." The Chinese was robbed, beaten and arrested. "Rot there," his captor told him as he threw him into a cell, "till ye lairn that there's no room in America for the likes of ye or your nation."[11]

In one chapter of *Roughing It,* Twain also referred to the fatal stoning of Wan Lee, and commented on the Chinese and those who persecuted them:

"They are a harmless race when white men either let them alone or treat them no worse than dogs; in fact, they are almost entirely harmless anyhow, for they seldom think of resenting the vilest insults or the cruelest injuries. They are quiet, peaceable, tractable, free from drunkenness, and they are as industrious as the day is long. A disorderly Chinaman is rare and a lazy one does not exist . . .

"He is a great convenience to everybody — even to the worst class of white men, for he bears most of their sins, suffering fines for their petty thefts, imprisonment for their robberies, and death for their murders. Any white man can swear a Chinaman's life away in the courts, but no Chinaman can testify against a white man. Ours is the 'land of the free' — nobody denies that — nobody challenges it. (Maybe it is because we won't let other people testify.) As I write, news comes that in broad daylight in San Francisco, some boys have stoned an inoffensive Chinaman to death, and that although a large crowd witnessed the shameful deed, no one interfered . . .

"No California *gentleman or lady* ever abuses or oppresses a Chinaman under any circumstances, an explanation that seems to be much needed in the East. Only the scum of the population do it — they and their children; they, and naturally and consistently, the policemen and politicians, likewise, for these are the dust-licking pimps and slaves of the scum, there as elsewhere in America."

Perhaps Mark Twain should have been a little less tender about the sensibilities of the quality folk. Naturally they were too genteel to heave a rock or paving stone at anyone, but they possessed the power and influence to see that the Chinese minority was protected, they were the masters of the "scum," the ultimate controllers of the police and politicians. But no cries of protest came from their pursed or withered lips. The Chinese were their lightning rod. In times of unemployment and mass suffering by the "scum," the Chinese problem distracted the mobs from firing their bricks at the stately homes on the hilltops.

2. *Literary Beachcombers*

The San Francisco literary vanguard was producing the most vigorous prose being written in America during the post–Civil War years. They pictured the Western frontier in all its crudity, violence and racial injustice. When they widened their horizons, Twain in particular, they were equally realistic in portraying the squalid underside of Gilded Age America. Yet when several of its members went wandering to Hawaii and the South Seas their critical faculties were seemingly paralyzed and their accounts of the Pacific world might have served as travel-poster advertising. Most were lured there by boyhood readings of Melville, as Jack London was a generation later, searching perhaps for their own version of the supple and seductive Fayaway whom Melville found in the valley of the Typees.

Even Mark Twain's calefactory pen was cooled as he described Hawaii, "tranquil as dawn in the Garden of Eden . . . the balmy fragrance of jasmine, oleander and the Pride of India . . . dusky native women swooping by, free as the wind on fleet horses." Charles Warren Stoddard, a poet with a delicate manner, hymned the pagan beauty of Polynesian manhood. Joaquin Miller composed purplish odes to the Hawaiian scenery. Later Jack London, wearying of the Frozen North, turned to his experiences in Hawaii and the South Seas for the material that provided him with the second stage of his career. Ambrose Bierce, as might be expected of his testy disposition, resisted the lure of the islands and referred to them contemptuously as "fly specks."

The enthusiasm of his colleagues, in print and on the lecture platform, contributed largely to the desirability of Pacific possessions in the American mind. They provided a gentler image, one more alluring to prospective tourists and merchants, than the occasional savagery glimpsed on Melville's pages.

Charles Warren Stoddard, though the least venturesome of the San Francisco literateurs (he wound up as an English professor), was the first to cast himself adrift in the Pacific world. His parents had brought him west when he was a boy of twelve, frail, introspective and shy. Early in his youth he began contributing poetry to the *Golden Era* under the pseudonym of Pip Pepperpod. His writing was wispy, elfin, often precious, but he was adopted as a ranking member of the group which produced the *Overland Monthly:* Harte, Twain, John Muir, Prentice Mulford. When he was in his early twenties he went to Hawaii to visit a sister who was living there and produced the first of his sketches, "Chumming with a Savage," for the *Overland*.

Then and in succeeding works Stoddard dwelled ecstatically on the beauty of the Polynesian males. Perhaps libellously, Mark Twain often referred to him as "such a nice girl." At any rate, such lyrical descriptions of lithe brown bodies as were to be found in *The Island of Tranquil Delights* and *Summer Cruising in the South Seas* were favorite reading in the homosexual underground early in this century.[12]

In 1870 Stoddard embarked on a voyage to Tahiti, where he hoped to support himself by working at whatever jobs were available while he studied the native customs. When he arrived in Papeete, he found there was no employment suitable for a gentleman. His money soon ran out, and Stoddard was reduced to the status of a genteel beachcomber, living in grass huts with the natives and sharing the food that dropped off the trees or was culled from the lagoons. He immediately and rather precipitously identified himself with the simple sunny life of the South Sea islanders, and later wrote almost swooningly of the friendships he formed with the (male) natives. "The simple and natural life of the islander beguiles me," he wrote in *Summer Cruising in the South Seas;* "I am at home with him; all the rites of savagedom find a responsive echo in my heart; it is as though I remembered something long forgotten; it is like a dream dimly remembered and at last realized; it must be that the untamed spirit of some savage ancestor quickens my blood."

His idyllic sojourn in the environs of Papeete ended when the white colony in Tahiti packed him off to San Francisco aboard an eastbound trading vessel. The lushly romantic pictures he composed of island life were published in the *Overland* and later in book form. They made a quick-blooming reputation for him. Perhaps his greatest influence, however, was on another writer — Robert Louis Stevenson. On his first visit to San Francisco in 1879, Stevenson was most eager to meet Stoddard, whose books had stirred his own interest in the South Seas. Stevenson and Stoddard, oddly matched as they were, became close friends. Stevenson often visited him at his rookery, "Plover's Nest," on Telegraph Hill and listened to Stoddard's accounts of his voyage to Tahiti. Stoddard's *South Sea Idylls,* along with his personal descriptions of island glamour, convinced Stevenson that he must follow his destiny into the Pacific.

A much lustier apostle of the beauties of Pacific-island life was Mark Twain, who sailed for Hawaii in 1866 under a commission from the Sacramento *Union* to write travel letters. Later he reworked the same material for a highly successful lecture tour, from which thousands of Americans gained an impression of the desirability of the islands such as he expressed in *Roughing It:* "How sad it is to think of the millions who have gone to their graves in this beautiful island [Oahu] and never knew there was a hell."

Twain's earthly "hell," as he made apparent in his first letters to the Sacramento newspaper, was the "cramped and crowded streetcars" of San Francisco, the city's "hurry and bustle and confusion" and the "combined stenches of Chinadom and Brannan Street slaughterhouses."

Twain spent his first infatuated days on Oahu riding around the countryside on a rented horse with "a convulsive sort of canter, which had three short steps in it and one long one, and reminded me alternately of the clattering shake of a great earthquake, and the sweeping plunge of the *Ajax* [the ship he took to Hawaii] in a storm."

With the iconoclasm which erupted periodically through the applied respectability of his character, Twain, on visiting the ruins of an ancient temple, reflected favorably on the old-time religion of the natives. He was not appalled by the human sacrifices made in that temple "in those old bygone days when the simple child of nature, yielding momentarily to sin when sorely tempted, acknowledged his error . . . and came forward with noble frankness and offered up his grandmother as an atoning sacrifice . . . In those old days the luckless sinner could keep on cleansing his conscience and achieving periodical happiness as long as his relations held out." He observed caustically that that was "long, long before the missionaries braved a thousand privations to come and make them permanently miserable by telling them how beautiful and blissful a place heaven is, and how nearly impossible it is to get there; and showed the native how dreary a place perdition is and what unnecessarily liberal facilities there are for going to it; showed him how, in his ignorance, he had gone and fooled away all his kinfolk to no purpose; showed him what rapture it is to work all day for fifty cents to buy food with, as compared with fishing for a pastime and lolling in the shade through eternal summer . . ."

He provided delightful descriptions of the people, the women with their "comely features, fine black eyes, rounded forms inclining to the voluptuous," the men in various costumes, "some with nothing on but a battered stovepipe hat tilted on the nose and a very scant breech-clout," the "smoke-dried children clothed in nothing but sunshine." The Honolulu marketplace "in the full glory of Saturday afternoon" delighted him, particularly the girls dressed in their black, red and white silken robes, though he conceded the coconut oil in which they drenched their hair smelled "like a rag factory on fire." Occasionally, Twain related, you caught sight of "a heathen from the sunny isles away down in the South Seas, with his face and neck tatooed until he looks like the customary mendicant from Washoe who has been blown up in a mine." He was less impressed with the edibility of *poi,* which "produces acrid humors, a fact which sufficiently accounts for the humorous character of the Kanakas." The eroticism of the hula dance had been suppressed by the missionaries, but Twain wistfully recounted the recollections of old-timers in Honolulu when that dance was "the very perfection of educated motion of limb and arm, hand, head, and body." Lissome unclad girls "waved, swayed, gesticulated, bowed, stooped, whirled, squirmed, twisted and undulated as if they were part and parcel of a single individual; and it was difficult to believe they were not moved in a body by some exquisite piece of mechanism."

Like most literary sojourners in the Pacific islands he was unimpressed by the efforts at Christianizing those children of nature and destroying such a beguiling remnant of ancient folk culture as the true, uncensored, unclothed hula. Such pastimes, he believed, had been prohibited because they "interfered too much with labor and the interests of the white folks." And all that the missionaries had succeeded in doing, he observed, was to "build up in the native women a profound respect for chastity — in other people." Sinful tendencies among the Polynesians would die only when the race was extinct, he believed, and "doubtless this purifying is not far off, when we reflect that contact with civilization and the whites has reduced the native population from 400,000 to 55,000 in something over eighty years!"

He also cast a shrewd eye over the government of the islands. The Hawaiian monarchy met with his approval because it gave precedence to the female line, sons inheriting from their mothers the right to the throne or other royal perquisites. "Their reason for this is exceedingly sensible, and I recommend it to the aristocracy of Europe: They say it is easy to know who a man's mother was, but, etc. etc. . . . ."

The legislative assembly, composed of whites and natives, was less impressive to Twain. Too many of its representatives resembled the "cow-county" members of the American Congress, only in Hawaii they might be called, he thought, "taro-patch members." Their pomposity, however, was amusing. "Now, on one occasion, a Kanaka member, who paddled over here from some barren rock or other out yonder in the ocean — some scalawag who wears nothing but a pair of socks and a plug hat when he is at home, or possibly is even more scantily attired — got up and gravely gave notice of a bill to authorize the construction of a suspension bridge from Oahu to Hawaii, a matter of a hundred and fifty miles! He said the natives would prefer it to the inter-island schooners, and they wouldn't suffer from seasickness on it." But that was no stupider, he thought, than a member of the Wisconsin legislature who rose during a debate over fixing the penalty for arson and "seriously suggested that when a man commits the damning crime of arson they ought to either hang him or make him marry the girl."

His Majesty's government was touched by vainglory which reminded him of "grandeur in a playhouse," complete with "nine-jointed titles and colossal magnates."

The prime minister was "a renegade American from New Hampshire, all jaw, vanity, bombast and ignorance, a lawyer of 'shyster' caliber, a fraud by nature, a humble worshipper of the scepter above him, a reptile never tired of sneering at the land of his birth or glorifying the ten-acre kingdom that has adopted him — salary, four thousand dollars a year, vast consequence, and no perquisites." The commander of the Household Troops was in charge of "about the number of soldiers usually placed under a corporal in other lands." The minister of war held sway over the royal armies consisting of "230 uniformed Kanakas, mostly brigadier generals, and if the country ever gets into trouble with a foreign power we shall probably hear from them." The minister of the navy was "a nabob who rules the royal fleet, a steam tug and a sixty-ton schooner." And the minister of finance "talks prodigiously of 'finance,' suggests imposing schemes for paying off the national debt (of $150,000) and does it all for $4000 a year and unimaginable glory."

With evident relief he turned from human folly to scenic grandeur, which inspired some fancy prose in his letters to the Sacramento *Union*. He wrote of "a laced and ruffled cataract of limpid water leaping from a sheer precipice fifteen hundred feet high; but that sort of scenery finds its stanchest ally in the arithmetic rather than in spectacular effect." He described a crater boiling with "a heaving sea of molten fire," white-hot chimneys of lava through which burst "gorgeous sprays of lava gouts and gem spangles, some white, some red and some golden — a ceaseless bombardment that fascinated the eye with its unapproachable splendor." Above was a gorge topped by "masses of white vapor hiding the turreted summits, and far above the vapor swelled a background of gleaming green crags and cones that came and went, like islands drifting in a fog."

But it was the earthier Mark Twain whom the respectable American colony had to contend with. His salty conversation and irreverent attitudes offended the pious folk, and there was one lady who made her daughter stuff her ears with cotton when she knew Twain would be calling. The lady's caution seemed to be justified when Honolulu residents later read reprints of his articles, including one which told how he watched girls frolicking on a secluded beach. "I observed a bevy of nude native young ladies bathing in the sea . . . but with a prudery which seems to be characteristic of that sex everywhere, they all plunged in . . . I was naturally irritated by such conduct, and therefore I piled their clothes up on a boulder on the edge of the sea and sat down on them and kept the wenches in the water until they were pretty well used up . . . I thought I could freeze them out, maybe, but it was impracticable . . . I went and undressed and went in myself. And then they went out; I never saw such singular perversity."[13]

His lecture titled "Our Fellow Savages of the Sandwich Islands" brought him his first taste of fame in the United States and Britain. For all his joshing, Twain had been deeply moved by his Hawaiian experiences and years later wrote an epitaph which still conveys — even against the touristic atrocities, commercialization and industrialization which have transformed the islands — a sense of what they must have been like a hundred years ago. "No alien land in all the world has any deep, strong charm for me but that one; no other land could so longingly and beseechingly haunt me sleeping and waking, through half a lifetime, as that one has. Other things leave me, but it abides; other things change, but it remains the same. For me its balmy airs are always blowing, its summer seas flashing in the sun; the pulsing of its surf-beat is in my ear; I can see its garlanded crags, its leaping cascades, its plumy palms drowsing by the shore; its remote summits floating like islands above the cloudrack; I can feel the spirit of its woodland solitudes; in my nostrils still lives the breath of flowers that perished twenty years ago."

In 1896, the self-glorifying poet Joaquin Miller was commissioned by the *Overland Monthly* and a number of newspapers to act as their correspondent during the political crisis then building up a head of steam. His journalistic sponsors favored annexation of the islands and they trusted that Miller, though a poet with an ego so vast that it astonished the pre-Raphaelites when he made a triumphal appearance in England, would provide them with good strong stuff to support their cause.

Miller was almost as great a disappointment to the people who paid his bills as he was a shambles of immorality to respectable Americans in Honolulu. He appeared in their midst with a young woman named Grace Oliver, who was pregnant with their third illegitimate child although Miller was almost forty years her senior. His dispatches to West Coast papers eager to prove to their readers that acquisition of Hawaii was a strategic necessity were a series of odes, paeans and pastoral pieces scribbled in his hotel room. The editors learned that Hawaii was "Sweet Arcadia," surrounded by an "argent, opal sea," with "cloud-capped peaks where thunders slept," but nothing about prospective naval bases or the attractions of low-cost Asian labor tilling the sugar and pineapple plantations. Molten lava swirling in the punchbowl of a volcano was "the dough of hell," as Miller put it, but he was silent on the attitude of Japanese immigrants toward the United States. The editors had to be content with warmed-over rhapsody.

They were probably undismayed by his comeuppance from the Hawaiian authorities. During a roundup of suspected counter-revolutionaries, Miller, as a poet, was naturally suspect and was accordingly arrested. The provisional government, however, was dismayed that a celebrity had been hauled in and he was released almost immediately. To make amends he was invited to dinner at the executive mansion by Governor and Mrs. Sanford Dole. Unwisely Miller brought Grace Oliver along and blithely introduced her to his hostess as "my plumber's wife." The story was so implausible that Mrs. Dole investigated it immediately after her guests left, and learned that Mr. Miller and Miss Oliver were occupying adjoining hotel rooms. Miller was ordered to leave on the first available ship —

which he did, after pawning his diamond ring — while Grace Oliver was permitted to stay in Honolulu until her child was born.[14]

The wayfaring tradition of American writers was continued into a third generation after Melville by the most robust and adventurous of them all — Jack London. As a boy on the Oakland waterfront, London had practically memorized Melville's novels, and shortly after he became a successful novelist himself he set out on the famous voyage of the *Snark,* his personally designed yacht. He sailed her straight for the Marquesas, the island of Nuku-hiva, and the valley of the Typee. London was bitterly disappointed by his visit to the scenes of Melville's first book. He found the valley being reclaimed by the jungle and only a few survivors of the warrior tribe, all of them suffering from elephantiasis, tuberculosis or leprosy.

A confused, self-made intellectual who claimed to be a revolutionary Socialist while operating one of the largest ranches in northern California, an equalitarian who also believed in Anglo-Saxon racial supremacy, Jack London was undoubtedly the most Pacific-minded of his profession — the only one who dwelled not only on the poetic enchantments of that ocean sea but America's political and military role on its littoral. The course of his involvement, however, comes later in the story of those who urged America to face westward.

Perhaps a more striking if less enduring impression was made on the mass imagination by several troupes of South Sea islanders brought over to America and placed on exhibition at the Chicago World's Fair of 1893 and the St. Louis World's Fair of 1904. Not everyone read books or attended lectures, but millions would go to the world's fairs and see the islanders in the flesh. Lorrin A. Thurston, an energetic promoter of Hawaiian annexation, a prominent Honolulu businessman and member of the "revolutionary" movement, brought a 420-foot moving cyclorama of the Kilauea volcano, backed up by a quartet of male Hawaiian singers, to the Chicago fair as a means of making propaganda for his cause. Neither the cyclorama nor the quartet of vocalists was exactly a smash hit. What the public wanted to see was hula-dancers. Thurston took his exhibition to the San Francisco Midwinter Fair the following year, and it was more successful among the annexation-minded Californians.

A more successful feature of the Chicago fair was the Samoan troupe imported by Harry J. Moors, an Apia trader. It was part of the Congress of All Nations, where various faraway peoples pretended to go about their daily routines while thousands gawked. The anthropological essays included Little Egypt dancing on the Streets of Cairo. Moors's Samoans set up a native village with a prefabricated hut, tapa-cloth costumes, spears, fire-sticks, war canoes, pottery and ceremonial headdresses. The girls, with covered breasts, performed a decorous version of their dances unlikely to offend any maiden aunts from Keokuk.

The Samoans proved to be a commercial enough attraction for Moors to import another troupe for the St. Louis World's Fair eleven years later. This time the crowds were given a more elaborate view of Samoan village life with the troupe climbing fake palm trees, cooking in underground ovens, staging ceremonial dances, making *kava* and selling handcrafted curios on the side. A Mexican orchestra was engaged to provide the musical accompaniment. It was all tame enough, compared to the Filipino exhibit, which featured the killing, cooking and eating of a dog, but the *Century Magazine* frowned on the "simply downright savage" dancing of the Samoans. Richard Harding Davis, however, was favorably impressed and wrote that the "imagination easily transports one to the little coral reefs on which these people live, and in their daily life do all they represent on the stage except to eat human flesh — they having abandoned cannibalism a quarter of a century ago and embraced Christianity under the teachings of French Catholic missionaries. So strong is their religion that they will not perform on Sunday and they are the only World's Fair company that keeps closed house on the Sabbath."[15]

Later the Samoans toured America from coast to coast for a year and a half, and were so adept at making friends — the dancing girls in the troupe, that is — that Moors had to "enforce strict rules against ogling acquaintances in the audience."[16] The Samoans "in person" probably made a greater impact on ordinary Americans than all the literary strivings and newspaper editorializing on the "Samoan question" combined.

3. *Bridges to Understanding*

In the 1890's Japan was making herself into a nation to be reckoned with. Industrially and militarily she was becoming a major power, and increasingly conscious of that power. She was industrialized, but not to any great extent westernized. American influence was waning as Japan began modeling her political system more on the German pattern than the American or British; her navy was being constructed and trained under British advice, and her army was being drilled by German instructors. Aside from those physical aspects, Japan had decided that she would take from Western thought only what she wanted and could use. There was no aping of Western customs, no echoing of Western platitudes, no self-abandonment such as characterized Japan during the occupation following her defeat in World War II. A misty Pan-Asianism was slowly developing, expressed most vividly in the observation of one Japanese intellectual that to the Western powers all of eastern Asia was "like a piece of meat thrown among a group of tigers."

During that decade of growing self-consciousness in Japan, Americans continued to view her indulgently, little aware of her diverging course.

Their simplistic picture of the Japanese was evident in the great popularity of *Madame Butterfly;* self-esteem could only be promoted by the scenario of Puccini's opera, with a bedraggled Japanese girl dying for love of the American navy lieutenant. It might have been more profitable if Americans had been able to read a translation of Nakae Chomin's pointed little fable, "Three Drunkards' Discussion on National Government," published in 1887.

In Chomin's story, three drunkards discuss the course which they believe the Japanese empire should take. The first drunkard declares that Japan should seize China and make herself impregnable in the Far East. The second takes an opposite view, that Japan should become less aggressive and link herself culturally and spiritually with the Western world. The third insists that Japan must take a middle-of-the-road position, expanding or contracting as warranted by the attitude of the Western nations. In all of their viewpoints, as Akira Iriye points out, there was no consideration of the morality of the actions they advocated. The three drunkards agreed that the outside world was immoral, and differed only on how to confront it.[17]

The Japanese attitude was skeptical, wary, fixed on the determination to choose an independent course. Japan adopted a constitution, convened a Diet, formed a cabinet, began building a telephone system, even tried coffee-drinking, but it was also to be remarked that she began curtailing the study of English, French and German in her schools and reemphasizing Japanese history and tradition in her educational program. Even among Japanese Christians there was a growing movement to make their churches independent of the American and other foreign missionaries.

In the closing decade of the last century American educators in Japan were placed on warning that Japanese tradition was regarded as more important by the new generation than an overlay of Western values. In 1892 there was a student walkout at the girls' school operated by American missionaries at Sendai. The girls protested that they wanted to learn more about their own country and its history and less about America. The missionary school promised to comply as best it could, but several girls still refused to continue their education there.

The Japanese were certainly not inclined to believe they could learn anything from China, but the educated classes would probably have paraphrased the optimistic statement of a Chinese commentator on westernization, Hsueh Fu-ch'eng, who wrote in 1890: "Learning from others does not necessarily mean that there is no chance to surpass them. How can we know that after several thousand years the Chinese cannot carry further the knowledge of the Westerners and develop once more the genius of creation, so that the Westerners will be astonished and dazzled by us?"[18]

During that final decade of the nineteenth century, when it became increasingly important for Americans and Japanese to arrive at a more intimate understanding than that conveyed in treaties and official documents, there were at least two Americans in Japan who sensed the need for building a cultural bridge across the Pacific, who saw that the channel of communication must be widened exactly because Japan became a power in Asia almost step by step with American growth as a colonial power. How else could a collision of interests be avoided?

Ernest Fenollosa and Lafcadio Hearn were both teachers, writers and Japanophiles. With so much in common, it was odd that the two expatriates did not become close associates and collaborators, but at any rate they worked in the same interest: that of explaining America to the Japanese, and Japan to the Americans.*

Ernest Fenollosa was an honored name in the scholarly world of Tokyo, partly because he successfully appealed to the Japanese government to save its priceless heritage of paintings, porcelains, bronzes, sculptures and rolls of calligraphy at a time when they were being thrown away as embarrassing relics of the backward centuries or sold in Oriental versions of the Flea Market because they weren't "modern." It must be noted that he profited personally by selling Japanese art objects to the Museum of Fine Arts in Boston and other American institutions.

Fenollosa envisioned a coalescing of Occident and Orient. They were two different types of civilization but he considered them compatible. In a poem titled "East and West" he described the East as feminine, the West as masculine, and considered their union as natural and inevitable as the marriage of male and female. They complemented each other, and when the One World he hoped for was achieved each would gain what was best in the other.

He developed this theme five years later, declaring East and West would be united through coalition rather than conquest. There had been a historic precedent, he pointed out, when Greece and India, through Alexander the Great, had achieved a cultural exchange "from which sprang modern Europe." (He did not pause to reflect that that contact had been brought about at spearpoint by Alexander's conquering army.) A still "broader" and more inspiring convergence, he predicted, would result from the fusion of the East and the West. "It is not merely that the West shall from its own point of view tolerate the East, nor the East the West; not even that the West shall try to understand the East from the Eastern point of view — but that both, planting their faith in the divine destinies of man, shall with cooperation aim at a new world-type, rich in those million possibilities of thought and achievement that exclusion blindly stifles."[19]

A more romantic and literary portrayal of emerging Japan, less concerned with an idealistic vision of the future, was presented by Lafcadio

* According to Lafcadio Hearn's latest biographer, Elizabeth Stevenson (*Lafcadio Hearn*, New York, 1961, p. 290–291), "Mr. and Mrs. Fenollosa courted Hearn, but he was embarrassed by their attentions and did not let them come close."

Hearn, who started out his career as a wandering and somewhat dissolute newspaperman and ended it as an educator, interpreter of Japan to America, and sober-minded essayist. His literary reputation has faded, his works placed in the category of the exotic and tributary along with those of Pierre Loti and others who, in the crude phrase of Old Asia Hands, "went Asiatic," but he was widely published and read in the United States before the turn of the century. In his highly individual way, as an American who settled for good in Japan and raised a Japanese family, he contributed much to the kindly feeling Americans had about the Japanese (those in Japan, not those in Hawaii or America) until their military and naval successes made them a little too impressive to be patronized.

Partly through his efforts the Japanese were seen in America to be an orderly, cultured people in contrast to the anarchic peasant masses of China. Something of the infatuation which began for him the day he arrived in Yokohama and caught his first sight of Mount Fuji, and which he conveyed to American readers, was expressed in his sketch, "My First Day in the Orient":

"There is some charm unutterable in the morning air, cool with the coolness of Japanese spring and wind-waves from the snowy cone of Fugi; a charm perhaps due rather to softest lucidity than to any positive tone — an atmospheric limpidity extraordinary, with only a suggestion of blue in it, through which the most distant objects appear focused with amazing sharpness . . . The street-vistas, as seen above the dancing white mushroom-shaped hat of my sandaled runner, have an allurement of which I fancy that I could never weary. Elfish everything seems; for everything as well as everybody is small, and queer, and mysterious; the little houses under their blue roofs, the little shop-fronts hung with blue, and the smiling little people in their blue costumes . . . And perhaps the supremely pleasurable impression of this morning is that produced by the singular gentleness of popular scrutiny. Everybody looks at you curiously, but there is never anything disagreeable, much less hostile in the gaze: most commonly it is accompanied by a smile or half smile. And the ultimate consequence of all the curious kindly looks and smiles is that the stranger finds himself thinking of fairyland. Hackneyed to the degree of provocation this statement no doubt is."[20]

Until the last years of his life, in fact, Hearn continued to convey that impression of an Oriental "fairyland" to his American readers. It was understandable enough to anyone who knew of the forty harried years of his life which preceded his journey to surcease and accomplishment in Japan.

Actually, it is claiming too much to label him an American writer, though he spent more time in the United States than in the Dublin of his youth or the Japan of his last fourteen years on earth. His Irish-Greek ancestry, at any rate, equipped him to be a citizen of the world. He was born on the Ionian island of Leucadia, the son of Dr. Charles Bush Hearn, an Irish surgeon in the British army, and Rosa Cassimati of the Ionian island of Cerigo. When his parents met, the British army was occupying certain of the Ionian islands. They christened their son Patrick Lafcadio Hearn. When Lafcadio was seven, his parents separated and were divorced; his father remarried in India and raised another family while his mother remarried back in her native islands and gave birth to four children by her second husband. Lafcadio and his younger brother, Daniel, were raised in Dublin by his father's family. The result, since he never saw his father or mother again, was a psychological trauma which took a lifetime of healing. "I was scarcely ever mentioned by name," he remembered in later years, "but only referred to as 'the Child.' "

He was adequately educated in church schools in France, England and Ireland. At the age of nineteen he was curtly informed that it was time to make his own way in the world, given passage money to America, and told to look up friends of the family in Cincinnati. He landed in the German-French-Irish city in 1869 and was plunged, penniless and unemployed, into what he later called "the wolf's side of life, the ravening side, the apish side; the ugly facets of the monkey puzzle."[21]

For a time he was sheltered in a coachhouse by a servant who fed him food stolen from his employer's pantry. He worked for more than a year in a boardinghouse as a handyman, meanwhile writing stories for the penny weeklies in Cincinnati. After three years of living from hand to mouth he landed a job as reporter on the Cincinnati *Enquirer* and was soon acquainted with the crime and squalor of the riverfront. "Beastly, practical, pork-packing Cincinnati," he called it, but he learned the writing trade on its newspapers. On the side he edited a humorous weekly, *Ye Giglampz,* observing the city with a savage humor. The weekly died after nine issues of "inanition and the bad taste of the great American people," as its young editor claimed.

His life was more feverishly disordered and Bohemian than that of most newspapermen of his time. When he was twenty-four he married a Negro woman and for that unforgivable breach of local custom was fired by the *Enquirer*. He was about to jump into a canal when he was hauled away by a friend. The editor who fired him later recalled: "He was as sensitive as a flower . . . The classics were at his fingers' ends. He was poetic, and his whole nature seemed attuned to the beautiful, and he wrote beautifully of things that were neither wholesome nor inspiring."[22]

Hearn eventually was hired by another Cincinnati paper, the *Commercial,* but his marriage to Mattie Foley broke up after three years. A few months later, in 1877, he drifted on to Memphis, "a dirty, dusty, ugly town," from which he wrote stories at space rates for the Cincinnati *Commercial.* One of his most striking was an account of the death of the Confederate cavalry leader Nathan Bedford Forrest, "one of these fierce and terrible men, who form in themselves a kind of protecting fringe to the borders of white civilization."

He moved on to New Orleans and its more antique Creole charm, "a dead bride crowned with orange flowers, a dead face that asked for a kiss." Somehow, living in the French Quarter, spending a total of thirty cents a day for his food, he eked out a living from writing sketches for the *Commercial*. In 1879 he was laid low by dengue, "breakbone fever," during a local epidemic. Still broken in health and looking like a ghost, he landed a job on the struggling *Item* and began eating regularly again. In addition to reporting, he translated stories by Zola, Daudet and Gautier. It was a pleasant, easygoing life that appealed to the Mediterranean side of his character. To a German-American friend up North who chided him for succumbing to the lazy charm of the Southern city, he replied, "You cannot make a Goth out of a Greek. Now I am with the Latin; I live in a Latin city . . . I eat and drink and converse with members of the races you detest like the son of Odin that you are. I see beauty here all around me — a strange, tropical, intoxicating beauty." That poetic sensitivity to atmosphere was a dominating element in his character, and his main strength as a writer.

What he had seen of the industrial North, of the lives degraded wherever men were merely the servants of machines, engines and turbines, had driven him to the backward South and would impel much wider wanderings. "In our great cities," he later wrote in *Gleanings in Buddha-Fields,* "beauty is for the rich; bare walls and foul pavements and smoky skies for our poor, and the tumult of hideous machinery — a hell of eternal ugliness and joylessness invented by our civilization to punish the atrocious crime of being unfortunate, or weak, or stupid, or overconfident in the morality of one's fellowman."[23]

As a roving observer of New Orleans life for the *Item* he composed many morbid little mood-pieces, in the manner of Poe, about the city's above-ground cemeteries, the shadowed courtyards of the French Quarter, the cafés and narrow streets. Later he worked for the *Times-Democrat,* continuing his efforts as a staff essayist whose work was beginning to be reprinted all over the country. He became an amateur Orientalist and wrote so frequently about Buddhism that the clergy became restive. His work began appearing in *Harper's Bazaar* and *Harper's Weekly,* mostly Oriental tales later collected in the volume titled *Some Chinese Ghosts,* which he objectively characterized as "early work of a man who tried to understand the Far East from books — and couldn't." His fascination with the East was heightened by his discovery of the works of Pierre Loti, the French naval officer, which he translated into English. When he finally went to Japan, he carried a copy of Loti's *Madame Chrysanthème* with him. Later he adored Loti less, and sized him up rather brutally as a man who had been a true poet in his youth but with the years had become "a little morbid modern affected Frenchman."

Late in the Eighties he spent a number of months on the French island of Martinique as the demand for his stories and sketches increased and he began appearing regularly in *Harper's* and *Lippincott's*. On his return to New York, still burning with curiosity about the Far East, he sold a publisher on the idea of a book about Japan (ultimately produced under the title *Glimpses of Unfamiliar Japan*) which would describe the life of the ordinary Japanese and attempt "thinking with their thoughts."

Hearn arrived in Japan on April 4, 1890, and at once felt himself at home for the first time in his life. Within a few months he knew that he would never return to the West. "Here I am in the land of dreams," he wrote an old friend in Cincinnati, "surrounded by strange gods. I seem to have known and loved them before somewhere: I burn incense before them. I pass much of my time in temples, trying to see into the heart of this mysterious people. In order to do so I have to blend with them and become a part of them. It is not easy. But I do hope to learn the language." He expected to be buried there, "under big trees in some old Buddhist cemetery, with six laths above me, inscribed with prayers in an unknown tongue, and a queerly carved monument typifying those five elements into which we are supposed to melt away."[24] Barely forty, he was anticipating death, and like most men half in love with death he was attracted by the fatalism of the East.

To support himself he began tutoring a boy of mixed parentage and working when he could on his book, which he now believed would take four or five years. He felt "indescribably" about Japan, he wrote. "This is a domesticated Nature, which loves man, and makes itself beautiful for him in a quiet blue-and-gray way like the Japanese women, and the trees seem to know what people say about them — seem to have little human souls. What I love in Japan is the Japanese — the poor simple humanity of the country. It is divine. There is nothing in this world approaching the naive natural charm of them. No book ever written has reflected it. And I love their gods, their customs, their dress, their bird-like quavering songs, their houses, their superstitions, their faults. And I believe that their art is as far in advance of our art as old Greek art was superior to that of the earliest European art-gropings . . ."[25]

With the help of Japanese friends he became a teacher at the Middle School in Matsue, in Shimane Prefecture, teaching English to a class of boys from twelve to sixteen years old. With all his poetic intelligence, his native sympathy and the energy of a scholar finally embarked on what he conceives to be a great work, he immersed himself completely in Japanese life. "To escape out of Western civilization into Japanese life," he wrote an acquaintance in Tokyo, "is like escaping from a pressure of ten atmospheres into a perfectly normal medium." He was not dismayed by the obliteration of the individual that characterized life among the Japanese, because "here the individual does not strive to expand his own individuality at the expense of everyone else."

He spent much time studying the "way of the gods" and its impact on the daily lives of the Japanese. In his two-volume *Glimpses of Unfamiliar Japan,* he dealt exhaustively with Buddhism and Shintoism, trying to understand and explain them from the Japanese viewpoint. Around Buddhism, he wrote, a vast theology had congealed, but "Shintoism has no philosophy, no code of ethics, no metaphysics; and yet, by its very immateriality, it can resist the invasion of Occidental religious thought as no other Oriental faith can. Shinto extends a welcome to Western science, but remains the irresistible opponent of Western religion; and the foreign zealots who would strive against it are astounded to find the power that foils their uttermost efforts indefinable as magnetism and invulnerable as air."[26]

When his Japanese friends pointed out that he now had a house but not a wife to go with it, he consented to the idea of an arranged marriage. The arrangements were made by a Japanese professor who was his closest friend in Matsue. The bride was Setsu Koizuma, the twenty-year-old daughter of an impoverished samurai family. He married her according to Japanese law and ritual, with the ceremonial exchange of rice wine in the presence of witnesses. The marriage was a success, despite or because of the initial lack of any Western nonsense about romantic love. He wrote a friend that the sweetness of the Japanese woman was unimaginable, that "all the possibilities of the race for goodness seem to be concentrated in her."

He was an accepted and respected member of the community, and his life settled into a productive routine of home, school, work on his writings. His sketches of Japanese life and essays on Japanese thought appeared in the American magazines and he published a book almost every year — *Glimpses* in 1894; *Out of the East,* 1895; *Kokoro: Hints and Echoes of Japanese Inner Life,* 1896; *Gleanings in Buddha-Fields,* 1897; *In Ghostly Japan,* 1899; *Shadowings,* 1900; *A Japanese Miscellany,* 1901; *Kotto,* 1902; *Japan: An Attempt at Interpretation,* 1904. As their titles suggest, they were warmly subjective explorations of the Japanese way of life, the Japanese mind and spirit. He was too infatuated to take an objective look at the changes — the hardening effects of militarization — which other Westerners observed and were dismayed by. He lived in happy removal from such distractions in the Japanese mainstream. When he did notice them, his wife wrote in her memoir, he would complain that "It is the Christians who are to blame."

Later he moved closer to those troubling currents when he was transferred to the Higher Middle School in Kumamoto. City life pleased him much less than the backwater of Matsue, but he took shelter in what he called his "little world of eleven people" — his wife and son, some of her family and the servants — and in wandering through the Kyushu country-side with its "little queer unknown towns, where there are no big vulgar hotels, and where one can dress and do exactly as one pleases."

He began to note in himself what other Westerners predicted he would, alternating optimism and pessimism about the future of Japan. "But with what hideous rapidity Japan is modernizing, after all," he wrote in 1894 after a vacation spent partly in the larger cities, "not in costume, or architecture, or habit, but in heart and manner. The emotional nature of the race is changing. Will it ever become beautiful again? Or failing to become attractive, can it ever become sufficiently complex to make a harmony with the emotional character of the West? . . . They have no reason to love us *en masse,* at least. Here, across the strait, is a city bombarded by us . . . Force sowed the seed; the future will gather the black crop. In the eternal order of things I suppose it is inevitable that every race should be made as wretched as possible; and all who cannot accept wretchedness as a necessary part of life must be exterminated."

Momentarily he considered returning to America and teaching in an American university, but almost as quickly knew it was impossible because "the cry would be raised that an atheist, a debauchee, a disreputable ex-reporter was corrupting the morals of the young under the pretence of teaching literature."[27]

He gave up teaching for a time to return to journalism on the staff of the Kobe *Chronicle,* edited by a tolerant Scotsman, writing editorials on subjects of interest to an Anglo-American readership by day and working on his own writings at night. The closer he examined Western influences in Japan, as in Kobe, the more convinced he was that Japan was passing from a racial childhood into "an adolescence which threatens to prove re-pulsive."

Nevertheless he became a Japanese citizen, and subsequently quit Kobe for the capital, where he became a professor of English literature at Tokyo University. He stayed there until about a year before his death in 1904. *Japan: An Attempt at Interpretation* was his last work, incidentally an answer to critics who charged that he had presented too "soft," romantic and charming a picture of Japan during the years when she was developing the industrial and military power which overwhelmed China in the middle Nineties and would soon shatter all the force the Russian empire could muster against her in Korea and Manchuria and on the high seas. In his final book, in fact, Hearn about-faced on many of his earlier conclusions about the Japanese. On first acquaintance he had admired the organization of their life and attributed it to their instinctive love of pattern, order and harmony; now he saw that it was achieved under the most intense discipline, imposed through centuries of pressure from the civil and religious authorities. Their beautifully ordered life was achieved at a psychological cost almost as great as its benefits. And there was more than a hint in his final work that the stresses of transforming their traditional society, of adapting its ancient and subtle harmonies to the grinding necessities of becoming a major power, might cause the Japanese to succumb to a national paranoia: a foreshadowing of Nanking, Pearl Harbor, Singapore and Manila, and all that those place-names were to signify in twoscore years.

When he died of a heart attack in 1904, a Tokyo newspaper reported there were only three foreigners among the hundreds who attended his funeral. He deserved better than that. A minor writer by the accounting of literary critics, he still taught the West more about the East, if the whole body of his work is studied, than any other Westerner. And he still had the modesty to sum up his achievements with the remark, "Of Japan I would say with Kipling's pilot: 'And if any man comes to you and says, *I know the Java currents,* don't you listen to him; for those currents is never yet known to mortal man!' "

9 🌿

"Advance Agent of the American Imperialism"

Whether they will or no, Americans must now begin to look outward.
— ALFRED THAYER MAHAN

To the bald, stately, middle-aged naval officer then serving as president of the Naval War College at Newport, Rhode Island, the world was a map of sea lanes, coaling stations and changing territorial boundaries brought about by conquest; a world of possible menace to the United States or, if she acted as he prescribed, one of awesome opportunity. Captain Alfred Thayer Mahan looked beyond the tranquil blue waters of the navy's torpedo station on Newport Bay, considered the professional dangers of becoming known as a visionary, a prophet, and nominated himself to supply "a voice to speak constantly of our external interests." In 1890 he would announce on the pages of the *Atlantic Monthly* that "whether they will or no, Americans must now begin to look outward."

Several years later, scoffed at as the "pedantic sailor" and the "amateur historian," denounced as "the advance agent of American imperialism" but heeded and studied by the most powerful men in America and the world, he would point to the manifest duty of our own expansion across the Pacific, blocked as we were to the north by "a body of states of like traditions to our own" and to the south by "the rights of a race wholly alien to us," adding:

"In our infancy we bordered upon the Atlantic only; our youth carried our boundary to the Gulf of Mexico; today maturity sees us upon the Pacific. Have we no right or no call to progress farther in any direction? Are there for us beyond the sea horizon none of those essential interests, of those evident dangers, which impose a policy and confer rights?"[1]

The dangers which Captain Mahan had in mind during the 1890's were so remote as to be unthinkable by the ordinary American. There was the doddering Spanish empire imposing its senile will upon the Cubans, but any other potential enemies were thousands of miles away. What riveted Captain Mahan's attention, of course, were the opportunities in the western Pacific and eastern Asia, the unsettled claims to territories and island groups of commercial and strategic value. The rivalry over Korea between Russia and Japan was approaching a flashpoint. Japan would soon detach chunks of Chinese territory as a result of the Sino-Japanese War of 1895. The French continued to gouge at Indo-China, had blockaded the Gulf of Tonkin during the Franco-Chinese War of 1883–1884 and fought a number of border battles to extend her control over the area. The extensive resources of Manchuria, the deserts of Inner and Outer Mongolia, were other possible prizes of war. And how long could the Philippine archipelago be held by the Spanish, with both the Americans and Germans ready to move in the moment the Spanish grip weakened? The only immediate danger was that the United States might lose out in the race for contested territories. The danger of the future was that she might not have the strategic bases to protect her interests overseas.

Captain Mahan was not the only prophet of Pacific Destiny. Others saw the opportunity, sensed the willing spirit of the present generation of Americans to assert themselves abroad. But it was Mahan who possessed the sense of history, the intellectual capacity and the moral authority to formulate the idea of moving across the Pacific in strength. He made it respectable as a consequence of historical necessity by his sober and restrained language. He concealed motives of self-interest — the conquering impulse — by asserting that the possible dangers of the distant future "impose a policy and confer rights."

There were other prophets of destiny who made similar proposals but lacked the ability to make them seem moral, righteous and therefore acceptable. Commodore Robert W. Shufeldt, for instance. He was the blunt old sea dog who finally negotiated our treaty with Korea in 1882. In a letter to Senator A. A. Sargent of California, Shufeldt declared that the United States should seek alternatives in the East; we should stop basing our policy on friendly relations with China because "all martial spirit" had died out in the Chinese — and besides the Chinese detested America. "Under these circumstances, portrayed without prejudice, even without sentiment, I am of the earnest conviction that the policy of the United States in China, and towards the Chinese in America, should be with us as with them — *purely selfish* — coming as it ought to, under the universal law of right and justice, but by no means governed by the fallacious idea of international friendship, or even the broader ground of a common brotherhood."[2] The Senator indiscreetly gave the Shufeldt letter to the newspapers, it was widely reprinted in the United States and Asia, and created a considerable, but temporary, stir.

A few years later, in 1885, the Reverend Josiah Strong anticipated Mahan with a widely read book titled *Our Country*. It is rarely recalled in the histories of that period but had a tremendous impact among ordinary people as Mahan was to have among men of high office, power and influence. Strong was Mahan in cruder popular form. He had been general secretary of the Evangelical Alliance for the United States and was now the pastor of the Central Congregational Church of Cincinnati. Asked to expand a pamphlet which promoted home missions, Strong inserted his own ideas and made a sizable book out of it. In five years *Our Country* sold 146,000 copies, which in today's terms would be a sale of half a million (more, that is, than the hard-cover sale of *Valley of the Dolls*).

Strong called for the forcible "evangelization" of the world by the Anglo-Saxon race, the only one he deemed fit to rule because of its moral superiority. He was outspokenly anti-Catholic, anti-Mormon, anti-immigrant and anti-Socialist. The fair-haired blue-eyed Protestant was his ideal. Even the isolationist heartland, the corn and wheat plains of the Middle West, warmed to his argument that "the highest Christian civilization" was destined to rule the benighted races.

To the English and American people, he emphasized, "we must look for the evangelization of the world . . . The Anglo-Saxon, as the great representative of these two ideas [the cultivation of civil liberties and 'spiritual Christianity'], is divinely commissioned to be, in a peculiar sense, his brother's keeper . . .

"It seems to me that God, with infinite wisdom and skill is training the Anglo-Saxon race for an hour sure to come . . . This powerful race will move down upon Mexico, down upon Central America and South America, out upon the islands of the sea, over upon Africa and beyond . . .

"God has two hands. Not only is he preparing our civilization the die with which to stamp the nations . . . he is preparing mankind to receive our impress."[3]

Strong became the intellectual hero of the church suppers and brought out a sequel titled *Expansion Under World Conditions,* which proclaimed: "We have already crossed the Rubicon that bounded our insularity." His career certainly did not suffer from his advocacy of using the Cross as a shield for annexing territories overseas, and he became a founder and moving spirit of the Federal Council of Churches of Christ in America and of the American Institute for Social Service. Nor was he condemned for declaring that the protection of American investments abroad called for the sternest measures. We have the moral right to impose ourselves on people less civilized than ourselves and uplift them, even against their wishes, as he asserted in his sequel. "The popular notion in this country that there can be no rightful government of a people without their consent," he baldly stated, "was formed when conditions were radically different, and peoples could live separate lives."[4]

Equally apocalyptic visions were summoned up in the writings of Brooks Adams, of the fourth generation of that notable family (he and his brother Henry were the grandsons of John Quincy Adams, the sons of Charles Francis Adams, the Civil War diplomat). Adams, as his biographer Arthur F. Beringause has written, became one of the "three musketeers in a world of perpetual war," the other two being Theodore Roosevelt and Henry Cabot Lodge. In *The Law of Civilization and Decay: An Essay in History* (1895) and *The New Empire* (1902), he propounded a historical "law" which tended to justify American expansion. Society, he held, "oscillated between barbarism and civilization, or, what amounts to the same thing, in its movement from a condition of physical dispersion to one of concentration." When a people became concentrated, as was happening in the United States with the passing of the frontier, it was governed by greed rather than fear and its energies came under the control of the "economic man," the banker. Energy declines, the arts deteriorate, and the people lose the vital force they need to maintain themselves in a world full of other races possessed of a barbaric vitality. For Americans this meant that a substitute for the frontier must be found to keep their martial spirit alive. America must become more centralized, with an aggressive leader in the White House. The United States must gain control of Asia, and make it serve as the American West of the future.

Both Strong and Adams recognized that Americans are the most restless people since the Phoenicians, and like other conservative intellectuals of the day evidently feared the time when they might start looking inward. They were counterrevolutionaries, in a sense, reacting against a revolution which had not yet occurred.

1. *The Thinking Man's Sailor*

To provide the strategic foundation for the New Navy, the government established a Naval War College at Newport in 1884. Its purpose was to provide naval officers with a postgraduate education in history, international law, tactics and the growingly complex fields of the naval art and science. As it turned out, the college served as the seedbed for what two naval historians have called "the far-reaching consequences that were to follow within a very short time."[5] These were embodied in the grave figure of Alfred Thayer Mahan, then forty-four years old, who was appointed the lecturer on naval history and tactics.

He was a tall, thin man with a long face, pale blue eyes set close together, a full beard and a high bald crown; very reserved, reticent and retiring, but occasionally capable of showing his temper by roaring out in what his wife called his "quarter-deck voice." One of his Annapolis classmates said Mahan was "the most intellectual man I have ever known." Undoubtedly he had always been an oddity in a service more notable for its thundering extroverts than for quiet reflective men.

Mahan was born September 27, 1840, on the West Point military reservation, where his father was professor of engineering. His father was the son of Irish Catholic immigrants, his mother of French and English descent. Though more Irish than anything else, Mahan considered himself to be English by temperament — and undoubtedly was. "I have none of the gregariousness of either the French or the Irish; and while I have no difficulty in entering into civil conversation with a stranger who addresses me, I rarely begin, having, upon the whole, a preference for an introduction."[6] He was educated at Columbia University and then at the Naval Academy. A rather priggish ensign, he joined the navy just before the Civil War and was assigned to serve on the steam corvette *Pocahontas* with smooth-bore guns on which "we looked with more curiosity than confidence." The corvette was employed on blockade duty along the Southeast coast. In 1867 he sailed with the *Iroquois,* a steam-driven vessel with auxiliary sails, to the China station.

He looked upon the Chinese and Japanese, as glimpsed in their port cities, with interest but without condescension. He would always remember "a party of two-sworded men," members of a faction which had lost out in a political uprising, to whom the *Iroquois* gave sanctuary while anchored at Osaka: "the poor fellows presented a moving picture of human misery, and certainly were under a heavy accumulation of misfortunes: a lost battle, and probably a lost cause; flying for life, and now on an element totally new; surrounded by those who could not speak their language."[7]

His service on the China station was as uneventful as duty during the wartime blockade. It would be hard to imagine anyone who served so long in the navy with so little excitement. On his return home, he was promoted to command rank but "the naval stagnation of that period was something now almost incredible." He deplored the "paralysis of idea, of mental development."[8]

It was time, he believed, for the country to rid itself of ideas dating back to 1812. "One was that commerce-destroying was the great efficient weapon of naval warfare . . . From that erroneous premise was deduced the conclusion of a navy of cruisers, and small cruisers at that; no battleship nor fleets. Then we wanted a navy for coast defence only, no aggressive action in our pious souls; an amusing instance being that our first battleships were styled 'coast defence' battleships, a nomenclature which probably facilitated the appropriations." Subsequently Mahan commanded the *Wachusetts,* part of a squadron based on the Pacific coast, and was dismayed at the lack of readiness for any serious business. The ships needed practice in working together, supporting each other, as they would in battle. Instead the *Wachusetts* and the rest of the squadron "all went out together, performed three or four simple evolutions, and then scattered. This was the only fleet drill we had in the two years, 1883–1885."[9]

Captain Mahan was exhilarated by news of the establishment of a Naval War College because it would provide for "the proper consideration and expert decision of strictly military questions, from the point of view of military experience and professional understanding," and for the study of "particular theaters of possible war in which the nation may be interested." He was even more pleased by news of his appointment to its faculty, largely because he had published a book on Civil War blockading, *The Gulf and Inland Waters.*

There were many who believed the naval school at Newport was a waste of time. He recalled a New York newspaperman who visited the installation "with all that magisterial condescension which the environment of the Fourth Estate nourishes in its fortunate members." Mahan had a map of the battle of Trafalgar hanging on the wall of his office. " 'Ah,' he said, with superb up-to-date pity, 'you are still talking about Trafalgar;' and I could see that Trafalgar and I were thenceforth on the top shelf of fossils in the collections of his memory." And a senior officer told him, "You won't find much to say about history."

His theory of the relation of seapower to history began to evolve, he said, from the recollection of reading Memmsen's *History of Rome.* "It suddenly struck me . . . how different things might have been could Hannibal have invaded Italy by sea, as the Romans often had Africa, instead of by the long land route; or could he, after arrival, have been in free communication with Carthage by water." An evaluation of the naval impact on history would have to be made from scratch. "There could scarcely be said to exist any systematic treatment, or extensive commentary by acknowledged experts, such as for generations had illuminated the theory of land warfare." He vowed to make his students realize what they were likely to overlook in their preoccupation with glory, blood and honors — that "War is not fighting, but business."[10]

The naval officers marked for future high command would be instilled with his pragmatic view of sea-fighting; his "self-assigned task," he said, was to "show how control of the sea, commercial and military, had been an object powerful to influence the policies of nations; and equally a mighty factor in the success or failure of those policies."[11]

His lectures soon were attracting attention not only within the navy but in the higher reaches of the government and among the country's opinion-makers. Expansionist politicians — growing in number and confidence — saw his lectures as providing a basis for their ambitions. Rising young Republicans like Henry Cabot Lodge and Theodore Roosevelt quickly adopted him as the prophet of a bigger navy and a revitalized imperialism. His ideas infected such relative innocents as John LaFarge, the artist friend of Lodge and Henry Adams, who would write during a sojourn in the South Seas: "I am impressed by the force that Americans could have for good, and by the careful calculation on the part of those who know us best, the Germans and the English, upon our weakness of action and irresponsibility, and our not knowing our enormous powers. The Pacific should be ours, and it must be."[12]

As a mark of his rising influence, Mahan was appointed president of the Naval War College when Admiral Stephen B. Luce was detached to take command of the North Atlantic Squadron. On parting, Admiral Luce warned him that "the College had many enemies and few friends." In 1887 it was threatened with the loss of its appropriation, and Mahan went to Washington to plead with the chairman of the House Naval Committee, who "set his teeth and compressed his lips" whenever Mahan appeared. "His argument was: Once establish an institution, and it grows; more and more every year. There must be economy . . . In vain did I try to divert his thoughts to the magnificent endings that would come from the paltry ten thousand the College asked. He stopped his ears, and kept his eyes fixed on the necessity of strangling vipers in their cradle." The college "lived from hand to mouth" for a year until it was decently funded. It did not come into its own, however, until Cleveland left office and President Benjamin Harrison almost immediately pushed through an appropriation for one hundred thousand dollars.

By then Mahan had decided to publish his lectures under the title of *The Influence of Sea Power on History,* but it took him three years to find a publisher. Little, Brown of Boston brought the book out in 1890. The reviews, he said, were "much more explicit and hearty in Europe," and especially in Great Britain, than in the United States; but its impact among Americans who counted, whether or not they wrote book reviews, was tremendous. Theodore Roosevelt wrote him that it would become "a naval classic." The *Forum* and *Atlantic Monthly* invited him to become a regular contributor. Harvard and Yale both made him a Doctor of Letters.

In *The Influence of Sea Power on History,* Mahan announced with a tremendous air of discovery that naval force was the crucial factor in achieving and maintaining a nation's supremacy. His study of military, commercial and diplomatic history of the seventeenth and eighteenth centuries convinced him that no nation could expand and prosper without a first-rate naval arm and a strong merchant marine. No nation could be strong without extensive foreign trade. It could not carry on such trade without its own merchant shipping. Because it would lose much of the profit if its products were consigned to foreign vessels, it was the "wish of every nation" to "confine this business to its own vessels."

Out of a wide-ranging merchant marine grew the necessity for whatever protection the government could afford it. Overseas trading firms needed secure ports in which to operate, which in turn required colonies on foreign soil. Their routes to those colonies must also be secure, which necessitated a strong navy. And the colonies, of course, provided secure bases from which the navy could operate.

He stressed the necessity for a large merchant fleet, a seafaring tradition to provide its manpower and maritime industries to support it, as "a shield of defensive power" behind which the nation could buy the time to "develop its reserve of strength." The combined maritime interests would also exert the necessary political pressure to keep the navy strong and efficient.

The United States was not yet a real maritime nation with the requisite overseas colonies, so its policy for the moment must be to insure neutral shipping access to our ports if we should be involved in a war. We must be able to prevent a blockade of our coasts such as the Union had applied to the Confederacy. Thus we needed high-seas squadrons to confront such an enemy blockading force far from our shores.

The United States accordingly must begin building capital ships, not merely cruisers designed to raid the enemy's commercial shipping, which was a "secondary operation." Battleships were needed to defend a wide area of the seas surrounding us. Discreetly enough, he emphasized the defensive role of the battleship, though its main role would be offensive. The battleships we built, obeying the law according to Mahan, thundered in Santiago Bay and off Manila, not in defense of the American coastline.[13]

There were some Americans, of course, who saw through the fabric of Mahan's argument that we needed a new naval doctrine, and the big-gunned ships to apply it, as an instrument of the reawakened national urge to acquire new territory in the Pacific. The inveterate anti-imperialist Carl Schurz obviously had Mahan in mind when he condemned "naval officers and others who advocate a large increase of our war fleet to support a vigorous foreign policy, and a vigorous foreign policy to give congenial occupation and to secure further increase to our war fleet."[14]

The idea that the United States should build capital ships and form them into far-ranging fleets was a wrenching experience for all but the New Navy advocates, the steel interests, the Roosevelt-Lodge group and other select circles. Until now — despite certain adventures in far parts of the world — Americans believed they were the most peaceful of nations, that they could maintain themselves and prosper without aggression, that they should serve as a model of the powerful but peace-loving republic for the less enlightened nations in Europe and elsewhere. Yet there was no great debate over Mahan's proposals. They probably reached a far smaller — but undoubtedly more influential — section of the public than the Reverend Josiah Strong's more inflammatory works. The Mahan book was something to be puzzled out by the elite. Its implications took time to sink in. A commentator who signed himself Nauticus observed that the world had been influenced by oxygen through the ages without understanding its properties until Priestley published his findings; similarly the historical impact of sea power had not been realized until Mahan demonstrated it.[15]

Mahan's influence swelled in proportion to his fame. His prestige increased in America as it became known that he was regarded as a prophet abroad, that his book was being studied by Kaiser Wilhelm of Germany, about to embark on a naval construction program himself; by Admiral Togo of Japan; by Lord Charles Beresford of England. It was quickly translated into French, German, Japanese, Russian, Spanish and Italian, and placed on the required-reading list of foreign naval academies.

2. *The Influence of Mahan Upon Sea Power*

The rise of Mahan's influence coincided with a favorable atmosphere in Washington, with the expansionist tendencies of the Harrison Administration, and a naval rebuilding program that had been started early in the 1880's as the need for replacing the surviving Civil War hulks became imperative.

Mahan's doctrine became a sort of foundation stone slipped in after rebuilding had begun. It provided the ideological basis for a report by Secretary of the Navy Benjamin F. Tracy, a forceful New Yorker who believed wholeheartedly in the necessity for rearming our sea power.

Echoing Mahan, Secretary Tracy declared that even a defensive naval policy required a "fighting force." Unarmored cruisers were capable only of raiding the enemy's commerce, he emphasized in his annual report. They could not "prevent a fleet of ironclads from shelling our cities." Steel-plated battleships were needed to "beat off the enemy's fleet on its approach." Our own forces must be able to deflect an enemy fleet from our coast "by threatening his own, for a war, though defensive in principle, may be conducted most effectively by being offensive in its operations." All these ideas, obviously, were cribbed from Mahan's book.

The Secretary of the Navy astounded Congress by making a series of breathtaking proposals. The United States, he said, should immediately begin building twenty battleships and sixty fast cruisers. Twelve of the battleships would be assigned to an Atlantic Fleet, eight to a Pacific Fleet. Both battleships and cruisers should be capable of "uniformly high speed" and "should equal the best in armament, armor, structural strength." In addition to the high-seas fleets, Tracy said, we must build "floating fortresses," at least twenty vessels for defending our coasts and harbors "with a powerful battery and the heaviest armor, combined with moderate draft." They would be "necessary components of a naval force which has a sea-coast to defend." The recommendation that a fleet of "floating fortresses" be built was more a political gesture, benefiting congressmen from seaboard states, than a naval requirement. It had not been recommended by Mahan, for the coast-defense vessels were actually the old unseaworthy, unwieldy monitors of Civil War fame. In any event, that part of the program was abandoned before any new monitors were built.[16]

Shortly after Tracy's report to Congress came an even more revolutionary document issued by the Navy Policy Board, which took national policy one large step farther: given a big navy, we should employ it with imperial energy. The board had been appointed by Tracy to recommend a new course of action, and it responded with a fervor that caused a backlash of congressional and public opinion.

The policy board's report conceded that there were few present dangers on the international horizon, that Great Britain had the only navy capable of posing a threat and that such an eventuality was unlikely. The chances of our becoming involved in a war appeared to be "at a minimum." Nevertheless, the board recommended that not eighty, but two hundred new warships of all classes be built immediately. The reason: we were entering an era of "commercial competition," this was certain to "reach out and obstruct the interests of foreign nations," and the building of a Panama Canal in the foreseeable future might be "a fruitful source of danger."

To keep such dangers from our shores, the board insisted on the need for a battleship fleet with a cruising range of fifteen thousand miles and the capability of staying at sea "during a long period." It must also be capable of "attacking points on the other side" of the oceans.[17]

This was the pedantically phrased Mahan doctrine taken off the book pages and given menacing substance. A discussion of history had been converted into a seascape of immense steel ships with their turrets delivering shells in thundering salvoes. Congress was taken aback by the vision summoned up by the Navy Policy Board. Secretary of the Navy Tracy disavowed it. Senator Eugene Hale of Maine, a Republican and the second-ranking member of the Naval Affairs Committee, declared it would be difficult to find one Senator or any "responsible government official" willing to endorse its conclusions. Even James Gordon Bennett, Jr.'s imperialist, navy-minded New York *Herald* balked at the report as "naval fanaticism" and predicted that it would "meet with slender approval unless the spirit and temper of the American people have suddenly and radically changed."[18]

Despite the initial outcry and the scores of petitions which deplored the report and were forwarded to Congress, the House Naval Affairs Committee approved the recommendation that battle fleets be formed to establish American naval supremacy in the western Atlantic, the Caribbean and the eastern Pacific. For openers, the committee appropriated funds for the construction of three battleships "designed to carry the heaviest armor and most powerful ordnance upon a displacement of about 8,500 tons, with a coal endurance of about 5,000 knots." They would constitute, according to Representative Charles A. Boutelle, chairman of the committee, "a squadron of defense that will be able to protect our own country from any assault that may be made by sea, but he added significantly that they must be "fighting ships."[19]

There was a continuing play on words — talk of "defensive" purposes coupled with a more menacing emphasis on aggressive characteristics. During the congressional debate on his appropriations bill, Representative Boutelle declared that the new battleships were designed not only to break a blockade of our ports but to "seize and hold those bases of supply in the immediate vicinity of the American coast" which would be "absolutely essential to the safety of our coast line." That sounded like possible aggression in the Caribbean but no one challenged Boutelle on the point. Congress finally approved the construction program, the Senate by 33 to 18, the House by 131 to 105. The *Congressional Record* indicates that most members believed they were voting for heavy ships which would provide a strictly coastal defense.

The American "temper" did change, and rather quickly, by becoming navy-minded to a degree even the New York *Herald* did not anticipate. The United States Navy's exhibition at the World's Fair in Chicago in 1893 was one of the most popular, particularly a newly developed "dynamite gun." This new terror weapon, which in practice turned out to be less formidable than its inventor hoped, was a sort of mortar which hurled a half-ton package of dynamite at its target (but without any great accuracy). A little later in the summer a navy review was held in New York and was so enthusiastically cheered that the *Herald* reported "it was a sight to stir men's souls, to send the blood tingling through their veins." Naval officers declared they were more popular with the public than at any time since the Civil War, and a certain amount of glamour began attaching itself to Annapolis and other naval institutions. Americans were becoming fascinated by the concept of naval power forwarded by giant steel ships, by the destruction that could be unleashed from rows of turreted guns. And when the depression that began in 1893 deepened, the boom in naval construction was seen as a source of thousands of jobs for the unemployed.

Within a few years the first results of Captain Mahan's historic speculations began sliding down the ways of Eastern shipyards — and they were somewhat more formidable than Congress had imagined. First into the water were three battleships, the *Oregon,* the *Indiana* and the *Massachusetts,* with a fourth, the *Iowa,* following in two years. They were ten-thousand-ton ships with an average speed of fifteen knots, a cruising radius of five thousand miles, each with four thirteen-inch guns and eight eight-inch guns. They were armored and gunned to match anything they might meet in battle. A British naval observer who witnessed the sea trials of the *Indiana* and the *Iowa* reported to the admiralty that they were equal to the new battleships of Britain's "Majestic" class, which displaced fifteen thousand tons and carried four twelve-inch and twelve six-inch guns.

Mahan continued to expound his theories and exerted an expanding influence on public opinion. When the question of annexing Hawaii arose, he plunged into the debate immediately in a letter to the New York *Times.* Hawaii must serve as an outpost of American civilization against the dangers presented by China. "It is sufficiently known," he wrote, "but not, perhaps, generally noted in our country, that many military men abroad, familiar with Eastern conditions and character, look with apprehension toward the day when the vast mass of China — now inert — may yield to one of those impulses which have in past ages buried civilization under a wave of barbaric invasion." In that event we would need European allies and "nothing more disastrous for the future of the world can be imagined than that general disarmament of Europe which is the Utopian dream of some philanthropists." To check any future Chinese aggression, he added, "a great, civilized, maritime power" must hold the Hawaiian islands."[20]

In a subsequent magazine article he developed his argument for annexation. Its essence was the strategic location of the Hawaiian Islands: "they form the centre of a large circle whose radius is approximately — and very closely — the distance from Honolulu to San Francisco. The circumference of this circle . . . will be seen, on the west and south, to pass through the outer fringe of the system of archipelagoes which, from Australia and New Zealand, extend to the northeast toward the American continent . . . To have a central position such as this, and to be alone, having no rival and admitting no alternative throughout an extensive tract, are conditions that at once fix the attention of the strategist." On the other hand, there would be an "immense disadvantage to us of any maritime enemy having a coaling station well within 2,500 miles." Admittedly to annex Hawaii and establish a base there would mean "a great extension of our naval power."[21]

Thus Mahan was the first to suggest the imminent presence of what would later be called the Yellow Peril, a resurgent China which one of his military idols, Napoleon, had warned against stirring into wakefulness. In the series of magazine articles he wrote during the Nineties he would also point to America's "broadening horizons." One of the key requirements of her position, not only to fend off possible "barbaric invasions" but to expand our commercial opportunities, was the construction of an isthmanian canal. It would "enable the Atlantic coast to compete with Europe, on equal terms as to distance, for the markets of eastern Asia." It would also "bring our Pacific coast nearer . . . to the great navies of Europe." Naturally that meant we would have to increase our naval strength to offset the possibility of European encroachment. "Except to those optimists whose robust faith in the regeneration of human nature rejects war as an impossible contingency, this consideration must occasion serious thought concerning the policy to be adopted by the United States."

We had to keep in mind that Britain had recently seized the Mosquito Coast of Nicaragua, possibly to build her own canal from Atlantic to Pacific. European powers were supreme in the Caribbean, but the United States had to start thinking about establishing its own presence in that area. Americans must realize that we had three seaboards, that communication between them would depend on "a strategic position hundreds of miles distant from our nearest post, the mouth of the Mississippi," and that coastal defense "has its application at points far away from our own coast."[22]

3. *The Prophet Honored*

Much against his will, Mahan was posted for sea duty late in 1892. He preferred lecturing, writing and brooding over strategy to commanding a ship, but even the navy's resident intellectual wasn't exempt from the alternations of ship and shore duty. A friend of Mahan's tried to arrange for a delay, but the new chief of the Bureau of Navigation — then the operating head of the navy — was unimpressed by Mahan's reputation and snorted, "It is not the business of a naval officer to write books." Furthermore the atmosphere in Washington had cooled again, temporarily, with the return of Cleveland to the White House.

Mahan was ordered to take command of the *Chicago,* the flagship of the European Station. He hoped to be able to find time to work on his writing at night but "Neither a ship nor a book is patient of a rival, and I soon ceased the effort to serve both." His service in Europe resulted in unusual honors for an American naval officer, so high was his standing with the British establishment. Queen Victoria invited him to Osborne for a dinner and he was the first foreigner to be guest of honor at the Royal Yacht Club, where he dined with a hundred admirals and captains. The prime minister, Lord Rosebery, invited him to dinner with John Morley the only other guest, and the three men talked until midnight. The queen invited him back for dinner at Buckingham Palace. Oxford and Cambridge conferred degrees on him, both in the same week, which was also said to be an unprecedented honor, and he had the grace to record his embarrassment at walking down the High Street, Oxford, on his way to the ceremony, with a red silk academic gown billowing over epaulettes, sword and "railroad" trousers. He maintained his composure when an irreverent Oxonian called down from the gallery, "Why don't you have your hair cut?" which Mahan took to be a "delicate allusion to my somewhat unparalleled baldness."

Mahan was also lionized by Kaiser Wilhelm, who invited him to dine aboard the royal yacht during Cowes Week. The German emperor, with devastating effects on European history, had been inspired to undertake the reconstruction of the German navy, with the aim of equaling the naval strength of the British, by his reading of Mahan's most celebrated book. The Kaiser, in fact, had been so overwhelmed by Mahan's doctrine — that no nation can be supremely powerful without a large navy — that he made it required reading for all his naval officers. Later Wilhelm telegraphed a friend that he was learning Mahan's book by heart. "It is a first-class book and classical in all points. It is on board all my ships and constantly quoted by my captains and officers."[23]

But while Mahan was being laden with honors and buttered by royalty, there were men in the United States who feared the consequences of what Mahan had wrought. The battleships were coming down the ways, and there was a spirit of "ferocious optimism," as E. L. Godkin called it, in the American atmosphere. Godkin, the champion of social and political reform as editor of the New York *Evening Post,* wrote a friend that the United States was becoming conscious of the "possession of enormous power and is eager to use it in brutal fashion against anyone who comes along without knowing how to do so and is therefore constantly on the brink of some frightful catastrophe." About the same time William James, then professor of philosophy at Harvard, was warning that once the American fighting spirit was aroused "there is no retreat."[24]

Mahan would have considered such premonitions unworthy of a great and powerful nation. More and more he was convinced that North America and Europe within decades would be engaged in a struggle for survival against the hordes of a reborn Asia.

Despite our rivalry with Great Britain, he believed the time had come to consider how she and the United States could jointly protect civilization. The maritime competition between the two was not a bad thing in itself. It led to the strengthening of both. He would not endanger the natural "working of kinship" between Americans and Britons by "premature striving for alliance, an artificial and possibly even an irritating method of reaching the desired end."

The British, he continued, would come to see the advantages of a close working relationship with the United States. In that article published in 1894, he foresaw the possibility that the British empire would disintegrate. "Disunion, loss of national identity, changes of constitution more than radical, the exchange of a world-wide empire for a subordinate part in the great federation — such *may* be the destiny of Great Britain in the distant future. I know not; but sure I am, were I a citizen of Great Britain, the prospect would not allure me an inch in such a direction."

An amalgamation between Britain and America must not be "forced," he emphasized. "The ground is not prepared yet in the hearts and understandings of Americans, and I doubt whether in those of British citizens . . . The difficulty is that the United States, as a nation, does not realize or admit as yet that it has any strong interest in the sea; and that the great majority of our people rest firmly in a belief, deep rooted in the political history of our past, that our ambition should be limited by the three seas that wash our eastern, western and southern coasts."[25]

He deplored what he called "our modern gods" — "ease unbroken, trade uninterrupted, all roughness removed from life." Such totems would not long protect us against "the vast outside masses of aliens to our civilization, now powerless because we still, with a higher material development, retain the masculine combative virtues." The continuing rivalry of the Western nations was good because it resulted in "the preservation of the martial spirit, which alone is capable of coping finally with the destructive forces that from outside and from within threaten to submerge all the centuries have gained."

America, he concluded, must forget past warnings against entanglement in European affairs because "now to take her share of the travail of Europe is but to assume an inevitable task, and appointed lot, in the work of upholding the common interests of civilization."

He wrote an introduction to the Reverend Josiah Strong's second book (*Expansion Under World Conditions*), approving Strong's prescription of strong medicine for "backward" nations, but in his own writings he was more discreet. Thus in an article published in 1895: "The inalienable rights of the individual are entitled to a respect which they unfortunately do not always get; but there is no inalienable right in any community to control the use of a region when it does so to the detriment of the world at large." Writing at the close of the Sino-Japanese War, he pointed with alarm at the "appearance of Japan as a strong ambitious state" as a "striking illustration of the somewhat sudden nearness and unforeseen relations into which modern states are brought"; and to the fact that the Hawaiian Islands were "occupied largely by Japanese and Chinese." America must keep encroaching races from her sea frontiers because "More and more civilized man is needing and seeking ground to occupy, room over which to expand and in which to live."[26]

In 1897, when most Americans were engrossed in the possibilities of war with Spain over Cuba, Mahan was looking ahead, with increasing concern, to a clash between the Western and Eastern civilizations. In a magazine article titled "A Twentieth Century Outlook," which was included in his book *The Interest of America in Sea Power,* he tried to foresee the future relations of a complacent West and a restive East. He was filled with foreboding about the renascent power of the Asian millions, which he regarded as a threat to Europe and America unless they were inculcated with Western values and rendered passive by acceptance of Christianity.

Mahan was depressed by the fact that Americans, "under the specious plea of peace and plenty," were hugging "an ideal of isolation" and refusing to "recognize the solidarity of interest" with European nations, so that together they could "go out to meet the future that . . . seems to await" them.

The quickening development of Asia from India to Japan brought forth his grimmest prophecies. Japan's rise was the most "astonishing," but India was also showing signs of "the awaking of political intelligence, restlessness under foreign subjection," and the "immense latent force of the Chinese character" was the most alarming of all. China, in fact, was his overriding obsession. Most Westerners had written her off, but Mahan was convinced of her tremendous potential.

"The collapse of the Chinese organization in all its branches during the late war with Japan," he wrote, "though greater than was expected, was not unforeseen. It has not altered the fact that the raw material so miserably utilized is, in point of strength, of the best; that it is abundant, racially homogenous, and is multiplying rapidly." It was far easier for the Japanese to "move and control an island kingdom of forty millions than a vast continental kingdom containing near tenfold that number of inhabitants." The Chinese might evolve more slowly but "that which for so long has kept China one, amid many diversities, may be counted upon in the future to insure a substantial unity of impulse which, combined with its mass, will give tremendous import to any movement common to the whole."

He was pessimistic about the possibility of Christianizing the East, of persuading it to accept Western morality as well as Western technology. "It is to be feared that Eastern thinkers consider it rather an advantage than a detriment that they are appropriating the material progress of Europe unfettered by Christian traditions — as agnostic countries. But, for the present at least, agnosticism with Christian ages behind it is a very different thing from agnosticism which has never known Christianity." The fact many were convinced Christianity was losing its grip on the West itself only reinforced the necessity for confronting the East in armed array. "If we have no higher sanction to propose for self-restraint and righteousness than enlightened self-interest and the absurdity of war, war — violence — will be absurd just so long as the balance of interest is on that side, and no longer. Those who want will take, if they can, not merely from motives of high policy and as legal opportunity offers, but for the simple reason that they have not, that they desire, and that they are able." The Eastern world was "rapidly appreciating the material advantages and the political traditions which have united to confer power upon the West; and with the appreciation desire has risen."

To counteract that "desire," Mahan stressed, the "great mission" of the West must be to "receive into its own bosom and raise to its own ideals those ancient and different civilizations by which it is surrounded and outnumbered . . . The history of the present century has been that of a constant increasing pressure of our own civilization upon these older ones, till now, as we cast our eyes in any direction, there is everywhere a stirring, a rousing from sleep, drowsy for the most part, but real, unorganized as yet, but conscious that that which rudely interrupts their dream of centuries possesses over them at least two advantages — power and material prosperity — the things which unspiritual humanity, the world over, most craves." The West must buy time by "force potential and force organized."

A semi-westernized East was more dangerous to the West than the formerly non-westernized East. Completing the westernization would need more time and effort than Mahan believed were available. We must guarantee that "generations" would elapse before "the barriers can be overcome behind which rests the citadel of Christian civilization." During that interval "force must be ready to redress any threatened disturbance of an equal balance between those who stand on divergent planes of thought, without common standards."

He despaired almost as much over the prospective decline of militant religious feeling in the West as the outside threat from the East. What good were battleships without righteousness, without a belief in Christian destiny? If the West was becoming irreligious, "a thing limited in hope and love to this world," he wondered "what we have to offer to save ourselves or others." He tried valiantly to reconcile his own religious feeling with what he regarded as an imperative duty to arm against the nonbelievers of the East. Anyone who believed that "God has made of one blood all nations of men" must repress feelings of hatred for men of other races. "But it is not necessary to hate Carthage," he added, "in order to admit that it was well for mankind that Rome triumphed."

It was the force of envy he feared would rise in the East and send her marching or sailing against the West. Less than a hundred years ago Americans had thought of the Orient as a treasure-house waiting to be entered and ransacked. Now Americans like Mahan saw that the industrial nations — possessing the ability to turn naval cannon on their lathes, for instance, instead of handcrafting silk screens and porcelain bowls — had become the grimy, utilitarian objects of envy.

"But men do not covet less the prosperity which they themselves cannot or do not create," he pointed out, "a trait wherein lies the strength of Communism as an aggressive social force. . . . Communities which want and cannot have, except by force, will take by force, unless they are restrained by force."

Our only hope of prevailing against the force of envy, the "flood of numbers," was to preserve the "proud combative spirit" and "warlike habits."[27]

It was oddly significant, perhaps, that nowhere in the hundreds of book and magazine pages Mahan covered with his words may the term imperialism be found. He was a master of the clotted euphemism: "outward impulses" was a favorite. And in this he displayed a shrewd understanding of the temper of his time. Many, perhaps most Americans wanted to see their country expand, acquire outposts, dominate distant seas, but only if it could be accomplished with sanctifying phrases. They wanted the game but not the name. "Liberate" was the code name for "occupy," "pacify" for "conquer." And there was a more old-fashioned but still influential group centered in New England, with its fulcrum located somewhere between the Harvard Yard and Walden Pond, which detested with a Founding Fathers' passion the evils of the European system, militarism, standing armies, far-ranging navies, the trappings of imperialism.

The intellectual descendants of the "old saints" of Boston and Cambridge regarded the rule of non-Americans by American proconsuls as a hideous prospect in any semantic guise. They held to the principle that America must demonstrate a better way of dealing with other nations, whether advanced or benighted. When it was proposed that Mahan and several others be given the rank of admiral — until now commodore had been the highest rank — one such traditionalist snorted, "Call them Admirals? Never! They will be wanting to be Dukes next."[28]

But Mahan did become an admiral if not a duke, and there were few in the New Navy who did not believe he deserved his two stars. Even President Cleveland's Secretary of the Navy, Hilary A. Herbert, was a Mahanite. After reading the gospel according to Mahan, Herbert came out more enthusiastically for capital ships than his Republican predecessor and followed the Mahan line precisely on how the navy would be rebuilt and redeployed.

Contrary as it was to recent Democratic opposition to any form of expansion, Herbert's opinion was that the navy must protect American interests everywhere in the world; it must be the instrument of national policy. "We must make and keep our Navy in such a condition of efficiency as to give weight and power to whatever policy it might be wise on the part

Admiral Alfred T. Mahan: Blueprints for Empire

of our government to assume," he stated in his annual report of 1893. Nor did President Cleveland disavow his last annual report three years later, which charged the navy with the duty to "maintain under all circumstances our national honor." With Cleveland's endorsement, he obtained congressional approval for three more battleships, the *Alabama*, the *Illinois* and the *Wisconsin*, all larger than those built before.

Mahan rendered further service to the naval establishment, and such political supporters as Lodge and Roosevelt, by pointing out the advantages of possessing Cuba in a magazine article published less than a year before that island was invaded. In "The Strategic Features of the Gulf of Mexico and the Caribbean Sea," he emphasized that Cuba would be more valuable to the United States than Jamaica was to Great Britain. "As a base of naval operations, as a source of supplies to a fleet, Cuba presents a condition wholly unique . . . The extent of the coastline, the numerous harbors, and the many directions from which approach can be made, minimize the dangers of total blockade . . . The positional value of Cuba is extremely great." Havana, he pointed out, was to the Caribbean what Gibraltar was to the Mediterranean. The island was also indispensable to defending the approaches to the projected Panama Canal, and it commanded the trade routes to Europe, North and South America.[29]

The war against Spain, spreading from the Caribbean to the Sulu Sea, not only confirmed Mahan's theories of naval warfare but speeded up our development as an imperialist power as advocated and propagandized by Mahan for almost a decade.

He was selected by President McKinley as the watchdog for American military interests at the first Hague Peace Conference in the spring of 1899. The chief of the American delegation to that conference on the possibility of preventing war was Andrew White, the former president of Cornell and presently ambassador to Berlin, who could be expected to represent the idealistic side of the American character while Mahan stood for realism. Considering his views, which had only hardened with the years, Mahan was a curious choice to help in the search for ways of limiting armaments and setting up a system to arbitrate international disputes. During the war with Spain, he had served as a member of the Naval War Board and behind the scenes had urged on the occupation of Cuba and Philippines as one of the most vociferous of the war hawks. Furthermore he had come to believe that an occasional war served as a tonic to the national character; that any form of pacifism was a deadly disease to the nation it afflicted. Modern war, he said, had acquired the "character of an occasional excess, from which recovery is easy," a statement confounded by the war which broke out in the year of his death and from which the world would never entirely recover.

Undoubtedly he would privately have echoed what the great German historian Mommsen, whose works in part had inspired his own, said in public about the conference at The Hague: "a printer's error in the history of the world." He sat in on the deliberations of the Commission on Armaments, at which the question of limitation on naval construction was the chief topic. Britain was pressing for naval limitation because she ruled the seas and hoped that German ambitions in that area could be tamped down. Mahan torpedoed the cause of naval limitation by informing the British that his government wouldn't even discuss the question. In view of the coming struggle for Far Eastern markets, he said, the United States would be undertaking a "very considerable" increase in its Pacific naval forces.

As for any American participation in arbitration schemes, Mahan was violently opposed and declared in a letter to a friend, "No greater misfortune could well happen than that civilized nations should abandon their preparations for war and take to arbitration."[30] Article 27 of the convention finally drawn up by the conference attracted his unqualified opposition. It would have required signatories to remind parties to an international dispute that a tribunal had been set up to arbitrate their grievances. Mahan stormed against that innocuous proposal on the grounds that it committed the United States to interfere in European affairs, and vice versa. The American delegation signed the convention only after a qualifying phrase had been inserted, at Mahan's insistence, in which the United States disclaimed any intention of becoming involved in European political disputes of any sort.

Until his life ended in 1914, Mahan continued to expound on his favorite themes, that an "honest collision" between nations — war — was an element of the "law of progress," that the United States must learn to recognize that the "profession of arms" was its "heroic ideal."

Close to the end of his seventy-four years he wrote an epitaph for American innocence, in which he presumably rejoiced: "The jocund youth of our people now passes away never to return; the cares and anxieties of manhood's years henceforth are ours."[31]

The schoolmasterly admiral, as the real architect of the New Navy, as the ideologue of American imperialism, had brought on those burdens as much as any man, perhaps more than any other. His great contribution to America's search for destiny in the Pacific was to make a radical alteration in our course. Until Mahan, we had viewed our role as merely the protector of open trade with the Far East. After Mahan, we looked upon the larger nations of the East as potential enemies, future threats to Western civilization, against whom we must build a remote line of outposts and station our dreadnoughts. He taught us that the best wars are those fought far from our own shores, and that lesson has remained indelible.

III. The Pest of Glory

Hard-headed old Benjamin Franklin hit the point when, referring back to the days of Marlborough, he talked about the "pest of glory." The thirst for glory is an epidemic which robs a people of their judgment, seduces their vanity, cheats them of their interests, and corrupts their consciences.

—WILLIAM GRAHAM SUMNER

10

The Philippine Pivot-Point

There is no gentle way of imposing alien rule upon a people. Nor is there any known race of humans so submissive that it will accept domination by strangers, no matter how piously they present themselves nor how heavily laden they are with gifts. Colonial administration is a history of repression, whether imposed by the Persians, the Romans or their successors in the Western world. The few who succeeded in that difficult art, keeping order without decimating the population, were generally men with equal portions of sternness, fairness and humor. If people must be dominated by foreigners, they like to know where they stand.

The Germans did not distinguish themselves in this field, but they produced one specimen in their short-lived Pacific empire whose name was long and wryly honored. Dr. Wilhelm Solf, the perennial governor of German Samoa, was physically the stereotyped Prussian with his granite face, dueling scar and monocle, but he was supple and scrupulous in his dealings with the Samoans. "Oldtimers in Apia," one South Seas historian has written, "still look back on his regime as a sort of grim Golden Age when, however arbitrary government was, everybody knew just where he stood, or at least could rapidly find out by stepping out of line. Solf did not fool, and knew just how to use the big stick that consisted of the German China Squadron." German plantation owners who tried to interfere with Dr. Solf's administration or stir up trouble among the natives were cooled off peremptorily, and could only protest by writing home and having questions asked in the Reichstag. At one inquiry into his conduct Solf was accused of having gone native, of lolling in a hammock with flowers in his hair. Solf's wordless reply to that charge was to stand at attention, sweep off his hat and display his large bald crown.

An American admirer related that he "did his best to honor German commitments to local politicians and to give the Samoans face-saving nominal participation in government." No one ever suspected him of disbelieving the Pan-German propaganda that the Kaiser was destined to rule the world but his governorship of German Samoa "worked as nothing had worked in Samoa before," and when New Zealand took over the protectorate at the end of World War I she was handicapped by "invidious memories of the great Dr. Solf" and his "grudgingly awarded halo."[1]

In the long American occupation of the Philippines there were few Wilhelm Solfs available to take up what Kipling advised us was the white man's burden. Our attitude was defined by the contrast in the phrase "little brown brothers," used with loving patronization back in the States, with "pockmarked kodiac ladrones," as Filipinos were identified in a song popular with American occupation troops. We seemed unable to strike a just balance between overflowing goodwill and brutal practice. We alternated between philanthropy and genocide, between spoiling them and wiping out whole villages with machine guns and dynamite. At one time we had seventy thousand troops marking paid to their aspirations for independence; a short time later ten thousand young American schoolmarms and experts on sanitation, nutrition, tropical medicine and agriculture were sent to the islands to improve their living conditions and wipe out disease.

Our invasion, liberation, pacification and occupation of the Philippines was a great pivot-point in American history. It signaled our determination to gain and hold supremacy in the Pacific and over as much of Asia as our military power could sustain. The consequences of that move have involved us in three wars so far and promise an unending, possibly unavailing conflict on the Asian littoral. It is the story of our lives. Yet our movement into the Philippines is one of the least understood phases of our history; one of those obscure episodes swept under the rug, for the best of psychological reasons, and forgotten. In the popular mind it survives, if at all, as a dreary sequel to the Spanish-American War.

To have buried the historic incident known as the Philippine Insurrection so deep in our consciousness obviously took an effort of the national will. Our war with Spain is remembered as one of those inexpensive but profitable operations, quickly accomplished with a few naval broadsides and a muralistic cavalry battle (Teddy Roosevelt charging over San Juan Hill and into the White House). Its sequel in Manila Bay is recalled by Commodore Dewey's order to Gridley, and the satisfying spectacle of a Spanish fleet sinking gracefully into the tropical waters.

Underneath those pretty finger paintings is a grimmer picture, which despite the explorations of historical novelists and film-makers in every other field has never been recalled to the popular imagination.* Yet a few facts and statistics will show that the Philippine Insurrection, aside from its impact on our policy in Asia, was no trifling affair to be recalled only in the gold embroidery of regimental streamers. It was a long hard guerrilla conflict, the first of our rice-paddy wars. A quarter of a million American soldiers and Filipino *insurrectos* were killed in the fighting between 1899 and 1902 — and the struggle went on for years, more remotely and obscurely, in the mountain jungles of the southern islands. The Philippines served as our laboratory for the study and practice of military government and colonial administration. Most of our military leaders in the two World Wars were products of that rigorous graduate school. (Generals Pershing, Harbord, Bullard, Billy Mitchell, among others in World War I, Generals MacArthur, Marshall, Eisenhower and Admiral Nimitz in World War II.) The idea that America was confronted with the problem of fighting guerrillas on a large scale for the first time in Southeast Asia is patently ridiculous. We have been fighting guerrillas of all colors and persuasions for more than a century — first the Indians, then various other dissident breeds, including the Haitians before World War I, the Mexicans in 1916 (when the Punitive Expedition into northern Mexico was launched in pursuit of Pancho Villa), and in Nicaragua (1927–1931) during the Sandino revolution. But our open-end conflict against the Filipino insurgents was our proving ground for all that; it went on vigorously until World War I in the Mohammedan territories of the south, and the Moro dissidents were never really conquered. It was one of the most deadly and prolonged wars — though never, of course, dignified under the title of a war — in the annals of empire. It confirmed us, in fact, *as* an empire.

That giant stride into imperialism, following such tentative toddling steps toward annexation in Samoa and Hawaii, was not taken without anguished self-questioning. There were no opinion polls to indicate the sentiments of the people as a whole, but there was a deep division among the political and spiritual opinion-makers in the nation. Protests against the conquest of the Philippines were strenuous and eloquent, enlisting liberal-

* One of the few exceptions was a film titled *The Real Glory,* produced by Samuel Goldwyn thirty-odd years ago, a fairly realistic account of the struggle against the Moros. There have been no important novels using the same background.

humanist figures such as Carl Schurz, Mark Twain and many others to contribute their rhetoric to the debate. Their proclamations echo strangely — and with the same futility — in the protests against the Viet Nam War sixty years later. Against their campaigning in hundreds of newspaper and magazine columns and lecture-platform appearances thundered the voices of expansion: Roosevelt, Lodge, Beveridge and others in high office. The parallels between that debate at the turn of the century and the Viet Nam protests and justifications of the 1960's are strikingly poignant and reflect one overriding circumstance: once a decision is taken by the monolithic United States government it can seldom, if ever, be reversed or even greatly modified by the most brilliantly organized and forcefully expressed opposition.

In all that echoing clamor from the early part of the century, amid all the emotionalism, there was at least one lucid, objective, astringent mind at work; one man capable of seeing what our course in the Pacific meant to us as a people and what its historic consequences would be. He was a crustily conservative Yale University professor named William Graham Sumner, who unlike most conservatives was adamantly opposed to American imperialism, on practical rather than humanist grounds. Sumner is an all but forgotten voice from the nineteenth century, though he coined the phrase "The Forgotten Man" in a different context than that to which it was adapted by President Franklin D. Roosevelt.* Sumner was a professor of political and social science and president of the American Sociological Society whose attitude toward his profession was marked, as a colleague with a gift for understatement noted, by "a certain austerity." He would have been outraged by the development of sociology along the course it has taken, which he apparently foresaw to some extent. "The field of sociology," he said shortly before his death, "is so raw that any crank can fasten on it from any angle."[2]

The Forgotten Man, to whom he referred continually in his essays, was not the slum-dweller but the person who paid the bills for what later sociologists would term the disadvantaged. The Forgotten Man of Sumner's canon was the one who "just when he wants to enjoy the fruits of his care, is told that it is his duty to go and take care of some of his negligent neighbors, or, if he does not go, to pay an inspector to go. No doubt it is often in his interest to go or to send, rather than to have the matter

---

* His common-sense approach to the question of American expansion was recalled, however, by Emmett John Hughes in an article in *Newsweek* magazine, August 21, 1967, which called attention to Sumner as a rational commentator on the events of that era. Mr. Hughes's article began: "The first massive American involvement in Asia came with the war against the Spanish Empire at the end of the nineteenth century. A small band of critics, unpopular but undaunted, assailed the adventure as folly. Among them there was no voice more rousing or relentless than that of William Graham Sumner — one of the nation's most famed teachers and essayists."

neglected, on account of his own connection with the thing neglected and his own secondary peril; but the point now is, that if preaching and philosophizing can do any good in the premises, it is all wrong to preach to the Forgotten Man that it is his duty to go and remedy other people's neglect. It is not his duty. It is a harsh and unjust burden which is laid upon him, and it is only the more unjust because no one thinks of him when laying the burden so that it falls on him. The exhortations ought to be expended on the negligent — that they take care of themselves."

That should serve as Sumner's credentials as a conservative.

Shortly before the Spanish-American War he opposed expansion into the Pacific or elsewhere on the most pragmatic grounds. "Any extension will not make us more secure where we are, but will force us to take new measures to secure our new acquisitions. The preservation of acquisitions will force us to reorganize our internal resources, so as to make it possible to prepare them in advance and to mobilize them with promptitude. This will lessen liberty and require discipline. It will divert the national energy from the provision of self-maintenance and comfort for the people, and will necessitate stronger and more elaborate government machinery. All this will be disastrous to republican institutions and to democracy . . . threatening a new cleavage within. If we had never taken Texas and northern Mexico we should never have had secession. The sum of the matter is that colonization and territorial extension are burdens, not gains."[3]

In an essay sardonically titled "The Conquest of the United States by Spain," written in 1898, he set forth the proposition that "We have beaten Spain in a military conflict, but we are submitting to be conquered by her on the fields of ideas and policies." He developed this theme with his customary unconcealed contempt for popular belief and prejudice. "Expansion and imperialism," he wrote, "are nothing but the old philosophies of national prosperity which have brought Spain to where she is now. Those philosophies appeal to national vanity and national cupidity. . . . They are delusions, and they will lead us to ruin unless we are hard-headed enough to resist them."[4]

He was certain that we would be haunted by the fate of the Spanish empire. "The Americans have been committed from the outset to the doctrine that all men are equal . . . In its absolute form it must, of course, apply to Kanakas, Malays, Tagals, and Chinese just as much as to Yankees, Germans and Irish. It is an astonishing event that we have lived to see American arms carry this domestic dogma out where it must be tested in its application to uncivilized and half-civilized peoples. At the first touch of the test we throw the doctrine away and adopt the Spanish doctrine. We are told by all the imperialists that these people are not fit for liberty and self-government; that it is rebellion for them to resist our beneficence; that we must send fleets and armies to kill them if they do it; that we must devise a government for them and administer it ourselves;

that we may buy them or sell them as we please, and dispose of their 'trade' for our own advantage. What is that but the policy of Spain to her dependencies?"[5]

He attacked the idea, often advanced by the expansionists, that "Americans can do anything." That, he said, was empty boasting. "There are some things that Americans cannot do. Americans cannot make 2 plus 2 equal 5. You may answer that that is an arithmetical impossibility and is not in the range of our subject. Very well; Americans cannot collect two dollars a gallon tax on whisky. They tried it for many years and failed. That is an economic and political impossibility, the roots of which are in human nature. . . . So far as yet appears, Americans cannot govern a city of one hundred thousand inhabitants so as to get comfort and convenience in it at a low cost and without jobbery."[6]

There was something ludicrous to Sumner about the spectacle of acquiring vast new responsibilities when we had not solved long-standing problems of national existence. "Three years ago we were on the verge of a law to keep immigrants out who were not good enough to be in with us. Now we are going to take in eight million [sic] barbarians and semi-barbarians, and we are paying twenty million dollars to get them [the purchase price for the Philippines paid to Spain under the Treaty of Paris]. For thirty years the negro has been in fashion. He has had political value and has been petted. Now we have made friends with the Southerners. They and we are hugging each other. We are all united. The negro's day is over. He is out of fashion. We cannot treat him in one way and the Malays, Tagals, and Kanakas another way . . . So the 'great principles' change all the time; or, what is far more important, the phrases change . . . the phrase-makers are always with us."[7]

It outraged the sensibilities of an old-fashioned American to be pelted with such neo-Napoleonic abstractions as talk of "glory" and "destiny." In his essay "The Predominant Issue," written in 1900, he presented the argument that "expansion may lower national vitality and hasten decay."

There was no glory in subduing poorly armed Filipinos; it was merely a dangerous delusion. "Hard-headed old Benjamin Franklin hit the point when, referring back to the days of Marlborough, he talked about the 'pest of glory.' The thirst for glory is an epidemic which robs a people of their judgment, seduces their vanity, cheats them of their interests, and corrupts their consciences."

He briskly disposed of the arguments of latter-day upholders of Manifest Destiny. Talking about destiny was "empty and silly" and "To invoke it in public affairs is a refusal to think . . . 'Destiny' is a name for the connection which unites the series of consequences upon an act . . . and it is invoked to prevent us from going back to see whether the consequences do not prove that the act was wrong and foolish."

He pointed to the dangers of that sort of illogical thinking, out of which we were entangled in the "risks and obligations" of pacifying and governing new territories. "A new doctrine of constructive obligation has been invented which is false and dangerous. A prominent newspaper recently argued that we are bound to protect the Chinese Christian converts because we allowed missionaries to be sent to China under our protection. This is but a specimen of the way in which false dogmas grow when statesmen begin to act from motives which are entirely foreign to statecraft. The arguments in favor of expansion all have the character of after-thoughts invented to excuse or defend acts which were resolved upon for other reasons."[8]

The United States, he said, was presented with an insoluble dilemma over "whether we shall govern them by our will or let them share in governing themselves and us" — the old vexation of colonialists anywhere. The only democratic approach would be to allow the Filipinos the same representation we fought the British for.

The United States, of course, chose the imperialistic method of ruling the Philippines; there were no Honorable Members of Congress representing the constituencies of Luzon, Samar and Mindanao. The handmaiden of that method, he predicted, would be militarism; the end result would be the garrison state. "The President will not wear a crown, and Congress will not introduce universal military service next winter. Derision of such fears is cheap, since nobody entertains them. In this world it is the little beginnings which tell; it is the first steps at the parting of the ways which are decisive. Militarism is a system. It may go with a small armament, or be absent with a large one, as in England. . . . This is a way of looking at State affairs, and it colors everything else . . . It is entirely opposed to the American temper which has been developed by industrialism and which does not believe in fighting methods."

His parting advice was that we should concentrate on the "development of our own country," instead of carrying our armed evangelism ten thousand miles away. He died in 1909 while the issue was still unresolved. How immeasurably saddened he would have been, since he had little of the vanity of a prophet, to know how his words might ring more than six decades later.

1. *Steps Leading Down*

The germinating point of great events is usually difficult to locate, often concealed by conflicting statements and self-serving evasions. In the case of the Philippine invasion, however, the train of events was set in motion late in December 1897, months before the United States forced a war on Spain. The plans for occupying the archipelago were developed long before the Asiatic Squadron's guns boomed in the bay of Manila.

All this, and much more, was the work of young Theodore Roosevelt, who at last had boosted himself into a position of secondary power from which he could promote the design of American greatness which he and his friend, Senator Lodge of Massachusetts, had perceived in the doctrines of Admiral Mahan. His ferocious energy, his willfulness, his ambitions for himself and his nation all contributed to the makeup of the man who within a few years would, almost singlehandedly, involve us in a war with Spain and the acquisition of an empire, take command of a volunteer cavalry regiment just before the glorious affray on San Juan Hill, and vault himself into the Vice Presidency and then into the White House. No more forceful man has ever attained the presidency. His impact was so stunning that it is still impossible to pass a magisterial opinion on whether his force was expended for the eventual good or ill of his country, but nobody can doubt that he loved her with a violent passion.

The fact that Roosevelt, as Assistant Secretary of the Navy, was able to exert such fateful influence was due in part to the vacuum of power he found in the McKinley Administration. President McKinley himself was immensely good-natured, permissive and lacking in force; a man who allowed himself to be manipulated by events and by other men. In the Navy Department itself, Roosevelt also found a passive, unadventurous atmosphere. His direct superior, John D. Long, was the former governor of Massachusetts, a gentle, scholarly Boston lawyer who seemed an odd choice for Secretary of the Navy. The professional operating head of the navy was Captain A. S. Crowninshield, the chief of the Bureau of Navigation, a cranky old fellow close to retirement who seemed more concerned with matters of rank and bureaucratic protocol than modernizing the navy and whipping it into fighting trim.

With such men to deal with, Roosevelt saw that he would have to take matters into his own hands, despite his sub-Cabinet rank. He gave fair warning of his intentions in an address before the Naval War College in June 1897, several months after assuming his duties. "All the great masterful races," he told the graduating class, "have been fighting races" and never lost their "proud right to stand as the equal of the best." He wanted a great navy, he said, not "primarily to fight, but to avert fighting." If we did not increase our naval power, we would invite aggression by making ourselves "an easy prey for any people which still retains those most valuable of all qualities, the soldierly virtues." Those who wanted peace for this country therefore would be wise to rely on "a first-class fleet of battleships."[9]

Despite Roosevelt's exhortations to President McKinley and Secretary Long, the administration recommended the construction of only one new battleship in that summer preceding the war with Spain. Long pointed out that American naval power had more than doubled in the past few years, and that there were no potential troublemakers on the horizon. His

young assistant, however, was　　　　　at the situation in Cuba would
explode and the United States　　　　　ne. He knew that Cuba would
be easy enough to grab, but wha　　　　　maining jewel of the Spanish
possessions, the Philippines? On　　　　　declared against Spain, our
Asiatic Squadron must steam imm　　　　Philippine waters and engage
the Spanish fleet there, and a vast　　　go of seven thousand islands
and almost ten million souls would be

The all-important question was　　　was to command the Asiatic
Squadron. The post was vacant, and　　sevelt wanted it filled by a man
with views similar to his own and the capacity to lead the squadron into
action. There were two candidates, both elderly commodores. One was
John A. Howell, commandant of the Philadelphia Navy Yard, whom
Roosevelt considered indecisive and afraid of responsibility — the worst
possible choice for the chores the Assistant Secretary of the Navy had in
mind. His rival for squadron command was Howell's opposite in temperament, George Dewey, then fuming at the inactivity of an administrative
post in Washington. The short, ruddy, high-tempered Dewey was sixty-one
years old but yearned for the glory of battle. He had served as a young
lieutenant under Farragut and modeled his career on that aggressive
pattern. And like Roosevelt he was convinced that war with Spain was
inevitable.

One autumn day in 1897 Roosevelt summoned Commodore Dewey
to his office and said he wanted Dewey for the command of the Asiatic
Squadron, but that the rival claims of Commodore Howell for the assignment were being pressed by a member of the Senate's Naval Affairs
Committee.

"I want you to go," Roosevelt told Dewey. "You are the man who
will be equal to the emergency if one arises. Do you know any Senators?"

Dewey properly, but doubtlessly with tongue in cheek, demurred that
he would not want to exert political influence on behalf of his own promo-
tion. After some coaxing, he confessed that Redfield Proctor, the Senator
from his home state of Vermont, was an old family friend.

Senator Proctor was only too pleased to intervene with President
McKinley — over the head of Secretary Long, incidentally — and obtain
Dewey's appointment as commander of the Asiatic Squadron. Dewey was
ordered to the Far East with instructions from Roosevelt to beef up the
Asiatic Squadron and prepare for action. But he was not given the rank of
acting rear admiral usually bestowed on the commander of a squadron.
Crowninshield and Long, annoyed at the way Dewey had been maneuvered
into the command, withheld the right to fly a two-star flag.[10]

In the Far East, meanwhile, the balance of power was shifting against
Britain, France and the United States. The public did not become aware of
the tilt in favor of Germany and Russia, but it was a matter of increasing
concern in the upper echelons of the United States government, goading us

toward decisive moves in the East. On March 6, Germany obtained a ninety-nine-year lease on the Shantung peninsula and showed its hostility to rival interests by refusing permission to an Anglo-American syndicate to build a railway from Tientsin to Tsingkiang. Two days later the Manchurian entry-ports of Port Arthur and Talienwan were taken over by the Russians, a move which the United States minister to China denounced in a cable to the State Department as "treacherous" and "morally base." The two ports had formerly provided the United States with an entrance to the increasing trade with Manchuria and North China. In the State Department it was suspected that Russia, France and Germany were conspiring to freeze Britain and America out of the China trade and eventually out of the Far East.

Later in the month, probably through confidential briefings by the State Department, American newspapers began raising the alarm. The Boston *Herald,* otherwise anti-interventionist, wondered whether we shouldn't cooperate with Britain in "preventing the closing of those faraway markets," the Philadelphia *Press* warned that "the future must not be put in peril," and the Pittsburgh *Press* denounced the "Muscovites" and declared the United States "should arm itself as soon as possible against European aggression."

By the time those events transpired Dewey had proceeded to Nagasaki and taken command of the Asiatic Squadron. He found the command in deplorable condition; the charts for the Philippine waters dated back to 1876 and the squadron didn't even have its full peacetime ammunition allowance. Under Roosevelt's instructions he refitted his ships — four lightly armored cruisers, two gunboats and a revenue cutter — obtained fuel and ammunition, and bought a British collier and a merchantman to serve as his supply train when and if the squadron was ordered to the Philippines. On February 25, 1898, he received the expected cablegram from Roosevelt:

ORDER THE SQUADRON TO HONG KONG. KEEP FULL OF COAL. IN THE EVENT OF DECLARATION OF WAR SPAIN, YOUR DUTY WILL BE TO SEE THAT THE SPANISH SQAUDRON DOES NOT LEAVE THE ASIATIC COAST, AND THEN OFFENSIVE OPERATIONS IN THE PHILIPPINE ISLANDS . . .

The order lacked precision, considering the importance of the step being taken, but it had been dispatched on one of the most hectic days the ordinarily somnolent Navy Department had ever seen. Secretary Long had absented himself, even though the battleship *Maine* had been mysteriously sunk only a few days earlier. Roosevelt promptly declared himself Acting Secretary for the day.

Long returned to his office the next day to find that Roosevelt had turned the place upside down. Roosevelt's activities, he wrote in his diary, almost caused "more of an explosion than happened to the *Maine* . . . Having authority for that time of Acting Secretary, he immediately began to launch peremptory orders; distributing ships; ordering ammunition, which there is no means to move, to places where there is no means to store it . . . sending messages to Congress for immediate legislation, authorizing the enlistment of an unlimited number of seamen, etc. etc."[11]

None of that flurry of orders was more consequential than the cable to Commodore Dewey, which placed his squadron in position to strike at the Philippines. It also placed him uncomfortably close to the Philippine Junta, a group of youthful insurgents headed by the fiery little Emilio Aguinaldo, who proposed to liberate the islands as soon as the means were available. They came aboard his flagship, the *Olympia,* and Dewey, in later testimony before a Senate investigating committee, was inclined to dismiss them as "all very young earnest boys. I did not attach much importance to what they said or to themselves . . . They were bothering me. I was getting my squadron ready for battle, and these little men were coming on board my ship at Hong Kong and taking a good deal of my time . . . Finally I would not see them at all, but turned them over to my staff." The commodore denied that he made any promises to Aguinaldo about returning the Philippines to native rule once the Spanish were dispossessed.[12]

From the importunities of native politicians, Dewey gratefully turned to studying the cables from Washington which indicated that war was swiftly approaching. His own squadron was ready to steam out of Hong Kong; it would include the flagship *Olympia;* three other cruisers, the *Baltimore, Raleigh* and *Boston;* two gunboats, the *Concord* and the *Petrel,* and the revenue cutter *McCulloch,* along with his supply train of two ships. As he studied intelligence reports from Manila, he was confident, as he said later, that he could sink the Spaniards and reduce their shore defenses in one day. His enemy-designate, Admiral Patricio Montojo, was barely equipped to fend off an invasion of Chinese junks. The Spanish squadron at Manila consisted of two armored light cruisers and five unarmored cruisers (three of them wooden, one of them an unseaworthy hulk used as a receiving ship). Montojo's collection of outmoded tubs totaled twelve thousand tons to the American squadron's nineteen thousand. In firepower the Spanish were even more outclassed. Montojo's heaviest batteries mounted 6.3-inch guns, seven of them, plus four 5.9's and twenty 4.7's — and that counted those on the receiving ship *Castilla.* Dewey's squadron boasted a total firepower almost double that, delivered by ten eight-inch rifles, twenty-three six-inch and twenty five-inch. Obviously an outgunned force like Montojo's would retire behind the range of Manila's land batteries, adding their firepower to its own, but Dewey learned that the Spanish shore batteries were equipped mostly with old smoothbores, some of them bronze muzzle-loaders that belonged in a museum.

His greatest worry was the mines the Spanish could be expected to plant across the entrance to Manila Bay. The menace of underwater explosives, plus the fire from the guns emplaced on the Manila waterfront, really shortened the odds, on the basis of what Dewey knew about the Spanish intentions. At the Hong Kong Club even the British friendly to Americans were betting heavily on a Spanish victory. A British regiment entertained Dewey and his officers at the club, and their attitude, Dewey later recalled, was "A fine set of fellows, but unhappily we shall never see them again."

On April 27, a cable arrived from the Navy Department:

DEWEY, HONG KONG. WAR HAS COMMENCED BETWEEN THE UNITED STATES AND SPAIN. PROCEED AT ONCE TO PHILIPPINE ISLANDS. COMMENCE OPERATIONS AT ONCE, PARTICULARLY AGAINST THE SPANISH FLEET. YOU MUST CAPTURE VESSELS OR DESTROY. USE UTMOST ENDEAVORS. LONG.

It took the eager Commodore Dewey only a few hours to clear Hong Kong. At 2 P.M. that day the Asiatic Squadron stood out into the China Sea, seven warships, 1743 officers and men, and Joseph L. Stickney, correspondent of the naval-minded New York *Herald*. Stickney stood on the bridge beside the publicity-conscious commodore, who appointed him a volunteer aide-de-camp. Thus Washington would learn the results of Dewey's sortie into Manila Bay first from the New York *Herald*'s dispatches — and thus also Stickney was the one to record the magnificent austerity of Commodore Dewey's order to his gunnery officer, "You may fire when you are ready, Gridley."

On the morning of April 30 the American squadron made landfall, with Cape Bolinao looming in the predawn darkness. They continued southward along the coast of Luzon until they reached Subic Bay thirty miles north of the entrance to Manila Bay. Two ships were detached to reconnoiter but could find no sign of the Spanish navy.

They waited until night to enter Manila Bay and negotiate the presumed menace of the Spanish mines. With the flagship *Olympia* leading, the American squadron passed in single file between the islands of Corregidor and El Fraile. Not a mine exploded. (Small chance, as the Americans later learned. On April 19, Admiral Montojo had been ordered by his Ministry of Marine to mine the entrance of the bay. He would need several hundred mines to do a proper job but had only fourteen. Even these lacked fuses and cables, so he improvised with a few torpedoes lowered into the channel near Caballo Island. Had the Americans used that channel, they still wouldn't have lost a ship, because the torpedoes were wrongly placed to make contact.)

In the damp heat of the tropical night the American force steamed slowly toward Manila. It was twenty-two miles from Corregidor to the waterfront, so Dewey arranged to stand off Manila and her frail defending forces just at dawn. The land batteries opened up on the Americans as they turned toward the southwest, but the shells fell short. From the bridge of the *Olympia,* Dewey sighted the Spanish squadron awaiting him at anchor under the shore batteries of the Cavite navy yard. With Spanish fatalism, Admiral Montojo had elected to engage the Americans at Cavite because the water was shallow and after his ships predictably were sent to the bottom the survivors could cling to their superstructures until they could be rescued. He had also moved his squadron away from Manila because the city's merchants, whose patriotism had evaporated, protested that if he took shelter under the more efficient and modern guns in position along the waterfront their property would be damaged by fire from the American ships.

The enemy rashly opened fire, to no effect. Dewey waited until his squadron came within range, maneuvering his column to starboard, parallel to the Spanish line. At 5:41 A.M., May 1, Dewey judged that his batteries were within range of the Spanish and ordered his turrets to open fire. For two hours the Asiatic Squadron steamed slowly up and down the Spanish line, firing steadily on each of five passes. The whole area was covered by smoke from the black-powder shells. The American ships had taken little damage, causing one death and minor wounds to eight other men, but it was impossible to see whether the Spaniards were still afloat. Some enemy shells were still falling here and there. Dewey fretted that, with his own ammunition supply running low, he hadn't managed to put Montojo's ships out of action. How would it look to Washington if he had to steam all the way back to Hong Kong for more ammunition, and repeat the performance?

A breeze came up the bay, and the smoke was dispelled enough for Dewey and his officers to see that the Spanish had been horribly battered. Several ships were on fire. Dewey moved in for the kill, and by noon the whole of Montojo's squadron had been sunk and several auxiliary vessels scuttled. The Spanish casualties totaled 381 killed and wounded. Their honor was intact, but their gunnery was a disgrace. The worst damage they had managed to inflict on the American squadron was a broken deck beam on the cruiser *Baltimore.*[13]

A shore party under Lieutenant B. A. Fiske, a future admiral, carried Dewey's demand that the Manila shore batteries stop irritating him with their occasional shelling. He also demanded of the Spanish governor the right to use the cable to Hong Kong. The Spanish agreed to stop firing, but denied him cabling privileges. Out of spite Dewey ordered the cable cut, which thus prevented him from broadcasting the news of his victory. He was forced to send the cutter *McCulloch* to Hong Kong with his report: "I control bay completely and can take city at any time, but I have not sufficient men to hold." He then occupied Cavite and settled down to wait for advice from Washington.

Washington and the nation received the news of Dewey's victory with elation. All but a few assumed that his dispatch meant that the Asiatic Squadron had somehow occupied Manila, though how this could be done without a sizable Marine detachment no one bothered to speculate. Nor was it considered just how a naval force could defeat the Spanish military occupying the islands, nor whether the liberation would be accomplished by American troops or Filipino insurgent forces under the impatient young Aguinaldo, who had been left on the dock at Hong Kong when Dewey's squadron majestically sailed forth to settle the fate of his people. The American press looked upon the Philippine venture favorably, but was more concerned with the outcome of the land and sea campaign being organized against the Spanish in the Caribbean. How odd that Manila should fall before Havana! And the nation chuckled over President McKinley's reported comment on hearing of Dewey's victory that he "could not have told where those darned islands were within two thousand miles."

The War Department, however, had already begun contingency planning for "those darned islands." On May 3, before confirmation of Dewey's destruction of the Spanish squadron had reached the United States, the army chief of staff, General Nelson A. Miles, recommended that three infantry regiments and three artillery battalions, about five thousand men, be sent to Manila to liberate and/or occupy the Philippine capital, with Major General Wesley Merritt, a veteran of the Civil War cavalry and the Indian campaigns, given the command. The directive handed General Merritt ordered him to restore order and security to the islands while they were "in the possession of the United States," to take over public property and collect taxes. The President did not state how long the islands were to remain in our possession. As for the Filipino insurgents, they were to be reminded that "the powers of the military occupant are absolute and supreme." General Merritt, however, was to impress on the Filipinos that we did not intend to "make war upon the people of the Philippines . . ."

Ominous words, but the country was too preoccupied with the coming invasion of Cuba to give much thought to the distant Philippines. Imperialism was in the saddle and issuing proclamations from the stirrups. Four days before the news of Dewey's victory reached the United States, Albert J. Beveridge, the eloquent young Senator from Indiana and an ardent apostle of expansion, was telling the Middlesex Club in Boston that "we are a conquering race," that we needed new markets and must occupy new lands. "American factories are making more than the American people can use; American soil is producing more than they can consume. Fate has written our policy for us; the trade of the world must and shall be

U.S. Asiatic Fleet takes on the Spanish hulks

Admiral Dewey, victor of Manila Bay

ours. . . . American law, American order, American civilization, and the American flag will plant themselves on shores hitherto bloody and be-nighted, but by the agencies of God henceforth to be made beautiful and bright . . .

"In the Pacific is the true field of our earliest operations. There Spain has an island empire, the Philippine Archipelago. It is poorly defended. Spain's best ships are on the Atlantic side. In the Pacific the United States has a powerful squadron. The Philippines are logically our first target."[14]

It was extraordinary how often in the next several weeks American politicians, soldiers, publicists and preachers informed their countrymen that we were "fated" to bring enlightenment to the Philippines; furthermore that, without explaining how they had been advised of divine intentions, God had willed it.

The will of God and the hand of fate, meanwhile, were being rein-forced by military preparation. With headquarters in San Francisco, Gen-eral Merritt was hastily assembling the men and ships for the first expedi-tionary forces to leave the North American continent.

Across the Pacific the political and military development of American plans for the Philippines was being briskly advanced. The first order of business was to put Aguinaldo and his junta in their place. One difficulty was that Aguinaldo claimed that Dewey and other American representatives in the Far East had given him to understand that Filipino self-rule would be applied as soon as the Spanish were dispossessed. Shortly after the news of the destruction of Admiral Montojo's squadron reached Hong Kong, Aguinaldo issued a proclamation to his people embodying his belief that the Americans had come to liberate, temporarily protect, and depart when the job was done. "Divine Providence is about to place independence within our reach. The Americans, not from mercenary motives, but for the sake of humanity and the lamentations of so many persecuted people have considered it opportune to extend their protecting mantle to our beloved country . . . The Americans will attack by sea and prevent any reinforce-ments coming from Spain . . . There where you see the American flag flying, assemble in numbers; they are our redeemers!"[15]

Aguinaldo's belief that the Americans were acting as liberators and protectors was bolstered by a letter he had received from Rounceville Wildman, the United States consul in Hong Kong: "Do not forget that the United States undertook this war for the sole purpose of relieving the Cubans from the cruelties under which they were suffering and not for the love of conquests or the hope of gain. They are actuated by precisely the same feelings for the Filipinos."[16]

In mid-May Dewey, now admiral at long last, summoned Aguinaldo and his staff of seventeen to Manila Bay on the cutter *McCulloch*. He advised Aguinaldo to "go ashore and start your army," and gave him arms and ammunition. In a few days he turned over more arms from the Spanish arsenal at Cavite. Except within the more heavily garrisoned Manila, the Spanish were no longer safe in the islands. Everywhere, armed by the Americans, Aguinaldo's insurrectos rose and attacked the Spanish. The admiral, as he made clear to a Senate committee later, knew exactly what he was doing; having no land forces of his own, he was allowing the Filipinos to wipe out whatever resistance the Spanish could offer — outside of Manila. "I knew what he [Aguinaldo] was doing — driving the Spaniards in — was saving our troops," Dewey testified. "They looked upon us as their liberators. Up to the time the [United States] army came he [Aguinaldo] did everything I requested. He was most obedient; whatever I told him to do he did. I saw him almost daily."

The reason for this collaboration, Dewey continued, was that "I was waiting for troops to arrive, and I thought that the closer they [the Filipinos] invested the city [Manila], the easier it would be when our troops arrived to march in. The Filipinos were our friends, assisting us; they were doing our work."[17]

By June 12 — with the first American troopships still en route from San Francisco — the Filipino insurgents had practically surrounded Manila. Perhaps they could have taken it, but Dewey warned Aguinaldo not to storm the capital until they were better prepared. That the Filipinos were doing an excellent job of liberating themselves was attested in a dispatch by John T. McCutcheon, correspondent for the Chicago *Record,* which stated: "Our respect for the insurgent prowess has grown a great deal . . . Over in Cavite the calm passionless statements of great victories that Aguinaldo gave us were being substantiated every day for hundreds and hundreds of Spanish prisoners were being marched in and placed in prison!"[18]

Aguinaldo issued the Philippine Declaration of Independence on June 18, 1898, and hastened to set up a de facto government. Undoubtedly he had begun to wonder about American intentions. His suspicions of American goodwill could only have deepened late in July when the transports bearing the VIII Corps, now increased to about 8500 men, began landing at Cavite. No longer was Dewey conferring with Aguinaldo "almost daily," but was immersed in constant planning sessions with General Merritt and his division commanders.

By August the Filipinos had surrounded Manila with fourteen miles of trenches. The first American troops, in fact, occupied part of that trench system. They then proceeded to ease the Filipinos out of their hard-won positions and move American troops into the siege lines around the capital. In a few days, with the Spanish resistance a hollow shell, they would take Manila.

Meanwhile, there was another sharp reminder that Germany considered the Philippines within the sphere of her interests in the Pacific. The rivalry between Germany and the United States for possessions in the western Pacific, spurred on by their struggle for Samoa, had again reached the flashpoint, and German boorishness was never more evident than in their activities that summer in Philippine waters.

The German Asiatic Squadron, Vice Admiral Otto von Diederichs commanding, sailed into Manila Bay practically in the wake of Dewey's task force. With him he brought seven of the eight ships comprising his squadron, which gave him more gun-power than Dewey's. All the time that Dewey was keeping an eye on the Filipino insurgents, making sure that they rounded the Spanish but stayed out of Manila, he was distracted from time to time by the German presence. Perhaps deliberately, Admiral von Diederichs ignored the book of naval etiquette as his squadron deployed itself in Manila Bay, unlike the British, French and Japanese warships which also sailed in to observe American imperialism at work.

French, British and Japanese officers paid polite calls on Admiral Dewey as he sat in his wicker chair under the *Olympia*'s forward turret. The blustery German, however, appeared on Dewey's flagship only after the American cruiser *Raleigh* fired a shot across the bows of a German ship which ignored a demand for identification. Von Diederichs had come to demand an apology. Instead he heard a frosty request from Dewey for an explanation of the show of strength in Manila Bay.

"I am here by order of the Kaiser, sir," the German admiral replied, adding that he was charged with protecting German interests in Manila (which totaled one trading firm).

Von Diederichs stomped down the *Olympia* gangplank without his apology. He and his captains continued to behave with Teutonic insolence. German warships insisted on cutting through the American flotilla without obeying the rules of the road; entertained Spaniards in their wardrooms, having discovered a sudden affinity for the lost Iberian cause; pointedly saluted Spanish flags wherever they flew and pointedly did not salute American flags; took soundings off the mouth of the Pasig River as though contemplating a landing on the Manila waterfront, and encouraged rumors that German sailors soon would be going ashore to protect European interests and make certain that the Spanish were not treated inhumanely by either the Americans or the Filipinos.

Admiral Dewey's testy temper managed to withstand the strain until early in July, kept below the boiling point by Captain Chichester, commanding the several British ships in the bay, who assured Dewey that the British would back up the Americans against the Germans any day. Then came word from Aguinaldo, who was still Dewey's little brown comrade-in-arms at that point, that a Filipino assault on the Spanish naval base on Grande Island, at the entrance to Subic Bay, had been prevented by the sudden intervention of the German cruiser *Irene*. Dewey immediately dispatched the *Raleigh* and *Concord* to Subic Bay with their decks cleared and their gun crews standing by. The *Irene* sighted the two American cruisers approaching at flank speed, slipped around Grande Island, and steamed off in great haste. The Americans proceeded to capture Grande Island themselves.

Once again Vice Admiral von Diederichs clambered up the *Olympia*'s gangway to complain. The ensuing dialogue was to the point:

DEWEY: "Do you want war with us?"

VON DIEDERICHS: "Certainly not."

DEWEY: "Well, it looks like it, and you are very near it . . . It matters little to us whether we fight Spain, or Germany, or the world; and if you desire war, you can have it right here and now."

Dewey's bellicose reply to the German admiral's demand for an apology was emblazoned across the American newspapers. None reflected that the Germans had as much right, or as little, to be cruising around Philippine waters as the Americans. Nor did any take alarm at an American admiral, claiming to speak for all his countrymen, threatening to take on "Germany or the world" so soon after dismantling the Spanish empire.

The Atlanta *Constitution* published an editorial which expressed American outrage at the German naval interference in terms which accurately reflected the position of Washington and the rest of the country: "Americans resent any kind of arrogance, but when it is displayed by a despot whose lunatic reign has excited the contempt and indignation of all who believe in human liberty, the feeling goes deeper . . . Who knows but the Imperial war-god of Germany may cause to be fired the shot that will be the signal of a conflict the result of which may be indirectly to redeem all Europe from the fraudulent government of kings and emperors."[19]

The nation would have to wait another nineteen years to put the Kaiser in his place. The *Irene* incident demonstrated that the Americans had staked out the Philippines for themselves, and Admiral von Diederichs and his squadron soon sailed away to snatch up the Caroline Islands, also a former Spanish possession. Their foray into Manila Bay had provided the United States with a moral obligation to take the Philippines before someone else did.

2. *A Pioneering in Counterinsurgency*

"The Filipinos," wrote Apolinario Mabini, perhaps the most literate and intellectual of the Aguinaldo insurgents, who was captured by the American forces in 1899 and exiled to Guam for two years, "realize that they cannot expect any victory over the American forces; they are fighting to show the American people that they are sufficiently intelligent to know their rights despite any pretense to hide these rights with able sophistry

. . . The Filipinos maintain their fight against the American troops, not because of an especial hatred, but in order to show the American people that, far from being indifferent as to their political situation they know how to sacrifice themselves for a government which assures them their individual liberty and which governs them in conformity with the wishes and needs of the people. They have been unable to avoid that fight, owing to the fact that they have been unable to obtain from the American government any kind of formal and clear promise regarding the establishment of such a kind of government. . . . The opinion prevailing among the impartial part of the American nation appears to tend toward adhering to its old traditions and the spirit of justice and humanity, which constitute at the present time the sole hope of all upright Filipinos."[20]

The forlorn dignity of that appeal, and the highly visible fact that the Filipinos were fighting for an independence which had been promised them in the days when their help was needed to end the Spanish resistance, did not prevail against the American determination to colonialize the Philippines. Nor was that decision stayed by the fact that Dewey and Merritt both frankly admitted in their dispatches to Washington that the Filipinos were an intelligent and disciplined people, as indicated by their restraint toward the thousands of Spanish prisoners they captured. The corollary was that such a people was capable of self-government. Washington, however, gave preference to reports from the American consulate in Hong Kong that wealthy Filipino emigrés there were clamoring for American rule — understandably enough — rather than trust their fortunes to a Philippine democracy.

Thus the McKinley Administration, having chosen to forget the President's own words in his message of December 1897 when he declared that "forcible annexation" would be "criminal aggression," signaled for the conquest of the islands. On August 13, 1898, the American commanders, by a secret agreement with the Spanish authorities, launched a mock assault on Manila, which the Spanish surrendered after a few hours of fighting. In came the American occupation troops, while the Filipino insurgents were kept on the outskirts of their own capital. The following month American commissioners began meeting in Paris with Spanish representatives on what became known as the Treaty of Paris, which after several months of bargaining was drawn up on terms highly favorable to the victors. Spain relinquished all claims to the Philippines in return for twenty million dollars. We had bought a whole nation, along with the real estate, at two dollars a head.

What had changed President McKinley's mind about the criminality of annexing the Philippines? Not long before he was assassinated, the President received a Methodist Episcopal missionary committee at the White House. Just as its members were turning to go, he stopped them and without preamble, with an eagerness that suggested the torments which had afflicted the conscience of a Christian gentleman, he blurted out, "I didn't want the Philippines, and when they came to us as a gift from the gods, I did not know what to do with them." He walked the floor nights, he said, and often dropped on his knees to pray for guidance. Then one night "it came to me," he recalled, that "(1) We could not give them back to Spain — that would be cowardly and dishonorable; (2) that we could not turn them over to France or Germany — our commercial rivals in the Orient — that would be bad business and discreditable; (3) that we could not leave them to themselves — they were unfit for self-government — and they would soon have anarchy and misrule over there worse than Spain's was; and (4) that there was nothing left for us to do but to take them all, and to educate the Filipinos, and uplift and civilize and Christianize them, and by God's grace do the very best we could by them, as our fellow men for whom Christ also died. And then I went to bed and went to sleep and slept soundly."[21]

The McKinley *mea culpa* was as sincere as it was naive and ill-informed. His military and naval representatives, hardbitten men whom no one could suspect of loving "natives" of any breed, had conceded the Filipinos' intelligence and self-control even in the moment they could have avenged themselves on their Spanish oppressors. And they had been Christianized for hundreds of years by the Spanish friars, with the thoroughness for which the Spanish were noted in religious matters. Presumably Mr. McKinley objected to the fact they had been converted by the wrong — Catholic — type of Christians. Rather than his own conscience, the President might better have consulted the barroom philosophy of Peter Finley Dunne's Mr. Dooley on the subject of the Filipinos: "We say to thim: 'Naygurs,' we say, 'poor, dissolute, uncovered wretches,' says we, 'ye miserable, childish-minded apes, we propose f'r to larn ye th' uses iv liberty . . . We can't give ye anny votes, because we haven't more thin enough to go around now; but we'll threat ye th' way a father shud threat his children if we have to break ivry bone in y'er bodies. So come to our arms,' says we . . . But, glory be, 'tis more like a rasslin' match than a father's embrace . . . An' there it stands, with th' indulgent parent kneelin' on th' stomach iv his adopted child, while a dillygation fr'm Boston bastes him with an umbrella . . . I'm not much iv an expansionist mesilf."[22]

President McKinley, coupling force with piety, ordered his commanders in the Philippines to break out from Manila and take over the "actual occupation and administration of the entire group of the Philippine Islands," to extend military government to "the whole ceded territory," but somehow to convince the Filipinos that "the mission of the United States is one of 'benevolent assimilation.' "

In accordance with that order, the American divisions in Manila began exerting pressure on the defense line of Aguinaldo insurgents drawn around the capital. The method was to keep seizing pieces of territory formerly held by the insurgents, who withdrew sullenly but without offering resistance. On the night of February 4, firing broke out all along the ten-mile front when an American patrol killed three Filipinos they found in disputed territory in the Manila suburb of Santa Mesa.

The Americans had their cause of war. That they had been looking for it was indicated when Aguinaldo sent an aide to the new United States commander in Manila, Major General Ewell S. Otis, and told him the night battle of February 4 had broken out against his wishes and suggested the establishment of a neutral zone to keep the two armies separated, General Otis stiffly replied that the fighting would have to continue to "the grim end." He was prepared for it, ready to take the offensive with his mixture of Regular Army and Volunteer (later known as National Guard) regiments organized into divisions commanded by Generals Arthur Mac-Arthur, father of Douglas MacArthur, and Thomas Anderson, the latter soon to be replaced by Major General Henry W. Lawton.

The military operations, at the outset, proceeded briskly and according to plan, thanks to the American superiority in training, equipment and firepower. The Filipinos were pushed out of the suburbs of Manila after heavy fighting. An expeditionary force was also sent to occupy the Visayan Islands and the city of Cebu. During the summer of 1899 the American forces began conquering all of Luzon, but only after bloody fighting that necessitated the dispatch of thousands of fresh troops from the United States. The Filipinos put up an expectedly bitter resistance, and the "insurrection," as the United States government preferred to label a full-scale war, became more brutal with every engagement. Behind the lines a prototype of the Viet Cong had been organized; it was called the Sandatahan. They had recruited hundreds of guerrilla fighters in Manila, staged an uprising in which parts of the New City were burned, and were dislodged only after American artillery leveled the structures from which they were fighting.

The Americans were beginning to learn the realities of operating against irregulars grouped in highly mobile formations, which kept attacking, then fading away into familiar terrain. They countered by devising "flying columns" and other innovations, but the clear-and-hold operations continued into 1900 without much visible success. General Lawton himself was killed only twelve miles from Manila. The American forces dissipated much of their offensive power in establishing garrisons by the hundreds, which gave them control of everything within rifle range but nothing beyond it. The American command claimed it was inflicting casualties on the insurgents at a ratio of twenty to one, but the correspondent of the New York *Evening Post* commented, "The twenty is guesswork."

Another correspondent, John Bass of *Harper's Weekly,* slipped a harshly critical dispatch past the stringent censorship in Manila by cabling it from Hong Kong. Despite all the proclamations of victory, Bass wrote, "we have been floundering about in the wilderness for months without accomplishing anything." Much of the blame rested with General Otis, who insisted on refighting the Civil War battles of his youth. "Why," he asked, "is the American outlook blacker now than it has been since the beginning of the war? . . . First, the whole population sympathizes with the insurgents . . . The second cause is that our army is ill-equipped and unwieldly in its management . . . The third reason is that the plans of campaign followed are not adapted to the nature of the country, the climate or the people . . . The sooner the people of the United States find out that the people of the Philippines do not wish to be governed by us, the better."

Worse yet, in Bass's opinio.., the Americans were introducing the Filipinos to "civilized" warfare by burning and looting many of the towns and villages they captured and teaching the insurgents the military value of a scorched-earth policy. "The insurgents are a good deal like children, and they imitated us; instead of leaving their towns for us to burn, they burned them themselves . . . Now there has been a great hue-and-cry made because the insurgents mutilated two of our dead by cutting off their ears, and yet one or two of our own scouts made a practice of cutting off the ears of the insurgents they killed, and preserving them as trophies." He believed that "the insurrection will prosper for some time to come," despite the hope of the Americans that it would "fall to pieces by natural disintegration."[23]

The Americans began replacing their disillusioned Volunteer regiments — some of them with seventy percent in the hospital from wounds, tropical disease and heat prostration — with Regular Army units expected to conclude the insurrection with professional dispatch. In the spring of 1901 Aguinaldo was captured and persuaded to order his forces to lay down their arms. The fighting continued, however, on Luzon and the southern islands, and the United States forces had been increased to 47,465 officers and men with 16,018 reinforcements on their way. Filipino casualties increased in proportion, General J. M. Bell, commander of the United States forces in the Luzon province of Batangas, reporting that one-sixth of the population of that island had been killed.[24] A short time later a visiting Congressman verified that estimate by noting that northern Luzon had been pacified most thoroughly. "They never rebel in northern Luzon," he was quoted on his return home, "because there isn't anybody there to rebel. The country was marched over and cleaned in a most resolute manner. The good Lord in heaven only knows the number of Filipinos that were put under the ground. Our soldiers took no prisoners, they kept no records; they simply swept the country, and wherever or whenever they could get hold of a Filipino they killed him. The women and children were spared, and may now be noticed in disproportionate numbers in that part of the island."[25]

To carry out a near-genocidal policy, the American fighting men convinced themselves they were exterminating subhumans. It epitomized the "gook-psychosis" which has so often afflicted Americans. Among American soldiers in the Philippines, the natives were usually referred to as "niggers," sometimes as "googoos." A popular song among the troops urged that the "kodiac ladrones," native bandits, be "civilized with a Krag [rifle]."

And the savagery of the combat troops was matched or exceeded by the ruthlessness of some of their commanders. A striking example was General Jacob Smith, soon to be notorious as "Hell Roaring Jake," who was the military governor of the island of Samar. Within ten days of his arrival on Samar, he ordered the population (about 250,000) herded into concentration camps.* According to an American newspaper in Manila, General Smith "ordered all natives to present themselves in certain of the coast towns saying that those who were found outside would be shot and no questions asked. The time limit had expired . . . and General Smith was as good as his word. The policy of reconcentration is said to be the most effective of the kind ever seen under any flag. All suspects including Spaniards and half-breeds were rounded up in big stockades and kept under guard."[26]

An insurrecto leader named Lucban retaliated by wiping out an entire company of United States infantry in a surprise attack on the garrison town of Balangiga. Whereupon "Hell Roaring Jake" issued a general order to his subordinates: "I want no prisoners. I wish you to kill and burn; the more you kill and burn the better you will please me." He further specified that all males over the age of ten be slaughtered and the whole island be made "a howling wilderness." There was an outcry of protest in the States when his activities were publicized, including a petition for an investigation signed by Mark Twain and thirty-six members of the University of Chicago faculty. The Army was forced to court-martial General Smith, whose real crime was to put his orders in writing, and the court reluctantly ordered that Smith was "to be admonished."

Similarly restrained punishments were meted to officers and men caught administering the "water cure" — a method of interrogation reportedly revived sixty-odd years later by American forces in South Viet Nam — to prisoners who refused to give information. A soldier wrote a New York newspaper that the water cure was "plain hell." As he described it, the prisoner's mouth was pried open with a piece of bamboo and up to

---

* This was an adaptation of the Spanish *reconcentrado* policy in Cuba, of which President McKinley several years before had told Congress, "It was not civilized warfare . . . It was extermination. The only peace it could beget was that of the wilderness and the grave."

Emilio Aguinaldo, leader of the Filipino resistance

Utah Light Artillery deploying on the Manila Front

five gallons of water poured into him through a funnel. "By this time the body becomes an object frightful to contemplate." Often the subject was dehydrated by jumping on his distended stomach. "I heard of one who took it [the water cure] three times and died." The soldier was concerned even more by the effects of such tortures on the men who performed them. "The unconcerned way in which the soldiers and civilians speak of the water cure, the exulting way in most cases, is the saddest phase of all."[27]

In Luzon and the northern islands the organized Filipino resistance had died out within three years of those first shots fired in a Manila suburb in February 1899. It had taken the American army 2811 separate battles and actions to subdue the people it had come to liberate.

3. *"We Risk Caesarism"*

One warm spring day when the sun shone brilliantly on Capitol Hill and the scent of cherry blossoms almost concealed the miasmic odors of the Potomac, the United States Senate listened to a continuation of the debate over our policy in the Philippines. It was largely a serial exchange between the ardent young Senator Albert J. Beveridge of Indiana, the leader of the hard-liners, and the elderly George F. Hoar of Massachusetts, who for several years had been trying to awaken his colleagues and the nation to the enormity of our actions and their implications for the future. Of that debate, Ambrose Bierce, the practicing misanthrope, then Washington correspondent for the Hearst newspapers, had written that he supposed Senator Hoar knew what he was talking about. "I dare say that is the right view to take of it. I am sure it must be wrong for nations to be wicked. But in the larger politics of this worst of all possible worlds it does seem as if ethical considerations had not more weight and influence than that to which their beauty entitles them. According to the principles so dear to the hearts of the worthy gentlemen who lift protesting hands when the rights of weak nations are invaded by strong ones, not a people on earth today has a right to be there."

On this day, Senator Hoar was discussing the consequences of the military victory which American generals were proclaiming from the field, and he would have none of the sophisticated evasions such as that expressed by the waspish Bierce.

"You chose war instead of peace," he told the Senate's expansionist faction. "You chose force instead of conciliation. . . . Had you made a declaration to Aguinaldo that you would respect their title to independence, and that all you desired was order and to fulfill the treaty and to protect your friends, you would have disarmed that people in a moment.

"Instead of that, the gentlemen talked of the wealth of the Philippine Islands, and about the advantage to our trade. They sought to dazzle our eyes with nuggets of other men's gold. Senators declared in the Senate Chamber and on the hustings that the flag never should be hauled down in the Philippine Islands, and those of you who thought otherwise kept silent and entered no disclaimer . . .

"Gentlemen talk about sentimentalities, about idealism. They like practical statesmanship better. But, Mr. President, this whole debate for the last four years has been a debate between two kinds of sentimentality.

"You, my imperialistic friends, have had your ideals and sentimentalities. One is that the flag shall never be hauled down where it has once floated. Another is that you will not talk or reason with a people with arms in their hands. Another is that sovereignty over an unwilling people may be bought with gold. And another is that sovereignty may be got by force of arms, as the booty of battle or the spoils of victory.

"What has been the practical statesmanship, which comes from your ideals and sentimentalities? You have wasted six hundred millions of treasure. You have sacrificed nearly ten thousand American lives, the flower of our youth. You have devastated provinces. You have slain uncounted thousands of people you desire to benefit. You have established reconcentration camps. Your generals are coming home from their harvest, bringing their sheaves with them, in the shape of other thousands of sick and wounded and insane to drag out miserable lives, wrecked in body and mind. You make the American flag in the eyes of a numerous people the emblem of sacrilege in Christian churches, and of the burning of human dwellings, and of the horror of the water torture."

We had turned the Filipinos into "sullen enemies," and he prophesied, "This war, if you call it war, has gone on for three years. It will go on in some form for three hundred years unless this policy is abandoned. You will undoubtedly have times of peace and quiet, or pretended submission. You will buy men with titles or offices or salaries. You will intimidate cowards . . . The land will smile and seem at peace. But the volcano will be there. The lava will break out again. You can never settle this thing until you settle it right."[28]

The Senator from Massachusetts spoke for a growing segment of the American people, sobered now as the men of nineteen different state Volunteer regiments returned home with their sick, wounded and mentally disturbed. Even more sobering were the thousands of others streaming westward in the troopships — more with each victory proclamation of the generals.

Half a million Americans had joined the Anti-Imperialist League founded by two Boston reformers, Moorfield Storey and Gamaliel Bradford. Its president was George S. Boutwell, the Secretary of the Treasury in the Grant Administration, and among its forty-one vice presidents were former President Grover Cleveland, former Secretary of War (under Cleveland) William Endicott, Senator Ben Tillman, President David Starr

Jordan of Stanford University, William James (who wrote that the United States had "puked up its ancient principles at the first touch of temptation" when it conquered the Philippines), Mark Twain, William Dean Howells, Jane Addams, Andrew Carnegie, Samuel Gompers, the president of the American Federation of Labor, and many other prominent politicians, writers, lawyers, clergymen and social reformers. From its first membership in Boston and Springfield the league grew branches in New York, Philadelphia, Baltimore, Washington, Los Angeles, San Francisco, Cincinnati, Cleveland, Detroit, St. Louis and Portland, Oregon. Among other things, the league exposed the fact that dumdum bullets had been issued to some American troops in the Philippines.

Certainly the anti-imperialist movement was able to muster the most eloquent speakers and the ablest writers in its cause. Peter Finley Dunne, the most popular of turn-of-the-century humorists, ridiculed the pretensions of the imperialists and kept reminding the country that few Americans knew whether the Philippines were "islands or canned goods" when they were first invaded. Mark Twain suggested that a new American flag be designed "with the white stripes painted black, and the stars replaced by a skull and crossbones."

Carl Schurz, whose liberalism had caused his banishment from the Republican establishment, delivered an address at the University of Chicago which was often quoted in the Senate debates for its acerb rejection of the argument that the Philippines must be occupied because the Filipinos were incapable of governing themselves. To that charge, Schurz said, "They may answer that this is their affair and that they are at least entitled to a trial. I frankly admit that if they are given the trial, their conduct in governing themselves will be far from perfect. Well, the conduct of no people is perfect, not even our own. They may try to revenge themselves upon their Tories in their Revolutionary War. But we too threw our Tories into hideous dungeons . . . we, too, have had our civil war which cost hundreds and thousands of lives and devastated one-third of our land; and now we have in horrible abundance the killings of lynch law . . . They may have troubles with their wild tribes. So had we, and we treated our tribes in a manner not to be proud of. They may have corruption and rapacity in their government . . . but Manila may secure a city council not much less virtuous than that of Chicago."

A Negro newspaper editor echoed Schurz's sentiments with the comment that it was "a sinful extravagance to waste our civilizing influence upon the unappreciative Filipinos when it is so badly needed right here in Arkansas."[29]

The campaigning in print and on the platform, one anti-imperialist Senator believed, at least had the effect of modifying the government's course in the Philippines. "It is a significant concession to public opinion that we no longer hear the argument of greed and avarice and the hunger for other men's possessions openly and defiantly proclaimed . . . It may not signify any change of heart or purpose, but it shows a realization of the fact that the public conscience is awake, and it shows that the authors of this policy begin to understand that they cannot justify 'criminal aggression' by pointing to the profits of the crime. It is a cheering sign that the second sober thought has come . . . when the party responsible for a bucaneering war is compelled to veil the grossness of its designs."[30]

Meanwhile, of course, the American public was subjected to a counterbarrage of propaganda from the other side, which was keynoted by such sonorous pronouncements as that of Senator Beveridge that the United States was the "trustee under God, of the civilization of the world," and more practically that "just beyond the Philippines are China's illimitable markets. We will not retreat from either. The Pacific is the ocean of commerce of the future and most future wars will be conflicts of commerce." And there was William Allen White's designation of Americans as "the chosen people" burdened with "the Anglo-Saxon manifest destiny to go forth as the world conqueror." White supremacy was being redefined as Anglo-Saxon superiority. The Anglo-American "race," together with the Germans, was "particularly endowed," as Professor John W. Davis explained it, "with the capacity for establishing national states, and are especially called to that work; and therefore they are intrusted, in the general economy of history, with the mission of conducting the political civilization of the modern world."[31]

The defenders of imperialism also grasped the propaganda value of pointing out that it was disloyal to question American motives while American soldiers were being killed. Generals Otis and Lawton both wrote from their Philippine headquarters that protests against the war were giving aid and comfort to the enemy and encouraging him to keep on fighting. General Lawton's meditations on this issue were published, with dramatic effect, shortly after he was killed in battle. His letter had charged that if he died in action his blood would be on the hands of those who protested against the war. "The continuance of the fighting," he explained, "is chiefly due to reports that are sent out from America." (This claim was given substance by the publication of Aguinaldo's memoirs, in which he admitted that "we hoped that the American people would soon demand an end to the war" because "the basic political principles on which the American government was founded were being violated and repudiated in the American action.") The dissent was even more vexing to President McKinley and his Cabinet; they debated whether to prosecute the *Nation* and several newspapers on charges of treason, but decided such a move would be politically unwise.

All the brooding over ethics and purposes seemed like ungrateful quibbling to "Marse" Henry Watterson, the fiery editor of the Louisville *Courier-Journal,* who thought we ought to be thankful that the invasion of the Philippines had given us the opportunity to change from a "nation of shopkeepers" to a "nation of warriors," and the risk of becoming a militarist force in the world was a small price to pay. In one of his more thunderous editorials, Watterson declared:

"We escape the menace and peril of socialism and agrarianism, as England has escaped them, by a policy of colonialism and conquest. From a provincial huddle of petty sovereignties held together by a rope of sand we rise to the dignity and prowess of an imperial republic incomparably greater than Rome. It is true that we exchange domestic dangers for foreign dangers; but in every direction we multiply the opportunities of the people. We risk Caesarism, certainly, but even Caesarism is preferable to anarchism. We risk wars, but a man has but one time to die, and either in peace or war, he is not likely to die until his time comes. In short, anything is better than the pace we were going before these present forces were started into life. Already the young manhood of the country is as a goodly brand snatched from the burning, and given a perspective replete with noble deeds and elevating ideas."[32]

Few of Watterson's persuasion would have put it so bluntly, but he expressed the mandate which they believed they had been given with the reelection of President McKinley in 1900.

We had acquired our India, and perhaps only the first of our Indias.

4. The First Peace Corps

With the end of organized resistance on Luzon and most of the northern islands, the administration in Washington, now Theodore Roosevelt's, began devoting itself to restoring order, reviving the economy and repairing the damage of three years of "insurrection." To this end, William Howard Taft was named civil governor of the islands and an earnest effort was made to provide a surface tranquillity. "The substitution of white duck in the place of khaki and brass buttons as the dress of the American official in the Philippines," wrote the bitterly anti-imperialist Moorfield Storey, "may be said to characterize Governor Taft's manner of quelling Filipino opposition . . . he proposed to establish Civil Government in order to pacify the natives and to assure the people at home that things were going along as they should . . . this policy was vehemently opposed by the military commanders whose real task was to combat the insurrection in some of the remaining islands."

The massively good-natured Judge Taft was eminently equipped to provide the required facade of democratic rule, behind which was the reality that Taft was as much the dictator of the Philippines as any departed Spanish captain-general, and that the next layer of authority was composed of the Philippine Commission, all Americans appointed in

Washington who were paid more than a Cabinet member out of the increased poll taxes levied on the Filipinos. And while the natives were being thus ministered to, Taft pointed out in a 1904 speech while back in the States on leave, American entrepreneurs would be advised to look for opportunity in "this pearl of the Oriental tropics." He added, "It is estimated that not more than five million acres of land are owned by natives in the islands, and that the remaining sixty-five million is owned by the government." If the American experience held true — and there was no reason it shouldn't be repeated in the Philippines — government land rapidly became private-owned land, with the proper exchange of inducements.[33]

Under these circumstances, the American bureaucracy in the Philippines, along with the military careerists and the incoming venture capitalists, naturally held a vested interest in keeping the Philippines in the status of a welfare client, little brown brothers who refused to grow up. This self-serving tendency was frankly exposed by W. Morgan Shuster several years after he served on the Philippine Commission. He wrote in a magazine article that the reports of the American proconsuls always showed "what the party then in power wanted the American people to think about the Filipinos." Anyone who tried to present a different picture "became at once, in official eyes, a dreamer, an anti-imperialist, or a demagogue. His opinions were taboo in high governmental circles, and he was deemed an unsafe man to hold important office. This was only natural and I recall it merely to show how the opinion of the American people on the question has really been formed." All the various governors, commissioners, generals and other functionaries, Shuster wrote, "took up the subject as I did, with a previously formed conviction that the facts were going to sustain the accepted government belief and policy, which were that the Filipinos were not fit to be, and should not of right be, independent, at least for a very long time to come. How long few ventured to predict. It is said that Mr. Taft when invited . . . to go to Manila . . . stated that he was opposed to our holding the islands. That, however, was before he had been intimately connected with the administrative policies already adopted, which were based on the opposite belief."[34]

With all their bustling, beaming, often naive goodwill, ordinary Americans enrolled in what they believed to be a worthy cause, risked their health and often their lives to civilize the Filipinos with something less lethal than a Krag. Most of them, perhaps, failed to see the irony in their efforts as perceived by more sophisticated persons, such as the caustic Englishwoman living in Manila who observed that it was the American program to "have lots of American schoolteachers at once set to work to teach the Filipino English and at the same time keep plenty of American soldiers around to knock him on the head should he get the notion that he is ready for self-government before the Americans think he is."[35]

That Filipinos should be forced to learn English — at their own expense as taxpayers — instead of the Spanish most adults already spoke also received the attention of Peter Finley Dunne, who observed through his Mr. Dooley: "In ivry city in this unfair land we will erect school houses an' packin' houses an' houses iv correction; an' we'll larn ye our language because 'tis aisier to larn ye ours than to larn oursilves yours. An' we'll give ye clothes, if ye pay f'r thim; an' if ye don't, ye can go without. And whin ye're hungry ye can go to th' morgue — we mane th' resth'rant — an' ate a good square meal iv ar-rmy beef. An' we'll sind th' gr-reat Gin'ral Eagan over f'r to larn ye etiquette, an' Andhrew Carnegie to larn ye pathriteism with blowholes into it."

The sheer physical effort of restoring the islands to productivity after years of a scorched-earth policy applied by both sides in the war was enough to confound a legion of Dooleys. In his 1902 report, Secretary of War Elihu Root surveyed the property damage, the broken "bonds of social order," the forgotten "habits of peaceful industry," and estimated that ninety percent of the islands' carabaos (the working animals of the rice paddies) had died of the rinderpest and that only twenty-five percent of the former rice crop was being produced.

The people who took over the reconstruction of the Philippines were, in effect, our first Peace Corps. Few of them ever walked the polished floors of the Malacanan Palace, the seat of colonial power in Manila, or were rewarded with anything but the personal gratitude of the people they worked among, but their history is one of the greathearted but unglorified experiences of the American people. If no great work of art has ever celebrated their achievements — the doctors fighting the plague, the teachers in the isolated jungle villages, the nutrition experts combatting beriberi and other diet-deficiency diseases — it is probably because their fellow citizens prefer not to have those years recalled and to dwell instead upon how we granted the Philippines their independence after World War II (after colonialism was found, on balance, not to be a paying proposition).

First the American volunteers had to tackle the health problem, the enormity of which was incredible to anyone who had not seen the fever-ridden, sunken-eyed veterans of the occupation forces coming down the gangplanks of the troopships in San Francisco. Malaria, dysentery, cholera, smallpox, tuberculosis and various skin diseases were endemic, and bubonic plague cropped up regularly because there were no safeguards against rats leaving ships arriving from Oriental ports. The Spanish had treated disease as an act of God; when a village was stricken by an epidemic, the image of San Roque was carried through the street, and the rest was left to Providence.

Army medical corps physicians began training Filipino doctors in more modern methods of attacking disease, but in 1905 a civilian bureau of health was established under one of the heroes of tropical medicine, Dr.

Victor Heiser, who was not only a great doctor but, equally important, capable of working with an alien race. "An accomplished linguist," wrote W. Cameron Forbes, a Bostonian who became governor general of the Philippines and a colonial administrator of the finest sort, "he soon learned how to deal with the Filipinos, discount their prejudices, and take advantage of their strong points to attain his objects, which were always directed with a single eye to the best interest of the Philippine people." A statistical measurement of Dr. Heiser's achievements was the fact that when he took over in 1905 the death rate was 27.46 per thousand; it was reduced to 18.82 during his eight years in the islands, and rose to 35.28 when he left. Dr. Heiser and his subordinates went to work immediately, cleaning up the streets, arranging garbage and sewage disposal, cleansing the drinking water, and ranging outward from Manila to the provinces and other islands with their vaccination kits. None of their labors were more heroic, however, than convincing the natives that diseases were not caused by exposure to the night air. In 1909 the Hamburg School of Tropical Medicine declared that the American efforts in the Philippines had been so remarkable that "Germany and all other nations having colonies in the far east will have to take lessons from the Manila sanitary authorities in dealing with the evils that beset us."[36]

Dr. Heiser and his aides also conducted a vigorous campaign against leprosy, and with an appropriation of fifty thousand dollars established a leper colony at Culion and obtained the use of the Coast Guard ship *Basilan* to gather together those suffering — without treatment of any kind — from the disease. Heiser himself boarded the *Basilan* and went from island to island in search of the "lion-faced." A magazine writer later told how Heiser had become legendary in the islands for his courage and humanity: "They say of Doctor Heiser that he has handled with bare hands from two to three thousand lepers in all the horrible stages of that most horrible of diseases; and I myself have seen him pick up a helpless leper in his arms and carry him aboard the leper ship to be taken to Culion with as little apparent concern for his own safety as he would display under the most ordinary circumstances."[37]

At Culion, Heiser gathered fifty-four hundred lepers in a city of clean barracks, shaded streets and flower gardens. Somehow he managed to convince them they were not outcasts but human beings and citizens. "The Culion Leper Republic," he reported in 1912, "is the only place in the Philippines where suffragettes and women's suffrage exist . . . Among the candidates for election as president is an American, who has the support of all the suffragettes and his election is almost conceded."[38]

An equally warming chronicle was the work of Robert R. Williams, a young organic chemist contracted by the army to work on beriberi, a wasting disease which caused an estimated twenty-five thousand annual deaths in the islands. It was early suspected that the disease was caused by the consumption of polished rice, which the Filipinos preferred to brown or unmilled rice. In the milling process, riboflavin and other vitamins which would build up resistance to beriberi were washed away. Williams and Dr. E. B. Vedder of the Army Board of Tropical Medicine began experimenting with the extracts of rice-polishings by feeding them to chickens and birds, then injecting a solution made from rice bran into humans suffering from beriberi. Williams often rushed to native barrios with his extract and treated children, blue and near death, who began recovering within several hours after receiving a few drops of the solution. Years later, on his return to the States, Williams continued to experiment in a laboratory built into the garage of his New Jersey home with the aim of synthesizing the life-giving vitamins. Twenty-six years after he went out to the Philippines as a young army chemist, in 1936, he isolated what became known as vitamin B-1.

Much of the profits from that discovery were channeled into the Williams-Waterman Fund, which financed further work on the beriberi problem. It was impossible to persuade most Filipinos to eat anything but white polished rice. The answer seemed to be to artificially enrich that product. As soon as World War II ended, Williams and his staff proceeded to the Philippines to conduct the Bataan Experiment, a rice-enrichment program with rigid controls which proved that beriberi and other deficiency diseases could be curbed by vitaminizing polished rice. Ten years later he was sent to Korea by the Defense Department to start a similar program. Through the efforts of the young man who went out to the Philippines in 1910, and of those who collaborated with him, the diseases which cause tens of thousands of Asian deaths annually are being steadily conquered. They also serve as a signpost to the kind of conquests for which Americans are peculiarly fitted.[39]

The American-run bureau of health also built the Philippine General Hospital in 1910 and made it one of the largest clinics in the world. The ranking genius on the staff was a German eye doctor named Rembe, who performed hundreds of operations which restored sight to persons who had been blind for years. "His fame swept through the provinces," Governor General Forbes later recorded, "and people came trooping in to place themselves in his care."[40]

An education program was instituted with the same fervor that characterized the medical and sanitation work. Many young soldiers became teachers the moment the shooting stopped, and took over the instruction at barrio schools with or without master's degrees. They were soon joined by qualified experts from the States, and the Department of the Interior began recruiting hundreds of American schoolteachers to go to the Philippines at the risk of their health and often of their lives.

The first supervisor of the Filipino educational system was Captain Albert Todd of the Sixth United States Artillery, and during the insurrection most of the regional superintendents of schools were army chaplains. General James F. Smith, who succeeded to the post of secretary of public instruction, claimed that the uniformed teachers were "an object lesson which, while it did not serve to convince the insurgents of the error of their ways, at least caused many of the better element among them to soberly inquire of themselves whether, after all, the United States might not have the welfare and well-being of the Filipino people very much at heart."[41]

The term culture shock had not yet been invented, but the teachers recruited for the Philippine educational system when civilian control was established often were confronted by problems never suggested in the curriculum of the normal schools back in the States. One was the custom of the Filipinos, adopted from the Chinese in their midst, of growing at least one fingernail to mandarin length as an indication of superior breeding. Americans made "very short work" of mandarin fingernails by introducing their pupils to manual training, agriculture and outdoor games.

Young Americans were plunged, with little preparation, certainly with none of the indoctrination given the present Peace Corps trainees, into an atmosphere that was always alien, sometimes bizarre and occasionally hostile. "At the outset," according to one report on their progress, "those who were sent into the more remote towns suffered certain hardships, not the least of which was their isolation. Their food was often such as they were unaccustomed to, and the change from the conditions which they had left was often such as to cause homesickness and a certain measure of dissatisfaction with their lot." Mail from home took months to reach them, and their pay, "by reason of the depreciation of the local currency," was "found to be worth less than at the time when they should have received it."

Once the initial difficulties were smoothed away, the report continued, "they became adjusted to their new surroundings, the civil supply stores made available a better quality of food, they became more intimately acquainted with the people . . . It might be added that the increases in a large number of salaries during the year tended to impress upon them that their services were, after all, appreciated. The strong desire on the part of the more intelligent Filipinos to have their children educated, and the aptitude of the children to learn have generally made the way of the American teacher easy, and given him or her a high place in the regard of those among whom they worked."[42]

When cholera epidemics closed the schools, almost all teachers stayed at their posts to help the public health doctors. Four teachers died of cholera. The willingness to share the lot of the people of the barrios, not strikingly evident among their Spanish predecessors, gave the teachers an almost "sacred" status with the Filipinos, which usually made them exempt from the banditry and violence of the countryside. Four American teachers, however, were killed by *ladrones,* bandits, while traveling in the mountains of northern Luzon because one was "mistaken for the provincial treasurer."[43]

Later many American teachers trained Filipinos to take over the classrooms and stayed on as supervisors, in which role they were often vexed by the casual attitude of the Filipinos toward their duties. After a big fiesta on Panay, one American reported, "I find my teachers are fully as badly demoralized as I expected they would be. Maria Garingales was the only one that came on time; Maria Girago came half an hour late and then wanted to get excused for the day. Francisco Girado came in an hour and a half late, and then only because I sent for him. Norberto Girado was at his home asleep and would not come at all, although I sent for him twice. He did not come to the school, but went to the cockfight instead, and as there is another cockfight tomorrow I have no reason to expect him at that time." Reflecting on the necessity to play truant officer with his own teachers, the American thought it "illustrates the fact that before anything in the way of social reform can be accomplished through the people themselves there must be breathed into them the spirit of a new life," they must be taught a "sense of moral obligation" toward their fellows, of which they had been deprived by Spanish colonialism.[44]

Filipino educational progress was surveyed constantly by the Philippine Commission and various official and unofficial investigators from the States. Within a quarter of a century, thanks to the effort poured into it by individual teachers and the money supplied partly by the Filipino taxpayer and partly by the American, more Filipinos were receiving a high school education, proportionately, than in England, Wales, Sweden or Spain, and almost as many as in Japan.[45] The Monroe Survey determined that Filipino children were learning to speak English "with sufficient clarity to make themselves understood either by other Filipinos or by Americans, but with an accent, tonal expression and rhythm that are thoroughly Malay," that in general attainment, however, Filipino children lagged "two or three years" behind the American.[46]

Another government report was certain that it was important for the Filipinos to learn a "civilized" language because "even if he has learned nothing else" he "has put himself en rapport with civilization." If learning English became the prerogative of the upper-class children in private schools, the report pointed out, it would "tend to perpetuate the prestige and domination of the present oligarchic element in Filipino society."[47]

Along with other aspects of Americanism, inevitably, came baseball. Governor General Forbes thought it "inspiring" the way young Filipinos took to the game. For a time it even competed with the cockfights as a sporting event. "Even in the hills the schoolboys took keenly to baseball and it was not uncommon to see an Igorot [aborigine] boy catching behind the bat, clad only in loincloth, baseball mask, and mitt." With lesser success, but with the same American promotional zeal, teachers tried to convert the native population to eating corn instead of rice by teaching girls in the domestic-science classes how to prepare it fifty different ways. They even resorted to the declaration of Corn Eating Week, but the Filipino continued to regard corn as something for the livestock.[48]

Importing baseball, corn-on-the-cob and other homely Americanisms was only another symptom of that defenseless sincerity which characterizes the American doing good abroad. It says something for the Filipinos that they did not mistake American openheartedness for sheer idiocy, as other peoples have; and that with the years, with the thousands of Americans who devoted part of their lives to the Philippines, something like a reconciliation took place. Without them, the Philippines might have been, not our India, but our Congo.

5. *In Moro Country*

While the northern islands were succumbing to Americanization, the southern Philippines, the Moro Province comprising the islands of Mindanao and the Sulu archipelago, were resisting the United States Army in a stubborn, intermittent swampfire war that continued until World War I. The Moros, in fact, were never really subjugated. Even the Japanese, during their occupation in World War II, were never safe on the jungle trails unless they traveled in convoys.

For the Americans, the Moro islands became a laboratory of colonial warfare, a proving ground for antiguerrilla tactics, a territory closed off to inquisitive civilians, muffled by military censorship, governed by army officers. A silent deadly war was conducted there, of which the American people heard little. Its lessons — principally that a determined native population, strongly motivated by religious or political doctrine, fighting on favorable terrain and using the tactics of the tribal wars in the bush with which they were familiar, could hold out indefinitely against a Western opponent fighting by the book — have never been fully comprehended.

The Moros came of the same Malay stock as the Filipinos. What made the difference, giving them their fighting creed, was the fact they had been converted to Mohammedanism centuries before. They kept their faith during the Spanish occupation, which was confined to Zamboanga, the chief port of Mindanao, and a few other fortified outposts. They also clung determinedly to such customs as piracy, the most respected of professions, slavery and polygamy. One of the more provocative summations of the Moro character was recorded in the diary of John J. Pershing, who probably got to know the Moros as well as any other American. "The almost infinite combination of superstitions, prejudices and suspicions blended with his character make him a difficult person to handle until fully understood. In order to control him other than by brute force, one must first win his implicit confidence, nor is this as difficult as it would seem. . . . He is jealous of his religion, but he knows very little about its teachings . . . As long as he is undisturbed in the possession of his women and children, and his slaves, there is little to fear from him. As a rule he treats his so-called slaves, who are really but serfs or vassals, as members of his family; but any interference with what he thinks his right regarding them had best be made gradually by the natural process of development, which must logically come by contact with and under the wise supervision of a civilized people."[49]

When they first arrived in the southern islands, the Americans hoped to bribe their way into domination of the estimated six hundred thousand population, which was partly Christian but completely ruled by the Moro chiefs. In 1900 they negotiated the Bates Treaty with the sultan of Sulu and lesser dignitaries. By its terms the sultanate was defined as a "protected sovereignty," whatever that meant; the sultan was to receive two hundred and fifty dollars a month for his good offices and lesser *datus* (chiefs) lesser subsidies. The sultan's writ, however, covered only about a third of the Moros and did not include the large island of Mindanao. In any case the real rulers of the Moro Province were the tribal chiefs and the *panditas,* Mohammedan priests. Nevertheless American forces began occupying the coastal towns of Mindanao, around which clustered the Christian minority and the pagans, while the Moros sullenly moved inland, up into the mountain jungles.

The Americans immediately offended Moslem tradition by decreeing an end to slavery and piracy. In reply, the Moros came down from their mountain strongholds and raided the coastal settlements for cattle and human captives. The raids were said to be led by a General Capistrano, whose fort was located on the lip of a mountain gorge above the Cagayan River. American headquarters in Zamboanga ordered a punitive expedition to invade the interior and scatter Capistrano's followers. It was accompanied by a mountain howitzer battery, which won for the Americans their first and cheapest victory over the Moros. The latter had never been shelled before and fled into the jungle after their mountain fort was bombarded.

But that still left an estimated three hundred thousand Moros living in the Lake Lanao district in a state of rebellion. Another punitive expedition was organized in 1901 when the Moslem tribesmen murdered several Americans traveling the jungle trails. That campaign ended successfully enough when the Americans stormed the sultan of Bayan's stronghold at Pandatahan and killed the sultan and more than two hundred of his followers.

Camp Vicars was then established in the heart of the lake country, much like a cavalry fort in the Old West, to keep an eye on the restive tribesmen. Captain John J. Pershing, the square-jawed veteran of the campaign against Geronimo and of the Battle of Wounded Knee, as well as the holder of the Silver Star for his participation in the charge up San Juan Hill, was appointed to take command of Camp Vicars and carry out whatever punitive actions against the Moros were required. Pershing, as a personal friend of President Theodore Roosevelt, was marked for higher command. He merited it as a highly capable career soldier who took his work seriously, who poured everything he had into each assignment that came to him, eventually, of course, including the command of the A.E.F. in France during World War I. A superior who recommended him for the post noted that in addition to the standard soldierly qualities Pershing had "infinite patience in dealing with these fanatical semi-savages, wise discretion, a serious desire to accomplish work set for him, and knowledge of the Moro character," and that was no more than just.[50]

Pershing learned the Moro dialects, played chess with their *datus,* and almost made himself into a Moro in his effort to understand that proud and passionate people. In the summer of 1902 he invited seven hundred Moros living around Camp Vicars to attend a Fourth of July celebration and mingle with his soldiers.

He could also be ruthless. When a number of Moro chiefs were threatening to go to war against each other, Pershing summoned them to Camp Vicars. First he astounded them by playing a record on an Edison "talking machine," a recording of barnyard noises which delighted the chiefs. Then he summoned two orderlies, one carrying a dead pig, the other a bucket of pig's blood. The Moros believed they would be barred from paradise if contaminated by a pig. Pershing took a dipper of pig's blood and threatened to spatter the lot of them if they didn't sign a peace treaty. They signed immediately.

The American military who were handed the job of keeping peace in the Moro Province had to ad-lib policy without much consultation with Manila or Washington, because of their isolation and uncertain communications. Their plan, in essence, was to break up the tribal system and destroy the authority of the *datus.* That was a simple, direct, military solution; the civilian method would have been to rule, if possible, through the people's rulers, rather than rend the whole fabric of their lives and try to abolish tradition overnight.

The strong-minded Brigadier General Leonard Wood, who had become military governor of the Moro Province, tried to explain the policy in a letter to an English friend: "It is a difficult proposition to establish the kind of government among these Moros which we Americans want . . . a government altogether different from the form of government which perhaps suggests itself to Englishmen under similar circumstances. You are quite content to maintain rajahs and sultans and other species of royalty, but we, with our plain way of doing things, find these gentlemen outside of our scheme of government . . . Our policy is to develop individualism among these people and, little by little, teach them to stand upon their own

feet independent of petty chieftains. In order to do this the chief or head-
man has to be given some position of more or less authority under the
government, but he ceases to have any divine rights." Each family was
being given forty acres, he added, and "The chiefs, big and little, we intend
to give an amount of land in accordance with their position and previous
authority. They will be made judges of the tribal courts, peace officers, etc.
and will be consulted in all affairs pertaining to their following . . . Municipal or town governments are being built up wherever there are enough
educated people to furnish the necessary personnel."[51]

Wood and his subordinates soon learned that forty acres of jungle
land were no compensation, from the Moro viewpoint, for the destruction
of their ancient society. Thousands of Moros defied the occupation laws,
refused to pay their poll taxes, and took to the bush in revolt. Late in 1902
Captain Pershing mounted a sizable expedition against the sultan of Maciu,
one of the leading dissidents, on the south shore of Lake Lanao. The sultan
was holed up in a fort with mud walls ten feet thick and surrounded by a
moat, but had only muzzle-loading rifles against the Americans' howitzers
and machine guns. Pershing took the fort at dawn after killing about fifty
Moros in the night battle, but most had escaped by wading along the
shoreline of the lake at their rear.

A few weeks later, however, Pershing was sending medical help to
scores of *rancherias* in his district when they were scourged by a cholera
epidemic that took fifteen hundred lives. He preferred to negotiate whenever possible, and there were grounds for suspecting he wasn't entirely
convinced that Wood's policy of trying to break the *datu* system was best,
but again in 1903 he was forced by increasing rebel activity to mount
another punitive campaign. Against warriors in buffalo-horn "armor" and
brass helmets and armed with bolos and muzzle-loaders, his troops performed with the professional and mechanical efficiency of a McCormick
reaper, storming mountain forts, taking few prisoners, scattering the followers of the dissident chiefs. His march around Lake Lanao was so
briskly conducted that Henry Savage Landor, the Tibetan explorer who
was allowed to accompany the column as a correspondent for the London
Mail, declared that Pershing was a "military genius" entitled to a "high
place among the military commanders of the world."[52]

At that stage of the "pacification" of Moro Province it was possible
to whip the Moros wherever they stood and fought, and take few casualties, because the Americans were equipped with modern weapons. Also the
Moros foolishly copied not only the Spanish weapons but the Spanish
tactics. Once they learned to strike, then fade away into the jungle, as
guerrillas must always fight, it wouldn't be quite so easy for an American
officer to win the reputation of being a military genius.

Again in 1906, when Governor Wood himself took the field against
rebellious Moros on the island of Jolo, it was demonstrated how the Moros

were defeating themselves by demonstrations of *machismo,* by preferring to stand and die because as warriors they were guaranteed passage to paradise, which was infinitely more attractive than being governed by Americans. About six hundred Moros had fortified the crater of Bud Dajo, a heavily wooded volcanic mountain that could be approached by only three trails. The Sixth Infantry, bolstered by a landing party from a destroyer and a detachment from the recently formed Moro constabulary, struggled up the steep flanks of the mountain. The ascent was so difficult that a mountain howitzer had to be hauled up by block and tackle. When they reached the crater, they were met with a shower of javelins, knives, bullets and boulders. Among the defenders were many women, who dressed themselves as men and fought just as bravely.

The Moros would not surrender, but fought to the last man and woman. Practically all of the six hundred rebels, male and female, were killed in the hand-to-hand fighting in the crater, and one-fourth of General Wood's troops were killed or wounded. When news of that bloody victory reached the States, there was an outcry of protest in the press and on the Senate floor. The War Department cabled Wood demanding particulars on charges that there had been a "wanton slaughter of men, women and children." John Sharp Williams of Mississippi read before the Senate a parody of the Tennyson epic which he titled "Charge of the Wood Brigade":

> *Chased them from everywhere,*
> *Chased them all onward,*
> *Into the crater of death,*
> *Drove them — six hundred!*
> *"Forward, the Wood Brigade!*
> *Spare not a one," he said.*
> *"Shoot all six hundred!"*[53]

Stateside claims that he should have surrounded the rebels and starved them into surrender displayed only an ignorance of the tactical situation, General Wood replied. "The mountain around the base is about eleven miles, most of it covered with a dense tropical forest. You can readily figure out the number of men it would have required to cover it. The renegades had from three to six months' supply on the mountain, with an abundance of water. There was nothing to do but take the place . . . I believe that some of our own hard-praying ancestors dealt with the Pequot Indians in a somewhat similar manner, and on a great deal less provocation."

Shortly thereafter Wood was transferred to command of the Philippine Division, with headquarters in Manila, and turned his attention from the Moro guerrillas to matters of strategy. The islands, he said, should be converted into a firm base for operations against whichever nation presented itself as an opponent of American expansion in the Far East. Wood nominated the Japanese, and he wrote President Roosevelt urging that a powerful naval base be constructed at Manila — not in Subic Bay as the navy proposed — to be ready for "any two powers while the war may last." He explained:

"Very few people who have lived in the East for any length of time take any stock in the idea that we shall be left free to work our will here. Japan is very anxious to be the new England, or England, of the East. She has unlimited coal and cheap labor, and she will soon be able to manufacture finished products from crude material almost as well as we can."[54]

With such eventualities in mind, it became all the more important that the Moro rebellion in the southern islands be suppressed and the whole Philippine base be made secure. In 1909 Pershing, who had been jumped from captain to brigadier general (coincidentally, perhaps, after he married the daughter of the Senate's Military Affairs Committee), was sent back to the Moro Province as military governor. The province was now listed as "pacified," but the Moslem priests and Arab missionaries were still stirring up trouble on the island of Jolo.

From his headquarters at Zamboanga, Pershing drew up a program for improving the living conditions of all the Moros, including a project to harness the Tumaga River and provide irrigation for year-round rice planting in the terraced fields of Mindanao. Yet even in Zamboanga Americans weren't safe on the streets. The more fanatical element among the Moros had devised a new weapon against the occupation forces and their families; it was called *juramentado*. A Moro whipped up into a religious frenzy by the priests would run amok with a bolo and cut down any Christian — man, woman or child — he could reach. The sudden attacks terrorized the resident Americans from Mindanao to the tailbone of the Sulu archipelago.

Just how frightening the atmosphere had become was described by the young wife of an army officer in a letter home: "Last December a Moro attacked a captain, who fired six .38 caliber shots into him. The Moro didn't stop running for a second; he came right on, cut the captain to pieces with his bolo and started on his way rejoicing, when a guard finally finished him with a .45 caliber bullet. That is the size of pistol everyone carries here. I am just beginning to go around without feeling scared to death. Joe says I will give him nervous prostration if I don't stop grabbing him and saying, 'What's that?' "[55]

Major General Tasker Bliss, then commanding the Philippine Division, suggested to Pershing that he adopt the methods of the British in India to halt the *juramentado* attacks. The British dealt with Moslem fanatics by burying them wrapped in a pig's hide. Pershing wisely refused to adopt the suggestion because he believed it would arouse an enduring bitterness among the Moros. He was determined to avoid a Sepoy Rebellion or any of the other bloody uprisings which had recently marked colonial administrations in North Africa, the Belgian Congo, Madagascar and Indo-China. He kept traveling over the Moro Province on horseback and between the islands on a cutter, urging the people to devote themselves to commerce and agriculture. As much as possible he wanted to subdue any unruly factions by employing a native cavalry force "mounted on hardy native ponies which require none of the expensive hay of the American horse."[56]

On the island of Jolo, however, his persuasions had little effect in countering the efforts of agitators who pointed out that the Joloanos had to pay American taxes yet were forbidden to own slaves or keep more than one wife. In 1911 he ordered the whole province disarmed. This caused such an uproar on Jolo that in December he had to organize a punitive expedition against the Moros of the Bud Dajo district. Once again the Moros took to the mountaintop. Pershing surrounded the crater with one thousand troops, half United States Regulars and half Philippine Scouts, and placed about three hundred Moros under siege. The Moros tried to break through the siege lines on Christmas Eve but the sortie was thrown back. The next day they surrendered, except for forty-seven who fled into the jungle and later were captured by the Philippine Scouts. The operation was performed neatly, humanely, almost bloodlessly.

The next year, however, trouble broke out again on Jolo, this time with the Moros of the Latiward district. The Moros retired to their fort on top of Mount Bagsak, and Pershing, after trying to talk them out of resisting, sent his troops up after them. He imposed the strictest kind of censorship, knowing that the Moros, "mostly notorious cattle thieves and murderers," would have to be rooted out with a heavy loss of life. The only correspondent who accompanied the force was a reliable type from the Manila *Times*.

At moonrise on the night of June 15, 1913, Pershing's Regular infantry and Philippine Scouts attacked the fortified crater on Mount Bagsak. They took it with only six of their own men killed, seven wounded, under the massed fire of heavy machine guns. In his report Pershing did not say how many Moro men, women and children were slaughtered, only that a "very severe punishment was administered." Some hints as to the extent of that punishment eventually leaked into the press. Several Manila-based correspondents reported that five hundred were killed.[57] A possibly more accurate estimate was given by John McLeod, a civilian employee of the Army Quartermaster Department, who returned to the States six weeks after the battle of Bagsak. He told a Washington newspaper that two thousand Moros had been killed, that women and children had been "mowed down by the scores" in a crossfire of machine guns. "The news of the fighting was strictly censored at Manila," McLeod was quoted as saying. "Three correspondents who managed to reach the seat of war were arrested on orders of General Pershing."[58]

There were good reasons not to upset the Washington of 1913 with the pacifist-minded Woodrow Wilson in the White House. Mindanao and the Sulu islands, in any case, continued to be the United States Army's experimental station, curtained off and soundproofed from sight and sound of the squeamish people back in the States. The armed resistance of the Moros was substantially reduced after the "punishment" administered by Pershing in 1913, but piracy, slavery and polygamy were never entirely stamped out, and the jungle trails of the mountainous interior of Mindanao and Jolo were never really safe for travel by Americans.

The Moros had demonstrated that brass helmets, blowguns, bamboo artillery and bolo knives could, if wielded by a determined and cohesive people, prevail against modern armaments. They could wait and stick it out while the Americans contented themselves — as elsewhere and later — with kill ratios and illusory victories.

From all but the most squalid financial viewpoints, the American seizure of the Philippines was simply a governmental crime. If it was necessary to extend our system of security into the western Pacific, we would have been granted bases in the Philippines, as Aguinaldo promised before the conquest began. We would also have been freely granted a preferred trading status in the Philippines simply by making it possible, through Dewey's destruction of the Spanish squadron in Manila Bay, for the insurgents to drive the Spanish out. We could have helped the Filipinos through the first stages of self-government by offering advice and counsel, without a prodding of bayonets. But we wanted it all, especially the heady sensations of conquest. The Assistant Secretary of the Treasury, Frank A. Vanderlip, made it plain enough in a magazine article published during the pivotal summer of 1898. Aside from the "alluring" strategic advantages of holding the Philippines, he wrote, the "undeveloped resources" of the islands were a "great opportunity for our genius . . . In a decade we might make a change greater than has been wrought since Magellan's discovery." He foresaw "great development companies formed to cultivate tobacco and sugar by modern methods, others formed to test the richness of the unknown mineral deposits, and still others to develop transportation or to reap the treasures of the forest."[59]

It all came to pass. Some of our people, and a lesser number of the Filipinos, became wealthy through exploitation. The incalculable weight is in the opposite balance of the scales, in thousands of deaths, thousands of sorrows, the dishonor of what we hoped to be as a nation. We had lost something more than our "jocund youth," as Captain Mahan put it, in exchange for national "manhood." We had struck a Faustian bargain we will never finish paying off.

11

The Testament of Homer Lea

Free China will yet perish unless there rises from your innermost bosom
the militant spirit of another Martial Monk.

— HOMER LEA, 1912

A California mining engineer named Red Wilson was prospecting mineral
formations west of Peking in May 1900 when a runner brought word that
the Boxer Rebellion had broken out. He knew enough of Chinese history,
and of the current mood of the Chinese people, to realize that such con-
vulsions could be dangerous to "foreign devils" as well as the natives
themselves.

Wilson started at once for Peking, where he believed he would be safe
behind the walled compounds of the foreign legations. That night he
paused in his journey at the village of a hospitable mandarin, from whom
he learned that the Boxers had become active all through the countryside
and might even now be storming the legations in Peking.

Wilson got up early the next morning to hurry on his way to the Chinese capital. He was just saddling his horse when a strange little figure appeared through the dawn mist. The man was a hunchback, no more than five feet tall, dressed in a Chinese robe and bearing a sword almost as long as he was tall. Even more oddly, the hunchback was a white man and spoke English.

"I've never had the pleasure of meeting you," he said, "but I know you by sight. You're Red Wilson. I'm a Stanford man myself — Homer Lea, Class of '99. I know all about you. Don't be worried about your trip to Peking. Word has gone on ahead, and you won't be molested."

Wilson and Lea discussed briefly various persons they had known at Stanford, and then the mining engineer, still puzzled by Lea's mysterious appearance and his strange, authoritative manner, rode off toward Peking. The countryside was in arms, but no one bothered him and he reached Peking in safety shortly before the Boxers laid siege to the foreign legations. Many times in succeeding weeks he puzzled over who Homer Lea was, what he was doing in China, how his writ could run through a countryside in which more than two hundred white missionaries would be killed and more than sixteen thousand Chinese Christians ("second-class red-haired devils," as the Boxers contemptuously classified the converts) would be massacred. Wilson would have been even more astonished if he had known that Lea was given the illusory rank of lieutenant general of the "Army of the Emperor" and at the age of twenty-four was making himself a factor in the history of modern China.[1]

1. *Birth of a "Martial Monk"*

Neither his contemporaries nor succeeding generations have known quite what to make of Homer Lea. He was an incredible figure — a half-blind, sickly hunchback who somehow became a Chinese general and one of the organizers of the revolution that finished off the Manchu dynasty. He also made incredible prophecies, which turned out to be incredibly accurate and may be still more so in the future — that Great Britain would lose her empire "east of Suez," that Japan would launch a war against the United States with sneak attacks on Hawaii and the Philippines, that the last great war would involve the Anglo-Saxon powers on one side and Russia on the other, that the "swarming of the Slav" eventually would present the West with its greatest political and military crisis.

Many historians have considered him a charlatan. He is rarely mentioned, or only in passing if at all, by scholarly historians of modern China. There has never been a biography of Lea himself. Any serious biographer would, in fact, be appalled at the task of making him believable. It was as though Toulouse-Lautrec threw away his paint pots and made himself a marshal of France.

Yet he cannot be ignored in any account of how the United States became transfixed by the idea of a Pacific empire. The Chinese revolution would have occurred, undoubtedly, if Lea had never lived. It was the impact of his ideas on his own country and others in the West that lent him a more than transitory importance. He was a direct influence on various American military leaders down to General Douglas MacArthur, on Kaiser Wilhelm, Adolf Hitler, Lenin, geopolitican Karl Haushofer, the British field marshal Lord Roberts and many others. The discomfiture of historians unable to credit his existence is evident in the conservative account of Lea's life in the *Dictionary of American Biography,* which says of him:

"He has been hailed as one of the great military geniuses of history, and he unquestionably impressed some observers with the right to this title. No one can doubt his uncanny skill in organizing and leading the forces of the Chinese people. Opinions as to his motives differ, and it is not easy to determine whether he was an unselfish enthusiast fascinated by the cause of Chinese freedom, or whether he seized an opportunity to satisfy his passion for military experience. At all events he is one of the most picturesque personalities of his generation and, perhaps, the most gifted American who ever joined a foreign legion."

To encapsulate his life as that of a "picturesque" adventurer who linked his fortunes to a foreign army is, I believe, to fall short of Lea's actual achievements. The reason he will be remembered, perhaps with great ruefulness, is not for his role as a prime mover in Sun Yat-sen's revolution but as a prophet of American destiny in the Pacific. As a top-drawer Pacificist, his influence was incalculable and undoubtedly extended to shaping certain attitudes which helped to bring about the events parenthesized by the attack on Pearl Harbor and the atomic obliteration of Hiroshima.

Homer Lea was born in Denver on November 17, 1876, and came of mettlesome Southern stock. His grandfather was a Tennessee-born physician who was killed in Missouri by border raiders because of his Confederate sympathies. His father joined the Colorado gold rush at the age of fourteen and staked out a number of profitable claims at Cripple Creek. Alfred Erskine Lea took his family, including Homer and two daughters, to Los Angeles when the boy was sixteen.[2]

By then Homer had developed a full set of defense mechanisms to protect any inferiority he may have felt over his small size, his curved spine and his myopia. Instead of shrinking from the sight of others, he made himself stand out. Instead of apologizing for his differentness, he made the most of it, he swaggered with self-confidence, he was a "brilliant but erratic student" at Los Angeles high school, as his classmates have recalled.

Early in boyhood he had become fascinated by military history, could reel off the details of all the campaigns of Alexander, Caesar and Hannibal. A boyhood friend has recalled that he showed an early talent for leadership by "drilling the kids with broomsticks in the backyard." His great ambition was to be a soldier, but he knew that he would never be accepted by any regular army in the world. Even in high school, one of his classmates had recalled, Homer continued to "play soldier," wearing self-designed uniforms, and "in his backyard he laid out replicas of the great battles and campaigns of the world . . . plotted and carried out the battles of Caesar, Napoleon and Robert E. Lee." Marshall Stimson also recalled that his friends "never allowed anyone to treat him as a cripple," and that he insisted on accompanying them on camping trips to the mountains. If he stumbled on the trail, he would rage at anyone who tried to help him up.[3]

As a teenager Homer also was engrossed in studying the Chinese and their language. He spent much time in the Los Angeles Chinatown, making friends and learning their customs. He studied the language with the family cook. In all this he showed a great deal of originality for a Californian of his time. In the 1890's the Chinese-American was regarded as a numskull capable of only the most menial labor, and certainly not worth any Caucasian's intelligent regard. Aside from intellectual curiosity, there was probably another reason for Homer's interest in the Chinese and his eagerness to share their company. The Chinese revered hunchbacks, believed they were specially endowed by heaven with wisdom and good luck. In China, too, tradition had it that scholars were generally bent-backed from their studies, which gave rise to the Chinese proverb that a man's brains are in his back. The Los Angeles Chinese were equally impressed by his large piercing gray eyes. "Homer Lea," they said, "can see fifteen feet into the ground." One Chinese friend said that "he had eyes that could bury you nine feet under the ground if you disobeyed him."[4]

By the time he entered college he had decided that since a military career was out of the question he would use his eloquence, his ability to sway the minds of others, as a lawyer. He attended Occidental College near Los Angeles for a year, then transferred to Stanford University at Palo Alto.

Entering Stanford with the Class of '99, he found himself, at first, a nonentity among a large assortment of vibrantly talented young men and women. Herbert Hoover would be leaving shortly to take up a mining career in China; he was director of the mining operations of the Chinese government when the Boxer Rebellion ended that phase of his career. Other big men on the campus included Will and Wallace Irwin, who became celebrated journalists and writers. An intellectual ferment was working on the campus; many of the students — definitely not including Homer Lea — were socialists, anarchists or pacifists, or all three at once. The

president of Stanford was Dr. David Starr Jordan, the renowned pacifist
and promoter of international arbitration, who would remember Homer
Lea as "vulgar, loud-mouthed, excessively war-like."

It was true enough that even when Homer Lea was immersed in the
prevailing liberal humanitarianism, the cultish pacifism at Stanford, he
stubbornly insisted on glorifying militarism. In the memory of the Irwin
brothers he lingered as a flamboyant little fellow, who dressed in strange
costumes accenting the Oriental and the military, lived in a room hung with
ordnance maps and called himself the "Martial Monk." He "acted like he
might be Napoleon himself," Wallace Irwin remembered.[5]

When the Spanish-American War broke out and hundreds of his
classmates enlisted, he was heartbroken to have the recruiting sergeants
shoo him away even during a war emergency. He joined a college cavalry
troop, Wallace Irwin recalled, that "included a thousand freaks — the
lame, the halt and the blind."

During his college years he survived an almost fatal bout with the
smallpox, which left his health even more precarious and further weakened
his poor eyesight. Yet he made himself one of the best fencers on the
campus, according to Wallace Irwin, as well as the canniest poker player.

Will Irwin remembered Lea the collegian as a pathetic but proud and
defiant youth. "His torso seemed only a bulb fastened on to his legs and his
face had that appearance of a wise child common among people with his
affliction. For all that, he carried himself with a defiant dignity. He seemed
to repel most advances toward intimacy, probably because he felt that pity
prompted them. But he played chess, and so did I; that led to acquaintance.

"He was always drawing the analogy between chess and war. A
clever move with his castle and 'See, I've brought my heavy artillery into
action,' he would say. I found, then, that war was his hobby — our American Civil War especially. Perhaps that was the prime reason why I began a
few years later to devour the political and military history of that period.
After a year or so, and so far as I know without taking anyone into his
confidence, he disappeared from Stanford. Someone said he had been very
ill and that upon his recovery he had gone to the Orient."[6]

One faculty member who was impressed by young Lea was Professor
Ray Lyman Wilbur, later president of Stanford and still later a member of
Herbert Hoover's Cabinet. Wilbur recalled him as a student of "great but
indefinable promise," and "one of those men who always question professors."

During his last year at Stanford, the Irwin brothers and his other
Caucasian friends saw little of Lea largely because he had formed a close
alliance with two Chinese-American students, Allen Chung and Lou Hoy.
The parents of both young men lived in China and were wealthy. At first
the three-cornered friendship was based on expeditions to the San Fran-

cisco Chinatown, where elaborate Chinese dinners and rice wine were consumed. Chung and Hoy, evidently, were feeling him out. Soon enough they were convinced that Lea's passionate interest in all things Chinese was sincere and profound; in vehemence it undoubtedly equaled theirs.

Chung and Hoy revealed that they were revolutionaries dedicated to driving the dowager empress Tzu Hsi from her Dragon Throne, that they were "members of a secret society whose purpose it was to overthrow the Manchus." Lea was introduced to more senior and influential citizens of Chinatown, who also looked him over and tested his sincerity. They decided he was trustworthy, and "one night in Chinatown Lea was secretly initiated into this undercover society."[7] Quite impulsively, he decided to quit college and throw all his energies into the cause of a republican China. His family was dismayed, and his father cut off his three-hundred-dollars-a-month allowance.

Before quitting the campus he announced with characteristic grandiloquence to Harry Carr, later a reporter on the Los Angeles *Times,* "All great careers are carved out by the sword. Mine, too, I shall carve out that way." Carr and others to whom he confided kept a straight face but inwardly considered him slightly mad. The idea of a deformed and myopic young man, barely five feet tall, turning soldier of fortune seemed quixotic at best. But not to the Chinese, who valued brains above brawn in a soldier, and besides Lea had the intrinsic value of being a white Caucasian, a possible bridge from the republican revolutionaries to the American sympathy and support they would need.

Lea applied to the State Department to send him to China as an official observer, but the government couldn't see any wisdom in financing the foreign travel plans of a twenty-three-year-old man who hadn't even finished his schooling. He would be given a passport and the government's unofficial blessings on his mission, whatever it was, but he was not to involve himself in the internal affairs of another government.

The money to send Lea to China was finally raised by the Los Angeles Chinese chamber of commerce. He was also given letters of introduction and instruction by the revolutionary secret society.* In June 1900, he sailed for Canton from San Francisco after telling friends, quite grandly, "I go to topple the Manchus from their ancient Dragon Throne." It is not difficult to believe that General Douglas MacArthur studied Lea, not only for his strategic concepts but his literary style.

As his ship sailed out through the Golden Gate, he later recalled, he thought of Kipling's comment on San Francisco: "What a wonderful place to loot!" It was the seedling of his conviction that the United States might one day be invaded from the West, from Asia.

---

* It was apparently a branch of the ancient White Lotus Society, which had brewed revolutions in China for centuries. Originally ·it was a secret Buddhist organization formed to drive out the Mongol overlords, and later the Ming dynasty.

2. *The Shadow Army*

For many years the Chinese empire had been enduring the rule of its own Victoria. Like the British queen, she was small, shrewd and willful. She not only had a whim of iron but the calcified heart required for the art of selective assassination. When anyone threatened her autocratic regime, he was eliminated with dispatch. Tzu Hsi, who had something in common with Catherine the Great and Cleopatra as well, had been ruling China for almost forty years of extravagant widowhood.

She had started out in a lowly position at the court of the Forbidden City, only a third-grade concubine, the daughter of an army captain. One night, according to legend, she had herself smuggled into the emperor's bedchamber. Rolled in a bolt of red silk, she had herself carried to the emperor's bed. The silk unreeled, and there lay Tzu Hsi, naked as a nightingale and blushing from head to foot. That Cleopatran maneuver resulted in the birth of a son, who became heir apparent to the throne. The emperor died in 1861, and Tzu Hsi became regent as mother of the future emperor. Anyone who stood between Tzu Hsi and the exercise of power was living in danger, including her own son. Rather than allow him to take that power, the eunuchs of her court were ordered to pander to all of her son's sexual fancies. The youth died of exhaustion. His widow was pregnant, but she died mysteriously before another claimant to power could be born.

That still left a nephew, Kuang Hsu, who was allowed to reach manhood with the understanding that he would ultimately be made emperor but would act only on the advice of his indomitable aunt. During his youth, however, Emperor Kuang Hsu fell under the influence of parties at the Imperial court who wished to see China reform and modernize herself. The dowager empress was outraged, but for some reason, possibly a sentimental one, she did not order her nephew to the chopping block. Instead, as a lesson in obedience, she had fifty-three of his servants executed. Kuang Hsu persisted in error, however, and appointed as prime minister Kang Yu-wei, a Western-minded progressive secretly working for the overthrow of the dowager empress. Again someone else had to suffer for Emperor Kuang Hsu's stubbornness; his aunt ordered two eunuchs to wrap the young man's favorite concubine in a carpet and drop her into the palace well while Kuang Hsu was forced to watch.

The youthful emperor, still under the influence of Prime Minister Kang Yu-wei and other members of the government, signed a series of edicts which, if placed into effect, would have transformed China into something resembling a modern state. The period of Kuang Hsu's brief self-assertion was known as the Hundred Days' Reform. It was abruptly terminated by the dowager empress, who had the emperor imprisoned in the palace and herself resumed ruling as regent. Some members of the government fled for their lives, six slower ones were beheaded, but Prime Minister Kang Yu-wei was either too canny or too prominent to be disposed of. He stayed in office, continued to intrigue against Tzu Hsi, and organized a sort of underground army to rise against her whenever the time seemed right.[8]

The next uprising, however, was staged by the Society of Harmonious Fists. Originally the Boxers were dedicated to destroying the Manchus, but the Empress Tzu Hsi managed by secret negotiation and possibly by bribery to divert the Boxers from their anti-Manchu activities to "driving out the foreign devils." She hated Westerners, and by this skillful maneuver would not only turn aside the native revolutionaries but, possibly, make China too uncomfortable for the merchants and missionaries who had acquired so much power over her country. For several months she was able to watch with satisfaction as the Boxers undertook their redhanded campaign of terror against the foreigners and their Chinese followers. In Tienstin, European women's breasts were cut off by the Boxers and the women left on the city wall to die. In Taiyuan a Chinese executioner, assisted by his Boxer comrades, hacked the heads off forty-five white missionaries, their wives and children. In other remote districts white women were doused with kerosene and ignited.

In the midst of all this terrorism, Homer Lea arrived in China and proceeded from Canton to Peking, where he had been ordered to report to the underground conspiracy Kang Yu-wei had organized before he was forced to flee for Hong Kong. An organization known as the Chinese Reform Army was waiting in the hills, Lea was told, waiting for the signal to strike. It would attack the Royal Manchu Army, the defenders of the dowager empress. Lea himself was appointed a lieutenant general and ordered to take command of what was styled the Second Division of the "Army of the Emperor." That would make the fourth military force to take the field. The "shadow army" sworn to loyalty to the imprisoned Emperor Kuang Hsu would take on the empress's Royal Manchu Army, while the combined expeditionary forces of the Western nations dealt with the Boxers besieging the foreign legations in Peking.

Young Homer Lea stepped into this confused situation with more courage than discretion. He must have loved every minute of it: the secret conferences, the conspiracies within the palace walls, the clandestine meetings with his new subordinates — and above all, perhaps, the gorgeously brocaded uniform of a Chinese lieutenant general.

He found his "division" — actually a rabble of ex-bandits and peasant youths looking for excitement and loot — waiting for its commander in the Shensi hills. Those amiable brigands would have frightened the wits out of anyone less confident of his power to command. Fortunately Lea had not been spoiled by a West Point education. He started drilling them as though he were the reincarnation of Chinese Gordon.

Meanwhile, his fellow Americans and other Westerners were fighting for their lives — and for once all on the same side — against the raging hordes of Boxers. The Siege of the Legations for several years was a heartwarming episode in the West; Germans and Frenchmen, Russians and Englishmen, Americans and Italians side by side in the firing line. And with them, those honorary Westerners, the Japanese, plucky little chaps who promised to be a credit to their patrons. The Peking Defense Force of 480 held off twenty thousand Boxers for fifty-five days. Then a relief column commanded by the German field marshal Waldersee and made up of troops of most of the besieged nationalities broke through and lifted the siege. Included in the expedition was the 14th United States Infantry commanded by General Adna R. Chaffee, which had been rushed from the Philippines to become part of a demonstration of colonialism at its apogee . . . the First Sikhs . . . the 24th Punjabs . . . the First Bengal Lancers . . . the Royal Welsh Fusiliers . . .

When the relief column entered Peking, Homer Lea and his Second Division of the Chinese Reform Army, about two thousand ragged and poorly equipped troops, marched in on the heels of the expeditionary force. Doubtless he and his troops presented a problem to the commanders of that force. If they were allowed to stay in Peking, they might yield to the temptation to loot. The place was overrun by soldiery as it was.

The problem was solved when the dowager empress fled from her palace with a large bodyguard of the Royal Manchu Army. Lea was ordered to take his ragtag legion and pursue her. The Second Division marched out of the capital with Lea at its head, riding in a gilded palanquin and dressed in mandarin's costume. The hardbitten old cavalryman, General Chaffee, must have shaken his head at that spectacle.

Lea's first campaign turned out to be a disaster. His troops chased after the dowager empress with a will, no doubt inspired by the thought of all the treasure she was carrying with her. Suddenly, however, they were attacked from the rear. The Second Division simply disintegrated. Those who escaped the enfilading fire of the Imperial troops fled into the Shensi hills, in which they could return immediately to their old calling of banditry.

Within a few hours Lea found himself downgraded from a lieutenant general to a fugitive. The empress particularly wanted him captured and punished, and placed a ten-thousand-dollar reward on his head. He found refuge in a Buddhist temple, where a courageous priest nursed him back to health. Meanwhile, the dowager empress was making peace with the Western nations and subsequently was allowed to return to her palace in Peking. An appearance of normality was restored, the boy emperor remained in his aunt's custody, but Homer Lea was still a fugitive with a price on his head.

Fortunately for him and the republican cause, the underground network of agents set up by Kang Yu-wei was still operative. Lea got word to them that he was hiding out in a Buddhist temple, and he was smuggled to Hong Kong and safety. There he joined Kang Yu-wei and another leader of the Reform party, Liang Chi-chao. In Hong Kong he also met for the first time Dr. Sun Yat-sen, the mild-mannered and idealistic founder of the "Association for Changing the Mandate," a polite Chinese euphemism for revolution. Sun Yat-sen had a political base in South China, the backing of thousands of members of the secret societies, and this gave him an advantage over such northern politicians as Kang Yu-wei and Liang Chi-chao, who had a conspiracy but no political organization. It was Sun Yat-sen's belief that China must acquire scientific knowledge from the West but "for the true principles of political philosophy, the Europeans need to learn from China."

As Dr. Sun described his first meeting with Lea in his autobiography: "I was speaking to a company of my fellows, when my eye fell on a young man of slight physique . . . Afterward he came to me and said: 'I would like to throw in my lot with you. I believe your ideas will succeed . . .' He held out his hand. I took it and thanked him, wondering who he was. After he had gone I asked, 'Who was that little hunchback?' 'That,' said the man who brought him, 'is Homer Lea, one of the most brilliant — perhaps the most brilliant — military genius now alive. He is a perfect master of modern warfare.' I almost gasped in astonishment, 'And he has offered to throw in his lot with me!' The next morning I called on Homer Lea. I told him in case I should succeed and my countrymen gave me the power to do so, I would make him my chief military adviser. " 'Make me that now,' Lea said, 'and you *will* succeed.' "

While trying to decide what to do next, Lea was approached in Hong Kong by several Japanese naval officers, who told him their country was also interested in the Manchu dynasty and wanted to help in that project. Japan then was hoping for larger trade concessions in China and arming to drive the Russians out of Korea and Manchuria, and a friendly government in Peking would greatly assist those covert designs. "Come to Japan," they told Lea. "There will be a haven for you. In Japan, with peace and quiet, you and your friends can go ahead with your plans for a revolution."

Lea conferred with Kang Yu-wei and Liang Chi-chao on the offer of Japanese hospitality, and all agreed that, suspicious as they were of Japanese friendship, they had no alternative but to accept.

A Japanese battleship took Lea and his colleagues to Tokyo, where they were received with flattery and lavish hospitality. The Japanese intimated that they would be willing to back a revolutionary movement. Lea spent three months in Japan sounding out officials of its government, trying

The Dowager Empress of China

to sort out hard guarantees from a chaff of promises and cloudy intimations. Finally he wearied of Japanese evasions and it was agreed that he
would continue on his way back to the United States while Kang Yu-wei
and Liang Chi-chao stayed in Tokyo and tried to persuade the Japanese to
make some concrete proposals.[9]

"But they had no intention of joining up the Japanese," Lea later told
a friend. "They were loyal to their native country, if not to the Empress
Dowager and the government in power. So we spent long hours together,
talking and planning what we would — or could — do next. We came to
one conclusion — the revolution must go on. Even though in exile — and
not daring to return to China to continue the fight — yet fight we would."[10]

Before Lea left Japan, yet another secret society was formed. It was
called the Po Wong Wui, or "Protect the Emperor Society." Kang Yu-wei,
a clever, adroit and ambitious man, assumed the offices of vice president,
secretary and treasurer, with the agreement that the presidency would be
left open for the leader of the revolutionary movement. Possibly that would
be Dr. Sun Yat-sen, though Kang Yu-wei undoubtedly had himself in mind
for the office.

Then Lea sailed for America to build a revolutionary movement
separated by the Pacific Ocean from the scene of its future endeavors.

3. *A Stirring in the Chinatowns*

Homer Lea returned to his native land with two passionate convictions.
The first and more immediate was that a Chinese republic must be estab-
lished for the sake of her people and for the preservation of peace in the
Orient. Only a strong and modern China could maintain a balance of
power. The second belief, and more important in the long run, was that the
United States must be awakened to the dangers it faced from an expanding
Japanese empire, must prepare to defend her possessions in the western
Pacific and even her own coast.

When he disembarked in San Francisco, Lea was met on the dock by
his two former Stanford classmates, Allen Chung and Lou Hoy.

Over dinner in Chinatown that night Lea informed his two old friends
that they must join the Po Wong Wui, that they would be his first recruits
on foreign soil.

"What, another Chinese secret society?" Chung groaned. "I already
belong to four!"

"This is different," Lea replied. "The other societies are negative in
their approach. They only want to overthrow the Dowager Empress. We
have a positive program, to liberate the Boy Emperor and modernize
China."[11]

Chung and Hoy signed on, and with Lea they toured all the Chinatowns of the United States from San Francisco to New York during the next months. In each Chinatown they first approached the secretary of the Chinese chamber of commerce and usually managed to persuade him to become the local organizer of a Po Wong Wui chapter in his town. The main object of each branch was to raise money. A war chest of $2,500,000 was needed immediately to forward the political and military objectives of the Po Wong Wui.

Lea cannily rejected the idea of seeking large contributions from the wealthier Chinese. This had to be a grass-roots movement, with membership equally as important as money. Each member accordingly was asked to pay fifty cents a month in dues. If they could manage to enlist a hundred thousand Chinese-Americans, the total dues would amount to fifty thousand dollars a month, six hundred thousand dollars a year. Later the Chinese communities in Canada and Mexico were visited by the Po Wong Wui recruiters and added their tithes to the war chest.

With the money beginning to flow in, Lea then turned his attention to more militant measures, intending to raise regiments of Chinese-Americans, with some Caucasian-American officers, to drill and train themselves for the day they would return to China as an army of liberation. He had already nominated himself as chief of staff of that army.

During this phase of his activities, in 1902, Lea began looking up his old college friends in the hope that he could imbue them with his own enthusiasm for liberating China. The response of his old opponent at the chessboard, Will Irwin, was probably typical. Irwin was working as a reporter on the San Francisco *Chronicle* when he received a note from Lea asking him to come to the Palace Hotel on urgent business.

"I found him established in a suite," Irwin recalled in his memoirs, "draped with Chinese hangings, hung with Chinese paintings. He had lost his shyness and acquired an air of authority. First pledging me to secrecy — thereby ruining the interview as a newspaper story — he plunged into business by offering me a commission as captain in the new Chinese army which was going to take over the country and put China on the map as a modern nation. 'I'm the generalissimo,' he added.

"Since my military experience was limited to a brief, inglorious service with the West Denver High School Cadets, I regarded the offer of a commission as fantastic. And I said so.

" 'Not at all,' he replied. 'This isn't any ordinary military situation. You were reared on the frontier. You can ride and shoot. You know how to get on with men. We'd expect you to spend two years in learning to speak Chinese — that's easier than you think — and studying military tactics under European instructors. Then you'd be ready to work. Also, remember this: you write, and China's an untilled field. Everything written about it by a European, so far, is childish — laughable.'

"This was one of the things to dream romantic dreams about, but not to take seriously. So I declined with thanks, as did several other Stanford men of my acquaintance to whom he offered commissions as captains or majors."

Irwin recalled that he was puzzled by Lea's own enthusiasm for liberating a foreign country until he talked to an American traveler just returned from China. "A prophet of the Chinese classics, he said, had written that a hunchback would come from afar to deliver China. I have wondered since if that was not only the answer to Lea's career but its first impulse. He had of course a complex of inferiority on account of his deformity. His military mania was his protective mechanism. Perhaps in his miscellaneous reading he had come across the prophecy and gone to China to capitalize on it."[12]

More promising material than his former Stanford classmates came Lea's way a short time later in the stalwart person of Ansel O'Banion, recently discharged as a sergeant in the Fourth United States Cavalry. O'Banion was a Nebraskan who had served in the Philippines, and came bearing a letter from Major General Adna R. Chaffee, which read: "The bearer of this letter is A. E. O'Banion, former 1st Sergeant of Troop A, 4th United States Cavalry, of whom I have previously written you. Without question he has all the qualifications you mentioned in your letter to the Auditor of the War Department."

General Chaffee had remembered meeting Lea in Peking during the Boxer Rebellion and sympathized with his plans for democratizing China. In the administration of Theodore Roosevelt this was quite permissible, apparently, though the War Department in effect would be cooperating in the attempted overthrow of a foreign government. Within a year General Chaffee would be promoted to lieutenant general and chief of staff of the United States Army, and would become one of the most fervent supporters of Lea's doctrines.

O'Banion met Lea by appointment in a Los Angeles hotel lobby, and was told that the Chinese revolutionary army needed an experienced noncom to help train the recruits. "I had one chap, a former West Pointer," Lea said, "who wouldn't use chopsticks and ate rice with his fingers. The Chinese didn't like him."

O'Banion was wary at first, but like most men soon succumbed to Lea's eupeptic personality. Lea admitted the service he required might be dangerous. "We are playing a hide-and-seek game with governments — and the secret controlling forces behind those governments. There may be times when we do not know exactly who are our friends — or who our enemies. We may ultimately land in jail, or even be murdered." The objective, Lea continued, was the Royal Manchu Army, which controlled China. "To rid China of this large standing army is one of the very first steps in our plan. We hope it can be done peacefully. We want to avoid bloodshed as much as possible. Rather than cut off heads, we'd prefer to cut off queues."

The odds admittedly were against a successful revolution, Lea added, but "We have one chance left . . . If we can enlist the aid and support of the Chinese living in America, there is some hope . . . We must work in America — there is no other place to go."

O'Banion took the oath of allegiance to the Po Wong Wui Society that night at a ceremony which combined the grislier aspects of a fraternity initiation and a voodoo ritual, but which Lea immensely enjoyed. (Uniforms, oaths, swords, secret societies, recognition signals, cloaks and daggers were the breath of life to Lea. They allowed him to escape into a sort of fictional existence. They also contributed to a feeling among the sober-minded that Lea was acting out a role in what should have been a private fantasy.) A live chicken was slaughtered and its blood drained into a bowl. O'Banion dipped his finger in the blood and signed his name on a paper on which the oath was inscribed.[13]

Lea had also rented a building in downtown Los Angeles which was converted into an armory and designated the Western Military Academy. Soon 120 recruits were drilling there every evening under O'Banion's command, and similar companies were being organized in cities throughout the United States. Each city was limited to one company of 120 men. Each man was equipped with a 7-mm. Mauser rifle. When room was needed for more complicated maneuvers, the old Stockade, a two-acre vacant lot surrounded by a ten-foot board fence at Apablasa and Juan streets, near Chinatown, was rented for the purpose. It was formerly a baseball field. There Lea's recruits were instructed in marching by columns and given bayonet drill.

There was a certain amount of snickering in Los Angeles and other cities with Chinatowns at the spectacle of laundrymen, cooks and waiters taking themselves seriously enough to claim to be soldiers. Both Lea and his recruits were accustomed to being laughed at, and doggedly continued with the training. Lea kept an eye on Los Angeles while in other cities the drilling was conducted by various United States Army veterans. Sergeant Francis Drischler, an architect, was in charge of the St. Louis contingent of the Chinese Reform Army; Sergeant William Donohue in Chicago; Corporal Frank C. Hardy in Denver; Sergeant Jim Bradley in New York, where the young men from Mott Street drilled in a vacant lot in downtown Manhattan; Sergeant Jim Littleton, in Boston; Sergeant Joe Miller, Spokane; Corporal William Grady, Portland, Oregon; Sergeant William English, in Hanford, California, and Sergeant Jim Healy in Seattle — many of them Old China Hands. Several other companies were commanded by Chinese, Ben Young in Fresno, Wing Lee in Phoenix, Wah Gee in San Bernardino, and Suey Wing in Santa Barbara.

Lea's influence over these scattered legions was so great that he even managed to persuade them to cut off their queues in mass ceremonies of defiance to the Manchus.

There was such a stirring in the Chinatowns across the country that the newspapers began taking note of the militancy which seemed at variance with the meekness of the Chinese, who had not tried to defend themselves years before when they were under attack by their fellow citizens. A newspaper in La Crosse, Wisconsin, reported that National Guard officers and noncoms were being approached to act as drill instructors. "It is said that none but Philippine veterans will be approached. Strict secrecy is being maintained."[14]

A scarehead in the Philadelphia *Inquirer* reported the existence of a vast conspiracy on American soil which had attracted the attention of the United States Secret Service. Agents of the Secret Service "acting under the personal direction of Chief Wilkie have discovered that a large proportion of Chinamen in this country are involved in a world-wide conspiracy to overthrow the present Chinese dynasty . . . In Philadelphia the revolutionary party has headquarters in the heart of Chinatown. In a house on Race Street, near Ninth, which is being watched night and day by the Secret Service men, a body of Chinamen is being drilled daily."[15]

Chief Wilkie eventually came to Los Angeles and interviewed both Lea and O'Banion, who were politely evasive. His investigation, in any case, came up with no startling revelations such as the newspapers predicted. It was quietly dropped. Higher authority than the Secret Service obviously was taking a paternal interest in Lea's revolutionary activities. They were extralegal, of course; officially the United States government could not permit an army to be organized on its soil to be employed against a friendly power. But a republican China, helped into being by Americans, would be an even friendlier power. Aside from commercial considerations, it could offset the growing power of Japan.[16]

Late in 1904 both Sun Yat-sen, based in Hong Kong and leader of the left wing of the republican movement, and Liang Chi-chao, Lea's old friend and a leader of the Po Wong Wui right-wing faction based in Tokyo, came over to inspect the Chinese Reform Army's various units. Liang Chi-chao arrived first in Los Angeles, and the publicity-conscious Lea announced to the newspapers that he was actually a Manchu prince. Royalty was always good for extended treatment in the American press, and "Prince" Liang Chi-chao got it. Lea greeted him in the full-dress uniform of the higher ranks of the Chinese Reform Army with its blue tunic decorated with self-awarded medals, its collar bearing the gold leaves of a general officer. A greatcoat was thrown around his hunched shoulders, and the hilt of his ceremonial sword came up almost to his collarbone. Liang Chi-choa inspected the Los Angeles troops and was honored by a parade through Chinatown. He was shocked, however, at the spectacle of respectable Chinese trotting around without their pigtails.

In February of the following year Kang Yu-wei, the titular head of the Po Wong Wui, came over from Tokyo and was the guest at a banquet attended by Harrison Gray Otis, the publisher of the Los Angeles *Times* and a patron of Lea's, the president of the Los Angeles chamber of commerce, and other Caucasian dignitaries. Among them also was the rising young novelist Jack London, who came down from San Francisco as a representative of William Randolph Hearst's *Examiner*.

Kang Yu-wei's principal objective on his visit was to deal with the hundreds of thousands of dollars collected by the Po Wong Wui chapters throughout the United States. Four hundred thousand dollars were invested in rubber plantations, on Kang Yu-wei's decision, and a trunk packed with thousands more was turned over to Lea for safekeeping under the trapdoor of a stable on Marchessault Street. Once the financial affairs were settled, Kang and Lea set out on a tour of the country, including Washington, where they were received by President Roosevelt, and ending up in New York. Kang told the New York *Times* that the President had been "very cordial" and "said he would do all in his power to further the better treatment of the Chinese, and would instruct all American consuls in China to make better arrangements . . . I told him we had military schools, and were trying to teach the young men English, and all he said was, 'Good.' . . . The Reform Association is growing throughout the world. We have several million members . . . a great change is coming in China."[17]

The revolutionary activity in the United States came to the attention eventually of the dowager empress, who strongly protested to Washington. The Roosevelt Administration was blandly unimpressed, and determined to ignore the law against an alien military organization. On being questioned about this by the Los Angeles newspapers, the United States district attorney for Southern California replied that such a statute existed but "I could not proceed without instructions from the Department of Justice. In such matters it is the Department of State that takes the first action . . ."

Until now Lea had tried to stay out of the internal politics of the revolutionary movement, but he became disillusioned with Kang Yu-wei on his visit to the United States. Somehow Lea got the impression that Kang was less interested in establishing a Chinese republic than in seizing power from the Manchus for himself. He was also repelled by Kang's refusal to consider linking the Po Wong Wui with Dr. Sun Yat-sen's faction of the revolutionary movement, believing that it could not succeed unless all parties were united. Sun Yat-sen, on the other hand, was firmly committed to a republican China. Furthermore, Sun Yat-sen had organized a widespread network of agents in China and had a large personal following in South China, which would necessarily be the base of any uprising against Peking.

The upshot was that when Dr. Sun arrived in Los Angeles from Hong Kong in the autumn of 1905, Lea met him secretly at a house in Long

Beach — the secrecy may well have been necessary, but in any case Lea loved midnight meetings — and they immediately came to an agreement. Lea would switch allegiance from Kang to Sun; a maneuver, recognizing Sun's superior ability as an organizer, which all Chinese could understand. He also recognized Sun Yat-sen's greater appeal to the masses, and it didn't lessen Sun's attraction for Lea that he was becoming known, prematurely perhaps, as "the George Washington of China."

Lea accompanied him to New York, where Will Irwin, now a reporter on the New York *Sun,* again caught up with his old classmate.

"The Chinese Washington," wrote Irwin in his autobiography, "and his suite were a group for the movies — long silken robes, pigtails, caps with the mandarin button and that air of class which makes the best-bred European seem a parvenu compared to a Chinese gentleman.

"Beside the Liberator marched an odd figure. He seemed hardly to come up to Sun's waist. He wore a pair of patent-leather hip boots and a blue cape with yellow lining and bindings which had the effect of being draped on the top of his boots, so short was the torso beneath it. I had to look twice at the tanned face squeezed between it and a military fatigue cap before I realized that this was indeed Homer Lea.

"The party proceeded to Chinatown, where, on the floor of a public hall, Sun's party reviewed two companies of volunteers for the Chinese Republican Army. Lieutenant General Lea marched down their lines, inspecting them. And his air of soldierly resolution, of dignity and of competence made one forget the oddity of his appearance."

That night Irwin and Lea met at the latter's suite at the Hotel Astor and talked for hours, off the record, about what Lea hoped would happen in China. "The giant was stirring. She could be the most powerful nation in the world . . . Someday China would rule all Asia."

Irwin asked, "By conquest?"

"How else," Lea replied, "does a nation ever achieve empire?"

Irwin said that Lea frankly told him he intended to "become the Napoleon of the Far East."[18]

4. *A Prophet Steps Forward*

A large amount of nervous and mental energy was packed into Homer Lea's tiny, ailing body. He was often so weak that Captain O'Banion had to carry him around like a child. Yet in the next several years he not only devoted himself to training his scattered army and raising funds for Dr. Sun but began a literary career that was to make him world-famous.

His first effort was inauspicious, a historical romance with a Chinese background and Chinese characters titled *The Vermilion Pencil.* He sent the manuscript to Will Irwin, by then an editor of *McClure's Magazine,* hoping it would be serialized. Irwin turned it down as a serial but recommended that McClure's book division publish it.

The Vermilion Pencil created little interest partly because the Orient had lost its fascination for America and partly because Lea was not a novelist. He often succumbed to a voluptuous style of phrase-making: "Her eyes became a perfect arsenal and the arched bow of her lips shot from some inexhaustible quiver shafts divinely smeared with a poppy that would lull into dreams the most valorously inclined defence . . . Weak governments and powerful gods sleep in the same bed . . . Sea-going junks hovered above the river like gigantic butterflies, their great ribbed sails turned into gorgeous, trembling wings of silk . . ." Lea the novelist also delivered a solemn warning against the underground forces which "exist to destroy," among which he listed the nihilists in Russia, the Socialists in Germany, the Clan-na-gael in Ireland, the Carbonari in the Latin countries.[19]

His apocalyptic vision became more specific and definitive, however, when he conceived the idea of what was published as *The Valor of Ignorance,* the main pillar on which his reputation as a prophet rests.

Valor was designed as an exposé of Japanese plans to conquer Asia and as a warning to the United States that her turn would come next. He hoped to awaken America to the dangers presented by a renascent East, and equally by its smugness, its lack of will to defend itself, softened by years of prosperity. "Opulence instead of being the foundation of national strength is liable to be the most potent factor in its destruction," he declared. "War between wealth and military energy has but one end, the old doom of the Purple Persian."

Two events had ignited his feeling that Japan was embarked on conquest, he told Captain O'Banion. One, he claimed, was a "secret map of Asia" he had been shown in the Japanese Naval Office when the Japanese were trying to persuade him to accept a commission; the map was inked with lines encompassing all of eastern Asia, and was supposed to convince Lea that he should join the "winning side." Two years before that, he said, his instincts had been alerted by reading Rudyard Kipling's *From Sea to Sea,* in which Kipling bluntly warned about the Japanese, "They are bad little men who know too much."

To support his belief that the Japanese could effect a landing on the Pacific coast, Lea wandered along the beaches north of Los Angeles, sometimes becoming so weary that Captain O'Banion had to carry him on his shoulders. Then he began writing the book, often scribbling away while he lay on an Indian blanket on the grass of Westlake Park in downtown Los Angeles, a few blocks away from where he lived with his younger sisters Ermal and Hersa. There he often conferred with General Chaffee, now retired as chief of staff; with Marco Newmark, a prominent Los Angeles financier, and Captain D. P. Quinlin of the United States Army.

The Valor of Ignorance was published in 1909 and created a stir with its prophecy of national decay, and even more of a sensation in military and naval circles which would use it as their testament — not long after the author's death — for a preventative war against Japan. Its credentials as a sober, highly professional essay in the developing field of geopolitics and a work of military strategy were attested in the introduction by General Chaffee:

"We do not know of any work in military literature published in the United States more deserving the attention of men who study the history of the United States and the Science of War than this."

Against the complacency of the Edwardian age, Lea summoned up the vision of a "dreaded *dreibund*" — alliance — which would eventually be formed by Russia, Japan and Germany and would crunch its way over the ruins of the Anglo-Saxon nations.

With the vehemence of an Old Testament prophet he inveighed against the lack of patriotism in the United States. "In peace, and not in war, is the time to judge the worth of a man's or a nation's patriotism. Those who are indifferent to their country's welfare in peace will be of no use to it in time of war."

America must grow, in the geopolitical sense, or perish. A nation, he believed, began to decline the moment it stopped expanding. As a political and social conservative to delight the heart of his contemporary, Ambrose Bierce, he declared that when the creative work of building an empire stopped, the state devoted its energies to caring for its "devitalizing elements — the social and economic parasites . . . It is in these, valorous with fat pride, that the nation takes its final and inglorious departure."[20]

It was his great fear that the United States would waste its substance on social welfare and other frivolities of the modern state, that the "true basis of national greatness," its military power, was being replaced by "a superstructure of papier-mâché, not unlike a Mardi-gras creation around whose gilded and painted exterior the nation is asked to dance in boastful arrogance." Its military history thus far was nothing to boast about, because "its conquests have been over nations and aborigines so disproportionately weak and incapable of waging war on a basis of equality that its wars have been destructive rather than inculcative of equitable military conceptions." From now on, America would be confronted by enemies of equal stature and strength, or perhaps of superior military capability.[21]

As he compared rival military forces among the leading nations, he cited the German general staff's own computations that it could transport 250,000 soldiers to the East Coast of the United States in two weeks, that the British fleet was three times stronger than the American in the Atlantic, that both Germany and France could deploy in the Pacific fleets four times stronger than the combined United States Pacific and Far East squadrons — all this to demonstrate that the United States was no longer protected by its two oceans, that "the airy bastions of space" would fall down around our ears in weeks or months if we persisted in the delusion.

The idea that Americans or any other people would "rise up" against an invader, in the old minuteman style, was ridiculous. "The more diffused national civilization becomes with the political elevation and liberty of the individual, the less probable is a unified resistance. . . . Such uprisings were possible only in primitive times, ceasing with the establishment of armies that required training and cohesion."[22]

He hammered at the theme that national "virility" was all-important, citing Japan and Germany as examples. "A few decades ago Japan was almost a myth and the German Empire only a geographical possibility. Today they are considered equal, and in many respects superior, in strength and greatness to the other powers of the world, and for no other reason than that they have not become top-heavy with industrialism . . . Should Germany on the one hand and Japan on the other continue to adhere rigorously to these laws, resisting the deteriorating influence of industrialism, feminism, and political quackery, they will, in due time, by the erosive action of these elements on other nations, divide the world between them."[23]

He had little faith in the "melting pot" theory, and believed that the Anglo-Saxon element in the United States must remain supreme. "A nation may be kept intact only so long as the ruling element remains homogenous." Once Anglo-Saxon domination ended, he said, "the ideal of national supremacy is lost in the endless controversies of internal legislation and petty ambitions." The influx of immigrants alarmed him because no "fidelity" could be expected of "a man who not only foreswears the land of his birth, but that of his forefathers, their dust and their deeds . . . American nationalization is not an antiseptic."

He was equally suspicious of the democratic process, which ultimately might destroy the national will to defend by expansion. "When the government of a country is the government of the masses, the number of negotiators is increased to the whole nation, and involves not only their mediocrity, but unending self-interests and prejudices."[24]

He devoted the first half of his book to inveighing against what he called the "decline in militancy," which he believed was fatal to a major power. In the second half, he took up the problem of fighting a war against the Japanese empire, which he believed was inevitable. Partly this was because of profound differences between the two nations. "One nation is a militant paternalism . . . the other an individualist emporium where aught that belongs to man is for sale." Japan had attained a commanding position in Asia through her victory over China in 1895 and her crushing defeat of Russia, on land and sea, in 1905. Meanwhile, Great Britain had become preoccupied in maintaining a balance of power with Germany, and was no longer a significant factor in Asian strategy.

That left the United States to confront Japan alone in the western Pacific. "Politically there are no conditions that can restrain Japan from entering into war with this nation." He scoffed at the theory of the Japanese economist Baron Kaneko that economic interdependence between the United States and Japan would prevent any possibility of conflict. The baron rather astonishingly had concluded that "the Japanese cannot live a single hour without American supplies." The interchange of necessary commodities would continue between the two countries even if they were at war, Lea rather cynically argued, "differing only in the route and the means of transference."[25]

Japan but not America was alive to the necessity of mastering the Pacific. That ocean and its littoral were the strategic key to world conquest. "Whether the world in the future is to be dominated, politically, militarily, or a coalition of them, in the dominion of the Pacific shall it be determined," principally because that ocean covers a third of the world's surface, half of the human race lived on its littoral and "two-thirds of the undeveloped resources of the earth are in the lands upon whose shores its waters break."

Then Lea proceeded to map out the sequence of Japan's march to supremacy. She would seize the Philippines because that would end American and European dominance in the western Pacific; "the channel of Balintang is the Rubicon of Japan." She would also occupy Samoa to dominate the South Pacific from Pago Pago, and Alaska to maintain control of the North Pacific.

The Japanese would easily invade the Philippines and defeat the American and Filipino defenders, he wrote, because it was "no complex military problem." With an accuracy that would encourage belief that the Japanese planners used Lea's book as a blueprint, he predicted that the Japanese would land at Lingayen Gulf and Polillo Bight; that the Americans would find Manila indefensible; that the Japanese would capture Manila in three weeks (it took them twenty-six days, actually).[26]

The Japanese, he said, would take the Philippines, Hawaii and Alaska and then proceed to the invasion of the American West Coast. As he analyzed it, the United States would be hard-pressed to fend off such an invasion, because "the long extent of the sea-coast constitutes three spheres of defence that are so widely separated as to be wholly independent of one another," which would each have to be defended by an army of two hundred thousand men. Because of her growing mobility, he added, "in a military sense Japan is one-third closer to Washington, Oregon and California than the military power of the United States."[27]

It was simple enough to attack Lea's book on moral grounds, as many outraged critics did, since it argued for a nation in arms and in a state of eternal belligerence. By Lea's prescription, the only security for the United States lay in conquering the world, if his concepts were followed to their logical end. While transforming itself into an Anglo-Saxon garrison, it would also have to ship back millions of Germans, Irish, Poles, Italians, Russians and all the other "heterogeneous" nationalities, along with all the Negroes and Orientals, to where they had come from — or whip them into docile battalions of Anglo-officered infantry.

Naturally enough his authoritarian views appealed to many Americans, particularly those who envisioned an American empire in the Pacific. *Valor* was, in fact, to be the handbook for a startling venture by the military and naval leaders of the nation several years hence. Its greatest initial impact, however, was in Europe and Asia, where it was received as the new Book of Revelations. Lea had become Europe's military prophet as Mahan had been adopted as its naval seer. Field Marshal Lord Roberts wrote Lea that "I could not rest until I finished it" and invited the author to visit him in England. Kaiser Wilhelm ordered all his senior officers to read the book and invited Lea to attend the next German army maneuvers. Lea accepted both invitations. Lenin read a translation in German, did not write a fan letter but commented, "This man knows more about politics than any cabinet officer now in favor." The book was placed on the curriculum of all German and Russian military academies.

But its most fervent readership was in Japan. There it sold forty thousand copies, went through twenty-four printings and was required reading for every army and navy officer. Something of a furor erupted when plans for its publication were announced by a Japanese firm in 1912 after the previous government had forbidden it. In Japan it was published under the title *The War Between Japan and America* and was falsely advertised as the work of an "American staff officer." Hoping to appeal to a general as well as a professional readership, the Japanese publisher proclaimed:

"More interesting than a novel, more mysterious than philosophy, this is really excellent reading matter for Oriental men with red blood in their veins."

The Japan *Chronicle,* as an English-language journal interested in Anglo-American and Japanese amity for the best of commercial reasons, editorially attacked the book as a "precious bundle of nonsense." The *Chronicle* also published a letter from Dr. David Starr Jordan, the president of Stanford and a leader in the peace movement, who denounced his former student as a poseur who had acquired his title from "some secret society of agitators," and his book as "mischievous in its influence." The book was "singularly worthless," Dr. Jordan wrote the *Chronicle,* and "It would be unfortunate if anybody in Japan should consider him [Lea] as a representative of the American army." Both the *Chronicle* editorial and Dr. Jordan's letter were included in a pamphlet titled *The Impudence of Charlatanism* and published by the World Peace Foundation.

The pamphlet was an emotional potlatch. If answer had to be made to Lea's call for a flexing of Anglo-Saxon muscle, it might have been done more effectively than Jordan's oddly sophomoric statement that "If a Great Nation like this decides it will live in peace, it will be let alone by other countries . . . Wars are mostly started by hoodlums, by those interested in causing military promotions."[28]

Such professional criticisms of *The Valor of Ignorance* as were made in the United States — largely by officers who did not believe the threat of a war with Japan was imminent, nor that a democracy composed of many nationalities and races was necessarily awaiting the "doom of the Purple Persian" — were handled by Lea's longtime patron, the retired General Chaffee. Marshall Stimson, a schoolmate of Lea's, recalls that Chaffee was particularly energetic in defending Lea's claim that the Pacific coast could be invaded. Chaffee acted as umpire in a sand-table war game with United States Army officers on one side, representing the defense, while Lea directed the movement of the "enemy." The result was that Lea (as the Japanese) was (theoretically) able to "take over every city on the Pacific Coast."

The Valor of Ignorance is forgotten now, but in her foreword to the 1942 edition Clare Boothe Luce recalled that when she visited the Philippines just before the Japanese onslaught her attention was called to *Valor* by members of General MacArthur's staff, who indicated that they regarded it as their Bible. So, unfortunately, did the Japanese.

5. *Closing In on the Empress*

It took more than a decade for the Chinese republican movement to prepare for the overthrow of the Manchus. Lea and his colleagues were determined that this revolution would succeed, and that no uprising would be signaled until everything was ready. If it failed, the cause might be set back another century.

There were many who regarded the task as impossible, who thought it ridiculous that a Chinatown army led by an amateur strategist could aspire to overthrow a vast empire. Those with an expert knowledge of China were less dubious. The republican movement was favored by such factors as the incompetence of the Royal Manchu Army, the corruption of the Manchu bureaucracy, the unreality of the dowager empress's court, which lived a fantasy far more narcotic than that of the Hapsburgs or the Romanoffs. Equally it was favored by the patience and diligence of the overseas revolutionaries, and the intelligence with which they were directed by Sun Yat-sen and Lea. Undoubtedly the revolution would have proceeded without a Lea, but it would have been delayed longer and might not have been so successful.

Even while tasting fame as a military prophet, Lea labored to make his legionnaries an efficient fighting force. The first class of graduates of his

Western Military Academy, in 1906, were sent over to China to enlist in the Royal Manchu Army; so would many more after they finished two years of training. They were to serve as privates until the revolution broke out. "Then they were to declare themselves for what they really were," as Captain O'Banion outlined the plan to his biographer, "come out in the open, and take command of the Royal Manchu Army as officers. When that happened, the Empress would find her army gone like a puff of smoke. She would have nothing with which to fight. Instead, she would be facing not her soldiers, but the Chinese Imperial Reform Army commanded by General Homer Lea."[29]

Several of Lea's agents were also sent to the port of Amoy, near Canton, where they settled down to vegetable farming and also set up a listening post from which they forwarded reports in code to Lea. In Macao and Hankow others established themselves as merchants for the same purpose of determining when the time would come to strike and also to organize an advance guard of the revolution.

During Dr. Sun's visit to the United States in 1905, he and Lea had devised the essential strategy for overthrowing the empress. They traced out on a map a triangle encompassing the rich Yangtze Valley between Hankow, Nanking and Shanghai. Whoever controlled that territory controlled China, and from that base the revolution could expand northward and westward.

The main elements of the Royal Manchu Army were stationed inside that triangle, while outside it were the bandit forces constantly waging guerrilla war against that army. Many of them were former members of the Second Division of the Chinese Reform Army which Lea had commanded during its brief uprising in 1900.

In 1907 Lea sent O'Banion over to China with $180,000 in cash to help cement his bonds with those brigands in the hills and also to bribe certain officers of the Royal Manchu Army whose names were given him by Dr. Sun as men of wavering, purchasable loyalty. "I am going to arrange this so it will be the nearest thing to a bloodless revolution that the world has ever known," Lea told O'Banion. "In many instances, we may be able to buy our way through. But it will be cheaper in the long run, for dollars are less valuable than the lives of men, and money spent is less messy than blood spilled."[30]

O'Banion slipped into China with his trunk full of American currency and operated from one of the vegetable farms near Amoy which had been established as listening posts. He found that both the bandit chieftains and the Manchu army officers were eager enough for the cumshaw from the States. The latter were told only to "Be prepared. It is for China. We shall let you know."

Approximately two thousand Chinese trained by Lea in the United States were sent over to China, some as agents, some as "sleepers" to await

The Day, some as recruits for the Royal Manchu Army. Many had to be smuggled over by professionals in the immigrant-smuggling racket, whose operations were reversed for Lea's purposes. The staging area was the beach near the coastal town of Watsonville, south of San Francisco; from there they were taken on small coastal craft to Matatlan, Mexico, where there was a large Chinese colony, and from there to Kobe, Japan, and to Amoy, China.

In 1908 the revolutionaries' plans were speeded up as a result of the news from Peking that the boy emperor, Kuang Hsu, had suddenly died, reportedly from poison administered by one of his aunt's eunuchs. The empress then named as his successor the five-year-old Prince Pu Yi, the son of Kuang Hsu's brother Prince Chun, shortly before her own death later that year. It was the beginning of a woeful life for the boy. Later Pu Yi was the puppet emperor of the Japanese; he died recently as a plain comrade of the People's Republic.

During the past several years Dr. Sun had been consolidating his control over the revolutionary movement, while the influence of Kang Yu-wei was waning. The latter favored retaining the imperial form. Dr. Sun, however, was opposed to keeping any vestige of the old system, preaching endlessly to the overseas Chinese that "Inasmuch as democracy is the political tendency of the day, China also should advance toward it." Lea threw all his influence, and that of the American Chinese, behind Dr. Sun. The power struggle between Sun and Kang went on for years, however, long after the revolution was an accomplished fact.

While he waited for the Chinese tinderbox to explode, Lea worked on a sequel to *The Valor of Ignorance* and married a young widow, Mrs. Ethel Powers, who had been acting as his nurse and secretary. The sequel, which was to be titled *The Day of the Saxon,* was urged on him by Field Marshal Roberts and other British devotees of Lea's earlier work when he and Mrs. Lea visited England and Germany in 1910. The Leas settled down in England while he worked on *The Day of the Saxon,* which was published the following year.

The main thrust of the book was that the then apparently healthy British empire was doomed because it failed to recognize the limitations of naval power or the "inability of the British Navy to prevent the destruction of the Empire east of Suez." His prevision was also twenty-twenty when in a few words he encapsulated the future course of world conflict: "In the past it was the individual who was the predominant factor; today, nations; tomorrow, races."

Lack of military preparedness, as in the United States, would cause the downfall of the Saxon, by which Lea meant the British people, not the Germans. "The thin, red Saxon line" stretched around the earth was made possible by the Englishman's "heroism and racial fealty," which had degenerated into "the pleasant security of their delusions."[31]

The British empire, he predicted, would crack up with the loss of India, which would create "a gap so vast that all the blood and fire and iron of the Saxon race cannot again bring together its broken ends. In the wreck of India is to be found the Golgotha of the Saxon." And Britain would lose India because she failed to grasp the fact that the Indian mind was ruled by "the most sublime and terrible forces in nature," and the restraint of British rule in India inspired only the contempt of the Indians.

India was the key to British expansion to the Pacific — "India, in a military sense, *is* the Empire" — and once it slipped away from British control, so would Australia and New Zealand. Britain's great mistake, he believed, was in allying herself with Japan rather than China, which Britain should have made into a "great continental power" in the years when it was still possible to do so. The Russian threat to India could have been neutralized by a strong China, whose borders with Russia had always made them natural adversaries.

The British also had reason to fear the modernization of Russia for its "glacial, timeless, measured movement, this calm and dreadful certitude, that even terrified Napoleon." Russia would expand east, west or south as circumstances dictated.[32]

The most immediate danger to Britain, of course, was Imperial Germany, which "has forgotten God in its exaltation of the Germanic race." The cause of a war between Britain and Germany would be the fact that "Germany is so tightly encircled by the Saxon race that it cannot make even a tentative extension of its territory or political sovereignty over non-Saxon states without endangering the integrity of the Saxon world." Waterloo, he said, was the "beginning of Germanic militant greatness and of Saxon militant decay."[33]

Britain and Germany, he predicted, would cancel each other out as world powers. Japan would develop the capability of invading and occupying the United States, but lacked the resources for world conquest. That left Russia, in Lea's opinion, as the ultimate ruler of the world.

The only way eventual Russian expansion over the entire surface of the earth could be halted, he said, was through an Anglo-American union, followed by the "complete separation of military and naval systems from the civil government," the introduction of universal military training, the organization of their armies into expeditionary forces capable of maintaining themselves anywhere in the world.

Otherwise he had one last axiom for the Anglo-American democracies: "Nations never advance to their doom. They retreat to it."[34]

6. *Double Ten*

An accidental explosion literally touched off the Chinese revolution of 1911–1912. Sun Yat-sen and Homer Lea had agreed that the signal for an uprising would be given in 1912, but the revolution did not wait for its leaders. On October 9, 1911, gunpowder secretly stored by the revolutionary movement in a house in the Russian Concession of Hankow blew up. The viceroy of Hankow investigated, announced the existence of a revolutionary plot and ordered a large number of suspects arrested. Somewhat prematurely, he then telegraphed Peking that he had smashed a rebel conspiracy.

That telegram had hardly arrived in the capital, the following day, when the garrison of Wuchang revolted. Units of the Royal Manchu Army in Hankow and Hanyang immediately followed suit. Most of their officers had been trained by Lea, had been promoted, thanks to the excellence of his Chinatown military academies, and had waited impatiently for the signal from Dr. Sun. They were convinced that conditions were right, and acted on their own.

The decisive day was October 10 — Double Ten, the tenth day of the tenth month, which later became the Chinese Fourth of July.

All over China, within three weeks after that cache of gunpowder accidentally exploded, there were riots and uprisings. Ten provinces were quickly won over by the republican revolution. Troops sent by Peking to suppress the disorders and engage rebellious garrisons simply vanished into the countryside or went over to the revolution en masse. It was a phenomenon of military disintegration which would be repeated, again to the world's amazement, during Chiang Kai-shek's last days on the Chinese mainland.

When these events took place, with their trainees effectively running the revolution to suit themselves, Lea was still in London, being lionized by the military (but not the naval) establishment, and Sun Yat-sen was in Denver rallying enthusiasm and raising funds for a cause which no longer needed them. They were in the position of having to catch up with events they had set in motion.

Lea cabled Dr. Sun to meet him in Marseilles as quickly as possible. He and the Leas then sailed for China, arriving in Shanghai on Christmas Eve. In the meantime, the Manchu resistance had all but collapsed. An armistice was requested, and in the negotiations that followed the Imperial representatives proposed that China be transformed into a constitutional monarchy. Sun's followers, however, insisted that the Manchus would have to abdicate in favor of a republican government.

Thus the fighting continued sporadically while the revolutionaries set up a provisional reform government in Nanking with Sun Yat-sen at its head.

Lea arrived in time to direct the last campaigning, as chief of staff of the republican army, from a palanquin.

It was a comparatively bloodless revolution; success won by long and

Sun Yat-sen and his cabinet

Homer Lea, the prophet of Pacificism

patient preparation had cost so much less than earlier failures to overthrow the Manchus.

Sun Yat-sen was proclaimed provisional president of the Chinese Republic, and Lea stayed on at Nanking as his military adviser, actually as commander of the republican army. He led the military escort which preceded Dr. Sun and members of his government three days after they took office on a pilgrimage to the tomb of Chu Yuan-chang, the founder of the Ming dynasty. Though a Christian, Dr. Sun made his obeisance to ancestor worship as he informed the spirit of the resident of that tomb that "everywhere reigns a beautiful repose . . . The dragon crouches in majesty as of old . . . Spirit, accept this offering!"

If that scene accorded with the most ancient of traditions, so did the compromise by which Dr. Sun was soon to be relieved of the presidency pro tem. The Manchus agreed to abdicate but only on condition that Yuan Shi-kai, a former member of their government but not a bitter reactionary, become president of the republic. Rather than subject the nation to more upheaval, Sun yielded to Yuan and accepted the post of director general of trade and transport. Later he broke with Yuan and in 1917 established the Republic of South China as leader of the Kuomintang (Nationalist Party). Shortly before his death, Sun presided over the first national congress of the Kuomintang and allowed the Communist Party of China to join it as a means of broadening his base of power.

During those few months he spent in his second sojourn in China, Lea began working on a third volume of military prophecy which he intended to publish as *The Swarming of the Slav*. From the notes he made for that work, it appeared that he considered the Russians the great menace to Anglo-American security. He believed that in the coming world war czarist Russia would be defeated by Germany, but that the setback would bring about "a great awakening of the Slav to his own power," that the old continental rivalries would be followed by a cataclysmic war between the United States and Britain on one side, Russia and her Slavic partners on the other.[35]

Oddly enough, for all his intimate concern with China, he made no prophecies regarding her future in any of his writings. Probably he considered that a republican China would simply become a docile but respected partner of Britain and the United States. Yet in his last days in China he was disturbed by a prevision of what might happen if the idealism of the republican revolution seeped away.

Called upon to speak at a presidential reception in Nanking, he had few comforting words to offer the assembled dignitaries. The great danger to the republic, he said, was a deep-rooted tendency toward "political corruption," and prophetically added: "Free China will yet perish unless there rises from your innermost bosom the militant spirit of another Martial Monk."

Ironically, a young republican officer named Chiang Kai-shek heard those words, but seemingly was not deeply impressed by them.

A few days later Lea suffered a stroke which paralyzed his left side and left him totally blind. Mrs. Lea took him back to the States. They arrived in San Francisco late in May, and Captain O'Banion was waiting on the dock when Lea was removed from the ship in a wheelchair. "Don't let this worry you, Captain," Lea told him. "I'll fool them yet. No man can die until his work is finished."[36]

He was taken to a seaside cottage at Ocean Park, where he lingered for months, that indomitable spark which made him one of the most remarkable Americans of his time refusing to flicker out.

Early that autumn Lea summoned O'Banion to his cottage. He acknowledged that he knew he was going to die and announced that he had made all the arrangements for his funeral. "It won't be long now," Lea said cheerfully. "I don't want to have a horse-drawn hearse and go poking along to the cemetery. I know automobiles aren't popular for funerals, but I want to be taken in an automobile, and no slow driving, either. Just go right along. I want only my family and closest personal friends — as few as possible. And please, no fuss. When a man's work is done, let's ring down the curtain quickly."

He died on November 1, 1912, only thirty-six years old.

"Must I die," he asked shortly before that, "not knowing if my work is finished?"[37]

Prophets always must.

12

The Yellow / Brown Peril

This rejuvenescent Japanese race has embarked on a course of conquest, the goal of which no man knows.

— JACK LONDON, 1910

For a century and a half the United States has maintained a striking ambivalence toward the two greatest nations of the Orient. Japan and China have alternated in our affections. We have never been entirely friendly toward both the dominant nations of eastern Asia at the same time, perhaps subconsciously following the dictates of a policy, never officially formulated, of keeping them apart. We have always taken alarm, too, at any steps toward a reconciliation between the two great Oriental powers. The thought of a highly industrialized Japan allied, for once, with the huge population of China is nightmarish. A Sino-Japanese alliance would eliminate forever the hegemony of any Western nation in the Pacific. Their historic rivalry, as much as American power, sustains the American presence in Asia.

The alternating current of our self-serving friendship was switched from Japan to China around the turn of the century, when it became apparent that Japan was the greatest danger to our new forward base in the Philippines. It was confirmed for decades to come by the Japanese victory over Russia in 1905. Americans generally supported the Japanese during that conflict because we regarded them as the underdog, but the efficiency with which Japanese armies steamrollered over the Russians in Korea and Manchuria and sank much of the Russian navy at Tsushima thoroughly alarmed the United States.

By then Washington was so impressed with the Japanese army that it sent two of its most promising officers — Pershing, and Captain Peyton C. March, the chief of staff during World War I — as military observers to report on the Manchurian campaigns. Pershing thought the Russians were defeated by their own stupidity as much as Japanese brilliance, but added, with the conviction of most American officers who had served in the East, that the Japanese might be encouraged by their success to consider moves against the American position in the Philippines. "Now it would be a weakness for them to possess the Philippine Archipelago," Pershing concluded in his report. "Yet there is no telling in the years to come in the Japanese rise to power."[1]

Anti-Oriental feeling in the United States thereupon subdivided itself. There was the old Yellow Peril sentiment about the Chinese, but that was now on the wane. Now there was also the Brown (Japanese) Peril, which was on the rise.*

In the aftermath of the Boxer Rebellion, there was a swelling friendliness toward China as a nation, though it was not matched by better treatment of the Chinese in the United States. The Chinese in China were fine fellows; those in America smoked opium, imported singsong girls, waged tong wars, and settled business disputes by dispatching hatchet men to eliminate their rivals. The official amiability was marked by a much-publicized disposition of the Boxer indemnity funds. The American government used those funds to bring over Chinese students and educate them, a gesture repaid when many of the "Boxer indemnity scholars" returned to China as a pro-American element. About the same time Secretary of State John Hay also proclaimed the Open Door policy, by which all nations were to have equal trading rights in China.

Again we covered ourselves with self-esteem. Throughout the nineteenth century we had shared in the exploitation of China, but not in the

---

* The Yellow Peril was, like so many other things, a German invention. Shortly after the Sino-Japanese War, Kaiser Wilhelm sent the czar of Russia a cartoon depicting an ogre rising in the East and menacing the West. In 1900 the Kaiser made a number of speeches warning of the Yellow Peril, and during the Russo-Japanese War he sided with the Russians by guaranteeing their western front. It was that guarantee, in fact, which helped bring on the war.

military measures which made it possible, meanwhile congratulating ourselves on a high standard of morality and posing as China's protectors. The
British, the French and the Japanese had fought the wars, the Russians and
Germans had seized areas of special influence but, as John K. Fairbank has
remarked, "The Americans had done none of these things and came up
instead with the 'open door' doctrine, which soon expanded to include not
only the open door for trade, but also the idea of China's integrity as a
nation. Thus we Americans prided ourselves on championing China's
modernization and self-determination. We considered ourselves above the
nasty imperialism and power politics of the Europeans. We developed a
self-image of moral superiority."[2]

The national change in attitude toward the Japanese was epitomized
by that of President Theodore Roosevelt. He won the Nobel Peace Prize
for negotiating an end of the Russo-Japanese War, but at the Portsmouth
(New Hampshire) Peace Conference in 1905 he was adamant in opposing
Japanese demands for a cash indemnity from Russia. The anti-Japanese
feeling was always more virulent in California than anywhere else in the
nation; a feeling so intense that Carey McWilliams characterized it as "the
California-Japanese War (1900–1941)" in his *Prejudice*. "For nearly fifty
years prior to December 7, 1941, a state of undeclared war existed between California and Japan," McWilliams noted. And Thomas A. Bailey
(*Theodore Roosevelt and the Japanese American Crisis*) emphasized that
"the general controversy lay not between the United States and Japan but
between Japan and California, with the federal government seeking to
secure justice for the aggrieved foreign power and at the same time
endeavoring to convince the state of its obligation to the rest of the union."

Californians were conditioned to respond quickly and vehemently to
any aspect of the "Oriental Question" by the many years of agitation
against the Chinese. Thus they were swift to react in 1900 when the
number of Japanese immigrants, following the annexation of Hawaii,
totaled twelve thousand against the previous annual rate of one thousand.
On May 7, 1900, an anti-Japanese mass meeting was called in San Francisco (usually more intolerant toward the Orientals than Los Angeles). It
was sponsored by the San Francisco Labor Council and its chief speaker
was Dr. Edward Alworth Ross, professor of sociology at Stanford. In one
newspaper account of his speech, he was quoted as saying that "should the
worst come to the worst it would be better for us to turn our guns on every
vessel bringing Japanese to our shores rather than permit them to land."
Dr. Ross objected to the Japanese immigrants on the grounds that they
were "unassimilable," that they worked for low wages and undermined the
living standard of American workmen, that they could not be converted to
democratic institutions.[3] A resolution was passed seeking the extension of
the Chinese Exclusion Act to the Japanese.

The agitation slackened somewhat when the Japanese government, by

Captain John J. Pershing with colleague in Japan

a gentlemen's agreement, announced that no more passports would be issued to contract laborers seeking to migrate to the United States. But it was revived in 1905 by the alarming swiftness of the Japanese victory over the Russians, when one Senator warned that Japan had become a "serious menace" to the United States and the chairman of the House Committee on Military Affairs declared that Japan was prepared to "fight a bloody war with the United States over the Philippines."[4]

The San Francisco *Chronicle* then launched an inflammatory series of articles under such headlines as:

CRIME AND POVERTY GO HAND IN HAND WITH ASIATIC LABOR

BROWN MEN ARE AN EVIL IN THE PUBLIC SCHOOLS

JAPANESE A MENACE TO AMERICAN WOMEN

BROWN ASIATICS STEAL BRAINS OF WHITES

"Every one of these immigrants," the *Chronicle* asserted, "so far as his service is desired, is a Japanese spy." Until now the Japanese were regarded as more diligent and friendly than the Chinese, but suddenly they were suspected of being the advance guard of the Japanese armed forces. Even as certain other prejudices aroused by the *Chronicle* series faded, that spy mania persisted among Californians. Anyone who lived in California before World War II will recall how native sons and daughters were generally convinced that the Japanese gardener clipping their hedges was actually a lieutenant commander in the Japanese naval intelligence making charts of gun emplacements in Beverly Hills. There was a genuine fear of the Japanese-Americans, as representatives of an expanding nation, that had never been extended to Chinese-Americans.

It was no coincidence that the most eloquent and dedicated propagandists of the Yellow/Brown Peril were Californians, and that they included such strange ideological bedfellows as Jack London, who considered himself a Socialist; Homer Lea, the imperialist, and William Randolph Hearst, press lord and multimillionaire — nor that they were all quite sincere in their warnings against the Asian menace.

The trade union movement around San Francisco and the corrupt politicians who ran the city for years were also united on the question. Labor was always strongly anti-Chinese, beginning with Denis Kearney and his Workingmen's Party in the 1870's. In July 1901 the Union Labor Party succeeded in electing its candidate, Eugene Schmitz, formerly a bassoon player in a San Francisco orchestra but now a henchman of Boss Abe Ruef, as mayor of San Francisco. In 1906, shortly after his reelection, Schmitz was under multiple indictment for malfeasance and misfeasance in office and sought to divert public attention from his misdeeds by launching a campaign against the Japanese in northern California. In this diversionary effort Schmitz and Ruef were supported, if not led, by such power-ful organizations as the California Federation of Labor, the California Grange and the Native Sons of the Golden West.

The Native Sons were and are a uniquely Californian ingroup pos-sessing a political, social and economic influence which non-Californians find difficult to comprehend. Their mystique of Californianism goes beyond mere boosterism, beyond the simple ancestor worship of the Daughters of the American Revolution. It reflects the belief of the native Californian, and many transplanted ones, that the state is somehow the epitome of the American Dream; a belief in Paradise Regained that is matched in fervor only by the less refined sense of statehood possessed by many Texans.

As a manufacturer of instant tradition, the Native Sons of the Golden West conferred upon themselves a special status wrapped in the folds of the flag of the short-lived Bear Republic. Until after World War II, they displayed a loathing for Orientals that was reflected in the legislation they proposed and usually succeeded in passing. Their leaders included such anti-Oriental figures with official status as United States Senator Hiram Johnson, Mayors Eugene Schmitz and James D. Phelan of San Francisco, Abe Ruef, State Senator J. M. Inman (president of the Cali-fornia Oriental Exclusion League), V. S. McClatchy, the publisher of a chain of newspapers in northern California, Anthony Caminetti, United States Commissioner General of Immigration, and Aaron Altman and James L. Gallagher of the San Francisco board of education.

Established California as represented by the Native Sons, rural Cali-fornia through the California Grange, and working-class California through the federated unions were all united on the "Oriental Question." They all solidified their memberships by campaigning for Oriental exclusion.

This atmosphere compounded of fear, suspicion and prejudice formed the climate in which the actions of the San Francisco board of education brought on a crisis in Japanese-American relations. On May 6, 1905, the school board placed itself on record as favoring the segregation of Oriental students in the city's schools. The resolution was not acted upon immediately. In April 1906 occurred the earthquake and fire which leveled large sections of the city. Anti-Japanese agitation ceased tempo-rarily when the Japanese government contributed more than a quarter of a million dollars toward the relief of its citizens. It came alive again during the post-quake building boom, when Japanese-Americans bought homes outside the Little Tokyo section. On October 11, 1906, the board of education took up the Oriental-segregation measure, apparently under pressure from Mayor Schmitz and Boss Ruef, who dominated the board and who needed an issue to distract the city from Schmitz's indictment.

As a first step in that program, the board of education ordered that ninety-three Japanese students be placed in a separate school, along with Chinese-American pupils, in Chinatown.

There was an immediate outcry from Japanese-Americans, from the Japanese government, and from American liberals. Secretary of State Elihu Root admitted that the action was a violation of the Japanese-American treaty of 1894 and cabled the American ambassador in Tokyo that "the United States will not for a moment entertain the idea of any treatment of the Japanese people other than that accorded to the people of the most friendly European nations." Japanese parents refused to send their children to the segregated school, and the San Francisco *Japanese-American* rather impetuously declared that "when National dignity is called to question, the sword of Masamune is unsheathed for action."[5]

On the other side of the Pacific, the Tokyo *Mainichi Shimbun* all but declared war on America: "Stand up, Japanese nation. Our countrymen have been humiliated . . . by the rascals of the U.S., cruel and merciless like demons. At this time we should be ready to give a blow to the U.S. Yes, we should be ready to strike the devil's head with the iron hammer for the sake of civilization."[6]

The San Francisco uproar, following so closely the much-praised Treaty of Portsmouth, greatly embarrassed the Roosevelt Administration. On December 3, 1906, President Roosevelt sent a message to Congress denouncing the action of the San Francisco school board as "a wicked absurdity." He also sent his Secretary of Commerce and Labor, V. H. Metcalf, to make an investigation on the scene. The Metcalf Report, hastily issued on December 18, condemned the segregation of Oriental students as unjustified and gave details of the assault by whites on nineteen Japanese residents in the San Francisco area. On January 17, 1907, the federal government filed suit in the California courts to enjoin the San Francisco school board from enforcing its segregation policy.

The administration dropped its suit, however, in the realization that Supreme Court rulings upheld the constitutionality of segregation of the races in American schools. A San Francisco literary journal had quickly pointed this out in a mocking editorial addressed to President Roosevelt: "Does President Roosevelt think Negroes freely exercise the right to vote in Southern States? We do not think so. It is thirty-eight years since the 14th Amendment gave to Negroes civil rights. Does President Roosevelt think Negroes are granted equal rights in theaters, hotels, railway trains, or streetcars in all the states, Southern or Northern? We do not think so. It may be said that the Federal Court can coerce the states into giving 'equal rights' to the Negroes. We do not think so. But if there may be those who doubt the soundness of our judgment, we may add that the U.S. Supreme Court . . . upheld the right of states to regulate domestic affairs; it decreed that there is a citizenship of the states as well as of the United States."[7]

Mayor Schmitz shouted at a mass meeting that he would gladly lay down his life in a war against Japan, upon which the Los Angeles *Times* commented that His Honor's promise "would almost reconcile anyone to a war with Japan." Another speaker bellowed that the Western states alone could "whip Japan at a moment's notice."

The San Francisco *Chronicle* declared that California would secede from the Union if the anti-Oriental measure was rescinded. The passions which inflamed the state against Japan and much of the rest of the United States (excepting the sympathetic states of the South) became so violent that *The Times* of London sent a correspondent out to investigate. "The whole agitation against the Japanese," he reported, "is causeless, artificial and wicked."

Undoubtedly it was the artificiality, the excessive passions aroused by the controversy which seemed the most striking aspect of the situation to most non-Californians. This air of unreality was heightened by the delegation which San Francisco, almost like the embassy of a sovereign state, sent to Washington to negotiate with President Roosevelt. It was headed by ex-bassoon player Eugene Schmitz, still plastered with indictments, accompanied by Superintendent of Schools Roncovieri, a trombone player and close friend of Schmitz's, and by Aaron Altman, president of the board of education, who happened to be Boss Ruef's brother-in-law.

The New York *World,* always anti-Roosevelt, was loftily amused at the spectacle of "the Mayor and the Board of Education of a single American city summoned to the White House, asked to approve the forms of a settlement with Japan proposed by the President and his Secretary of State, and allowed to make conditions and changes of international policy with the manner of an independent power."[8] The imperialist-minded New York *Herald,* on the other hand, thought it no laughing matter, and pointed out that Japan was using the issue to whip up anti-American sentiment. It also quoted Captain Richmond P. Hobson, the naval hero now retired to the lecture platform: "We know that the Japanese in California are soldiers organized into companies, regiments and brigades."[9]

Mayor Schmitz and his colleagues were persuaded by President Roosevelt to withdraw the Oriental-segregation ordinance, in return for which Roosevelt issued an executive order stopping Japanese immigration by way of Hawaii, Canada and Mexico. Public opinion in San Francisco was outraged by the settlement and street mobs assaulted Japanese-Americans.

The Japanese reaction to the harsh treatment of its people in San Francisco, as reflected in newspaper editorials undoubtedly inspired by the government, was exceedingly militant. The Tokyo papers hinted that war might result. In the United States, too, there was an incipient war hysteria. The *Literary Digest* conducted a public opinion poll and reported a consensus that war between the United States and Japan was inevitable. The New York *Sun* editorially agreed. The New York *Times* published an article outlining how the Japanese might invade the Philippines as the first stage of a war against the United States, and the New York *Tribune* serialized a quickly concocted novel detailing such a conflict.

The anti-Japanese sentiment in the press throughout the country, and among California officials and opinion-makers in particular, became so feverish in the fall of 1907 that President Roosevelt felt called upon to denounce the "jingoism" of "certain California mob leaders and certain yellow [*sic*] journals."

In Japan, too, there was a strong current of hostility sent rippling the other way across the Pacific, but it was more an expression of governmental policy than of popular indignation. There it was referred to in the newspapers as the "California situation." But it was "used by the bureaucratic authorities as the basis of constant and insistent demands for military and naval expansion," as one historian has observed. "The furnace of popular indignation was deliberately fanned by the militarists for the rolling of armour-plate and the drawing of heavy cannon."[10]

Almost every year, from then until World War I, there was a new Japanese war scare, rumors of secret bases established in Mexico, whispers of Japanese naval intelligence officers active in the various Little Tokyos, relentless agitation against the "little brown men."

1. *The Propaganda of Jack London*

In one of the lesser known short stories of Jack London, titled "The Unparalleled Invasion," London pictured a China with her population swollen to over a billion. Driven to desperation by the necessity of feeding all those people, she threatens to conquer all of Asia and then the rest of the world. The West accordingly is driven to the necessity of waging bacteriological warfare on China, and her whole population is wiped out by disease.[11] That nightmarish exploration of the future was published more than forty years before Communist China accused the United States of dropping "germ bombs" during the Korean War; before, in fact, bacteriological warfare was a reasonable possibility.

London was a very busy young man, turning out two or three books a year on the average, but he found energy to spare for several conflicting enthusiasms. He was a firebrand Socialist who professed a belief in the brotherhood of man and always signed himself "Yours for the Revolution," but he was also, and equally, a fiery advocate of Anglo-Saxon supremacy who often larded his stories with the plaint of the California working class, which he expressed as "We're the white folks that lost out . . . that was too busy being good to be smart."

Already the best-selling author of *Call of the Wild* and *The Sea Wolf*, he was confirmed in his prejudices against Orientals when he agreed to cover the Russo-Japanese War for the Hearst newspapers. In Japan, where spy-catchers were suspicious of every Caucasian face, he was arrested as a Russian agent when he wandered with a camera into a fortified zone. He and the other correspondents were kept under irksome surveillance when they moved over to Korea to cover the campaigning. When he quarreled with the groom he engaged to tend his horses and struck the man, he was arrested again and held for a court-martial by the Japanese army. He was released after President Roosevelt himself protested to the Japanese government, and then only on the condition that he leave Japanese territory.

London returned to the United States detesting everything Japanese, and compared the vaunted courage of their infantry to the "South American peccary pigs in their herd charges." The Oakland chapter of the Socialist Party was shocked by his denunciation of the Japanese in racial as well as political terms. One of those present at the meeting recalled that "he cursed the entire yellow race in the most outrageous terms. Some of the comrades present were somewhat embarrassed. The struggle against race prejudice, especially against hatred of the 'yellow' races, was part of the daily work of the Socialist branches on the West Coast and it was hard to conceive of Jack London, one of the foremost members of the branch, evincing race chauvinism."

His comrades tried to reason with him, but only made London angrier. "Convinced that there was some misunderstanding, one of the comrades began talking to him about classes that exist in Japan as everywhere else. Another called his attention to the slogan decorating the wall over the portrait of Marx: 'Workers of the world, unite!' But this did not touch him in the least and only served to increase his passion. Pounding his fist on the table, Jack met their arguments with, 'What the devil! I am first of all a white man and only then a Socialist!' "[12]

In his first novel, *A Daughter of the Snows,* published in 1902, London had served notice that whatever direction his political radicalism took in other ways, he wasn't prepared to swallow the Socialist doctrine that all races are equal. The idea of Nordic racial supremacy was, in fact, his ruling passion. The heroine of his first novel was a sinewy blonde who could have served as the model for a recruiting poster for Hitler's *mädchen* in uniform. In hymning her virtues, he asserted that the "dominant races come down out of the North"; the Nordic was "a great race, half the earth its heritage and all the sea! In three score generations it rules the world!"

For all his belief in Nordic supremacy, however, he deeply feared it might be engulfed by the Asian masses. For several years, the Yellow/ Brown Peril became an obsession with him. He made several trips to Los Angeles to confer with Homer Lea, about the time the latter was writing *The Valor of Ignorance,* on their mutual conviction that Japan intended to attempt a conquest of the world.

As London saw it — and there were many in high official places who would agree with him — the Japanese would become supremely dangerous when and if they formed an alliance with the Chinese; together they might be unconquerable. A quarter of a century before, that more professional strategist, General Grant, had worked for such an alliance on the grounds that it would preserve peace in the Orient and prevent the exploitation of the Asian nations — but that was before Japan had attained military and naval power. London, however, believed that Chinese-Japanese collaboration would be disastrous for the rest of the world.

In an essay titled "The Yellow Peril," first published in the receptive Hearst newspapers and later collected in *Revolution and Other Essays,* London pointed out that the Chinese and Japanese were both descended from the Mongols, but "The infusion of other blood, Malay, perhaps, has made the Japanese a race of mastery and power, a fighting race through all its history, a race which has always despised commerce and exalted fighting."

Now that it had borrowed from the West all the necessary military and industrial techniques, "handling machines and systems with remarkable and deadly accuracy, this rejuvenescent Japanese race has embarked on a course of conquest, the goal of which no man knows. The head men of Japan are dreaming ambitiously, and the people are dreaming blindly, a Napoleonic dream. The soldier shouting 'Nippon, Banzai!' on the walls of Wiju, the widow at home in her paper house committing suicide so that her only son, her sole support, may go to the front, are both expressing the unanimity of the dream."

Japan had been confined until now by the meagerness of her resources, her cramped living space and small population, "but given poor, empty Korea for a breeding colony and Manchuria for a granary, and at once the Japanese begins to increase by leaps and bounds."[13]

By himself, London wrote, the Japanese "would not constitute a Brown Peril. He has not the time in which to grow and realize the dream." The West was exploiting the East so swiftly that "before he could attain the structure requisite to menace, he would see the Western giants in possession of the very stuff of his dream.

"The menace to the Western world lies, not in the little brown man, but in the four hundred millions of yellow men should the little brown man undertake their management. The Chinese is not dead to new ideas; he is an efficient worker; makes a good soldier, and is wealthy in the essential materials of a machine age. Under a capable management he will go far. The Japanese is prepared and fit to undertake this management. Not only has he proved himself an apt imitator of Western material progress, a sturdy worker and a capable organizer, but he is far more fit to manage the Chinese than we are. The baffling enigma of the Chinese character is no baffling enigma to him. He understands as we could never school ourselves nor hope to understand. Their mental processes are largely the same. He thinks with the same thought-symbols as does the Japanese, and he thinks in the same peculiar grooves. He goes on where we are balked by the obstacles of incomprehension."

The Japanese as an imitator of Western materialism was inhibited from further progress, he believed, by an inability to comprehend what lay behind it. "Things spiritual cannot be imitated; they must be felt and lived, woven into the very fabric of life, and here the Japanese fails. It required no revolution of his nature to learn to calculate the range and fire a field-gun or to march the goose-step. It was a mere matter of training. Our material achievement is the product of our intellect. It is knowledge, and knowledge, like coin, is interchangeable. It is not wrapped up in the heredity of the new-born child, but is something to be acquired afterward.

"Not so with our soul-stuff, which is the product of an evolution which goes back to the raw beginnings of the race. Our soul-stuff is not a coin to be pocketed by the first chance comer. The Japanese cannot pocket it any more than he can thrill to short Saxon words or we can thrill to Chinese hieroglyphics."

The Japanese worshiped the State, and therein lay their strength. "The Japanese mind does not split hairs as to whether the Emperor is Heaven incarnate or the State incarnate. So far as the Japanese are concerned, the Emperor lives, is himself deity. The Emperor is the object to live for and die for. The Japanese is not an individualist. . . . The honor of the individual, per se, does not exist . . . He does not look upon himself as a free agent, working out his own personal salvation. Spiritual agonizing is unknown to him. He relates himself to the State as, amongst bees, the worker is related to the hive; himself nothing, the State everything; his reasons for existence the exaltation and glorification of the State."[14]

He thought it foolish of the Western world to "rhapsodize" over the intensity and purity of Japanese patriotism, "unwittingly measuring the Japanese patriotism by its own conceptions of patriotism." The "blind and unswerving loyalty" to what was "practically an absolutism" was the greatest danger the West had to face.

"No great race adventure," he continued, "can go far nor endure long which has no deeper foundation than material success, no higher prompting than conquest for conquest's sake and mere race glorification. To go far and to endure, it must have behind it an ethical impulse, a sincerely conceived righteousness. But it must be taken into consideration that the above postulate is itself a product of Western race-egotism, urged by our belief in our own righteousness and fostered by a faith in ourselves which may be as erroneous as are most race fancies. So be it."

The motive power of Western expansion in Asia thus far had been provided by Christianity, by a nominal desire to proselytize the heathen, but London as a professed atheist was not prepared to endorse it as a countervailing force against Japanese emperor-worship. He could suggest no faith or ideology — not even socialism — as a stiffening element for Western determination to confront the Yellow and/or Brown Peril. He was opposed to the American occupation of the Philippines, though it provided us with the forward bases which military experts insisted were necessary for that purpose.

Nor did he venture any prediction on the outcome of a collision between East and West. "The world is whirling faster today than ever before," he concluded in his essay. "Affairs rush to conclusion. The Far East is the point of contact of the adventuring Western people as well as of the Asiatic. We shall not have to wait for our children's time nor our children's children. We shall ourselves see and largely determine the adventure of the Yellow and the Brown."[15]

As in his youth London had made himself the "Kipling of the North" for his Klondike tales, he devoted much of the balance of his short life (ended by suicide when he was forty) to fictional explorations of the Pacific. Many of his South Sea stories were of enduring interest because he undertook, in his venturesome fashion, to pick up where Melville left off. He sailed his own yacht into the South Seas and visited the valley of the Typee where Melville had spent his youthful idyll. He found no more lissome maidens or stalwart warriors in that valley, only death and disease brought by the white man, and could only mourn that "all this strength and beauty has departed . . . Life has rotted away in this beautiful garden spot . . ." In the Solomons he sailed with what was politely known as a labor-recruiting ship, heavily armed and with her deck protected by barbed wire. The ship was wrecked and London barely escaped with his life when the labor recruiters were besieged by thousands of ungrateful Solomon islanders. His experiences provided him with the material for *Adventure,* a novel which depicted with brutal realism the life on a copra plantation in the Solomons, and for scores of short stories.

Both as a prophet of the dangers of a reborn East, and as one of the most popular fiction writers of his time, Jack London was enormously influential in shaping American attitudes toward the Far East. Until the last year of his life he considered himself first of all a Socialist revolutionary, but those convictions were conveyed to people of similar beliefs. His Pacific-mindedness and his devotion to the idea of Anglo-Saxon domination threaded through much of what he produced for the mass consumption in national magazines and books.

It was one of the consummate ironies of his career that as a Hearst star he produced work that entirely pleased William Randolph Hearst, while Ambrose Bierce, the archconservative and a Hearst stablemate of London's, was bitterly contemptuous of all concepts of American superiority and once wrote that "we belong to a race of gluttons and drunkards to whom dominion is given over the abstemious. We can thrash them consummately and every day of the week, but we cannot understand them;

Lafcadio Hearn, who explained Japan

Jack London, always alert to the Yellow/Brown Peril

and is it not a great golden truth, shining like a star, that what one does not understand one knows to be bad?"

2. *The Great White Fleet*

At the height of the Japanese war scare of 1907, President Roosevelt decided to send "the great white fleet" — sixteen assorted warships — on a cruise around the world to demonstrate our naval might. It would visit six continents, leaving in its wake the debris of a notable series of barroom brawls, but its principal purpose was to overawe the Japanese. The little black ships of Commodore Perry were an image on which Roosevelt intended to superimpose the more menacing apparition of long, heavily gunned battleships and cruisers. He had tried to moderate the anti-Japanese sentiments of the Californians, but now judged, apparently, that it was time to demonstrate that he had not forgotten how to brandish his metaphorical big stick. The President announced his plans for the supercruise just at a time when rioting had broken out again in San Francisco, Japanese immigrants were being beaten by mobs, Japanese property was being wrecked, and when *Collier's Weekly* was serializing the translation of a German novel picturing a Japanese task force wiping out the United States Navy in half an hour and then landing an army on the California coast.

As far as Japan was concerned, the visit of the Great White Fleet was not intended as a goodwill gesture. Rear Admiral Robley D. (Fighting Bob) Evans, a gouty, testy-tempered old sea dog of the Farragut school, intimated that he was prepared to shoot his way into Japanese harbors. "Whether it proves a feast, a frolic, or a fight, we are prepared," he proclaimed.

Meanwhile President Roosevelt was receiving a tip from Kaiser Wilhelm — they were on excellent terms — through his ambassador in Berlin that the Japanese were "drilling thousands of soldiers in Mexico." Earlier that year (1907) Ernst von Reventlow, president of the German Navy League, had produced his hair-raising novel *Banzai,* which ended with the German High Seas Fleet steaming at flank speed across the Atlantic to save America from the Japanese. Germany was determined to drive a wedge between Britain's alliances in Europe and Asia, as well as between Britain and America. The Kaiser even forwarded to President Roosevelt the promise that his navy would protect America's east coast while the Great White Fleet was plowing its way around the world, and pledged that his Wehrmacht would come rushing across the Atlantic to fight beside the Americans if they were attacked from Mexico or Canada. All this, and building his dream railroad from Berlin to Baghdad . . .

The French, who had also formed an alliance with Japan, were horrified by the American naval junket. André Tardieu wondered whether the

United States was really foolish enough to test the "brave, stout, disciplined, enthusiastic" Japanese Imperial Navy. That navy had sunk a Russian fleet at Tsushima, while the most recent exploits of the Americans had consisted of blasting apart the antique Spanish fleets. The French press called Roosevelt a demagogue and an imperialist, denounced the United States for its mad-dog chauvinism, and predicted France and the United States would come to blows before the cruise ended.

Both the English and French newspapers gloated over the probability that Japan, boiling with resentment over the uninvited appearance of the American warships in her waters, would provide a watery grave for the Great White Fleet in Tokyo Bay or elsewhere. "This American fleet would crumple up and disappear," declared the London *Daily News,* "before the forces of the nation which hitherto has never thought it necessary to declare war before commencing hostilities." *La Libre Parole* of Paris licked its chops over the question: "Is the [American] fleet being watched by the Japanese from some dangerous ambush? Will Admiral Evans, when he arrives in April or May, find the Japanese already occupying Hawaii or the Philippines? Edward VII, Japan's ally, could possibly answer these questions. Wilhelm II, who we believe is united by secret treaty with Washington, may have a fine opportunity to try his new fleet."[16]

Undeterred by any of his own forebodings, the warnings of the over-friendly Kaiser, the qualms of the British, the annoyance of the French or the possible hostility of the Japanese, President Roosevelt sent the Great White Fleet on its way December 16, 1907, from Hampton Roads with the bands on shore playing the quickstep "The Girl I Left Behind Me" and the men on the ships defiantly singing:

> *Old Japan can lick our navy,*
> *She can? Yes? Like hell she can!*[17]

The hundred-million-dollar fleet steamed south in splendid array with fourteen thousand men aboard the *Connecticut, Kansas, Louisiana, Vermont, Georgia, Virginia, New Jersey, Rhode Island, Minnesota, Ohio, Missouri, Maine, Alabama, Illinois, Kentucky* and the *Kearsage,* in addition to auxiliary vessels and a torpedo-boat flotilla.

Latin American ports were visited first, and despite the fact that the ships' libraries included books on etiquette available to the crews, there were a number of liberty-party brawls on shore. The cruise of the Great White Fleet, in fact, was responsible for the organization of the Shore Patrol to keep American swabbies from tangling with the natives and each other. Down the east coast of South America, up the west coast, then to San Francisco, the fleet proceeded without serious incident, although attended by spy scares and threats of sabotage.

In midsummer 1908 it headed westward across the Pacific, despite hundreds of pleas to the White House asking that the Japanese visit be called off because the treacherous Nipponese might be waiting in ambush. The German press was giddy with predictions that the Americans would be waylaid by the Japanese navy. Count von Zeppelin, busy with his own preparations for the dirigible fleet which would bomb London and Paris a half-dozen years hence, took time out to express the hope that the United States fleet was ready to "strike where strategy demands." A Karlsbad journal viewed the Pacific voyage as the beginning of "the important part of the war or peace drama — the demonstration against Japan."

Already fearing Japanese encroachments, the Australians gave the American ships an almost hysterical welcome. Along the parade routes of Australian cities they raised banners reading "Yellow Peril," "Big Brother" and "White Australia." An Australian newspaper suggested that the United States should formulate "a new Monroe Doctrine" for the Pacific, which would protect Australia from Japan, now that Great Britain was a Japanese ally. To such suggestions there was a warm American response, the New York *Sun* assuring the Australians they would one day be part of the American system but pointing out, "The only possibility is for us to admit them as states within our Federal Union."[18]

Meanwhile diplomatic arrangements had been made for the fleet's reception in Japan. The Japanese guaranteed a friendly welcome provided that the whole fleet would go to Tokyo rather than carry out a previous plan to split it between visits to China and Japan; this apparently was calculated as an affront to the Chinese at a time when the Japanese were maneuvering for an enlargement of their Manchurian holdings.

As it turned out, the American fleet sailed into Tokyo Bay to be welcomed with a warmth exceeded only by that of Australia. A Yokohama newspaper greeted them with a "Fleet Banzai Number!" Ten thousand schoolchildren singing "Hail, Columbia!" in English greeted the 150 seamen carefully selected for shore leave on the basis of their reputations for sobriety and nonviolence. Fifty thousand citizens of Tokyo saluted the fleet with a torchlight parade. All the admirals were given living quarters in the ancient Shiba Palace and captains were put up at the Imperial Hotel.

An even more extraordinary honor was tendered the visitors when the emperor Meiji unexpectedly appeared at a luncheon given for the admirals and captains at the Imperial Palace. The American officers were agreeably surprised that the emperor turned out to be an affable, Edwardian-type monarch in a Vandyke beard, dressed in a military uniform, instead of a Gilbert and Sullivan mikado, and that he discussed armor-plate and muzzle velocities with an intelligent interest.

Admiral Togo, the most prestigious naval officer in the world for his Tsushima victory, received all the officers at a garden party, and Premier Katsura entertained them at a formal ball. Even luckier, perhaps, were the newspaper correspondents who had accompanied the fleet. Each was presented with a small paper house, a kimono and a beautiful girl. With each girl came a packet of official papers attesting to the fact that they were married to the newspapermen to whom they were assigned for the duration of the fleet's visit. Understandably enough, at least one of the correspondents confessed in print that he had "fallen in love" with Japan.

The enlisted men behaved admirably, though they had reason to be annoyed by the fact that their activities were limited to trolley-car riding and feasting on ice cream. But that wasn't the fault of the Japanese. They had recruited 250 geishas to entertain the sailors and raised funds for hundreds of barrels of beer to slake the naval thirsts. An American missionary named A. W. Woodworth, however, wrote a series of urgent letters to the Japan *Times* declaring that the "morality" of American seamen would be affronted by offering them geishas because most of them "belong to the Y.M.C.A." A beer-bust was out of the question, he said, because American seafaring men preferred ice-cream socials. American wives living in Japan supported the missionary, and all those charming Japanese plans had to be canceled. Instead of drinking beer and submitting to the attentions of the geishas, the American sailors were surrounded by Japanese Christians wearing Y.M.C.A. armbands who pressed ice cream on them day and night.

The only casualties were a sailor who sought an antidote to ice cream by drinking lemon extract and who was given a military funeral ashore, and Rear Admiral Charles S. Sperry. The admiral and other officers were given a tour of the battleship *Mikasa* by Admiral Togo. As an extraordinary gesture of goodwill, the officers of the Imperial Navy seized Admiral Sperry and tossed him in the air three times in a blanket, resulting in various contusions and abrasions. The American officers then accorded similar honors to Admiral Togo. One of them was a young ensign named William F. Halsey, better known during and after World War II as Admiral "Bull" Halsey. "If we had known what the future held," Halsey said many years later, "we wouldn't have caught him the third time."

Once the fleet sailed away, fairly convinced of the sincerity of the Japanese welcome, foreigners living in Japan learned how carefully and stringently the whole affair had been stage-managed by the government. Evelyn Adam, an Englishwoman living in Tokyo, discovered that Japanese cities had been plastered with a "police proclamation" a month before the Great White Fleet appeared, in which the citizenry was warned: "People shall not crowd around foreigners in the streets. Sticks and stones shall not be thrown at dogs accompanying foreigners . . . No comments or ridicule or mean words shall be given in regard to the dress, bearing and words of foreigners. . . . Impediment shall not be given to the foreigner at play or on bicycle by the throwing of fragments of tile, stone or stick or by arraying children in the streets."[19]

It was not announced until a month later, in November 1908, that all during that love feast in and around Tokyo Japanese diplomats were negotiating a treaty, later called the Root-Takahira Agreement, which historians have generally condemned as yielding too much to the Japanese in exchange for their goodwill during the visit of the Great White Fleet. A "terrible diplomatic blunder to be laid to the door of T.R.," Willard Straight, then the United States consul at Mukden, Manchuria, called it.[20] Its principal clause was an agreement by both powers to maintain the status quo in the Orient, which was taken to include Japanese expansion in Manchuria.

The agreement was signed, the *Army-Navy Register* reported from Washington, as part of a bargain by which the United States Fleet would be welcomed in Japan and Roosevelt's grandiose naval parade around the world would be unmarred by a hostile reception. Britain was delighted because it eliminated any fruition of the proposed German-American-Chinese alliance against Britain, France and Japan, which might have disturbed the balance of power in the Far East.

If all the speculation about the American motivation for signing the Root-Takahira Agreement was true — and the fact it was signed just about the time the Great White Fleet was sailing into Japanese waters lends weight to the conjecture — then that globe-girdling voyage provided a significant addition to Japanese self-confidence about their plans for further aggression. It was in any case one of those rare occasions when T.R.'s big stick turned into a twig.

One offshoot of the Root-Takahira Agreement, and the resentment it aroused in Washington, was a clandestine American effort to undermine Japan's intention of monopolizing and taking over Manchuria. It was largely undertaken by Willard Straight, the young upstate New Yorker who had recently been posted to Mukden as consul-general. If it was the State Department's policy to thwart Japan in Manchuria as much as possible, then Straight had been an excellent choice for the assignment. He was strongly biased in favor of China and against Japan.

An orphan who had been raised by an Oswego doctor and graduated from Cornell with an architectural degree, Straight joined the Chinese Maritime Customs Administration in 1901 at the age of twenty-one. Subsequently he became United States vice-consul at Seoul. When the Russo-Japanese War broke out, the venturesome young man had himself appointed a war correspondent by Reuters'. Like his fellow correspondent Jack London, he experienced an obsessive suspicion of the Japanese, whose military and naval victories had changed them into strutting Prussians of the Orient. Regarding the Japanese military in Korea, Straight wrote in his diary, "They all hate us, all of them, officers and men. They have been the underdog until now, they have been the scholars, we the masters, and now they're going to show us a thing or two if it can be done. They hate us. God knows the feeling is mutual."[21]

Eager, hardworking and ambitious, Straight returned to diplomacy after the war and from 1906 to 1908 was United States consul-general at Mukden, the center of Japanese intrigue to overspread all of Manchuria. His view of such ambitions accorded with American policy following the Japanese defeat of the Russians, which was to build up China through loans and railway construction as an offset to Japanese imperialism. Straight was a hardheaded visionary who saw trouble ahead with the Japanese. Undoubtedly, too, there was an element of racism in his detestation of the Japanese and his resentment of their successful exploitation of Korea and South Manchuria. He admitted as much in a letter to a friend:

"For no particular reason, with no real cause for complaint, I now find myself hating the Japanese more than anything else in the world. It is due I presume to the constant strain of having to be polite and to seek favors from a yellow people. We cannot know them or understand them and they dislike us thoroughly. Kipling was absolutely right when he wrote 'The East is East and the West is West, and never the twain shall meet.' " The overlay of Westernism which some Japanese displayed, he explained, was "essentially that of a man who keeps a new suit and rides a new horse — his character won't change."[22]

Straight was summoned home to serve as chief of the new Far Eastern Affairs division of the State Department from November 1908 to June 1909. In that position he was able to guide and influence the "dollar diplomacy" of the Taft Administration. The State Department hoped that American capital investment in China would be increased and act as something of a bulwark against Japanese expansion. Acting as liaison with the great private banking houses of New York, Straight was invaluable to the department. He believed that "diplomacy and commerce should go hand in hand," that the "political prestige so necessary to the future of America in the Far East could only be secured by the creation of substantial vested interests." Bluntly stated, he was convinced that the United States would act forcefully in China and Manchuria only if the interests of American capitalism required protection. He had become so anti-Japanese that he was willing to consider an alliance with Britain, or even Germany or Russia, to thwart Japanese ambitions.

Straight left the State Department in 1909 to participate more directly in the economic struggle in the Far East. By that time Wall Street's interest had been intermittently attracted to its possibilities since 1895, when the China Development Company was formed to secure railway construction rights in China by James Stillman of the National City Bank, Charles Coster of J. P. Morgan, Edward H. Harriman, and Jacob Schiff, the senior partner of Kuhn, Loeb & Co. By then, too, the American railroads had acquired shipping interests to extend their operations from the

American continent to the Orient, the Union Pacific holding half the stock of the Occident & Orient Steamship Co., the Southern Pacific buying control of the old Pacific Mail Steamship Co. in 1900, and James J. Hill of the Great Northern forming an association with a Japanese line for shipment of flour, cotton goods and steel rails to Japan and China. There was considerable jockeying for a preferred position in the trans-Pacific trade between the Japanese and the Americans and the Americans among themselves. Kuhn, Loeb had floated loans for Japan during its war with Russia, and naturally considered that this entitled them to preference. Harriman of the Southern Pacific turned down an offer from Japanese interests to buy out his share of the Pacific Mail. Big money was scented, and vast schemes were being conceived.

Harriman, the aggressive entrepreneur who had dismantled Jay Gould's empire, took Straight on as his adviser and they proceeded to Tokyo. There was nothing small about Harriman's aspirations. He told Lloyd Griscom, the United States minister in Tokyo, that "if I can secure control of the South Manchuria Railway from Japan, I'll buy the Chinese Eastern from Russia, acquire trackage over the Trans-Siberian to the Baltic, and establish a line of steamers to the United States. Then I can connect with the American transcontinental lines and join up with the Pacific Mail and the Japanese trans-Pacific steamers. It'll be the most marvelous transportation system in the world. We'll girdle the earth."[23] The Japanese, however, were too canny to part with the South Manchuria Railway, the linchpin in the Manchurian economy, much as they needed capital. Harriman then approached the Russians with an offer to buy their holdings in the Chinese Eastern Railway. Harriman's death on September 10, 1909, wrote off that project. Undeterred, Straight organized an international consortium and tried to wangle a concession in Manchuria for the construction of a railroad by British and American interests, but couldn't make headway against the combined opposition of Japan and Russia.

He was dedicated to the idea that only by restoring China to national health and independence could Japan be thwarted and the Western powers maintain their dominance in the Far East. "The more I see of Manchurian affairs," he wrote, "the more I am convinced that we, the Americans, are favored above all others and that ours is the opportunity to befriend China in this her time of need and to aid her in straightening out her affairs . . . [Once] we had established ourselves in Manchuria, we could do a tremendous work in furthering the Chinese Renaissance. The task not of Empire building, but of Empire shaping could with proper handling be ours."

Straight rightly divined that the possession of Manchuria was essential to military or commercial expansion on the Asian mainland, but he gave up his attempts at "Empire shaping" to become a Morgan partner at the unprecedented age of thirty-two shortly after marrying Dorothy Whitney, the daughter of William C. Whitney. A man of remarkable intellectual breadth, he also established the liberal *New Republic,* largely because he admired the work of Herbert Croly, who became its editor, and also the *Journal of the American Asiatic Association* (later the prestigious *Asia Magazine*). He was only forty when he died in France during the postwar flu epidemic, but he had won a high place among the prophets of a coming conflict with Japan. He had exerted his greatest influence at a time when Japanese-American relations were becoming politely hostile and mutually suspicious.

4. *A Real-Life Sequel to "Valor"*

"We were near war with Japan in 1913," wrote Secretary of the Navy Josephus Daniels in his memoir *The Wilson Era.* How near, perhaps, the nation never realized. One contributing factor was the raging temper of the Japanese government. Another was the equally bellicose mood of the United States military establishment, particularly its naval arm, which was urging a preventative war against Japan.

Six months after the death of Homer Lea and a year after the publication of his *The Day of the Saxon* with its dire prophecies of the Anglo-Saxon future, coupled with his earlier warnings in *The Valor of Ignorance* of Japanese plans to strike without warning, the Lea influence on American strategists was stronger than it had ever been before, or would ever be again. Military and naval leaders in the United States, wrote Jonathan Daniels (*The End of Innocence*), the son of the Secretary of the Navy, were "giving belligerent attention to the warnings of Homer Lea, an eccentric or prophetic soldier of fortune, about the dangers of the 'yellow peril.' "

The immediate cause of Japanese resentment, exacerbating a national conviction that they were a great power and were destined to be the greatest, was the Alien Land Act passed by the California legislature. In effect, it was the first official act of discrimination aimed at the Japanese, and was far more humiliating than the rescinded ordinance of segregation adopted by the San Francisco board of education several years before. The Alien Land Act forbade Japanese to own or lease any land in California; its sponsors openly admitted that its purpose was to drive the Japanese from the state.

The Japanese ambassador delivered a note from Tokyo protesting the legislation as "obnoxious, discriminatory, unfair, unfriendly, and in violation of the treaty between two countries." Strong language for a diplomatic message, but even stronger was used by Japanese officials in both Tokyo and Washington. President Wilson agreed that the law was "unfair," and sent Secretary of State William Jennings Bryan to Sacramento to plead with the legislature to reconsider and with Governor Hiram Johnson not to sign the law. Both the legislature and the governor refused to yield to Bryan's well-advertised eloquence, and Bryan returned to Washington to report to President Wilson that there was nothing the federal government could do about it.

When the President passed along that word to the Japanese ambassador he was appalled at the latter's reaction. "It never occurred to me that war could be possible between the two countries," Wilson told his Secretary of the Navy, "until I observed the manner of the Japanese Ambassador, who was very nervous and gave evidence that his country looked for war."[24]

The ambassadorial reaction was only the mildest reflection of an aroused public opinion in his home islands, where the militarist faction was whipping up the mob into a frenzy of anti-Americanism. On April 18, 1913, a throng of twenty thousand in Tokyo "hysterically cheered the demand that Japan resort to arms," according to a press report. "Revelling in the recent discovery of its power, the mob, inflamed by the opposition [to the ruling government], endeavored to use the same methods to force a settlement of the California question as it had employed in bringing down the previous Katsura Ministry," A. M. Pooley, an American observer, noted. "More unfortunate still," Pooley recorded, "the wave of excitement grew under the stimulus of anti-American societies formed by men in responsible positions. The agitation of April and May, 1913, became a national movement and of such volume that the Government had to pay respect to it. The anti-American movement spread, associations sprang up like mushrooms to deal with the matter . . . National demonstrations were held in the principal cities to protest and to threaten. The leaders of the mobocracy boasted of their late victory over the clans, and asserted that the time had come to settle once and for all the question of racial prejudice.

"Members of Parliament invoked the old *jio* (anti-foreign spirit), advocated a policy of *yakiuchi* (incendiarism), and invited the people to burn the American embassy. Insulting placards were posted on its walls and a police guard without."[25]

The Marquis Okuma demanded the expulsion of American missionaries as an essential first step in convincing the United States of Japanese wrath. And, according to Mr. Pooley, "The missionaries, as usual, blew the Japanese trumpet, conferred together and with the authorities, and enriched the cable companies by innumerable cablegrams to the States denouncing their own countrymen and eulogizing the Japanese." Japanese embassies in Europe put out feelers for a large foreign loan, but the European countries were arming themselves as fast as they could and the money couldn't be spared for a Far Eastern adventure.

Meanwhile, by mid-May, the American admirals and generals, along with their supporters in the press, were pumping up the war scare for all they were worth. Some favored a preemptive strike against the Japanese home islands, others suggested that threatening moves by the American forces in the western Pacific might goad Japan into moving against the United States.

In this lowering atmosphere one of the more brazen trumpets was sounded by the New York *Herald,* long regarded as the house organ of the Navy Department. Its absentee publisher was the high-handed Commodore James Gordon Bennett, Jr., who sailed around the world on his yacht and cabled his alcoholic inspirations to his newspapers in New York, London and Paris. Bennett was a naval buff who had served for exactly two months as an officer with the blockading squadron off Port Royal until he annoyed his superiors by complaining endlessly about shipboard cuisine and was goaded into resigning.

In mid-May 1913 the New York *Herald* published a story under tall headlines about a supposed "leak" in the war plans of the joint Army and Navy Board, which then functioned much like today's Joint Chiefs of Staff. The story was written by Joseph K. Ohl, the *Herald*'s former Far Eastern correspondent but now a senior editor in New York. The story read in part:

"At a meeting held this date [May 13, 1913] the Joint Board unanimously decided in consequence of urgent presentation made by the army member of the board that it is a matter of the utmost military importance that the United States cruisers *Saratoga, Cincinnati, Albany, Rainbow* and *Helena* now on the Yangtze River be moved immediately to Manila to reinforce and cooperate with the Army there as well as to insure the safety of the vessels themselves.

"In view of existing conditions, the Joint Board recommends most strongly that the following disposition of the ships of the Pacific station be made at once: first, that six armored cruisers of the *West Virginia* class, four submarines and five destroyers be ordered to the Hawaiian Islands; that the *Oregon* and *Cheyenne* be ordered to Panama."[26]

By the *Herald*'s account, Admiral Dewey, as senior member of the board, raised the question of what should be done to prepare against the Japanese threat. The army chief of staff, General Leonard Wood, who had been warning about Japanese intentions ever since he served in the Philippines, reported that the "Japanese notes were becoming more and more insistent," that the army had been moving supplies to Hawaii and the Philippines in case those possessions were attacked. General Wood then recommended that the navy take similar precautions.

The story exploded over Washington like a projectile from one of the new fourteen-inch guns. The knowledgeable realized that the story must have been planted; the armed forces weren't very security conscious in those days, but such crucial decisions didn't just happen to provide scoops for Washington correspondents. It was also significant that the story was written, not by the *Herald*'s correspondent in the capital but Editor Ohl in New York. "This publication," wrote Secretary of the Navy Daniels later, "was believed by the President and me to have been made in order to force the hand of the Commander in Chief."

Only after the story was leaked, Rear Admiral Bradley A. Fiske, a dapper, quick-tempered bantamweight who had served with Dewey in Manila Bay and was now the chief of the navy's bureau of operations, came to Daniels with the Army and Navy Board's recommendations for a naval concentration at Manila, which could very well have provoked the Japanese into hostile action.

"I suggested to him," Daniels wrote in his memoirs, "that it was unprecedented for an Army officer [General Wood] to be initiating Naval activities, and that if there were to be any movement of Naval ships, it could not be done without the order of the Secretary of the Navy or the Commander in Chief. I also told him I thought nothing could be more injurious to peaceful negotiations than the movements recommended and that the Board had exceeded its functions because what it recommended might precipitate war.

" 'But Secretary of War Garrison has approved the prompt sending of Army forces, and the Navy should act quickly,' said the Admiral.

" 'That is a matter for the President to decide,' I answered. 'Personally I think the Board has erred and I cannot approve the warlike recommendations. I have no criticism of the Secretary of War, but I will not be a party to such an ill-considered course taken without consultation with officials who are looking for a peaceful solution.' "

Admiral Fiske, he recalled, was "militant" and "would like to have seen war with Japan."[27]

At the subsequent Cabinet meeting Daniels and Secretary of War Lindley M. Garrison had "quite a debate," as Daniels described it. Garrison defended the actions and intentions of the Army and Navy Board and declared that precautionary measures had to be taken unless we were willing to risk losing Hawaii and the Philippines to Japanese aggression. "Garrison was somewhat of the same mind as the imperialistic members of the Joint Board. He nearly always sided with the plans they mapped out for military preparation and action . . . he looked at matters from the same standpoint as men like General Wood."[28]

Daniels was critical of the Joint Board's contingency planning because "it would be most unwise for any large movement of the Army or Navy in Far Eastern waters to take place while negotiations looking to a peaceful solution were pending . . . It would strengthen the hands of those Japanese who wanted war and would weaken the hands of those who . . . hoped for peaceful adjustment." Although his background was journalistic rather than military, Daniels did not hesitate to criticize the proposed movement of ships on tactical grounds. "I took the ground that if the Japanese were so minded, the very minute the ships (which were of an old type with guns of short range) left Chinese waters, it would be the easiest thing in the world for the Japanese to sink them before they could reach the Philippines." Even with the reinforcements advocated by the admirals and generals, he added, "we would still be unable to prevent the taking of the Philippines with our little force in the Far East, if the Japanese were determined to take them — we were so far from any base of supplies — and it would be a dangerous, provocative, and impotent gesture."[29]

Secretary of State Bryan supported Daniels and vigorously objected to the independent action of the Joint Board as an effort to take over control of government policy. "While we were discussing how to prevent a threatened war, these men were busy with plans of how to get us in. It is time enough for the Army and Navy to make plans when the Commander in Chief calls upon them to do so."

When Secretary of War Garrison again urged the necessity of protecting our Philippine interests, Daniels replied that our conquest of the islands had been unwise from the strategic as well as the moral standpoint. "Just as a chain is only as strong as its weakest link, so no country is stronger than its remotest and weakest possession. The sooner we repair the wrong done under McKinley and give the Philippines their independence, the sooner we will return to real democracy and insure ourselves against the necessity — if it is necessary — to hold them in our possession."

At the end of the Cabinet meeting President Wilson, who had thus far leaned to Daniels's side of the argument, asked Daniels and Garrison to meet with him that afternoon for a more thorough discussion of the problem. Both repeated their arguments, with Daniels elaborating on the tactical weakness of the Joint Board's plans. He emphasized that "any movement of ships or troops which was not large enough to make victory certain was worse than no movement; that if the Japanese situation was so critical, we ought to send our dreadnoughts over to the Philippines and have them ready to protect the smaller ships when they left the Chinese waters."

President Wilson then ordered that no action be taken until the matter had been threshed out. He was "greatly outraged," Daniels said, by the apparently calculated leak of the Joint Board's recommendations and "was ready to take summary action" against the officers responsible because "he thought it was an attempt to forestall action by the Commander in Chief."

With schoolmasterly severity, President Wilson then proceeded to deal with the Joint Army and Navy Board.

Henceforth, and until it was reactivated by his direct order, the Joint Board was to go into hibernation. A comparable gesture today would be a presidential order disbanding the Joint Chiefs of Staff. Such a drastic action was possible, of course, only in that time more than half a century ago when years of peace had made the military establishment slightly less important than, say, the Bureau of Fisheries.[30]

President Wilson informed the generals and admirals of the Joint Board that he wanted no more war planning by a council which could not even keep its own deliberations secret. As the Secretary of the Navy gleefully recalled, "From the moment the President directed the Joint Board to meet no more, it went into innocuous desuetude — that is to say, it was as if it did not exist — suspended between heaven and earth, and its members out of commission for more than two years." Wilson's own interventions in Mexico and later his decision to enter World War I resulted in the Joint Board's hasty resuscitation.

The war scare of 1913 evaporated, and later that year the Japanese sent a mission to this country to ameliorate the justifiable anger of the Japanese in California. One member of that mission published a pamphlet urging the Japanese-Americans to assimilate, to abandon old-country habits and customs which set them apart from other Americans, and conduct themselves as good citizens even though they were denied citizenship.* [31]

And as the magazine *Independent* reported, the phony war scares continued to crop up in the several years following. There were reports, assiduously published in the California papers, that the Japanese navy was secretly charting California harbors, and "Then there were numerous plottings with Mexico for a position from which this country could be attacked. A combination with Germany to destroy the Monroe Doctrine was the Pablum served up to the American public . . . In the same year Japan was forming an alliance with the West Coast Indians to gain a military foothold in this country. In 1915 Japanese spies were seen in the Panama fortifications and in the next year Japan was found conspiring to get a foothold in Panama by getting control of the San Blas Indian lands. Japan's diplomats penned Carranza's protests against our invasion of Mexico [the Punitive Expedition of 1916], after there had been landed in that country two hundred thousand Japanese troops, who had already fired on American troops at Mazatlan."[32]

The easing of the tensions of 1913 did not entirely relieve Secretary of the Navy Daniels of his troubles with the militant admirals. The chief of operations, Admiral Fiske, pressed for a general-staff system, which would "Prussianize" the navy in Daniels's view and eliminate civilian control of the naval firebrands. "He and Richmond Pearson Hobson [the ex-naval

---

* Even this tactful and large-minded work attracted the scorn of Hearst's Japanese-baiting San Francisco *Examiner*. On October 2, 1913, it published an editorial sneering that the pamphlet "informs us that Honorable Japanese is truly morally superior to unfortunate American inhabitableness . . . therefore is perfectly agreeable to naturalization and intermarriage."

hero now a member of the House Naval Affairs Committee] were obsessed with the yellow peril. They sat up nights thinking how Japan was planning to make war on America and steal a march on us by taking the Philippine Islands and going on to Hawaii. Hobson made speeches about it, which the President regarded as in bad taste at a time when critical matters were at issue between two countries."[33]

Daniels complained in his memoirs that Admiral Fiske took up much of his time with his arguments for preventative action against Japan. "One day while he was telling me of the imminence of the yellow peril, a Japanese photographer . . . came by appointment . . . to take my picture at my desk and a picture of the room. Before he came within earshot I said to the admiral, 'You are right. The yellow peril is on us. Here comes a Jap with a bomb. You had better get out.' He was so serious and so confident that whatever he thought was right and so lacking in humor that he was shocked at my levity, but he retired while the photographer did his best."[34]

In fairness to Admiral Fiske's memory, Daniels might have added that he lived to see the day when the Japanese provided an admittedly belated confirmation of Fiske's apprehensions with their assaults on Hawaii and the Philippines. Fiske, in fact, was one of the most forward-looking and scientific-minded officers in a navy that lacked professionalism. He was a pioneer enthusiast of naval aviation, having taken up the study of aeronautics in 1910 when most people thought the airplane was a ridiculous toy. "My idea," he wrote, "was to prevent the Japanese from landing [in the Philippines] at all by using aeroplanes against them while they were trying to land."[35] He envisioned air strikes against the Japanese transports while they approached the coast of Luzon. Torpedo bombers were not even conceived on the aeronautical engineers' drawing boards then, but he urged that the navy proceed with their development as a strategic advance in combining air and sea power. Most of his colleagues on the board which governed the navy, Admiral Dewey excepted, viewed his proposals for ships that would extend their striking power by launching planes as "wildcat schemes." The Admiral Rickover of his day, Fiske nevertheless persisted. More than any other man he was the father of the fleet air arm. Seven years after the Wright brothers' experimental flight Fiske, as commander-in-chief of the Atlantic Fleet, supervised the landing of a plane on the deck of the cruiser *Birmingham,* thus proving the practicability of the aircraft carrier. Two years later, in 1912, Fiske obtained the basic patents for the torpedo-launching plane, a weapon largely responsible for the crucial victory at Midway thirty years later. Surely the forgotten Admiral Fiske deserves a prominent niche among those who turned the United States westward on its geopolitical axis.

If the Japanese war scares were at least partly a sequel to the tocsins sounded by Homer Lea, Jack London and other literary prophets, there was also a footnote to that sequel which concerned the role of Franklin D. Roosevelt, then Daniels's ambitious young Assistant Secretary of the Navy, and more particularly the fateful attitudes it may have shaped.

Daniels's son, in his recapitulation of the era (*The End of Innocence*), suspects that the leak to the New York *Herald* may have been F.D.R.'s office, via Roosevelt's own chief assistant, Louis Howe, who "wanted nothing so much as pushing the earthly fortunes of FDR." Jonathan Daniels points out that Howe had been a reporter for the New York *Herald* for twenty years and "Howe often used the *Herald* as a paper in which to plant kind words and trial balloons about his ambitious young boss."

During that brief conspiracy of the Joint Board, Daniels continues, "Franklin's sympathies were entirely with the militant generals and admirals. This was, moreover, the first occasion, as one of Fiske's close colleagues, Admiral William F. Fullam, later reported, in which the admirals got the Assistant Secretary to pretend to the Secretary that memoranda prepared by them were suggestions of his own. Fullam had already found that the Secretary did not always embrace his proposals, as when he told the new Secretary he thought it would be better if he addressed new recruits not as 'young gentlemen' but as 'my lads.' Fullam remembered later that Franklin took his memo to the Secretary's office and, in a contortion characteristic of the time; put it on the floor beneath his feet and, through his knees, read it as his own. The Admiral said that 'coming from him as a civilian to the Secretary of the Navy, it had some effect.' Nothing resulted, however, which might provoke war. The purpose of the Navy was peace."[36]

The historic importance of young Franklin D. Roosevelt's minor involvement in the Joint Board's cabal, however, was its influence — perhaps only in the subconscious — on Roosevelt's later attitudes and policies toward Japan. Historians are divided on the subject of whether Roosevelt, as President, goaded Japan into the climactic events of December 1941, but it is certain that he could have exerted himself more effectively to head them off.

Possibly part of his antipathy for the Japanese was grounded in those years before World War I. Even before he became Assistant Secretary of the Navy, Roosevelt was sensitive to the possibility of Japanese aggression. In 1923 he wrote a magazine article that "outside the executive departments at Washington it has never been known in this country that, during the ten nervous days in the early summer of 1908" — that is, when the Great White Fleet was approaching Japan and the Root-Takahiri Agreement was being negotiated under pressure — "the United States hovered on the edge of an ultimatum from Japan."[37] Possibly he received that information firsthand from his cousin, President Theodore Roosevelt, or he may have come across documents relating a Japanese threat of war in the

Josephus Daniels: Dove among the Hawks (1912)

Navy Department files when he took over as Assistant Secretary. At any rate his statement in the magazine article reflected a continuing concern over Japanese enmity for the United States.

This is confirmed by Sumner Welles, his Undersecretary of State during the World War II years. "Purely personal reasons," Welles wrote, were partly responsible for Roosevelt's intense interest in the Far East.

"As Assistant Secretary of the Navy for more than seven years," Welles explained, "he had become imbued with the Navy's conviction that Japan was America's Number 1 antagonist. And no one close to the President could have failed to recognize the deep feeling of friendship for China he had inherited from his mother's side of his family. His mother, in fact, had lived in China as a small girl, and he himself loved to tell over and over again stories of the dealings members of his family had had with various Chinese dignitaries and merchants in the earlier decades of the nineteenth century."

Roosevelt's pro-Chinese, anti-Japanese bias, rooted both in his family background and his participation, whatever the degree, in the events of the years of the Yellow Peril, thus became of crucial historical importance. "A personal equation of this kind," Sumner Welles noted, "undeniably influences the thinking of a man even in high office . . . He became ever more incensed by Japan's conduct as the years passed."[38]

For Roosevelt as well as many of his contemporaries the decade of the Yellow/Brown Peril was a prefiguration of the atomic cloud which erupted over Hiroshima.

13 🌿

Walking on Eggs in Siberia

Watch your step; you will be walking on eggs loaded with dynamite.

— SECRETARY OF WAR NEWTON D. BAKER *to* MAJOR GENERAL
WILLIAM S. GRAVES

American interventions in Asia have usually been characterized by a confusion of motives, a crosscurrent of purposes. In the simplest terms, we have often interceded professing highly idealistic reasons for our military or naval presence but acting covertly out of self-interest. In taking the Philippines, we proclaimed that we had come to liberate the islands, and kept on saying it long after liberation had turned into repression. After that lengthy schooling in the disciplines and realities of colonialism, we told ourselves and the world that whatever actions we took in the Far East were in defense of our unwilling wards.

There was to be no facing up to the fact that so long as we held such advanced positions — even though we refused to spend the money to defend them properly, with a large modern Asiatic fleet and two or three army corps, the cost of which would have been insupportable before World War II — we were committed to protecting them against whichever power, Asian or European, was strongest in the Pacific. The result was half-measures, contrivances, occasional bluster and a tentative aggressiveness.

Such circumstances inevitably attended the Siberian Expeditionary Force of 1918–1920, when we invaded the mainland of Asia for the second time (the Boxer Rebellion being the first) and occupied parts of the Russian Maritime Provinces.

In the climactic summer of the war, when every division was needed for the Western Front in Europe, we hastily launched that expeditionary force across the Pacific into a situation of the greatest complexity. Communist propaganda since then has depicted that intervention as an attempt to crush the Russian Revolution. It was anything but that. The American commanders in Siberia were hardly sympathetic to the Bolshevik forces struggling to gain power, but they were openly hostile to many of their enemies. The Americans were the best friends the Bolsheviks had in Siberia.

But it was understandably difficult to tell friend from foe in all that confusion. There were so many flags flying over Siberia that it looked as though flag-making were the national pastime. Among the interests fighting and conspiring to gain supremacy in the years following the revolution of 1917 were the Czechoslovak Legion, the Japanese, the Chinese, the French and British, German war prisoners, a White (Russian) army under Admiral Kolchak, displaced Cossack forces turned to brigandage, the Bolshevik partisans, Pan-Mongols dreaming of Genghis Khan, and a notable array of freebooters shooting up the countryside in armored trains.

Into this resounding chaos was plunged an American expedition guided by little more than the several paragraphs of an *aide-mémoire,* equipped with more sturdy common sense than its government had any right to expect, and led by men whom George F. Kennan (in *The Decision to Intervene*) has characterized as possessing "the unquestioning fidelity to technical purposes and the high-minded impatience with the domestic-political conflicts of other nations which have marked the American mind in all ages . . ."

1. *Eggs Loaded with Dynamite*

July 1918 was an exceedingly anxious month in Washington. On the Western Front the last great German offensives had been hurled back, but only after they had almost succeeded in breaking the Allied lines. No one, of course, could be sure that was Germany's last gasp. The American Expeditionary Force in France until now had fought under French and British supervision, and would not conduct its first independent operation, the reduction of the St. Mihiel Salient, until mid-September. Even while the Allies were pleading for every available half-trained unit of American troops so they could regain the initiative, the Supreme War Council was proposing that the United States join in a Siberian intervention.

Britain, France, Japan and the United States, under this proposal, were to send forces to Siberia to consolidate an eastern front against Germany after the Bolshevik government negotiated a separate peace. Another factor was a large body of Czechoslovaks, who had fought in the Austrian army, had surrendered to or been captured by the Russians, and were now trying to fight their way out of Russia to join the Allies. One body of Czechs had reached Vladivostok, another was bogged down in the Urals fighting with the counterrevolutionary White Russians against the Bolsheviks. The project of rescuing the Czechoslovak Legion naturally appealed to President Wilson.

Another angle, discussed sotto voce, was the French and British determination to do in the Soviet government; Allied forces, including an American detachment, had already occupied parts of North Russia. Still another facet — and not the least important, particularly to the British — was the eager participation of the Japanese in the proposed expedition to Siberia. It was believed, with good reason, that Japan would use the occasion to expand her holdings in Manchuria, extend her influence to the two Mongolias and perhaps try to carve out a new colony from the Russian Maritimes. The French and British would be able to send only advisers to Siberia, so they wanted the United States to provide the troops, guided by French and British "advice," to act as a counterweight to the Japanese and keep their ambitions tamped down.

The celebrated Colonel R. H. Bruce Lockhart, British agent in Moscow, cabled the British Foreign Office on March 5, 1918, warning against allowing Japan to make her unilateral moves against eastern Russia. "If the Allies are to allow Japan to enter Siberia, the whole position is hopeless. Every class of Russian will prefer the Germans to the Japanese [because of Russian bitterness over the Japanese victory in 1905]. . . . I feel sure that you can have no idea of the feeling which Japanese intervention would arouse. Even the Cadet Press [more or less representative of the Russian middle class], which cannot be accused of Bolshevik sympathies, is loud in its denunciation of this crime against Russia, and is now preaching support of any party that will oppose Germany and save the revolution . . . And now when Germany's aims have been unmasked to the whole world [Germany occupied the Ukraine following the peace of Brest-Litovsk], the Allies are to nullify the benefits of this by allowing the Japanese to enter Russia."[1]

Another motive for sending American troops to Siberia was to reclaim and protect the mountain of war supplies which the United States had sent to the Kerensky regime in Russia, shortly before it was undermined by the Communists, with the understanding that they be used in maintaining the war against Germany. Now those supplies might fall into the hands of the Bolsheviks, the Japanese, or the various freebooters operating within striking distance of the Vladivostok warehouses where they were stored.

On July 5, 1918, President Wilson announced to his Cabinet that he had decided to dispatch a Siberian Expeditionary Force. An advance-guard of sorts was already in Siberia. The Soviet government had requested American assistance in restoring railroad service in eastern Russia. This unit, designated as the Russian Railway Service Corps, was based in Harbin, Manchuria, and consisted of 110 engineers. They had arrived in Harbin in March 1918 and taken over the supervision of the Trans-Siberian and Chinese Eastern railroads. Control of the railroads was as essential to any operations in northeastern Asia as it was complicated in management and financing. The only alternative to rail travel was carts, horseback or camel caravan. So it was of great help to the Americans that they had secured a considerable share in the control of the rail lines extending from Vladivostok to Harbin, Mukden, Chita, Irkutsk and Khabarovsk.[2]

Other than to succor the Czechs and protect those American supplies in Vladivostok, the idea of American intervention was abhorrent to President Wilson, even including, at the time, the necessity for curbing Japanese aspirations in eastern Russia. Yet he was harshly criticized. Justice Louis D. Brandeis wrote a friend that Wilson "should be judged by what he was and did prior to August 4th, 1918, the date of the paper justifying the attack on Russia. That was the first of his acts which was unlike him; and I am sure the beginning of the sad end." The *New Republic,* then edited by Walter Lippmann, opposed military intervention and insisted that the United States should stick to its original position of "no interference in Russia's internal affairs"; so did the *Nation* and most liberal publications. The elderly George Kennan, who had explored Siberia years before and written a book about the political exiles, warned in the *Outlook* of the dangers of "a conflict with the power and authority of the Bolsheviki."[3]

Public opinion generally was so distracted by events in western Europe that a Siberian intervention seemed a sideshow of little importance. The fate of a few thousand Czechs, or the security of American munitions dumps in Vladivostok, seemed a piddling concern compared with the thousands killed daily on the Western Front.

On August 2, President Wilson stopped in at the State, War and Navy Building — all three departments were then under one rococo roof — on his way back to the White House from his morning round of golf, and with the casualness of most of his military appointments agreed that the Siberian Expeditionary Force would be commanded by Major General William S. Graves.

However casually it was made, it was an excellent choice. Graves was one of those scholarly, sober-minded, well-educated soldiers, in a tradition later epitomized by George C. Marshall, who probably outweigh the Custers and Pattons in our military history, even though they fail to receive and would probably be dismayed by the garlands of legend. He was grave and almost professorial in manner and fittingly wore steel-rimmed spectacles; more important, he was cool-tempered, deliberate and possessed the capacity for seeing around sharp corners. When the United States entered the war, he was a lieutenant colonel and secretary to the general staff. At his own request, hopeful of being sent to France, he was transferred from staff to line, and took command of the Eighth Division at Camp Fremont, Palo Alto, California. The Eighth Division was scheduled to leave for France in October.

On August 2, a few hours after the President had conferred with the Secretary of War and the chief of staff, General Graves received a message in code from the War Department instructing him to "take the first and fastest train out of San Francisco and proceed to Kansas City, go to the Baltimore Hotel, and ask for the Secretary of War." Two hours later he was on his way, still mystified by the abrupt summons. "I tried to figure out what this very secret mission could be, and feared it meant Siberia," he later recalled, "although I had seen nothing in the press indicating that the United States would possibly send troops to Russia."

Graves arrived in Kansas City at ten o'clock at night. A redcap met him and announced that Secretary of War Newton D. Baker was waiting for him in a room in the station. Baker had to rush back to Washington and couldn't wait to confer with him at the Baltimore Hotel. It was typical of the offhand manner in which the military establishment operated in those unpretentious pre-Pentagon days that Graves was sent halfway around the world as casually as if he had been a quartermaster assigned to count underwear in a Salt Lake City warehouse. By Graves's brisk account, the Secretary of War "said he was sorry he had to send me to Siberia. As always, he was very generous and expressed his regrets and said he knew I did not want to go and he might, some day, tell me why I had to go. He also wanted me to know that General March [the Army chief of staff] tried to get me out of the Siberian trip and wanted me to go to France. He said: 'If in future you want to cuss anybody for sending you to Siberia I am the man.' "

Baker then handed him a sealed envelope, saying, "This contains the policy of the United States in Russia which you are to follow. Watch your step; you will be walking on eggs loaded with dynamite. God bless you and goodbye."

General Graves hurried to the hotel and opened the envelope the moment he was alone in his room. The guidelines by which he was to conduct himself in distant, revolution-torn Siberia were contained in a few sheets of paper headed *Aide-Mémoire,* with "Department of State, July 17, 1918," inscribed at the bottom.

The instructions were so sketchy that he went sleepless that night, "kept wondering what other nations were doing and why I was not given some information about what was going on in Siberia." Certainly it was a curious document, which Wilson himself had composed on his rickety old typewriter. It told more about Wilson's grievous state of mind than how, and to what effect, Graves and his troops were to interpose themselves between the Russians and the anarchy enveloping them. It went on rather pointlessly excusing the necessity for intervention. Wilson's *aide-mémoire* admitted that "military intervention there would add to the present sad confusion in Russia rather than cure it, injure her rather than help her, and that it would be of no advantage in the prosecution of our main design, to win the war against Germany . . . a method of making use of Russia, not a method of serving her."[4]

Wilson then reversed himself and declared an expedition to Siberia was "admissible" from the American viewpoint "only to help the Czecho-Slovaks consolidate their forces and get into successful cooperation with their Slavic kinsmen and to steady any efforts at self-government or self-defense in which the Russians" — he did not say which Russians, Red or White — "themselves may be willing to accept assistance. Whether from Vladivostok or from Murmansk and Archangel, the only legitimate object for which American or allied troops can be employed . . . is to guard military stores which may subsequently be needed by Russian forces and to render such aid as may be acceptable to the Russians in the organization of their own self-defense." The reiterated concern for military aid to the Russians was especially puzzling, since they were fighting each other and he did not specify which side, the revolution or the counterrevolution, was to receive that aid.

He emphasized the tentative, utterly discreet manner in which the American forces were supposed to operate in eastern Russia. The American government "hopes to carry out the plans for safeguarding the rear of the Czecho-Slovaks" — again there was a confusion; the Czechs had no "rear" in the military sense, one body being in the Urals and the other in Vladivostok — "operating from Vladivostok in a way that will place it and keep it in close cooperation with a small military force like its own from Japan, and if necessary from the other Allies, and that will assure it of the cordial accord of all the allied powers; and it proposes to ask all associated in this course of action to unite in assuring the people of Russia in the most public and solemn manner that none of the governments uniting in action either in Siberia or in northern Russia contemplates any interference of any kind with the political sovereignty of Russia, any intervention in her internal affairs, or any impairment of her territorial integrity either now or hereafter."

Either President Wilson was misinformed or he had ignored the latest intelligence from the Far East regarding Japanese intentions. Japan sent an expeditionary force of seventy-two thousand to Siberia, not the seven thousand she had been requested to send.

Wilson ended his memorandum on a customary note of piety. "It is the hope and purpose of the Government of the United States to take advantage of the earliest opportunity to send to Siberia a commission of merchants, agricultural experts, labour advisers, Red Cross representatives, and agents of the Young Men's Christian Association accustomed to organizing the best methods of spreading useful information and rendering educational help of a modest sort." The thought of Y.M.C.A. "agents" proselytizing over coffee and doughnuts among the vodka-swilling Cossacks and Mongol cutthroats must have warmed General Graves on many a cold Siberian night.

2. *Off to Vladivostok*

The day after General Graves puzzled over that presidential memorandum, the army began moving its forces toward the port of Vladivostok. The only troops close to that destination were in the Philippines. The War Department cabled the Philippine Department to dispatch on the first available transports the equivalent of a brigade: the 27th and 31st Infantry Regiments, an ambulance company, a field hospital and Company D, 53rd Telegraph Battalion of the Signal Corps. With the usual perversity of military administration, troops acclimated to the tropical jungle and clothed accordingly were sent to serve in the subzero cold and Arctic winds of the Siberian tundra. Both Philippine regiments were considerably under-strength, so General Graves was ordered to select five thousand men of his Eighth Division, "strong, hardy, fit for service intended" and "representing all parts of the United States," to beef up his composite forces. To tame the forces of anarchy, Graves would have an under-strength division.

It was a rush job. The 27th Infantry arrived in Vladivostok from the Philippines on August 16, the 31st Infantry a few days later. General Graves and his leading echelon reached the port on September 1.

Graves was admittedly ill-equipped to deal with the situation he found there so far as military or political intelligence was concerned. The only information given him just before leaving San Francisco was a State Department dispatch forwarded from Washington. It warned him that there were indications that "Japan's policy would be to keep the various Russian forces apart and oppose any strong Russian central authority, but to support a number of weak Russian forces which could not form more than a screen for Japanese action." Graves commented:

"If I had known as much about the Japanese Military when I received this information from Washington as I knew later, the message would have conveyed much more information to my mind. I have often thought it was unfortunate I did not know more of the conditions in Siberia than I did when I was pitchforked into the melee at Vladivostok. At other times I have thought that ignorance would not only be bliss in such a situation, but was advisable."

Thus he arrived in Vladivostok ill-informed but "without any preconceived ideas as to what should or should not be done. I had no prejudice against any Russian faction."[5]

The city itself was being governed by the two regiments of Czech ex-prisoners which had prevented a Bolshevik takeover. The American headquarters were located in a building owned by a German trading company. And the strongest force around was the Japanese Imperial Army. Those were just a few indications of the international scramble in Siberia.

The Japanese lost no time in letting General Graves know, very politely, that the Americans would have to fit themselves into Japanese planning. The Japanese General Otani was senior in rank on the scene and immediately after Graves had presented himself, Otani wanted to know whether Graves had received orders from Washington placing the American troops under his control. Otani styled himself as "Commander-in-chief of Allied Armies."

Graves replied that he had received no such orders, and the matter was dropped. On the personal level, Otani proved to be a "very agreeable man." He told Graves anecdotes about General Grant's visit to Japan, when Otani was a young officer just out of the military academy. He didn't know whether it would be more respectful as a member of General Grant's official escort to carry his saber in his hand or keep it in its sheath. He kept switching back and forth until one day Grant patted him on the shoulder and said, "Young man, you had better put that in the scabbard, you might stick someone with it."

On the official level, however, the Japanese proved themselves to be difficult and devious from the outset, indicative, Graves thought, of the fact "they always hoped to occupy eastern Siberia." The American commander made an inspection tour of the Trans-Siberian Railroad as far north as Khabarovsk, one of the largest cities in Siberia, where a sizable American detachment was posted, and found the countryside swarming with Japanese soldiery. Supposedly they were being deployed to "defeat the Austro-German prisoners and Bolsheviki troops" along the Amur branch of the railroad, as one of their general orders stated.

Aside from trying to divine the exact scope of Japanese ambitions Graves was baffled by the Russians themselves. When he arrived in Vladivostok, he recounted, Allied representatives in speaking of the Russians "meant the old Czarist officials, who felt it was then safe enough for them to appear in their gorgeous uniforms every evening, and parade down

Svetlanskaya, the principal thoroughfare. The other class was called 'Bolsheviks,' although, as a matter of fact, the old Czarist officials did not claim to be in favour of the reestablishment of a Czar in Russia, and the Russians who were called Bolsheviks did not claim to be in favour of the Soviet Government. The line of cleavage between these two classes, however, was distinct enough for anyone to recognize . . . As the Allies were so opposed to bolshevism, and every form and degree of liberalism was classed as such, they were dealing almost exclusively with the former Czarist officials . . . [who] were not slow to organize so as to make the most of this advantage and were soon reaping their revenge on Russians who had dared to act contrary to their beliefs."[6]

Shortly after his arrival Graves was informed by the local Czech command that the Czech forces west of the Urals were in grave danger and needed Allied assistance. Graves, however, was instructed by Washington that his troops were to venture no farther west than Lake Baikal and that his main task was to keep the Trans-Siberian line open for them. He was immediately placed under pressure by the French and British missions to act more forcefully on behalf of the Czechs and criticized by his nominal allies for not vigorously supporting the czarist faction. Graves could only reply that he wasn't supposed to take sides, and within a month after his arrival was noting that there was a complete lack of unity between the Americans, the Japanese, the British and French. The Japanese were intent on carving out an eastern Siberian colony for the Rising Sun. The British and French were obsessed with smashing communism.

Graves was determined to stay neutral between czarism and bolshevism, and followed to the letter the statement President Wilson was to make June 26, 1919, to the United States Senate: "The instructions to General Graves direct him not to interfere in Russian affairs."

Meanwhile the American troops were being introduced to the Siberian winter, by which time warmer clothing was arriving from San Francisco. The lucky ones were those stationed in Vladivostok, where they occupied the huge, well-built barracks constructed for the czar's garrison. Others who were guarding bridges and culverts on the Trans-Siberian lived in boxcars from which the wheels had been removed. Among the many far removed from the warm barracks in Vladivostok the suffering was intense when temperatures sank to thirty and forty below. Other allies shared that suffering when contingents arrived from Canada and China (the Chinese were allies during World War I). A few shivering Italians also arrived on the scene as a token of the facade of "unity" the Supreme War Council fabricated in Paris.

That winter of 1918–1919, following the Armistice of November 11, Graves and other Americans began making the acquaintance of various bloodthirsty personages involved in the struggle for Siberia. Undoubtedly they were the most villainous assortment ever to confront an innocent

American abroad. That they claimed to be anti-Communist was probably the best advertisement communism ever had.

The first of these adventurers to present himself hopefully at Graves's headquarters was a former Cossack captain named Grigori Mikhailovitch Semenov, the commander of an independent force equipped with armored trains. He was an Asiatic Russian, partly of Mongol descent, with tigerish eyes and what was described as a "basilisk grin."[7]

On further acquaintance Graves found Semenov, who now called himself a lieutenant general and ataman (chief) of all Cossacks in Siberia, "a murderer, robber and a most dissolute scoundrel . . . He was financed by Japan and had no convictions that would interfere with his doing as the Japanese directed. He always remained within striking distance of Japanese troops. As a matter of fact, he had to do this because he could not have existed one week in Siberia, if he had not had the protection of Japan. He was always talking about 'the restoration of the Motherland.' "

Actually Graves's characterization of Semenov was an understatement compared to what most other people said about him. With his subsidy of between $100,000 and $150,000 monthly from the Japanese, Ataman Semenov moved around the countryside on an armored train called, with good reason, "The Destroyer." His private car was furnished with Oriental rugs, velvet tapestries, silk bedsheets, and always a mistress or two. Semenov's Massacre Special would steam up to a settlement, and members of his Savage Division — Mongol cavalrymen with a sprinkling of Chinese and Russian adventurers — would round up the inhabitants. The place was quickly looted. The men were accused of aiding the Bolsheviks, lined up and shot. The more attractive women were raped. Then "The Destroyer" pulled away firing its three-inch automatic cannon and machine guns as a farewell salute to the smoking ruins of the settlement. Foreign observers at Chita, which he made his headquarters, once watched his troopers selling 348 bloodstained suits of clothes while Semenov smiled down from a window overlooking Ataman Square.

To Semenov the orgy of looting, bloodletting and rape was serving a purpose. His ambition was to rape the whole world, and pillaging Siberia was simply good practice for his followers. Under his towering red-fox shako was a brain, fevered with cocaine and vodka, dreaming mightily of a Pan-Mongol empire. Its seedling was the forty thousand Buriats (Mongol tribesmen) who entered Outer Mongolia in 1918 to checkmate Chinese plans to occupy the deserts from which Genghis Khan and the Golden Horde sprang. Ostensibly they were now colonizing it for the Japanese, but Semenov, while taking Japanese gold, had his own ideas. With Japanese help he would establish control over Mongolia, then proceed to conquer Siberia, and then move westward with a vast Asiatic army. "The whole world is rotten," as one of Semenov's officers expressed it. "Greed, hatred and cruelty are in the saddle. We intend to organize a new empire, a new civilization. It will be called the Middle Asiatic Empire, carved out of Mongolia, Manchuria and Eastern Siberia." The trouble with Semenov — as the Japanese well knew — was that his intellect was so much smaller than his appetites.

They would use him until his bloodthirst made him a liability. In one day at Adrianoka he executed sixteen hundred persons he accused of befriending the Bolshevik partisans. Late in 1918 his men killed a Swedish physician attached to the International Red Cross near Transbaikalia, and the Japanese once again had to defend him against the outraged protests of their allies. There was also a scandal over the members of the Manchurian Soviet who had been captured and taken to Chita in a sealed train; all had been tortured to death.

On an inspection trip to the American garrison at Khabarovsk, General Graves also made the repellent acquaintance of one Ivan Kalmikov, a former Cossack officer who had served on the Caucasian front with Semenov before coming to Siberia. Kalmikov had murdered the legitimate candidate for ataman of the Ussuri Cossacks and taken his place. The Ussuri Cossacks trekked to Siberia on the promise of White leaders that they would be given land if they fought the Bolsheviks for Admiral Kolchak's White army based on Irkutsk. Kalmikov quickly sold out to the Japanese, and at their instigation moved with his Cossack regiment to Khabarovsk, where their orders were to make life miserable for the Americans and help persuade them to sail back to America.[8]

Graves considered Kalmikov an even worse blackguard than Semenov, a "notorious murderer, robber and cutthroat . . . the worst scoundrel I ever saw or heard of and I seriously doubt, if one should go entirely through the Standard Dictionary, looking for words descriptive of crime, if a crime could be found that Kalmikov had not committed. He was warmed and financed by Japan in their efforts 'to help the Russian people.' I say this advisedly, because I have evidence that would satisfy any open-minded person. Kalmikov murdered with his own hands, where Semenov ordered others to kill, and therein lies the difference between Kalmikov and Semenov."[9]

Perhaps it was Kalmikov's insolent proximity which excited General Graves's greater wrath, because most foreigners considered Semenov by far the more vicious and dangerous of the two *hetmen*. Kalmikov, for instance, had the audacity to arrest an American officer and his patrol on the outskirts of Khabarovsk and charge them with "not having Russian passports." The officer was released, but another American detachment had to be sent to retrieve the enlisted men, who were beaten with Cossack knouts before Kalmikov would turn them over.

The fact that all the Allies, the Japanese in particular, officially supported Semenov and Kalmikov as anti-Bolshevik stalwarts was disgusting to General Graves. He was outraged by two incidents reflecting the anti-

Communist atmosphere in the United States after the Armistice, the density of which he did not appreciate in his remote headquarters. A Russian representing the Siberian cooperatives, stigmatized as a Bolshevik "because he was not in the Kolchak boat and pulling," according to Graves, was denied admittance to the United States by the immigration authorities. A few weeks later a captain on Semenov's staff was warmly welcomed and escorted around Washington by a War Department colonel even though "he boastingly claimed that one object was to get me relieved from command of American troops." It seemed to General Graves that his country was losing its moral balance over the question of which faction came out on top in Russia. "This man," he wrote, "represented Semenov and it is certainly fair to assume that he had the same moral and criminal character as his chief, whom he represented. Semenov's character was well known in Washington, therefore one can only assume that character was ignored, and political classification alone considered, in determining whether a Russian should be permitted to enter the United States."[10]

Personally less repulsive to Graves and other Americans than Semenov and Kalmikov was another megalomaniac, General Dmitri L. Horvath (sometimes spelled Horvat), whose official title was general manager of the Chinese Eastern Railway but who in moments of excessive optimism about his prospects called himself "Ruler of All the Russias." His actual domain was limited to the railroad zone, the capital of which was the Manchurian city of Harbin. Horvath, a tall heavy man with a white beard that extended to his waist, had ruled the Chinese Eastern and its right of way for twenty years after the Russo-Asiatic Bank was given the right to build and operate the C.E.R. between Chita and the South Ussuri Railway. The Chinese Eastern was a factor in power politics because of its strategic importance; the key to dominating Manchuria, Inner Mongolia and the Russian Far East.

Horvath's sense of importance was swollen by the fact that he commanded the loyalty of twenty thousand railway employees, including a heavily armed corps of guards required to patrol every mile of its track. He made a lunge for personal power when the successive central governments in Petrograd and Moscow lost control of events in the Russian East, but eventually the foreign and domestic anti-Bolshevik elements settled on Admiral Kolchak as the leader of the White Forces east of the Urals. "The interests, pressures, and considerations bearing on the possible creation of a government by Horvat were so varied and conflicting," George F. Kennan (*The Decision to Intervene*) has written, "and the real prerequisites for any such undertaking present only in so small degree, that nothing at all emerged . . . The Japanese, who had initially promised Horvat support in most categoric terms, became increasingly cool to his fortunes as the weeks wore on . . . with the evident intention of promoting disunity in the Russian camp — a process that required little outside stimulus in any case." But Horvath, with his firm hand on the Chinese Eastern, was still a considerable factor in the turmoil, a comparatively stable element, though he believed Americans to be soft on communism.[11]

Still another but much more volatile, if not completely demented, figure the Americans had on occasion to reckon with was an incredible character named Alexander Vasilievich Ungern-Sternberg. A baron of Baltic German descent whose ancestry was traced to the Teutonic Knights, Ungern-Sternberg would have taxed the literary skill of a Dostoievsky to make credible in print. He was wounded and distinguished himself during the Japanese attack on Port Arthur, rendering heroic service to the crown prince's Nerchinsk Regiment of the Ussuri Cossack Division. He also became notorious as a duelist and drunken brawler. His behavior became more erratic after his skull was cracked in a brawl, and his virility was marked even in a Cossack regiment by his habit of sleeping in a tent during subzero weather and riding naked on horseback into the river on frosty mornings.

The Baron Ungern-Sternberg, as a Harbin-born fellow officer, Dmitri Alioshin, described him, was "tall and slim, with the lean white face of an ascetic. His watery blue eyes were steady and piercing. He possessed a dangerous power of reading people's thoughts." Alioshin attended an inspection at which the baron winnowed out what he considered the unfit among his followers, including all Jews (his anti-Semitism would have qualified him for high command in the Nazi SS, which fortunately he did not survive to know about), the disabled and the sickly. "Hundreds of innocent people," Alioshin wrote, "were 'liquidated' by the time the inspection was closed."

The baron was said to be a favorite of the German-born czarina's, but his dangerously antisocial personality made it necessary to post him to the remotest garrisons in the empire. On at least one occasion he would have been cashiered without the czarina's intercession.

During the war against Germany and her allies, he served with the Cossacks on the Galician front, won the Cross of St. George for valor and was promoted to major general. After the revolution he headed east and took over Dauria Province, on the Mongolian border, as his personal satrapy. Like Semenov, he conceived the idea of reviving the Mongol empire and gathered a large following which ultimately (in 1921) swept on to Urga (now Ulan-Bator) and wrested the capital of Outer Mongolia from the ten thousand Chinese troops occupying it.

By the time he seized control of Dauria he was a homicidal maniac who, as Alioshin observed, "firmly believed that in killing feeble people he only did them good, as they would be stronger beings in their next life . . . In his unbalanced mind he became convinced that he was the world's salvation." He financed himself and his troops by removing persons, whom his agents in Harbin had singled out as traveling with money or valuables, from the train at Dauria station, robbing them and shooting them. Jews, of course, were shot for being Jewish. Once in an eastern Siberian town he saw a beautiful Jewish lady whose profile he admired in spite of himself. As a measure of his aesthetic appreciation, he offered one thousand rubles to anyone who would bring him her head — and gladly paid the reward.[12]

3. *The Squeamish Americans*

The principal *stated* reason for American intervention in Siberia, the "rescue" of the separated Czech forces, was eliminated shortly after the arrival of the Siberian Expeditionary Force when the advance-guards of both Czech bodies linked up at Chita. Originally the Supreme War Council had planned that the Czechs be evacuated to France, but that idea was dropped when the Czechs involved themselves in the Russian civil war by enthusiastically joining their forces with the Whites — the Soviet government, not Germany, had become the more hated enemy. The American troops, however, stayed on after the Armistice as a stabilizing force, long after most of the A.E.F. went home.

General Graves in his memoirs bluntly stated that about all the American forces could do in Siberia was to stand by and watch the slaughter. "Semenov and Kalmikov soldiers, under the protection of Japanese troops, were roaming the country like wild animals, killing and robbing the people, and these murders could have been stopped any day Japan wished. If questions were asked about these brutal murders, the reply was that the people murdered were Bolsheviks and this explanation, apparently, satisfied the world . . .

"There were horrible murders committed, but they were not committed by the Bolsheviks as the world believes. I am well on the side of safety when I say that the anti-Bolsheviks killed one hundred people in Eastern Siberia, to every one killed by the Bolsheviks. It was my judgment . . . Japan always hoped . . . the United States would become disgusted with conditions, withdraw her troops and request Japan to go in and clean up the situation."[13]

The Whites were making it increasingly apparent that the American forces were unwelcome because of their refusal to take sides against the Bolsheviki. Their newspapers outspokenly criticized American policy for not taking part in the struggle against Bolshevism. A report to Admiral Kolchak in Irkutsk from his agent in Vladivostok charged that "The United States soldiers are infected with Bolshevism . . . most of them are Jews from the East Side of New York City who constantly agitate for mutinies." Actually most of the American soldiers serving in Siberia came from the two Philippine regiments and were professional soldiers, and

Major William S. Graves and the Cossack Ataman Semenov

those who reinforced the two regiments from the Eighth Division came mostly from the Western states.

The charge was made, Graves believed, because "Kolchak supporters had given up any hope of receiving active military support from American troops, and if the world and especially Czarist officials surrounding Kolchak could be made to believe that the United States had sent a command composed of Russian Jews to Siberia, the reason we did not support Kolchak would appear evident."[14] This particular charge was reiterated in the White Russian press, and Graves put a stop to it only by threatening to arrest one editor and suspend publication of his journal. The only way the Americans could have made themselves popular with the Whites was to join Semenov and Kalmikov in their massacres of the Siberian population, most of which was neither Red nor White and only hoped to survive the civil war.

Why, then, wasn't the expeditionary force withdrawn from Siberia instead of being allowed to stay on until 1920? Secretary of War Newton D. Baker urged withdrawal late in November 1918 in a letter to President Wilson. "Two reasons are assigned for our remaining in Siberia. One is that having entered we cannot withdraw and leave the Japanese. If there be any answer to this it lies in the fact that the longer we stay, the more Japanese there are and the more difficult it may be to induce Japan to withdraw her forces if we set the example. The second reason given is that we must have a military force to act as guardians and police for any civil relief effort we are able to direct toward Siberia. I frankly do not believe this, nor do I believe we have a right to use military force to compel the reception of our relief agencies."[15]

President Wilson, however, was soon preoccupied with the Paris Peace Conference and felt he could not take unilateral action regarding the Siberian Expeditionary Force. In the spring of 1919 he was forced to throw himself into the unsuccessful campaign to win acceptance of the League of Nations — and in the middle of that unsuccessful effort he suffered a stroke. For many months thereafter the American government was almost as paralyzed as its leader. Meanwhile anti-Bolshevik forces in the State Department and throughout the country were gathering strength. They insisted that the S.E.F. stay on the scene and if Admiral Kolchak's campaigns turned out to be successful they could be supported by General Graves and his troops. Thus Washington temporized, and its distant, discomfited and ill-conceived expedition stayed where it was.

4. *Dealing with the Atamans*

By early December of 1918, General Graves and his command were seriously at odds with the brutish Ataman Kalmikov and his Cossack division, most of which was posted around Khabarovsk and its coal mines. The Cossacks were "advised" by a major of the Japanese army, who apparently did nothing to halt their excesses. Hardly a day passed, Graves reported to Washington, without some atrocity committed by Kalmikov or his men. He protested to the Japanese and was solemnly promised that Kalmikov would reform.

"It was evident that Kalmikov did not kill, after that, where Americans could verify the murder," Graves wrote later, "but it was also evident that he was taking his victims where Americans could not see their bodies. Two women came to my office from a town two or three hundred miles from Vladivostok, and told me Kalmikov had come through their village and taken their husbands. They begged me to help find out if these men were alive and if alive, where Kalmikov had taken them."[16]

Graves ordered an investigation, only to be informed by Kalmikov that the two prisoners had "escaped." Graves later learned that "when his train was passing a lake, Kalmikov had it stop while he had stones tied to the necks of these men, and they were thrown into the lake."

Under the pretense of combatting Bolshevism, Kalmikov arrested people suspected of having money or possessions worth stealing, tortured them to make them reveal their hiding-places, and then executed them. The whole population was "terrorized," Graves said, after two or three hundred persons had been tortured and killed.

Kalmikov's brutality extended even to his own Cossack troopers, whom he had flogged in wholesale lots whenever they failed to exhibit enthusiasm for his firing squads and village liquidations. On December 28, a number of his men appeared at the headquarters of the 27th Infantry in Khabarovsk and asked to be allowed to enlist in the United States Army. A month later, on January 27, 1919, seven hundred of his troops deserted. About half went into hiding, and 398 marched in a body to the headquarters of the 27th Infantry — along with their horses, four field guns, three machine guns and all other weapons — and sought the protection of the Americans. They surrendered their arms and were placed under guard.

An immediate protest was presented to General Graves by the Japanese high command, which demanded that the mutinous Cossacks be returned to the care of their "little father," Ataman Kalmikov. Graves sternly replied in a letter to the Japanese chief of staff:

"Such soldiers will not be delivered, by the American forces, to Kalmikov, Horvath or the representatives of either at Khabarovsk, or elsewhere, but will be released at Khabarovsk and permitted to go where they please . . . Upon such release, they will be given reasonable protection against persecution by Kalmikov, or his forces, on groundless charges, or charges of desertion, rebellion or mutiny . . . While yet under control of American forces, any of such soldiers will be delivered to local civil authorities upon service of Judicial warrants . . . provided that there shall accompany such warrants a synopsis of the evidence against the accused person indicating prima facie evidence of guilt. . . . All this is but reasonable protection to prevent ruthless sacrifice of human lives, and for the proper protection of our own soldiers and property."[17]

The Japanese, through a general-staff colonel, then demanded that Kalmikov's deserters be turned over to them, but General Graves bluntly told him he "would not discuss this matter again with any representative of Japan." The deserters were released within the next few weeks to go where they pleased.

But the cost of maintaining the American presence continued high. Diseases were epidemic because of the large number of refugees drifting around Siberia and the fact that drinking water had to be obtained from surface wells. The chief surgeon of the S.E.F. reported that it was impossible to describe the "sanitary situation" in Siberia because "practically none exists," and that hundreds in the American command were stricken with "plague, typhus, relapsing fever, typhoid fever, scarlet fever and malignant sore throat."

A new and muddling factor in the anti-Bolshevist "front" appeared in the person of General Ivanoff-Rinoff, a czarist officer appointed to command all Russian troops in the eastern provinces of Amur, Primorskaya, Sakhalin and Kamchatka. Ivanoff-Rinoff immediately placed the provinces under martial law, a measure which Graves saw as an attempt to restore the old autocratic rule. The American commander was discomfited by reflections that his forces were being kept in Siberia as an instrument of the czarist regime's repressions. He could see no reason why American troops should stay and serve such a purpose, thereby "delaying the settlement of Russian questions by the Russian people . . . We could not escape responsibility for some acts against the Russian people that could not have been committed if foreign troops had not been in Siberia."

As he spelled it out in a dispatch to the War Department, "The effect of keeping troops in Siberia is to permit the crowd of Reactionaries, headed by General Horvath, supported by former Russian officers, to try to firmly establish themselves while the Allied troops are in Siberia."

Even under General Ivanoff-Rinoff, the brutality of Russians against their own people continued, in the style of Kalmikov and Semenov, and if anything increased. In March 1919 Graves's intelligence officers learned of the descent of Ivanoff-Rinoff troops on the village of Gordyevka. They came looking for recruits, and when the young men of the Siberian village fled into the forests at their approach, ten older villagers were tortured and killed.

An American officer was sent to investigate. He found that the Ivanoff-Rinoff troops had left Gordyevka, and the villagers had armed themselves with old army rifles to defend themselves in the schoolhouse if the Ivanoff-Rinoff troops returned. The officer's report to General Graves continued:

"The first woman interviewed said her husband was on his way to the schoolhouse with his rifle to turn it in to the Russian troops, as ordered. He was seized on the street, beaten over the head and body with his rifle, and then taken to a house a short distance from the school where he was stretched on his back to a pin on the rafter, his hands tied, and terribly beaten about the body and head until the blood was splashed even on the walls of the room, and the marks on the body showed me that he had been hung by his feet also."

"Later he was among those shot to death," the American officer learned. "There were ten men in line and all were killed but one, he being left for dead. . . .The next woman I interviewed was the woman in whose house all the men were beaten, and in the back of whose barnyard the men were shot . . . A number of Ivanoff-Rinoff's men came to her house and made her take her husband to another house, and about 11:30 they took her husband back to her house and beat him . . . also broke one of his arms and cut out his fingernails, and knocked out all of his front teeth. Her husband was an invalid and a cripple. . . .

"I found that the floor of the room these men were beaten in was covered with blood, and the walls in the room were all splashed with blood. The wire and loops of rope that were used around the men's necks were still hanging from the ceiling and covered with blood. I also found that some of these men had been scalded with boiling water and burned with hot irons, heated in a little stove I found in the room.

"I visited the spot where these men were shot. These men were lined up and shot, and each body had at least three holes in it, and some as many as six or more. They were apparently shot in the feet first and then higher in the body."

On submitting his report to General Graves, the investigating officer added in a trembling voice: "General, for God's sake, never send me on another expedition like this. I came within an ace of pulling off my uniform, joining those poor people, and helping them as best I could."

Graves believed that the objective of the terrorism was to force the Siberian peasants to defend themselves and "this would justify calling for more Allied troops to put down the Bolsheviks."

In mid-February partisan bands struck back at the Japanese forces near Blagoveshchensk. Several Japanese patrols were wiped out or decimated. Then on February 16, 1919, two companies of Japanese infantry, plus an artillery company, a total of perhaps four hundred men, were attacked by the partisans. Only three Japanese escaped with their lives. The Japanese command in Khabarovsk appealed to the 27th United States Infantry to rush a company to the rescue, but the American commander referred the request to Graves, in Vladivostok, who countered by demanding proof that the attacking partisans were Bolsheviks and not simply enraged peasants fighting in self-defense. By the time the Japanese request was bucked up and down the line it was too late to rescue their troops.

American newspapers, particularly those taking a strong anti-Communist line, reprinted charges in the Japanese press that Graves stood by while a Japanese contingent was wiped out. The general was easily able to defend his position on that Japanese military disaster, pointing out that, as the Japanese knew, there were no American troops within four hundred miles of the action, and inquiring, "Why didn't the Japanese send their own troops to the assistance of their men? They had an entire division in Khabarovsk and vicinity, while the Americans had but two battalions." The Japanese request for reinforcements, as General Graves considered it, was a trap. "Americans would no longer have been pacific observers of the atrocities being committed in Siberia, but we would have been participants in them."

Graves insisted on being guided by the original presidential directive, which emphasized that the United States forces would not interfere in Russian internal affairs. It had never been rescinded or amended, so he stood on firm ground.

Furthermore, he was perplexed by the various definitions of a Bolshevik which his allies tried to impose on him. "According to Japanese representatives and her paid puppets in Siberia, all Russians were Bolsheviks if they were not willing to take up arms and fight for the Semenovs, the Kalmikovs, the Rozanovs and the Ivanoff-Rinoffs . . . According to British and French representatives, all Russians who were not willing to take up arms and fight for Kolchak were Bolsheviks." Yet "no nation in the world" was willing to "recognize any of the above named men, or any other man," as the rightful head of the Russian government.

The British, in particular, were vigorous in pressing Graves to adopt a more sympathetic attitude toward Admiral Kolchak and his efforts to extend White domination from the Urals to the Pacific. General Alfred Knox, head of the British mission and a man of fervent old-regime sympathies traceable to his years as military attaché in Petrograd, wrote the American commander that he hoped American and British policies wouldn't continue to diverge because "The policy of our government is to support Kolchak, and I believe in that policy, for if he goes there will be chaos. I don't for a moment pretend that Kolchak is the Angel Gabriel, but he has energy, patriotism and honesty and my eight years in Russia has taught me that when you get these qualities combined in one man he is a man to keep. There is widespread propaganda to the effect that your Countrymen are pro-Bolshevik. I think in the interest of Allied solidarity, and of the safety of Allied detachments, you should try to contradict this."

Replying to that letter, Graves wrote Knox that his orders forbade taking sides and as for anti-American propaganda "I am sure the propaganda is more from the anti-Bolshevik crowd than from the Bolshevik crowd."

That was cool enough, but Graves's temper rose higher some months later when he learned that the British were exerting pressure on Washington to replace him. Graves then understood more completely a rather cryptic note he had received early in 1919 from the army chief of staff, General Peyton C. March. "Keep a stiff upper lip," General March advised. "I am going to stand by you until hell freezes over."

During the summer of 1919, the United States ambassador to Tokyo, Roland S. Morris, arrived in Vladivostok to investigate the possibilities of a successful resistance by the White forces to the larger and better organized Bolshevik units then beginning to move eastward from the Urals. (The State Department was firmly anti-Communist in its stance, while the War Department insisted that its forces in Siberia must remain neutral.) Graves accompanied the ambassador to Omsk, then the headquarters of the Kolchak regime, to determine just how firmly the Whites were standing up to the increased Red pressure. They found that Kolchak's army had already, as Graves said, become "a retreating mob." The Whites were trying to reform along the line of the Ishim River and begin a counteroffensive which they boasted would "drive the Bolsheviks into the Volga."

Leaving Ambassador Morris in Omsk, Graves journeyed by automobile to Petropavlosk, the supposed concentration point for the White counteroffensive. Quickly enough, he learned it was all bluff, a military version of Potemkin's villages. Graves and his companions came across only three soldiers on the long road to Petropavlosk. In that town he found a Russian general who threw his arms around the American commander and offered all kinds of hospitality, but was forced to admit he had no troops for the counteroffensive supposed to begin in two weeks. And that was the army which the Allies were urging the United States to back to the hilt; the army that was going to save the world from communism.

His field trip verified exactly what Graves had suspected when he cabled the War Department on August 7, a week before he journeyed to Petropavlosk: "The Kolchak forces are still retreating and it looks as if the demoralization is such that the hope of reforming the Army and renewing the offensive must be based on the weakness of the Bolsheviks, and lack of their desire to come to Omsk, which I cannot assume to be the case. Well authenticated reports justify the statement that officers are leaving the troops and fleeing to the rear, staff officers preceding line officers in this flight, soldiers are throwing away their arms and ammunition . . . so as to enable them to move more rapidly to the rear. I have been unable to discover any enthusiasm for the Kolchak Government." After his return from the Ishim River "front," Graves added that thirty trains were hauling White troops eastward. He inspected some of the trains at Omsk and found sick or wounded soldiers lying in boxcars without medical attention while a few minutes' walk from the marshaling yards a band was playing in a park and a thousand people were dancing. Graves had to confess his bewilderment at the Russian temperament, "which probably could not be duplicated in any other country in the world."[18]

On the way back to Vladivostok, Graves halted their special train at a village which had often served as one of Ataman Semenov's "killing stations," where Semenov blocked the tracks and "inspected" trains passing through. Semenov was stepping up his terrorist activities even as the White cause was crumbling. Two Americans attached to the Russian Railway Service Corps boarded the special train and gave the general an account of how Semenov and his followers had stopped a train with 350 persons aboard. The Americans tried to follow when Semenov's officers shunted the Russian train down the tracks a few miles, but were ordered to turn back. "In one hour and fifty minutes the empty train returned to the station. The following day these two men went out to the killing place, and saw evidences of the wholesale execution and it was evident from the shells on the ground that the prisoners had been killed with machine guns, as the empty shells were in piles just as if they had been ejected from machine guns. The bodies had been placed in two ditches which had been freshly dug. In one ditch the bodies were entirely covered, in the other ditch many arms or legs were left uncovered."

It was evident to Graves and most Americans by then that no matter how much military and diplomatic assistance was given Kolchak, how much effort was put into keeping the Trans-Siberian and Chinese Eastern railroads functioning and under the control of anti-Bolshevik elements, or how many troops the Japanese imported to protect the operations of anti-Bolshevik forces, the White cause was doomed. After all the horrors committed by Kolchak's forces and their Cossack and Mongol allies, "no power on earth," Graves believed, "could have driven the peasant to support his cause."

The fact that the United States State Department still insisted that some way must be found to support Kolchak and prevent the anti-Bolshevik front from collapsing, in which it sedulously followed the Franco-British-Japanese line, could only be attributed to its refusal to believe reports from the commander of the S.E.F.

5. *The Law of the Jungle*

Apologists for the hostility Soviet Russia has consistently shown the West, particularly America, claim that the Soviets for half a century have been suffering from the traumatic effects of the Allied intervention. One facet of this argument, which echoes the Russian propagandist-historians, is that the Siberian Expeditionary Force was an important element in the attempt to make the counterrevolution successful. In this the apologists and propagandists are surely mistaken. Graves and his command tried to stay aloof from the revolutionary struggle, but whenever they did become involved, and shots were fired and casualties suffered, it was invariably in confronting the anti-Bolshevik freebooters financed by Japan. They strived with remarkable patience to maintain their absolute neutrality, but the brutality of the anti-Bolsheviks against the Siberian population, who were as innocent of political bias as the Americans, could not help but warp their attitudes. And those attitudes were bent *against* the anti-Communist front fabricated by Japan, Britain and France in Siberia. If the Soviet government had any sense of historical justice, it would erect a towering monument to the Siberian Expeditionary Force in the main square of Vladivostok.

The only discoverable instance in which Americans fired upon Bolshevik partisan bands was in the Suchan coal-mining district near Vladivostok. Atrocities committed by Kalmikov's Cossacks in the neighborhood caused the forming of partisan bands, which fell under Bolshevik influence. The Americans knew that if fighting broke out around the mines between the partisans and the Cossacks, the coal needed for fuel and railroad operation would be cut off. They refused to allow Cossacks to enter the district because a strike would result, but agreed in return that all Bolshevik activities around the mines would be prohibited. Securing that area resulted in a few minor skirmishes. Otherwise the scattered units of the American force simply didn't come in contact with Bolsheviks.

But there were repeated, often violent confrontations with the brutalized soldiery of Kolchak, Semenov, Kalmikov and other more or less White leaders. One such encounter took place in the railroad station in Vladivostok. An American soldier was returning from furlough, waiting for a train to take him back to his unit, when an officer in Kolchak's army went up to him and called him a "damned Bolshevik."

The American swung at the Russian, but the blow never landed. The Russian officer had drawn his pistol, with which he shot the American through the head.

A group of Japanese officers who smilingly witnessed the murder went over to the Russian and shook hands with him over the corpse and congratulated him on his patriotism.

The Russian officer then gave himself up to a sympathetic Russian civil court, was tried immediately, acquitted and released within an hour.

This occurred at a time when General Graves was being forced to turn over to Kolchak a shipment of arms and ammunition which had just arrived on United States transports, under an agreement by which the Wilson Administration promised on June 12, 1919, to "assist the Government of Admiral Kolchak and his associates with munitions, supplies, and food."

Under the changed circumstances since the signing of that agreement — especially the anti-American activities of Kolchak and his allies and the impending collapse of the White government — General Graves was extremely reluctant to hand over the arms shipment. The chief of ordnance for Kolchak's army came to Graves's headquarters in Vladivostok with one million dollars in gold to pay for the shipment. Despite the outraged protests of the British mission headed by General Knox, Graves refused the gold and halted the transaction, cabling the War Department his explanation that "on account of anti-American activities of Kolchak agents here I have refused to take the gold, and have refused to give up the rifles." He added that he would withhold any military supplies "as long as Kolchak agents in the East are threatening to use military force against the United States."

There was a sound military reason for General Graves's refusal to help rearm the White army. He feared that most of the rifles would fall into the hands of Semenov and other irregular allies of the Whites and Japanese. They would give the Cossacks, who in Graves's mind had become the enemy, a marked superiority over the outnumbered and widely dispersed American brigade. The "enemy" was equipped with field artillery, which the Americans weren't, and armored cars, which the Americans also lacked. The Semenov forces coursed over the Siberian landscape in steel-plated armored trains called *bronevicks* while the "armor" on American-operated trains consisted of sandbagging.

It weighed heavily on Graves and his staff that they had a total strength of about seven thousand men broken up in many detachments along a two-thousand-mile stretch of the Trans-Siberian. If the anti-American feeling of the Whites should become more militant, the "enemy" could destroy the innumerable small bridges which carried the Trans-Siberian over the soggy tundra and prevent Graves from concentrating his forces. Thus, as he admitted in his memoirs, he "deliberately and wilfully would have refused to turn the rifles over to any Russian in Vladivostok, no matter from whom the order came." Strong words from a man indoctrinated all his life with the necessity for obeying orders.

He cabled the War Department: "The Cossacks, under the leadership of Kalmikov, are threatening to commence action against Americans. This action is supported by Semenov and I believe instigated by Japan. These Cossacks have armored cars which our present arms will not pierce. Request one battalion three-inch or mountain artillery be sent to report to me . . . I feel absolutely sure nothing will happen to Americans if sent."

He finally negotiated a settlement with Kolchak's representatives in Vladivostok. The million dollars worth of rifles would be sent to the White headquarters in Irkutsk, west of the Cossacks' zone of operations.

The first munitions shipment reached Irkutsk without interference from Semenov, through whose domain the train passed. The second train, however, was stopped in Chita, Semenov's headquarters, when it reached there October 24. Semenov boarded the American train and arrogantly demanded that fifteen thousand of the rifles be turned over him before the train would be allowed to proceed — just what Graves feared might happen.

One Lieutenant Ryan was the train commander, with a mere fifty soldiers behind the sandbagged barricades of his flatcars, and he was in a very tight spot with the nearest American detachment hundreds of miles away.

Semenov gave him thirty hours in which to surrender the fifteen thousand rifles, then moved up two armored trains to block the Americans from advancing or retreating. He also surrounded the American train with a battalion of wild-looking Cossacks.

Lieutenant Ryan wired S.E.F. headquarters for instructions, to which General Graves immediately replied that he was not to give up a rifle, to open fire if necessary. According to Graves's intelligence officers, General Oi, then Japanese commander in Siberia, was in Chita with Semenov. The American command was certain the Japanese would not allow Semenov to go to the extremity of attacking the American train.

So Ryan held firm in Chita; thirty hours passed without an attack, and finally, ten hours after the ultimatum expired, he was allowed to continue the journey to Irkutsk.[19]

Later Graves learned, through a Russian informant, that the White government in Irkutsk had turned over four carloads of the American arms to Semenov.

The "law of the jungle," Graves said, now ruled the Siberian tundra. He heard reports that the Cossacks were conducting a pogrom in the Ekaterinburg district and that three thousand Jews had been massacred. An American liaison officer in Omsk investigated the report at Kolchak's headquarters, where officers admitted "something had occurred at Ekaterinburg that would give the Jews something to think about." Anarchy was replacing the ramshackle, unpopular and corrupt government of Admiral Kolchak, and the sounds of a breakup, like the cracking of the ice on a Siberian river, even reached the Foreign Office in London. One day late in 1919 the British high commissioner in Siberia came to Graves's headquarters and showed him a cable of instructions from the Foreign Office:

YOU GET OUT OF SIBERIA ON THE FIRST SHIP LEAVING VLADIVOSTOK DO NOT WAIT FOR A BRITISH SHIP.

A virulent disease known in a later Asian war as bugout fever was almost as endemic in those last weeks of 1919 as the spotted typhus felling the soldiers of the retreating White army. In and around Irkutsk, the Czechs and the Cossacks were contending for the power — and the treasury — of the collapsing Kolchak regime. The Bolsheviks were advancing steadily from the west. There was little to stop them except Semenov's and Kalmikov's mercenaries.

Within four months, the short-lived autonomous Far Eastern Republic would be established with Lenin's approval. The "independent" republic was authorized by the Supreme Soviet in Moscow because it was realized that the Japanese, still clinging to the Maritime Provinces, would attempt to crush any Communist government in the Far East. Its strongman was Alexander M. Krasnoshchekov, a Russian Jew, who had fled Russia in 1905 after his brother was hanged. Krasnoshchekov had spent a dozen years in Chicago as a labor lawyer and leader of the International Workers of the World. Shortly after returning to Russian soil, he remarked to an American officer who was amazed that a Soviet official should speak such excellent English: "It is going some to change from a bum lawyer in Chicago to a Commissar of the Soviets in Eastern Siberia in two months."[20]

By the time the ex-"bum lawyer" took over in Siberia and issued a "Siberian Declaration of Independence," it was no longer any direct concern of the Siberian Expeditionary Force. The S.E.F. had sailed away, leaving things a little worse than they had found them.

6. *A Farewell Blaze of Gunfire*

On December 27, 1919, Graves cabled the War Department suggesting the advisability of immediate withdrawal of the Siberian Expeditionary Force. With Washington in a state of semiparalysis and a stricken President serving out the last weeks of his term, the War Department took almost three weeks to reply in the affirmative.

One week before it was announced that the S.E.F. would be evacuated, on January 9, 1920, an incident occurred at Verkhne-Udinsk in the sector of the Trans-Siberian under American control that underlined the urgency of withdrawal unless the expeditionary force was to be caught in the maelstrom of White disintegration and Red takeover.

Verkhne-Udinsk was the headquarters of the American sector, with Colonel C. H. Morrow and a battalion of the 27th Infantry stationed there. Because of its comparative strength, it was an odd choice of places for Semenov to demonstrate his furious displeasure. On the afternoon of January 9, his notorious death-dealing "Destroyer" armored train steamed into the Verkhne-Udinsk station with its steel turrets bristling with machine guns and its rapid-fire cannon fully manned.

The "Destroyer" was under the command of Semenov's chief lieutenant, General Bogomolets, who climbed off the train with his bodyguard and seized the stationmaster. The latter had irked Semenov by protesting to the Americans a week earlier about the theft of railroad property. Now General Bogomolets was charging him with being a Bolshevik. Before he could haul off the stationmaster, Colonel Morrow arrived on the scene and ordered a company of infantry to set up heavy machine guns sited on the armored train. He informed Bogomolets that the stationmaster was under American protection and demanded the reason for the attempted arrest.

"I am not supposed to give any account to you of our actions," General Bogomolets replied. "I will not converse any more on the subject."

"Let me tell you this," Colonel Morrow snapped. "I do not want to cause any trouble for you. However, I have twenty-five hundred men here [a slight exaggeration] to carry out my orders. I must know why this man was arrested. He is under my protection."

"I was told he was a Bolshevik," the Cossack haughtily answered, "and I want to kill him tonight. But if you insist I will release him. It is immaterial to me. If the stationmaster is guilty we will get him sooner or later."

General Bogomolets climbed back on the "Destroyer" in a rage of frustration, and the armored train steamed off westward. Sixty miles down the track, at Posolskaya, was another American detachment on guard duty. The United States outpost consisted of one officer, Lieutenant Paul Kendall, and thirty-eight enlisted men. They were equipped with rifles and grenades, against the three-inch guns and machine guns on the "Destroyer."

The Americans were asleep in a railway car used as a barracks when the armored train pulled in about 1 A.M. and started firing with everything it had into the Americans' sleeping quarters. Besides being taken by surprise, the Americans were outnumbered more than two to one by the seven officers and eighty-three men under Bogomolets as well as being seriously outgunned.

In this first and last serious clash between Americans and Russians, the United States troops proved the value of their training and discipline. An American sergeant clambered up on the locomotive of the "Destroyer" and dropped a grenade into its boiler just before he was fatally wounded. The fire from the American rifles was so accurate and intense that Bogomolets decided to pull out before he took a worse beating.

The armored train wheezed away with just enough steam left in its ruptured boiler to carry it about five miles down the track. The pursuing Americans surrounded it and took Bogomolets and his remaining troops into custody. Two Americans had been killed and several wounded. Five of the Cossacks were killed, several wounded and twelve disappeared in the heat of the battle at the station. The rest were taken prisoner, and their train was towed to Colonel Morrow's headquarters at Verkhne-Udinsk.[21]

General Graves was elated by the dispatches telling of the one victory in battle gained by his troops on the very eve of their departure. "I was sorry that Lieutenant Kendall, who first got hold of Bogomolets," he later wrote, "did not hang him to a telegraph pole, but he acted within the law and really exhibited better soldierly qualities in doing as he did."

He ignored Semenov's demands for the return of his armored train and the prisoners until January 23, when Colonel Morrow and his command evacuated the American sector of the Trans-Siberian. The prisoners, questioned separately, confessed that between January 1 and 10 (as Morrow reported to Graves) they "robbed and brutally murdered over forty men and three women were raped and brutally killed." The next General Graves heard of Semenov was back in the States, two years later, when he was officially received in Washington as a brave crusader against communism.

With the bitter aftertaste of men whose military services have been employed for obscure political purposes — yet with great honor for having carried out their duties with forbearance, for having kept their hands clean — the Siberian Expeditionary Force sailed from Vladivostok, the first contingent leaving February 15. The last echelon embarked April 1, with General Graves among them.

Graves, the man who bore all the responsibility with a soldierly sense of justice and fidelity to his mission, could not help but feel that he and his troops were somehow the victims of a political betrayal back home. As he summed up his attitude in his memoirs, he was never "able to come to any satisfying conclusion as to why the United States ever engaged in such intervention." The reasons given in the presidential directive, he felt, "were not frank and complete." As of a month before he received his orders, the "rescue" of the Czechs, the principal objective given him, was no longer necessary; they had rescued themselves and joined in the Russian civil war. As for the other assigned reason: "The Americans were also sent to guard the military stores, that might be needed in future by the Russian forces, but the lack of cooperation by the various representatives in Siberia made it impossible to accomplish much in this respect."

The State Department complained that Graves had not supported Admiral Kolchak as self-styled "Supreme Ruler," but: "It seems to me very evident that it was never contemplated by the War Department that the Military should pick out a faction of Russians and extend help to that faction." He believed that such help as was given Kolchak and the other proclaimed anti-Bolsheviks was deeply and bitterly resented by ninety percent of the Siberian population, because "by this interference the United States helped to bolster up, by its military forces, a monarchistically inclined and unpopular Government."

One result of the intervention was that it succeeded in "placing the mass of Russians even more solidly behind the Soviets." Nor was there any justification for intervention under international law. "There was no question as to the protection of life or property of American citizens involved

. . . nor can the United States plead the act of intervention was a war measure, as it definitely refused to look upon it as such."* [22]

An even bitterer pill for Graves to swallow was that on his return to the United States he was accused of having favored the Bolshevik cause. The charge had been made repeatedly by that inveterate troublemaker on the Washington scene, Colonel George Harvey, in his then-influential *Harvey's Weekly*. Such charges found a receptive audience in the days of the Red Scare when hundreds of suspected radicals were deported or inprisoned.

General Graves and his comrades learned that they were under suspicion by the government they had served with great distinction when a group of about sixty men who had been in Siberia held a banquet at the Commodore Hotel in New York one evening in November 1921. Admiral Austin M. Knight, commander of the Asiatic Fleet, which had given naval support to the S.E.F., also attended. The arrangements committee noted that a man unknown to any others at the banquet had taken a seat at the table. A member of the committee asked the stranger to identify himself. "The man showed him a Department of Justice badge and said he had been ordered from Washington to be present at this meeting, that he was going to remain, and he advised the representative of the committee not to cause any trouble."

Graves was convinced that the government agent was sent to cover the dinner because of "fear of subversive activity against the United States," from which it could only be inferred that certain officials believed those who had served in Siberia might have become infected by the Bolshevist virus. The men attending the banquet felt they had served their country well and were "mortified and hurt" that they should be spied on.[23]

All that was in the future the day Graves and his staff embarked with the final echelon of the Siberian Expeditionary Force. Two days before the embarkation of April 1, 1920, he and his intelligence officer, Colonel Robert Eichelberger, who more than a score of years later commanded one of the two armies under General Douglas MacArthur in their campaigns through the Southwest Pacific, toured the outskirts of Vladivostok in an automobile.

Along the heights of the First River they saw Japanese troops filling sandbags and digging trenches. The Japanese commander, General Oi, had

---

* Confirmation of Graves's views came from an odd source, a book titled *Japan's Pacific Policy*, by the Japanese journalist K. K. Kawakami. "From the beginning the American idea of the Siberian undertaking was different from that of the Japanese. The Americans believed they had nothing to do with the internal political conditions of Russia . . . Japanese soldiers were made to believe they were sent to Siberia to combat Bolshevism. On the whole the American attitude was wise and right . . . America should have stood firm upon her original stand, refusing to subscribe to any idea of intervention."

intimated that his forces would soon be pulling out, but it was evident that they intended to dig in and stay as long as it was possible to hope to profit from the revolutionary turmoil in eastern Siberia. From their experience of a temporary alliance with the Japanese from 1918 to 1920, the Americans could only expect more trouble from that source if they intended to maintain a superior position in the Far East.

A Japanese military band came down to the docks to serenade the last Americans to leave Siberia aboard the transport *Great Northern*. As the ship pulled away from the dock, the Americans heard one last tune from the Japanese band and wondered whether it was trying to tell them something.

The farewell tune they played was "Hard Times Come Again No More."

IV. The Blunted Sword

14

Shanghai Nights

There was nothing healthy or good about Shanghai life.
— PEARL BUCK, *My Several Worlds*

During the Twenties and Thirties the real university of many ordinary Americans, particularly the majority unable to attend college, was the motion picture theater. Unwittingly they were receiving an education of sorts while under the impression they were being entertained. It was not altogether a pitiable way of absorbing knowledge. The movie theater did not produce scholars but at least it provoked curiosity, and most people whose formative years fell in the two decades between the World Wars will admit they retained more of the flickering images from the local Bijou or Rialto than the more formal schooling they received. The film's unofficial role in the educational process is just beginning to be understood and evaluated.

One of the staples in the cinematic curriculum was the Eastern, always a popular subject with the undergraduates of the University of Hollywood. Warner Oland, Anna May Wong, Sessue Hayakawa, Boris Karloff, Lon Chaney, Sidney Toler — only one of whom, Miss Wong, was of genuine Oriental descent — were among the favored instructors from the days of D. W. Griffith's *Broken Blossoms* on through the Fu Manchu-Charlie Chan (Middle Kingdom) period to the later and more sophisticated *Shanghai Express, The Good Earth* and *The General Died at Dawn.*

The Good Earth conveyed more propaganda for the dignity of the Chinese people than *Gone With the Wind* for the plantation aristocracy of the Old South, and Marlene Dietrich as Shanghai Lily, the seductive drifter of the China coast, imparted more of the cosmopolitan glamour of her operating base in *Shanghai Express* than a shelfful of Old China Hands' memoirs.

Our grandfathers considered the local Chinese a tribe of helots, sneaky, depraved and subhuman, but we acquired a more respectful view. The Chinese we studied on the screen was capable of more than ironing shirts. He might be a hatchet man for a warring tong, a bloodthirsty warlord with a rattail mustache or a monstrous villain scheming to make the world his empire. He might even be an amiable Chinese detective from Honolulu who quoted Confucius. Whether he carried a cricket cage or a machine gun, he was a figure worthy of respect.

The most fascinating of all were the adventure films based on Shanghai, which had become the capital of a dream, the Paris of the East, the most fascinating, sinful, violent and picturesque city in the world. In the cinematic vision of that city, it was the true cosmopolis teeming with beautiful and mysterious White Russian girls, firm-jawed American adventurers, drunken Englishmen on remittance bellowing for a whiskee-soda, Chinese warlords and lovely slant-eyed girls (often born in Berlin or Budapest) with lacquered hair and gestures copied from the American-born Anna May Wong.

The composite film with that locale might have been titled *Shanghai Nights.* Opening montage of the brilliant night lights of Bubbling Well Road, the bund, the Avenue Joffre; skyscrapers and luxury hotels rising above the native huts surrounding them on the mud flats of the Whangpoo. The principal characters would be an American good-bad guy running guns to a warlord in the north, a good-bad girl with a lurid past but not beyond redemption, assorted European villains, and a beautiful Chinese girl hopelessly in love with the American. The plot would be an inverted horse opera, with the Chinese assuming the role of the Indians, turning on whether or not the American would carry through his gun-running scheme or suffer an attack of Christian conscience. A rousing battle scene, with a few Westerners chopping down native hordes, preferably on a fleet of river junks, topped it off.

Historical or literary truth were of small consideration. What counted was the atmosphere — the Blue Express hurtling through the night to Peking, the bars and nightclubs thick with intrigue and overrun by sinister characters, the contrasts between Western wealth and native poverty and between ancient China of the walled cities and the overlay of Western industrialism. Such films as *The General Died at Dawn,* with a screenplay by the late Clifford Odets, conveyed a sense of what Americans now wanted to believe about China; it had changed from an Oriental treasure-house to an Occidental playground full of sex and violence, with the Chinese no longer cast as victims but as playmates.

During the years before World War II, Paris served as a Mecca for the writers and intellectuals but Shanghai was the place where more venturesome youth dreamed of going and where tourists in search of certified depravity headed first of all.

Aside from the prospects of adventure or profit, Americans were lured by the availability of women. Shanghai between the World Wars was a saturnalia, participation in which was easily financed by the exchange of American dollars for Chinese (Mex.) dollars. "A veritable army of prostitutes swarmed over the cities of China," wrote Edgar Snow, who went over as a serious-minded young newspaperman. "The sale of women was a major industry . . . Pretty girls were selected for distribution to metropolitan markets . . . In 1929 the Shanghai International Settlement and French Concession together held 48,000 'piao-tzu.' There were in addition fifty to a hundred thousand unlicensed women operating on the streets and sidewalks, accompanied by voracious amahs whom you could see dragging still-bargaining customers into back-lane lairs."[1]

To an equally dedicated Sinophile, Pearl Buck, the daughter of a missionary, it was also disturbing that Americans and other foreigners looked upon Shanghai as a glamorously sinful city without bothering to peer behind the facade. "There was nothing healthy or good about Shanghai life," as she remembered. "Its Chinese city was filthy and crowded, and the foreign concessions were hiding places for criminals of all countries, behind their facades of wealth and magnificence. Upon the streets the beggars and the struggling people pushed and hurried. If I had to draw a cartoon of Shanghai at that period, I would draw a wretched riksha puller, his vehicle piled with five or six factory workers on their way home after work, being threatened by a tall English policeman, or a turbaned Sikh in the British Concession, while he made way for a car full of satin-clothed people of any nationality that one might mention."[2]

Shanghai then was an island ruled by the Western nations even though it was Chinese soil, "a political exoticism, a hippgriff," as one American journalist called it. "No other city quite like it ever rose on the earth before or is likely to appear again . . . White men built it out of nothing and made it the fifth busiest seaport in the world."[3] It was an

international city-state, protected by foreign troops backed up by a private
army called the Shanghai Volunteers, in which Chinese were not permitted
to live. There were lanes that looked like part of London, boulevards of
Parisian design, steel and glass buildings that seemed to have been transplanted from New York City's skyline.

The city was a jumble of races and the pursuits that brought them to
Shanghai — twelve thousand British, four thousand Americans, thirteen
thousand White Russians, three thousand French, two thousand Germans,
twenty thousand Japanese, fifteen thousand other nationals, all imbedded
among and surrounded by more than six million Chinese. Over them
fluttered the flags of thirteen nations. The Chinese looking in, second-class
citizens in their land, "resented every flag and inch of Shanghai," as it
has been recalled by Relman Morin, who went to China as a student and
stayed on as a newspaper correspondent. "Many of them benefitted by the
city's existence . . . but many more resented it. They resented it as a
symbol of China's humiliations and as a fact of foreign privilege. They
resented the soldiers, sailors and marines in the streets and the warships off
the bund. They resented having no Chinese members on the Municipal
Council. Most of all, they resented 'extrality,' the treaty provisions that set
up special courts for foreigners with foreign judges interpreting a case
under foreign codes of law."

To the visitor it seemed that one only had to turn a corner to enter a
different world. There were the skyscrapers of the International Settlement
and the beautiful homes of the French Concession; the Broadway blaze of
Bubbling Well Road by night; the Walled City built eight centuries before;
the thousands of sampans encrusting Soochow Creek; penthouses looking
down on the curling tiled roofs of pagodas and the thatch of native huts;
the factory district of Yangtzepoo with its textile mills, chemical plants and
other industries and its warehouses crammed with products from all over
the world, which looked to some Americans like Chicago before the Hay-
market riot, all its buildings fortresslike with high walls and massive iron
gates built to withstand a mob.

With the warlords of the north and the revolutionaries of the south
both needing munitions, many Americans and Europeans with some experience in filling such needs in Latin America and the Middle East drifted
into Shanghai and made it their headquarters. So did demobilized soldiers
willing to sell the techniques of slaughter learned on the Western Front to
the highest bidder. There was Two-Gun Cohen, who was Dr. Sun Yat-sen's
bodyguard, a genuine Jewish gunfighter, of whom it was said more or less
affectionately, "That bastard would take your eye and peel it for a grape."

Shanghai was crowded with picturesque and legendary characters; it
was also the "last port of call for the derelict, the floater, the broken-
hearted, the defeated and despairing," according to one American correspondent headquartered there for many years. "Oh, yes," he added,

"there was a Beat Generation in the 1930's . . . you were more aware of it in Shanghai than elsewhere because of the high saturation there. For years Shanghai had been the world capital of the Beat Generation."[4]

Those who wanted to drop out of the America of the 1920's or '30's placed Shanghai high on the list of places in which to disappear. Its romantic squalor was more appealing than the glittering perversities of Berlin after the Kaiser and before the Fuehrer, less expensive than Paris's "moveable feast," less enervating than Tahiti. And it was very difficult for a white man or woman to get into serious trouble under the benevolence of "extrality."

Among the more exotic outlanders recalled by the American journalist quoted above were a tall, severe-looking American woman always seen with a pretty Chinese girl. "She was a teacher of Romance languages in an expensive finishing school for girls somewhere in the States. Seems she took to seducing the young ladies, right and left, and the word got around. Now she's the *amah* for her Chinese girl-friend, who is a prostitute . . . There was the tall, grave-faced Englishman, almost a ringer for Cordell Hull, who had been a great lawyer until he stole an estate. There was the ex-clergyman, now a professor of religion, who drank himself silly every night . . . There was the American who shaved his head and showed up at the tea dances in the Astor Hotel, wearing the robes of a Buddhist monk."[5]

Shanghai had something for everybody. For those with low tastes in night life there was "Blood Alley," on which military and naval personnel converged, where the services of the cheapest, most bedraggled whores in the world, white and colored, were available. It was also the arena in which the American Marines and the Seaforth Highlanders staged some of their most memorable brawls. When those contingents met in a bar, the furniture and glassware of the establishment was immediately written off as a total loss. Every form of gambling was available day or night at whatever scale you could afford. There was an establishment on the Rue Cardinal Mercier that provided opium and girls for those who wearied of roulette or fan-tan.

There were as many rackets operating in Shanghai as in Chicago. The most profitable and dangerous was gunrunning, but those with more refined talents could turn to counterfeiting (in all known currencies), forging of passports and identification papers (a sizable industry in itself in a city crowded with "stateless" persons), smuggling, floating stock companies based on mines or oil wells with dubious production records. There was an open traffic in all forms of narcotics. There were ingenious swindles which usually required a Chinese partner.

For an American with liberal principles, Shanghai required a certain amount of adjustment, of course, to the prevailing racial attitudes. Those attitudes were summed up by two signs in the Bund Garden, one of the parks along the riverfront where foreigners were permitted to stroll or listen to band concerts. One sign warned against taking dogs into the park, the other read, "No Chinese, excepting work coolies, are admitted." Chinese agitators later claimed there was one sign in the Bund Garden reading "Dogs and Chinese Not Admitted," but that was not true; the effect was the same, and the Chinese have never forgotten. The American with some degree of racial tolerance also had to make himself callous to the way Westerners treated the Chinese working for them, to the grinding, hopeless poverty of the Chinese masses and the endemic diseases of typhoid, cholera and dysentery which were "so prevalent," as John B. Powell (*My Twenty-five Years in China*) observed, "that one wondered what prevented the entire population from being swept away by epidemics." If he had any preconceived ideas about sanitation, the American also had to accustom himself to the Shanghai belief that there was something unhealthy about indoor plumbing and flush-toilets. Anyway the "night-soil" collected from the International Settlement was used in fertilizing the truck gardens surrounding Shanghai and was the basis of one of the staple industries.

Shanghai was not only the Paris of the East, as promoters of tourism maintained and as motion pictures and popular fiction testified, but the Bowery, the Skid Road, the Scollay Square or Barbary Coast, on a cosmopolitan scale. "Escape?" Relman Morin wrote. "You escaped when you got off the ship here, mister. Now the problem is to escape Shanghai."

1. *Open and Closed Doors*

The high life for privileged Westerners in Shanghai and the treaty ports whirled on during the post-World War I years. Those Americans who participated in its pleasures and profits seemed unaware, generally, that they were the citizens of an Asian Pompeii. Underneath them, rumbling with long-stored resentment, was a volcano called Chinese nationalism. For a century Old China Hands had been assuring each other and themselves that the volcano was a myth told by nervous diplomats and missionaries who kept their ears too close to the ground. The Chinese would never unify themselves; they were split by too many loyalties, corrupt and quarreling factions, secret societies, and above all the determined individualism of the Chinese temperament. Even a man like Dr. Sun Yat-sen could prevail only in his native south, around Canton, because there were regional prejudices added to all the others.

"China isn't a nation," was a favorite saying of the Old China Hands. "It's just a hell of a lot of people." The Chinese had no conception of patriotism in the nationalistic sense, no comprehension of the necessity for the rule of law, no regard for equal justice; they were hundreds of millions of people, each imbued with one overriding passion, that of survival.

Yet China too was infected by the postwar obsession with nationalism that swept from Prague to Shanghai, was eager to test Woodrow Wilson's proclamation of self-determination for all nations. She wanted the treaties imposed on her by the major Western powers modified if not revoked. Perhaps it was time that the earlier American diplomatic invention called the Open Door — a device which opened the Chinese door for the Western nations on an equal footing, but shut out China's national interests completely — be slammed shut. Already a startling idea was gathering force in China: why not turn from Washington to Moscow?

The pivot-point on which the new Chinese attitude turned was the "Shantung Question," an incident largely ignored in the West but indicative to the Chinese of how little hope they had of protection against Japanese aggression from the Western nations. In 1898, Germany, acting on the pretext of the murder of two German Catholic missionaries in Shantung Province, had proceeded to carve out a sizable holding. She seized Kiaochow Bay, the best harbor on the coast; the fishing village of Tsingtao, and the right of way for a railroad built from Tsinan, the capital of Shantung Province, to connect the main-trunk Tientsin-Nanking Railroad with Tsingtao. The Kaiser then sent his best city planners to convert Tsingtao into a model German city — clean streets and "Keep off the Grass" and *Verboten* signs all over the place — within a few years. By 1914 Tsingtao was the showplace of the China coast.

The Japanese admired it so much that, immediately after their opportunistic entry into World War I, they moved to seize Tsingtao. A Japanese naval expedition ran up against German forts with revolving turrets and was driven off, but Japanese infantry finally attacked from the land side and took the city. The Japanese then overran the entire province and introduced not only opium but morphine and heroin (which they manufactured in the Tientsin Concession), to the Chinese population. It was a clear violation of the Open Door policy, but that was made in Washington, not Tokyo. Even more alarming to the United States, particularly, was the seizure of the mandated islands from Germany — the Marshalls, the Carolines and the Marianas — which Japan proceeded to fortify as a barrier between the United States and the Philippines despite its agreement not to do so.

Just after the World War, the United States itself had moved decisively toward making the Pacific an "American lake." Only a few weeks after the Armistice, Secretary of the Navy Daniels, now more alert to the Japanese danger, appeared before the House Naval Affairs Committee and asked for a naval construction program which would add ten battleships, six heavy cruisers and 140 smaller vessels to the fleet. Many of the new ships were earmarked for the Asiatic and Pacific forces, though as Daniels explained it the program would provide the League of Nations with "tremendous police power of protection."

A Pacific naval race soon developed. Early in 1919 the main elements of the United States Navy were transferred from the Atlantic to the Pacific fleets. As he explained that move while reviewing the augmented Pacific Fleet at San Diego, Daniels was "acting on a hunch." A little later a dry dock capable of repairing battleships was opened at Pearl Harbor, where the facilities were being expanded to handle "any movement, offensive or defensive, across the Pacific," as the Navy Department phrased it. The total tonnage of American warships in the Pacific now approximated that of the entire Japanese navy, which had been supreme in that area during the World War years. In July 1920, the Japanese Diet accordingly authorized the construction of sixteen battleships and heavy cruisers. The Japanese militarists were also clamoring for means of defending the home islands from the air, and the Imperial Aviation Association produced a film prophetically showing Tokyo in ruins after being attacked by an enemy aerial armada.

Diplomatically, too, the atmosphere was thickening by 1921. China was demanding that Japan evacuate the Shantung peninsula, with the United States readily concurring. Soviet Russia was insisting that Japanese forces join the Allied exodus from Vladivostok. By then, too, Japan's only allies, Britain and France, were disassociating themselves in alarm at her appetite for more territory.

The only solution to the perennial Far Eastern Question seemed to be another international conference. Such conclaves, however, were no longer regarded as mankind's last best hope. President Harding as Wilson's successor wanted to avoid any further adventures in power politics; nor were most of the other postwar national leaders, who had witnessed the divisive results of the Versailles Conference, confident of amelioration through a Versailles of the East. But the effort had to be made.

Even the Japanese, who could hope for little at a bargaining session except demands to disgorge, felt it necessary, with dragging footsteps, to seat herself at the table.

Japan realized that she was temporarily blocked from pursuing her aggressive policy. The firmness of American policy, as embodied by the granitic Major General William S. Graves in Siberia, made it apparent Washington was in a less permissive mood. Financing for other military adventures, furthermore, would have to be arranged through the United States, the only power left with that kind of money, and she wasn't likely to capitalize designs inimical to her own interests. Admiral Kato Tomosaburo had proclaimed in 1917 that Japan must prepare herself for an eventual war with the United States, but in 1921 he was declaring it was "imperative to avoid war with the United States."[6] The Japanese were realistic enough to know that now was the time for consolidation rather than lunges against the perimeter of other nations' interests, and the gains they had made during the war years might be legitimatized by the conference — if not Shantung, then the mandated islands.

Despite his party's aversion to "foreign entanglements," President Harding called the Washington Conference into session late in 1921. The Republicans, from Harding on down, had succeeded in winning the election of 1920 largely by pointing to the Shantung Question as a means of discrediting the Versailles Treaty and the Democratic policy of attaching American signatures to the Covenant of the League of Nations. The "rape of China," Harding and his cohorts declaimed, proved that the League of Nations could not halt aggression among its members. Now Harding felt obligated to solve the Shantung Question and incidentally the problem of reducing naval armament.

The conference served as a marvelously revealing index to national attitudes in the postwar decade. The Japanese delegation came, as one observer said, "somewhat in the mood of a naughty child called to the teacher's desk for a reprimand." The British appeared as tightrope walkers, having assured the Japanese that they wouldn't be punished too severely if only they would show up for the conference, and at the same time realizing that if the conference succeeded to any degree the Japanese-British alliance would in effect be abrogated. The Canadians came hoping that the Anglo-Japanese alliance would indeed be terminated because she was having the same difficulties over Japanese immigration the United States had experienced in the first decade of the century. The Americans tried to play the role of benign host while intent on curbing the outward thrust of the Japanese empire. France, Italy, the Netherlands, Belgium and Portugal were also invited but took no great interest in the proceedings.

After some hesitation and much debate in the State Department, an invitation was also extended to China. That China, as a "free and independent Power," should be asked to take a place at the table was a tremendous boost to Chinese official self-esteem. Chinese dignity suffered, however, in the events which followed the invitation to Peking. The rival Kuomintang regime in Canton, headed by Dr. Sun Yat-sen, howled in protest at being ignored. They sent a delegation of their own, which sniped at the Peking group throughout the conference. As an answer to that sniping, there was an attempt to assassinate Dr. Sun in Canton during the conference.

China's diplomatic recognition as a sovereign power engendered so much enthusiasm that the Peking delegation swelled to three hundred persons, and the Chinese embassy in Washington was hard-pressed to arrange for their living quarters. There were undiplomatic snickers among their fellow conferees at the bustling self-importance of the Chinese, and *sotto voce* suggestions that the Yellow Peril had descended on Washington in swallowtail coats. The British commonwealth nations also had taken a sudden interest in international diplomacy — particularly the Canadians,

Australians and New Zealanders, all of them animated by an anti-Japanese spirit — so the British delegation was almost as large and clamorous as the Chinese. Arthur James Balfour, the chief British delegate, received frequent nudges and unsought advice from his colonial colleagues.[7]

Considering the circumstances, the Washington Conference accomplished much — for good or ill — with surprising dispatch. At the opening session on November 12, Secretary of State Charles Evans Hughes rose to announce that the United States, as a gesture toward world peace (and in the hope of cutting its budget), was willing to call a halt to naval construction. "The way to disarm," he bluntly proposed, "is to disarm." We would scrap a number of ships on which construction was almost completed. No vessel larger than ten thousand tons, no guns larger than the eight-inch, would be added to the fleets of the United States or its rivals.

His fellow delegates, unprepared for the sweep of the American disarmament proposal, stared at each other in wonderment. Japan, having been alarmed at the size of American naval construction in recent years, regarded it as a windfall. Colonel Repington, the London *Times*'s military expert, noted that Hughes in his half-hour speech had "sunk more ships than all the admirals in the world have sunk in a cycle of centuries." In the corridors of the Navy Department, American naval officers greeted each other with a parody, "We who are about to be abolished salute you." Others less directly concerned observed the paradox in the fact that President Harding, the successor of McKinley and Roosevelt, the member of a party which had championed expansion in the Pacific, had engineered a great turnabout. It was in line with Harding's and the nation's yearning for "normalcy," but the United States Navy believed its effect would be to cede the Atlantic to British control, the western Pacific to the Japanese. Our Asiatic Fleet was always a lightweight, and the American gunboats constituting the Yangtze River patrol, close to the Japanese zone of influence in Manchuria, would operate under the sufferance of the Japanese Imperial Navy.

Japan was less pleased by a codicil to the American proposals. It was the famous 5:5:3 parity. Under it a ratio would be established among the three leading naval powers in the Pacific of five American tons to five British to three Japanese.* To sweeten that pill, the United States agreed not to continue fortifying any positions west of the 180th meridian.

---

* The Japanese delegation tried to bargain over that point, but the Americans knew that they would yield. Tokyo cabled its delegation to try for a 10:10:7 ratio but to give in if the United States was obdurate. The State Department, as was later revealed, was looking over the shoulders of the Japanese delegation. It had established a secret code-breaking operation in New York City, the famous "black chamber," which had cracked the Japanese diplomatic code. Every day during the conference a courier arrived from New York with a diplomatic pouch containing translations of all messages between the Japanese delegates and their superiors in Tokyo.

The central document of the Washington Conference was the Nine-Power Treaty, also known as the "Chinese Charter of Liberty," which foreswore all sphere-of-influence meddling with Chinese affairs and ended the threat of Chinese dismemberment. The signatories also pledged themselves to help China achieve an independent, unified state. The Japanese had to agree to withdraw their troops from Shantung Province, and turn over the German-built port of Tsingtao and the railroad inland to the Chinese government.

A resolution was also adopted to send an international committee to China to work out a way for the Western nations to end their extraterritorial privileges and place all foreigners on Chinese soil under Chinese law. Nothing said and done at the conference was to cause so much trouble as that implied promise to the Chinese.

Once they had pushed across the main objectives of American diplomacy in the Pacific, which were to curb Japan, get her out of Siberia and bolster Chinese hopes for sovereignty, the Americans could lean back and take a detached and amused view of the conference, the first large diplomatic effort in its history, aside from Wilson's disillusioning participation at Versailles. One observer at the various plenary sessions recalled moments of high comedy not on the agenda. "One occurred when the gallery shouted for Aristide Briand, head of the French Legation. William Jennings Bryan, ex-Secretary of State and outstanding pacifist, sat in the front row of the visitors' gallery facing the press. Bryan's benign countenance had become familiar at receptions. He was quite happy over the arms-scrapping phases of the conference, and insisted that this was a direct result of his efforts on behalf of world peace. When the crowd yelled for Briand, Bryan thought they were calling for him and was on his feet before a friend seized his coattail and pulled him down."[8]

The French, being forced to return the territory they had leased at Kwangchowan, southwest of Canton, were in a bilious mood at the conference. Almost equally offensive to Gallic sensibility was the fact that this was the first important international conference at which French was not the official language. All other delegations delivered their remarks in English. The French insisted on speaking French. Their insistence on using their own language caused a considerable delay. The next day one of the Washington columnists referred to the French as the "only foreigners at the conference." This statement, plus a cartoon in one of the Baltimore papers showing France trying on the old German spiked helmet, caused the French to lodge a protest with the State Department.

Secretary of State Hughes was determined that the details of the Japanese evacuation from Shantung Province be settled on the scene between the Chinese and Japanese delegates, with American and British delegates sitting in as observers and referees. "I am an old man," Hughes acidly remarked, "and I want to see the Shantung Question settled before I die." Many of the Sino-Japanese sessions were concerned with the disposal of German properties seized by the Japanese. For some reason the Japanese were stubborn about possession of the municipal laundry in Tsingtao which had been established by the Germans. After much bickering, Dr. Alfred Sze, chairman of the Chinese (Peking) delegation, turned to John V. MacMurray, the United States observer, and whispered, "Let the Japanese have the laundry. The Chinese have always had the reputation of being the world's laundrymen. We are now glad to permit the Japanese to share some of that reputation."

At the Washington Conference the United States was able to do the Soviet Union one more favor regarding Siberia. Hughes maneuvered the Japanese into agreeing to evacuate their forces from Vladivostok, Russia then being too weak to force the issue. The Russians, to show their peaceful intentions toward China and Japan, immediately scrapped the old czarist fortifications. A few years later, however, the Soviet government changed its mind about adopting a passive attitude in the Far East, revived the Vladivostok shipbuilding industry and machine shops, and began building a large fleet of submarines.

Few international conferences have settled so much — as it appeared on the surface — in so short a time. The Washington Conference concluded its sessions on February 6, 1922. Whether its decisions would work, of course, depended on the goodwill of the nations involved. If each lived up to its word, the Pacific navies would be limited and the fortification of Pacific islands halted, and perhaps more importantly China would be given a chance to pull itself together with help from abroad.

That its resolutions were not enforced was probably due to the cynicism and war-weariness of the whole world. America sought a quick, easy solution to Far Eastern problems because it wanted to reduce taxes; it was willing to settle for Japanese promises because a continuing surveillance of Japanese performance would have taken too much energy and money. "We were all responsible for the failure of the Washington Conference," said one Washington official, "because we were a disillusioned people. The let-down and disillusionment which followed the war were so complete that we permitted the pacifists and internationalists and paid propagandists to dominate our national policy. The Japanese were quick to take advantage of this situation, ready-made for their purposes. It was estimated that they expended no less that $10,000,000 annually in the United States on their various propaganda schemes."[9]

As far as its measures to mend relations between China and the West were concerned, they came too late, promised too little, and produced even less.

Many months elapsed before the United States finally appointed a delegation to the conference at which extraterritoriality was to be studied. Not eliminated, but ways of eliminating it examined. To the Chinese it seemed an elaborate stall. The Chinese suspicion was confirmed when Silas H. Strawn, the head of the American delegation, himself denounced the State Department for its dilatory attitude. "They gave us a charter of liberty," a Chinese official complained to John B. Powell, the Shanghai editor, "but failed to provide the means for making our new independence effective."

American officials responsible for Far Eastern policy considered that the first priority was to stem Japanese expansion. It should have been to rebuild China, for an effective and democratic China would by its existence serve as the counterweight to Japanese ambitions. Already it was too late to appease the Chinese by talking about eliminating the extraterritorial courts, extending a vague sympathy, and mumbling promises to help China build a stable government.

2. *A Protégé Turns Sour*

Americans living in Shanghai, and elsewhere in China, may have sensed that there were volcanic heavings underfoot, but they continued to enjoy the privileges of what amounted to a colonial style of life. It has always been surprising how quickly Americans manage to adapt themselves to such conditions and ignore the human exploitation on which they are founded. Within a few months they are commanding the services of "the natives" with all the aplomb of a genuine sahib or memsahib. "Housewives who had always done their own work and looked after their own children at home," as one American observed, "suddenly found themselves surrounded by servants. In our home we had two female servants or amahs, a cook, houseboy, and coolie. They all lived somewhere in the rear, which we never visited." Americans had organized their own businessmen's and social clubs, had established a Community Church and the American School, located in the French Concession, to which a certain percentage of other nationalities were permitted to send their children. Naturally enough, Americans developed a compound psychology similar to that of other Westerners, a feeling for the superiority of white skin, a determination to keep the natives, or wogs, at a respectful distance.

The natives, however, were becoming less awed by presumptions of Western superiority, less willing to believe in democratic solutions or the advantages of being Christianized. One probable cause was World War I. Dr. Sun Yat-sen and the Kuomintang had unsuccessfully opposed China's nominal participation in that conflict, in which she had no direct interest; she had been roped in by the instinctive tendency of nations at war to make alliances with any neutral, no matter how ineffectual, as proof of the worthiness of their cause. Significantly enough, Dr. Sun had warned that "the Chinese people may not be able to distinguish between foreigners of different nationalities and if the simple and honest people are taught to kill Teutons, they might be led to slaughtering all white foreigners in the country."

Several incidents before and after the Washington Conference showed that the Chinese were becoming restive under foreign domination and dissatisfied at the pace with which their government — or governments, one in Canton, the other in Peking — were arriving at a new understanding with the West. In 1922, a world congress of Christian students was scheduled to be held in Shanghai, which a nationwide movement sprang up to protest. In the same nationalistic spirit, Chinese Christians were demanding that foreign preachers be replaced by Chinese.

That same year, in December, an American trader in Kalgan was shot to death by Chinese soldiers for no other apparent reason than that he was American. The American State Department took a strong, even a haughty line regarding the incident, reflecting its lack of understanding of how things were changing in China. Secretary of State Charles Evans Hughes declared the murder was "further evidence of increasing disregard by Chinese authorities for the rights of American citizens in China." Quite right, but Hughes's instructions to Jacob Gould Schurman, the United States minister in Peking, were phrased with a lordliness the Chinese would find galling and offensive: "Should the Government fail to deal with the case promptly and energetically, you may indicate that this Government regards the matter as a test of confidence which may be placed by it in the Government of China." Dr. Schurman, a former president of Cornell and ordinarily sensitive to Chinese feelings, drove the message home with added impact by warning that Sino-American relations had reached a critical point. "The attitude of the United States toward China," he added, "had always been one of benevolent helpfulness . . . The American government now wishes to know whether it is the intention of the Chinese Government to prevent the United States from continuing that attitude."

In their present moods, both China and the United States were expecting too much of each other. China hoped for, even demanded that a United States weary of all foreign associations immediately help to lift China into modern statehood. The United States expected China to be patient. A nation so long-suffering, so noted for its ability to take the view of centuries and millenniums, could suffer a little longer.

But China suddenly, shockingly, was unwilling to wait, suffer or tolerate any longer. Revolution was preferable to gradual change, and an immensely sympathetic Soviet Russia was more worthy of emulation than an aloof, coldly condescending America. And the most impatient, as well as the most influential of all Chinese leaders was Dr. Sun. Suddenly he had acquired the power — after a decade of ruling in opposition from Canton — to turn the whole of China in a new and dismaying direction.

The reconstituted parliament had elected him as the first legal and constitutional president of China.

His first formal diplomatic contact was with Adolf Jeffe, the representative of Soviet Russia, in the Palace Hotel at Shanghai. Significantly, the new president of China preferred to meet the Russians, including Michael Borodin, who was to be the most influential of all the Soviet representatives on Chinese soil in the years to come, not in his home base of Canton but in Shanghai, among the watchful bastions of Western commerce.

Dr. Sun, however, made several efforts to arrive at an understanding, an equal footing, with the United States. In 1921 he had sent a direct appeal to President Harding, asking American support for his republican cause, referring to the United States as "the champion of liberalism and righteousness, whose disinterested friendship and support of China in her hour of distress has been demonstrated to us more than once." In February 1923, even after accepting Soviet financial assistance and advice, he asked that the United States "send a strong man" — Secretary of State Hughes preferably, for all his icy hauteur — "who as a neutral person would be able to bring together the now mutually suspicious leaders of China and make it possible for them to unite for the carrying out of some scheme of Government."

He made other efforts, according to Edgar Snow, to interest a consortium of the major Western powers in modernizing China and helping in her unification. The trouble was, principally, that there was a touch of the grandiose to his scheme for international development of China, particularly just after World War I when most of those nations were trying to recover from the devastation extending from the Belgian coast to the Black Sea.

Edgar Snow, however, has recorded that "even after Dr. Sun reached an agreement with the Russians he made a final appeal to the American minister in China . . . to ask for international intervention on a scale which even Russia never attempted. He proposed that Britain, France and the United States occupy China for five years, eliminate the warlords, and jointly with the Kuomintang set up an honest administration, industrialize and modernize the country, and prepare the people for democratic elections."[10]

The lords of the north, with their private armies and private ambitions, were Dr. Sun's most urgent problem. From 1922 to 1928 they would dominate much of the country, just as in America they became household words — Marshal Chang Tso-lin in Manchuria, General Wu Pei-fu in North China and the "Christian general" Feng Yu-hsiang. All the regional tyrants fought with each other on occasion, but never more bitterly than they opposed an incursion into their territories by forces dispatched by a central government. To eliminate them would take long and bloody campaigning. It would take a larger inter-Allied expeditionary force, which was just about as likely a project for the war-weary West of the 1920's, remembering a similar venture in Siberia, as the reincarnation of Chinese Gordon.

By late 1923 Dr. Sun had definitely turned to Soviet Russia for inspiration and support. His most promising young officer, Chiang Kai-shek, had been sent to Moscow for training in revolutionary warfare and returned to establish the military academy at Whampoa. The only opposition to his alliance with Russian communism came from the right wing of the Kuomintang Party.

Late that year the Chinese Customs Incident occurred when the Nationalist government announced that it would take part of the customs revenue for various municipal projects. The West, with an attitude virtually unchanged since the Opium Wars, overreacted as usual. A combined fleet, including ships of the United States Navy, collaborated in a "demonstration" off Canton. Until then Dr. Sun had hoped the United States would see the justice of his claims to a share of the customs receipts.

"America was the inspiration and example," he wrote in his bitter valedictory to the nation from which he had expected so much, "when we started the revolution to abolish autocracy and corruption in high places. We might well have expected that an American Lafayette would fight on our side in this good cause. In the twelfth year of our struggle towards liberty there comes not a Lafayette but an American admiral with more ships of war than any other nation in our waters."

Before a Canton Christian College assembly he predicted another world war in ten years with China, Russia, Japan, Germany and India fighting the United States and other imperialist nations, then "the United States would see how it feels to have a Chinese fleet in San Francisco harbor." The Chinese George Washington's viewpoint had become so warped by the Soviet military and political advisers who wrapped him in a cocoon that he had lost sight of the fact that China's number-one enemy was Japan, not the United States, and his talent for prophecy did not come close to the standard set by his old friend Homer Lea.

3. *Warlords and Rice Christians*

Sun Yat-sen died in 1925, leaving his country more bitterly and dangerously divided than ever. His own party was split between the left wing, dominated by the Communists, and the right wing, which still hoped for completely democratic solutions. There was still a rival regime in Peking. Most of northern and western China was held in a fiefdom of terror by regional despots. The Japanese were backing Marshal Chang Tso-lin, the "Manchurian Tiger," and planning their conquests of the following decade. The Russians were busy trying to convert the Kuomintang into a branch of the Communist International, training and organizing its forces under Chiang Kai-shek and other apolitical officers for the campaign to the north. And where neither warlords nor contending political factions held sway, there were always bandits watching the roads from their mountain hideouts.

While their government in Washington merely wrung its hands and loudly deplored the "lack of stability" caused by what amounted to a civil war, thousands of Americans stayed on in China. They were living dangerously, but the fleshpots of Shanghai stayed open for business, trade was booming, the American navy and army maintained their presence in the coastal enclaves, and the missionaries were still laboring in the vastest vineyard ever subjected to the organized efforts of Christianity.

Americans had been involved in that effort since 1829, when David Abeel, representing the American Seamen's Friend Society, and Elijah C. Bridgman, sponsored by the American Board of Commissioners for Foreign Missions (at first auxiliary to the London Missionary Society), had been assigned to work among the Chinese and also American sailors in constant danger of being led astray ashore. Abeel and Bridgman were provided with free passage to China and given other help by D. W. C. Olyphant, the merchant from New York whose Canton factory was known as "Zion's Corner" for the piety of its proprietor and his abhorrence of the opium traffic. Abeel returned home after a year's tour of duty, but Bridgman stayed on to open a school for Chinese boys and establish the celebrated *Chinese Repository,* a periodical which disseminated not only news of missionary activities but information on the laws, customs, literature and history of the Chinese people.

A half-dozen years later, in 1838, Dr. Peter Parker, the medical missionary who later turned diplomat and advocated the American seizure of Formosa, established an opthalmic hospital in Canton because of the prevalence of eye diseases among the Chinese. In the decades following Dr. Parker's pioneering efforts, about a tenth of all American missionaries sent over were medically trained; by 1905 their work had been extended up and down the China coast and into the interior, with more than a million patients treated that year. The missionaries had established 330 hospitals by 1905, and one of the more notable examples of their diligence was Dr. Elizabeth Reifsnyder of Shanghai, who ministered to more than two hundred thousand patients in fifteen years.

In the years following World War I, Christianity was still confident that in China it would win its greatest victory over superstition and heathen doctrine. During the decades following the Boxer Rebellion, Christian influence in China reached its apex; the years when the Chinese at last seemed ready to accept Western benevolence, especially American, and adapt themselves to Christian principles. With the missionaries, of course, came education, food and clothing as well as medical services. There were material benefits obtainable through acceptance of Christianity; for many

Chinese, somewhat after the fashion of the Jews in pre-Bismarck Germany, conversion offered the only hope of rising in the world. And during the Twenties and Thirties many of the American missionaries regarded themselves not only as evangelists but, with equal importance, educators, social workers and public-health specialists. The program of which they were a part, one authority claims, predated "the Point Four program, ECA, UNESCO, the State Department's information and cultural services."

Much of the residual idealism of the West was channeled into the missionary endeavors. Two to four million dollars a year was collected in Sunday church offerings, and much more came from the Rockefellers', the Edward Harkness and other great fortunes. This unofficial benevolence more than matched the politically calculated military and economic assistance given the Kuomintang by Soviet Russia, but the slow patient effort to conquer illiteracy and disease was never so impressive as an array of guns and marching troops.

The massiveness of the American effort to Christianize the East after World War I is hard to comprehend now that so much of it has lain in ruins for twenty years. In China the missionaries almost formed a parallel, but not rival government; which is probably why the Communists moved so quickly and ruthlessly to exterminate the last shred of their influence. They assumed, in fact, many of the functions of a modern, welfare-minded government. By 1925 there were twenty-seven missionary colleges and universities in China, all but six founded since the turn of the century. In Christian secondary schools there were 300,000 Chinese students in Protestant institutions and 260,000 in Catholic. Throughout China the Protestants claimed 700,000 followers, the Catholics about a million and a half.[11]

Even in Korea, under Japanese occupation, there were 40,000 professed Christians in Pyongyang, now the capital of North Korea, and there were 290 Protestant churches in Seoul alone.

Throughout the East, however, the influence of Christianity was greater than could be indicated by statistics. Those who accepted the Holy Spirit also could accept the better food, health and education which allowed them to surpass the non-Christians. The Christian-educated became part of the moneyed and influential class; the doors to achievement opened on mission schools rather than the Forbidden Palace or the old Manchu bureaucracy.

Old China Hands could mock that the missionaries had only managed to convert a flock of "rice Christians," who would vanish the moment the fires under the rice boilers were extinguished, but the "Christian adventurers," as Pearl S. Buck has characterized her own missionary parents, were convinced they brought a spiritual flame to the East that would light the world. They believed that once they had set the example for China, their millions of Chinese followers, with all the ardor of converts, would refurbish Christianity and inspire the materialistic West. "I can only believe," Pearl Buck wrote in her autobiography, "that my parents reflected the spirit of their generation, which was of an America bright with the glory of a new nation, rising united from the ashes of [civil] war, and confident of the power to 'save' the world. Meantime they had no conception of the fact that they were in reality helping to light a revolutionary fire, the height of which we still have not seen, nor can foresee."[12]

In many cases, perhaps most, the stereotype of the long-faced, platitudinous Christian shepherd, lording it over his compound and choking Bible lessons down his flock, was undoubtedly an unforgivable libel. The people who went East as representatives of the various mission boards and religious orders were young and ardent, not old and tiresome. They were receptive and openminded, as willing to be changed by the East as they were eager to help the Easterners. In many ways, like those who flooded the Philippines earlier in the century, they were a prototype of the Peace Corps, with a less secular indoctrination, perhaps, but the same animating impulses. It was little wonder that they helped to change the American image of China, or wherever they were stationed, from that of a vast grasping body of clients to a more human and respected status.

The process by which a missionary was transformed by his experiences in China, how he himself underwent a sort of conversion, was described by Earl Cressy, a prominent missionary teacher, on his return for home leave. The missionary, he wrote, "had come to the Far East with a message that he was on fire to give, but in the process of transmission the East had spoken its message to him. He had gone out to change the East and was returning, himself a changed man . . .

"The conversion of the missionary by the Far East results in his being not only a missionary but an internationalist, an intermediary between the two great civilizations that inherit the earth. Abroad he represents a universal religion, and is himself an embodiment of the strivings of the West to attain its ideals of social justice and world brotherhood; at home he is constantly changing the attitude of the millions of his constituency, bringing to them something of his new breadth of vision, and helping them to a larger appreciation of the greatness and worth of the civilization of the Far East."

The broadening of missionary activities beyond the nineteenth-century concentration on "saving souls for the Lord Jesus" brought them into closer contact with Oriental life. The educational process, bringing a warmer appreciation of the intelligence of the natives, was more conducive in a way to human understanding than preaching to and exhorting them from the pulpit. A classroom contains a less captive audience than a church. Many missionary teachers like Earl Cressy felt themselves expanding as human beings under the influence of their eagerly receptive pupils. During his furlough home Cressy particularly missed the courtesy given their preceptors by Chinese students. The American teacher became "accustomed in the Orient to seeing students rise and bow at the beginning of the recitation, and he feels ill at ease when no one at the occidental university takes note of the entrance of the professor, and the opening sentence of the lecture cuts across a buzz of conversation."[13]

His experience as a lecturer in Peking impressed John Dewey with the greater maturity of Chinese students compared to Americans of the same age. The Chinese "listened soberly and intelligently to lectures on subjects that would create nothing but bored restlessness in an American school. There is an eager thirst for ideas — beyond anything existing, I am convinced, in the youth of any other country on earth."[14]

Harold R. Isaacs (*Scratches on Our Minds*), who was a correspondent in the Far East for many years before taking up an academic career, observed that the new breed of missionaries was much more tolerant and understanding toward non-Christian societies than those predecessors who brought visions of hellfire and the wrath to come. "A more inquiring and respectful attitude toward Chinese society became more common. This was more than an intellectual pose; it came to some out of living experience. In the more relaxed and friendly circumstances, many a missionary was almost insensibly acclimatized. He began not only to learn more about the life of the people around him, but also to savor it and once in a while even to become part of it. For some missionaries, at least, the First World War contributed much to this onset of greater humility. It made some Christians less supremely confident of their own virtue and rightness. It severely shook the conviction of invincible progress always held up hitherto as a contrast to the dying stagnation of China and Chinese outlooks."[15]

Some missionaries branched out in ways that might have alarmed their governing boards back in the States. One of the more intrepid was the father of John C. Caldwell. The senior Caldwell was a Southern Methodist missionary at Fooching, south of Shanghai. "Father always got furious," Caldwell recalled in his memoir, "when he encountered the idea, held by so many Americans, that a missionary was a serious, doom-faced gentleman with a Bible under one arm and a black umbrella under the other, interested in nothing but preaching and saving souls. But he was also troubled when he gained more and more fame as tiger hunter, scientist, pacifier of bandits. He began to fear that people might misunderstand the true nature of his activities, the end towards which all his activities were directed. Tigers, expeditions into Mongolia, bandits — these were things that provided recreation, true; but far more important, they opened a door into the minds and hearts of people held in the thrall of superstition."

Aside from being the regional white hunter called upon whenever a tiger or a wild boar was sighted in the district, the Reverend Caldwell was a highly effective, if somewhat fundamentalist preacher in the Tennessee hills tradition. At the end of one of his high-decibel sermons, his son recalls, "converts would bring their household gods and ancestral tablets with them, and when the suppliants had been accepted there would be a great bonfire of gods and goddesses of every description."

From the observations of his childhood and youth in China, Caldwell believed that many of his father's and other missionaries' converts were "rice Christians," or those who pretended to accept Christianity in hopes of getting an education and a better job, but "there were thousands for whom conversion meant a totally new life, a life free of devils and demons, free of the myriad ancient superstitions that bound their minds as well as their feet. It meant an opportunity for children, especially girls, to get an education. It meant a new viewpoint on matters of public health — and above all it meant a new awareness of the importance and dignity of the individual, of his obligations to society."[16]

The fact that so many children of missionaries became prominent in American life, seldom as members of their fathers' profession but notably often as writers and publicists, was probably due in part to the broadening and deepening of their childhoods in China. From their various memoirs, it is apparent that they absorbed much of enduring value from the Chinese soil, and more particularly from the Chinese people. For most it was undoubtedly a strange, exotic childhood, which was poor preparation, at first, for being plunged into the brisk, pragmatic American atmosphere. No matter how poorly their parents were paid by the mission boards, they were immeasurably richer than the people around them. Yet the impressionable young often acquired Chinese attitudes from their playmates. "From the secret thoughts of the Chinese," Pearl Buck wrote, "thoughts often confided to me by my Chinese playmates who caught them from the talk of their elders, these westerners were 'foreigners' as my playmates called them and as I thought of them, too, and they were potential enemies." As a child Miss Buck learned to accept horrors which would have scarred the mind of a child brought up in more sheltered circumstances, the sight of lepers with their rotting flesh and of dead children lying on the hillsides. She was abruptly made aware of the difference between herself and her Chinese playmates during the Boxer Rebellion, when she and her parents were forced to flee to the safety of Shanghai.[17]

Even for missionaries, bandits and warlords were a constant reminder that the veneer of civilization was nowhere thinner than in China. The bandits specialized in kidnaping. They were part of John Caldwell's earliest memories of a boyhood spent on the Fukien coast. "I remember the sensation in the American community," he has written, "when Jay Dinsmore, an American lumber merchant, was killed in the mountains above Nanping. There was the kidnapping of two missionary ladies for ransom, with a bloody finger of one of the ladies enclosed with the ransom note. Mother was once captured and held for four hours. John Pilley, my brother-in-law, suffered the indignity of having his pants taken away by bandits and walking ten pantless miles home."

As a renowned tiger hunter, Caldwell's father was asked by the Chinese provincial government to become the Bandit Pacification Commissioner of Fukien, an appointment which shocked the American consul in Foochow. "He warned Father that no American should interfere in the internal affairs of the Chinese. If they wanted to go about killing and robbing each other, that was their business. Father took a somewhat different view of the matter. To him, this was another opportunity to do the Lord's work. In spite of dire warnings that he would lose the protection afforded him by his American citizenship, if he went ahead, Father plunged into his new task, and kept at it until the day he left China."[18]

Many of the bandit chiefs were allied to neighboring warlords, who were also familiar figures, seen or only heard about, in the lives of the missionaries and their families. Some of the warlords were comic-book villains, but often, according to one rather fond reminiscence, they were "strong, wilful, humorous, rough-and-ready individuals, afraid of no one and often very funny. One of our neighbouring war lords was famous because of three things he did not know — how many soldiers he had, how much money he had and how many wives he had.

"I remember the war lord in the next province who was twice defeated by another war lord. At last he declared in loud and public tones that he intended to fight once more and if he were defeated he would come home in his coffin. We all waited the outcome of this much-touted battle, and when it ended as the others had, in defeat, an elaborate funeral was prepared for the return of the body. The funeral went off in high humor with every detail complete, except that instead of a corpse in the enormous coffin, the old war lord, very much alive though vanquished, was seated therein, dressed in his best robes and grinning at the astonished crowds while he smoked a large foreign cigar. The people burst into roaring laughter and instantly forgave the old ruler all his sins because he had made such a good joke."[19]

Obviously it would have been difficult not to love a people like that. Many were stubborn in their paganism, obdurate in their belief in demons and devils, and probably less than one-half of one percent ever responded to the call of Christianity. Of all the world's people, in fact, they were probably the least susceptible to Christian evangelization. There was both comedy and pathos in the missionaries' unending struggle with the Chinese soul, or psyche, and the unfailing politeness of the Chinese resistance to that struggle.

Everything considered, the struggle would have to be considered a magnificent failure. Yet as John Caldwell pointed out in 1953, when the missionary effort in China had reached its tragic and often violent end, there were lessons to be learned from it. He contrasted the millions spent on foreign missions and the results they obtained with the billions being spent overseas in various forms of aid by the United States government without any highly visible success. "The missionaries had no mansions in which to live, no PX's and vast commissaries in which to buy their supplies, no beautiful restaurants or cafes in which to take refreshments, no cars to travel, indeed no roads on which cars could operate. In spite of these difficulties these men and women of all faiths and denominations did succeed in making friends where America's official billions have often failed . . . They succeeded because they lived close to the people, because they learned the languages and customs, because they lived not only in the great cities but in fishing villages and mountain hamlets throughout Asia. But above all they succeeded because they had that missing ingredient — *a spirit of dedication*."[20]

Former missionaries are convinced that there are still Chinese secretly faithful, untrampled by the Red Guards. But which faith is stronger, that of the missionaries' in their flock or that of their old converts?

4. *"So Gallant in Their Deed"*

Across the street from the main building of the infantry school at Fort Benning, Georgia, from which so many thousands of young Americans have proceeded in recent years to fight in Asia, a white-marble memorial gate stands. It was presented to the infantry school when the 15th Infantry returned to the States in 1938 after being stationed in Tientsin for twenty-six years.

The inscription on the gate, in Chinese characters, explains that it was presented to the regiment by the grateful people of Tientstin because the American troops defended the city in 1925 from marauding Chinese forces. The poem below the inscription reads in part:

> *The sons of Uncle Sam so gallant in deed,*
> *Day and night to strict defense took the greatest heed.*
> *And through their strenuous efforts and suffering*
> *Peace among all was kept and maintained.*

The 15th Infantry was one of the more notable of American army, navy and Marine units posted on Chinese soil up to World War II to protect American interests in China. In Tientsin and other enclaves along the China coast they tried to preserve a sense of order in a China disintegrating into revolution and anarchy. Often their services, both to Americans and Chinese (as the memorial gate indicated), were heroic and self-sacrificing, but their purpose, their reason for being, was nakedly imperialistic.

One of the great Marine heroes of the China station was Major General Smedley D. Butler, who first served there during the Boxers' siege of the Peking legations and later during the crisis of 1927–1928, and who was twice awarded the Congressional Medal of Honor. No one knew more about the purposes to which the American forces were committed from the turn of the century to World War II; he was the Marshal Lyautey of American colonialism, and a blunt, high-tempered, outspoken man.

On retirement — military men, unfortunately, can speak out only when it is too late — General Butler decried American policy in the Pacific, the policy for which he had so often risked life and honor. In a little book forthrightly titled *War Is a Racket,* he wrote:

"Back in 1904, when Russia and Japan fought, we kicked out our old friends the Russians and backed Japan. Then our very generous international bankers were financing Japan. Now the trend is to poison us against the Japanese. What does the 'open door' policy in China mean to us? Our trade with China is about $90,000,000 a year. Or the Philippines? We have spent $600,000,000 in the Philippines in thirty-five years and we (our bankers and industrialists and speculators) have private investments there of less than $200,000,000.

"Then, to save that China trade of about $90,000,000, or to protect these private investments of less than $200,000,000 in the Philippines, we would be all stirred up to hate Japan and to go to war — a war that might well cost us tens of billions of dollars, hundreds of thousands of lives of Americans, and many more hundreds of thousands of physically maimed and mentally unbalanced men."

Interventions abroad, as General Butler wrote in 1935, were profitable to only a few. The nation itself was weakened. "At the end of the World War period, as a direct result of our fiddling in international affairs, our national debt jumped to over $25,000,000,000. Our total favorable trade balance during the twenty-five-year period was about $24,000,000,-000. Therefore, on a purely financial bookkeeping basis, we ran a little behind year for year, and that foreign trade might well have been ours without the wars."

As a self-appointed revisionist of Captain Mahan and the big-navy propagandists, General Butler declared that the American people were being deceived about the purposes for which military and naval appropriations were made. "The swivel-chair admirals of Washington (and there are always a lot of them) are very adroit lobbyists. And they are smart. They don't shout that 'We need a lot of battleships to war on this nation or that nation.' Oh, no. First of all, they let it be known that America is menaced by a great naval power. Almost any day, these admirals will tell you, the great fleet of this supposed enemy will strike suddenly and annihilate our 125,000,000 people. Just like that . . . Then, incidentally, they announce maneuvers in the Pacific. For defense. Uh, huh. The Pacific is a great big ocean. We have a tremendous coastline on the Pacific. Will the maneuvers be off the coast, two or three hundred miles? Oh, no. The maneuvers will be two thousand, yes, perhaps even thirty-five hundred miles, off the coast. The Japanese, a proud people, of course will be pleased beyond expression to see the United States fleet so close to Nippon's shores. Even as pleased as would be the residents of California were they to dimly discern, through the morning mist, the Japanese fleet playing at war games off Los Angeles."

It was Butler's simplistic, but not necessarily mistaken belief that if we didn't threaten any other nation, no other nation would be a threat to us. The United States Navy, by his prescription, "should be specificallly limited, by law, to within 200 miles of our coastline . . . And the army should never leave the territorial limits of our nation."[21]

What, then, were all those American troops and naval forces doing in China, those regiments of soldiers and Marines, those American gunboats patrolling the Yangtze, those cruisers of the Asiatic Fleet which appeared off the coast in times of trouble, all those imperial representatives of a professedly anti-imperialist nation? The soldiers and Marines added a few pages, some glorious and some not, to the American military legend, the gunboats were handy for occasional rescue operations and inspired a fine novel (*The Sand Pebbles*), the navy acquired a large body of technical information for the future operations of the Seventh Fleet, which cruises those waters now but with more trepidation.

But if their presence was designed principally to protect American lives and property in the sprawling expanse of revolutionary China, it was generally futile. Nor did it prevent the Japanese from expanding their foothold in Manchuria, nor the Russians from conspiring to take over the Chinese revolution. American military power in China was just strong enough to be resented, but insufficient to undertake any decisive interventions.

In 1926 and 1927, Chiang Kai-shek, as successor to Sun Yat-sen at the head of the Kuomintang, along with his Russian mentors, advisers and suppliers, launched his Northern Expedition to clear the country of all rival factions. On March 24, 1927, after an impressive series of victories from Canton to the Yangtze Valley, Chiang Kai-shek's army entered Nanking. His troops got out of hand (or were turned loose) and began attacking foreigners, stripping white women on the streets, killing white men, looting and burning foreign property.

Days of terror followed for the white residents, among them Pearl Buck and her family. Most had refused to flee because, like Miss Buck's father, they "refused to believe that the new revolutionists would also be anti-foreign, for by this time he refused to believe anything evil of the Chinese, and had become far more Chinese than American." When the violence broke out, the Bucks took refuge with a Chinese family and "outside the hut we heard the firing of guns and the howls of the crowds."

Just when the Bucks and all the other Americans and Westerners who had thus far escaped the slaughter thought they were certain to be found and killed, foreign warships appeared in force on the Yangtze and shelled the Nationalist-Communist forces. Under cover of that bombardment, they reached the riverbank and were evacuated on American gunboats, but it was too late for many others lying dead in their looted and burned homes. The sailors who rescued them, Miss Buck has recalled, were "harsh and some of them even contemptuous" because the missionaries had not left Nanking months earlier when the United States consul warned of the danger from the advancing revolutionary army.* [22]

Even in dealing with the warlords and bandits who occasionally molested, kidnaped or killed American citizens, the American forces in China, necessarily operating from their coastal enclaves, were not strikingly effective. Their writ did not run far inland, and meant little to cutthroats who had been holding sway from their mountain headquarters for generations, some of them actually for as long as six centuries. Compared to them, the Sicilian Mafia were diffident newcomers to the profession of banditry.

Perhaps their greatest coup was accomplished on the night of May 5, 1923, when the leading bandit gang of Shantung Province held up the crack Blue Express on its run between Nanking and Peking. Among the passengers they robbed and forced to accompany them on a long grueling march up to their mountain headquarters were Miss Lucy Aldrich, daughter of the late Senator Nelson Aldrich of Rhode Island and sister-in-law of John D. Rockefeller, Jr., and her French maid. Other victims included tourists, businessmen, journalists, and a mysterious Italian named G. D. Musso who had amassed a fortune in Shanghai and was one of Mussolini's early supporters. Unfortunately for Signor Musso, he weighed three hundred pounds and suffered terribly during the climb into the mountains.

John B. Powell, the Shanghai editor, who was one of the captives, has described how whole villages on their route turned out to "see the spectacle of the captive foreigners." They were taken to Mount Pao-tzu-ku, about forty miles from the railway station of Tsaochwang. Weeks passed, during which the Western powers fumed and the Japanese newspapers snidely reminded them that such a thing would never have happened if the Japanese army had not been coerced into leaving Shantung Province. Negotiations began between the bandits and consular representatives in Tientsin,

---

* A month after the Nationalist-Communist terror in Nanking, Chiang Kai-shek broke with his Communist supporters and killed many of them. A Chinese authority, Dr. Hu Shih, writing in an American periodical many years later, declared the Nanking Incident had been deliberately planned by the Russians to provoke Western intervention and forcibly to unify China under Communist control. They aimed to "create a situation of a real 'imperialist war' . . . The commanding general of the offending army in the Nanking Incident was General Ch'en Ch'ien, who is now with the Chinese Communist regime . . ."[23]

the former threatening to kill all the captives if any forcible means of rescuing them were attempted. Furthermore the bandit "army" demanded a considerable ransom: the top officials of the provincial government were to resign and be replaced from governor on down by the bandits themselves, and the main-line of the railroad running through the province was to be turned over to them.

About all the American garrison in Tientsin could come up with was a harebrained rescue operation which would probably have succeeded in getting everyone killed. A note was smuggled in a food parcel from a United States Army officer who had come to Tsaochwang to speed their release. It was addressed to Powell and suggested that revolvers and ammunition be smuggled up to the mountain camp in boxes of raisins brought by carrier coolies. The captives would arm themselves, shoot it out with the bandits, and barricade themselves in a cave. Meanwhile a force of fifty American soldiers, disguised as civilians, would come from Tientsin and storm their way up to the mountaintop.

Fortunately this scheme was never attempted. Provincial officials finally effected the captives' release through negotiations, in which the bandits were promised a large sum of money and the opportunity to join the provincial army. Some months later Powell learned that the governor of Shantung had tricked the bandits into disarming and slaughtered six hundred of them with machine guns.[24]

Generally, military service in China entailed few opportunities for the derring-do suggested by the officer who hoped to rescue Miss Aldrich and her companions in the best frontier-cavalry tradition. But it was undeniably picturesque, a throwback to the age of a Kipling, with officers playing polo, enlisted men brawling in bars and whorehouses, sunset parades, much spit and polish, much flashing of sabers and trotting of cavalry squadrons on review (in the day, well marked by all but the ineffably nostalgic military, of the machine gun and the tank).

As of the mid-Thirties there was actually a colorful but militarily useless outfit called the Horse Marines, a detachment of Marines mounted on Manchurian ponies, as part of the United States garrison in Peking. Its commander in 1933 was Lewis B. "Chesty" Puller, later a three-star general renowned for his exploits in the Pacific war and his combative retreat from the Chosin Reservoir during the Korean War.[25]

And then there was the crack 15th "Can Do" Regiment stationed at Tientsin for twenty-eight years, until it had become an institution with traditions so exotic it was the dismounted American version of the Bengal Lancers. Many of its enlisted men served so long in China that they took their discharges in Tientsin and lived off pensions inflated by exchange into Chinese currency. They had established their own Old Fogies Club and took an avuncular interest in the regiment. Most of them married Chinese, Korean, German or White Russian "squaws." They regarded themselves as infantrymen emeritus and were allowed the privileges of the Post Exchange and the Post Hospital.

Aside from Old Fogies, the 15th Infantry also graduated a notable array of officers who distinguished themselves in more serious endeavors later in life. Its roster of onetime lieutenants, captains and field officers included General of the Army George C. Marshall, four-star Generals Joseph W. Stilwell and Matthew B. Ridgway, Lieutenant Generals L. L. Williams and Rueben E. Jenkins, and Edwin F. Harding, Jens A. Doe, Hayden L. Boatner, John R. Deane among the one- and two-star generals to achieve later prominence.

Since they represented the threat of force rather than force itself, the officers were imbued with a sort of casual aptitude for outfacing the Chinese hordes. The swagger-stick spirit is admirably conveyed in General Ridgway's account of one such encounter in 1927 when a force of twelve thousand troops under Marshal Chang Tso-lin were advancing on Tientsin, which Chinese forces were forbidden under treaty to enter. "I was told to take as many men as I thought I would need to go out and divert them. Since not all the forces of the 15th, and the British regiment combined, could have done much 'diverting' a force of twelve thousand if they had chosen to come in, I picked two men to go with me . . .

"It was a clear, bitterly cold day. Bundled in furs, mounted on shaggy Manchurian ponies of the breed that had carried the cavalrymen of Genghis Khan, we rode out, our feet freezing in the steel stirrups. Soon across the plain to the north we saw the dust of the marching column. To my considerable relief, I saw it was skirting the restricted zone. We shadowed that force all day, staying well away on the flanks but keeping the column in view. We were not molested, nor did we make any attempt to molest them . . . I went back that night to report my day's observations to Lieutenant Colonel [George C.] Marshall. He merely nodded. It was a routine contact."[26]

One of the hardest battles that engaged American forces in China, in fact, was a magnificent brawl between the 15th Infantry and the Marines. In the summer of 1928, when the northern warlords were combining to resist Chiang Kai-shek's all-out attempt at unification, the Fourth Marine Brigade, under General Smedley D. Butler, arrived to bolster the American forces in Tientsin. The old spirit of service rivalry flared up immediately, culminating in a bar brawl that expanded into several thousand soldiers and Marines slugging it out on the streets. The brawlers covered much of the downtown area, and merchants lost a small fortune in broken glass. General Butler himself finally halted the fighting by promising his Marines that he would take up their grievances with the colonel commanding the 15th and that if the matter wasn't settled "I myself will lead you to clean up on the 15th Infantry."[27]

Of greater historic impact than any of the skirmishes in which American troops were engaged during their long stay on the China coast was that of the Chinese revolution on two American officers. One was Captain Stilwell, of the 15th Infantry, the other Captain Evans F. Carlson, the intelligence officer of the Fourth Marine Regiment. Both were serious-minded soldiers who studied the development of the indigenous Communist movement after Chiang Kai-shek broke with the Russian Communists and their Chinese comrades undertook the Long March to the north. Carlson, who was killed on Saipan while leading his Marine Raider battalion, and Stilwell, who struggled to organize an effective Chinese army during World War II, were the only American military men, according to Edgar Snow, who "grasped the significance" of the disciplined and dedicated Chinese Communist cadres being formed outside the territories held by Chiang Kai-shek and the Japanese.

Carlson made the long journey to the headquarters of the Communist Eighth Route Army and returned greatly impressed by its potential fighting power. "Other American military observers in China ridiculed Carlson for his enthusiasm," Snow has written. "It particularly irritated them that he thought *we* had anything to learn from *any* Chinese. But he had one intensely interested listener. He was sending confidential personal reports to the White House, for the President's very interested eye, alone."[28] The sympathetic observations of Stilwell and Carlson on the incorruptibility of the Communists, in contrast to the greed and opportunism which soon corroded Chiang Kai-shek's government, were to greatly influence American attitudes toward China in the crucial Forties.

5. New China Hands

Back in the States, during the Twenties and Thirties, the attitude, as always during a period when the Japanese were being regarded with fear and suspicion, had become admiring and respectful toward the Chinese. In those two decades thousands of Americans went to China not only as merchants, soldiers and missionaries, but as educators, businessmen, scholars and tourists. At the peak of American influence in China during the Thirties there were more than thirteen thousand Americans living there. China, in effect, was rediscovered. Again, as during the first years of the China trade, things Chinese became something of a craze. Suburban matrons clacked away with the tiles of a million mah jong sets. Chinese restaurants became immensely popular. Such cultural transferences as Chinese checkers, puzzles, lanterns, architecture and clothing took place.

An image was created of the Chinese as wise, enduring, somehow more human than other people. At first this was largely a literary creation. The American fascination with China made Alice Tisdale Hobart's *Oil for the Lamps of China* a best seller, along with *The Bitter Tea of General*

Yen and other novels directed at the mass-circulation magazines. In the nonfiction field books like Carl Crow's *400 Million Customers* and Carl Glick's *Shake Hands with the Dragon* and the early works of Lin Yutang (*My Country and My People*) were immensely popular.

Charlie Chan, the Chinese detective based in Honolulu, became a sort of folk hero after his creator, Earl Derr Biggers, introduced him in the *Saturday Evening Post* in 1925. As the hero of *Post* serials, a string of books and forty-eight films, Charlie Chan became a household figure in the United States — the epitome of the wisdom, conveyed in rather simple-minded aphorisms, of the Chinese.

About the same time Charlie Chan's opposite number, Dr. Fu Manchu, was also a totem of the literary and cinematic imagination. Significantly, perhaps, the same actor (Warner Oland) played both characters from time to time. Fu Manchu was a green-eyed monster of villainy, who with a horde of murderous Burmese dacoits and other followers to do his bidding was perennially trying to conquer the world for his own satanic, but ill-defined purposes. His perennial opponent was the brave and dashing Commissioner Nayland Smith. At the end of almost every encounter the Englishman managed to finish him off, but like Frankenstein's monster he was too valuable a property for his fabricator, Sax Rohmer, to keep in the great beyond.

Even the dastardly machinations of Fu Manchu contributed to the feeling that the Chinese were worthy of respect. So did a sensational novel published in 1929 by Floyd Gibbons, the most celebrated war correspondent of his time, who wore an eye-patch and dashed around the world like a reincarnation of Richard Harding Davis. Gibbons naturally popped up in China from time to time to cover the only war going in a largely peaceful world. In *The Red Napoleon,* serialized in the mass-circulation *Liberty Magazine* and later published as a book, he created an even more monstrous villain than Fu Manchu. The novel has been recalled as a prophesy of the rise of Mao Tse-tung. Actually his central figure was a Mongol, a new Genghis Khan, who suddenly burst upon the world at the head of a horde of warriors. The East would go Communist under his influence and the Red Napoleon would be prevented from world conquest only in the last Western ditch. Gibbons portrayed those horrendous events as occurring between 1933 and 1938.

The one book which struck the deepest roots in the American imagination, however, was the entirely sympathetic novel by Pearl Buck, *The Good Earth,* published in 1931 just as the Japanese began their course of aggression in Manchuria and American sympathy for the beleaguered Chinese was about to reach its peak. "It can almost be said," Harold Isaacs has written, "that for a whole generation of Americans she 'created' the Chinese, in the same sense that Dickens 'created' for so many of us the

General Smedley D. Butler, outspoken marine in Shanghai (1926)

people who lived in the slums of Victorian England."[29] Miss Buck's novel, treating the ordinary Chinese in a maternal but not a condescending manner, described the lives of a peasant, Wang, a stubborn durable sinner, and his wife O-Lan, the patient and devoted wife, mother and grandmother, and their mutual struggle to survive against war, famine, flood and all the adversities the Chinese peasant is heir to.

Both the novel and the film based on it, with the late Paul Muni and Luise Rainer portraying the leading characters, were tremendously influential in casting a new light on the Chinese people and enlisting American sympathies for the Chinese against the Japanese. The book sold more than two million copies, and the film was seen by twenty-three million Americans (and an estimated forty-two million people all over the world).* In these and other novels, Pearl Buck has conveyed her own long-considered impressions of the Chinese, which she herself has defined: "He is not poetic, but extremely realistic, practical rather than artistic. The Chinese artist is never an artist for art's sake. Art is always a means or a philosophy with the Chinese. China could not produce a Matisse or a Gaugin, certainly not a Picasso. There are no Chinese cubists. The Chinese is a loyal father and friend. But this has its limits. He is not fantastically loyal. The loyalty will come to an end if occasion demands it. He is common-sensible about everything . . . He will never die of love. He is not egocentric. He is remote from the maudlin in everything. He is a man of principle, but not to the point of folly."[30]

Another missionary's child, born in China and destined to influence American attitudes toward China with an incalculable force, was the late Henry R. Luce, whose *Time, Life* and *Fortune* have exerted a considerable leverage on public opinion. Luce was an inveterate Sinophile, and his strong-minded opinions were reflected in his publications and their support of the Nationalist cause in all its travail. He never forgot the land of his birth, and though he became, to some extent, a man of the world, he was invariably influenced by his missionary parentage. A Christian and democratic China was his great hope, the eventual atheistic and Communist China his great tragedy.

Doubtless, as publisher of *Time,* he was greatly pleased by the choice of Chiang Kai-shek and his American-educated bride, Soong Mei-ling, to grace the cover of that news magazine as Man and Woman of the Year in 1938. It did not hurt Chiang's cause in the slightest, so far as most Americans were concerned, when he was converted to Christianity on

* "No one was more astonished than I," Pearl Buck has written of *The Good Earth's* success, and she made an "apologetic" appearance in American literary circles. Nevertheless she was dismayed at the "blast from my fellow writers" when she was awarded the Nobel Prize in 1938. Their reaction ever since has made her reluctant to mingle with writers.

Warner Oland as Fu Manchu, one-man Yellow Peril

marrying the daughter of the rich and conservative Soongs, who also happily was the sister of the revered widow of Sun Yat-sen.

During the Thirties the Chinese people rapidly assumed a new and more admirable shape in the eyes of the Americans. They were no longer a horde of heathen but a vast and heroic peasantry resisting both the calamities of their lot and the invasions of the Japanese. A prospective ally naturally is seen in a kindlier light.

The Shanghai Nights had come to an end, and such denizens as Shanghai Lily and Mother Goddam were superimposed with the more virtuous image of O-Lan and her sisters.

15 🌱

The Excluded Japanese

The anti-Japanese feeling of Californians before World War II was almost incredible to outsiders. Native sons, and many adopted sons, regarded Japanese-Americans as both contemptible subhumans and devilishly clever plotters of the coming Japanese attempt at a takeover.

Most of the southern-California Japanese lived either in Little Tokyo in downtown Los Angeles or on their small truck gardens between the western edge of the city and the beaches, where they worked from before sunup to after sundown scratching a living out of the sandy soil, with oil pumps laboring on the Baldwin Hills and Iowa tourists gawking at them from the highways which bisected their fields.

To the small, earth-colored figures bending over their rows of vegetables, boys on bicycles would shout, "Hey, Itchy Scratchy, get a horse."

"That ain't no horse," others would shout, "that's his wife."

After years of hard work, the Japanese truck gardeners and flower growers gradually began to prosper a little. They came to the downtown markets in secondhand trucks instead of pushing their produce into town on carts. The flower shops on San Pedro Street downtown grew larger and more prosperous. A branch of the Yokohama Specie Bank opened up. Japanese manned many of the fruit, vegetable and flower stalls at the Farmers Market on the edge of Beverly Hills.

Still, as they attained the equivalent of middle-class status in the Thirties, they were not respected, trusted or liked. They were always called "Japs." Their hard work, lawfulness and honesty were only resented. If the police rarely had to invade Little Tokyo — even less often than China-town, where fan-tan was as popular as the numbers in Brooklyn — people whispered that the quarter, always dark at night except for a few restaurants, was full of Japanese intelligence officers evaluating the day's intake of military and naval information.

Anyone who lived in Los Angeles, or in other California cities with Japanese communities during the Thirties will recall the silent groan that went up from the rest of the population when the newspapers published the list of valedictorians and other students with the highest scholastic attainments, and invariably they contained twice as many Japanese names as their share of the high-school graduating classes warranted.

The Japanese simply couldn't win. Their response to the demands of American citizenship, their diligence and quietness counted for little or nothing. Their virtues could have been summed up for most other Californians in two words: cheap vegetables. They were restricted from owning homes in most parts of the cities by zoning ordinances. When there were reports of a Japanese family trying to buy a house in one of the Los Angeles suburbs, the whole dreary tract suddenly sprouted signs reading JAPS, KEEP MOVING! And California, it should be added, exhibited only the more virulent aspects of anti-Japanese prejudice in the United States which, in the years following World War I, was probably more deeply felt than anti-Semitism or anti-Negro sentiments.

The prejudice extended to the Issei, first-generation Japanese, and the Nisei, or second-generation, alike. Of all immigrants who came to America, they alone were to be denied the possibility of Americanization, despite all the solid evidence that no nationality, not the blondest, fairest or bluest-eyed, made better or worthier citizens. It was partly racial, of course; partly a reflection of American resentment of Japanese policy; partly an economic matter, rooted in the Japanese ability to outwork native Americans, and later the fact that Japanese-owned farmland around the cities, once almost worthless, was becoming valuable with the growth of those cities, especially Los Angeles.

And yet, for all the contempt with which they were treated, they loved California and America. It was a pity more Californians couldn't have read the letter written by Tani Koitabashi, a Nisei, on the occasion of his return to California after a stay in Japan:

"Sayonara, Japan, I am going home. Farewell, O nation of age-old traditions . . . where a coalition government fails to coalesce and politics is still in its rompers stage; where the uniform is a badge of superiority and gold-teeth a sign of affluence . . .

"Goodbye to garret-like apartment houses and match-box homes, to high-walled gates and foot-square gardens. I am going to a land of spacious gardens . . . where baths are taken individually and not collectively, and are a glory to the plumber's art . . .

"*Domen-nasai* to bulky and unsatisfactory meals; and heaped-up rice bowl and the byproducts of the prodigal bean . . . Farewell, O anemic coffee, you deserve a better fate . . . I am going to a land of sublimated viands, of thick wedges of apple-pie and the juicy steaks on the plank; where asparagus is harvested from the field and not from a tin, and lettuce is a whole meal instead of a garnish; of scrunchy celery and the melting melon; the five-layer cake with its inch-thick chocolate frosting.

"Goodbye, O land of contradictions, where the soda bottles pop down instead of up; where theater box offices offer reductions at premieres instead of demanding a premium . . . where self-deprecation is virtue and bluffing a sin. Goodbye, Topsy-Turvy Land.

"I am leaving you for a far-off land where they believe all Japanese are inherently honest and always polite; to a place where all Japanese women are judged by Madame Butterfly standards and considered very cute . . .

"I am going back to a people who are your best friends and yet who keep antagonizing you; who always are trying to understand your viewpoints . . . but who usually end up by misunderstanding you. I long for America. Farewell!"[1]

No homesick tourist from Indiana could have written a more stirring tribute to his native land, and one can only hope that Tani Koitabashi was not rewarded, eight years later, by being "relocated." His attitude, incidentally, was not singular among second-generation Japanese, some of whom were sent to Japan by their parents as students or merely to visit their grandparents. A Tokyo University professor, in an interview published by the *Japan Chronicle* of Kobe, complained that young Japanese-Americans "persist in looking at the Sino-Japanese crisis with American eyes. Even worse, many of them cannot think of the Far East except from the Chinese angle, and the professor has confessed himself at a loss as to how to bring his charges over to the Japanese way of thinking."[2]

1. *Singling Out the Japanese*

Newspapers and magazines, particularly those circulating in the Western states, found it profitable to condemn and ridicule the Japanese. One of the more popular magazine series was Wallace Irwin's "Letters from a Japanese Schoolboy," published in *Collier's* and later in several hard-cover editions. Irwin created the comic figure of Hashimura Togo, the garrulous, arrogant, buck-toothed student. Mostly his stories were good-humored enough but they made a stereotype of the Japanese which the public was willing or eager to accept as a valid generalization. A fair sample of Hashimura's thoughts: "Some frequent Professors are asking the question now: Will White Men and Yellow Man ever Mix? Yes because I have knowledge of the affair. They mix once in San Francisco; they mix once in Vancouver. But such mixing is not good-healthy for the human race because it make broken-glass, pistol-shot, outcry, militia and many other disagreeable noises. Japanese gentleman mixes race with Jiu Jitsu, Irish gentleman with gas-pipe."

During and after World War I, the anti-Japanese campaign became more vociferous in its clamor for further restrictions on Japanese immigration. Much of this sentiment was whipped up by various books which raised the issue of miscegenation. A number of authors, who reached a large audience, were convinced that the Japanese in particular were determined to "pollute" the purity of the Caucasian bloodstream in this country. Shuddering deliciously, Americans read of the "race-mixing" on which Orientals were intent, the result of which would be a race of degenerate, saffron-hued Eurasian-Americans so weak and demoralized they wouldn't be able to hold off the Siamese navy. This specter was raised in particular by three books published in 1916, Madison Grant's *The Passing of the Great Race,* James F. Abbott's *Japanese Expansion and American Policies* and Carl Crow's *Japan and America*. All viewed the Japanese-Americans as the advance-guard of the Japanese army and navy.

Following the war, America lapsed into xenophobia, suspicious and resentful of all foreigners and foreign influences. Our adventures abroad had soured us on relations of any kind beyond our coasts. The mood was receptive for such jeremiads as that of Valentine S. McClatchy, the scion of an Irish-American family with considerable influence over the San Joaquin Valley and the rest of northern California, who was publisher of the Sacramento *Bee,* Modesto *Bee* and Fresno *Bee*. The McClatchy newspapers were liberal-minded on almost every subject except Japanese immigration, which of course was a burning issue in the agricultural valleys of northern California. In 1919 he made a trip to the Orient and came back impregnated with the conviction that the Japanese were planning to "penetrate" the United States. His impressions of a bellicose Japan were conveyed in a long series of articles for his own papers which were reprinted elsewhere and later collected into a pamphlet, *The Germany of Asia,* which was circulated throughout the country.

On his voyage of discovery, McClatchy found the Japanese "ambitious," "courteous," "literate," "generally superior in physical fitness to other peoples." But Japan was "the Germany of Asia, with an ambition somewhat similar to her model . . ."; the samurai spirit survived, and she was planning the conquest of all the Far East. He was particularly outraged by Japanese propaganda-making and the government control over the news which Japan maintained through arrangements with Reuters' and other news agencies allowed to operate only by presenting a favorable view of Japanese actions. He and his wife were visiting Seoul March 1, 1919, when the Japanese military broke up the huge Korean independence demonstrations with "clubbed muskets and swords" and watched "girl students being set upon by Japanese coolies with clubs and stamped upon."[3]

In an editorial published in the Sacramento *Bee,* he warned that the gates must be slammed against further Japanese immigration, particularly the "picture brides" who were allowed to come over and marry Japanese men already in the United States, because "our Japanese population . . . has multiplied six-fold since 1900" and "It has been conclusively proved that the two civilizations will not exist together; that under economic competition, and because of difference in standards of living and in racial characteristics, the Anglo-Saxon is displaced by the Japanese."[4]

The Japanese was undesirable because "he does not assimilate." On the other hand, it was a good thing he didn't intermarry with whites. He simply meant to outbreed us. In his native land, McClatchy pointed out, "they forbid by very stringent laws the immigration into Japan of Chinese and Korean labor." If we were to continue granting Japan privileges she didn't extend to other countries, he warned, the Japanese population in the United States would rise to two million by the 1960's and one hundred million by the mid-twenty-first century. "Long before then the white race would have succumbed in the economic competition and the world's glorious Republic would have become a province of Japan!"[5]

McClatchy was so consumed by the righteousness of his cause that he resigned his position as the publisher of his family's three newspapers, established the California Joint Immigration Committee and devoted the rest of his life to agitating against the Japanese in America. He was not the usual racist, never indulged in name-calling or advocated violence of any kind, but was simply obsessed by the menace of a growing Japanese-American population.

Under his influence, according to one authority, Wallace Irwin produced a widely circulated novel, *Seed of the Sun,* serialized in the *Saturday Evening Post* in 1920 and published as a book a year later. Certainly it was part of McClatchy's anti-Japanese campaign, as was *The Pride of Palomar,* a novel written by another best-selling California-based author, Peter B. Kyne, which was serialized by Hearst's *Cosmopolitan.* The Anglo hero of *The Pride of Palomar* observed that "when a member of the great Nordic race fuses with a member of a pigmented race, both parties to the union violate a natural law," and argued that "we ought to have Jim Crow cars for these cocksure sons of Nippon."[6]

Those same years following World War I saw a number of "scientific" attempts to prove that intermarriage between the races — with particular reference to the Asian, rather than African — would bring eventual disaster to the whites. Anthropologists since discredited were studying various races and primitive societies, analyzing bone structure and speech patterns to show that the Nordic race was superior to the others. One anthropologist confirmed a considerable body of prejudice when he testified before a congressional committee that the Negro's mental capacity was only eighty percent of the white man's, the yellow and brown races ninety-five percent. The easy conclusion was that the children of mixed marriages would be that much less intelligent than their parents, and back down the ladder of evolution.

One of the more dramatic literary interventions on this subject was Lothrop Stoddard's *The Rising Tide of Color,* published in 1920 and so immediately popular that new printings came off the presses in three successive months. A veteran worker in the same vineyard, Madison Grant, contributed an introduction warning that "for the white man to share his blood with, or entrust his ideals to, brown, yellow, black, or red men" was "suicide pure and simple."[*]

Stoddard's own rhetoric was more restrained and "scientific," which of course made his argument all the more credible. He believed that the Western nations could not maintain their supremacy in the Orient forever, but that when they were forced to withdraw they should make certain that the Asians would not expand into other parts of the world; tit was not for tat. If Westerners tried to hold back the Asian resurgence, he wrote, the result would be a welding of "Japanese imperialism and Chinese nationalism in a 'sacred union' " which would lead to "at the very least the prompt expulsion of the white man from every foothold in eastern Asia." (The bugaboo of an alliance between China and Japan has always been the secret nightmare of Pacificists. It still is, and should be.)

He quoted the pronouncement of the Japanese military in 1916, in which it was boasted that "we are now well astride of our steed, China . . . As for America — that fatuous booby with much money and much sentiment, but no cohesion, no brains of government; stood she alone we should not need our China steed. Well did my friend speak the other day when he called her people a race of thieves with the hearts of rabbits. America, to any warrior race, is not as a foe, but as an immense melon, ripe for the cutting . . . North America alone will support a billion people; that billion shall be Japanese with their slaves. Not arid Asia, nor worn-out Europe . . . but North America is fit for our people . . . That

---

[*] It didn't hurt Stoddard's cause that his book was published by the respectable and prestigious firm of Charles Scribner's Sons.

continent so succulently green, fresh, and unsullied . . . It shall be ours by the higher, nobler right of conquest."[7]

The late World War had immeasurably weakened the West in its ability to withstand such onslaughts. "It was the Nordics — the best of all human breeds who suffered far and away the greatest losses . . . Everywhere it was the same story: the Nordic went forth eagerly to battle, while the more stolid Alpine and, above all, the little brunette Mediterranean either stayed at home or even when at the front showed less fighting spirit, took fewer chances, and oftener saved their skins." He quoted with approval the statement of his mentor, Madison Grant, that "as in all wars since Roman times, from the breeding point of view the little dark man is the final winner."

Even after that disaster in Europe, the white race still had a chance of survival but "decisions — firm decisions — must be made." In America, particularly, "our very race existence" must be preserved as "the sacred heritage of our children." He then launched into his pseudoscientific argument against a fusion of white and colored bloods:

"We have already seen that nothing is more *unstable* than the racial makeup of a people, while, conversely, nothing is more *unchanging* than the racial divisions of mankind. We have seen that true amalgamation is possible only between members of the same race-stock, while in crossings between stocks even as relatively near together as the main divisions of the white species, the race-characters do not really fuse but remain distinct in the mixed offspring and tend constantly to resort themselves as pure types by Mendelian inheritance. Thus a country inhabited by a mixed population is really inhabited by different races, one of which always tends to dominate and breed the other out — the outbred strains being lost to the world forever."[8]

The point of all his hastily ingested anthropology and biology was that "the admission of aliens should, indeed, be regarded just as solemnly as the begetting of children, for the racial effect is essentially the same." After much more discussion of "race-values," "race-heritage," "crossbreeding" and "alien blood," he asserted that the hope of the American future was its undefiled "colonial stock," which was "immensely prolific before the alien tide wrought its sterilizing effect." Half the American population could boast of that sacred "old blood," and he was willing to concede that "many millions of the immigrant stock are sound in quality and assimilable in kind."[9]

But now was the time to "stabilize our ethnic being," and refuse to "lay any sacrificial unction to our souls," by which he apparently meant a stronger resistance to liberal or humanitarian ideas about immigration. Barriers must be erected against "a perfect deluge of colored men into white lands," and hearts must be hardened against "the desperate seekers after fuller life," many of which already had "crept and crawled through every crevice" in the immigration laws. If Americans yielded to compassion, "the diminished white world would be faced with an even louder clamor for admittance — backed by an increased power to enforce the colored will."

He was fascinated by the faddish new science of eugenics, which he interpreted in ways that must have annoyed or alarmed at least some of the eugenicists. The conclusion he drew from their findings was that "the more primitive a type is, the more prepotent it is. This is why crossings with the negro are uniformly fatal. Whites, Amerindians, or Asiatics — all are alike vanquished by the more primitive, generalized, and lower negro blood." The more imminent danger, however, came from the possibility "the white stocks may be swamped by Asiatic blood." Stoddard's stern prescription: "rigid Oriental exclusion"[10]

The missing ingredient in most of these horror tales of mass miscegenation was the easily provable fact that Orientals, particularly the Chinese and Japanese, were even less eager for intermarriage than Caucasians. They had their own theories, much deeper-rooted in their traditions, about the purity of Chinese or Japanese blood. Those who married whites were considered to have dishonored themselves and their ancestors.

2. *The Exclusion Act*

After twenty years of earnest effort, the anti-Japanese forces in the Western states began making their point with the rest of the nation in 1923–1924. The result was the Immigration Act of 1924, better and more accurately known as the Japanese Exclusion Act. Few congressional measures have matched it for unabashed racial discrimination.

Recognizing the seriousness of the anti-Japanese sentiment in this country, the Japanese government adopted a flexible stance, particularly in regard to the "picture bride" system by which passports were given Japanese girls who had been selected for marriage by Japanese immigrants in the United States. The arranged marriage had always been repugnant to the stubborn American belief in romantic love and marriages based, whether anyone admitted it or not, on sexual attraction, though a study of Japanese divorce statistics would have convinced anyone that picture brides were more likely to stay married than American girls smothered in orange blossoms and high expectations.

There were other than sociological objections to the system, however, as the most influential newspaper in the Southwest, the Los Angeles *Times,* bluntly stated them: "There are now more than 30,000 children in the State of Japanese parentage, native-born; they possess all the rights of leasing and ownership held by white children born here. . . . The birth statistics seem to prove that the danger is not from Japanese soldiers, but

Lothrop Stoddard, racial alarmist

from the picture brides. The fruitfulness of those brides is almost uncanny . . . Here is a Japanese problem of sufficient gravity to merit serious consideration. We are threatened with an over-production of Japanese children. First come the men, then the picture brides, then the families. If California is to be preserved for the next generation as a 'white man's country' there must be some movement started that will restrict the Japanese birth-rate in California. When a condition is reached in which two children of Japanese parentage are born in some districts for every white child, it is time something else was done than making speeches about it in the American Senate."[11]

When the chairman of the House Committee on Immigration began writing a bill calling for total Japanese exclusion, the Japanese government agreed not to give any more passports to picture brides. But that didn't satisfy the exclusionist movement. The immigration bill presented to Congress for passage in 1924, with all its juggling of statistics and euphemistic evasions, would in effect shut off all but a handful of immigrants from Japan.

Newspapers all over the country supported the proposed legislation, including those in communities without a single Japanese resident. The Syracuse *Post-Standard* declared that Representative Albert Johnson, of Washington, who was the author of the measure, "is writing a bill for all states, not for the Pacific Coast alone." To the Chicago *Tribune,* the leading organ of isolationism, "The industry, thrift and ability of the Japanese have already put many American farmers and small tradesmen out of business. Do we want this to continue?" One of the few papers to raise a strong objection was the independent Springfield *Republican,* which claimed that Western Congressmen were "imposing their will on the enormous majority of the American people." That "enormous majority," however, was apathetic and if it was opposed it certainly did not make itself heard.[12]

There were other opposing voices raised, however, both in Congress and in the Executive Department of the government, John V. A. MacMurray, the chief of the State Department's Far Eastern division, who had always advocated firm resistance to Japanese expansion, wrote that Japan could hardly be expected to live up to the agreements reached at the Washington Conference if she were insulted by having her people entirely barred from entering the United States. He warned in January 1924 that if the Japanese provisions in the immigration bill were not liberalized, the measure would "make difficult, if not impossible, that sympathetic and wholehearted cooperation, in the area of the Pacific Ocean, which the results of the Washington Conference have brought within the range of practical realization." Senator McKeller of Tennessee warned that "holding Japan down to 246 [immigrants] is virtually an exclusion law; to all intents and purposes it is an exclusion law."

Professor A. A. Smertenko of Hunter College testified at a congressional hearing that the "scientific" bases of arguments for Japanese exclusion were unsound, citing the works of Houston Chamberlain, Madison Grant and Lothrop Stoddard, "Consciously or not, they base this fantastic farrago of cephalic indices, skull sutures, brain weights, intelligence tests, and cultural stages on the very earliest and most antiquated ethnological postulates and shun the later investigations and demonstrated conclusions . . . The situation has no parallel in science; it is as if some radio amateur, troubled by a nightmare, had studied the lightning experiments and accepted the conclusions of Benjamin Franklin and on the basis of that knowledge had published books and magazine articles alarming the public with his hysterical dread of the dangers of electricity."[13]

Senator Reed of Pennsylvania also tried to counteract the anti-Japanese current in Congress with an eloquent plea for more generous treatment of the Japanese on April 8, 1924. "The Japanese government does not wish to colonize the United States," he declared on the Senate floor, "and does not wish to force her emigration into our ports. But they are a proud people, everybody knows that, and they would resent an exclusion law just as we would resent an exclusion law passed by Japan. They would resent it particularly because they realize as we must that there is no sense in it, that we do not need an exclusion law in order to keep down the number of Japanese in this country. They would resent it finally because it is the same thing as saying to them that they do not keep their plighted word with this country."

Just two days later, on April 10, the Japanese Ambassador to Washington, Masanao Hanihara, unwittingly killed off all chances that the bill might be defeated. That day he wrote Secretary of State Charles Evans Hughes, who had already deplored the bill as unnecessary and of doubtful legality, that "to Japan, the mere fact that a few hundreds or thousands of her nationals will or will not be admitted into the domains of other countries is immaterial so long as no question of national susceptibility is involved. The important question is whether Japan, as a nation, is or is not entitled to the proper respect and consideration of other nations."

The Japanese exclusion clause in the new immigration bill, he wrote, singled out the Japanese "as a nation, stigmatizing them as unworthy and undesirable in the eyes of the American people."

Then he added the fateful paragraph: "I realize, as I believe you do, the grave consequences which the enactment of the measure retaining that particular provision would inevitably bring upon the otherwise happy and mutually advantageous relations between our two countries."

Two words, "grave consequences," were pounced upon by Senator Henry Cabot Lodge and other members of the Pacific-minded group in the Senate and denounced as a "veiled threat." Ambassador Hanihara tried to repair the damage by protesting that he had not intended to make any threats, but Lodge and the other Pacificists were in the saddle. Even Senator Reed changed his mind and voted for exclusion, though it meant "the waste of much of the results of twenty years of excellent diplomacy . . . a loss of part of the good relations that followed the prompt and friendly action of America after the Japanese earthquake of last year."

The bill was passed, and President Calvin Coolidge refused to veto it, though regretting "the impossibility of severing from it the exclusion provision which, in the light of existing law, affects especially the Japanese." The reason, guessed the Baltimore *Sun*, was political, rather than moral. Coolidge recognized the injustice of the measure and had worked hard behind the scenes to persuade Congress not to pass it. "There is some doubt," the *Sun* added, "whether a veto would be sustained. Consequently, in asking that he veto the bill, it is asked that he pursue a policy which may have no parliamentary effect. And at the same time it may have a far-reaching political effect, for it would be likely to injure the President on the Pacific Coast in the fall campaign."[14]

With little regard for the humiliation it inflicted on the Japanese so quickly after they had shown a conciliatory attitude at the Washington Conference, the United States rejoiced in its small, mean moment of discrimination. To us it was merely one of those temporary triumphs of unreason, which could be rectified in time. Madame Butterfly had become a picture bride in the American imagination, but American generosity would triumph in the end.

In Japan, now so impatient, sensitive to slights and full of national pride, the news struck like a shock wave. The evidence on the Japanese reaction was unanimous: it was the bitterest insult ever offered the nation. Both the Japanese and Americans in Japan testified to that.

"By a curious coincidence," Yusuke Tsurumi wrote in *Contemporary Japan,* published in 1927, "the Immigration Act broke in upon the meditations of the Japanese people at a moment when the nation was bleeding from the wounds inflicted by the greatest calamity ever visited upon mankind by earthquake and fire . . . A tremendous amount of the national capital lay in utter ruins, more than two hundred thousand people had been killed by falling buildings or burnt to death in a raging whirlwind of fire, industries were prostrate, vast regions devastated, and national economy subjected to awful strains at every point. In the midst of our afflictions, the nation that had literally shaken open our gates — waved aside a long standing agreement with us and slammed its own gates in our face."

Attempts to explain the congressional action as a result of sectional prejudice — as a phase of the old California-Japan War — were met with incomprehension. A few years before the act was passed, Henry W. Taft had accompanied a party of prominent Americans, mostly financiers involved in Far Eastern trade and banking operations (Frank A. Vanderlip, president of the City Bank; Lyman J. Gage, former Secretary of the Treasury; George Eastman, Seymour L. Cromwell and others with substantial reasons for fostering Japanese-American friendship), on a goodwill visit to Japan.

Taft had tried to explain to his hosts the narrow geographic range of anti-Japanese prejudice in the United States, though looked at another way it meant the Japanese were disliked most by the people they lived among. The Japanese, Taft wrote, could not understand that "under our Constitutional system where the rights or convenience or prosperity of the several states are directly involved it is only in the most extreme cases, and reluctantly, that the national government will intervene under the treaty-making power to render nugatory what an individual state regards as wise domestic policy. Japan being used to a consolidated and centralized system of government, having no feature of confederation by which, as in the United States, constituent political units retain a part of their sovereign powers, it was not surprising that even intelligent Japanese . . . should not understand why when a single state enacts laws threatening the good feeling with a foreign country, the federal government should not at once intervene."[15]

California's anti-Japanese legislation could thus be explained away, but not the action of the Congress. There was, in fact, no explaining it away. It had to stand as a calculated insult. Arnold J. Toynbee, then professor of international history at the University of London, wrote that "The cloud that descended upon Japanese-American relations in 1924 cast its long shadow over Australia and India and Kenya and the South African Union . . . if the storm broke in the Pacific, there would be heavy weather in the Indian Ocean."

Toynbee considered that the American action was all but intolerable to the Japanese. "In the Washington Conference, the United States cooperated with the British Empire to restore, politely but insistently, the balance of power in the Pacific and the Far East. The earthquake followed the clump as a crowning economic blow. The United States Restriction of Immigration Act of 1924 followed the Washington Conference as an overt political humiliation."

The agitation in Japan, as Toynbee observed, was alarming. "In Japan the news of the enactment aroused the nation for several weeks to a dangerous pitch of excitement. On the 31st May and the 4th June two persons committed suicide as a protest against the passage of the Act, and on the 10th June the funeral of one of them was the occasion of a great popular demonstration. On the 5th June, when Mr. Woods sailed for the United States, crowds attended to bid him farewell as a mark of esteem for his person and of regret for the good-will between the two nations which seemed to be departing with him. In Tokyo, on the 7th June, a dance at the Imperial Hotel, at which Japanese as well as Westerners were present, was interrupted by a party of men, several of them dressed in Samurai costume, who protested to their fellow-countrymen present against dressing and dancing like Americans and keeping Western company. On the 1st July an unknown Japanese entered the precincts of the American embassy, lowered the American flag, cut it in two, and escaped without being arrested. These were a few incidents which stood out against a background of public agitation."[16]

American observers were also impressed by the bitterness and depth of the Japanese reaction. They saw signs on Japanese storefronts reading: "Yankee, don't come here. I sell no American goods." The Associated Press correspondent in Tokyo reported that "nation-wide demonstrations and mass prayer meetings" were being held "at all the Shinto shrines throughout the country." In his study *The Far Eastern Policy of the United States,* A. Whitney Griswold summed up the damage done Japanese-American relations. "It seems safe to say that the American people have never resented any policy pursued by Japan in China or elsewhere as deeply, as unanimously, and with as poignant a sense of injustice as the Japanese have resented the statutory exclusion of 1924."

The most dangerous aspect of Japan's justified resentment was the encouragement and added support it gave the right-wing, militarist faction. The Japanese militants sponsored mass meetings and stepped up the dissemination of propaganda urging that Japan renounce all allegiances to the West, unite the colored races and proceed forthwith down the road to conquest.

For fifty years the military faction in Japan had been working to prepare the nation for a war against the United States, an effort in which their most valuable and most unwitting collaborators were the anti-Japanese propagandists in the United States. They kept reprinting Satori Kato's *Mastery of the Pacific,* originally published in 1909 and only one of a large number of such books and pamphlets in which the authors boasted of what Homer Lea, Jack London and others warned against. In *Mastery of the Pacific,* Kato boasted that "In the event of war Japan could, as if aided by a magician's wand, overrun the Pacific with fleets manned by men who have made Nelson their model and transported to the armadas of the Far East the spirit that was victorious at Trafalgar.

"Whether Japan avows it or not, her persistent aim is to gain the mastery of the Pacific. Although peace seems to prevail over the world at present, no one can tell how soon the nations may be engaged in war. It does not need the English alliance to secure success for Japan. That alliance may be dissolved at any moment, but Japan will suffer no defeat. Her victory will be won by her men, not by armor-plate — things weak by comparison."[17]

Ten years later, in the same vein, the militarist Tokyo *Hochi* warned, "That age in which the Anglo-Japanese alliance was the pivot and American-Japanese cooperation an essential factor of Japanese diplomacy is gone. In future we must look not eastward for friendship but westward. Let the Bolsheviki of Russia be put down and the more peaceful party put in power. In them Japan will find a strong ally. By marching then westward to the Balkans, to Germany, to France, to Italy, the greater part of the world may be brought under our sway. The tyranny of the Anglo-Saxons at the [Versailles] Peace Conference is such that it has angered gods and men."

Even less restrained was the fulmination of another Japanese prophet: "Fifty millions of our race wherewith to conquer and possess the earth! To begin with, we now have China! Far shall we ride upon her! Even as Rome rode Latium to conquer Italy, and Italy to conquer the Mediterranean; even as Napoleon rode Italy and the Rhenish States to conquer Germany, and Germany to conquer Europe; even as England today rides her colonies and her so-called allies to conquer her robust rival, Germany — even so we shall ride China. So becomes our paltry 50,000,000 race 500,000,000 strong; so grow our paltry hundreds of millions of gold into billions . . .

"But, using China as our steed, should our first goal be the land? India? Or the Pacific, the sea that must be our very own, even as the Atlantic is now England's? The land is tempting and easy, but withal dangerous. Did we begin there, the coarse white race would too soon awaken, and combine, and forever immure us within our long since grown intolerable bounds. It must, therefore, be the sea; but the sea means the Western Americas and all the islands between; and with those must soon come Australia, India. And then the battling for the balance of world-power, for the rest of North America. Once that is ours, we own and control the whole — a dominion worthy of our race!"[18]

The bluster of Japanese militarists was quickly picked up and translated in the United States, much of it by the anti-Japanese *Literary Digest* — the *Time* or *Newsweek* of its day — and reached a mass audience. It was also quoted by such commentators as Lothrop Stoddard, with predictable effect. Thus prejudice fed fear, and fear nourished hatred with all the consequences such hatred entails.

3. *Japan Breaks Loose*

Seven years after the Japanese Exclusion Act was passed by Congress, after long and careful preparation, Japan demonstrated to the world that she would follow the path indicated by her jingoists and militarists. In the fall of 1931, she broke all previous agreements by forcefully expanding her holdings in Manchuria. Under the protocols of the Portsmouth Peace Conference of 1905, Japan leased Port Arthur from Russia and received control of the South Manchurian Railway between Port Arthur and Chang-

Chung. Later agreements extended Japanese control over railroads in that area, mining and agricultural ventures, and trading rights in northern Manchuria and eastern Inner Mongolia.

For a long time, however, the Japanese had believed Manchuria should be hers entirely, regardless of Chinese and Russian interests. She had stationed the Kwantung Army there and allowed it to become an independent satrapy, a power unto itself, with only the loosest control from Tokyo. The Kwantung Army, however, was Japanese and no amount of polite shrugging in the foreign ministry in Tokyo could excuse its actions. Japan, in fact, was just as responsible for the Kwantung Army as the American people were for the Japanese Exclusion Act.

The overt aggression in Manchuria had long been foreshadowed by the psychosis of nationalism developing in the islands, encouraged by military and naval successes, provoked by British condescension and American racial hostility, inflamed by the opportunities presented by a crumbling of the old order in the Far East (particularly the weakness of Soviet Russia, with her Siberian defenses still in disarray). As far back as 1915, Thorstein Veblen, in an essay titled "The Opportunity of Japan" (no echo of Homer Lea but a foreboding of trouble nonetheless), noted the advancing "spiritual disintegration" brought on by Japan's rapid industrialization and too-rapid modernization.

Veblen foresaw that the dynamics of change would compel Japan to move aggressively within a decade or two.

"If this new-found efficiency," he wrote, "is to serve the turn for the dynastic aggrandisement of Japan, it must be turned to account before the cumulatively accelerating rate of institutional deterioration [by which Veblen meant the "Spirit of Old Japan," the true strength of its people] overtakes and neutralizes the cumulatively declining rate of gain in material efficiency; which should, humanly speaking, mean that Japan must strike, if at all, within the effective lifetime of the generation that is now coming to maturity . . . the imperial government must throw all its available force, without reservation, into one headlong rush; since in the nature of the case no second opportunity of the kind is to be looked for."

Veblen looked even farther into the future when he foresaw the ease with which Japan, at the insistence of a victorious United States, would abandon the concept of the emperor as divine. "As soon as her people shall have digested the western state of science and technology and have assimilated its spiritual contents, the 'Spirit of Old Japan' will, in effect, have been dissipated. Ravelings of its genial tradition will still trail at the skirts of the new era, but as an asset available for the enterprise of dynastic politics the 'Spirit of Old Japan' will have little more than the value of a tale that is told. There will doubtless continue to float through the adolescent brain of Young Japan some yellow vapor of truculence, such as would under other skies be called *el valor español,* and such as may give rise to occasional exploits of abandon, but the joy of living in obscure privation and contumely for the sake of the Emperor's politics and posthumous fame will be lost to the common man."

Education and the spread of knowledge would "unavoidably act to dissipate all substantial belief in the opera bouffe mythology that makes up the state religion and supplies the foundation of the Japanese faith in the Emperor's divine pedigree and occult verities; for these time-worn elements of Shinto are even less viable under the exacting mechanistic discipline of modern industry than are the frayed remnants of the faiths that conventionally serve as articles of belief among Christian peoples."[19]

The leaders of the Japanese government realized in 1931 that what Veblen glimpsed in 1915 was coming true; that they had to exploit the remaining medievalism in the Japanese character, the residue of the samurai spirit, before chauvinism began its irreversible decline.*

Thus the outbreak in Manchuria. On the night of September 18, 1931, the Kwantung Army, supported by the Japanese army of occupation in Korea, drove into northern Manchuria and occupied Mukden, the Manchurian capital. The excuse was that Chinese soldiers had blown up a stretch of track on the South Manchurian Railway, and the Kwantung Army was forced to protect Japanese interests. (An investigating commission from the League of Nations later found that an express train traveling fifty miles an hour had passed over the "wrecked" section of track twenty minutes after the explosion was supposed to have occurred.) American correspondents arriving in Japanese-occupied Mukden learned that Japanese in plain clothes, but carrying rifles and wearing armbands, had infiltrated the capital several days before the railroad incident they manufactured. At 10 P.M. September 18, thousands of Japanese soldiers were in position to occupy all the strategic points in Mukden in one rush.

Tokyo's protests that the hotheads in command of the field army in Manchuria had taken matters into their own hands were unacceptable to the West. It was generally recognized that a dangerous situation had been created, with Japan pressing against Soviet territory in northern Manchuria and beginning the dismemberment of China. But the rest of the world had been presented with a *fait accompli,* and there was no determined effort made to discredit Japanese claims that they had acted in self-defense against Chinese "banditry."

President Herbert Hoover, an Old China Hand but no sentimentalist, believed that the United States, struggling with an economic crisis, could not afford to identify herself with Chinese interests to the extent of

---

* Carl Randau and Leane Zugsmith in their *The Setting Sun of Japan* (1942) reported that in the decade before World War II began ordinary Japanese were becoming Americanized. "They like American movies, American slang, American baseball. They like their American relatives."

threatening intervention. His attitude remained passive even as the Kwantung Army expanded its holdings throughout Manchuria and proclaimed the autonomous state of Manchukuo.

Others in the administration and in his party were more actively alarmed by the Japanese action. "That," wrote Senator William E. Borah in a magazine article early in 1932, "is what Japan is today, an outlaw nation. In face of increasing evidence that the leading countries of the world are entirely opposed to its war in Manchuria, Japan steadily goes ahead completing its conquest."[20]

Hoover's Secretary of State, Henry L. Stimson, went as far as he could, presumably, by declaring a "non-recognition" policy. No forceful means would be used to turn the Japanese out of Manchuria, but her conquest would be frowned upon continually as ungentlemanly and unacceptable. His idea, as one historian recently has viewed it, was the seedling of global morality; the eventual fruit of which, perhaps, was the American intervention in South Viet Nam and the conviction that the United States must keep the peace wherever it is broken or threatened.

Stimson, Akira Iriye has written, "saw little distinction between Asia and Europe as theaters of international conflict. His policy of non-recognition implied that he would not recognize any Japanese rules that were not universally applicable. Just because Japan was an Asian nation, it did not follow that it had the right to enunciate new principles and policies and disregard the existing precepts, however Western oriented these might be. . . . Throughout the Manchurian episode Stimson phrased his policy primarily in the form of rebuking Japan, not of helping China . . . Once aggression was checked, he assumed that things would return to normal."[21]

No American interests were directly threatened in the Japanese takeover of Manchuria, but Stimson was determined, in the little time left to the Hoover Administration, to make the Japanese suffer for their conquest. Embargoes, economic sanctions, boycotts were considered, but President Hoover remained impassive and the cooperation of other nations was not forthcoming. "I was soon to realize," as Hoover wryly recalled in his memoirs, "that my able Secretary [of State] was at times more of a warrior than a diplomat."

More than a warrior, however, Stimson was trained as a lawyer and was convinced that nations had to abide by the legalities. He tried to persuade the rest of the Cabinet that sanctions against Japan, at least, should be attempted, but seemingly he was the only high official in the Hoover Administration who sensed that the night the Japanese suddenly swarmed over Mukden was, as much as any other precursive event, the beginning of the Second World War. Even the flamboyant Secretary of War, Patrick J. Hurley, opposed him. At one Cabinet meeting, Stimson noted in his diary, Hurley "gently turned to Manchuria and suggested that we were making a mistake to get into it at all; that the Japanese were going to seize Manchuria anyhow, and we were simply letting our country in for a rebuff and a loss of prestige. He did it gently but gave the army view which he had evidently been getting from some of his generals. So it was necessary for me to give a pretty thorough talk in reply, which I did with some vigor."

Other Western governments, however, were also cool to Stimson's proposals for proceeding against Japan. They were not convinced, as he was (rightly), that Japan was unprepared to take on any greater military tasks at the moment than the "pacification" of Manchuria. Documents since uncovered showed the Japanese war and naval ministries were both fearful of becoming engaged in hostilities with the United States at that time. They needed years to expand their base on the mainland and develop the resources of Manchuria to build up their war machine.

Only Stimson among the world's statesmen seemed to grasp the fact that aggressors must be punished quickly, for the price of their aggressions will be much greater in the long run. The same international lassitude prevailed when Hitler marched into the Rhineland a few years later.

Though few seemed to realize it at the time, the incident was also a crucial point in America's passage to a Pacific Destiny. Particularly in regard to China, the United States in the past had passively benefited from British imperialism even while piously denouncing it. The decisions and actions had been undertaken by Britain, which now refused to decide or act. The matter was lamely referred to the League of Nations, which was even more impotent; the Chinese forces under the regime of Chiang Kai-shek, now established in Nanking, retreated below the Great Wall, and the dithering of the great powers only encouraged Japan to stay on course.

Public opinion in the West simply refused to take Japanese aggression in such a remote corner of the world, with all the complications of railway agreements and zones of influence and treaties dating back to 1905, as a matter of present or future concern. The American attitude was most pungently expressed, perhaps, in the jazzy isolationism of the New York *Daily News,* which editorialized, "Let's shinny on our own side of the street . . . we have no right to sit on the safety valve of Japanese expansion." Even the Pacific-minded Hearst press was undismayed by the dismemberment of China: "We SYMPATHIZE. But it is NOT OUR CONCERN." Pacificism was at its lowest ebb since the sailing of the *Empress of China.*

Edgar Snow, as a correspondent long based in China, believed that Japan would have moved earlier toward expanding on the Asian mainland if it had not been for fearing an American punitive reaction. "She had waited years to see what choice America would finally make; to renounce her part in the European overlord position in China, leaving the colonial powers to find their own way out of Asia; or to accept the role of leading overlord and herself become the outright surviving champion of colonialism; or to conciliate and support Japan as the last best hope of imperialist leadership and countervailing power against the 'menace of Russia.' Japan's conquest of Manchuria was the big test. With that the United States had to put up or shut up about the future of the Western Pacific."[22]

When Franklin D. Roosevelt took over the presidency in 1932, Japan hoped for a relaxation of tensions with the United States, during which she could prepare further incursions against Chinese territory. United States Ambassador Joseph C. Grew in Tokyo wrote that "the Japanese press is unanimously pleased with the election results, first because they foresee a tariff policy more favorable to them, and second because it means the passing of Mr. Stimson whom they consider personally responsible for most of their troubles with the world over Manchuria."[23]

President Roosevelt soon disappointed them. Always a Sinophile and long suspicious of Japanese intentions, he was convinced that Stimson's firm-as-possible policy in the Far East was right. Raymond Moley, then one of his closest advisers, wrote that shortly before the inaugural he and Rexford G. Tugwell, another adviser, spent hours arguing against the Stimson policy. "Roosevelt," he recalled in *After Seven Years* (1939), "put an end to the discussion by looking up and recalling that his ancestors used to trade with China. 'I have always had the deepest sympathy for the Chinese,' he said. 'How could you expect me not to go along with Stimson on Japan?' "

During the Shanghai Incident of 1932, when a Japanese expeditionary force fought with Chinese troops, Roosevelt immediately demonstrated the firmness of his attitude. Always a frustrated admiral, as Winston Churchill so shrewdly recognized, he ordered a naval concentration on the Pacific coast. That ominous maneuver caused a split in Japanese militarist circles. The Japanese navy believed that it would have to confront the United States soon or later, but preferably later when the high-seas fleets were built up to parity with the American navy. The army, particularly the aggressive officers of the semi-autonomous Kwantung Army, held that the sudden Russian buildup of their forces in Siberia made the Soviet enemy the more immediately dangerous.

President Roosevelt's firmness, however, had to be limited to strictures on international morality, governed as it was by the political realities of an America struggling to recover from the worst depression in its history. More than any of his predecessors in the White House, he was the self-conscious inheritor of Wilson's moralistic attitude toward foreign affairs.

4. *Undeclared War*

For a half-dozen years Japan digested its Manchurian conquest, then felt the appetite for more Chinese territory. During those years Soviet Russia had reappeared as a power in Far Eastern affairs, its authority bolstered by a sizable army along the southern borders of Siberia; and Mao Tse-tung's Eighth Route Army had disengaged from Nationalist China to conduct its Long March north and recruit new divisions—another power soon to be reckoned with. But Japan proceeded with her plans in the summer of 1937.

"Day and night the *'banzai* parties' escorted soldiers to the trains," as Relman Morin, the chief Associated Press correspondent in Tokyo, wrote. "Cheers and shouting echoed and re-echoed through Tokyo Station. The departing man went directly into the car and stood stiffly at attention in front of the open window. His family, friends, neighbors, and co-workers at the office crowded close to the window. Individuals made little speeches of exhortation. After each one the group would shout *'Banzai'* three times in unison, waving the white flags with the blood-red ball in the center. The soldier neither smiled nor spoke. From time to time he saluted and bowed. The farewell might go on for as much as an hour. Finally, when the train slowly moved, a fierce explosion of *'Banzai'* thundered in the station. The whole length of the boarding platform thundered in the station. It felt and looked like a football rally, the send-off for the Big Game. This ceremony bade the Japanese soldier not Godspeed but glory in China."[24]

The ferocious exploits of those soldiers departing for the Chinese front in an undeclared war soon stunned the Western world. They started with one of those "incidents" so artfully manufactured by the Kwantung Army. On the evening of July 7, 1937, the Japanese forces were conducting maneuvers near the Marco Polo Bridge, twenty miles west of Peking, when they claimed they were fired upon by soldiers of the Chinese 29th Army. On that pretext, the Japanese forces marched down from Manchuria and occupied Peking and Tientsin while Chiang Kai-shek's Nationalist army retreated to the Yellow River line. Japanese bombers destroyed Nankai University while supposedly striking at military targets. The Japanese, with scant regard for world opinion, closed the Yangtze River to foreign shipping and blockaded the coast south of Shanghai. They also bombed Chinese cities with sizable foreign colonies.

Yet, with their curiously convoluted thinking, the Japanese still looked upon the United States as a continuing source of materials to keep their war machine going; United States protests were regarded as knee-jerk reflexes of its moralistic, but militarily supine attitude. A memorandum circulated among officers at the headquarters of the Kwantung Army, which did not hesitate to make its own foreign policy, urged that American rights "in the Philippines and Kwantung" must be respected and it must be the Japanese aim to "promote economic and cultural cooperation," and, it naively added, "if necessary bring about an improved atmosphere by proposing a Pacific defense agreement solely between the two countries."[25]

But American public opinion, indifferent until now to the struggle so dimly perceived, largely because of a mental resistance to Oriental place-names and haphazard instruction in geography, began to sharpen as the Japanese suddenly moved against Shanghai. Every American knew where Shanghai was. It was part of his cinematic dreamworld, as familiar as the smell of candy wrappers and dusty plush.

Again the Japanese fabricated an incident, this time at Shanghai shortly after their war minister declared that China must be "chastized for her insincerity" in not knuckling under to the Imperial Army. There was a shooting scrape at an airdrome outside Shanghai, in which an officer and sailor of the Japanese navy were killed. With suspicious promptness, the Japanese landed troops at Woosung, ten miles north of Shanghai, and the battleship *Idzumo* steamed up the Whangpoo to anchor opposite Shanghai's International Settlement.

On "Black Saturday," August 14, 1937, an air battle erupted over Shanghai as an estimated 1,500,000 Chinese refugees from the countryside being occupied by the Japanese army thronged into the International Settlement. Bombs fell on the crowded streets, some from Japanese planes and others from crippled Chinese bombers attempting to attack the battle-ship *Idzumo,* and two thousand civilians were killed and another twenty-five hundred wounded. A rather high price for the killing of two Japanese. The rest of the world was outraged, and said so loudly and futilely. The Japanese merely went on with the work of occupying more of eastern China.

More eloquently, but with equal futility so far as changing the course of Japanese aggression was concerned, President Roosevelt made his famous quarantine-the-aggressors speech in Chicago on October 5.

"War is a contagion," he declared, "whether it be declared or unde-clared. It can engulf states and people remote from the original scene of the hostilities . . . It seems unfortunately true that the epidemic of world lawlessness is spreading. When an epidemic of physical disease starts to spread, the community approves and joins in a quarantine . . . Peace loving nations can and must find a way to make their wills prevail."

That speech might have fully roused the country, and perhaps other nations as well, if Roosevelt had not suddenly become evasive about how a "quarantine" could be applied and what it would consist of. The motives behind the speech are still a mystery; possibly it was a test of public opinion, or perhaps the President and his advisers hadn't thought out the implications of his suggestion. He had a habit of turning airy — it would have been coyness in a less masculine man — when White House corre-spondents tried to learn the exact meaning of his pronouncements, and this was no exception. He simply refused to spell out what he meant by a quarantine. Others volunteered to give form to the President's proposal. The American Federation of Labor called for a boycott of Japan. Henry L. Stimson, retired to private life, suggested in a letter-to-the-editor two days after the Roosevelt speech that Japanese silk — this was the pre-nylon era — be boycotted in the United States and shipments of oil and rubber to Japan be embargoed. "Let me make it perfectly clear," he added, conscious of his hawkish reputation, "that in my opinion this is not a case where there should be any thought of America sending arms to participate in the strife going on in Asia."[26]

President Roosevelt dropped whatever idea he might have had about "quarantining" Japan, and public opinion subsided. The China coast, after all, was terribly remote; it is always ten times more distant in the American mind when isolationism is the governing mood. Few Americans had more than the faintest idea of how the train of events in the Far East had been placed in motion; some began wondering whether Commodore Perry's mission hadn't all been a mistake, but few realized that, for instance, American financiers had supplied the loans which made the Japanese war against Russia possible thirty-odd years before, that the resultant occupation of Korea and Port Arthur led inescapably to Mukden, Shanghai . . . and very shortly to the ghastly assault on Nanking. Many would have agreed with a carefully thought-out memorandum ex-President Hoover had written during an earlier crisis:

"We must remember some essentials of Asiatic life . . . Time moves more slowly there; political movements are measured in decades or centuries, not in days or months; that while Japan has the military ascendancy today and no doubt could take over parts or all of China, yet the Chinese people possess transcendent cultural resistance; that the mores of the race have carried through a dozen foreign dynasties over 3,000 years . . . No matter what Japan does . . . they will not Japanify China and if they stay long enough they will be absorbed or expelled by the Chinese. For America to undertake this on behalf of China might expedite it, but would not make it more inevitable."[27]

American doubts remained in suspension while the Japanese increased the scope of their aggression and the Nationalist armies began fighting back as hard and well as they knew how. "We were trying to make foreign policy out of morality and neutrality alone," as Herbert Feis observed in *The Road to Pearl Harbor*. President Roosevelt, according to Undersecretary of State Sumner Welles, began considering an embargo against Japan to be enforced by a quasiblockade by British and American naval forces stationed at strategic locations in the Pacific, in the belief that "Japan was already so heavily committed in China that her economy was stretched to the breaking point." He abandoned it, Welles believed, because "he finally decided that public opinion would refuse to support any action that entailed even the remotest possibility of war."

Before that year ended, however, there was to be a jolting reminder from the Japanese that they were finding other interlopers in China intolerable, particularly in the Yangtze Valley. In mid-December 1937 the

Japanese air force was engaged in heavy bombing operations around Nanking, the capital Chiang Kai-shek was forced to abandon at the beginning of his own "long march," which finally ended on the island of Formosa.

The afternoon of December 12, a Sunday, the gunboat U.S.S. *Panay,* the small tanker *Mei-an* and two oil-company launches were anchored about twenty-five miles above Nanking, near the village of Hohsien. The gunboat had retreated upstream after being endangered by Japanese shells during the assault on Nanking. It had removed some members of the American embassy staff and other foreign refugees just before the capital was sacked, many of the women forced into prostitution and thousands of men and boys executed by machine gun squads.

About noon that day two British gunboats and five river steamers, all with the Union Jack painted on their decks, were attacked from the air and bombarded by Japanese shore batteries about twenty-five miles farther up the river. Then came the turn of the *Panay* and her tiny flotilla. A flight of nine Japanese navy planes bombed the gunboat, then strafed her with machine guns while the Americans fought back with armament designed to quell Chinese bandits. Three Americans were killed and many wounded before the gunboat sank. The Japanese planes then machine-gunned the lifeboats pulling away with the survivors, and were joined in the attack by a Japanese army launch. Evidently they hoped to kill off all the witnesses, but among the refugees aboard the *Panay* were American correspondents and a newsreel cameraman who provided irrefutable evidence of the deliberate assault. Ironically, one of those killed was a correspondent for an Italian newspaper who was also the leader of the Fascist party in Shanghai's Italian colony.

That woke up America. Photographs and newsreels showed how the Japanese had attacked an American ship with two large flags spread on her awnings as well as the usual one on her flagstaff. Since the Japanese dropped their bombs from an altitude of seven thousand feet, the *Panay* incident also destroyed the myth that Japanese couldn't possibly make good pilots because of their weak eyesight. The United States demanded indemnity, which the Japanese government quickly granted. As one historian has observed, the Japanese "undoubtedly would have been delighted to pay for the entire [U.S.] Navy on the same basis."

The civilian public in Japan seemed to have taken alarm at the sinking of the *Panay,* according to an American correspondent stationed in Tokyo, who related that "in the days immediately following, individual Japanese men and women stopped Americans on the streets of Tokyo to apologize." Admiral Harry E. Yarnell, commanding the Asiatic Fleet, declared in Shanghai, "United States naval vessels are in Chinese waters for the protection of American citizens, and will remain here as long as the necessity exists."

American indignation mounted when it became known that the Japanese were informed of the *Panay*'s position upriver from Nanking just to prevent such "accidents," and was hardly cooled down by the admission of the Japanese ambassador to Washington that the sinking of the gunboat was a "grave blunder." But the America of 1937 was ill-prepared to make anything more than threatening noises in the aftermath of the sinking of the *Panay*. From their attitude, Homer Lea might have been convinced, if he had lived that long, that the Americans were simply waiting for what he had called "the old doom of the Purple Persian." He would have been dismayed by the Purple Persian attitudes in the War and Navy Departments. In the army and navy high commands, Welles recalled, "the feeling prevailed that anything that might touch off a showdown should be postponed," and only Admiral William D. Leahy, then chief of naval operations, urged that American diplomatic activity be "followed up by the imposition of trade sanctions."

In America, the people awaited the next turn of events in a mood wavering between apathy and apprehension.

In Shanghai, the capital of the Old China Hands, the mood was more hectic. The French Club, Ciro's, Farren's, the Cathay Tower were never gayer or more crowded with big spenders. The profit motive was still highly operative. "While the American government gave abstract rebukes to the Japanese invaders," one American in Shanghai observed, "most American business with China was with the sections they invaded. A similar amount of relief and missionary money went to occupied territory. Everything Americans living under the Japanese did to preserve 'normalcy' in their own affairs, doing the Lord's work or turning an honest penny, helped the Japanese restore 'normalcy' among the conquered Chinese. Furthermore, almost all American organizations in China kept to their pre-war headquarters, in Shanghai, Peking, or the other big cities of the coast. Their top men were stationed there and made trips to Chungking only occasionally, to save the face of the Kuomintang."[28]

5. *"Orange" into "Rainbow"*

A sizable literature exists on the subject of how Japan was persuaded that there was no alternative to attacking American and other nations' possessions throughout the Pacific, and on whether the United States deliberately fostered the sentiment. Much of it is incredibly biased, either defending President Roosevelt's actions or virtually convicting him as a war criminal. In the latter view, Roosevelt was guilty of having "maneuvered" the Japanese into attacking us, even of so deploying the Pacific Fleet that the Pearl Harbor disaster was made inevitable.

There is some substance to the argument that, taking a long but not very humane view of history, war with Japan could have been avoided by a policy based on hard-headed realism. This essentially was Herbert Hoover's attitude — that China could never be "Japanified," though she would suffer enormously in the attempt. All the controversy came down to a question of morality — whether we could abandon the whole of Asia to a brutally militaristic Japan — with an added tug at the other largely emotional issue of giving up the idea of a Pacific Destiny almost as old as the nation itself.

There was also the carefully reasoned disengagement program suggested to the State Department by John V. A. MacMurray, retired United States minister to China and former head of its Far Eastern division, who pointed out that since 1931 China had become a commercial and diplomatic wasteland so far as the United States was concerned while Japan was now "a jealous and irascible and dangerous claimant to the estate." It was time, MacMurray indicated, to reappraise our relations with China and possibly write off the attempt to block Japanese designs west of the Philippines.

"We might in our minds," he wrote, "(1) abate somewhat the rather exaggerated zeal with which we have been accustomed to afford 'protection' to citizens whom we are no longer actually in a position to protect. We might (2) let the other most interested Powers carry the heavy end of the log, go along with them as best we can, and take no marked initiative of our own. While having it in mind (3) to take our superfluous military forces out of China, we might let them dwindle until there comes a time at which to remove them without antagonizing others or breaking too obtrusively with our own practice. And (4) our Asiatic Fleet might similarly be reduced, ship by ship, kept more and more away from Chinese waters and perhaps indeed (now that the Philippines are entering a phase of qualified independence) withdraw practically in toto from the Far East."

As for the Japanese, he added, "We can deal with them fairly and honorably and in a friendly spirit, and we can dispel some of their groundless suspicions — since China is no longer a game worth the candle — we can so deal with that situation as to remove all ground for the jealous fear that we are secretly inciting the Chinese against them; and we can similarly let our conduct make it evident to them that we are not intriguing to egg Russia against them."[29]

Those were the more or less conservative views, cool, detached, realistic. Once the conservative American had been the most vigorous advocate of expansion, because it seemed to be good business. With Japan now a major power, expansion was impossible without a war which cost-accounting analysis indicated would be unprofitable. Let Japan go up against the other long-established power in eastern Asia, Soviet Russia, and the two would knock each other out.

The U.S.S. "Panay," Yangtze gunboat

But it was too late for cold-blooded detachment. Powerful forces of public opinion had been mobilized on behalf of Nationalist China, and they operated on terrain suddenly favorable to them. The sinking of the *Panay* and the rape of Nanking had convinced Americans, possibly a majority of them, that Japan was a villain among nations. Between the summer of 1937 and the spring of 1939, the Gallup public opinion poll showed that the number of Americans regarding themselves as "pro-China" increased from forty-three to seventy-four percent.

Probably many of those becoming pro-Chinese had been converted by the graphic newsreels — the pre-television image-maker — which showed Chinese resistance to the Japanese invaders, the heroism of the Chinese, the brutality of the Japanese. One particularly memorable shot showed a naked Chinese baby sitting alone, wailing, in a street which had just been turned into rubble by Japanese bombers. There were also such documentaries as Joris Ivens's and John Ferno's *The Four Hundred Million* (1938) portraying the Chinese withdrawal inland; factories and universities literally being hauled on bearers' backs.

And there was the incessant drumming of missionary propaganda, now an organized and potent force. After almost a century of laboring in the Chinese vineyard, the American missionaries combined with their sympathizers at home to become a factor in history — the Lord's work had now metamorphosed into the nation's duty. The missionary's voice, raised in condemnation of Japanese aggression, was the most penetrating of all. It was God's will, he contended, that he work and live in zones occupied by the Japanese army, and the United States was duty-bound to protect his person, his missions, his churches, schools and hospitals.

The missionary wielded more political power than might have been imagined. His voice was amplified by the churches and congregations supporting him, and no Congressman could afford to ignore the thousands of letters that flooded his office urging aid for the Chinese cause. Even more pressing were the appeals for protection of the missionaries and their families. The State Department from 1937 onward urged them to leave coastal China and the areas occupied by the Japanese. Some sent their wives and children home, but almost all of them considered it their duty to stay at their posts. Instead of abandoning their Chinese flocks, they declared, they should be protected by the United States Army and Navy, and their government should find a way to halt the Japanese conquest.

During 1938 a highly organized and effective campaign was launched by the missionary interests to halt shipment of raw materials used in manufacturing munitions and military equipment in Japan, to boycott Japanese products, to send medical and other aid to China, to combat a countermovement for the United States to order its citizens and armed forces out of China. In a 1941 survey of the combined efforts of these groups, John W. Masland noted that they succeeded in presenting a highly idealized image of Chiang Kai-shek and his wife to the American people.

The missionary propagandists also centered on picturing the Nationalist government and its officials as valiant and dedicated figures. "They have never failed to point with pride to the fact that a high percentage of the officials of the [Chinese Nationalist] government have been educated in Christian institutions, and that many of them are themselves Christians, including Generalissimo Chiang Kai-shek. Madame Chiang has practically become a saint to them."[30]

Not the least powerful chords struck in this diapason issued from Henry R. Luce's publications. While many Americans accused the President of dragging us into war, the Chinese-born missionary's son believed that Roosevelt was "overcautious . . . At no time did he take the lead. I think he was an isolationist."[31] And his three widely read magazines reflected this opinion.

Thus there was mounting pressure on President Roosevelt to take sterner measures against Japan. At first an ambiguous "moral embargo" to discourage the shipment of aircraft and aircraft parts to Japan was instituted, then controls over the export of scrap iron and steel. Any eagerness on Roosevelt's part to "drag" American into a war was outstripped by events over which he had no control, the agreement between Hitler and Stalin, the start of war in Europe, the Axis formed by Germany, Italy and Japan, the Japanese invasion of French Indo-China.

In the opinion of Herbert Feis (*The Road to Pearl Harbor*) there was little President Roosevelt could have done, given the circumstances, to halt or dissuade or deflect Japan from the course she took. A more forceful attitude would not "have caused Japan to slow up. . . ." Feis wrote. "More probably, I think, it would have caused it to move farther and faster . . . the crisis in the Pacific might well have come during the winter of 1940–1941, instead of the next one."

By then, of course, the army and navy had begun contingency planning in line with those events in Europe and Asia. Before 1938 American planners had prepared for a war against Japan only. The code name for those plans was "Orange." Now it had become apparent that the United States might have to fight a war on two widely separated fronts. The new code name was "Rainbow." Under the conditions of a Rainbow war, the United States would have to devise a global strategy. Of five contingency plans drawn up for Rainbow, three were based on American naval and military forces standing on the strategic defensive in the Pacific, two for offensive action. Despite the fact we were attacked by the Japanese, the decision was made to hold off the Japanese while throwing everything we could spare into the war against Germany and her allies. It was the last great victory for the Atlanticists.

After V–E and V–J Days, the Pacificists came into their own. A new Pacific Destiny was just around the corner, the corner we have yet to turn after three Asian wars within one generation.

16

Ocean of Destiny?

> We must carry out our general task with the tactical purpose of *getting
> the enemy out of his natural environment* . . . make him feel like a
> cornered beast wherever he may move. Then his moral fiber will begin
> to decline.
>
> — CHE GUEVERA, 1967

Shortly after the beginning of this century, President Theodore Roosevelt,
as the standard-bearer of Pacific expansion in his time, proclaimed that
America would find imperial greatness in the Pacific world. "The Mediterranean era," he said in 1903, "died with the discovery of America; the
Atlantic era is now at the height of its development and must soon exhaust
the resources at its command; the Pacific era is destined to be the greatest
of all, is just at its dawn."

Roosevelt, however, flung out his banners of rhetoric at a time when

Americans believed that they had invented a new, benevolent form of imperialism. They subjugated people against their will, but only for their own good; they foreswore acquisition of overseas territory, but built naval bases and military installations; they encouraged the rise of democratic aspirations, but on a graduated scale. Since then, benevolent imperialism has been exposed as a contradiction in terms. In the modern world, you cannot impose your will on other peoples and maintain a benevolent posture. Under its semantic finery, American policy viewed from overseas constitutes imperialism unqualified, whether it bears arms, builds a bridge of food ships or concocts vast plans for the development of the Mekong River. Since the time of the first Roosevelt, and more particularly since the second Roosevelt, Asia has become the graveyard of imperial ambitions: the British in India, the French in Indo-China, the Dutch in the East Indies, czarist Russia in Manchuria.

The closer the world has come together through the swiftness of communications, the stronger the urge to differentiate among peoples. Imperialism dissolves into nationalism, which breaks up into tribalism. The Asian peoples resent the indigenous imperialism of other Asians almost as fiercely as that of Western intruders. They were happy to be released from Japan's Co-Prosperity Sphere and welcomed Western expeditionary forces as liberators from their fellow Asians. Even the Chinese of Singapore urge American resistance to Chinese communism in South Asia.

Ten years after the end of World War II, the Bandung Conference, now a half-forgotten event in Western minds, signaled the unmistakable change of mood in the East. Its aim of constructing an Asian-African neutralist world, aloof from the two major opposing ideologies, as sufficient unto itself as possible, has seemingly fallen short of accomplishment. The alarm that surged through foreign offices in the West now seems to have been exaggerated.

Bandung, in the Western mind, symbolizes a failure, a comforting indication that fecklessness is still one of the more imperishable characteristics of the Asian mind; of a piece with sacred cows, temple dancers and ivory back scratchers; a flashback to the heyday of its flamboyant host, Bung Sukarno of Indonesia.

But the animating spirit of Bandung is merely sleeping and can be awakened when present crises fade and a longer view of the future can be taken. In 1955, certainly, it did not seem merely a pretentious Afro-Oriental powwow. It alarmed the superpowers, both of which were excluded. America and Russia were dismayed not only by their exclusion, but more importantly because Communist China seemed to be the chief beneficiary of the conference held on the south coast of Java.

Something of the hope with which Asia viewed the China of 1955 was measurable in an editorial published in the leading Indian newspaper shortly before the Bandung Conference opened. "Much will depend on whether Peking considers itself more Asian than Communist or *vice versa*. If the Asian-African Conference accomplishes nothing more than reveal to what extent the Communist is willing to cooperate with its Asian neighbors and Arab States, it will be a worthy attempt on behalf of Asian solidarity. Peking will then be given an opportunity to establish its *bona fides* and if possible to confound those sceptics who feel that, by the fact of being Communist, China is nearer to its fellow Communist States in Europe than to its Asian neighbors with which it has racial and cultural ties."[1]

The Soviet Union was rejected for membership despite her claim to being a protector of Asian and African states fearful of neocolonialism because for most of the participating nations, as Ronald Segal has written, she was "white and rich and powerful . . . a member of the race that had for so long dominated, and dominated still — if not politically, then economically; if not directly, then by the mere fact of its superior wealth and power — the coloured world."[2]

In its open sessions, there was no doubt of the color-consciousness of its participants, or their eagerness to disengage themselves in every possible way — except for a necessary economic dependence — from the white nations of the West. They included such allies of the United States as the Philippines and Thailand. The racial resentments that burned even, or perhaps more especially, in the breasts of America's client-nations were indicated by the surprising source of one of the most scathing attacks on white prejudices. It was voiced by the Philippine representative, Carlos P. Romulo. Until he had been plunged into the heady, liberating atmosphere of Bandung, Romulo had always been regarded as one of the most pro-American political figures in the Far East.

The racial aspect of Bandung and its loathing of colonialism, whether directed at other nations or a minority in its midst, was emphasized in the report of Richard Wright, the expatriate American Negro novelist. "The overwhelming majority of the Asian and African countries and peoples have suffered and still are suffering from the calamities under colonialism. This is acknowledged by all of us. If we seek common ground in doing away with the sufferings and calamities under colonialism, it will be very easy for us to have mutual understanding and respect, mutual sympathy and support, instead of mutual suspicion and fear, mutual exclusion and antagonism . . . We Asian and African countries, China included, are all backward economically and culturally."[3]

When the time came for a second Afro-Asian conference, this time in Algiers, it was indefinitely postponed. Hope was deferred but the optimism and fellow-feeling engendered by the first conference at Bandung has not been forgotten in the East as it has been in the West. And a "second Bandung," no matter how long delayed, may reap what was sown at the first, when the deprived, once-colonized nations not only realized how weak they were individually compared to the great nations of the West but glimpsed the possibilities of how strong they could be if they acted in unison.

Even with a semblance of unity, however, their combined power would be a puny thing compared to the American military presence in Asia. Before World War II, we held forward positions, from which an antiquated Asiatic Fleet operated; now in addition to bases in the Philippines, on Japan and Formosa, we occupy the Micronesian heartland of the western Pacific. It has been an article of faith with Americans in this century that we have profited from none of our wars, that we make peace with clean, unsticky hands, and have never aspired to acquire territory as a result of our victories. True enough so far as World War I was concerned. At the end of the Second World War, however, we found ourselves the unembarrassed proprietors of vast new tracts of real estate.

We did not, of course, seize all those formerly Japanese-held islands by right of conquest. They were mandated to the United States as a trust territory, in the case of the Micronesian islands, and the Ryukyus and the Bonins were simply taken over from Japan. Iwo Jima in the Bonins has recently been returned to Japan, and eventually the Ryukyus, including Okinawa, will probably also be restored to Japanese rule.

Since the Korean War, Okinawa, the largest of the Ryukyus, has become our great forward base, advancing the military power center in the Pacific from Hawaii to the island located between Japan and Formosa. Okinawa's strategic importance can be measured by its central position on an arc extending from Tokyo to Saigon; it is 950 miles from Tokyo, 800 from Seoul, 400 from Taipei (Formosa), 900 from Manila and 1800 from Saigon. It is the unofficial capital of the Southeast Asia Treaty Organization, able to furnish conventional or nuclear military support to Japan, Formosa, South Korea, South Viet Nam and any SEATO allies. Nuclear bombs are stored on the island to arm the F–105's of the 18th Tactical Fighter Wing, and the 498th Tactical Missile Group is equipped with Mace–B intermediate-range missiles which could hit targets on mainland China. It is also the headquarters of the Third Marine Corps.

Since the islands are inhabited by a million Japanese-speaking people, Japan has been pressing as hard as diplomatically possible for their return to a Japanese administration. In 1960 the Okinawans staged riots and street demonstrations in demanding reversion to Japanese rule. It is a knotty situation, though the United States under the peace treaty with Japan was given complete administrative control over both the Bonins and the Ryukyus, with Japan retaining a residual sovereignty. Okinawa is the keystone of American nuclear capability in the Far East, as well as providing logistic support for American forces in Viet Nam; its value as a staging area, supply and repair base and an unsinkable aircraft carrier is also immense. A Far Eastern correspondent recently reported, however, that "there is an understandable but dangerous tendency in the United States to take Japanese support and cooperation for granted. It is dangerous, because if we do not move toward an amicable reversion agreement now, the issue may get out of control in Japan and we could find ourselves forced to withdraw our bases not only from Okinawa but from Japan as well."[4]

Obviously the political complications growing out of policing the Orient, a largely self-assumed role, rise in geometric proportion to the military and naval bases we build, the bombing squadrons we station, the fleets we operate. In the past several years the once-glowing promise of a Pacific Destiny has been shadowed by foreboding over the tensile strength of American military power, the exhaustion of our will to rush in full force to every trouble spot west of the Japan-Australia axis. There is such a delicate balance between the desire of even our allies and other friendly nations to be protected, and their fear of the consequences of that protection with nuclear weapons as the ultimate resort. More that a decade ago Sir Ivone Kirkpatrick, then permanent undersecretary of the British Foreign Office, expressed the American — and Western — dilemma. "If this thing we call 'the West' is to survive," he was quoted as saying, "we must decide not only what to save but also what *not* to save. We cannot arm, educate, industrialize and inspire every country on earth. We must judge certain places worth little enough to say to the Communists: 'It's yours. Take it. Spend your rubles, send your technicians, pick your puppets — and waste your time!' We cannot be — or do — all things with all nations. We must fix priorities. We must make choices. What else lies within reason?"[5]

The sobering second thoughts about the inexhaustibility of American military resources have arisen most disturbingly since the confrontations with the regular or guerrilla forces of China, North Korea and North Viet Nam, all of them nations with a previously despised military record, on the peninsulas of mainland Asia. In less than two decades the image of the mainland Asian warrior has changed from that of a figure exceedingly quick to flee before any determined opposition to a bitter-end fighter who uses inferior weapons with great skill; a lightly armed, quick-moving soldier who can bog down Western military machines and techniques in the jungles and rice paddies, who has demonstrated the utility of cheaply made mortars, rockets, mines, grenades and machine pistols against the most advanced technology the West can employ. In 1931 an American military observer in China, Brigadier General Thomas Magruder, wrote that "the Chinese have never been and are not now a warlike people . . . they have developed no scientific military traditions. At heart the Chinese believe that the continuance of their race will not be accomplished by the exercise of military qualities." He believed that developing a martial spirit in the Chinese would be an exceedingly slow process, that spiritually and intellectually the Chinese exhibited "those racial qualities which create a natural antipathy for joining battle with an enemy" instead of "a relish for combat."[6]

Regarding that picture of the Chinese as a dispirited sad sack among the world's soldiery, Hanson Baldwin, the eminent military commentator, offered a revision just twenty years later, "That the world no longer thinks of the Chinese in terms of pacifism is a measure of the change in China . . . The picture we once entertained of the somewhat benign, inscrutable but wise and civilized Chinese, too intelligent for war — an oversimplified caricature twenty years ago — has even less validity today. For the future China is in the hands of peasant stock, of patient men who have shown on many battlefields that they *will fight*. We have learned this, somewhat to our surprise and at heavy cost, in Korea."[7]

The transfiguration of the Chinese soldier, and that of his North Vietnamese and North Korean satellites, along with the emergence of Communist China as a nuclear power, has shockingly changed the American concept of China. No great nation has transformed itself in such a short time from welfare client to menacing giant; no one speaks of the Chinese anymore as "coolies," or regards the Asians as an inert defenseless mass. Similarly, the Pacific has swiftly changed from a world of opportunity, an arena in which the American reservoir of goodwill can be tapped at American pleasure, and with American self-congratulation, into the menacing lands of which Mahan, Lea, Stoddard and other advertisers of the Yellow Peril had stridently warned.

On the optimistic side might be chalked up the fact that the great bugaboo of almost a century of American diplomacy in the Far East — and never has it operated with more ingenuity and subtlety than in this aspect — has not yet manifested itself. That is the alliance of Japan and China. It is a natural linking by geopolitical and strategic standards; as natural as an alliance between Germany and Russia, the specter which has for so long haunted European diplomacy.

The dynamic energy of such an alliance, which would combine Japanese technology with Chinese population and other resources, might well make the Yellow/Brown Peril something to turn the Western nations from a hedonistic materialism to contemplation of the problems of survival. After the long Saturday night of Western self-indulgence, sermons and soda water . . . and a struggle with a destiny suddenly turned inside out.

1. *Still Westward the Course*

A little more than two centuries ago George Berkeley, the bishop of Cloyne, advised his contemporaries that "Westward the course of empire takes its way; / The four first acts already past, / A fifth shall close the drama with the day: / Time's noblest offspring is the last."

If this is the fifth act in the drama of America's westward course, it seems quite possible as this is written, in the summer of 1968, that the final scenes will be anticlimactic, even antidramatic — a sullen ebbing of American force, a bitter vaporizing of the dreams of a Pacific empire stretching from San Francisco to Shangri-La which had once seemed so substantial. The technology which seemed to have promised us the fulfillment of dreams as old as the Republic now appears to have betrayed us; a situation graphically symbolized on television for its mass audience by a multi-million-dollar aircraft crammed with the most sophisticated electronics gear and weapons systems shot down over an Asian jungle by peasants not much advanced from the age of the musket and the blowgun.

Our "noblest offspring" may be yet to come, but it does not seem now that it will be born of military solutions.

Instead our long infatuation with Asia as a sort of treasure-house, whether in terms of trade or territorial acquisitions, or an arena in which to confront the expanding ambitions of other nations, seems to have come to an end. The SEATO obligations remain, the Seventh Fleet continues its ceaseless parade up and down the China coast, strongly held outposts along the Japan-Okinawa-Philippines-Australia axis will be maintained. So will the installations costing almost a billion dollars in Thailand, including air bases, port facilities and the most elaborate highway network ever built in Asia, and the $150,000,000 communications system linking Bangkok, Manila and the United States.

But the readiness to intervene on the Asian mainland has vanished, perhaps for all time. In less than three decades we have become involved in three Asian land wars; our infantry and Marine regiments have fought in the Philippines, the Pacific islands, China, Burma, New Guinea, Korea and Viet Nam, with results that have not been encouraging. We supported Chiang Kai-shek, only to watch his Nationalist regime crumble and take flight to Formosa. We fought a series of costly campaigns in Korea only to reestablish the sanctity of the 38th Parallel and keep a small army of occupation on hand to enforce the stalemate. No sooner had we restored peace of a kind to Korea than we began pouring supplies into Indo-China to support a French colonial regime until it collapsed after Dienbienphu. Then when the two Viet Nams failed to coexist we built up a massive expeditionary force in South Viet Nam, almost company by company, until the demands of sustaining that effort against an elusive and persistent enemy ulcerated our national existence.

It was not that a totally united and determined America could not subdue a guerrilla army, no matter how remote or plentifully supplied by its Russian and Chinese backers, but the cumulative weariness and disillusion of fighting one war per decade under ground rules conceived and enforced by the enemy drained our militancy and enthusiasm. The significance of fighting a limited war, with objectives more political, psychological and moral than military, had not yet been absorbed by the pragmatic American mind. Nor had it accepted the necessity of heavy costs in blood and treasure for gains which cannot be measured by any military yardstick. A war in which the enemy has privileged sanctuaries (Korea) or in which his lines of supply and communication cannot be directly attacked even while he is sending rockets and mortar shells into our bases (South Viet Nam) cannot easily be explained or justified to the ordinary American.

Through the ironical workings and turnings of circumstance the liberal and antiwar elements in the United States found themselves quoting such conservative, more or less expansionist military men as General of the Army Douglas MacArthur who, bitterly reflecting on the Korean experiences which tarnished his career, warned that American troops must never again be employed against massed Asian armies. Similarly, General Mark Clark, after his own experience of commanding the United States forces in Korea, cautioned that "never again should we be mousetrapped into fighting another defensive war on that peninsula." Perhaps the operative word in General Clark's warning was "defensive."

A similar feeling was expressed by President Eisenhower when he recalled that "I remarked [to Undersecretary of State W. Bedell Smith] that, if the United States were, unilaterally, to permit its forces to be drawn into conflict in Indo-China, and in a succession of Asian wars, the end result would be to drain off our resources and to weaken our overall defensive position."

Those views of professional military men dovetailed rather neatly, if coincidentally, with what the late Che Guevera was supposed to have written in an article prepared for the 1967 Havana congress:

"We must carry out our general task with the tactical purpose of *getting the enemy out of his natural environment* . . . make him feel like a cornered beast wherever he may move. Then his moral fiber will begin to decline."

It was a graphic description of the military bog in which the American forces were soon to find themselves, tactically and psychologically — also of the world's televised view of them as six-foot beasts ravaging the villages of South Viet Nam, being outwitted and outfought by the five-foot heroes of the Viet Cong.

It takes no military prophet to foresee that it will be a long time, and then only in the direst circumstances, before the United States sends its ground forces deep into the Asian mainland, its airmobile units into the rice paddies, its airpower against the impenetrable camouflage of the jungle, its intricate weaponry against mud and monsoon rains.

2. *The Next "Ocean of Destiny"*

When President Theodore Roosevelt talked about America's "ocean of destiny" he was referring to the Pacific Ocean. The Pacific, however, is no longer an area of opportunity; all claims have been staked out and only a general war would uproot them. Within the last few years it has begun to appear that the thrust of American imperialism, to use a phrase many still find indelicate, will be still further westward.

Jumping the barrier we have erected against the possibility of Chinese expansion, leaving behind a growingly redoubtable Japan and an almost miraculously reborn Nationalist China on Formosa, the sea road now leads us into the Indian Ocean.

Once the repercussions over Southeast Asia subside, the United States will probably be occupied with advancing a "third-ocean" strategy. Such presently obscure islands in the vast empty seascape of the Indian Ocean as Socotra, the Comoro group, the Chagos Archipelago, the Seychelles and the Cocos will become as familiar to Americans as the Philippines and the Ryukyus. A glance at a map will show how American military and naval power has been shifting ever westward: from the eastern coast of Asia and into the South China Sea. The next step is through the Indonesian straits and into the wide lonely Indian Ocean, the newest and largest vacuum of power.

Merely because the United States decides to abandon deep penetrations of the Asian mainland is no sign we have given up a global, superpower posture. Thwarted momentarily by the problem of rooting guerrillas out of the jungles, our imperialistic impulses will satisfy themselves elsewhere. Already new logistics systems have been devised in the Pentagon to support such far-ranging ventures. One such scheme is the "Fast Deployment Logistic" (FDL) system which could airlift and sealift American troops and supplies anywhere on the earth's surface in a matter of hours. A fleet of fully equipped supply ships would be stationed all over the world-ocean to provide quick support for American forces anywhere from Pole to Pole. The air arm of such a system would be the giant C–5A transport planes just going into production, which could be correlated with the FDL system.

If the Indian Ocean, rimmed by underdeveloped and overpopulated countries (India, Pakistan, Burma, Ceylon, Tanzania, Kenya, Indonesia, Malaysia), seems a poor choice for expansion, it should also be considered that one of its sleeves is the Persian Gulf, on which the world's greatest oil reserves are located.

Both Russia and the United States are now edging toward that vast area of the world's third largest ocean above and below the Tropic of

Capricorn. If there is a future collision between the growing maritime power of Russia and that of the United States, it might well be in the Indian Ocean, rather than the Pacific or the Mediterranean where the rival fleets now circle each other warily. Symptomatic of the great Soviet naval expansion are the fleet it has suddenly placed in the Mediterranean, its sea-train now making a regular route of the Bosporus, its trawlers and survey ships off the American coasts, its naval units appearing suddenly all over the Pacific. A hint of the ubiquitous presence of the Russian naval forces was noted a half dozen years ago during the 1963 maneuvers of the United States Pacific Fleet. A Russian submarine suddenly surfaced in the midst of that fleet and snatched a mini-buoy, a newly invented device for detecting enemy subs, which had been dropped by a plane. The Russian submarine disappeared with its prize almost before the American commanders realized what had happened.[8]

One objective of the massive Russian naval buildup undoubtedly is to expand Soviet power into the Indian Ocean, enabling it to penetrate the underdeveloped world — the world of the Bandung Conference — from the sea. Russian power expands slowly, on a monolithic scale, what Homer Lea called a "glacial, timeless, measured movement" almost imperceptible to the impatient eye. It has been sixty years since Lea predicted that the basic line of Russian expansion would be "through Persia [Iran] to the Plains of India, where are found both the Pacific and the Bosphorus." Does that still hold true? Apparently it does.

Secret documents brought to light since the end of World War II indicate Russia's continuing interest in moving southward to the Indian Ocean. The fourth article of the so-called Ribbentrop Plan, in which the Nazi foreign minister carved up the world, was one indicator. Ribbentrop came up with his master plan in the summer of 1939 when Stalin made the deal with Hitler to permit Nazi Germany to begin its conquest of western Europe. Under that plan "spheres of interest," according to Sumner Welles, were allotted Japan, Germany, Italy and the Soviet Union: "A. the South Seas region for Japan; b. Central Africa for Germany; c. North Africa for Italy; d. the Middle East, including Iran and India, for the Soviet Union."[9]

Russian foreign policy is the one constant in its national life. Regimes may change, and Stalinism may be qualified, but Russian ambitions are unmalleable and inflexible. The warm seas have lured them as irresistibly as Germans yearn for a strip of Mediterranean coast. Russian actions, the thrust of Russian diplomacy since World War II indicate that Iran and India, with the Indian Ocean beyond, still provide a polar attraction for the Soviet Union; a continuation of the czarist fixation on the Bosporus, Russia's sea-lane to the Mediterranean, the Red Sea, the straits of Aden and out into the Indian Ocean, and on India, the focus of years of intrigue and covert operations against the British presence in the Khyber Pass.

Immediately after World War II, Russia made a smash-and-grab attempt against Iran's northern provinces, which was thwarted with American moral and material support. After that crude Stalinist power play failed, she resorted to subtler means. Never has Communist diplomacy exerted itself with such delicacy and tact as in succeeding relations with Iran and India. Russia has been unstinting in providing aid — no apparent strings attached — to Afghanistan and India. In the last year or two she has succeeded in thawing out almost completely the suspicions of the Iranians. Iran now is submitting, with the complaisance of a Persian odalisque, to the Russian embrace.

Meanwhile, all but unnoticed in the rush and clamor of other, possibly less crucial events, the United States has not been unaware of the strategic necessities of the Indian Ocean area. The Indian Ocean is the world's third largest body of water and covers an area of twenty-eight million square miles, with the African continent on the west, Asia on the north, Australia on the east and Antarctica on the south. It is the ocean on which almost a billion people live, mostly in India, Pakistan and Indonesia. The only land on its huge expanse are scattered dots of islands. Strategically it could be dominated by a strong India. Until a few years ago it was largely a British domain, but the British withdrawal from their great naval base at Singapore and from secondary bases on the Seychelles and Mauritius, following the departure from India, have left the vacuum which attracts Russian and American power.

Aside from an India able to dominate the ocean which washes both flanks of the subcontinent, the second strategic key to controlling the area is the groups of small islands, most of them only a few acres of sand and jungle, little more than atolls, which lie athwart the sea-lanes. An Indian strategist has noted that the islands' naval value "lies either in their being so remote from the mainland as to constitute valuable potential advanced bases or in being in sufficient proximity to a major land mass or maritime or air route as to block it without the costly occupation of large areas of territory and continued contact with an enemy by the land forces."[10] Thus Socotra, an island in the Gulf of Aden, controls the eastern approaches of the Suez Canal. The Cocomoro Islands in the Mozambique Channel dominate traffic along the coast of East Africa. The Chagos Archipelago, located almost in the middle of the Indian Ocean, could provide a naval base to dominate the whole area. The Cocos Islands stand athwart the route from India to Australia.

To the naval strategist it is also evident that the Indian Ocean contains one of the four bottlenecks — the Panama Canal, the Strait of Gibraltar, the Suez Canal and the Strait of Malacca — control of which means dominance over the world's maritime commerce. Western command of the bottlenecks has been steadily eroding. Our control of the Panama Canal is threatened by political unrest. The Suez Canal has been taken over by a hostile United Arab Republic. The Russian fleet in the Mediterranean, on the verge of acquiring a large base in Algeria, is edging closer to Gibraltar.

So far the Western powers have managed to hang onto the Strait of Malacca, the narrow channel between Malaysia and the Indonesian island of Sumatra (so narrow the largest oil tanker now in operation cannot negotiate it). On the eastern approaches to that strait stands the United States Seventh Fleet; the western approaches were formerly guarded by the British base at Singapore. A friendly government in Singapore and another in Malaysia seems to guarantee the strait will stay under Western control, but a strong American naval presence in the Indian Ocean would certify it and in addition would provide an outlet for an imperialism which may ebb from Viet Nam but will renew itself in short order.

The dangers to that control were underlined several years ago, before the downfall of Bung Sukarno, when he proclaimed the Indian Ocean would be known as the "Indonesian Ocean." In 1964 Hanson Baldwin noted that "the increasing threat to the Strait of Malacca and to the vast vacuum of power that extends from Southeast Asia westward to the Red Sea and the African continent is the background reason for the U.S. Navy's desire to establish a fleet in the Indian Ocean . . . Here, too, as in Panama, there will be no peace in our time, for the Communist drive for political hegemony is directed against a maritime focal point of high strategic importance."[11]

As military commentator for the New York *Times,* Hanson Baldwin's views often reflected the high-level thinking in the Pentagon (or perhaps, as some would have it, vice versa). By the time Baldwin wrote those cautionary words, the United States Navy was already making a rather stealthy approach to the Indian Ocean problem. It escaped the world's attention, but not the Kremlin's, that in the summer of 1964 an American naval unit casually, with as little publicity as possible, took a leisurely cruise on the Indian Ocean. It was before the United States became deeply involved in Southeast Asia and the navy was able to detach the aircraft carrier *Bonhomme Richard,* three destroyers and an oil tanker for this summer cruise. The unit was designated the "Concord Squadron" — and any feelings that its activities were reminiscent of Commodore Perry's four black ships and their visit to Tokyo Bay 110 years earlier were probably well founded.

The Concord Squadron called at Madagascar, Kenya, Aden and Iran. Off Iran, significantly, it conducted a weapons display for the shah, then sailed on across the Indian Ocean. Later that summer its activities were revealed in the *Economist* of London and the Washington *Post,* in which it was demonstrated that the cruise was a more or less covert search for island bases in the Indian Ocean which could be fitted into overall American strategy. Specifically mentioned in the articles as possible future sites of American bases were Diego Garcia, an island in the centrally located Chagos Archipelago, and Aldabra, near Madagascar; the proposed facilities would include a naval communications station, air bases, resupply facilities for naval task forces and nuclear-powered submarines, and staging bases for amphibious landing forces. Presumably such ambitious plans were delayed by more urgent developments in Southeast Asia, and American installations in the Indian Ocean were limited to a missile-tracking station on Madagascar and a similar facility on Mahe in the Seychelles.

The reconnoitering mission of the Concord Squadron was rather quickly followed up by the Russians. First an oceanographic survey ship, the *Vitiaz,* made its soundings and other scientific observations. Then a fleet of five Russian trawlers sailed in March of 1965 from their Baltic port to the Indian Ocean, where they hoped to establish a firmer Russian presence there than anything the Americans had managed through the cruise of the Concord Squadron. An agreement for a trawler base and fishing rights had been negotiated with Mrs. Sirimavo Bandaranaike, the leftward-leaning prime minister of Ceylon. That clandestine arrangement for a fishing-trawler base, which of course could have been rapidly expanded to include everything up to submarines and heavy cruisers, was ruined while the Soviet trawlers were en route to Ceylon. Mrs. Bandaranaike had been thrown out of office by the electoral victory of her pro-Western opposition, and the first Russian foray into the Indian Ocean ended in a humiliating failure.

Recovering from those setbacks, the Russians in the spring of 1968 managed to move forward diplomatically on both the Iranian and Indian fronts. Premier Kosygin was welcomed to Teheran on a visit to the $300,000,000 steel mill the Russians had begun building, and before leaving he persuaded the shah to quintuple Iran's trade with the Soviet Union, which would make Russia its best customer and biggest supplier. The shah had begun turning from a traditional friendship with the United States over our refusal to support his claims that the whole Persian Gulf belongs to Iran.

That same week, British intelligence leaked a story that the Russians had just succeeded in persuading Premier Indira Gandhi to grant them the right to use the strategic Andaman and Nicobar islands in the Bay of Bengal as Russian fleet bases. Obviously the Russians are preparing to rush in when the British complete their withdrawal from the Indian Ocean area in 1971. A Russian-built factory near Bombay is making late-model MIG fighters for the Indian air force, and the Indian navy was awaiting the arrival of three Soviet-made submarines. Several months earlier the commander-in-chief of the Soviet navy had visited India, reportedly to discuss cooperation between the Indian and Russian fleets in the Indian Ocean. The Russian influence on India has been greatly forwarded by multiple programs of economic assistance.[12]

The only countermove from the United States in that area has been to discuss with Britain, Australia and New Zealand the construction of a huge air and naval base in northern Australia, where a mobile strategic force could be stationed, but those plans were contingent on developments in Southeast Asia.

"The Indian Ocean is immensely important," wrote C. J. Creekmore in 1965, "not only for what it is — our means of communication and trade with Australia and New Zealand, and repository of a significant percentage of the free world's oil reserves — but for what it could be: a base for projecting our influence into all the new nations of East Africa and maintaining a western presence on the Indian subcontinent. Will it thereafter be seen that, as a tide already begun to ebb sometimes sends a small wave back above the highwater mark, the cruise of the *Bonhomme Richard* marked the limits of our attempt to establish peace and security in a most crucial area of the world?"[13]

It hardly seems likely. The geopolitical realities dictate that American power must replace the British, if power politics continue to dominate the world's affairs. Withdrawal from Southeast Asia under whatever foreseeable circumstances, whether an unlikely military victory or an equally unlikely Oriental Dunkirk, will urge upon American planners the necessity of securing the Malacca Strait and sharing, if not absolutely controlling the islands, the waters and the oceanographic deeps of the Indian Ocean, and of influencing the nations on its littoral. If so, a Pacific Destiny becomes somewhat passé. In the last half of the twentieth century, the oil domes of the Persian Gulf may lack the glamour of that largely ephemeral "wealth of the Indies" which once bedazzled us, but they surpass it in strategic importance.

3. *The Good American Earth*

There was no second Bandung Conference to continue the work of uniting the nations around the Indian Ocean, but shortly before it was indefinitely postponed there was a conclave of equal importance and greater urgency. At Geneva, the stately mausoleum of so many international hopes, the rich nations confronted the poor nations to decide what could be done about the worsening condition of the have-nots. Predictably, the chief result was a series of ringing manifestoes all but promising a global redistribution of wealth — without suggesting how that was to be accomplished. Another was the institutionalizing of the effort — almost a sure sign that it would end in yet another stately Geneva impasse, complete with permanent secretaries, staff experts and committees — under the title of the United Nations Conference on Trade and Development. UNCTAD has churned out millions of words, but not one step has been taken toward carrying out its recommendations.

Three years after that first meeting of UNCTAD a restive sector known as the "Group of 77" — actually eighty-six of the have-not nations — met in the fall of 1967 at Algiers to urge that the rich nations finally do something about what was called a "class struggle" on an international scale. The present economic order, with underdeveloped nations receiving less and less for their raw materials from the industrial countries, was condemned by the delegate from Madagascar as "a source of perpetual misery . . . the scandal of the century." The Liberian delegate declared that the present inequities were "the key question of our time; it will decide the issue of war or peace." Peru's delegate complained that the rich nations "won't let us into the twentieth century." The most passionate outburst came from President Boumedienne of Algeria, who charged that "Europe and the U.S. have plundered the natural wealth of the Third World," that they were "veritable octopi whose tentacles are drawing ever tighter on the developing world . . . We should consider whatever contribution the industrialized countries make as a simple restitution of a tiny part of the debt the Western countries contracted by their odious exploitation."[14]

The outcries in Geneva and Algiers are merely one chord in a rising lament from the tier of overpopulated, underdeveloped nations largely located in the southern hemisphere. In the past several years they were largely unregarded in our preoccupation with the war in Viet Nam and the internal disorders. Despite our unwillingness to listen, their voices threaten to grow in volume and desperation.

Very soon the stark problem of survival for hundreds of millions of people around the world will be confronting us. In that probable catastrophe, the matters which have concerned us for almost two hundred years — destiny, prestige, trade, territory, democracy, all the words and symbols — will seem trivial by comparison. The projections of the geopoliticians and the deliberations of Pentagon strategists will be wildly out of sync with reality; in any case the orbiting of a military space platform would make all their plans obsolescent.

By 1975, according to Paul Paddock, a United States Foreign Service veteran, and William Paddock, an agronomist, the world will face the converging disasters of famine and overpopulation, and the major problem of the superpowers will not be war or a continuation of their rivalries but how to deal with the unprecedented question of feeding the lesser nations. In their recent and highly controversial work, *Famine — 1975!,* they forecast a crisis that will "last for years, perhaps several decades, and they are, for a surety, inevitable. Ten years from now parts of the undeveloped world will be suffering from famine. In fifteen years the famines will be catastrophic and revolutions and social turmoil and economic upheavals will sweep areas of Asia, Africa and Latin America.

"The locomotive roaring straight at us is the population explosion. The unmovable landslide across the tracks is the stagnant production of food in the undeveloped countries, the nations where the population increases are greatest. The collision is inevitable. The famines are inevitable."[15]

The same problem was confronted in 1954 by Harrison Brown (*The Challenge of Man's Future*), and has been warned of with increasing vehemence since World War II. "The victory in the fight for world supremacy," Brown wrote, "may not go to the one who has accomplished the most spectacular fireworks, but rather to the party which does something to alleviate the distress among peoples of the earth. . . . When you look at the historic record of the United States, the American people, once confronted with a famine, have never really debated what to do. We have just responded . . . We in the United States are in a position of overwhelming responsibility . . . for in a very real sense the destiny of humanity depends upon our decisions and upon our actions."[16]

Under that unimaginable weight of responsibility — literally the decision on who shall live, who shall die, since we could not save more than a fraction of the peoples doomed by famine — other national concerns dwindle into insignificance.

Our yearnings for an empire in the Pacific will seem puerile illusions too long sustained; an insupportable vanity. We will no longer attempt to provide the world with an easily summoned constabulary, nor will we be able to afford the short-lived ambition for a Pax Americana.

Then perhaps we will realize, as we should have more than a century ago when we began succumbing to the manifestations of destiny, that the real treasure of America is not far across the Pacific but the prosaic wheat-covered plains and the black earth of its Middle Western farmlands.

Notes

Notes

1. America's Marco Polo

1. Helen Augur, *Passage to Glory, passim,* and Jared Sparks, *The Life of John Ledyard,* 9–11.
2. Sparks, *The Life of John Ledyard,* 10–11.
3. Ledyard Collection at Dartmouth College library.
4. *A Chronological History of Northeastern Voyages of Discovery.*
5. Ibid.
6. Ledyard, *A Journal of Captain Cook's Last Voyage to the Pacific Ocean, passim.*
7. Ibid.
8. Ibid.
9. Ibid.
10. Ledyard Papers, New York Historical Society.
11. Ibid.
12. Ibid.
13. Sparks, *The Life of John Ledyard,* 209–210.
14. Ledyard Papers.
15. Ibid.

16. Ibid.
17. Ledyard's Siberian journal is part of the Ledyard Collection at the Dartmouth College library.
18. Letter in Jared Sparks Collection, Dartmouth College library.
19. Ledyard's Siberian journal.

2. Opium for the Pipes of China

1. Jefferson to Gallatin, Aug. 15, 1808, Jefferson Papers, Library of Congress.
2. Charles H. Carey, *The History of Oregon*, 23.
3. Joseph Quincy, editor, *The Journals of Major Samuel Shaw, passim*.
4. William C. Hunter, *Bits of Old China*, 63–67.
5. Related by Mrs. Richard O'Connor (the author's wife), a descendant of Elias Hasket Derby.
6. Samuel Curwen's journal and letters, MSS. in Essex Institute, Salem, Mass.
7. James Duncan Phillips, *Salem and the Indies*, 77.
8. Letter in the Derby Collection, Essex Institute.
9. Robert E. Peabody, *The Log of the Grand Turks, passim*.
10. Ibid.
11. Ibid.
12. Letter in the Derby Collection, Essex Institute.
13. Hunter, *Bits of Old China*, 44.
14. Bowditch background, Robert E. Berry, *Yankee Stargazer, passim*.
15. Phillips, *Salem and the Indies*, 329.
16. Providence *Gazette*, May 11, 1793.
17. Foster Rhea Dulles, *The Old China Trade*, 47.
18. G. G. Putnam, *Salem Vessels and Their Voyages*, 145.
19. Benjamin Morrell, *A Narrative of Four Voyages*, 57–59.
20. Ibid., 211–214.
21. Thomas Jefferson Jacobs, *Scenes, Incidents and Adventures in the Pacific Ocean, passim*.
22. Edmund Fanning, *Voyages Around the World*, 74.
23. Samuel Eliot Morison, *The Maritime History of Massachusetts, 1783–1860*, 70–73.
24. Hunter, *Bits of Old China, passim*. William C. Hunter, the author of this fascinating volume, was one of the earliest American traders on the China coast.
25. Robert Bennet Forbes, *Personal Reminiscences, passim*.
26. *North American Review*, October 1834.
27. Ibid.
28. Forbes, *Personal Reminiscences, passim*.
29. Ibid.
30. Captain's Letters, Navy Department, May 28, 1839, National Archives.
31. Quoted in Tyler Dennett, *Americans in Eastern Asia*, 121.

3. "To Establish on Earth the Noblest Temple"

1. John B. McMaster, *A History of the American People*, IV, 109.
2. G. E. Woodberry, *The Life of Edgar Allan Poe*, I, 353.
3. Ibid., II, 123.

4. Julius W. Pratt, who investigated the matter thoroughly, reported in the *American Historical Review,* July 1927, that he was unable to "find any substantiation" for legends attributing the phrase to Webster.

5. New York *Morning News,* Jan. 5, 1846.

6. Richard O'Connor, *The German-Americans,* 126–127.

7. Benjamin Morrell, Jr., quoted in Irving B. Richman, *California under Mexico and Spain,* 300.

8. Richard Henry Dana, *Two Years Before the Mast, passim.*

9. Ibid.

10. Ibid.

11. Ibid.

12. James D. Richardson, *Messages of the Presidents,* IV, 399.

13. James K. Polk, *Diary,* I, 397.

14. John Lloyd Stephens's career is definitively recorded in Victor Von Hagen, *Maya Explorer.*

15. Postscript to the later editions of Dana, 312–313.

16. Ibid.

17. House Document 123:33–1, 224.

18. C. Bradford Mitchell, "Pride of the Seas," *American Heritage*, December 1967.

4. "The Curse of a People Calling Themselves Christians"

1. Lewis Mumford, *Herman Melville,* 66.

2. Dana, *Two Years Before the Mast,* 206.

3. Herman Melville, *Typee,* 3.

4. Ibid., 8–9.

5. Ibid., 86–87.

6. Ibid., 213.

7. Ibid., 287.

8. Mumford, *Herman Melville,* 76–77.

9. Quoted in Basil Lubbock, *Bully Hayes,* 5.

10. Ibid., 45–46.

11. *Queensland Official Gazette,* Aug. 28, 1875.

12. Lubbock, *Bully Hayes,* 19.

13. Honolulu *Advertiser*, Sept. 24, 1859.

14. Lubbock, *Bully Hayes,* 29–34.

15. Ibid., 40–42.

16. San Francisco *Bulletin,* Aug. 31, 1859.

17. Sydney *Empire,* July 6, 1860.

18. Lubbock, *Bully Hayes,* 95–97.

19. Auckland *New Zealander,* Feb. 1, 1865.

20. Quoted in Lubbock, *Bully Hayes,* 115–116.

21. Louis Becke in *Adventure Magazine,* September 1914.

22. Quoted in Lubbock, *Bully Hayes,* 299.

23. The details of Hayes's death were reported in the San Francisco *Post,* June 2, 1877.

5. Onward Christian Soldiers, Sailors and Marines

1. House Report 596, 30th Congress, 2nd session, 30–31.

2. Ibid.

3. Senate Executive Document, 34th Congress, 2nd session, 49:32–2.
4. Akira Iriye, *Across the Pacific,* 14.
5. Parker Correspondence, Senate Executive Document, 35th Congress, 2nd session, 22:35–2, 1211–1218.
6. Senate Executive Document, 35th Congress, 2nd session, 1218.
7. Senate Executive Document, 35th Congress, 2nd session, 14.
8. Dennett, *Americans in Eastern Asia,* 260.
9. Senate Executive Document, 33rd Congress, 2nd session, *passim.*
10. William E. Griffis, *Matthew Calbraith Perry,* 307.
11. Quoted in Arthur Walworth, *Black Ships off Japan,* 16.
12. Ibid., 28–31.
13. Marie H. Taylor and Horace Scudder, editors, *The Life and Letters of Bayard Taylor,* 250.
14. F. W. Williams, editor, *The Life and Letters of S. Wells Williams,* 197.
15. J. W. Spalding, *Japan and Around the World,* 165.
16. S. Wells Williams, *A Journal of the Perry Expedition,* 259.
17. "A Paper Read Before the American Geographical and Statistical Society," quoted in Walworth, *Black Ships off Japan,* 129.
18. Ibid.
19. Fosco Maraini, *Meeting with Japan,* 178–179.
20. Iriye, *Across the Pacific,* 11–12.
21. Carl Crow, *He Opened the Door of Japan,* 14–17.
22. Ibid., 33–34.
23. State Department Archives, Japan Dispatches, Vol. I, June 2, 1856.
24. Mario Emilio Cosenza, editor, *The Complete Journal of Townsend Harris,* 195.
25. Ibid., 225.
26. Ibid., 231–232.
27. Ibid., 246.
28. Ibid., 308.
29. Ibid., 316.
30. Ibid., 377.
31. Ibid., 377.
32. Ibid., 440.
33. Ibid., 440.
34. Quoted in Crow, *He Opened the Door of Japan,* 214–215.
35. Harris to Kate Drinker, Manuscript Division, New York Public Library, July 1, 1861.
36. J. H. Longford, *The Story of Old Japan,* 302.
37. Dennis Bloodworth, *The Chinese Looking Glass,* 173.
38. Hallett Abend, *The God from the West,* 22–29.
39. Ibid., 22.
40. North China *Herald,* Mar. 14, 1860.
41. Abend, *The God from the West,* 11–20.
42. State Department Archives, Diplomatic Correspondence, 1864, 851.
43. Paul Charrier, *Gordon of Khartoum,* 41.
44. *Chesney's Chinese Miscellany,* II, 408.
45. Quoted in Abend, *The God from the West,* 230–231.

6. Little Wars with the Heathen

1. Iriye, *Across the Pacific,* 37–38.
2. Earl Swisher, *China's Management of the American Barbarians,* 690–691.

3. F. W. Williams, *Anson Burlingame and the First Chinese Mission,* 138–139.
4. Alfred Stead, editor, *Japan by the Japanese,* 166.
5. William H. Seward, *Works of William H. Seward,* I, 250.
6. Frederick W. Seward, *Seward at Washington as Senator and Secretary of State,* 383.
7. State Department Correspondence, 1867, I, 414.
8. Tyler Dennett, "Seward's Far Eastern Policy," *American Historical Review,* October 1922.
9. A detailed account of the expedition may be found in "Our Little War with the Heathen" by Albert Castel and Andrew C. Nahm, *American Heritage,* April 1968.
10. Frederick W. Seward, *Seward at Washington,* 348.
11. James G. Blaine, *Twenty Years in Congress,* II, 334.
12. Edward L. Pierce, *Memoir and Letters of Charles Sumner,* II, 318–319.
13. Foster Rhea Dulles, *America in the Pacific,* 92.
14. Frank A. Golder, "The Purchase of Alaska," *American Historical Review,* XXV (1920), 423–424.
15. Olive Risley Seward, *William H. Seward's Travels Around the World,* 89.
16. John Russell Young, *Around the World with General Grant,* II, 550–551.
17. State Department Archives, Japan Dispatches, Vol. XVIII, July 6, 1871.
18. Ibid., Nov. 22, 1872.
19. Quoted in Dennett, *Americans in Eastern Asia,* 443.
20. Legendre Collection, Manuscript Division, Library of Congress.
21. Quoted in *Time* magazine, Mar. 31, 1967.
22. Young, *Around the World with General Grant,* II, 167.
23. Ibid., 372.
24. Ibid., 410–412.
25. Ibid., 443, 451.
26. Ibid., 480–481.
27. Ibid., 543–546.
28. John Russell Young, *Men and Memories,* II, 294.
29. Dennett, *Americans in Eastern Asia,* 445. "Grant's visit to the East," Dennett comments, "may be reckoned as a very important date in the history of American policy in the East."

7. The Furor of the Consuls

1. Quoted in Iriye, *Across the Pacific,* 60.
2. Ibid., 58.
3. S. Wells Williams, *The Middle Kingdom,* I, 833–836.
4. Arthur Smith, *Some Chinese Characteristics,* New York, 1894, *passim.*
5. Quoted in Iriye, *Across the Pacific,* 63.
6. Harold and Margaret Sprout, *The Rise of American Naval Power, 1776–1918, passim.*
7. Robert Louis Stevenson, *A Footnote to History,* 391.
8. Ibid., 303–304.
9. Quoted in Arthur Johnstone, *Recollections of Robert Louis Stevenson in the Pacific,* 92.
10. Charles Wilkes, *Narrative of the U.S. Exploring Expedition,* II, 80.
11. House Executive Document 161, 44th Congress, 2nd session, 5.
12. Ibid., 76.
13. Ibid., 125.

14. Frederick W. Seward, *Reminiscences of a Wartime Statesman and Diplomat,* 437–441.
15. Charles Oscar Pullin, *Diplomatic Negotiations of American Naval Officers,* 350.
16. Foster Rhea Dulles, *The Imperial Years,* 26.
17. Stevenson, *A Footnote to History, passim.*
18. Quoted in Dulles, *America in the Pacific,* 115.
19. Quoted in Dulles, *The Imperial Years,* 115.
20. *Nation,* XXVIII, 84.
21. Stevenson, *A Footnote to History, passim.*
22. Quoted in J. C. Furnas, *Voyage to Windward,* 402.
23. *Forum Magazine,* March 1893.
24. New York *Commercial Advertiser,* Apr. 14, 1893.
25. House Report 243, 53rd Congress, 2nd session, 59.
26. Allan Nevins, *Grover Cleveland, passim.*
27. Boston *Herald,* Jan. 30, 1893.
28. State Department Archives, Papers Relating to the Foreign Relations of the United States, 1899, 626.

8. "For Ways That Are Dark"

1. The Elsie Sigel murder is detailed in Richard O'Connor, *Hell's Kitchen,* 154–157.
2. Quoted in Harold R. Isaacs, *Scratches on Our Minds,* 116.
3. *Literary Digest,* Mar. 12, 1927.
4. Oscar Handlin's introduction to Gunther Barth, *Bitter Strength,* Vol. XIV.
5. Isaacs, *Scratches on Our Minds,* 111.
6. B. J. O. Schrieke, *Alien Americans,* 11–12.
7. Bret Harte, *Selected Stories of Bret Harte,* 148.
8. Richard O'Connor, *Ambrose Bierce,* 71–74.
9. Barth, *Bitter Strength,* 145.
10. *Overland Monthly,* September 1870.
11. Quoted in F. L. Patee, *Mark Twain,* 98–104.
12. Furnas, *Anatomy of Paradise,* 436.
13. Mark Twain, *Letters from the Sandwich Islands,* edited by G. Ezra Dane, *passim.*
14. M. M. Marberry, *Splendid Poseur,* 233–234.
15. Furnas, *Anatomy of Paradise,* 418–420.
16. Ibid., 421.
17. Iriye, *Across the Pacific,* 67–68.
18. Ssu-yu Teng and John K. Fairbank, *China's Response to the West,* 150.
19. Quoted in Iriye, *Across the Pacific,* 64.
20. Lafcadio Hearn, *Glimpses of Unfamiliar Japan,* 4.
21. Quoted in Elizabeth Stevenson, *Lafcadio Hearn,* 30.
22. John A. Cockerill, "Lafcadio Hearn," *Current Literature,* June 1896.
23. Lafcadio Hearn, *Writings,* VIII, 51.
24. Milton Bronner, editor, *Letters from the Raven,* 94.
25. Hearn, *Writings,* XIV, 102.
26. Ibid., V, 242–243.
27. Elizabeth Bisland, editor, *Japanese Letters of Lafcadio Hearn,* 411.

9. "Advance Agent of Imperialism"

1. Alfred T. Mahan, *The Interest of America in Sea Power*, 35–36.
2. Quoted in Dennett, *Americans in Eastern Asia*, 463.
3. Josiah Strong, *Our Country*, 209.
4. Josiah Strong, *Expansion under World Conditions*, 227.
5. Sprout and Sprout, *The Rise of American Naval Power, 1776–1918*, 202.
6. Alfred T. Mahan, *From Sail to Steam*, xii.
7. Ibid., 243.
8. Ibid., 266–267.
9. Ibid., 269–271.
10. Ibid., 277–279.
11. Ibid., 283.
12. John LaFarge, *Reminiscences of the South Seas*, 43.
13. Alfred T. Mahan, *The Influence of Sea Power upon History, passim.*
14. *Harper's Monthly*, October 1893.
15. Quoted in Barbara Tuchman, *The Proud Tower*, 132.
16. House Executive Document 1, 51st Congress, 2nd session, 1889.
17. Senate Executive Document 43, 51st Congress, 2nd session, 1889.
18. New York *Herald*, Jan. 31, 1890.
19. *Congressional Record*, Vol. XXI, 3163.
20. New York *Times*, Jan. 31, 1893.
21. Alfred T. Mahan, "Hawaii and Our Future Sea Power," *Forum*, March 1893.
22. Alfred T. Mahan, "The Isthmus and Sea Power," *Atlantic Monthly*, October 1893.
23. Quoted in Charles C. Taylor, *The Life of Admiral Mahan*, 131.
24. Tuchman, *The Proud Tower*, 138.
25. Alfred T. Mahan, "Possibilities of an Anglo-American Reunion," *North American Review*, November 1894.
26. Alfred T. Mahan, "The Future in Relation to American Naval Power," *Harper's Magazine*, October 1895.
27. "A Twentieth Century Outlook," *Harper's Magazine*, September 1897.
28. Taylor, *The Life of Admiral Mahan*, 12.
29. Mahan, *The Interest of America in Sea Power*, 288–289.
30. Quoted in Captain William D. Puleston, *Mahan*, 171.
31. Quoted in Leon Wolff, *Little Brown Brother*, 364.

10. The Philippine Pivot-Point

1. Solf's career is described in Furnas, *Anatomy of Paradise*, 240–241.
2. Introduction to William Graham Sumner, *War and Other Essays*, edited by Albert Galloway Keller, xxiii.
3. Ibid., 292–293.
4. Ibid., 297–298.
5. Ibid., 309–310.
6. Ibid., 329.
7. Ibid., 328–329.
8. Ibid., 342.

9. Henry Pringle, *Theodore Roosevelt, passim.*
10. Walter Millis, *The Martial Spirit,* 85–86.
11. John D. Long, *America of Yesterday,* 169–170.
12. Wolff, *Little Brown Brother,* 169–170.
13. Authoritative accounts of the battle of Manila Bay may be found in the memoirs of two leading participants, Admiral George W. Dewey, *Autobiography,* and Admiral Bradley A. Fiske, *From Midshipman to Rear Admiral.*
14. Wolff, *Little Brown Brother,* 63.
15. Moorfield Storey and Marchial P. Lichauco, *The Conquest of the Philippines by the United States,* 45. Hereafter cited as Storey.
16. *Congressional Record,* Apr. 17, 1900, 4287.
17. Senate Document 331, Part III, 2928–2936.
18. Chicago *Record,* June 24, 1898.
19. Quoted in Millis, *The Martial Spirit,* 116.
20. Quoted in Maximo Kalaw, *The Case for the Filipinos,* 79–80.
21. Quoted in Millis, *The Martial Spirit,* 383–384.
22. Quoted in Wolff, *Little Brown Brother,* 273.
23. *Harper's Weekly,* June 1899.
24. New York *Times,* May 3, 1901.
25. Boston *Transcript,* Mar. 4, 1902.
26. Manila *Times,* Nov. 4, 1901.
27. New York *Evening Post,* Apr. 8, 1902.
28. *Congressional Record,* May 22, 1902.
29. Quoted in James Shirley, "War Protest in Wartime," *New Republic,* May 6, 1967.
30. Quoted in Storey, 177–178. Senator Carmack delivered his speech before the Senate on May 31, 1902.
31. Quoted in Walter Lord, *The Good Years,* 7.
32. Quoted in Wolff, *Little Brown Brother,* 270.
33. Speech delivered before the New York chamber of commerce as reported by the New York *Times,* Apr. 22, 1904.
34. *Century Magazine,* January 1914.
35. Quoted in James H. Blount, *American Occupation of the Philippines,* 340.
36. W. Cameron Forbes, *The Philippine Islands,* I, 333. The Forbes and Blount books form a definitive history of the United States occupation of the Philippines before World War I.
37. Article by Eleanor F. Egan, *Saturday Evening Post,* Feb. 2, 1918.
38. Interview with Dr. Heiser carried by the *Cablenews-American,* July 4, 1909.
39. Interview with Robert R. Williams in New York City, May 7, 1956.
40. Forbes, *The Philippine Islands,* I, 349.
41. *Report of the Philippine Commission,* 1903, 673–674.
42. Ibid., 1902, 869–970.
43. Ibid., 1903, 679–680.
44. Ibid., 1902, 872.
45. Forbes, *The Philippine Islands,* I, 435.
46. Ibid., 438.
47. *Report of the Philippine Commission,* 1902, 880–881.
48. Forbes, *The Philippine Islands,* I, 455.
49. Pershing Papers, Box 1, Manuscript Division, Library of Congress.
50. O'Connor, Richard, *Black Jack Pershing,* 60.

51. Letter to J. St. Loe Strachey, Jan. 6, 1904, quoted in Hermann Hagedorn, *Leonard Wood*, II, 14–15.
52. O'Connor, *Black Jack Pershing*, 70–72.
53. New York *Sun*, Mar. 16, 1906.
54. Quoted in Hagedorn, *Leonard Wood*, II, 70–71.
55. New York *World*, Sept. 21, 1913.
56. O'Connor, *Black Jack Pershing*, 96–97.
57. Ibid., 102–104.
58. Washington *Herald*, Sept. 21, 1913.
59. *Century Magazine*, August 1898.

11. The Testament of Homer Lea

1. Will Irwin, *The Making of a Reporter*, 19.
2. Clare Boothe Luce's introduction to Homer Lea, *The Valor of Ignorance*.
3. Interview with Marshall Stimson in 1954.
4. Ibid.
5. Quoted by Mrs. Luce, introduction to Lea, *The Valor of Ignorance*.
6. Irwin, *The Making of a Reporter*, 19.
7. Carl Glick, *Double Ten*, 36–37.
8. Bloodworth, *The Chinese Looking Glass*, 92–93.
9. Glick, *Double Ten*, 43–44.
10. Ibid.
11. Ibid., 49.
12. Irwin, *The Making of a Reporter*, 19–20.
13. Glick, *Double Ten*, 27–45.
14. Ibid., 63.
15. Ibid., 114–115.
16. Ibid., 124–125.
17. New York *Times*, June 27, 1905.
18. Irwin, *The Making of a Reporter*, 20–22.
19. Homer Lea, *The Vermilion Pencil, passim.*
20. Lea, *The Valor of Ignorance*, 5–12
21. Ibid., 19–25.
22. Ibid., 29–49.
23. Ibid., 76–101.
24. Ibid., *passim.*
25. Ibid., *passim.*
26. Ibid., *passim.*
27. Ibid., *passim.*
28. *The Impudence of Charlatanism*, World Peace Foundation pamphlet series, Vol. II, 1912.
29. Glick, *Double Ten*, 223.
30. Ibid., 210.
31. Homer Lea, *The Day of the Saxon*, 4–5.
32. Ibid., 117–118.
33. Ibid., 180–205.
34. Ibid., 239–240.
35. Quoted by Mrs. Luce, introduction to Lea, *The Valor of Ignorance*.
36. Glick, *Double Ten*, 275–276.
37. Recollection of the late Harry Carr, then a reporter on the Los Angeles *Times* and a personal friend of Homer Lea's, to the author.

12. The Yellow/Brown Peril

1. O'Connor, *Black Jack Pershing*, 84–85.
2. *Hearings Before the Senate Foreign Relations Committee,* 89th Congress, 2nd session, March 1966, 103.
3. San Francisco *Call,* May 8, 1900.
4. Quoted in Carey McWilliams, *Prejudice,* 19.
5. San Francisco *Japanese-American,* Oct. 25, 1906.
6. Quoted in Robert A. Hart, *The Great White Fleet,* 32.
7. *Argonaut,* Nov. 10, 1906.
8. New York *World,* Feb. 14, 1907.
9. New York *Herald,* Feb. 3, 1907.
10. A. M. Pooley, *Japan's Foreign Policies,* 122.
11. *McClure's Magazine,* July 1910.
12. Richard O'Connor, *Jack London,* 220–221.
13. Jack London, "The Yellow Peril" in *Revolution and Other Essays,* 279–287.
14. Ibid.
15. Ibid.
16. Quoted in Lord, *The Good Years,* 206–207.
17. Quoted in Hart, *The Great White Fleet,* 55–60.
18. Ibid., 197.
19. Evelyn Adam, *Behind the Screens in Japan,* 262.
20. Hart, *The Great White Fleet,* 233.
21. Iriye, *Across the Pacific,* 103, 121, and Kenneth Scott Latourette, *The United States Moves Across the Pacific,* 23–24.
22. Latourette, *The United States Moves across the Pacific,* 23–24.
23. Lloyd Griscom, *Diplomatically Speaking,* 263.
24. Josephus Daniels, *The Wilson Era,* 161.
25. Quoted in McWilliams, *Prejudice,* 46–47.
26. New York *Herald,* May 15, 1913.
27. Daniels, *The Wilson Era,* 164–165.
28. Ibid., 164–165.
29. Ibid., 165.
30. Ibid., 165–167.
31. McWilliams, *Prejudice,* 47.
32. Quoted in Henry W. Taft, *Japan and America,* 111.
33. Daniels, *The Wilson Era,* 1968.
34. Ibid.
35. Fiske, *From Midshipman to Rear Admiral,* 478.
36. Jonathan Daniels, *The End of Innocence,* 107–108.
37. *Asia Magazine,* July 1923.
38. Sumner Welles, *Seven Decisions That Shaped History,* 68.

13. Walking on Eggs in Siberia

1. Quoted in William S. Graves, *America's Siberian Adventure,* 21–22.
2. George E. Sokolsky, *The Story of the Chinese Eastern Railway, passim.*
3. Quoted in George F. Kennan, *The Decision to Intervene,* 405.

4. Graves, *America's Siberian Adventure*, 3–5.
5. Ibid., 55–56.
6. Ibid., 65–66.
7. Semenov's career is described in Graves, *America's Siberian Adventure;* Clarence A. Manning, *The Siberian Fiasco:* Dmitri Alioshin, *Asian Odyssey;* J. A. White, *The Siberian Intervention,* and Erwin Lessner, *Cradle of Conquerors.*
8. White, *The Siberian Intervention,* 198.
9. Graves, *America's Siberian Adventure,* 90–91.
10. Ibid., 104–106.
11. The character and activities of General Horvath are discussed in Alioshin, *Asian Odyssey,* and Sokolsky, *The Story of the Chinese Eastern Railway.*
12. Alioshin, *Asian Odyssey, passim.*
13. Graves, *America's Siberian Adventure,* 108–109.
14. Ibid., 110.
15. Frederick Palmer, *Newton D. Baker,* II, 394.
16. Graves, *America's Siberian Adventure,* 128.
17. Ibid., 131–132.
18. Ibid., 235.
19. George Stewart, *The White Armies of Russia,* 292.
20. Graves, *America's Siberian Adventure,* 39.
21. Manning, *The Siberian Fiasco,* 156.
22. Graves, *America's Siberian Adventure,* 343–348.
23. Ibid., 122–124.

14. Shanghai Nights

1. Edgar Snow, *Journey to the Beginning,* 6.
2. Pearl Buck, *My Several Worlds,* 229.
3. Relman Morin, *East Wind Rising,* 160.
4. Ibid., 170.
5. Ibid., 171.
6. Iriye, *Across the Pacific,* 144.
7. John B. Powell, *My Twenty-five Years in China,* 72–77.
8. Ibid., 78–80.
9. Ibid., 79–80.
10. Snow, *Journey to the Beginning,* 93.
11. *China Year Book,* 1925, *passim.*
12. Buck, *My Several Worlds,* 4.
13. Earl Cressy, "Converting the Missionary," *Asia Magazine,* June 1919.
14. John Dewey, "New Culture in China," *Asia Magazine,* July 1921.
15. Isaacs, *Scratches on Our Minds,* 147–148.
16. John C. Caldwell, *China Coast Family,* 161–162.
17. Buck, *My Several Worlds,* 7.
18. Caldwell, *China Coast Family,* 90–93.
19. Buck, *My Several Worlds,* 124.
20. Caldwell, *China Coast Family,* 226–227.
21. Smedley D. Butler, *War Is a Racket,* 7–10.
22. Buck, *My Several Worlds,* 205–216.
23. *Foreign Affairs,* October 1950.
24. Powell, *My Twenty-five Years in China,* 92–124.

25. Burke Davis, *Marine!*, 87.
26. Matthew B. Ridgway, as told in Harold H. Martin, *Soldier*, 35–36.
27. Charles G. Finney, *The Old China Hands*, 164.
28. Snow, *Journey to the Beginning*, 194–197.
29. Isaacs, *Scratches on Our Minds*, 155.
30. Quoted, ibid., 158.

15. The Excluded Japanese

1. *Pacific Citizen*, November 1933.
2. Quoted in the *Pacific Citizen*, June 1938.
3. Valentine S. McClatchy, *The Germany of Asia*, 34.
4. Sacramento *Bee*, June 17, 1919.
5. McClatchy, *The Germany of Asia*, 35.
6. McWilliams, *Prejudice*, 60–61.
7. Lothrop Stoddard, *The Rising Tide of Color*, 44–51.
8. Ibid., 183, 251.
9. Ibid., 252, 266, 268.
10. Ibid., 301.
11. Quoted in *Literary Digest*, Aug. 9, 1919.
12. Quoted in Morin, *East Wind Rising*, 30–32.
13. *Congressional Record*, April 8, 1924, 5809.
14. Baltimore *Sun*, May 11, 1924.
15. Taft, *Japan and America*, 138.
16. Ibid., 192–194.
17. *Literary Digest*, Nov. 13, 1909.
18. Quoted in *The Military Historian and Economist*, January 1917.
19. Thorstein Veblen, *Essays in Our Changing Order*, 255–265.
20. *Nation*, Jan. 6, 1932.
21. Iriye, *Across the Pacific*, 179.
22. Snow, *Journey to the Beginning*, 99.
23. Quoted in Morin, *East Wind Rising*, 290.
24. Ibid., 294.
25. Quoted in Iriye, *Across the Pacific*, 195.
26. New York *Times*, Oct. 7, 1937.
27. R. L. Wilbur and A. M. Hyde, *The Hoover Policies*, 600.
28. Graham Peck, *Two Kinds of Time*, 59.
29. Quoted in Morin, *East Wind Rising*, 323–324.
30. John W. Masland, "Missionary Influence Upon American Far Eastern Foreign Policy," *Pacific Historical Review*, September 1941.
31. Quoted in John W. Kobler, *Luce*, 122.

16. Ocean of Destiny?

1. *Times of India*, Dec. 28, 1954.
2. Ronald Segal, *The Race War*, 325.
3. Richard Wright, *The Colour Curtain*, 135–136.
4. Martin E. Weinstein, "Okinawa's Future and Far East Security," *Reporter*, Nov. 2, 1967.
5. Quoted by Emmett John Hughes in his *Newsweek* column, Oct. 2, 1967.

6. Thomas Magruder, "The Chinese as a Fighting Man," *Foreign Affairs,* January 1931.
7. Hanson Baldwin, "China as a Military Power," *Foreign Affairs,* October 1951.
8. Boston *Globe,* July 13, 1964.
9. Welles, *Seven Decisions That Shaped History,* 78–79.
10. Quoted by C. J. Creekmore, "Decision East of Suez," *Reporter,* June 1, 1965.
11. Hanson Baldwin, "Red Flag over the Seven Seas," *Atlantic Monthly,* March 1968.
12. *Chicago Daily News* dispatch by Ernest Weatherall, Apr. 13, 1968.
13. Creekmore, "Decision East of Suez."
14. *Newsweek,* Oct. 30, 1967.
15. Paul and William Paddock, *Famine—1975!,* 8.
16. Harrison Brown, *The Challenge of Man's Future,* 266.

Selected Bibliography

Selected Bibliography

Abend, Hallett, *The God from the West,* New York, 1947.
Adam, Evelyn, *Behind the Screens in Japan,* New York, 1910.
Alioshin, Dmitri, *Asian Odyssey,* New York, 1940.
Augur, Helen, *Passage to Glory: John Ledyard's America,* New York, 1946.
Barth, Gunther, *Bitter Strength: A History of the Chinese in the United States, 1850–1870,* 2 vols., Cambridge, Mass., 1964.
Berry, Robert E., *Yankee Stargazer,* New York, 1941.
Beston, Henry, *The Book of Gallant Vagabonds,* New York, 1925.
Bisland, Elizabeth, editor, *The Japanese Letters of Lafcadio Hearn,* Boston, 1910.
Blaine, James G., *Twenty Years in Congress,* 2 vols., Norwich, Conn., 1884.
Bloodworth, Dennis, *The Chinese Looking Glass,* New York, 1967.
Blount, James H., *American Occupation of the Philippines,* New York, 1913.
Bronner, Milton, *Letters from the Raven,* New York, 1907.
Brown, Harrison, *The Challenge of Man's Future,* New York, 1954.
Buck, Pearl S., *My Several Worlds,* New York, 1954.
Butler, Smedley D., *War Is a Racket,* New York, 1935.
Caldwell, John C., *China Coast Family,* Chicago, 1953.

Carey, Charles H., *The History of Oregon,* Portland, Ore., 1922.

Charrier, Paul, *Gordon of Khartoum,* London, 1965.

Chesney's Chinese Miscellany, Shanghai. No date.

Christy, Arthur H., editor, *The Asian Legacy and American Life,* New York, 1942.

A Chronological History of Northeastern Voyages of Discovery, London, 1819. Pages unnumbered.

Cosenza, Mario Emilio, editor, *The Complete Journal of Townsend Harris,* New York, 1930.

Crow, Carl, *He Opened the Door of Japan,* New York, 1939.

Dana, Richard Henry, *Two Years Before the Mast,* New York, 1947.

Daniels, Jonathan, *The End of Innocence,* Philadelphia, 1954.

Daniels, Josephus, *The Wilson Era,* Chapel Hill, 1944.

Davis, Burke, *Marine!,* Boston, 1962.

Dennett, Tyler, *Americans in Eastern Asia,* New York, 1922.

Dewey, George W., *Autobiography,* New York, 1913.

Dulles, Foster Rhea, *America in the Pacific,* Boston, 1932.

——— *China and America,* New York, 1946.

——— *The Imperial Years,* New York, 1956.

——— *The Old China Trade,* Boston, 1930.

Fairbank, John K., *The United States and China,* Cambridge, Mass., 1948.

Fanning, Edmund, *Voyages Around the World,* New York, 1833.

Feis, Herbert, *The Road to Pearl Harbor,* Princeton, 1950.

Finney, Charles G., *The Old China Hands,* New York, 1961.

Fiske, Bradley A., *From Midshipman to Rear Admiral,* New York, 1919.

Forbes, Robert Bennet, *Personal Reminiscences,* Boston, 1878.

Forbes, W. Cameron, *The Philippine Islands,* 2 vols., Boston, 1928.

Furnas, J. C., *Anatomy of Paradise,* New York, 1947.

——— *Voyage to Windward,* New York, 1951.

Glick, Carl, *Double Ten,* New York, 1945.

Graves, William S., *America's Siberian Adventure,* New York, 1931.

Griffis, William E., *Matthew Calbraith Perry,* Boston, 1887.

Griscom, Lloyd, *Diplomatically Speaking,* New York, 1940.

Hagedorn, Hermann, *Leonard Wood: A Biography,* 2 vols., New York, 1931.

Halle, Louis J., *Dream and Reality,* New York, 1959.

Hart, Robert A., *The Great White Fleet,* Boston, 1965.

Harte, Bret, *Selected Stories of Bret Harte,* London, 1875.

Hearn, Lafcadio, *Glimpses of Unfamiliar Japan,* Boston, 1904.

——— *Writings,* 16 vols., Boston, 1922.

Heiser, Victor G., *An American Doctor's Odyssey,* New York, 1936.

Hirsch, Mark D., *William C. Whitney: Modern Warwick,* New York, 1948.

Hunter, William C., *Bits of Old China,* Shanghai, 1911.

The Impudence of Charlatanism, World Peace Foundation pamphlet series, Vol. II, 1912. Place of publication not given.

Iriye, Akira, *Across the Pacific,* New York, 1967.

Irwin, Will, *The Making of a Reporter,* New York, 1942.

Isaacs, Harold R., *Scratches on Our Minds: American Images of China and India,* New York, 1958.

Jacobs, Thomas Jefferson, *Scenes, Incidents and Adventures in the Pacific Ocean,* New York, 1844.

Johnstone, Arthur, *Recollections of Robert Louis Stevenson in the Pacific,* London, 1905.

Kalaw, Maximo, *The Case for the Filipinos,* New York, 1916.
Kennan, George F., *The Decision to Intervene,* Princeton, 1958.
———— *Russia and the West,* Boston, 1961.
Kobler, John W., *Luce,* New York, 1968.
LaFarge, John, *Reminiscences of the South Seas,* New York, 1891.
LaFeber, Walter, *The New Empire,* Ithaca, 1963.
Langer, William L., *The Diplomacy of Imperialism, 1890–1902* (2nd edition), New York, 1951.
Latourette, Kenneth Scott, *A History of Christian Missions in China,* New York, 1929.
———— *The United States Moves Across the Pacific,* New York, 1946.
Lea, Homer, *The Day of the Saxon,* New York, 1942.
———— *The Valor of Ignorance,* New York, 1942.
———— *The Vermilion Pencil,* New York, 1908.
Ledyard, John, *A Journal of Captain Cook's Last Voyage to the Pacific Ocean,* Hartford, 1783.
Lessner, Erwin, *Cradle of Conquerors,* New York, 1955.
London, Jack, *Revolution and Other Essays,* New York, 1910.
Long, John D., *America of Yesterday,* New York, 1923.
Longford, J. H., *The Story of Old Japan,* New York, 1910.
Lord, Walter, *The Good Years,* New York, 1960.
Lubbock, Basil, *Bully Hayes: South Sea Pirate,* Boston, 1931.
———— *The Opium Clippers,* Boston, 1933.
Mahan, Alfred T., *From Sail to Steam,* New York, 1907.
———— *The Influence of Sea Power upon History,* Boston, 1897.
———— *The Interest of America in Sea Power,* Boston, 1911.
Manning, Clarence A., *The Siberian Fiasco,* New York, 1952.
Maraini, Fosco, *Meeting with Japan,* New York, 1960.
Marberry, M. M., *Splendid Poseur,* New York, 1953.
Martin, Harold H., *Soldier,* New York, 1956.
May, Ernest R., *Imperial Democracy,* New York, 1961.
McClatchy, Valentine S., *The Germany of Asia* (pamphlet), Sacramento, 1919.
McMaster, John B., *History of the American People,* 7 vols., New York, 1913.
McWilliams, Carey, *Prejudice; Japanese-Americans: Symbol of Racial Intolerance,* Boston, 1944.
Melville, Herman, *Typee,* New York, 1951.
Millis, Walter, *The Martial Spirit,* Boston, 1931.
Moley, Raymond, *After Seven Years,* New York, 1939.
Morin, Relman, *East Wind Rising,* New York, 1960.
Morison, Samuel Eliot, *John Paul Jones: A Sailor's Biography,* Boston, 1959.
———— *The Maritime History of Massachusetts, 1783–1860,* Boston, 1921.
———— *Old Bruin,* Boston, 1967.
Morrell, Benjamin, *A Narrative of Four Voyages,* 1932.
Morse, H. B., *In the Days of the Taipings,* Salem, 1927.
Mumford, Lewis, *Herman Melville,* New York, 1929.
Neumann, William L., *America Encounters Japan,* Baltimore, 1963.
Nevins, Allan, *Grover Cleveland: A Study in Courage,* New York, 1932.
O'Connor, Richard, *Ambrose Bierce: A Biography,* Boston, 1967.
———— *The German-Americans,* Boston, 1968.
———— *Hell's Kitchen,* Philadelphia, 1958.
———— *Jack London: A Biography,* Boston, 1964.
———— *The Scandalous Mr. Bennett,* New York, 1962.

Paddock, Paul, and William Paddock, *Famine — 1975!,* Boston, 1967.

Palmer, Frederick, *Newton D. Baker: America at War,* 2 vols., New York, 1931.

Pattee, F. L., *Mark Twain,* New York, 1935.

Peabody, Robert E., *The Log of the Grand Turks,* Boston, 1926.

——— *Merchant Venturers of Old Salem,* Boston, 1912.

Peck, Graham, *Two Kinds of Time,* Boston, 1950.

Phillips, James Duncan, *Salem and the Indies,* Boston, 1947.

Pierce, Edward L., *Memoir and Letters of Charles Sumner,* 4 vols., Boston, 1893.

Pitkin, Walter B., *Must We Fight Japan?,* New York, 1921.

Polk, James K., *Diary,* 4 vols., Chicago, 1910.

Pooley, A. M., *Japan's Foreign Policies,* New York, 1920.

Powell, John B., *My Twenty-five Years in China,* New York, 1945.

Pratt, Julius W., *America's Colonial Experiment,* New York, 1950.

——— *Expansionists of 1898,* Baltimore, 1958.

Pringle, Henry, *Theodore Roosevelt,* New York, 1931.

Puleston, William D., *Mahan,* New Haven, 1939.

Pullin, Charles Oscar, *Diplomatic Negotiations of American Naval Officers,* Baltimore, 1912.

Putnam, G. G. *Salem Vessels and Their Voyages,* Series 1, Salem, 1924.

Quincy, Joseph, editor, *The Journals of Major Samuel Shaw,* Boston, 1847.

Richardson, James D., *Messages of the Presidents,* Washington, 1899.

Richman, Irving B., *California under Mexico and Spain,* Boston, 1911.

Schrieke, B. J. O., *Alien Americans,* New York, 1936.

Segal, Ronald, *The Race War,* New York, 1967.

Seward, Frederick W., *Reminiscences of a Wartime Statesman and Diplomat,* New York, 1916.

——— *Seward at Washington as Senator and Secretary of State,* New York, 1891.

Seward, Olive Risley, *William H. Seward's Travels Around the World,* New York, 1873.

Seward, William H., *Works of William H. Seward,* 8 vols., Boston, 1884.

Smith, Arthur, *Some Chinese Characteristics,* New York, 1894.

Snow, Edgar, *Journey to the Beginning,* New York, 1958.

Sokolsky, George E., *The Story of the Chinese Eastern Railway,* New York, 1928.

Spalding, J. W., *Japan and Around the World,* New York, 1856.

Sparks, Jared, *The Life of John Ledyard,* Boston, 1847.

Sprout, Harold, and Margaret Sprout, *The Rise of American Naval Power, 1776–1918,* Princeton, 1939.

Stead, Alfred, editor, *Japan by the Japanese,* London, 1904.

Stevenson, Elizabeth, *Lafcadio Hearn,* New York, 1961.

Stevenson, Robert Louis, *A Footnote to History,* Vol. XVIII of *Collected Works,* New York, 1892.

Stewart, George, *The White Armies of Russia,* New York, 1964.

Stoddard, Lothrop, *The Rising Tide of Color,* New York, 1920.

Storey, Moorfield, and Marchial P. Lichauco, *The Conquest of the Philippines by the United States,* New York, 1926.

Strong, Josiah, *Expansion under World Conditions,* New York, 1900.

——— *Our Country* (revised edition), New York, 1891.

Sumner, William Graham, *War and Other Essays,* New Haven, 1911.

Swisher, Earl, *China's Management of the American Barbarians,* New Haven, 1953.

Taft, Henry W., *Japan and America,* New York, 1932.

Taylor, Charles C., *The Life of Admiral Mahan,* New York, 1920.

Taylor, Marie H., and Horace Scudder, editors, *The Life and Letters of Bayard Taylor,* Boston, 1884.

Teng, Ssu-yu, and John K. Fairbank, *China's Response to the West: A Documentary Survey,* Cambridge, Mass., 1954.

Tripp, Bartlett, *My Trip to Samoa,* Cedar Rapids, 1911.

Tuchman, Barbara W., *The Proud Tower,* New York, 1966.

Twain, Mark, *Letters from the Sandwich Islands,* edited by G. Ezra Dane, Palo Alto, 1938.

Veblen, Thorstein, *Essays in Our Changing Order,* New York, 1934.

Vevier, Charles, *The United States and China, 1906–1913,* New Brunswick, N.J., 1955.

Von Hagen, Victor, *Maya Explorer,* Norman, Okla., 1947.

Walworth, Arthur, *Black Ships off Japan,* New York, 1946.

Welles, Sumner, *Seven Decisions That Shaped History,* New York, 1951.

White, J. A., *The Siberian Intervention,* New York, 1924.

Wilbur, R. L., and A. M. Hyde, *The Hoover Policies,* New York, 1937.

Wilkes, Charles, *Narrative of the U.S. Exploring Expedition,* 5 vols., Philadelphia, 1845.

Williams, F. W., *Anson Burlingame and the First Chinese Mission,* New York, 1912.

———, editor, *The Life and Letters of S. Wells Williams,* New York, 1889.

Williams, S. Wells, *A Journal of the Perry Expedition,* New York, 1856.

——— *The Middle Kingdom* (revised edition), 2 vols., New York, 1883.

Wolff, Leon, *Little Brown Brother,* New York, 1961.

Woodberry, G. E., *The Life of Edgar Allan Poe,* 2 vols., Boston, 1909.

Wright, Richard, *The Colour Curtain,* London, 1956.

Young, John Russell, *Around the World with General Grant,* 2 vols., New York, 1879.

——— *Men and Memories,* 2 vols., New York, 1901.

Index

Index